Advance Praise for *Healing the Heart of Humanity*

An important, indeed a necessary book in these difficult times. While unflinchingly illustrating the devastation of gender injustice, the authors offer an original and inspiring path to hope and healing. Their program, so vividly and movingly described, could change the world.

—**Jean Kilbourne, Ed.D.**, Senior Scholar, Wellesley Centers for Women, creator of the film series, *Killing Us Softly: Advertising's Image of Women*

Healing the Heart of Humanity is overflowing with ancient spiritual wisdom and contemporary insight into the tragic interplay between gender and violence. As such it is an invaluable resource for those of us who struggle to help others see the deep connections between men's violence against women, other men, and themselves. Even more importantly, it offers men, women, and others creative and compassionate strategies for moving forward, together.

—**Jackson Katz, Ph.D.**, activist on gender, race, and violence, and author of *The Macho Paradox: Why Some Men Hurt Women and How All Men Can Help*

Truly inspiring—for the chronicles of GERI's positive impact across six continents, for the research highlighting the efficacy of the GERI methodology, and for inviting us to "*transcend* the past and *rewrite* the gender future of humanity."

The GERI process of "collective alchemy" uses the dross of patriarchal oppression to fuel the alchemical heart fire and process of transmutation and transformation. Fault lines give way to etheric lines of sacred interconnectedness between hearts, and gender wars abate in recognition of our mutuality, our "interbeing." So simple, yet so profound—according empathic resonance, grace, and forgiveness.

—**Annette Williams, Ph.D.**, Associate Professor, Women's Spirituality Ph.D. Program (Chair), and Women, Gender, Spirituality, and Social Justice MA Program, California Institute of Integral Studies

The authors have written "the bible" on the topic of gender and healing. Their expertise is world class as is this absolutely remarkable book. We ALL need the insights, information, challenging truths, comprehensive understandings and profound healing power of this book. I celebrate the scholarship contained in this work but most of all, the LOVE they have so deeply expressed through this book on the most vital topic of our age.

— **Lynne Twist**, Co-Founder of Pachamama Alliance, author of *The Soul of Money*

Profound crisis in realtions between men and women in today's world takes many different forms in different continents and countries, and causes enormous suffering. This extraordinary and groundbreaking work holds great promise as a way to its alleviation.

— **Stanislav Grof, M.D.**, author of *Psychology of the Future* and *Healing our Deepest Wounds*

Unless we make the 21st century the feminine century, our humanity is at stake. This book shows the important steps to cultivate feminine values and how to lead with them for the ultimate good for all.

— **Zainab Salbi**, Humanitarian, author, TV Host, and founder of Women for Women International

The majority of men want to be "Better Men," but don't know how to go about it. [When] men heal and connect to their hearts, true equality and partnership will reign. The Gender Equity and Reconciliation work is a key that helps train men to become the *better men* they long to be, not just for themselves, but for their loved ones and colleagues.

— **Ray Arata**, Founder, Better Man Conference, author of *Showing Up: How Men Can Become Effective Allies in the Workplace*

Advance Praise for *Healing the Heart of Humanity*

Young and old, working for justice must rank as our highest priority. The brave accounts in this volume across many divides are inspiring, demonstrating that we can successfully step up and show up to do this courageous work, and reclaim our humanity. We must continually make this work accessible, to reach every neighbourhood. It is that urgent.

— **Lechesa Tsenoli**, Deputy Speaker, National Assembly, Parliament of South Africa

A deep and powerful exploration of gender opposition, gender injustice, and the pathway through this suffering to a vision and life as one human family.

— **Rev. Joan Jiko Halifax**, Abbot, Upaya Zen Center, Santa Fe, NM

In a world that pushes us towards polarities of differences, this pivotal work celebrates those differences and helps us find common ground. The book is full of new approaches practiced over decades and a wealth of experiences gathered from across the world that have fostered genuine healing and reconciliation between men, women, and people of all gender identities. It is a must read.

— **Vishal Talreja and Suchetha Bhat**, Co-Founder and CEO of Dream a Dream, Bangalore, India

An experiential methodology called "Healing of Memories" was developed as a parallel process to South Africa's Truth and Reconciliation Commission. Our work of Healing of Memories resonates profoundly with this magnificent work of *Healing the Heart of Humanity*, which shows that wounds can heal, and a new humanity is possible.

I am of the view that the woundedness and oppression in the relationship between women and men is the oldest wound in the human family. This magnum opus is a testament that holds out before all people an invitation to participate in the work of redemption that will liberate all of us.

— **Fr. Michael Lapsley**, President, Healing of Memories Global Network

Magnificent heartfelt healing work that is leading us toward the love we long for. It gifts us a map of deep positive transformation we can use in these troubled and divisive times.

— **Jack Kornfield**, Founder of Spirit Rock Meditation Center, author of *A Path With Heart*

Whenever I talk with girls in middle or high school about their empowerment, a young man always asks, "What about *us*?—don't you have a program for us boys?" I am startled when they say, "we need help as well. I want to grow into a loving man." GERI is a resource and gift to young men as well as women. Gender Equity will be the lighthouse that young people are yearning for. I am excited!

— **The Honorable Jacquelyne K. Weatherspoon**, Former Member, New Hampshire House of Representatives

The authors have devoted decades to addressing the scars of gender imbalance through their reconciliation work. For humanity to progress, and even survive, the millennia-long era of domination must give way to a new era of collaboration and balance. *Healing the Heart of Humanity* shows the way forward—how to bring hidden gender wounds to the surface so they can be addressed and healed. I have no doubt that this book will serve as a lifeline to thousands of people around the world.

— **Dena Merriam**, Founder, The Global Peace Initiative of Women, author of *The Untold Story of Sita: An Empowering Tale for our Time*

Advance Praise for *Healing the Heart of Humanity*

Many admirable people and organizations are devoted to making the world a better place. High on that list is the courageous work described in this volume. The stories and events recounted here are immeasurably inspiring. There is scarcely any more important work going on today than the effort to heal and transform the relationships between men and women, between people of all genders: and from there, to accept responsibility, grieve, ask for and offer forgiveness. The hard-won achievements of such work ripple out to the larger human society, and to the many other species that constitute our Earth community. I hope this book is read by many, and its work will be taken up by all who are moved by the depth of its heartful wisdom.

— **Richard Tarnas, Ph.D.**, author of *The Passion of the Western Mind* and *Cosmos and Psyche*, Founder of Philosophy, Cosmology, and Consciousness Program, California Institute of Integral Studies

Healing the Heart of Humanity is a groundbreaking guide for all of us who want fulfilling relationships and a more caring and equitable world.

— **Riane Eisler**, author of *The Chalice and the Blade*; co-author of *The Partnership Way* (with David Loye), and *Nurturing Our Humanity* (with Douglas Fry)

For 30 years, GERI has been reaching to the root of and dismantling the social construct [of gender] that has been institutionalized at so many levels, and giving us new tools for identifying and resolving the connections between gender, race, and inequality. This book is an alchemy of cultural stories spanning the gender spectrum and its intersectional ties. It serves as a blueprint to move forward as one equal family. What a gift we have been given in this volume.

— **Marilyn Turkovich**, Executive Director, Charter for Compassion

This book is a powerful and timely contribution to breaking the tyranny of silence and exposing the hidden truths, harmful stereotypes, and trauma of gender oppression. This global repertoire of activist voices spanning three decades has redefined the contours of our gendered political and social landscape in a remarkable manner. The imperative of the book is a deliberate intersectionality of reconciliation, mindful action, inclusive practice, resilience, respect for diverse realities, and a more radical humanism.

— **Professor Rajendra Chetty**, post-colonial scholar, University of the Western Cape, South Africa

With its boldly audacious goal to address the deepest, most insidious and universal trauma that pervades our human species, this book shares stories and methods that have proven effective in creating transformations rippling in societies around the globe. It speaks to thousands of years of gender bias and violence—a root cause of all the issues we face. Integrating multiple modalities into a holistic framework, working with people of all genders, the authors co-evolved a method to reach deep into people's hearts, shed conditioning, and transform for the sake of the beloved community that's possible on the other side.

If you're called to help heal our world from a root cause of human suffering, read this book! It's deeply applicable, timely and useful, in any profession.

— **Nina Simons**, Co-Founder of Bioneers, author of *Nature, Culture, and the Sacred: A Woman Listens for Leadership*

Advance Praise for *Healing the Heart of Humanity*

If there was ever a need for a book with a bold mission it is now. With empathy, compassion, and bravery, *Healing the Heart of Humanity* tackles the most pressing issue of our day by seamlessly melding the micro with the macro level of analysis to "rewrite the gender story and reinvent the gender future of humanity." It would be impossible to read this book and not be profoundly changed in how we think about gender inequality, and the ways we can lovingly work together to create a new way of being that is transformative.

— **Gail Dines, Ph.D.**, Professor Emerita of Sociology and Women's Studies, Wheelock College in Boston, MA, and President of Culture Reframed

When I learned about this gender equity and reconciliation work several years ago, I had never seen anything quite like it. The engaging and compelling approach, developed over 30 years of rigorous research and practice, is not about policy or politics. It's about people.

It's about how we as a society—through universal human values of compassion, empathy, and forgiveness—can create safe spaces for women, men, and people of all gender identities, backgrounds, cultures, and ethnicities to come together as equals to explore the taboos, vulnerabilities, violations, and conditions that are at the root of gender inequity. It is work that we can all support. It is work that will change our world.

— **Suzanne Lerner**, President and CEO, Michael Stars, activist for gender equality and equity

For 30 years, the authors have worked on illuminating and redressing gender conditioning, oppression and injustice. Of particular note is GERI's consideration of the role of patriarchy in established religions, and the disproportionate negative impact on women, and LGBTQ+ communities.

Much reconciliation and healing needs to be done, and GERI has been at the foreground of engaging with these issues. Essential reading for anyone interested in addressing these significant imbalances.

— **Rev. SeiFu Anil Singh-Molares**, Executive Director, Spiritual Directors International

This book is an inspiring and intersectional approach to gender healing and reconciliation. It underscores the transformative power of gender justice movements as it provides practical tools toward gender equity and healing.

— **Latanya Mapp Frett**, President and CEO of Global Fund for Women

At last we have a book that tells the life-changing stories of GERI's global, ecumenical, cross-cultural and healing work, with a track record of impact. We hear narratives of how GERI facilitates and holds space to address gender wounds in individuals, relationships, systems and cultures. This book invites you on a thoughtful, safe and holistic journey to hope, healing, understanding, empathy, and gender reconciliation. Thank you GERI.

— **Rev. Dr. Doug Calhoun, Rev. Adele Calhoun**, co-authors, *Spiritual Rhythms for the Enneagram: A Handbook for Harmony and Transformation*

The GERI leaders are pioneers in a world-wide battle to prevent crimes against women. This book is thoughtful, brilliant, and brave. They and their fellow warriors and co-authors have personally traveled the globe educating and healing. This book captures their vast compassion and intelligence.

— **Delia Ephron**, novelist, screenwriter, and author of the memoir, *Left on Tenth: A Second Chance at Life*

Advance Praise for *Healing the Heart of Humanity*

I am a disabled woman of colour, who survived Apartheid. I hail from a small rural area in South Africa. As an activist who spent most of my life in pursuit of equality for all, I must acknowledge that after all the talks, awareness programs, public demonstrations and noises we collectively make, still today, we face the toxic contagions of vast imbalance. The big question confronting us all is how we collectively approach a beast that is so multi-faceted, multi-layered and complex.

I congratulate the authors of this book, as their work over many years has made an important contribution to our struggle against patriarchy and injustice. The book aims to empower girls and women, educate boys and men, and people of all genders, challenge gender norms, and social attitudes. This is the work required to transform the judicial systems, healthcare, disability networks, and ultimately society.

— **Dr. Marlene Le Roux**, Chief Executive Officer of Artscape, and a global leader in the disability and the arts sector, South Africa

The vision and methodology of this book is medicine for activating hope in anyone concerned with healing traumatized and militarized masculinity. As someone committed to men's work—the lifelong work of deconstructing the "Man-box" and healing the harms of patriarchy in all genders—I cannot think of any better work than GERI to engage in. This book promises to deepen and broaden the transformative efforts of all people determined to achieve gender healing and justice.

— **Terry Symens-Bucher, J.D., M.Div.**, Illuman—Men's Rites of Passage—Board of Directors and Former Chair

Hold, Hear, and Honor . . . this (deceptively) simple formula has shaped both the structure and the spirit of GERI events from the very earliest days. It has enabled participants to free themselves and one another from so many of the dark and damaging lies about gender we've all inherited, that I wonder whether it's time to tweak this a bit: *Hold, Hear, Honor . . . and Hope.* Because as you turn the pages of this extraordinary account, and hear one voice after another describe the transformative powers of GERI, something very like *hope* does begin to stir. What a gift!

— **Carol Lee Flinders, Ph.D.**, author of *At the Root of This Longing: Reconciling a Spiritual Hunger and a Feminist Thirst*

Studies suggest that the gender archetype is the deepest in the human psyche. Healing the gender wound is among the most important and systemically transformative acts we can take. This gripping book is a master work, a field guide to one of the most hopeful initiatives in the world today. It offers nothing less than a page-one rewrite of humanity's gender story and a pathway to the reinvention of the gender future of humanity. Changing that will truly change everything.

— **Kenny Ausubel**, Co-Founder of Bioneers, Producer of *Changing of the Gods*

Not every organization and movement that claims "Beloved Community" status deserves to do so, but GERI does. In summarizing its work over thirty years, its founders have included extensive contributions by GERI's facilitators and distinguished collaborators. In this volume, each contribution uniquely reveals the proven transformative power of GERI's methodology developed and applied in service of truth, reconciliation, and love.

— **Robert McDermott, Ph.D.**, Professor Emeritus, former President, California Institute of Integral Studies (CIIS), author, *Steiner and Kindred Spirits*

Advance Praise for *Healing the Heart of Humanity*

In this impactful, comprehensive, and deeply personal book, the authors invite us to step forward with them into a post-patriarchal world of gender healing and reconciliation. In a time when our culture of masculinity is in crisis, men and boys need new stories and models of masculinity that are creative, connective, and life-affirming. The authors of this book don't just provide theories and concepts, they invite us into the practice of divesting from domination-based culture and investing in a thriving and equitable human future. May we step forward wholeheartedly into this emerging world together.

— **Dan Mahle**, Founder, Wholehearted Masculine

Imagine a world where our differences as people catalyze connection and spark generative action—[creating] communities that bring their trouble, trauma and triumphs to the center, together, for witnessing, healing and justice. This work provides a masterful map for us to navigate the terrain between a culture of cold concern for liability to one of warm, welcoming accountability. This book and the work it underscores is medicine for heart and soul—individual and collective. Never has there been a more timely and potent contribution to healing the gender wound in our society.

— **Nicky Wilks**, Co-Founder, Journeymen Institute

Transforming… This work is about a safe space where one enters to explore inherent feminine and masculine energies, embracing both with openness in a trusted community, and sharing heart-rending stories. One exits this sacred space with the truth, beauty, and goodness of self, of others and of creation as one. A most excellent program and read.

— **Charles Barker M.D., M.P.H, Th.M.**, Past Chair, International Charter for Compassion

This book and the GERI work is a journey of discovery for men—about their relationships with, and impact on, women; and about the feminine within themselves. Bridging deep work in men's and women's circles, and sharing the depths of ourselves in a vulnerable way helps all of us to connect more authentically and intimately. This is vital work for all of us engaged in men's work, in growing in ourselves, and in deepening our connections with women.

— **Paul Samuelson**, ManKind Project, Board Member and Past Chair

As a striking number of societies remain mired in gender con flict, I am thrilled to endorse *Healing the Hart of Hum anity*, which propels the reader to a unique level of awareness as it uses a fresh and invigorating approach to achieving gender parity. This practical workbook will allow men and women to move beyo nd poli tical, gender, and theological differences and embrace a common vision of hope and prosperity.

— **Dr. Daisy Khan, D.Min.**, author, *Born with Wings*; Founder, Executive Director, Women's Islamic Initiative in Spirituality and Equality

We are one human family. The variety of our diversities is a great strength, and to view them as problematic reduces what we are, what we can be, and what we need to be. We've all had experiences beyond our physical reality, and we perceive and name them in different ways. GERI assists us in the essential journey of our transformation, not only to understand our actual reality, but to act on it in ways that benefit us all.

— **Carl Murrell**, Advisory Board of A Call to Men, Principal Representative to United Nations of U.S. Baha'i community, former Board Member of the Parliament of the World's Religions

Healing the Heart of Humanity

The Outer and Inner Alchemy of Reconciliation between Masculine and Feminine

William Keepin and Cynthia Brix

with

Desireé English ▪ Garrett Evans ▪ Karambu Ringera ▪ William Diplock ▪ Esther Diplock ▪ Lucille Meyer ▪ Silvia Araya ▪ Myra Kinds ▪ Tristan Johannes ▪ Hugo Sanchez ▪ Michele Breene ▪ Ansar Anwar ▪ Laurie Gaum ▪ Harin Jeong ▪ Samantha Van Schalkwyk ▪ Antonia Porter ▪ Jorge Rico ▪ Jabu Mashinini ▪ Julien Devereux

HOHM PRESS
CHINO VALLEY, ARIZONA

Cover Design: GRworld.org

Interior Design and Layout: Kubera Book Design, Prescott, Arizona

Library of Congress Control Number: 2022939113

ISBN: 978-1-963433-16-6

Hohm Press
P.O. Box 4410
Chino Valley, AZ 86323
800-381-2700
http://www.hohmpress.com

This book was printed in the U.S.A. on recycled, acid-free paper using soy ink.

Dedication

To all who have engaged in this pioneering work with remarkable courage and compassion, and to those yet to come,

To our spiritual teachers and mentors who bless us and the GERI community with their wisdom, light, and love,

To the Nameless One who holds our community and this work with immeasurable grace . . .

CONTENTS

SPECIAL HIGHLIGHTED SECTIONS:

FOREWORD

...what creation strains towards,
what all that is yearns towards, what salvation
bends towards is love. Love is
the point and the purpose of every life and is
all of the meaning of life...

Trauma and drama seethe below the surface of all our relationships. Patriarchy has penetrated the sacred dimensions of our lives, leeching the joyful certainty of dignity and mutual respect from people of all genders and every race. Our world is writhing through the turmoil of another Western war that comes hard on the heels of wars that have ravaged and are raging in other parts of the world. These violent conflicts were sparked or spurred on by patriarchal greed and power grabs. Our planet is gripped by catastrophic climate change that we have the ways but not the will to avert. In different parts of the world at disparate speeds we are emerging from a global pandemic of Covid-19. War, disease and violence, human induced climate crisis; it is hard to escape the verdict that we are ailing from a deep sickness that plagues the planet.

Will Keepin, Cynthia Brix and their colleagues in the Gender Equity and Reconciliation International (GERI) community have come together to document thirty years of healing offered across diverse communities around the world. Their work addresses the original wound to which all other traumas can be traced. It is our dysfunctional gender relationships that form the foundation of all other disordered power relationships: our drive to exert power over one another, and our wanton disregard of the other inhabitants of our planet can be traced to the injury inflicted by patriarchy. This book describes the multifaceted modalities of gender reconciliation that help to heal the, sometimes invisible, hurt.

Gender reconciliation recognizes the essential humanity of all participants regardless of gender identity or sexual orientation. This foundation of *ubuntu* (interdependence of all life) for GERI helps to unwind the hurt and reweave society in an inclusive tapestry that honors our individuality and our interdependence.

Many modern healing modalities offer chemical medicines for the body, or therapeutic conversations in pairs that engage the mind. To address gender-related traumas, practitioners usually work in single-sex groups. GERI draws from a richer palette to offer a more profound hope for healing: the work engages body and mind, soul and spirit: storytelling, role playing, witnessing, worshipping, silence and song, all these form part of the GERI workshop. Rather than isolated pairs, participants join the workshops as individuals in a community, and this communal aspect of the work creates a healthy container for witnessing, sharing and healing. GERI recognizes that the patriarchy has wounded gender non-binary and gender non-conforming people, cis-gender women and men, so all genders participate in these workshops as equal partners. Sometimes as storytellers, sometimes as witnesses, always as partners. For many participants it is through the GERI workshops that they first fully see their own woundedness and how, from the foundation of their own hurt, they have inflicted hurt on others. For many participants, the GERI workshop is the first time that they come to know that we are all survivors of systemic mutilation of our essential identity.

The past 30 years of GERI are a golden beacon that offer us hope for healing our wounded world. In the next 30 years, I pray that GERI is a wave of wellbeing that washes over our world.

Mpho Tutu van Furth
Amstelveen, Netherlands, 2022
Author of *Forgiveness and Reparation*; co-author (with Desmond Tutu) of *The Book of Forgiving* and *Made for Goodness*

Note to Reader: All the stories and experiences recounted in this book are true, and are recounted here with permission. Unless otherwise noted, names of individuals have been changed for confidentiality.

INTRODUCTION

My Dear Brothers and Sisters,
We are ONE human family . . .
—Archbishop Desmond Tutu

The late Archbishop Desmond Tutu announcing a partnership with Gender Reconciliation International (Media launch, August 20, 2013, Cape Town, South Africa)

We are one human family. Could anything be more obvious? We are brothers and sisters and non-binary siblings of the *one* human family. No matter how much we dwell on our differences (which are important), we are ultimately far more alike than different. We are similar siblings who have fashioned a fractured world of disastrous divisions.

We have divided our family in many tragic ways, and one of the most ancient and destructive is along gender lines. The entire human family suffers from the devastation of gender oppression and injustice—regardless of race, culture, nationality, or religion. It's been going on for thousands of years, in every country and continent, in families and institutions alike, across all social strata—from leaders to laborers, from wealthiest to poorest, from our intimate bedrooms to corporate boardrooms, and everything in between. Humanity is deeply divided, under a kind of "gender apartheid" of our own making. The time has come for this tyranny to end, once and for all.

Gender oppression is as deep as it is universal. Yet for this very reason, bringing "truth and reconciliation" to gender relations—between women and men, and people of all genders—can become a diamond pivot for leveraging systemic transformation on a large scale. "Gender reconciliation" can be a vehicle for profound liberation, individual and social healing, and unprecedented cultural transformation across the entire human family.

This book documents thirty years of sustained work in "Gender Equity and Reconciliation" that was inspired early on by the principles of the Truth and Reconciliation Commission (TRC) led by Archbishop Desmond Tutu in South Africa. When we started our gender healing work, we initially called it "Gender and Ecology," with the byline: "Are there parallels between exploitation of the Earth and exploitation of the feminine?" Unbeknownst to us, at the same time we launched our first gender healing programs in September and October 1992, Archbishop Tutu was speaking at Johns Hopkins University (October 1992). "South Africa will be free," he proclaimed, a full two years before this became a reality in 1994. "Injustice and repression and lies cannot have the last word."

So too with gender injustice. The central purpose of the TRC was to "promote reconciliation and forgiveness ... by the full disclosure of truth." This was precisely the methodology we had been developing in our gender work. We were also inspired by the spiritual principles of reconciliation and forgiveness implemented by the TRC. As Archbishop Tutu often emphasized, "We live in a moral universe." The TRC was not just a secular process but invoked the moral and spiritual dimensions of healing and consciousness, just as we were striving to do in our gender healing work.

So, in 1996, we renamed our program "gender reconciliation." As we wrote in the first edition of this book,

> Led by Archbishop Desmond Tutu, the TRC represents one of the most unique experiments in human history on a national scale working explicitly with reconciliation and forgiveness. While the process was not without its flaws, the TRC fostered remarkable healing in a country that had been severely ravaged by systematic racial violence. The mandate of the TRC was not only to discover the truth, but also to go beyond truth finding to "promote national unity and reconciliation in a spirit of

> understanding which transcends the conflict and divisions of the past."[1]

In a direct parallel, our work seeks not only to reconcile and forgive the egregious gender injustices of the past. We also work to transcend the gender conflicts and divisions of the past altogether—and *rewrite* the gender story and *reinvent* the gender future of humanity. Since its inception in 1992, the Gender Equity and Reconciliation International (GERI) project has convened over 375 intensive workshops and trainings, for more than 10,000 people on six continents—to engage in a deep process of unraveling the systemic knots of gender conflicts, and develop new practical skills for transforming gender relations from the inside out. Another 24,000 people have been introduced to the GERI process in conference sessions and introductory trainings.

In 2013, Archbishop Desmond Tutu formally endorsed the GERI program, and announced a partnership between GERI, the Desmond and Leah Tutu Legacy Foundation, and Stellenbosch University. "We are inaugurating and announcing this collaboration with an outstanding group [GERI] that has done wonders in helping to recover the humanity of women," said Archbishop Tutu at the media launch [photo above], which was covered by national South African news and internationally via Reuters. "We have undermined our humanity by the treatment that we have meted out to women," he said, "just as much as racists undermine their humanity by treating others as less than human." Tutu was also a vocal advocate for the rights of LGBTQ+ persons. "Gender Reconciliation is the logical next step for our country," said Rev. Mpho Tutu van Furth, former Executive Director of the Desmond and Leah Tutu Legacy Foundation, and Tutu's daughter. "The work of racial reconciliation will never be complete without the work of gender reconciliation."

The purpose of this partnership was to implement GERI programs for qualified university students. An important follow-up from this partnership was the first research project on the GERI methodology carried out over two years at the University of the Free State and Stellenbosch University, led by Dr. Samantha van Schalkwyk and Professor Pumla Gobodo-Madikizela. The auspicious results of this research are published in summary form in Chapter 24 of this book.

To date, GERI programs have been introduced in 21 universities: five in South Africa, six in the United States, three each in Canada and Costa Rica, two in Colombia, and one each in Kenya and Italy. Full GERI workshops have been conducted at seven universities: California Institute of Integral Studies and Pacific Lutheran University in the United States; Universidad de la Salle in Colombia; and Stellenbosch University, University of KwaZulu-Natal, University of the Free State, and University of the Western Cape in South Africa.

Why Are There So Many Authors of This Book?

We, the authors of this book, are leaders of a global community of people committed to transforming gender oppression and injustice, and striving to "replace" this disastrous legacy with transformed societies rooted in compassion, wisdom, mutual reverence and respect. We work *together* toward this goal, catalyzed by the grist of gender, through a process we call Gender Equity and Reconciliation International (GERI).

Why are there so many authors of this book? The late Vietnamese Zen master Thich Nhat Hanh answers this question well:

> We desperately need love. … It is possible the next Buddha will not take the form of an individual. The next Buddha may take the form of a *community*; a community practicing understanding and lovingkindness, a community practicing mindful living.[2]

This principle applies to the human family as a whole (not only Buddhism). This book and the GERI project are the product of just such a community—comprised of committed souls who are together practicing lovingkindness, deep understanding, and unflinching truth-telling—all in service of transmuting gender injustice into what is often called "Beloved Community."

The work recounted in this book is made possible by the entire GERI community, and not just a subset of this community. *Have all these authors made a substantial contribution to this book?* Yes, and so have others too numerous to name and list as authors, although many are named throughout the book. Beyond the original authors of the first edition of this book (Keepin and Brix), each author of this volume has been deeply engaged in the GERI program for anywhere between 5 and 20 years, and each has made a unique and original contribution to the evolution and implementation of this work within their particular communities and cultures.

Without these diverse contributions, the GERI program and its global implementation would not have been possible. Taken together, the 22 authors of this book are representative of the primary, active leaders who have built this global movement, and they constitute a relatively balanced representation of the more than 330 facilitators and trainers that have been certified in the GERI process since the first professional training began in 2001.

In order for this book to represent the GERI program and community accurately, it is essential that the authorship include the representative leaders who have built this work and global community into what it is today. These authors come from diverse cultures and continents around the world, and from multiple ethnic, racial, religious, and cultural backgrounds. They have taken this work deeply into their hearts and have worked tirelessly and against all odds and cultural barriers to implement this mission in their own communities and cultural contexts. Their sacrifices have brought deep healing in an arena where many people understandably fear to tread, or have given up all hope. Together, these authors are the co-*pioneers* who have built the magnificent intersectional global community that GERI is today.

Gender Equity and Reconciliation ~ Five Parts

Part I: *Untold Stories Keep Gender Oppression Invisible*

Chapter 1 introduces the background and history of the GERI program, the current cultural context and shifting gender landscape, with attention to various aspects of the contemporary gender conversation, including the #MeToo movement, the non-binary and transgender dimensions, emphasizing recent developments and movements. Also introduced is the GERI methodology, the nature of reconciliation, inner and outer alchemy, the spiritual dimensions of this work, and the implementation of GERI in diverse social contexts and cultures.

Chapters 2 through 9 introduce the GERI process, elucidating the methodology of collective alchemy with detailed narrative accounts of each element and stage of the GERI process.

Part II: *Ubuntu in Action*

Ubuntu is an African term for the fundamental principle of interdependence of all of humanity (often taught by Desmond Tutu). Chapters 10 through 16 address the application of the GERI process in various segments and sectors, including: LGBTQ+, BIPOC, religious and spiritual communities, government and politics, the corporate sector, and the United Nations.

Part III: *Transforming Gender Injustice into Beloved Community: Voices of Victory from Around the World*

Chapters 17 through 23 present inspiring stories of transformation from different countries and regions around the world, and also from the online implementation of GERI programs. Numerous stories are recounted—both heartrending and deeply inspiring—many in the words of the people themselves who experienced the impact of the GERI process in their lives.

Part IV: *Academic Research on Gender Equity and Reconciliation*

Chapter 24 summarizes academic research on GERI. A two-year longitudinal study at two South African universities concluded that students "began to free themselves from lifelong patriarchal conditioning," and that "[GERI] programs should be mandatory for students entering into the university environment." Another research study at the University of the District of Columbia in the USA concluded that GERI creates "new experiences of gender equity," and that "GERI is a proven catalyst for social change."

Part V: *Re-Writing the Gender Future of Humanity*

Chapters 25 and 26 explore the expansion and future of the GERI program. The GERI professional training is outlined, which has certified over 330 facilitators to date and is steadily expanding. The final chapter illuminates key learnings from three decades of the GERI initiative, and how this work relates to other forms of intergenerational trauma healing. We are focused not only on healing the past, and re-writing the gender story of humanity, but also we are already birthing the future today. Despite the constant and inevitable setbacks, and millennia of gender oppression with its ties to militarism, this work and related initiatives are slowly but surely moving humanity toward a new civilization of love.

Special Highlighted Sections

Gender Equity and Reconciliation features special highlighted sections from prominent leaders in various fields, who write about their experience of GERI and its potential for making an important contribution in their professional field. Ten special sections include reflections from each of the following leaders:

- Stanislav Grof, M.D. and Brigitte Grof. Stan is a co-founder of transpersonal psychology, author of 27 books on psychology, psychiatry, and clinical practice of non-ordinary states of consciousness
- Jetsunma Tenzin Palmo, leading Western Tibetan Buddhist nun, founder of Dongyu Gatsal Ling nunnery that is re-claiming the lost *Togdenma* yogini lineage
- Peter Rutter, M.D., Jungian psychiatrist, leading authority and author of several books on sexual harassment and exploitation
- Pat McCabe, a leading Diné (Navajo) elder; provides an indigenous perspective on gender reconciliation, and the urgent need to rebalance the feminine and masculine
- Sr. Lucy Kurien, founder, Maher Ashram, which has established 63 homes across India for rehabilitating battered women and children
- Nozizwe Madlala-Routledge, former Deputy Minister of Health, Deputy Minister of Defence, and Deputy Speaker of Parliament, South Africa
- Stuart Sovatsky, Ph.D., yogi, psychotherapist, and former professor, author of several books on gender, sexuality, and spirituality
- Jenny Wade, Ph.D., researcher, professor, and author of books on transcendent sexuality, and transpersonal psychology
- Mark Greene, author of *Remaking Manhood, The Little #MeToo Book for Men*, and consultant on relational practices, diversity/inclusion and masculinities
- Ken Kitatani, Director General, ICEED, United Nations Environment Programme, Board member of U.N. Committee of NGOs.

PART I

Untold Stories Keep Gender Oppression Invisible: Breaking Thousands of Years of Silence in Thirty Years

CHAPTER 1

Oases of Truth and Reconciliation: Three Decades of Gender Healing

The Beloved is with those whose hearts are broken for the sake of the Beloved.
—Sufi saying

"Can a woman become enlightened?" asked the bright, aspiring student with keen enthusiasm. Her shining eyes revealed her heart's exuberant passion for spiritual realization. This burning desire had led her to northern India, where she had joined the exiled Buddhist community that had fled Tibet to escape Chinese persecution.

"No," came the solemn reply from the wizened senior lama. He was one of the most venerated masters in the Tibetan Buddhist tradition, and his sonorous voice imparted a commanding authority and measured calm. "A woman can advance to a very high spiritual stage, just prior to enlightenment," he continued in deep resonant tones. "Then she must die and be reborn as a man, in order to attain enlightenment."

Why? wondered the young woman inwardly, her crestfallen heart sinking rapidly with profound disappointment. She reluctantly accepted the answer from the wise old lama with quiet resignation. She had no choice: the lama's spiritual integrity, depth, and authority were beyond question. He was a highly revered teacher whose very presence exuded profound qualities of deep wisdom and compassion, qualities to which her yearning heart ardently aspired. She could even feel his compassion for her tragic plight, as a woman aspiring for the impossible. The very word for "woman" in the Tibetan language means literally "lesser birth."

But why must a human being be a man in order to become spiritually enlightened? She continued to puzzle over the question, deeply in fact, for many years. The more she pondered the question, the less sense it made. She tried to rationalize it, comforting herself with the thought that the enlightened state is beyond all reason and sense of mind, so perhaps this deep truth could only be realized after a woman dies and is reborn a man and becomes enlightened herself—er... *himself*! Or perhaps it's like a Zen koan, she mused, something that transcends all logic and mental comprehension altogether. Meanwhile, like the other Tibetan nuns, she was relegated to cooking, cleaning, and supporting the monks. But the question would not let her rest, and she continued to wrestle with it for years, from many different angles.

She found another lama who initiated her into the esoteric practices of Tibetan Buddhist meditation. Her sincerity and depth of commitment led her to move into a cave, high in the Himalayas at thirteen-thousand feet, where she lived alone for twelve years. There she meditated for twelve hours every day, spending a total of more than fifty-two thousand hours in meditation. Profound depths of spiritual and mystical consciousness were awakened within her. Over those twelve years, she almost died twice, first when her cave was sealed shut in a huge snowstorm, but she was able to dig herself out. The second time was from a large falling rock. She was sitting quietly when suddenly she heard an inner voice say, "Move." When she did not respond immediately, the voice repeated itself urgently. "Move, *now*!" She moved, and a gigantic boulder suddenly fell exactly where she had been sitting.

But the voice was silent on other matters, such as her dilemma of being a woman striving in vain for spiritual enlightenment. Her commitment to spiritual realization was absolute. Yet she could not attain the ultimate goal. Why? Because she was a woman. Not because she was perhaps insufficiently pure of heart. Not because she was maybe not committed deeply enough, or insufficiently disciplined in her meditation practice. Not because she was imperfect in her austerity or aspiration or prayers—all of which were plausible reasons she could readily accept and understand. But because she was a woman. She carried her dilemma into deep meditation. Yet, unlike other quandaries or issues that she took inward into deep contemplation, this one did not resolve itself. The situation did not become ever clearer and self-evident. Instead it became all the more bewildering and confusing. The more she pondered it, the more befuddled it became—even ludicrous. The bottom line boiled down to a simple, ridiculous question that posed itself in her mind starkly: *What is so spiritually special about a penis that it is impossible to become enlightened without one?*

Finally, one day she had the opportunity to ask her question of other senior lamas. She had come down from the mountain after twelve years in meditation, having achieved something that few senior lamas had ever done. Indeed, her intensive solo retreat high in a mountain cave for twelve years was something all the lamas had been convinced was impossible for any woman to accomplish. She was now afforded tremendous respect among the leaders of the Tibetan Buddhist tradition. At one point, she was invited to a high-level meeting of many of the highest lamas in the tradition. She was the only woman present.

There she again asked the same question: "Can a woman become enlightened?" And again, three of the senior lamas told her, "No." So she asked them to please go into meditation, and in all seriousness to ponder this question in earnest: *Why is it that a woman cannot attain enlightenment? In particular, what exactly is it that is so spiritually special about the male reproductive organs that it is impossible to become enlightened without them?*

The three lamas went away and duly meditated upon the question for several days. Then they came back and told her, "We do not know." The woman gazed intently at each lama in turn, searching for any further clues or insights. None were forthcoming.

"We could not discover the answer," they concluded.

"Ah, yes," she responded, "and this is because it isn't true." She then announced to these senior lamas that she was making a firm commitment to continue to incarnate in female form until she became a fully enlightened buddha in a woman's body.

This is the true story of Jetsunma Tenzin Palmo, a Tibetan Buddhist nun born in Britain who still lives in northern India today, where she runs a nunnery she founded to train Tibetan nuns in the esoteric Buddhist practices that have been denied women for more than a thousand years. Tenzin Palmo's Dongyu Gatsal Ling Nunnery, together with a few other pioneering projects, is reversing centuries of patriarchal precedent in Tibetan Buddhism. And the nunnery has received the blessing of the Dalai Lama, who, by the way, has told Tenzin Palmo that a woman can indeed become enlightened.

Essence of Gender Equity and Reconciliation

The foregoing anecdote reveals, in its bare essentials, the nature of gender healing and reconciliation between women and men, and people of diverse gender identities. In essence, the process is simple: women and men gather together—on equal terms, in integrity, dropping the usual conditioned denials, taboos, and excuses—and jointly explore the truth of their gendered experiences, vulnerabilities, conditionings, violations, insights, and aspirations. Through this process, they make discoveries together and allow new awareness to dawn. These new revelations change them, as they embrace whatever healing is required and take full responsibility for the consequences of whatever is jointly discovered and experienced. When this work is conducted with integrity and sensitivity by even a small number of people, the resulting benefits are not for them alone, but also filter back into the community to benefit the larger society.

While Tenzin Palmo's story is charming, almost whimsical, and certainly comical in hindsight, living through those challenging years was very real and deeply painful for her. She was denied the transformative esoteric practices of Tibetan Buddhism—one of the most profound and beautiful schools of spiritual wisdom in human history—simply because she was a woman. Those were the loneliest years of her life, far lonelier than her extended solitude in the cave. Meanwhile, the Tibetan people—men and women alike—had never questioned the gender inequity in their tradition because for them it was based on the "reality" of who women and men are. Yet, it was sheer illusion, sitting right there at the core of a tradition committed to dispelling illusions—and for many centuries this illusion had unjustly denied Tibetan women, and especially Tibetan nuns, their spiritual birthright.

Neither Jetsunma Tenzin Palmo nor the lamas could have achieved this breakthrough on their own. They needed each other. She needed sincere, well-intentioned male lamas to whom to pose the question. The lamas needed her to ask the question in earnest in order for them to even embark upon the inquiry. She further needed the men to respond with integrity, and they did so—thereby honoring her and upholding the spiritual principles of their tradition. Together, Tenzin Palmo and these few lamas achieved a profound breakthrough—not only (or even primarily) for themselves, but for the Tibetan people and the entire Vajrayana Buddhist tradition, as women are admitted into the ranks of spiritual mastery. This breakthrough has helped change the Tibetan Buddhist tradition forever.

Of course, in other cases of gender reconciliation the process can and usually does look very different, depending on the circumstances. It may entail cathartic emotional releases, or powerful dynamic energies coming into play, or the profound spiritual grace that pours forth at times. But the process is basically the same: women and men—inclusive of sexual orientation and gender identities—join together as equals, speak their gendered truth, and are thereby mutually liberated and transformed.

Oasis of Truth: The Need for a New Forum for Women and Men

The forum that Jetsunma Tenzin Palmo was finally afforded—a context in which she was taken seriously and where she could ask the unaskable questions—is something that every human being longs for: an oasis of truth where the deep questions can be asked in earnest and where one can drink directly from the wellsprings of truth, free of the conditioned responses and cultural thought forms that shape and distort so much of our experience of being human. In the case of gender, such an oasis would be a forum in which people of all genders can gather in integrity, raise challenging questions about gender and sexuality, discuss the undiscussable, and allow healing and reconciliation to unfold naturally. Societies everywhere need just such a forum—yet virtually nowhere does it exist. Even in spiritual communities or groups or similar contexts where we might expect such an open forum to be present, frequently there are taboos on speaking openly about gender issues and dynamics, particularly in cases where the leadership may be engaged in gender power dynamics or sexual activities that are kept hidden from view.

Gender equity and reconciliation work seeks to provide this needed forum—an oasis of truth and reconciliation in which issues relating to gender and sexuality can be addressed openly and honestly by people of all genders. Every voice is welcome in this work. We often use the abbreviated traditional terms "men" and "women" (irrespective of sexual orientation) for people who identify within these categories. For people of other gender identities, we recognize that the landscape of gender identity, expression, and sexual orientation is constantly shifting and evolving, as are the associated terminologies, and this has resulted in a wide range of increasingly varied and complex acronyms in recent years. In this book we follow a recent trend toward simplification, by adopting the acronym LGBTQ+ to represent lesbian, gay, bisexual, transgender, queer, plus *all* other gender identities and gender expressions. In places where greater specificity is required, the appropriate specific term will be used, but otherwise the acronym LGBTQ+ is understood throughout this book to include the above gender identities as well as intersexed, asexual, questioning, ally, genderqueer, demisexual, pansexual, non-binary, two-spirit, and all other existing and future gender identities and expressions.

The purpose of Gender Equity and Reconciliation work is to provide a forum where real stories can be told, from the heart, in uncensored detail, and be truly heard. It is a forum that is not limited to dialogue alone but also navigates the psychic terrain that opens through asking the deep questions—and embraces the tears, outrage, embarrassment, anguish, shame, absurdity, as well as forgiveness, compassion, and spiritual grace that all come forth in their innate wisdom. A place where the heart can melt or soar as needed, and the human spirit can triumph through the trials and tribulation of thousands of years of gender oppression and injustice.

Such a forum is needed in every culture across the globe. It must go beyond mere verbal exchange and conceptual understanding into a place of mutuality, compassion, forgiveness, and communion. This book documents a concerted initiative in this direction over three decades that has produced remarkable results, and points to the need for much wider implementation of such work.

Gender Equity and Reconciliation International Project

To begin creating a forum for gender healing and reconciliation, the authors and various colleagues founded a project originally called Gender Reconciliation, focused on the healing and reconciliation of gender-based conflict and injustice, and hosted by the Satyana Institute, a nonprofit service organization based in

Colorado and Washington. The process was founded on universal principles of love and forgiveness, and the methodology integrates a broad mix of modalities, including psychological and therapeutic techniques, contemplative disciplines, experiential exercises, and transpersonal and spiritual approaches. This integral methodology has proven vital to the success of the work. To limit gender healing to cognitive or dialogical modalities alone would tend to derail the process and preclude a deeper, transformative process.

During the first 15 years of this project (1992-2007), over 40 intensive events were convened to delve into gender reconciliation, most of which were 5-day intensive residential workshops. These gatherings provided a unique forum for women and men to jointly confront the realities of gender disharmony and engage in constructive dialogue and healing work on some of the most divisive and seemingly intractable gender issues. The process was found to work equally well both in affluent Western countries and in many other countries across a diverse cultural and economic spectrum.

Over the past 19 years (2007-2026) since the first edition of this book was published, the Gender Reconciliation project has expanded at least tenfold, spread across 22 countries, and its name was changed to Gender Equity and Reconciliation International (GERI). More than 375 intensive workshops and trainings have been conducted to date, serving more than 10,000 people. Another 24,000 people have been introduced to GERI in conferences and introductory workshops. The professional training component of the project has also expanded greatly, and there are now approximately 330 certified GERI facilitators around the world. Specialized programs have also been developed to serve specific segments of the population, particularly LGBTQ+ communities and BIPOC communities (Black, Indigenous, and People of Color). This book describes in detail the results from these GERI programs conducted over three decades on six continents, with a specific focus on results in different regions of the world, and for different segments of the population.

The fundamental premise underlying GERI work is that women *and* men, and people of all gender identities, suffer the effects of gender injustice, and that each needs the other for a true and complete healing and reconciliation. Although major strides forward have been taken by the women's, men's, and LGBTQ+ movements in the past several decades, no group working alone can create full gender balance in society. The genders must work together for this balance to be realized, collaborating in courageous new forms of experimental and transformative modalities. A whole new approach is needed that goes beyond the more traditional methods of social and political reform.

In this book, we sometimes use the abbreviated term "Gender Reconciliation" to refer to this particular form of healing and reconciliation work in the Gender Equity and Reconciliation program. The international organization that delivers this work is Gender Equity and Reconciliation International, often denoted by its acronym: GERI. Several other organizations are also authorized or licensed to deliver this work in various countries. As explained in the Introduction, the methodology of Gender Reconciliation was inspired by and modeled after the principles of truth and reconciliation applied by Archbishop Desmond Tutu in the Truth and Reconciliation Commission of South Africa. The term "Gender Reconciliation" can potentially be interpreted in a variety of ways, and may have different meanings in other contexts. Sometimes when people hear this term they assume it has to do with reconciling conflicts about personal gender identity, but this is not what is intended here. For this reason, to minimize confusion, the name of our program was later changed to Gender Equity and Reconciliation. Nevertheless, we still often use the term "gender reconciliation" as a shorthand way to refer to the particular form of cross-gender healing work described in this book.

The purpose of GERI, or gender reconciliation, is to transform the roots of gender imbalance at multiple levels: within the individual, in interpersonal relationships, and in the larger society. Gender reconciliation seeks to provide a safe and skillfully facilitated forum where women and men, and people of all gender identities, can jointly examine the subtle knots of cultural conditioning around gender and sexuality, support each other in healing the roots of negative gender dynamics, and address the associated inequities and injustices in the world. In carefully designed and facilitated group process exercises, issues rarely discussed aloud are openly shared and collectively addressed. The process entails the power of mindful, heartfelt truth-telling in community coupled with the mysterious grace of loving witness, forgiveness, and compassionate presence to facilitate deep healing and reconciliation.

The gender issues and dynamics that arise in GERI programs are nothing new in themselves. Gender injustice is age-old and universal, and the key issues have been frequently addressed in women's and men's groups, LGBTQ+ groups, and social justice and diversity and intersectional groups of all kinds—typically working in relative isolation from each other—as they strive to bring greater consciousness to the hidden gender injustices of our society. The separation of women's groups and men's groups was historically necessary because authentic gender healing work could not have begun in any other way, and indeed this work continues to be important today. For example, the importance of separate women's and men's support groups was highlighted yet again by the #MeToo movement.

Nevertheless, the time has come to take a next step: to forge creative new ways for men and women, and people of all gender identities, to collaborate *together* on mutual gender healing.

Powerful new dimensions of transformative work between women and men become possible when difficult gender issues are confronted with integrity and sensitivity in mixed groups. To our knowledge, the work reported in this book represents one of the very few organized, sustained efforts in collaborative gender healing with women and men working together.

Earlier examples of gender healing work that bore some relation to our work, although utilizing quite different methods, are summarized in the first edition of this book.[1] Riane Eisler and David Loye pioneered what they call the "partnership" model for gender relations in their book *The Partnership Way*.[2] Beyond these, there are innumerable popular books on gender and intimate relationships, most of which are less directly relevant to our work. Other books or projects relevant to various aspects of our work will be cited as we proceed.

Theories of Gender and the Heart of Gendered Experience

The work reported in this book is practical and experiential in nature, rather than analytical or theoretical, and the results are applicable in a wide range of theoretical or philosophical contexts. Theories abound about the nature of gender differences, and of course these theories often contradict each other. For the present work, although we value this spectrum of perspectives, it matters little which theoretical, philosophical, or spiritual perspective the reader holds about the nature of gender, or related questions. Individuals and communities from vastly diverse philosophical backgrounds have found deep meaning and value from the insights and transformations they experienced through the GERI process. As the reader will discover, what transpires in the events reported in this book does not depend for its validity on any particular philosophical perspective, theory of gender, or spiritual orientation. For this work, what is more important than any particular perspective or intellectual framework is the sincerity of each individual's heart, and the willingness to enter deeply into a process of personal and collective truth-telling, discovery, and transformation.

Casualties in the "Gender War"

While this book presents an optimistic and positive message, it is nevertheless important to begin by acknowledging the extremely painful manifestations of gender injustice in our society today. Although many of us are familiar with the realities of gender violence, it is instructive to review a few of the sobering statistics, focusing in particular on the distinct ways in which different subgroups of the population are afflicted.

Women's Gender-Trauma Statistics

- In the United States, a woman is raped or sexually assaulted every minute—usually by a friend or acquaintance. One out of every five women is a victim of rape in her lifetime. Worldwide, 40 to 60 percent of sexual assaults are committed against girls fifteen years of age or younger, regardless of region or culture.
- Domestic violence is the leading cause of injury and death to women between the ages of 15 and 44 worldwide. At least one out of every three women and girls worldwide has been beaten or sexually abused in her lifetime (WHO). These rates are highest in Sub-Saharan Africa, Southern Asia, and Oceania, where UN statistics indicate 33 to 51 percent of women have experienced intimate partner violence.[3] Over half of all female murder victims are killed by their intimate partners, according to the Centers for Disease Control and Prevention.[4]
- "Honor killings" by male family members claim the lives of five thousand girls and women in Hindu, Middle Eastern and Asian cultures every year.[5]
- Each year in India, over five thousand women are doused in kerosene and set ablaze by their husbands or in-laws.[6] These heinous "bride burning" murders are often dismissed as kitchen accidents by a patriarchal justice system.
- In the United States, nearly twice as many women as men suffer from depression each year.[7]
- Teen pregnancies have risen sharply in Africa during the Covid-19 pandemic. This is attributed to the closure of schools and drop-in crisis centers during pandemic lockdowns.[8] Furthermore, the pandemic has significantly impacted child marriage. As UNICEF notes, "Over the next decade, up to 10 million more girls will be at risk of becoming child brides as a result of the pandemic." This number is in addition to the "100 million girls at risk of becoming child brides before the pandemic began."[9]

Men's Gender-Trauma Statistics

- The victims of men's violence are mostly other men, accounting for 80 percent of male violence.
- Men commit suicide about four times more often than women.
- In the United States, more than 6 million men suffer from depression each year.[10] Male depression more often goes unrecognized and untreated.
- In 2021, the Boy Scouts of America reached a $850 million settlement with more than 60,000 men who sued the iconic institution over alleged sexual abuse over several decades.[11] In 2007, the Boy Scouts of America had first revealed its secret archives on sexually abusive scout leaders, exposing a vast history of pedophilia that required the dismissal of at least 5,100 scout leaders since 1946.
- Among teenagers, males account for fully 90 percent of completed suicides,

a statistic that speaks volumes about the pressures on young men coming of age.

- Men have higher death rates than women for all 15 leading causes of death.
- Men account for 60 percent of traffic fatalities, 79 percent of murder victims, 95 percent of workplace fatalities, and 99.993 percent of deaths in armed combat.
- In the U.S., the average life span for men is five years shorter than for women, and seven years shorter globally.[12] Male stress is the decisive factor.

Lesbian-Gay-Bisexual-Transgender-Queer+ Trauma Statistics

- LGBTQ+ people experience about four times more violence than non-LGBTQ+ people, and they are twice as likely to have mental health issues.[13] Over 16 percent of hate crimes are based on sexual orientation.[14]
- In 16 U.S. cities, reported incidents of violence against LGBTQ+ individuals recently increased by an average 242 percent over a single year. Incidents of further harassment and abuse of LGBTQ+ victims by police increased by 155 percent over the same period (NCAVP study).
- In some 77 countries, discriminatory laws criminalize private, consensual same-sex relationships—exposing individuals to the risk of arrest, prosecution, imprisonment, and in at least five countries, the death penalty (U.N. Free and Equal Campaign).[15]

Black, Indigenous, and People of Color (BIPOC) Trauma Statistics

- Domestic violence is higher in BIPOC communities.[16] Women of color experience about twice as much domestic violence as white women.
- 60 percent of Black girls are sexually abused before their 18th birthday.[17]
- Native Americans experience more than twice the rate of sexual violence in other racial groups. Over 84 percent of Native American women have experienced violence in their lives.[18]
- In 2019, Black males were twice as likely to die from gun violence than white males in the U.S.[19]
- In the U.S., roughly 32 percent of multiracial men, 23 percent Native American men, 19.4 percent of Black men, 18.5 percent of Hispanic men, and 9.4 percent of Asian/Pacific Islander men (compared with 16.5 percent of white men) experience sexual violence in their lifetime, according to the CDC's National Intimate Partner and Sexual Violence Survey 2010-2012.[20]

These statistics reflect grim social realities of gender injustice and associated human rights violations. In societies across the globe, people of both sexes and every gender identity and race and ethnicity are boxed into narrowly defined roles, and in most countries there are strong reprisals for those who dare to step beyond these rigid restrictions. These pressures inevitably produce widespread self- and gender conflict, which takes an incalculable toll on all societies. Even in the West, despite the supposed emancipation of the feminine, there are strong cultural forces and pressures that favor men and uphold masculine values. Western societies are far from gender balanced, and the pretense that they are is one of the obstacles to making further headway.

Domestic Misery: The Iceberg Underlying Domestic and Intimate Partner Violence

Terrorism is a widely publicized threat in many countries of the world today. Yet, this danger is miniscule compared to the daily terrorism of domestic violence and intimate partner violence, which plagues at least one in three households across the globe. In the United States today, for example, the public is traumatized by the huge increase in mass shootings, or potential threats from terrorists whether foreign or domestic. Yet in purely statistical terms, most citizens have a far greater chance of being murdered or attacked by their own intimate partners or family members than by a terrorist or anonymous mass-shooter. Where is the public outrage about this? How are people mobilizing to ameliorate this more urgent threat that claims far more lives every year?

The Covid-19 pandemic of the early 2020s exacerbated this already urgent crisis, with major spikes in domestic violence reported across the globe, plus increased difficulty in accessing help for victims. In a U.N. gender equality survey of 13 countries, 7 out of 10 women reported that domestic violence increased in their community since the pandemic began, a phenomenon dubbed the "Shadow Pandemic."[21] In South Africa, President Cyril Ramaphosa likened the increased Gender Based Violence (GBV) and domestic violence in that country to a "second pandemic."[22]

In any war, the wounded far outnumber the dead. Whatever number of people are killed, there are always many more who are wounded, usually by a factor of ten or more. And the wounded are yet again far outnumbered by those who are psychologically damaged or stricken. Moreover, it is well known that cases of domestic and intimate-partner violence are vastly under-reported. A U.S. study conducted by the Bureau of Justice Statistics in 2017 estimated that 40 percent of domestic violence incidents go unreported to police.[23]

Consider what all this means for the "gender war" of domestic violence. As reflected in the statistics above, domestic violence is the leading cause of murder for women in the United States. Similar patterns hold in most other countries across the globe. Tragic as they are, these deaths are only the most severe casualties in the gender conflict. Beyond these "war dead," there are many thousands or millions more who are wounded and injured every year through physical and sexual abuse perpetrated by those who supposedly love them most. And quite beyond these "wounded" are many more millions, or rather billions, who are psychologically damaged, depressed, stricken—living under oppressive or threatening conditions in their own homes and communities. Thus, massive numbers of people are suffering deeply in their closest intimate and family relationships.

What we call domestic violence is but the tip of an iceberg of vast suffering that afflicts billions—a phenomenon that could be called "domestic misery." Precisely in those relationships where one is supposed to feel the most loved and accepted, many people are the most miserable and vulnerable—all across the globe. Much of this domestic misery is created and sustained by dysfunctional relations between women and men, or between heterosexual and LGBTQ+ family members—often held in place by oppressive gender, social, and religious conditioning within the society from which its hapless victims know not how to escape.

This vast collective misery is then projected outward, which fuels corresponding forms of misery and oppression in social institutions and in relations among nations. It is a cliché, but true, that "peace begins at home." Yet "home" is precisely where billions experience no true peace whatsoever. As Mahatma Gandhi emphasized, if we practice love and nonviolence in the outer world but we don't manifest these principles in our daily home life, then any success in the outer world is a chimera. This is confirmed anecdotally in our work in multiple countries and cultures, where we frequently hear exasperated comments or reflections from astute local professionals. "Costa Rica has no military," a professor in San Jose remarked to us, "but there is a war in every household." A Japanese social activist told us something almost identical, "Japan is a peaceful country, but there is a gender war in every home."

What all this points to is a global crisis in "right relations" of such gigantic proportions it is almost inconceivable. This crisis cries out for a massive societal response, yet compared to the magnitude of the suffering involved, it still receives woefully inadequate attention. Domestic and gender-based violence are continuing to devastate our communities, and although this is more widely recognized than it was 10 or 20 years ago, many people still live in relative oblivion or denial about this—like living next to a gigantic mountain that is so huge everyone takes it for granted, and barely even notices it.

Hidden Truths Keep Oppression Invisible—and Intact

A major factor that helps keep all this domestic misery firmly in place is not talking about it. Individuals, families, and society collude to keep this stupendous suffering well hidden. For example, a key lesson borne out for the authors from years of facilitating gender reconciliation work is that there exist large and crucial gaps in women's awareness of men, and in men's awareness of women. These gaps in mutual awareness are kept in place by all manner of taboos and forbidden topics of conversation or inquiry in society—especially in mixed company, but also within each gender grouping. As a result, men do not realize the depth and nature of the suffering endured by women, nor do women realize the nature and depth of men's suffering, nor do heterosexuals realize the nature and extent of suffering in LGBTQ+ populations.

Although this situation has improved significantly in recent years, due largely to initiatives such as the #MeToo movement and growing awareness of LGBTQ+ rights, there is still a *long* way to go. Women generally do not grasp the devastating pain and incapacitation that boys and men suffer as they are conditioned to become "real men": how their emotions are denied them, how their inner sensitivities are bludgeoned in masculine competition, how their sexuality is brutalized and desacralized through masculine conditioning—be it in the schoolyard, the family, the church, the military, or the workplace. Nor do men realize the magnitude of women's and girls' suffering in relation to the incessant threat (or experience) of rape, physical abuse, and psychological violence; the denial of girls' and women's authentic voices and intuitive powers; the oppressive conditioning around female beauty; fears around body image; the painful realities of sexual harassment and the glass ceiling in the workplace—to name a few. In all societies, despite the awakenings and breakthroughs of #MeToo, both women and men remain powerfully conditioned to repress the daily realities of these experiences and to collude with the rest of society in keeping these dimensions of shared experience hidden. Similar patterns apply in relation to the suffering of LGBTQ+ populations, to which the heterosexual population is often completely oblivious.

Yet it is precisely in bringing courageous and compassionate light to these taboo arenas that deep healing and transformation of social gender conditioning can take place. As the Rev. Dr. Martin Luther King, Jr. emphasized, social change does not happen by keeping corruption and injustice hidden, but rather by bringing darkness into the light and confronting it with the power of love. No matter how challenging the ensuing process may become at times, the inner light and love in the human heart always has the power to dispel darkness and ignorance. The process calls forth—indeed *demands*—the highest from the human heart, which for lack of a better term we can call "divine consciousness," something that dwells deeply within every human being regardless of race, culture, or religious heritage. This divine consciousness manifests as the awakening of a universal love, the *agape* that transcends all human weakness, darkness, and obscurity. Gender healing and reconciliation consciously invokes this universal love of the heart, which in the end has the capacity to overcome the very real and formidable challenges of gender oppression and injustice that have tormented human societies for literally thousands of years.

If "pessimism concerning human nature is not balanced by an optimism concerning divine nature," observed Martin Luther King, Jr., then we "overlook the cure of grace."[24] The power of love invokes this grace, which in turn facilitates deep healing and fosters authentic social transformation and change. Without conscious cultivation of love, the grace does not come, and the social change does not last. Although Martin Luther King, Jr. spoke of this process in Judeo-Christian terms, precisely the same process is described in Hindu terms by the twin principles of *ahimsa* and *satyagraha*, articulated by Mahatma Gandhi. Gandhi emphasized that *ahimsa* and *satyagraha* confer a "matchless and universal power" upon those who practice them. Similarly, the Buddha taught that: "Hatred never ceases by hatred, but by love alone. This is an ancient and universal law."[25] The GERI work draws upon these universal spiritual principles, which are found in every faith tradition. As such, our work draws from all spiritual traditions, and is not beholden to any one tradition. This spiritual orientation is addressed more fully below and in later chapters.

The Outer and Inner Alchemy of Gender Reconciliation

How is the power of this universal love activated and invoked in practice? We draw upon the ancient tradition of alchemy to describe how healing and transformation take place in the gender reconciliation process. Alchemy has long been discredited and mischaracterized in contemporary Western societies as an arcane physical science that sought to turn lead into gold. Yet the deeper significance of alchemy has little to do with physical transformation, and is instead a spiritual process in which the "lead" of the human psyche—the inner darkness and repressed "poisons" lodged in the mind and heart (called *prima materia*)—are confronted directly and transmuted into the golden light of love. As the thirteenth-century Persian mystical poet Rumi puts it, "When the dross of the false self burns, it becomes part of the light." Alchemy refers to this process, which operates by the unfathomable power of love. This process has long been known by spiritual masters in various traditions, yet only relatively recently, through the work of pioneers such as Carl Jung, has alchemy been recognized in the West as having any legitimacy. Traditionally, alchemy refers to a process of spiritual transformation that takes place within an individual. As Sufi teacher and Jungian scholar Llewellyn Vaughan-Lee describes the process, the divine light or spark of the soul is directed to areas of blocked awareness or unconsciousness within the individual. As the light of the soul is directed inward, it illuminates and eventually dispels the darkness within. At first this process brings to conscious awareness what has been repressed and pushed away. This is often quite a painful and humbling process, because it typically unmasks a large amount of repugnant "shadow" material in the consciousness of the individual. Yet deep within this very darkness dwells an innate light, which Jung termed the *lumen natura*. As the alchemical process continues, this latent inner light is awakened, and over time it completely transforms the individual into a being of light. Although greatly oversimplified in this description, in essence the darkness within is transmuted into light and love. This is the *inner alchemy* of spiritual transformation.

In gender reconciliation work, an analogous process of *outer alchemy* takes place on a collective or community level. We gather in a diverse group—as women and men, for example—and after setting the context and creating a safe space for the work, we begin by skillfully exploring arenas that are usually avoided or unacknowledged in relation to participants' experiences of gender in their lives. We confront the collective darkness in our society in relation to gender conditioning, sexuality, and the oppression of the feminine that has predominated since antiquity. The process is initially painful, which is why it is usually avoided in our society or, if entered, rarely carried beyond this stage. In gender healing work we keep going and continue to examine key issues directly and openly, without flinching, yet with compassion, as men and women together. In so doing we bring the light of our personal and social consciousness to dark corridors of human pain that have long been neglected and suppressed. As the process continues, something remarkable eventually begins to happen. There is an awakening of a new light, an unexpected healing energy and grace that arises in some form. This is surprising to many participants because often, just when it appears that the group is beginning to tread the most intractable or hopeless territory, seemingly beyond our limited capacity to embrace, there is an infusion of healing presence and grace that suffuses each person with love and opens the door to new pathways together as a group. This ushers in powerful group experiences of healing, reconciliation, and forgiveness that constitute the "gold" of this collective alchemy.

This process of outer (or "collective") alchemy takes some time to understand and must be witnessed repeatedly to be understood deeply. Although it takes place within a group and includes a strong element of healing, it is fundamentally different from a collective psychological process such as group therapy. In group therapy, the therapist is a trained professional who holds clinical authority in the group and works with each individual as the group process unfolds. The role of the therapist is, in part, to point out what needs healing in each individual and to be the "expert" on each person's process.

In gender reconciliation work, if there is a "therapist" present at all, it is the group wisdom itself. When someone bares their soul before the rest of the group or community, it is not the role of the facilitators or other participants to analyze that person's story or experience. Rather, the story is witnessed and received by everyone in the group, which often precipitates some further opening or sharing from others in the group. The process then evolves organically within the group, building a synergistic momentum that may unfold in any number of creative directions. Over time, as trust builds in the community, the personal disclosures and stories begin to unmask ever more vulnerable truths or hidden secrets, and as the community attends to these, the alchemical nature of the process begins to unveil itself. From within the inevitable darkness and distress, light begins to shine forth.

This bears similarity to a process the Sufis call "light upon light," in which the inner light of the soul is met and amplified by a corresponding light from the Divine. The Indian sage Sri Aurobindo describes this same process in his Integral Yoga, where the grace of spiritual aspiration stretching "upward" from the human heart is met and greatly amplified by a spiritual grace that "descends" from the Divine plane. In gender reconciliation work, this process takes place within a group or community rather than in one person's interior spiritual journey.

As people turn the light of collective attention toward their interior vulnerabilities and hidden secrets, the initial shock and outrage they may feel soon dissolves into a deep, abiding comfort that comes with facing truth directly. Then a sense of the *real* begins to take hold, and people are comforted and even nurtured by this unmasked truth far more than they are scandalized by whatever disclosed secrets or illusions are unveiled, most of which they already knew deep down in their hearts anyway. The power of the work comes through this alchemical process in which the darkness is transmuted into light, and the energy that was trapped in maintaining rigid social strictures and toxic cultural conditioning becomes freed up and released.

This alchemical process characterizes truth and reconciliation work in groups generally, but it is especially intensified when working with gender issues. This is because in gender and sexuality the intimacy of the heart is involved as well as the body and mind. Wrapped up in gender is the longing of the human heart for love and intimacy, embracing all levels, from the desire for a beloved partner to universal forms of love for God or the Divine.

The *outer alchemy* reconciles polarities and differences among human beings, and unites them in a 'beloved community' of mutual compassion, trust, and philial love. The *inner alchemy* reconciles polarities within the individual human being, which ultimately leads to transcendent union with the Divine Source (by whatever name or concept is conceived). In short, outer alchemy creates beloved community, and inner alchemy creates communion with the Beloved. These two alchemies intersect in the depths of the heart, which becomes the foundation for the total transformation and liberation of humanity.

Although this might sound implausibly idealistic, it is actually how love functions. Love flows from the heart of the divine Source into the heart of every human being, and sustains and nurtures each person. Depending on how open and attuned the heart is, love flows out from the human being to other humans and other living beings. As Rumi expresses this transformation, we step out of the sphere of time, and into the sphere of love. This 'sphere of love' operates both outwardly (beloved community) and inwardly (divine love). This is how we are intended to live, and it is also *why* we exist. Human beings are created to be instruments of love, to nourish and engage with all of life.

Masculine, Feminine, and Gender

Because we are a community of authors working in multiple cultures and social and psychological contexts, we hold a diversity of perspectives and philosophies relating not only to gender, but also other dimensions of life. We also hold diverse spiritual beliefs and commitments, and we span a broad spectrum of experiences and backgrounds in relation to gender and sexuality. We don't necessarily agree on all aspects of the contemporary gender conversation, which is dynamic and rapidly shifting at this time.

Nevertheless, we do hold certain basic convictions in common, and perhaps the most important is the deep need today for creating special forums in which people can safely share the deep truths of their hearts in relation to gender and sexuality, and be truly heard and met with compassion. This is foundational.

In the course of our gender reconciliation work we strive to maintain an open mind to the intrinsic value inherent in all spiritual and philosophical perspectives; our work is practical and does not seek to advance any particular theoretical or spiritual position. We acknowledge the complementarity of masculine and feminine archetypes and principles, more as a spectrum than a duality, and that masculine and feminine principles or qualities dwell together in every human being. A corollary of this perspective is that a dynamic balance between masculine and feminine principles and qualities is necessary for a healthy functioning person, relationship, or society. When there is a systematic imbalance between masculine and feminine, as has been the case in Western culture for more than three millennia, profound social malaise is the inevitable result, and this is the condition we find our society in today.

A healthy balance between masculine and feminine dimensions of life is fluid and dynamic, rather than fixed and static. At times the masculine principle prevails, at other times the feminine principle prevails, and the two energies are mutually interpenetrating (masculine) and mutually inter-receptive (feminine) in their eternal dance. Esoterically, masculine and feminine energies are linked together in the abandon of a profound love, rather than a struggle for power. Exoterically, the dynamic balance of feminine and masculine manifests at multiple levels simultaneously: from the innermost solitude of the individual, to the family and community, and on up through the broadest domains of culture and civilization. Just as a bird can fly only by using both wings in a coordinated, dynamic *balance*, humanity can soar to its highest potential and live in lasting peace only when a harmonious balance between feminine and masculine is fully realized.

Our work has focused extensively on creating forums for people who identify as women and men, irrespective of sexual orientation. GERI programs attract people of diverse sexual orientations and gender identities, including lesbian, gay, bisexual, transgender, and queer persons (LGBTQ+). We value all of these diverse gender identities and sexual orientations, as addressed more fully in later chapters. In recent years we have found it helpful to develop multiple forms of our programming, to better meet the specific needs of diverse communities. Currently GERI has three primary program areas; one for people who mostly identify as men or women (inclusive of sexual orientations), another for LGBTQ+ persons, especially those who identify as gender fluid or queer or otherwise outside the traditional "gender binary," and a third for BIPOC communities (Black, Indigenous, and People of Color). The boundaries between these programs are not rigid, and participants choose which program feels most appropriate for their needs.

The purpose of our gender reconciliation work has not been to analyze or theorize about the nature of gender differences, but rather to convene forums in which women and men, and people of all genders, can enter into a deep exploration of and openhearted communication about their experiences of gender and sexuality, and to move from this foundation through creative dynamic interaction to a place of mutual healing, forgiveness, and reconciliation. The core of this work is the inner work of the heart, which transcends sexual orientation, gender identity, body identification, and lifestyle and philosophical differences. The "inner alchemy" of the heart transcends all such categories.

The Need for Change

It almost goes without saying that the work reported in this book is just a beginning step. The need for gender healing and reconciliation is vast and multidimensional, extending to virtually every human society across the globe. The key issues of gender imbalance and injustice in individuals and society are deep, ancient, and complex, reaching to archetypal proportions that span all cultures and eras throughout human history. While acknowledging the magnitude of the daunting challenge, this book outlines an initial, admittedly humble, step that can be taken toward this larger goal of social and cultural healing between the genders. Although it is impossible to know exactly how such a comprehensive healing might eventually unfold, we do believe the approach and methodology documented in this book offer a skillful place to begin.

Collective Healing of Gender Injustice

No human being escapes the affliction of cultural gender conditioning and associated injustice. It is so pervasive that it is often taken for granted and assumed to be a normal and inevitable part of life. Most people are at least vaguely aware that our society tends to value the masculine over the feminine, with its many correlates of rational over intuitive, heterosexual over LGBTQ+, and other lopsided values. Yet few of us are aware of how powerfully this imbalance shapes our personal, family, and social realities daily. After thousands of years of structural injustice related to gender and sexuality, the level of systemic healing and transformation required to properly address this cultural imbalance can only be done in the collective—in the society from which it has emerged. Our culture cannot thrive, nor even *survive* longterm, unless a profound balance of masculine and feminine is restored. As the Diné (Navajo) elder Pat McCabe (Woman Stands Shining) emphasizes in her brilliant indigenous teaching on gender reconciliation (p. 165): the ancient cultures warn us that earlier indigenous civilizations were destroyed because "Men's Nation" and "Women's Nation" believed they could live without each other.

However, because no forum or vehicle exists for the multidimensional reconciliation of masculine and feminine values in our culture, this burden falls inadvertently upon every marriage and intimate partnership, as well as every professional or interpersonal relationship. These avenues are of course woefully inadequate to the task, through no fault of their own. In the privacy of every intimate couple's bedroom, for example, the entire archetypal history and drama of the "battle of the sexes" is present. Every couple is saddled with a burden they can barely discern or comprehend, much less transform on their own. Having little or no direct awareness of this collective human pain, the couple nevertheless experiences its power and negative impact. Typically, they do not recognize when the conflicts and tensions arising between them have little or nothing to do with their personal lives but rather are a manifestation of this collective human pain being channeled through them.

To escape from the pressure of this isolation, the burden of gender healing needs to be placed back where it belongs —in the collective, with women and men and people of all genders working together in conscious community to foster the necessary healing. The possibility of such collective healing holds tremendous transformative power that remains untapped. Our society is thus called to embark upon a new venture of systemic cultural gender healing and transformation. After decades of separate women's, men's, and LGBTQ+ movements—valuable though they have been—another step is urgently needed: the time has come for women and men to band together to jointly create gender harmony. We must gather in mixed groups to plumb new depths of relational awareness, courageous truth-telling, compassionate listening, empathic sensitivity, and mutual healing. This form of gender work is almost entirely absent in our society, even in progressive social change movements and otherwise highly conscious spiritual communities. Yet there is a powerful yearning on the part of women and men of all sexual orientations—many of whom have done years of work in separate women's or men's groups—to now take this next step.

Reconciliation: Moving Beyond Conflict Resolution

There is a growing body of literature today in the emerging field of reconciliation, which is becoming recognized as a crucial step beyond conflict resolution. Detailed review of this literature is beyond the scope of this book, but a few summary observations are appropriate.

Reconciliation is a step beyond the domain of conflict resolution, which, as traditionally defined and practiced, is increasingly recognized as inadequate for creating true healing, harmony, and effective community in arenas where there has been longstanding conflict. Reconciliation recognizes that a deeper level of community healing and bonding work is required that goes beyond agreements and resolutions between adversaries. An altogether different kind of leadership is required to create pathways for relationships to flourish, and to heal wounds so as to support mutual growth between parties that have traditionally been in conflict.

A phenomenon reported in the reconciliation literature is that the leaders in this new field are rarely the same leaders who prevailed during processes of negotiation and conflict resolution. We have observed a parallel phenomenon in the field of gender reconciliation. Leadership in gender reconciliation is not necessarily coming primarily from leaders in the women's, or men's, or LGBTQ+ movements, as might be expected at first blush. Rather, the leadership is coming from small groups of people who are moving beyond the frameworks and agendas of these movements, and embarking upon an unprecedented level of healing and reconciliation across the gender categories. These pioneering individuals are not interested in mere conflict resolution, nor in winning concessions from the "other side," but rather in building an altogether new level of integrity and harmony between women and men, and across all genders, that will one day enable humanity to reclaim the magic of a unified "Beloved Community." The term "Beloved Community" was coined by Josiah Royce and popularized by Dr. Martin Luther King, Jr., and refers to a new human civilization that creates peace and justice for all. As King said, "Our goal is to create a beloved community and this will require a qualitative change in our souls, as well as a quantitative change in our lives."[26]

Emerging leaders in reconciliation frequently have a strong commitment to spiritual transformation in their personal and professional lives and to manifesting an inclusive vision of social harmony for all. They are striving for practical unity and oneness within the entire human family—across all divisions of gender, race, religion, nation, creed, and class. In short, they align closely with Archbishop Desmond Tutu's insistence that "We are ONE human family." The principles of Truth and Reconciliation applied to gender were foundational to our intention and methodology from the outset, and this has remained consistent over the 34 years of this project. In 2013 and 2014, we were blessed to meet with Archbishop Tutu several times, and he formally endorsed our methodology and initiated a collaborative partnership with our GERI project and Stellenbosch University. We were introduced to him by his daughter, Rev. Mpho Tutu van Furth, who had attended our GERI programs in Cape Town.

Just as the TRC in South Africa was underpinned by potent religious principles, so the Gender Equity and Reconciliation work is grounded in spiritual principles of a universal nonsectarian nature, with a similar goal of fostering deep healing and reconciliation that creates a fresh beginning and transcends the conflict and divisions of the past.

Working with Shifting Sexual Orientations and Gender Identities

Traditional gender identities and sexual orientations are being profoundly questioned and widely deconstructed today, particularly among younger generations in Western societies. Within a few short decades, the cultural dominance of heterosexuality has come under increasing scrutiny and criticism, and many societies across the globe have embraced a greater level of acceptance of diverse sexual orientations and LGBTQ+ persons.

These sweeping changes have made a major contribution to dismantling some of the most destructive forms of gender conditioning. Alternatives to the traditional rigid masculine and feminine gender roles are emerging, giving people greater freedom to express their uniqueness and explore new forms of gender identity and sexuality beyond heterosexual norms and constricted conceptualizations of gender. As a result, there is a vibrant "queer revolution" happening today. Simultaneously, there is also a "masculinity revolution" happening, as men are increasingly recognizing and breaking out of the narrow "Man Box" of traditional male socialization, which has forced men to deny key parts of their humanity. There is also a "femininity revolution" continuing to happen, as women continue their struggle for justice and equality, and the entire culture embraces feminine values more fully. This multifaceted gender revolution is gradually freeing the entire human population from the stranglehold of rigid roles and rules of the gender orthodoxy that has dominated human societies for millennia.

Over the years, we have worked with participants spanning a vast array of sexual orientations and gender identities, although the majority of our clientele have identified as heterosexual women and men. We have always welcomed LGBTQ+ individuals to our programs. In our first yearlong professional training program in gender reconciliation, which began in 2001, 11 out of 33 trainees identified as LGBT. This provided deep contributions to the development of GERI which have continued to grow over the years. The GERI certified facilitators today include numerous LGBTQ+ facilitators.

The dynamics within a gender-diverse group have the potential to become a source of creative tension within the group, and if properly handled, this can serve to move all participants into a powerful experience of awakening, healing, and transformative learning. In most GERI gatherings that have combined heterosexual and LGBTQ+ participants, a profound level of gender healing work has resulted that would not have occurred in the same way had the group not been so diverse. At the same time, it has also been important to develop specialized GERI programs to meet the unique needs of different groups and populations, including the LGBTQ+ community for which our dedicated program is described in Chapter 10.

Spiritual Basis of Gender Reconciliation

Our work regards the spiritual dimensions of human consciousness and society as fundamental to gender healing and reconciliation. This commitment is not rooted in any particular religious ideology or spiritual philosophy. Rather, we seek to invoke universal spiritual values that are not tied to any particular tradition, but which underpin all authentic spiritual traditions. Such an inclusive perspective is becoming increasingly recognized as vital to the understanding of spiritual consciousness in human society. It represents what is sometimes called "the perennial philosophy," "interfaith spirituality," "integral spirituality," or "ageless wisdom"—terms that refer to a broad synthesis of universal truths in cross-cultural spiritual wisdom. Such a synthesis of the world's wisdom traditions is certainly not new, but is today slowly gaining a much wider recognition as vital to awakening a deep and urgently needed level of global consciousness and human unity. This is another aspect of our work that Archbishop Desmond Tutu resonated with, and he gave his endorsement and blessing to our "Dawn of Interspirituality" series of conferences on multi-faith spirituality which we organized in 2013 and in 2018.

This book is not a theoretical volume, and our purpose is not to argue for any philosophical or spiritual framework over another. We simply draw upon the primacy of Spirit in human consciousness as reflected throughout the world's wisdom traditions, and affirm that for authentic gender reconciliation to take place—whether on the individual, family, societal, or cultural level—it is essential to include the spiritual dimension of human consciousness. Without consciously taking account of Spirit and invoking this transformative dimension of human existence, the dilemma of gender disharmony and injustice—which has afflicted human societies across the globe for thousands of years—will never be resolved. Psychological, social, and political reforms alone, although essential, will not suffice.

In our work, we draw upon many different spiritual traditions and practices, applying them as appropriate to our task of cultivating the domain of gender reconciliation. All cultures and societies—from the most ancient to the most industrial or the most esoteric—have grappled with the polarity and complementarity of masculine and feminine, and each has contributed important insights and practices. We draw on specific contributions from different traditions and perspectives as appropriate, including, for example: silent meditation practices (such as Vipassana meditation), the yin-yang duality of Taoism, the lover/Beloved of Sufism, the male-female divinity and esoteric wisdom of Hindu and Buddhist traditions, Judeo-Christian mystical symbolism, the Divine Feminine across the religions and Goddess traditions, and the indigenous Native American traditions, including the tradition of two-spirit persons (third or fourth genders).

Certain archetypal representations of masculine and feminine polarity are relevant in gender reconciliation work, such as the half-male/half-female deity of Ardhanarishvara in Hindu mysticism, the *conjunctio oppositorum* of alchemy, the Christian tradition of bridal mysticism, the rich symbolism of the *Mahabharata* in Hindu mythology, Mother Earth and Father Sky in indigenous wisdom, the complementarity of *ejiwapo* (balanced twoness) in Yoruba, the tree of life in the Jewish Kabbalah, the Gnostic gospels' representations of male and female, the *heiros gamos* (sacred marriage), and the tantric union of male and female deities in Hinduism and Vajrayana Buddhism. Recognizing that spiritual wisdom itself evolves, we do not limit ourselves to these codified traditions alone, because new insights are emerging all the time.

In this process, we invoke specific insights or archetypes at points where they emerge through the work naturally, but we are careful never to impose any particular perspective. Our goal is not to propose a definitive universal model of the spiritual dimensions of masculine and feminine across different cultural traditions and contexts. On the contrary, we sense that, ultimately, feminine and masculine aspects of existence are portals to a larger mystery whose deepest roots are utterly sacred and far beyond any capacity for expression in conceptual models or archetypal frameworks. Thus, "gender" is but a doorway to a vast inner universe of ultimate relationships between oneness and duality, manifest and divine, being and nonbeing, temporal and eternal. Just as in Taoism, the *real* secret of yin-yang is neither yin nor yang, but their profound union, which transcends both.

We have found that this eclectic spiritual approach works well in practice, but we invoke this inclusive pluralism without making a dogma of such a model or framework. "All models are wrong, but some are useful," as the saying goes. We draw upon universal models as potentially insightful frameworks, but we do not impose them as a set of universal truths that must be accepted before the work of gender reconciliation can begin.

Gender reconciliation work is not for everyone. It requires a willingness to be open and vulnerable. As one colleague said to us wryly with a sheepish grin, "I'd sooner lie down naked in a pit of scorpions than do gender reconciliation work." Yet for those who are ready for it, the process is profoundly liberating and transformative.

Our work in gender reconciliation has been hands-on and experiential, not theoretical or conceptual. Participants do not require a common spiritual framework to embark upon gender reconciliation work together. We have worked equally comfortably with staunch Catholics, Protestants, Evangelical Christians, devout Muslims, Zen meditators, Hindus and Buddhists, secular humanists, Western scientists, clergy of various denominations, New Age visionaries, atheists, as well as with groups that mix all of these up together. The gender conditioning we have all experienced cuts across these categories, and unites us in a common humanity, with a common work to be done together. From this foundation, gender healing and reconciliation work proceeds naturally.

For participants who do not have a strong spiritual background or orientation, gender reconciliation work can sometimes serve as a natural pathway to awakening spiritual insight. To give an example, when a community of women and men explore gender dynamics together, contradictory truths and perceptions often emerge—both across the sexes and within each sex grouping. Such moments of apparent impasse provide significant opportunities for breakthrough. As Blaise Pascal says, "The heart has reasons of which reason has no knowledge." As the community stays with the uncomfortable tension of contradiction, individuals begin to perceive the truth of "the other" as their own experience, and the polarities of conflicting positions often dissolve into an unexpected emergence of a deeper underlying unity: a profound recognition that, ultimately, there is no "other." We are all one. This remarkable realization occurs not infrequently in the course of gender reconciliation work—as a direct perception, rather than as a mere concept or philosophical principle. Thus the heart of gender reconciliation serves as a powerful vehicle for awakening transformative insights and experiences of human unity.

Widespread Implementation and Testing of GERI

This book documents a 30-year initiative. Only a fraction of the many experiences and stories can be included here, for obvious space reasons. We have sought to choose representative examples, to span the breadth and depth of what we have experienced. Much of this material is presented in summary form in Parts Two and Three of the book, which include diverse examples and stories of gender challenges and experiences that have arisen in GERI programs over the years. These accounts speak to diverse gendered experiences and circumstances that people have encountered, and how GERI helps them transform themselves and these conditions. A number of these accounts exhibit broad similarities, which in itself is an important finding from our work.

As outlined in the Introduction, the book is structured in five parts. To reiterate briefly: Part I (Chapters 1 – 9) provides a first-hand experiential overview of the GERI process, almost as if the reader was in the room (or online), taking part in a GERI program. Parts Two and Three address the broad applications of GERI: Part II (Chapters 10-16) explores implementation of GERI in diverse sectors (politics, religion, corporations, NGOs, etc.) and Part III (Chapters 17-23) documents applications of GERI in different regions and countries of the world. Part IV (Chapter 24) summarizes two research studies on GERI, and Part V (Chapters 25-26) covers the GERI professional training program, and the major conclusions from this 30-year initiative.

Taken as a whole, we have observed two key patterns that seem to be demonstrated phenomenologically in our work over 30 years:

First, gender dysfunctions are "alive and *un*well" in very similar ways across all the different societies and cultures in which we have worked around the world, *and* across the many different sectors *within* each society and culture. Broadly interpreted, this suggests that across the globe, people everywhere are living the same (or very similar) gender-dysfunctional nightmares. This is not to deny important differences across cultures, particularly in the nature and severity of the 'symptoms' of gender injustice in different cultures. Nevertheless, gender injustice and its social dysfunctions are basically universal, and operate strongly even in societies that regard themselves as more progressive and advanced.

Second, the methodology of GERI is yielding remarkably similar results of breakthrough and transformative experiences—across all these cultures and sectors. In making this observation, we are not suggesting that GERI is the *only* way this could happen, or that it is a comprehensive solution to the many facets of gender injustice. Nevertheless, we do affirm that the basic methodology and unique contribution of GERI—convening circles for deep truth-telling and healing in community

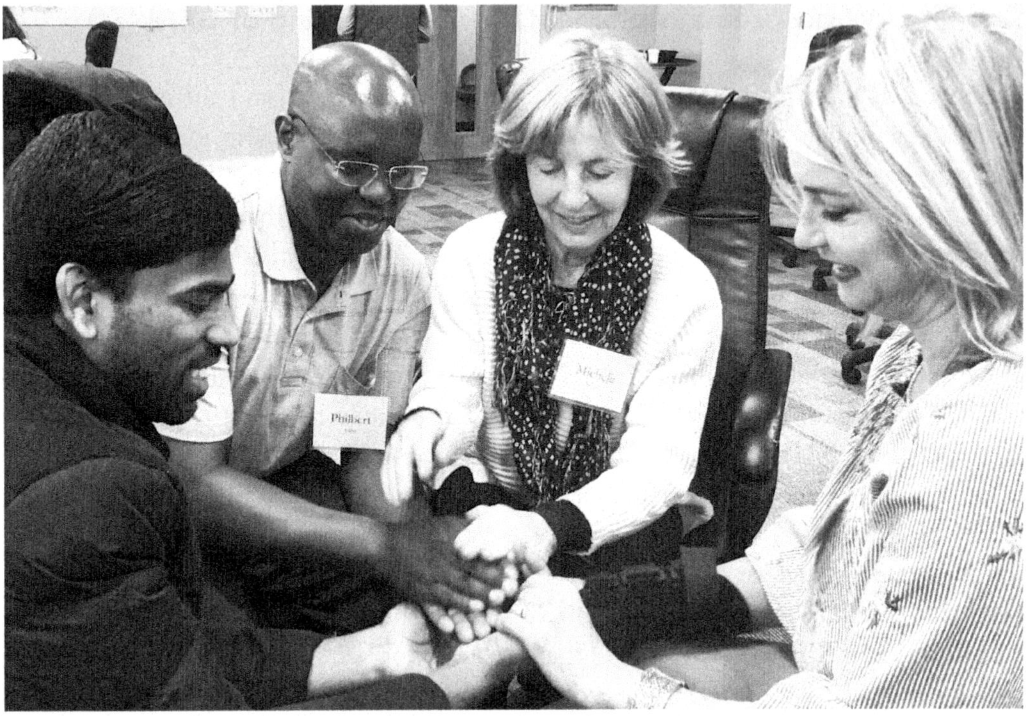

GERI workshop outside Boston, Massachusetts, 2018

across the gender divisions of society—has profound beneficial impacts that have the potential to transform and rejuvenate human communities everywhere.

These results were not a foregone conclusion. The GERI model had to be tested widely to determine whether it was effective or not, and if so, whether it was transferable to diverse contexts and cultures. For this purpose, it has been essential to implement the GERI work in a broad range of countries, and in various sectors and demographic segments of society, to assess how it performed in each case. This careful testing was all the more important given the intricate nature of this particular work, because it enters directly into one of the most delicate, intimate, vulnerable, and potentially volatile domains of human experience: gender injustice and gender relations in society, which go to the very depths of human experience.

This explains why this book is necessarily detailed, and provides so many examples from different countries and sectors, some of which may seem repetitive at times, particularly in Parts II and III of the book. Yet this repetition is actually *replication* of the efficacy of this approach, and demonstrates the consistency and robust effectiveness of the GERI methodology for transforming gender injustice.

It might well have happened that the GERI methods worked well in some countries but not in others, or in some sectors or demographics, but not in others. If so, that would have been an important finding in itself. But this has not been our experience. The fact that such similar transformative experiences have emerged from such widely diverse cultures and demographics is itself a key discovery of the GERI initiative over 30 years.

Let us now enter into this work by invoking a prayer from the great mystical poet Jnaneswar:

I honor the God and the Goddess,
The eternal parents of the Universe . . .
What beauty! Both are made of the same nectar,
And share the same food.

Out of Supreme Love,
They swallow each other up,
But separate again,
For the joy of being two.

They are not completely the same,
But neither are they different.
None can tell exactly what they are.

How sweet is their love!
The entire universe is too small to contain them,
Yet they live happily together
In the tiniest particle,
and in the heart of every being.
They dwell together,
Both wearing a garment of light.
From the beginning of time they have been together
Reveling in their own Supreme Love . . .[27]

CHAPTER 2

Cultivating Compassion: Principles of Gender Equity and Reconciliation

When you make the two into one, and when you make the male and female into a single one, so that the male will not be male nor the female be female, then shall you enter the Kingdom of Heaven. —Gospel of Thomas (Logion 22)

In the Jain spiritual tradition there is a parable about a man who becomes very ill. His wife cares for him diligently, the doctor gives him medicine, and family members visit, showering him with loving attention. In spite of all this, he gets worse and worse. Then one day he experiences a powerful opening in his heart to the presence of God, and when this happens, he is healed. As he quickly recovers, all those who cared for him feel vindicated that their loving ministrations finally succeeded. The doctor smiles confidently in the conviction that his medicine has been effective, and the wife rests assured that the healthy food and loving massage she gave her husband are responsible for his recovery. Yet all of them are mistaken in attributing the healing to themselves. The man's inward opening to the presence of Spirit actually created the healing.

This parable underscores the essence of healing, which is intrinsically mysterious to our cognitive minds. We do not know how healing "works." It is quite beyond our rational capacity to understand. We cannot direct it, yet we can participate in its unfolding. We may develop certain theories about it, and we can learn to recognize various aspects of the process and ways to support it, but, in practice, the most we can actually *do* is to align ourselves with the deeper wisdom of the healing process. We invite and invoke and support the healing process, and then it inevitably takes its own course.

Just as a physical wound knows how to heal itself, so too the human psyche instinctively knows how to heal itself. This principle is foundational to gender reconciliation work, and perhaps to all healing work, as it reflects the existence of a larger force or mystery that is responsible for healing. Our task in gender reconciliation work is to allow this mysterious healing process to unfold in its own organic, natural manner—and to be directed *by* it rather than attempting to direct it.

The metaphor of a physical wound is apt. When we get a cut or laceration, we keep it clean and covered to keep the dirt out. The wound then heals of its own accord; we don't do the healing ourselves. We could not even begin to tell the blood vessels how to reconnect, or the skin how to regenerate itself. The most we can do is create an environment conducive for the healing to take place. Our bodies, not our minds, know internally what to do to heal.

The process of healing the human psyche is much the same. We do not have to consciously understand all the subtle intricacies of the healing process in order to participate effectively in it. Nor can we consciously direct the healing in the way we are accustomed to orchestrating or managing other endeavors. The invisible fuel for this healing process is our heartfelt compassion and loving presence and the sincerity of the collective intention that we bring to it.

Principles of Gender Reconciliation

Five foundational themes have arisen over the years in our work with gender reconciliation—key understandings that have emerged through observation and experience. These ideas ground the philosophical underpinnings of the work and motivate its practical application. All five reflect basic principles or patterns we've witnessed repeatedly, or aspects that have emerged frequently in 30 years of working with thousands of women and men and LGBTQ+ people of many different cultures, ages, and countries.Taken together, these five principles contribute to our emerging perspective about working together across the genders, and the manner in which the overall process of gender reconciliation unfolds. We offer these principles here, not as definitive truths or axioms, but rather as guidelines gleaned from years of engagement in the rich domain of gender reconciliation.

1. *Transforming the cultural foundations of gender imbalance is best done in groups or communities.*

Because gender disharmony is a cultural affliction or intergenerational trauma that affects the entire collective consciousness of humanity, gender reconciliation is necessarily collective healing work. To find genuine resolutions to gender challenges, we must seek solutions at their root, within the collective social and cultural context from which those challenges have emerged. Gender reconciliation asks participants not only to consider their individual experience but also to align with collective energies and work with the diversity and range of perspectives that each individual brings to the group. Working in groups and communities, participants find that their boundaries begin to expand outward from the personal dimension, to embrace a collective synergy and energetic spaciousness. When gender issues are introduced into this context, individuals begin to realize that many of the gender challenges they struggle with are systemic: hidden forces operating in the collective that are quite beyond their own personal failings or understandings. For many, this is a major revelation—a shocking realization of the extent to which they have been socialized and conditioned at every stage of life, from earliest childhood onward.

In today's world, when we encounter challenging gender dynamics in personal relationships, we generally seek to resolve these struggles on a personal or interpersonal level. We reflect on our personal issues and failures, or we focus on the limitations of our partners and friends, or we may go into couple's therapy. All this has its place, of course, yet in so doing, we often collapse the situation into the private and the personal sphere, giving insufficient attention to the fact that we are all profoundly impacted by social and cultural conditioning in relation to gender. This conditioning is so ubiquitous and longstanding that we often take it for granted, and are hardly aware that it exists.

No one escapes gender conditioning. Most of us unwittingly carry the cultural gender trauma into our important relationships, and we end up in struggles with our partners, family members, friends, and colleagues that aren't really about us as individuals. When women and men do gender reconciliation work in community, they begin to see the power of this cultural baggage in a new light. They realize the prevalence of overarching social patterns and conditioning in much of their experience, and comprehend that, in this larger context, they are not alone in what happened to them. This is a profound realization that has to be embraced holistically. It is not enough to understand it cognitively; it must be experienced emotionally, physically, and psychically. It must become wisdom of the heart. Gender reconciliation potentially allows each individual to see in a deeper way just how great a disservice their cultural conditioning has been.

Another key reason that gender reconciliation work is best done in groups or communities is that communities are the fertile ground for the coming era of humanity's awakening. As noted earlier, Zen master Thich Nhat Hanh has said that the next Buddha will come not as an individual but in the form of a community—a group of people living together in loving kindness and mindful awareness. Many contemporary mystics are echoing this view, including Sufi teacher Llewellyn Vaughan-Lee, who says there is a new divine energy coming into humanity that will operate only in communities and groups, and the "rules" for spiritual awakening have changed. Communities are now fundamental vehicles for that awakening.

Indeed, humans have reached a point where different forms of synergistic cooperation may be the only way to survive. This awareness points to the need for us to join in community and discover together the ways in which the collective gender shadow, or intergenerational gender trauma, has made itself manifest. Gender reconciliation work, and the power of our collective intention, create a crucible for catalyzing the necessary transformative healing in the entire human community.

2. *A spiritual foundation is essential for gender reconciliation.*

Gender imbalance is, at its root, a collective spiritual crisis. Hence, spiritual principles and practices, universal and nonsectarian, are essential to transforming gender relations. By "spiritual foundation" or "divine consciousness," we simply mean recognition of the existence of some form of larger presence or higher wisdom that is fundamental to all life and existence. It is something beyond what the mind can comprehend directly, but this makes it no less real. No matter how it is named—whether we call it God or Goddess, the Divine, Tao, Spirit, or simply the Universe—there is an essential mystery of consciousness, creative genius, and universal love that permeates all of existence. In gender reconciliation work, this ineffable mystery is consciously invoked and embraced, and we rely upon and align ourselves with it.

Every religious tradition affirms some version of this mystery. There is something "out there" or "in here" that is omnipresent and all powerful, and which must be our guide if we are to be instruments for the transformation of the unhealthy dynamics at play in our species. If we ignore this hidden mystery and depend solely on our own intelligence, skills, and intellectual resources, our vision is myopic and our work is rendered ineffective or incomplete.

A striking contemporary formulation of this universal consciousness or wisdom is given in the work of the Snowmass Conference, a pioneering group of spiritual leaders from nine major world religions. Convened by the late Benedictine monk Fr. Thomas Keating, this group met annually over a period of 32 years and was comprised of leaders from diverse religions, including Protestant, Catholic, Eastern Orthodox, Islamic, Jewish, Native American, Hindu, Theravadan Buddhist, and Tibetan Buddhist. This group created a list of eight points of universal agreement shared by all. The first of these points is the existence of an Ultimate Reality to which different names are given in various traditions, but which cannot be limited by any name or concept and which is the source of the infinite potentiality and actualization of all humanity and existence. The seventh point is that human suffering, ignorance, weakness, and illusion are the direct result of our experiencing the human condition as *separate* from this Ultimate Reality.[1]

Thomas Berry reiterated this principle, stating that in order to grapple effectively with the destructive conditions that are engulfing the planet we must "lean on the Universe." This is another way of saying, "Not my will but Thy will," or in nontheistic traditions "not following personal desires but the *Dharma*"—which requires surrender to the larger wisdom of the forces that gave rise to all existence. This same truth is found across all spiritual traditions; we must invoke and take refuge in the supreme reality, whether it is called the Dharmakaya, the Great Spirit, the Divine Mother, or Universal Love, or any other name. There is an Ultimate Reality beyond the human being that we must embrace if we are going to find our way to genuine healing or positive change that will endure.

This is not to say that agnostics, atheists, and others who consider themselves "nonspiritual" cannot participate in or benefit from gender reconciliation work. Indeed, the work itself generally entails an opening of the heart, which speaks in its own language to a deeper universal experience. Keating's Snowmass conference affirmed in the final point of agreement that, "Ultimate Reality may be experienced not only through religious practices, but also through nature, art, human relationships, and service to others." Gender reconciliation is a form of training that begins by moving individuals out of their own self identifications and into a kind of empathic connection with "otherness," and from there eventually into an experience of Oneness. In many traditions, a practice of "formative community" can facilitate initiatory experiences of deep insight or awakening, and this is frequently experienced in the work of gender reconciliation.

Lasting harmony across the genders cannot be achieved through social, psychological, or political reform alone. These modes are certainly valuable and necessary for realizing gender equality in society, but they are not sufficient in themselves because gender reconciliation entails an inherent spiritual dimension. Gender disharmony is vast and pervasive; its symptoms are manifest in myriad ways in virtually every culture across the globe. For authentic gender reconciliation, we aspire to a comprehensive approach that includes but also transcends traditional modes of social change, invoking a larger universal intelligence or grace. For this, we must consciously place ourselves in relationship to that larger wisdom.

In the Gospel there is a parable about a sick woman who reaches out as Christ walks by, and she touches the hem of his robe. He spins around and says, "Who touched me? Power has gone out of me." Trembling, the woman acknowledges her action—and, in fact, she is healed. Her action, her faith, and her conviction—not the robe of Jesus—brought about her healing, which was beyond her capacity but within her reach.

When we convene a group for gender healing and reconciliation, we are collectively taking similar action. We stretch ourselves to a larger consciousness and ineffable grace that is *beyond our capacity, but within our reach*. This action and experience is related to what mystics speak of in referring to union with the Divine: an annihilation of self in which the "I" is dissolved altogether and merged into a higher experiential unity. All true healers know that when healing unfolds at its best, there is no egoistic self that does the work; rather it is simply being done, as the spirit or Divine moving on earth. In gender reconciliation groups, we collectively reach for an unknown power or grace that has a healing potential far beyond our own capabilities or understanding. We invite this power and presence, knowing from experience that something transcendent and universal can and does work through us and it dwarfs our own mechanisms for healing, thinking, fixing, and/or reconstructing what needs to be healed. As with all spiritual healing, the gender wound of humanity will one day heal not because we know how to fix it, but through its own mysterious capacity, coupled with our collective intent, consent, and openness to the process.

3. *"Gender" represents a vast spectrum of personal, social, and collective identities and expressions that are rapidly shifting today across the globe. It is essential that equal value be placed on different gender perspectives and identities. Gender is in turn interconnected with intersectionalities of race, culture, ethnicity, and other diversities.*

"Gender" and "sex" are not the same, and gender identity is distinct from sexual orientation and gender expression. Gender identities are expanding in many contemporary societies beyond the fixed, binary categories of male and female. Gender identities, sexual orientations, and gender expressions are becoming increasingly diverse and complex, and are classified into multiple categories including but not limited to: heterosexual, lesbian, gay, bisexual, transgender, queer, cisgender, intersex, asexual, non-binary, gender fluid, two spirit, and more. Communities of gender identity are thus diverse and complex—each one having its own specific needs. We honor them all, and every human being has a voice in the larger emerging gender conversation. For an overview of some of the key current issues in the ever-shifting gender landscape, see the Appendix.

Given this rich diversity, we respect the needs and concerns of different gender identities and communities. While the Gender Equity and Reconciliation work evolved originally from working with people who identify as men and women, inclusive of all sexual orientations, this has expanded into multiple program areas, each designed to serve the needs of particular groups and communities. Our signature program continues to focus primarily on healing between women and men, inclusive of all sexual orientations. While people of all gender identities are welcome to join and participate in this program, it emphasizes the experiences of women and men, and the reconciliation of relations across the sexes. Another of our program areas, "LGBTQ+ Healing Across the Gender Spectrum" is a specialized form of the GERI process held by LGBTQ+ GERI facilitators that creates an intimate and unique space designed to support LGBTQ+ participants of all gender identities and expressions in unpacking and exploring sensitive issues of gender and sexuality (details in Chapter 10). A third specialized GERI program area is designed specifically for Black, Indigenous, and People of Color (BIPOC) communities (details in Chapter 11). GERI's leadership team and certified facilitators include a diversity of gender identities, sexual orientations, races, cultures, and ethnicities.

In gender reconciliation work, it is crucial to maintain a dynamic balance between the masculine and feminine perspectives and to avoid any systematic bias toward either. All people are afflicted by gender injustice, and we each need the other for true and complete healing. The work requires that we embrace difference and "hold the tension of opposites," which supports the emergence of a deeper unitive truth and/or a transformational breakthrough. This is the "outer alchemy" of reconciliation. It means giving equal support to fundamentally different or opposing views in a collective container, so the alchemy of opposites can work its creative magic. Indeed, diverse gender perspectives make for synergistic depth and clarity, creating something that neither perspective could accomplish on its own. As physicist Neils Bohr has expressed this principle, "The opposite of a profound truth is often another profound truth."

Still, a bias toward either a masculine or feminine perspective can creep into this work. Much has been done in the past several decades to articulate an essential feminist critique of our culture, yet this critique can inadvertently leave us failing to recognize the damage that has also been done to men. We have often seen reflected in our gender workshops the impasse that currently exists between the women's, men's, and LGBTQ+ movements. Each side demands to be heard by the other; then, not feeling heard, each side reiterates the same points again and again. To break through this impasse, it is helpful if each group can clear its collective mind of its own gender-focused bias or agenda and listen deeply to receive the other.

Too often, when engaging in dialogue across the genders, the result is merely cognitive exchanges of information, heard by each "side" through the filters of its own gender lens and conditioning, and often dismissed without being truly received. When women and men or people of diverse gender identities listen with the heart, however, a liberating or cleansing process comes about in the collective, and a transformative current begins to move through the various parties and into the dialogue.

In personal development and spiritual work, awareness of one's own "shadow" is essential to the process, serving as grist for the mill of transformation. In the same way, a collective awareness of the gender shadow is grist for the mill of gender reconciliation. It is essential that we look at this shadow directly, without denial or defensive posturing. It is vital that we learn to listen to each other in a deep and authentic way. To do so we must look together at what each of us carries in our collective shadow and examine the parts of ourselves that we don't necessarily want to share. If we can create forums where such sharing is possible, in an atmosphere free of judgment and blame, we can then begin to create the conditions for a collective transformation around gender consciousness that our culture urgently needs.

Every human being embodies both masculine and feminine qualities. To be whole, each person must ultimately create a balanced integration of these qualities that is unique to her- or him- or themself. As Jung and many others have emphasized, every individual integrates a combination of personal qualities drawn from a broad spectrum ranging from the "essential" masculine to the "essential" feminine. And because each individual integrates masculine and feminine characteristics differently, a rich diversity and collective power emerges in a group or community of people that brings these multiple combinations into dynamic synergy. When these qualities are well integrated and balanced in any human being, the result is a dramatic rise in empowerment, creativity, and well-being.

As Gerda Lerner has pointed out, "when we see with one eye, our vision is limited in range and devoid of depth." Just as visual acuity and depth are achieved by combining the information coming through both of our eyes, so depth of human experience arises from synthesizing the gifts of both masculine and feminine qualities.

4. The process of gender reconciliation requires the fullness of our humanity—integrating physical, emotional, intellectual, and spiritual dimensions—to create the conditions for genuine transformation.

If any essential aspect of our humanity is omitted in gender reconciliation work, the resulting transformation will be neither authentic nor lasting. Our society often ignores or sidesteps challenging truths, dilemmas, or difficult emotional expressions when they arise. Entire institutions are created to formalize and reify these omissions. Our religious institutions frequently deny the physical or sexual dimension in an attempt to "transcend" this "lower" part of ourselves. Our academic and political systems tend to downplay our intuitive or spiritual faculties in a quest to be "rational" or scientific. Many social institutions tend to inhibit our emotional and artistic expression and often systematically suppress the uniqueness of each human being. This is equally true of gender conditioning, which often tends to restrict our full potential and creative expression in various ways, sometimes over- or de-emphasizing certain aspects of our being.

This socialized repression helps to keep structural gender injustice and imbalances in place. As a corrective, we must develop constructive ways to give full voice and expression to the spectrum of responses associated with our gendered experience, including the challenging emotions of anger, grief, fear, sorrow, shame, despair, and vulnerability. Indeed, a critical aspect of gender work is skillful facilitation of intense emotional process. This means embracing our humanity in its own experiential currency, and not rationalizing, repressing, sublimating, or denying the emotional or less "tidy" parts of ourselves.

Over the years, we have encountered numerous attempts at gender healing work that limit their methodology to dialogical or cognitive modalities alone. We have found that restricting the work in this way often derails the process entirely. For example, two psychotherapist colleagues, a man and a woman, had each been running separate men's and women's groups for several years. The two colleagues decided to initiate a gender reconciliation process for their clients by combining their two groups. After only two meetings, and a classic gender confrontation, the project came to an abrupt end. What happened? At the first meeting, one of the men told one of the women that she had beautiful hands. The woman felt objectified, rather than seen for who she really was. The man felt he was innocently reaching out in sincerity to give an innocuous compliment to the woman. A verbal exchange between the two spread into the larger group and rapidly escalated into a heated conflict that divided the group along gender lines and was left unresolved. The same discord arose again in the second meeting, and the ensuing dialogue deteriorated into a gridlock from which the group simply could not recover, despite the genuine goodwill that had brought the two groups together. The organizers felt they had no choice but to abandon the project altogether. From our perspective, this outcome was the result of the process being limited to dialogue and verbal exchange. The tensions that were triggered in the mixed group required a deeper level of processing that could not be reached through words alone.

To take another example: one of the authors (Will Keepin) once attended a workshop on Bohmian dialogue led by Lee Nichol, a skilled facilitator who presented dialogue workshops all over the United States and abroad. Developed by physicist David Bohm, Bohmian dialogue is a powerful method designed to support collective inquiry and creative communication in groups. One of its foundational principles is that there is never a prescribed agenda for the dialogue—the focus of the conversation must be free to go wherever the group takes it. After the workshop, Will asked Nichol if he ever intervened on the content or topic of the conversation, rather than merely on process. Nichol replied that there is only one area in which he does intervene: the "man/woman issue." As Nichol explained, this is the one issue with the capacity—if not the tendency—to draw the group into a destructive quagmire in which the dialogue process itself breaks down.

This anecdote hints at two telling realizations: first, that to explore the "man-woman issue" is precisely what many groups need to do in order to discover a whole new level of group consciousness and depth of experience; and second, that dialogue alone is not an adequate methodology to work with gender issues in a group.

In gender reconciliation work there are times when powerful emotional expression and releases of various kinds are necessary. To inhibit them is to obstruct or block the reconciliation process. There are other times when contemplative silence, group meditation or prayer, breathwork, psychodrama, spontaneous ritual, or other forms of nonverbal group work are essential to the skillful resolution of what arises in the process. Throughout this book we describe some of the practices we have employed that go beyond the cognitive and verbal levels to help free up the psychic and energetic blockages that inevitably surface in gender healing work.

The need for nonverbal forms of group process and facilitation applies not only to creating a safe space for the release of challenging emotions but also to allowing the presence of ecstatic dimensions of consciousness. These aspects of the work can be tremendously healing and arise in ways that are often quite startling to those who have little experience in deep group-process work. Indeed, a primary motivation for insisting on appropriate experiential avenues for processing challenging emotional energies is not for their own sake alone but also because, in so doing, we simultaneously create the possibility for the expression of highly benevolent emotional and spiritual energies, which often follow naturally on the heels of deep emotional-release work. Such positive energies can manifest in a variety of ways, including richly moving or inspiring forms of creative, artistic, or ecstatic expression. It is not enough simply to tell inspiring stories or read beautiful poems celebrating the qualities of the masculine and feminine and their eternal dance. It is vital to create experiential contexts in which people can actually touch these dimensions directly, witness them living in one another, and celebrate the birthright of our full humanity as human beings on the earth.

5. *Transforming gender relations is uncharted territory. No experts, road maps, or guidebooks exist, and no major society on Earth is gender-healed.*

Gender disharmony is vast and ancient, and the implications touch every aspect of human society. As conveners and organizers of gender reconciliation work, we make no claim to have found definitive answers for transforming gender relations. After 30 years of facilitating gender work, our methods and approaches continue to evolve, and there is certainly no definitive formula that applies to all situations. Yet, one thing we have learned is this: bringing compassionate, unflinching awareness to gender dynamics in groups and communities is a remarkably powerful place to begin. As in all spiritual practice, deepening awareness is itself transformative.

There are myriad ways in which gender injustice is unconsciously supported and perpetuated in society. We mentioned in Chapter 1 a few ways in which the genders are unaware of one another's social reality. Beyond this, we are often socialized to unconsciously perpetuate harmful myths within our own gender. For example, men need to examine among themselves the insidious ways in which men are conditioned to ridicule or dominate women and reject the feminine through habitual socialized behavior and humor, and to foist reprisals upon those men who don't buy into the dominance model of male socialization. And women need to examine their complicity in exploiting and enforcing injurious cultural norms around physical beauty and sexual attractiveness, sometimes using these energies to manipulate men and each other, thereby exacerbating the very objectification from which women seek to escape. These and other learned socialized behaviors are so routine and pervasive they often escape our conscious notice. As a result, many of us unwittingly perpetuate gender disharmony in innumerable subtle ways, while holding the sincere conviction that we are not personally complicit in the spread of gender injustice.

Today's widespread social disharmony in relation to gender is not inevitable for human society, although it is the inevitable product of thousands of years of systemic gender injustice across the globe. Because we have never known anything else, it is difficult or impossible for us to imagine what life would be like if we had grown up in a society that was truly integrated and healthy in relation to gender and sexuality. The entire fabric of human society would be vastly different from what we know today. The forums for social interaction, the depth and intimacy of interpersonal relationships, the structure and roles of family and community, the exalted expression and celebration of the erotic, the nature and forms of religious worship and spiritual ceremony—all these aspects of life would likely be profoundly different from today's cultural norms and socialized patterns. Taken together, these elements would comprise a rich and fulfilling community life that we can only guess at yet is often glimpsed in gender reconciliation work.

Perhaps there do exist a rare few individuals who were fortunate enough to grow up in a truly gender-healed community, tucked away somewhere in an isolated society far removed from the cultural mainstream. But the vast majority of us—whether from the West or the East, North or South—have no experience of life in such a harmonious social context, and we carry the multiple wounds and confusions of an unhealed humanity deep in our hearts. We carry this challenging burden not only in the form of our own personal histories and socialization, but also in the larger archetypal legacy of generations of humanity's collective pain around gender and sexuality. This leads to an incredible challenge when it comes to unraveling and healing these issues in society.

Yet, despite this daunting morass and unenviable cultural heritage in relation to gender, it is also true that we are all experts on what needs to be healed, because we all have direct personal experience of the inequities and injustice. As spiritual ecologist Joanna Macy has observed, "Our wounds are our credentials." Indeed, we are collectively quite astute about the specific challenges and subtleties of what needs to be transformed in society. Yet, precisely because we have not lived in a gender-healed society, none of us are experts on how such a society would actually look, or what new forms healthy social organization and interpersonal relations might take. Nor do we know how to accomplish the necessary healing and transformation to get us there. In short, we know what needs to be done, but we don't know *how* to do it.

For all these reasons, we must begin with the recognition that there are no experts in gender reconciliation, because (to borrow the vernacular) no society has "been there, done that" yet. This is equally true of the authors of this book. We make no claim to have found definitive "answers" for gender reconciliation, and we see ourselves as beginners rather than "experts" in this nascent field. From our perspective, no such experts currently exist. Nor are there maps or handbooks that can lead us out of the dense forest of gender injustice into the promised land of a healthy society of gender harmony.

However, that said, we do believe we have found a way to begin the process. And we don't believe it is necessary or even desirable to know in advance the details of where the process will ultimately lead. What is essential is to stay present for the task and maintain impeccable integrity in the gender healing process as it unfolds.

In the face of so many unknowns, how can we ensure even this integrity? How do we proceed in practice? The answers are simple enough, if challenging to implement at times: speaking our truth, witnessing with compassion, staying present throughout the process, bearing with its agonies as well as its ecstasies; not flinching from the difficult realities; trusting the emerging wisdom of the community; leaving nothing out, including anyone who participates in earnest; and, perhaps most of all, maintaining an unshakable faith in the human spirit. As facilitators and organizers, we have lived through many challenges in this work over the years. Yet, the healing moments have always outweighed the difficulties and provided the inspiration and confidence that helps us persevere on a path that will lead to the reconciliation and harmony that we all yearn for and which is our birthright as human beings.

Ethical Guidelines and Agreements

To help support the implementation of the above principles of gender reconciliation in practice, we have developed a set of ethical guidelines and agreements that we ask participants to uphold throughout our events. These protocols or community rules support the integrity of the gender reconciliation process and help to ensure a safe, effective "container" in which to engage the group work. When registering for a workshop or training, participants are asked to commit themselves to these community agreements.

For the most part, our guidelines and agreements reflect the kind of protocol often found in experiential healing or group-process work in community. They include agreements to maintain confidentiality about what transpires during the event, to take responsibility for one's own experience and to respect the experience of others, to be mindful about one's own communication style and allow room for others to share, to come with the sincere intention for healing and upholding the safety of the process, and to stay present for the duration of the process.

In addition to these more typical agreements, there are also some agreements or practices specific to this work that we ask participants to commit to during our time together. These include honoring the power of silence and recognizing that moments of silence often reveal deeper levels of meaning and subtlety in what transpires. We also ask participants to recognize that gender reconciliation work is uncharted territory for all of us and so it is essential to allow for ambiguity and uncertainty as we proceed, and to learn to "hold the tension of opposites"—sitting with discomfort without necessarily rushing in to try to resolve or "fix" things.

Finally, we make an unusual request: we ask participants to refrain from romantic or sexual interactions during our gender reconciliation workshops, except in cases of established couples with a longstanding prior commitment. There is much to be learned about intimacy that cannot be experienced in the face of powerful forces of cultural conditioning around sexuality and intimate relations. By temporarily suspending society's unwritten rules of engagement pertaining to romantic and sexual pursuits, participants are supported to step beyond habitual behavior and familiar territory and enter into something altogether different.

The purpose of this temporary sexual moratorium is not to deny or denigrate sexuality in any way. Quite the contrary, it serves to create an exceptionally safe and intimate environment for comfortable discourse and collective inquiry on highly delicate or vulnerable matters relating to gender and sexuality. It also cultivates a deeper mindfulness of this powerful arena of life. When a group of people choose to consciously step back from habitual cultural conditioning around sexual energy and relations, a remarkable opportunity emerges to witness the profound impact of the daily onslaught of sexual innuendo and romantic ideals that are promulgated in mainstream society.

In our culture, the vast domains of spiritual and human intimacy—both immanent and transcendent—have been largely collapsed into the merely erotic. And the rich spectrum and expansive depths of the erotic have been collapsed into the merely sexual. And the deep ecstatic energies and life-giving powers of sexuality have been collapsed into the merely physical coupling aspect. And the intensive nurturing and intricate ecstasies of physical sexuality have been largely collapsed into merely genital stimulation and response. And finally, these in turn have often been further minimized, trivialized, or pathologized in different ways through our various social customs, and religious, philosophical, and educational conditioning. So, we have suffered a catastrophic collapse of intimacy on all these levels. By entering into this shared commitment together, we are enabled to begin reclaiming these different dimensions of intimacy that have been largely lost in contemporary society.

If the sun never set, we would have no perception of the vast depths of space, which becomes visible only at night when we are able to see what is obscured by the bright daylight. In similar fashion, we refrain from sexual interaction in gender reconciliation work in order to discover hidden depths of intimacy and subtlety that are otherwise obscured in our daily lives. Over the years, we have found that working in community with this agreement tends to cultivate new modes of shared intimacy, mutual inquiry, and collective healing on levels that are rarely experienced otherwise in normal social environments.

These guidelines and agreements have served to strengthen the gender reconciliation process, and of course they become particularly important when a crisis or

William Keepin leading a GERI breakout session, State of the World Forum, 1998, San Francisco. Seated adjacent is Susan Bailey, then Director of the Wellesley Centers for Women.

Men sensitively honoring and anointing the women (with their permission); GERI workshop in Valencia, Spain, 2022

shared agreements as a foundation to maintain the integrity of the community as we carefully explore difficult and potentially divisive issues.

In closing this chapter, we quote the mystic poet Rainer Maria Rilke, who expressed in this poem the general philosophy underpinning our gender reconciliation work with great eloquence:

> Have patience with everything unresolved in your heart, and try to love the questions themselves, as if they were locked rooms or books written in a very foreign language.
>
> Don't search for the answers, which could not be given to you now, because you would not be able to live them. And the point is, to live everything.
>
> Live the questions now. Perhaps then, someday far in the future, you will gradually, without even noticing it, live your way into the answer.[2]

CHAPTER 3

Bearing Witness to Gender Injustice

The world situation today, where sex is concerned, is so critical and so serious that there are no thinkers to be found who can yet see the solution, or who can find—no matter how clear their brains or erudite their minds—the way out of the present impasse.
—Djwhal Khul (Alice Bailey)

Looking out at some two hundred upturned faces, now divided into separate women's and men's groups, we asked everyone in the auditorium to turn their chairs so they were no longer facing the podium, but rather were facing the other group across the aisle. There had been a general commotion only moments before as the conference participants had risen to their feet and walked to the side of the aisle where their gender group was gathering. This partition alone ushered in a tangible presence of archetypal energies as the men gathered on one side and the women on the other.

The setting was an international conference entitled "The Alchemy of Peacebuilding," held in Dubrovnik, Croatia, in June of 2002. The conference brought together activists, politicians, academics, and concerned citizens from several countries to explore new pathways to peace. Included among the participants was an impressive contingent of youth from around the Balkan region and an equally impressive group of young American Black leaders from the Watts neighborhood in Los Angeles. Many of these young people had experienced firsthand the violence of war or civil conflict. It was humbling to hear their stories, and inspiring to see their commitment to building a just peace in the world.

The energy level in the room intensified, and people were stimulated with both the curiosity and the slight trepidation that always accompanies the beginning of gender reconciliation work. We had opened with a brief introduction to the wider cultural and historical context of gender injustice, and our goal was to give this group an experiential glimpse of the process of gender equity and reconciliation as a component of building peace in the world.

As the men and women turned to face one another, a paradoxical combination of heightened tension and deeper intimacy could be felt as the group began a subtle shift toward becoming more of a community and less of an audience. We asked people to pay attention to how it felt to consciously sit within their particular "gender group," and to notice whatever feelings arose from being placed in these groupings, opposite one another. We asked them to reflect on whether they felt at home within their ascribed gender group and to become aware of the tremendous gender diversity inherent within each group, acknowledging the broad range of life experience, sexual orientation, and body biology that each group embodied.

Next, we asked the participants to close their eyes and reflect inwardly on their experience of the world through their particular body and mind, including their unique biology, sexuality, gender identity, and spiritual orientation. During this silence we gently guided participants to be mindful of the inner terrain of their own private and personal feeling states, taking note of whatever awareness or inner dialogue was present within them. We then invited a deepening of the silence, asking participants to enter into any practice of silence, meditation, or contemplation they found comfortable.

After sitting together in silence for several minutes, we read a poem from the Indian poet Jnaneswar celebrating the union of the sacred masculine and the sacred feminine (quoted at the end of Chapter 1). As we opened our eyes some minutes later and looked about the room, there was a sense of clear recognition that we were a group of earnest women and men who had gathered to explore and discover how to build bridges across diversity and difference in order to create more peace in our war-weary world.

Silent Witnessing

The conference community was now prepared to move into a process we call "silent witnessing." This practice tends to elicit complex emotional energies, memories, and insights as individuals bear witness to formative or challenging experiences in their personal lives relating to gender and sexual conditioning. Silent witnessing brings forward an immense degree of mutual awareness and unusual kinds of information in a group—minus the specific details—about the reality of gender conditioning in human society.

Silent witnessing is an exercise in which a series of questions is put forward pertaining to peoples' life experiences related to gender. Depending on the context, the plenary group is often divided into subgroups according to gender identity. In this case, the conference community was divided into two groups, identified as men and women, and questions were asked first of one group and then the other. After each question, individuals are invited to stand in silence if the answer to that question is "yes" in their personal history. The rest of the community remains seated in quiet acknowledgment of those standing, and everyone is asked to be sensitive and mindful of their own feelings and reactions. Those who are standing remain for a few seconds, until the facilitator says, "Thank you," and they sit back down. Then follows the next question, and the process is repeated until the questions are complete. A key guideline for this exercise is that we stand not as victims, but rather to bear witness to the gender injustices present in our lives and in our world as a whole. Behind each person standing is a unique story, and we recognize the experience in that person's life without knowing the particular details. Moreover, when we stand, we do so not only for ourselves, but also for countless others who have similar stories but may never have an opportunity to be witnessed. Thus, each person standing is bearing witness for millions of others with the same or similar experience.

The questions begin with the simplest forms of gender imbalance: "Have you ever felt your needs came second to a man's?" (for the women) or "Have you ever felt your needs came second to a woman's?" (for the men). Gradually, the questions become more challenging and pointed: The women are asked if they have ever been afraid to walk the streets alone because they are women. Similarly for the men. We ask about violence and sexuality, both from the point of view of the victim and of the perpetrator: "Have you ever feared for your life or your physical safety in your own home?" "Have you ever been hit or physically abused by a man—or by a woman?" "Have you ever hit or physically abused a man—or a woman?" As the process continues, the questions and responses become increasingly revealing.

At the conference in Croatia, when we asked the question, "Have you ever been forced sexually against your will?" nearly half the women stood up, as well as three men. The emotional atmosphere of the whole room was charged, as the men sat in silent acknowledgment, bearing witness to this profound violation of nearly one hundred women and three men standing before them. In our work throughout the United States and in several other countries, we have found that this stark reality is not unusual: generally, one-third to one-half of the women present stand for this question, and not infrequently two-thirds or more. In Croatia, when we asked, "Have you ever feared that you might have to die fighting in the armed services for your country?" every single man stood, but only two women. And when we asked, "Have you ever fought in a war?" at least a dozen men stood, but none of the women.

The impact of witnessing so many people stand in response to these questions moved the group profoundly. Waves of grief and compassion were palpable in the hush that followed. We asked each person to turn to someone near them and share what they were experiencing—first within their own gender group. In general, both women and men are often surprised by the shared reality—across the gender divide—of pain and suffering. Women, for example, expect to revisit the familiar pain of women during this process, but they are often startled to witness the pain of men. Men are startled that it is the women actually present in the room, rather than some remote victims in a newspaper article or statistic, who have suffered violation. For everyone, the fact of violation shifts from the abstract to the concrete, and this very awareness is transformative in itself.

After the separate gender groups have had a chance to process the exercise among themselves, each group is given an opportunity to present their reflections to the whole community. The insights that came forward at the peace-building conference were similar to those that emerge in our other gender reconciliation programs. A sense of collective compassion was born in this community, and with it a very tender warmth. The women and men were surprised by the degree of pain and victimization experienced in the room and were aroused to feelings of empathic solidarity—both within and across the gender divide.

As the last stage of the witnessing process, we asked participants to begin milling slowly about the room, mixing women and men back together again, and to pay particular attention to the subtle energies and feelings as the community reformed. Then we asked people to pair up with a partner of either sex, and each person was invited to share a personal story with their partner from their own background that represented one of the questions for which they had stood. Each partner spoke in turn, uninterrupted for several minutes, while the other listened. Speaking and hearing these stories further deepened the intimacy and compassionate presence in the community, and the dyad process concluded with mutual blessings and heartfelt affirmations between partners.

To close the morning, the entire group gathered into a large circle, joined hands, and sang a simple healing chant. There was a strong presence of interconnection in this community that was now awakened, at least a bit more deeply, to the profound need in our time for social healing and cultural transformation in relation to gender. We had experienced together a natural heart opening, and there was an uplifted sense that the needed changes in our society are actually feasible.

Silent Witnessing in Community

The same silent witnessing exercise is conducted in all our events as a standard part of the gender reconciliation process. In a group of 20 to 30 people the process is also very powerful, in some ways more so, because it becomes more intimate and personal. In smaller groups, the individuals who stand in response to each question are in much closer physical proximity to those who witness. People can see more clearly, and affectingly, one another's faces and nuances of body language. The responses to the questions comprise a kind of intimate revelation, and it can be shocking to see most or all of the other gender group stand for certain questions, as well as to see them all remain seated for other questions.

Participants take different lessons from this exercise. As one South African woman exclaimed after our gender reconciliation workshop in Cape Town, "The silent witnessing exercise was powerful, and it gave me an opportunity to acknowledge what I have been through, and also to 'stand up' against it. For me, it was to say, 'No More!'"

For others, silent witnessing serves as an opening to new levels of awareness and empathic awakening to the pain of other gender groups. Women are often surprised to discover the degree of men's wounding and violation around gender conditioning, and men are frequently amazed to see how many women have suffered different forms of abuse or sexual violation. Heterosexuals are often surprised to witness the degree of suffering that LGBTQ+ people have experienced.

At the same time, the exercise reveals striking differences in participants' behavior and life experience. People often comment that the exercise is a poignant reminder not to lump all men (or women) together. Women are often surprised to see men standing for experiences which they believed applied only to women, such as sexual coercion and manipulation, or vulgar harassment on the streets. Similarly, men do not always stand for behaviors that women believe apply to all men—and the same holds for women. As one participant observed, "In seeing each other as individuals, we were reminded to not—*indeed we really cannot!*—write the other gender off as a collective group that all acts a certain way."

Thousands of Years of Lived Experience

In a typical workshop group of 20 to 30 adults of diverse ages, there are somewhere between 800 and 1200 years of lived human experience sitting right there in the room. From this perspective, every group has all the "data" it needs relating to gender conditioning and experience, firsthand. Collectively, the group knows very well what needs to be healed and transformed, and it also encompasses a depth of wisdom and healing potential to become a kind of alchemical universe unto itself. As gender reconciliation proceeds, every group unfurls its own unique dynamics and psychic energies, as well as its own "shadow" that gender work tends to discover and unveil. Of course, every group is different, particularly in terms of the precise content of what emerges, yet most groups of well-intentioned participants are similar in having the resources and wisdom within their own ranks to effectively navigate the collective healing process.

Levels of Gender Conditioning: From Planetary to Personal

The silent witnessing process described above asks participants to bear witness to how gender injustice affects them within their own communities and within the workshop community. To set the stage for this and other experiences that follow, we first prepare the field by introducing participants to the larger social and historical context of gender injustice, raising awareness of what might be called "the collective gender shadow" (to borrow from Jungian terminology). This introductory phase includes a series of video clips meant to stimulate, evoke, and articulate several key gender issues—generally relating to gender disharmony in the larger society and the world.

Some examples of these video clips include:

- Excerpts from Jean Kilbourne's Media Education Foundation video, *Killing Us Softly*, which documents the exploitation of women's bodies, sexuality and dignity in the mainstream media.
- Sections of Tony Porter's TedTalk, *A Call to Men*. Sharing powerful stories from his own life, he shows how the "act like a man" mentality, drummed into so many men and boys, can lead men to disrespect, mistreat and abuse women and each other.
- Clips from the 2010 film adaption of Ntozake Shange's choreopoem *For Colored Girls Who Have Considered Suicide / When the Rainbow is Enuf.* The film depicts the interconnected lives of ten women exploring their lives and struggles as women of color.
- Sections from the Media Education Foundation documentary *Bro Code*, which examines pornography and the ways that popular culture continues to reinforce and reward sexism, as cool, desirable, and normal, particularly among boys and young men.
- #MeToo at the United Nations—Excerpts of a 2018 CNN report by Christiane Amanpour who interviews a UN employee who says she was assaulted by a top UN official.
- Clips from the *The Invisible War*—a personal story from a man who had served in the US military. He shares the secret he held for most of his life about the sexual violation he experienced early in his military career.
- Trailer of Media Education Foundation's *SPEAK UP!* and selected videos from the Human Rights Campaign, which document the unique challenges of violence and harassment faced by gay, lesbian, bisexual and transgender students.
- Film clips from *Flirting with Danger*, a Media Education Foundation film that illustrates Power & Choice in Heterosexual Relationships and explores how young women navigate heterosexual relationships and hookups in a culture that sends conflicting messages about women's sexuality, consent, and coercion.

These are just several examples of the many film clips we draw from to more fully bring to awareness gender disharmony on a global and community level. The clips are adjusted for each particular cohort of participants to best represent the diverse cultures, contexts, and experiences present in the room. Other video clips may be shared here to cover a diverse range of topics including: sexual abuse in religious communities "#ChurchToo"; abuse and compulsory military service for men in South Korea; "corrective rape" of lesbian women in South Africa; the practice of female genital mutilation in East Africa; Latino men discussing vulnerability and machismo culture; challenges of Black trans women in the United States South; and others, depending on the group.

These multimedia presentations demonstrate the global dimensions of gender injustice and different ways in which women, men, and people of all genders are afflicted. As participants discuss among themselves their responses to these presentations, they naturally begin to examine the effects of such injustice in their own lives. After a short break and silent meditation, the process of silent witnessing described above flows naturally.

In the structure of our gender reconciliation work we begin the process of raising awareness around gender dynamics at a broad level by examining gender injustice in human culture and society. This is the "safest" and least threatening context in which to examine this material. From there, we gradually narrow the focus, first to the collective experience of the participants attending the event, through the silent witnessing exercise described above, and then further still to the more intimate and vulnerable domain of participants' personal histories.

For this last step of the process, we ask participants to share their own "gender biographies," usually in small groups. This provides an unusual opportunity for people to explore their particular life story in relation to their personal gender experience and history, and the unique experiences and struggles they encountered in relation to societal gender conditioning. Proceeding in guided stages from birth through childhood, adolescence, young adulthood, and onward to the present, people often discover certain recurring themes or patterns throughout their lives that are highlighted when viewed through the lens of gender. Participants are then invited to share their stories in small groups at whatever level of depth and intimacy feels appropriate. For many people, the details of their particular gender biography include some of the most intimate, humbling, or vulnerable aspects of their personal life experience, as will be clear from examples given in later chapters. We always caution participants to honor their own boundaries, and not to share any information that feels too personal or private. At the same time, we encourage people to use this opportunity for sharing in a substantive way that may stretch them beyond their usual comfort zones.

Not surprisingly, one of the powerful results of this process is that people with particularly challenging or painful personal histories often discover that others in the group have had similar or related difficulties in life. This stark recognition is often an enlightening moment that awakens tremendous compassion and empathy. It also ushers in strong feelings of relief, as well as a shared solidarity in wanting to collaborate to transform the damaging gender dynamics that remain so prevalent in society.

We close this chapter with a special highlight on the impacts of the *#MeToo* movement and its relationship to GERI, written by Jungian psychiatrist Peter Rutter, who is a leading authority and expert witness on sexual harassment.

GERI, #MeToo, and Sex in the Forbidden Zone

Peter Rutter, M.D.

Many clients in my 45+ years of clinical psychiatric practice have been traumatized by gender oppression, and gender violence—as is our entire culture. Gender Equity and Reconciliation International (GERI) offers a practical methodology that builds cross-gender empathy and understanding on personal, social, and cultural levels.

I recall during one of the GERI workshops at Ghost Ranch when a conflict emerged in the group. One of the male participants had been "coming on" to two of the women, and this became a major rift in the community. The women processed this in the women's group, and then brought it forward to the entire community. The facilitators orchestrated a remarkable resolution of this situation, with structured support for the man and for the two women, and skillful engagement of the rest of the community in compassionate presence. This collective healing process was reminiscent of a clinical process called "impasse resolution" that I sometimes apply in my clinical practice, in cases of a significant violation or breach of trust of some kind. Impasse resolution was developed by a colleague in the Bay Area, Dr. Sue Nathanson Elkind, and provides a way to navigate the tensions of intersecting primary vulnerabilities, and secondary wounding, in an attempt to resolve the impasse.[1] Elkind's work focuses primarily on rifts between clients and therapists in clinical settings. Here in the GERI workshop, I witnessed a similar approach in this collective gender healing work.

Impacts of the #MeToo Movement

People sometimes ask me what has changed in regard to sexual harassment in society, as a result of the #MeToo movement. Of course, it has been a crucial awakening to a much broader recognition of structural gender injustice and sexual harassment in our culture. Throughout history, victims of sexual harassment or exploitation have been blamed, and ruthlessly silenced if they dared to speak out. Any woman who spoke up against a powerful man was severely disempowered or humiliated, often literally murdered. For this reason, the majority of victims of sexual harassment or exploitation never spoke out. Sometimes it took a while for a victim to gain the strength to speak out, and then the response would be, "Well, why didn't you complain at the time? Why are you bringing this forward now, after several years?" And the woman would explain, "Because I was afraid for my safety, or well-being, or my family, or my life." That argument has credibility today, but it did not for millennia. Women who spoke up later, after time had elapsed since their violation, were thoroughly discredited for not having spoken up at the time. So "case closed," and it became a double violation.

A clear example is Anita Hill and the Clarence Thomas confirmation hearings of 1991. Two years earlier, my book *Sex in the Forbidden Zone* had been published.[2] I was able to reach Professor Hill's lawyer, Charles Ogletree, and discussed with him studies about the intensive shaming and blaming that women are subjected to when they speak out about sexual harassment, which was an important aspect for my own clients and research. Mr. Ogletree requested a memorandum for the hearing, which I sent to him, but he never had the opportunity to introduce it, because the hearings were suddenly terminated prematurely.

I recall that sometime after one of the GERI workshops I co-facilitated around 2000, I received a phone call from one of the women in that workshop, who was suddenly being harassed by a top male leader in her corporation. She was a middle manager, he was the corporate board chair, twenty years her senior. He had begun pressuring her for sexual intimacy, and manipulating her in ways that have now become much more widely recognized and understood because of #MeToo. At that time, these behaviors were still much hidden in so many seemingly upstanding corporations and institutions. I became part of her support and legal team, as the corporation started down the predictable path of defaming her and building its legal case against her. She was forced out of the job, but because she quickly found another position, she decided not to pursue the sexual harassment case legally, primarily to save herself the personal stress and expense it would entail. Such injustices still occur today, but there is so much more awareness now, and stronger support both within and outside organizations for people who are harassed in this way. All this has come about because of the #MeToo movement.

A Personal Example of Professional Awakening (As Related In Sex In The Forbidden Zone*)*

In my own case, I lost my professional innocence during an incident that came upon me suddenly, dangerously, in the closed chamber of my first psychiatric office. A patient I will call Mia came to her appointment one evening with the unspoken, unplanned agenda to offer herself sexually. Over the previous five months as my patient, we had identified her pattern of becoming sexually intimate with men quickly, because she felt she had no other way to keep them interested. Mia was a woman of 25 whose bright clothes and quick pace masked her severe chronic depression. She had a painful personal history that included sexual molestation, and episodes of street life and drug abuse.

Mia had never been seductive with me. But that night, without warning, I felt her sexuality directed toward me from the moment she stepped into the room with an intensity beyond anything I had yet experienced. As she tearfully recounted a humiliating rejection from a man she'd been dating, Mia slid off the patient's chair, and sat cross-legged in front of me. The sexual posturing grew more intense, as she began to edge closer toward me.

As Mia reenacted her role as victim, all she needed was my participation. Nothing in my training had prepared me for this moment. In those days, little if any attention was given in clinical training to these delicate situations, and there was even a rather lapse attitude within the profession about therapists having intimate relations with their clients.

I sat frozen, neither encouraging nor stopping Mia. I felt the intoxicating mixture of the timeless freedom and danger that men feel when a forbidden woman's sexuality becomes available to them. I also sensed that if I went ahead with this sexual encounter, I could count on Mia, as a well-trained victim, to keep our illicit secret.

Another part of me, however, remained separate from this sexual intrigue. This part was trying to understand what was going on inside Mia and searched for a way I could help her. I made a choice in that moment: I asked Mia to return to her chair. In our respective seats, we then began a therapeutic exploration of the way she was bringing her self-destructive pattern, in the only way she knew how, by replicating it with me.

I realized that at the critical moment, the path taken depended not on her, but on me. I had to fight off some typically masculine components of my sexuality that were all too ready to accept Mia's self-destructive offering. From this experience I discovered just how passionate and dissolving the erotic atmosphere can become in relationships in which the man holds the power and the woman places trust and hope in him. It was more readily available and powerfully alluring than I had ever admitted or recognized. In that early and naive stage of my clinical formation, I shudder to think how close I came that evening to harming both of us. But my decision in that critical moment enabled the therapeutic work with Mia to continue in a constructive direction, and I never forgot this crucial lesson.

Fostering Gender Safety in Society—Summoning Healing Moments through the Power of Restraint

Day after day we men sit in inviolable privacy with women who trust, admire, and rely upon us. If we have been working together for some time, a familiarity and trust develop that start to erode the boundaries of impersonal professional relationships. As a result, we find ourselves experiencing a closeness, a completeness, with these women; and many of them begin to feel the same way about being with us.

As one professional man recounted about an unacknowledged mutual attraction with a female business colleague that reached a critical point, "I was going crazy with tension that night. I was ready to just take her in my arms. But when I saw how unprotected she was, I suddenly realized that she was my spiritual daughter. This meant I would have to give up the idea that we would ever have a sexual liaison." The woman later recounted, "I was shocked, but relieved, when he directed us back to our work. I didn't think it was possible for a man to turn away from that kind of sexual energy. It was as if a spell had been broken." The two continued a long and productive professional relationship thereafter that never extended beyond the office. After giving up his fantasies, the man found that "I have access to a strength and inner satisfaction that I had never known before."

Because so many women have been injured by the uncontained sexuality of men who have had power over them, the potential healing power of restraint is enormous. Not only is the woman made safe from being exploited, but the healing moment kindles the promise that she can be valued entirely apart from her sexuality. In these moments, life takes a new turn, and the wounds from past injury as well as hopelessness about the future can be healed. For the man, there is a new form of empowerment and integrity, and these qualities can readily extend to his relationships with other women in his life, contributing to build greater gender safety and trust throughout his professional and personal networks. This contributes to building a society that is safer and more respectful for all.

I have continued to follow GERI over the years, as its work has gone out to South Africa and India and several other countries. What I particularly appreciate is witnessing GERI's mission of training qualified people in those cultures and communities to become the leaders of their own movements for gender reconciliation in their cultures. The GERI program is unique, and uniquely valuable to the world.

Peter Rutter, M.D. is a Jungian psychiatrist, and a leading authority on sexual harassment and exploitation. He is author of *Sex in the Forbidden Zone* (1989); *Sex, Power, and Boundaries* (1996); and *Understanding and Preventing Sexual Harassment: The Complete Guide* (1997).

CHAPTER 4

Deepening into Separate Gender Circles

The shortest distance between a human being and the truth is a story.
—Anthony de Mello

Having experienced the intensity and vulnerability of the silent witnessing exercise described in the previous chapter, there is often a strong wish in a community of people to break into separate gender-specific circles for a period. These might be women's and men's circles, or perhaps circles of men, women, and LGBTQ+ participants, or whatever breakout configuration makes sense given the composition of the group. Participants may be feeling sheepish or vulnerable in view of what they have silently revealed about their personal histories. Some may be feeling uncomfortably lumped together, perhaps feeling implicitly associated with identities or behaviors that do not apply to them personally. The intensity of what has just been witnessed, the commonality and specificity of human pain in relation to gender injustice, and the degree of personal and collective exposure, all point to the need for supporting a sense of safety. Same-sex groups or other gender-specific groups often provide this safety, where people can take refuge in their separate gender circles to explore the often raw and delicate emotions or experiences that can be difficult to address in the full plenary group.

The nature and function of these sub-groupings in the context of gender reconciliation is generally quite different from what many people are used to from previous experience. For example, in a group that separates into women's and men's circles, the dynamic character of the women's circle will be shifted to a large degree by the presence of the men—and vice versa. Even though the women's and men's circles meet in separate spaces, entirely out of earshot of each other, the two groups affect each other greatly.

To elucidate a bit: in a conventional women's group the women may speak about their relationships with men—husbands, sons, fathers, lovers, and so forth—but there is no active engagement of these relational dynamics because no men are actually present. By contrast, in gender reconciliation work, when the women's circle meets, the women have all experienced one another in the presence of men, and they will soon be moving back into community with those same men. Behavior speaks louder than words, and the women's behavioral patterns and dynamics in relation to men will tend to be reproduced right there with the men present in the workshop. And, of course, this same process will also be going on among the men in relation to the women in the workshop. So, in both cases, ingrained patterns of behavior in relation to the opposite sex will naturally arise, and these patterns will be observed by others within the same-sex group.

All this creates valuable grist for the mill of *intra*gender work, which plays out in innumerable ways. Competitive dynamics often surface. In a group of men, when even one woman comes onto the scene, a whole new dynamic immediately comes into play—especially if she is regarded as attractive. Traditionally, the men begin to compete for her attention—often unconsciously attempting to outshine one another. In gender reconciliation work this competition may not be overt or play out along traditional macho masculine lines of physical prowess or brilliant intelligence. Some men might jostle and maneuver themselves so as to be seen as the most "sensitive," "compassionate," or "heroic" advocates of women's plight, thereby seeking to draw to themselves adoration and respect from the women.

A similar dynamic often emerges in a group of women when a man enters upon a scene where previously only women had been present. The resulting dynamics vary depending on the man, and are often influenced by where the different women's alliances lie. Women are socialized to create alliances with men in order to substantiate and advance their own positions. The more skilled a woman is at creating alliances with men, the better she is likely to fare in society at large. In a mixed group, women often seek to form alliances with men even at the expense of the other women in the group. It's another form of competition. Later, when the women gather back into the women's group and expect and ask for allegiance among the women, an interesting tension can arise. It often becomes quickly evident how much value each woman places on sisterly allegiance, and which women will readily sacrifice this allegiance to establish deeper alliances with men. And the true alliances become plainly visible for all to see.

In short, it is evident that gender reconciliation work sets in motion a complex process that interweaves both intergender and intragender dimensions of interaction and conditioning. By working both within and between two (or more) gender subgroups, rich and revealing dynamics often surface rather quickly. Participants' individual behavior patterns are inevitably exposed on various levels, often unwittingly, which frequently brings invaluable insights and learnings. It is crucial to keep in mind that many ingrained patterns of behavior and interaction between women, men, and other gender groups are socialized and culturally learned, and the only place to start unlearning unhealthy patterns is to see them with unflinching clarity—as they emerge in real time. This is where much of the richness and power of gender reconciliation work is often found.

We now explore two specific examples of what transpires in same-sex circles—one anecdote each from a men's circle and a women's circle. These examples are drawn from two different events, and, in each case, the process that began in the same-sex circle became a pivotal element in the unfolding process and outcome for the entire event.

The Men's Circle

The first example comes from a workshop held in a large ranch house, which lent a certain informality to the gathering.[1] Participants found themselves in a cozy, intimate situation that left them feeling rather like housemates. Meals were catered, but participants did the dishes and helped keep the kitchen and house clean. This was an intergenerational workshop that included both teenagers and adults, which added a wonderful dynamic to the group and increased the sense of being in a large family gathering atmosphere.

About two days into the retreat, the women's and men's lunch times were staggered to allow each gender circle to meet for the entire day without encountering the other. As it happened, the men ate their lunch after the women on this day, and they decided afterward, as a service to the community, to do the dishes and clean up the kitchen.

When the men finished the cleanup, one of them—we'll call him Sam—wanted to leave a note for the women —"as a joke"—saying that since the men had cleaned up the kitchen, they expected sex from the women later on. Two of the other men began to laugh and hoot and chimed in their enthusiastic support for Sam's suggestion. But the proposed prank quickly met with resistance from several of the other men, who were concerned that the women would be offended by the note, especially in the context of a gender healing workshop. Sam protested that it was only a joke and would certainly be received as such by the women—all the more so *because* it was a gender workshop. He insisted on going forward with his idea.

The resulting rift in the men's group rapidly escalated into a crisis, polarizing the men into two camps: Sam and his two supporters on one side, and the rest of the men, to varying degrees, on the other. In an attempt at compromise, Sam and his team proposed they leave the note and sign only their three names to it, making it clear that it wasn't from all of the men. But several men objected. They felt the note would still affect the whole course of the workshop and would be seen by many women as a betrayal, typical of the ways in which women so often experience men. The men as a group would all be tainted with the same negative brush, they argued, even if they did not all sign the note—a reenactment of an age-old dynamic between the sexes.

It quickly became clear to the male facilitators that they had to address this issue head on; indeed, to do so *was* the men's work in that moment, and it took precedence over our existing agenda. So, we announced that the men's group was reconvening to address this issue among the men. Sam was visibly irritated; he just wanted to leave the note and get on with whatever was next on the agenda. His critics were equally irritated, and several of them groaned out loud as they realized the afternoon's program for the men's circle was now in jeopardy because of the need to address what seemed to them an inane issue coming from just a few individuals within the men's group. Despite almost unanimous resistance among the men, we insisted and reconvened the men's group to address this issue.

As we opened with a simple council process, there was a lot of energy and tension in the room. Several of the men began expressing serious concern about how some of the women in the group would likely react when they found this note. Meanwhile, Sam and his cohorts kept insisting the women would take it as a joke. "And if they don't," Sam exclaimed at one point, "they have a lot to learn!"

This remark outraged a couple of the men, who demanded, "What exactly are the women supposed to learn!?"

"About sex!" shot back Sam.

"And what is your note going to teach the women about sex?!" the opposing men persisted.

Witnessing this heated exchange and the rising tension it was generating, we conceived the idea of delving more deeply into this conflict and having the men act it out. So we proposed a spontaneous psychodrama process in which several men would play the various roles of the women reacting to the note. We explained our idea to the group: "Let Sam and his cohorts make their case and defend it however they see fit, and let the men who are expressing concerns about the reactions they think the women might have actually *play* the roles of those women in the psychodrama."

The men set up the imagined confrontation that would ensue after the women had found the note. Sam and his two supporters were playing themselves, and six other men were playing the women—with the rest of the group in witness. Each of the latter six chose a specific woman in the group whom he thought he could accurately portray, including a fourteen-year-old boy who played one of the young teenage girls. The fourteen-year-old boy did a masterful job of portraying a particularly tender, innocent ninth-grade girl in the group. Another man played the part of an outraged feminist activist. "She'll be fit to be tied!" he exclaimed, and he dove into the role. Still another played one of the older women facilitators, a circumspect and loving matriarchal figure who could understand the joke from one perspective but also see its potential harm. He thought she would try to orchestrate all the conflicting views to create harmony.

Three or four of the men played angry women who were basically saying, "Not again! We came here to do a new and different form of gender healing work, and what we get is the same old abuse and patriarchy all over again—right in our face!"

As the psychodrama proceeded, the facilitators supported both sides of the confrontation, encouraging full expression of all views and feelings. Sam and his team played their roles adamantly, insisting the note was harmless and just good fun, while the other side countered with how offended they felt by the note. The situation heated up, with passionate arguments on both sides. Sam insisted that if the women didn't find the note funny, then they needed to "loosen up" around sexual matters. This outraged many of the "women" [played by men], who called for a retraction and apology from Sam, pointing to centuries of sexual violation, rape, and other abuses committed against them by men.

As the arguments were hurled back and forth, the "women" portrayed a rich tapestry of reactions. Many were vocal in their outrage, and two demanded some form of retribution for this latest patriarchal abuse. One conceded that she found Sam's note amusing herself but was concerned for how her sisters were feeling. Some expressed total loss of hope in gender reconciliation because this incident had reenacted yet again what men always do to women. The circumspect, wise crone could see all sides of the conflict and sought to bring resolution and harmony back into the community.

Over time, Sam's cohorts slowly began to soften their position, as they realized the note actually *was* likely to elicit a strong reaction and sense of betrayal among at least some of the women. Deciding that this possibility was not worth the risk, one of Sam's cohorts switched camps about halfway through the psychodrama. Toward the end, Sam's other supporter followed suit, leaving Sam to argue his case alone. Sam eventually came around to the view that leaving the note was not such a good idea after all because it carried a significant risk of precipitating a crisis, which was not his intention. In the end, Sam not only withdrew his proposal, but expressed gratitude for what he learned in the process. This feeling of gratitude and deep learning was mutual as the men debriefed the intensive experience, which had lasted nearly two hours. They had become truly empathic as they delved deeply into their roles and began seeing things from the women's perspective. A number of the men were amazed at how strongly they identified with their roles as women, and at the passion for justice that inspired and energized them. In the end, all the men felt a sense of great achievement and grace at having handled a potential crisis internally among themselves, and at having come through it with deeper insights and compassion for the women.

The men were beaming as they came back into the mixed group that evening, and the feeling among them persisted throughout the rest of the workshop. The women could feel the men's positive energy and were eager to know what had happened in the men's group that had brought about the heightened intensity of the men's warmth and affection, attentiveness, and *presence*. But the men had made an agreement of total confidentiality, in part to protect Sam and his cohorts but also to maintain the integrity of the process in the men's group and in the workshop itself.

On the last morning, to his credit, Sam elected to reveal what had happened, and his disclosure opened up the space for the rest of the men to share. The women were deeply moved by their story. The positive energy that arose from the men's group work had spread so tangibly out into the larger circle that the women had taken notice and were favorably impacted throughout the event. As the event came to a close, the women expressed their gratitude, and many felt deeply honored by the way the men had handled the situation and by their capacity to empathically identify with the women's concerns. To a large extent, the men's work had shaped the entire workshop, transforming what might have been a textbook replay of abrasive sexism into a powerful healing event that lifted the entire group to a high level of sensitivity, caring, and collective intimacy.

Before proceeding to the next example, an important reflection about what happened in the men's circle needs to be made. If, as in most men's groups, the circle of men in the above example had not been accountable to a larger mixed community—then a joke along the lines of Sam's proposed note would not likely have been processed by the men to any significant degree. Typically, when a crude or unconscious sexual joke is made among men, the response is that those who find it funny laugh out loud, while others who may find it offensive either feign a laugh, say nothing, or at most mutter something to themselves under their breath, eager to move beyond it. But rarely does any conversation or processing beyond this take place, and thus old patterns remain unexamined and thereby reinforced. This same response would probably have occurred in this men's circle had it not been for the gender reconciliation context. Indeed, neither Sam nor his adversaries wanted to delve into the issue, and both sides would have avoided it if they could have. But the need for accountability and integration with the women led them into it, and this in turn led to the unexpected breakthrough of what emerged in the men's group, followed by the discovery of a bit of alchemical gold that this ushered into the full community.

The Women's Circle

"I almost died; I have to remember that!" Carolyn stammered. "And I know I'm not an isolated case. It sounds dramatic, but it has to be said: I almost died, and I know that if pornography hadn't been involved, I would not have gone off the deep end the way I did."

Carolyn was beginning to share her personal experience with pornography, following a group exercise that dealt with the effects of pornography. A vibrant and keenly insightful professional woman around forty years old, Carolyn had never shared this part of her personal history with any group before. In fact, she had never told it to anyone.

"I was very armored around this. I don't know of any arena, other than this gender reconciliation work, that could have broken this open for me. Pornography is not some little thing we can just banter around. It's a gigantic thing that is having a huge impact—a hugely negative impact—on many people's lives. And I felt a need to say, '*Look people, we can talk about pornography up here* [in our heads] *all we want, but the bottom line is that people are dying from it.*' I know that sounds extreme, but I also know that was my experience."

Carolyn took a deep breath and recounted the following story. When she was in her early twenties, she had married a young officer in the U.S. Air Force and moved with him to an airbase in the South where he was training as a fighter pilot. She had met her husband while working for a civilian company that ran the recreation center at a top-secret site where they were testing the stealth fighter bomber. "I knew what pilots were like. I knew what went on because I was the bartender there. There was plenty of stuff [pornography] around there," she said. "They would come to the bar; I would see it, but I wasn't affected by it. My husband didn't seem like that kind of guy. He was a nice guy. He was friendly, and he was funny. We played a lot. People who would see us together would say, 'Oh yeah, good match.' He was my best friend.

"So when he introduced pornography into our home, I said, 'Wait a minute, what is this? What is this about?' and I expected him to understand." Carolyn and her husband were young newlyweds and had only been at the base for about a month when, "All of a sudden, boom! He brought home all this stuff, and I was shocked. I was really firm. I said, '*No, this isn't coming into my house. I'm sorry, this is not okay.*' I put up a strong front. I thought, if he loves me, if he's a good husband, he's going to say, 'Okay, I get it.' He's going to see that this is wrong. Instead, just the opposite happened. He really jerked the rug out from under me. I can still pinpoint the moment—I can tell you exactly what I was wearing, exactly where I was standing, everything, because that's the moment I realized I didn't count, I didn't matter. This other thing [pornography] was much more important."

"The reason we *needed* pornography in our house, he explained to me, was because he was in pilot training, and he was at the top of his class and wanted to stay at the top of his class. In order to do that, every week each of the guys would cut out the most disgusting picture they could find, laminate it onto a dollar bill, and turn it in. Whoever had the picture that was the most offensive—or as they thought of it, most titillating—would win extra flight time. And of course, if you got extra flight time, you would be the better pilot."

The pornographic dollar bills were laminated and submitted every week by the young training pilots to their elder, higher ranking officers, who judged them and duly awarded extra flight training hours accordingly every week. Carolyn's husband often won, but the price of his winning was a growing preoccupation with pornography. "He'd go through the magazines all the time. He'd have to go through them several times just to figure out which pictures he liked. So we had magazines all over the house—not just *Playboy*, *Penthouse*, and *Hustler*, but all kinds of other obscure ones, too. He would drive off base to the next town to buy them, where they had a bigger selection."

All the training pilots would get together a couple of times a week in Carolyn's home and go through the magazines and laminate their dollar bills. "It was hard to hear him sit with his buddies around these magazines going, 'Ooh, look at this one! AHH, look at that one!' All I could think about was, what can I do to look like them, so he will look at me the way he does at them? There was a lot of time spent on it.'

"Everyone thought it was funny," Carolyn recalled, including the other wives. When Carolyn tried to discuss her objections with the other women, they told her, "Oh, just chill out, it's no big deal." The women were right in line. When Carolyn persisted, some of the women stopped being friends with her. In fact, one night when the men had gathered to make their dollar bills, the wives showed up at Carolyn's house carrying stacks of *Playgirl* magazine. "We thought we'd come over and lighten you up," they told her, "so we're going to make our own dollars."

"That was the hardest thing, I think, to have the women come over and tell me that I needed to lighten up, that it was no big deal." As time went on, Carolyn was admonished in no uncertain terms and told to step in line and be a team player. "The peer pressure was so great that even if my husband had realized it was hurtful to me and had stopped wanting to participate, he would have been dropped to the bottom of his class, which would have affected the rest of his career life in the Air Force. That was made clear to him again and again. They called him in to reprimand him about me. The message to him was very clear: *Toe the line, you're one of our top guys here, we want to keep you there. You could even make colonel early on. But you have to get your wife under control.*

Carolyn's husband hardened his position. "He just kind of shut me down," she said. "He wasn't mean about it, we didn't fight, he just left the magazines out everywhere and told me, 'You need to deal with it. You need to get over it. This is something I have to do.'

"So I shut up," Carolyn explained. "It was hard, though. We'd been buddy-buddy, hanging out and doing things together until we got married, but then after we got married, I couldn't go out with him anymore because it wasn't okay for the wives to go. It was okay for me to go when I was his friend, but then everything shifted and all of a sudden I was on the back burner. That isn't the way he wanted things, that's just what was expected, and he wanted to be good. He wanted to be the best."

Carolyn was chastised not only for her objections to the pornography, but when the colonel's wife determined that the colonel was spending an inordinate amount of time at the swimming pool gawking at women in bathing suits, Carolyn's employment there as a lifeguard was suddenly deemed "inappropriate" for an officer's wife, and she was forced to quit through internal pressure on her husband. "I was confused," Carolyn explained. "There were so many things I seemed to be doing 'wrong,' yet there in front of me was this thing that was 'right'—because *it* [the pornography] was what got the extra time on the flight plan; *it* was what we spent all of our time on."

Carolyn became increasingly insecure. "I was so afraid that I was going to lose him, that I wasn't good enough, wasn't pretty enough, that I had nothing to offer." When her husband's training started to include more special assignments and temporary duty, the situation deteriorated further. "I knew that when they went on special assignments or on temporary duty, they spent their time in the strip clubs, hitting on women. That's just what they do," and on one occasion she inadvertently found confirmatory photographs in his bag.

Gradually, Carolyn turned to the models in the pornographic magazines, believing they had what she needed in order to secure her husband's love. "I thought if my body could be that perfect, I wouldn't lose him, and it would be okay." She found a job teaching aerobics five times a day. "In between, I would bike or run. I started spending my whole day doing workouts. I knew the calorie and fat count of every single thing that went in my mouth, and how much exercise I needed in order to offset anything I ate. At first I was eating, but then I stopped and started living on four liters of Diet Dr. Pepper a day. That's all I would put in my body." By this time Carolyn was looking at herself constantly in the mirror "to see what was wrong, comparing myself to the pictures, picking myself apart, and never really seeing myself. Seeing only parts."

The pattern continued to develop over the ensuing months. "I remember pulling out the magazines and comparing myself to the pictures, even to the point of putting myself in different poses, to see what was so enticing in the magazines and to see if I was there yet. It got to where I would do that four or five times a day, at least. It's what I did during the day when he was gone, and on the weekends, too, if he was on travel. Then I would step on the scales and see how much I weighed and how much more I needed to lose."

By this point Carolyn was drinking so much caffeine that she couldn't feel her body anymore. "I couldn't feel a thing," she told us. "I remember praying one night that somehow I could be zero weight and just start over; then I could rebuild my body and make it perfect. That was informing everything I was doing. I know that's not a rational thought, but at the time it just seemed that if I could go all the way to zero, I could make it better."

When Carolyn, who is five feet, nine inches tall, got down to ninety-seven pounds, she had a split-second epiphany one day when she actually saw her true reflection in the mirror. "I could see every rib and every vertebra. Then when I blinked and looked again, I couldn't see it anymore." She had a moment of panic and called her mother, asking her to come get her and take her home. "Two minutes later I called her back and told her I was just kidding and not to worry about it." Fortunately, Carolyn's mother realized something was amiss and immediately booked an airplane ticket to visit her daughter.

Two days later Carolyn and her mother were back home. "When I checked into the hospital, I weighed ninety-four pounds. I had a heart murmur, one of my kidneys was operating at 30 percent, and the other at 70 percent. Between the two of them, I had only one kidney, and all sorts of other physical ailments were going on. The doctor told me that my body was literally shutting down, and if it continued I would die. He said it would continue to shut down until I started building it up. He said, 'That's how you die, not from starvation per se, but from the shutdown of all of your systems.' When I saw it on paper, I started to cry. I was thinking, *Oh my God, what have I done to myself? What am I doing to myself?*"

Carolyn was in the hospital the first time for four months. The staff tried to make her eat frequent, substantial meals, which was extremely difficult for her, which is why it took four months before she was ready to leave. "When I got out of the hospital, I made the mistake of going to the mall with a friend. It was like I was a huge walking bruise. We walked into the mall and—you know what a mall looks like—there were tons of pictures in every store telling me what I needed to look like to be beautiful and successful. I couldn't handle it. I couldn't deal with it. I got angry again, and I looked at all those pictures and I thought, *Damn it, I want to be beautiful! I have a right to be beautiful! I have a right to look like that. Who are these people trying to make me ugly, trying to make me unacceptable?* And I stepped right back into it—the anorexia—at that moment. Even now, there are times when that's still my knee-jerk reaction if I'm not on top of things. It's still a struggle," Carolyn explained. "I'm not talking about an isolated incident that occurred only once in my life."

Carolyn had to return to the hospital a second time for another month and a half. During both these hospital stays, her husband never once visited her, and Carolyn came to the realization that her marriage was finished. She filed for divorce and traveled to Germany, where she lived for four years. In Germany, where she found less emphasis on women's bodies, she came to feel stronger and more certain of her choices around her body and food. But, as she was quick to point out, anorexia changes the brain chemistry, and one has to confront an ongoing range of psychological symptoms. "I'm lucky," she told us, "because many women with anorexia don't make it, they don't kick it, they end up dying.

"There was discomfort in the group after I spoke," Carolyn reported, "because it does change things if we face rather than deny this kind of information" about pornography and anorexia. "There's so much at stake. There was so much at stake for my husband. For him to actually start looking at this he'd have to reevaluate himself as a human being, and I think that would be too much for him. He couldn't do it in that context. There would be no support for it. There's a lot of activity within that little cult, especially among the higher officers and pilots. They get in less trouble. The more elite they are, the less trouble they will get in, and the more deviant it seems they're allowed to be.

"When I was working at the test range, the base commander raped one of the maids," Carolyn continued. "There was nowhere she could turn for justice. She went to the military police and they basically told her, 'What do you want us to do about it? He's the base commander. He did it because he knew he could and get away with it. He thought it was funny.' So she said, 'I'm going to go to the police down south,' which was what we called the city, and the police told her, 'If you do that, it's a breach of the oath that you swore to come up here to this top-secret base, and you will go to jail.' We were at a top-secret site. We all had top-secret clearances, and so we swore an oath. And part of the oath is agreeing never to reveal that it's there. They told her that if she went down south to the city police, she would go to prison. So she could say nothing, and do nothing about it.

"My husband was one of the nicer guys. One time we drove up and dropped him off in Washington at a camp where they train officers how to deal with torture by an enemy without disclosing military secrets. When he came back, I was really upset because it took him so long to recover, especially when he was telling me what happened. I had never seen him cry, and there were a couple of times when he broke down and cried as he talked about it. I was so angry. I remember thinking about the kind of people that they train and hire to staff this camp. These men, their jobs—my tax dollars pay them—is to hurt, to torture somebody's mind. I was so angry, and there was nothing I could do."

A postscript to this story occurred about ten years later, when, after years of no contact, Carolyn had lunch one day with her ex-husband. It was early winter 2003, just weeks before the start of the Iraq War. As they sat down to lunch, Carolyn wondered how he had changed and grown over the years. They had a friendly social chat. With the country on the brink of war, Carolyn was surprised that he made no mention of it, and she wondered how he really felt about it, being an officer in the armed forces. She hesitated for a moment as a memory flashed through her mind of their early days as best friends, laughing together. She recalled the warmth and beauty of his youthful, innocent spirit. Then she lowered her voice and gingerly changed the subject, asking him how he felt about the current political situation and the impending possibility of war. He replied casually, "Oh, I'm glad all this is happening."

Carolyn was stunned. "Why?" she asked him.

"Because it means I get to fly more," he replied flatly.

From the "winning" pornographic dollar, to the loss of his best friend and later his marriage, to his nation going to war—these things were all good, if it meant that he got more flight time. He had not changed one bit, except perhaps for how much more he was prepared to sacrifice in order to fly more.

First ever GERI Professional Training, Loveland, Colorado, 2001

CHAPTER 5

Speaking Truth to Unspoken Truths

True reconciliation exposes the awfulness, the abuse, the hurt, the truth. It could even sometimes make things worse. It is a risky undertaking but in the end it is worthwhile, because in the end only an honest confrontation with reality can bring real healing. Superficial reconciliation can bring only superficial healing.

—Archbishop Desmond Tutu

Things were getting off to a rough start for the men. For the first several minutes all they could do was express their frustration—and, in some cases, anger—at the fact that they were sitting in a circle talking to each other, while stationed all around them were the women, silently listening in. Earlier the men had called an emergency meeting to consider the strong resistance several of them had to this whole idea of a "men's truth forum," as the facilitators were calling this exercise. There were complex dynamics, including secrets of different kinds, some involving particular individuals in the community. Three men had specifically requested that what they had shared earlier in the men's circle must be kept strictly confidential, not to be disclosed in this new context with the women witnessing. The men were faced with the necessity of trusting one another at a new level and remembering which aspects of their earlier men's circle were not to be repeated here—creating a vulnerability to mutual trust that was unnerving. Adding to the tension, the facilitators had decided to let the women (who had somehow known to ask) go second. This felt like a familiar refrain—safety first for women and children when the ship is going down; but otherwise, it's men who are supposed to test the dangerous waters of the unknown.

For most of the men, it was unthinkable that they could speak even remotely as honestly as they'd been doing all afternoon, when no women were present. The instructions for the men's truth forum were to continue with their men's circle as if the women were still absent, even though the women were sitting all around them, quietly listening in. The men were convinced the process would be utterly contrived. The stakes were high. Nothing real was likely to happen, and that too would be classic—the men would get nailed for being superficial. Obviously, doing the forum poorly would be more destructive to this gender reconciliation process than doing nothing at all. The men felt trapped.

As the talking stick went around the men's group, gradually some of the men who had less resistance began to model ways of sharing authentically. Building upon the cumulative courage of one another, a few men gingerly entered into a discussion about sex and their attitudes toward women in general, continuing on a theme they had been discussing earlier in the men's circle. Their honesty gradually deepened as they began to speak about lust and desire, acknowledging their preoccupation with female bodies and physical beauty. Yes, they imagined having sex with the pretty women they passed on the street or saw in a bar. Yes, they ranked women at parties and gatherings—from the one they most wanted to the one they would settle for if she was all they could get. Yes, they imagined larger breasts or smaller hips as "needed," or added a more elegant nose or wider-set eyes.

Several men acknowledged that they habitually sexualized their encounters with women, implicitly measuring the value of every interchange by its sexual charge. "Attraction is not a matter of rational choice," exclaimed Charles, a lanky, sharp-witted law student. "It's a matter of biology. Men are hardwired to respond sexually to attractive women," he concluded in passionate earnestness. "It's an incontrovertible fact of life." Expounding on similar themes, others spoke of how they inevitably compared the women in their lives to images in the media. Yet the media were not necessarily to blame, they explained, because the media were simply reflecting back what men instinctively already knew: perfect female bodies and youthful beauty were in fact what captured men's attention and motivated their desire. "In fact," intoned a reflective man with chagrin, "given how men are—that is, hardwired to pursue women merely on the basis of their sexual desirability—this attempt at 'gender reconciliation,' noble as it sounds, is probably a complete waste of time."

As several men seemed to nod in agreement, others began shifting in their seats, preparing for their chance to speak. The women witnessing outside the circle remained quiet, though hardly calm. They had been asked to listen deeply with their hearts, to bear witness in silence to whatever the men shared. Listening quietly was the women's only task during the men's truth forum, and the women had been advised that the better they were able to do this, the more their energetic presence would actually create the support to allow the men in the inner circle to go deeper. It was not an easy task: on the one hand, every woman in the room was deeply moved, gratified to be privy to such frank male honesty. Most would later report that they had never heard a group of men share so candidly. On the other hand, many of the women would also report that what the men were sharing was very difficult to hear—reinforcing their nightmare images of men. One woman later said that the only thing she heard in the men's truth forum that she completely agreed with was the remark that we might as well all give up and go home—that the gender divide was too wide, and true reconciliation was a hopeless chimera.

But then, as so often happens when raw honesty prevails, something remarkable occurred. John, the only gay man in the group, had become increasingly quiet as the conversation progressed. But suddenly he interjected, "I need to say something about my experience—as a gay man." He paused to collect himself, acutely aware that he was entering treacherous waters. "I get sized up all the time," he began cautiously, "by men who are awash in the same kind of sexual lust that you're talking about here in relation to women." John glanced around the circle of men, looking for silent permission to continue, which they gave him. He then proceeded to explore the ramifications of men who unconsciously indulge their sexual appetites. "In the gay culture," John explained, "men's sexual desirability is measured by a crude term known as the 'Fuckability Quotient.' Many gay men quickly assess the Fuckability Quotient of every man they meet as a means of determining who they will pursue for even the simplest exchange. In fact, there seldom are simple, honest exchanges—almost every nuance is a calculated invitation or measured rebuff.

"Furthermore," John continued, finally casting off all self-consciousness, "some very specific components determine the FQ (as it is known for short), none of which have anything whatever to do with a person's soul or true self. High ratings are conferred for good looks, for how well someone is dressed, for handsome bodily proportions—for how hard and muscled they are—or for how well they return a sexually suggestive stare." John explained that FQ also increases with evidence of apparent wealth or other emblems of social status and success. "The bottom line is that specific, unwritten 'standards' are operative in various domains of the gay culture. The more a man fits those standards, the higher is his FQ and, consequently, the more attention he commands, and hence the more potential he has for selecting lovers and for a host of other social and even professional opportunities."

A few of the men stiffened as John spoke, and the women inched forward, making sure not to miss a word. The attention of everyone in the room was riveted on this lone gay man as he challenged the heterosexual men in the circle and expressed disdain for the superficiality of unbridled forms of raw male sexual energy. "Whether we're heterosexual or gay," John continued, "it seems that such crass frameworks for pursuing sexual intimacy are utterly misguided, and they are demeaning and hurtful to all parties involved. For me personally, my deepest desire is to discover true intimacy, and I know for certain that the profundity of sexual intimacy transcends the mechanics of physical passion and the functional release of body fluids."

As John spoke the energy in the room began to shift. One could almost hear the women in the room wanting to shout "Yes!" in appreciation of the fact that this man was naming something they too experienced. His words somehow exposed the offensiveness of objectification—the ruthless trivializing it entails. That it was a gay man speaking to this experience was profound; it opened the space in a unique way. There was something in John's stance, in his acknowledgment. Here was a man saying, I know, from experience, that exploitative male sexuality is hurtful, and it's a travesty of the true purpose and promise of authentic intimacy.

John's challenge opened the space for the men to drop inward to a deeper level of honesty and self-critical reflection. Some of the men conceded their own complicity in this kind of behavior. And rather than continuing with the shared rationalization that "that's just the way men are" and nothing can be done about it, the men began to examine and explore their sexuality and how they had grappled with it in different ways. Some spoke about how they were conditioned to think about male sexuality in the crude ways they had been describing. Others spoke of unacknowledged initiation processes that went on in school locker rooms—boyhood rituals in which they were taught what it is to "be a man."

A stocky, bright-eyed man named Jerry who had been quiet during much of the earlier discussion suddenly opened up with an insightful perspective. He explained that he had been very active in the "mythopoetic" men's movement in years past, from which he had benefited a great deal. Yet there were some aspects of the male experience, including sexuality, that were not adequately addressed in the men's movement, he said. Jerry then proceeded to offer a soliloquy of sorts on the effects of pornographic pictures passed around at school by adolescent boys. He spoke with conviction:

> There is a kind of false imprint on the young male psyche about the nature of sexuality that is crystallized in adolescent masturbation experiences with pornographic pictures and videos, which nowadays are channeled online directly into his bedroom. Those moments are devastatingly formative in his innocent psyche. As a result, the young boy then falsely believes that he knows what sex feels like, what women are supposed to look like and act like, and what it's all about—when actually he doesn't have a clue.
>
> And all this backlog of charged energy and expectation gets carried into his first sexual encounters with an actual girl or woman. Even as a young man falling in love for the first time, he is carrying all this pornographic conditioning without even realizing it's there. It's a kind of contamination, or a deflowering of his innocence and purity that happens long before he ever gets to that first sexual experience as a young man. And of course it's been constantly reinforced in the media, in the schoolyard, and especially on the internet ever since he could walk. So the impressionable young male coming of age never has a

chance; there is a kind of toxic poisoning of his intimate heart in relation to sexuality that starts in childhood, and then gets strongly reinforced in adolescence. And there it stays stuck, for most men—it's rarely healed after that. I think many men in society are still frozen at that adolescent stage, and it explains the continual obsession so many of us men have with young, naked women throughout our entire lives.

Many of the men nodded in agreement, and the room grew silent. One of the facilitators rang a bell chime to respect and sustain the charged silence for a few moments. As the men began speaking again, they slowly started to examine their sexual histories more deeply through this new lens. The word "wounded" entered the conversation for the first time. The emotional energy shifted—softened and became more tender—as several men shared experiences they'd had as boys that left them feeling devalued and damaged. Several spoke in hushed tones, others choked back tears.

Howard was a striking man in his mid-forties who was very active in men's work. He commanded a particular power and respect in the group, in part because he was a senior leader for a major national men's project. "When I was eight years old," he began slowly, "my mother was terrified of sexuality. Neither she nor my father ever talked about it with me or my sister. One day I was playing with some kids in our backyard, and after a while they all left except for a little girl named Janice. We kept on playing, and soon we got into that game, you know, where you show me yours if I show you mine. It was exciting, and I remember we both knew we had to be careful not to be seen. So we went behind the bushes at the back of the yard, where we'd be all alone.

"We hadn't been there very long when suddenly my mother appeared—like out of nowhere—towering above us in a raging fury. She sent Janice off scurrying home, yelling at her never to do that again. And then she took me inside and really let me have it."

Howard's lip began to tremble as the painful memories bubbled back up. He lowered his voice. "She had spanked me before, but this time she made me take off my pants, and she went at me with my Dad's thick leather belt on the bare butt. She kept shouting over and over—driving in each word with every thwack of the belt—'*Don't – you – EVER – do – that – again!*'"

Howard sat silent for a moment, and large tears began rolling down his trembling face. The man next to him reached out, gently placing his hand on Howard's shoulder. This gesture gave silent permission for Howard's grief and he broke into sobbing, but then quickly pulled himself back together again, and blew his nose.

"I've done a lot of therapy around this," Howard continued, "but it's amazing how that pain is still right there. Just under the surface." He paused, and then looked down. "The whole episode had a major debilitating effect on my later relations with girls, and basically destroyed my first marriage. And never, to this day, has my mother been able to talk about it with me. She just can't face it. I eventually gave up trying to address it with her."

Howard's tale struck a nerve and further dissolved the men's fear and self-consciousness. Other stories started coming out as the men became more forthright. The women listened ever more intently, and several quietly sniffled or choked back tears. There was a baseball coach who had used dirty jokes as a way to separate "the men from the boys." One boy had been repeatedly shamed by his sister and both parents for liking to play with girls. Another had been sexually violated by his priest when he was in junior high school, something he had only come to terms with in recent years.

A vibrant, athletic man named Mark reached for the talking stick. "When I was in eighth grade, I started 'going steady' with my first girlfriend. My parents became concerned and sat me down for a serious talk. I was raised Catholic, and they spoke about religious values, using big words like 'concupiscence,' which I didn't understand at all. But the message was clear. My mother got all tied in knots trying to say that sex was dirty and demeaning; not appropriate behavior for Christians like us. But then my father was saying it's different when you're older, and you're in love with your wife. It was obvious that neither of my parents was the least bit comfortable with the conversation, or with each other on this one. It was totally weird, and I knew they weren't giving me the whole story."

Mark started shaking his head, and then began to chuckle. His face suddenly lit up. "The absurd double message," he said, with a gleeful twinkle in his eye, "was this." He ceremoniously mimicked the unveiling of a somber proclamation: "Sex is disgusting, nasty, and immoral. Therefore, save it for someone you truly love!" Laughter filled the room, and with it came a wave of welcome relief to the intensity we had all been sharing.

As one man's revelation led to another, the power of each person's story was amplified by the others. The themes shifted beyond sexuality to include other issues. Many felt they were pushed to fulfill functional and disposable roles in society: as moneymakers, sperm donors, and child support providers (rather than fathers), as well as cannon fodder for the military machine. The silences between the words were thick, filled with irony and mutual recognition. Taken together, what became conspicuously clear was the massive conditioning the men had been subjected to in their lives as boys and as men. One way or another, most of the men in the group felt they'd been used or manipulated by the culture, coming not only from their childhood and parental upbringing but also from peers and social influences in their adult lives.

When the time for the men's truth forum was completed, the women were given an opportunity to reflect on what had been said. They began by honoring the men. For many women this experience was a first, and they felt privileged to have witnessed the men speaking so frankly, authentically, and searchingly about these aspects of their sexuality and conditioning. The men were genuinely surprised and touched by the women's reflections. They had not expected the women to be so appreciative; they had been more prepared for judgment and criticism. As the women spoke, expressing their feeling that the men had given them a gift by being so open, everyone in the group began to understand something about the work that needs to be done between women and men. The men felt they had accomplished something significant in their forum, and we all knew that we had, collectively, begun an important piece of healing work.

The irony, however, was that for many of the women, portions of the men's sharing represented a devastating confirmation of their concerns about male sexuality. This was doubly ironic because the confirmation had arisen precisely because the men had chosen to make themselves vulnerable by sharing candidly. An attractive, fiery woman in her mid-thirties named Julia spoke to this paradox. Carefully, but with determination, she said she feared the men were justifying their behavior to each other. "As a woman, I have to constantly compensate for the way my true being is trivialized by superficial lust. Men who desire me because they find my FQ sufficient are rarely available in any authentic way." She went on to explain that unbridled male sexual energy was ultimately assaulting. She was distressed that the men's truth forum seemed, even in the end, to have concluded that male sexuality is an unchallengeable reality—whether conditioned or biological—that women just have to accept. Her conclusion was abrupt and blunt: "I find it difficult to believe there isn't a more fundamental connection between men's hearts and their penises."

Others began to respond, but the hour was late, so the facilitators brought closure to the day with a silent meditation and honored the group for the unique and difficult nature of the work they were doing. As a way to respect the delicate place we were in as a group and to support deep integration of the work done so far, the facilitators requested that everyone in the group maintain silence until we met again the next day.

The Women's Truth Forum

In the morning, it was the women's turn to be in the inner circle while the men, seated around the outer edges of the room, listened in silent witness. The women's and men's roles were now reversed for the women's truth forum. As the talking stick went around, many of the women spoke about the power of the previous evening, and about the complex layers of gratitude, poignancy, and anger they were feeling as a result. Then Susan, a self-confident woman in her late twenties, interjected her thoughts.

"I totally identified with some of the men. When they defended their appreciation of female beauty and of evaluating women on a purely physical basis—I think this is perfectly natural, and what's more, I do it all the time myself—with both men and women. I often see men or women on the street and wonder what it would be like to have sex with them. I think this is perfectly normal, basic human behavior—sizing up potential mates. I don't mind that men do it to me, and it doesn't feel wrong when I do it, either."

An elegant older woman named Harriet bristled, and angrily challenged the whole idea of either gender sexualizing the other. "I find it unhealthy and dehumanizing," she exclaimed, "and I don't buy the idea that it's for potential mate selection." Harriet explained that the Fuckability Quotient more accurately described a system by which both women and men are manipulated, and coerced into manipulating each other. "We are essentially turned into commodities, and we exchange our quotient of desirability for whatever else we want—sex, power, position, even cash!

"Desirability is a kind of currency, almost like money," she prickled. Then she turned to Susan, who had spoken earlier, "and you're feeding the system. You are complicit in your own exploitation. You're attractive now, so it's to your advantage to stay in the game. But that won't always be the case. Eventually your FQ will drop, from aging if nothing else. What will you do then?"

The mounting tension among the women was forceful, so much so that one of the facilitators briefly interjected and encouraged the women to take some deep breaths and join hands in order to stay present with the intensity. Silence settled back in, and then Sally, a thirty-something self-identified feminist, took the talking stick. She urgently implored us to look more carefully at the ramifications of a society obsessed with the selling power of sex. Referencing video footage we had watched on the first day—testimonies of rape and related gender violence presented during a UN tribunal on human rights—Sally became adamant. "Rape is born from precisely the kind of sexual objectification that the men were talking about and that some of us have been romanticizing. Men are habitually aroused, not by relating or by imagining an actual relationship with the personhood of a woman. What arouses them—habitually and obsessively—is looking at a woman's body as something to possess, as a thing."

There was silence for a few moments as Sally's words sunk in. Then Julia, the woman who had expressed her dismay at the end of the previous evening, reached out resolutely and practically seized the talking stick. "Nancy Raine wrote a book called, *After Silence—Rape and My Journey Back*. She writes about living with fear the way others live with cancer."

Julia's eyes dropped toward the floor. "I know exactly what she's talking about."

Julia then began to describe how, some years earlier, a man had broken into her apartment at night while she slept, grabbed a jacket from her closet, and used it to cover and hold down her head. Her first awareness, she said, was of struggling to awaken from a terrible nightmare. But then Julia realized that this was no dream: "Whatever I was trying to wake from was actually happening in reality. My head was in some kind of grip. I spit and hissed and fought my way up until I could feel the windowsill against my back. It was my first contact with substance, a point of reference: Yes, I was awake in my bed, in my apartment, in Oakland, California, in the United States, on planet Earth."

She managed to sit up, she said, but could not free her head. Until the man spoke—threatening her life—she wasn't sure what she was fighting, or why. "Stop fighting me, bitch! . . . or I'll kill you!" Julia's voice rose to a near scream as she repeated his threat. All attention was riveted upon her as she stopped herself, drew in a deep breath, and became almost unbearably calm.

"It wasn't until he spoke that I understood that a man was in my bedroom, holding me down with something that he'd put over my head, that it was his hands and arms that were forcing me down as I tried to fight my way free. I couldn't see. I was trapped in the dark. The whole sequence of events was so abrupt and unexpected, so wrenching and incomprehensible, so the way violence is—changing everything in a heartbeat—that the truth of my experience simply overwhelmed me. I collapsed inwardly. Like everything else about being raped, it's hard to describe the sensation of deadly surrender. It felt like the space between my vertebrae gave way, like my body simply crumpled into half its size. I became inexplicably compliant and cooperative. I went limp.

"The next few minutes and hours are there inside me. I know, because whenever something wakes me in the night—my heart pounds, my body goes rigid."

Julia paused and took a deep breath. "I always want to stop the story right here. I never want to say what happened next. I don't want to talk about his penis, or the way it felt to have my face forced into a pillow so I could barely breathe. I want to end the story with the relief I felt when I realized my attacker was human. But, in fact, the rest of what happened is there, the events I didn't tell the police, although they tried to get me to. Events I didn't tell my mother, my father, or my brother. Events I've never laid out for any of my close friends, not even for a therapist, because every time I get to this place in the telling, I feel the shame crawling up the side of my neck and I feel the difference between the fear, which I can talk about, and the degradation, which I cannot."

Julia was silent for a time. Then, using her hands to shield her face, as if it weren't enough that her eyes were closed, she slowly began to relate a full description of the rape and the psychological annihilation she had experienced. As she spoke, Julia's outrage grew. Rape, she told us, is an experience of utter obliteration. No words could convey the dehumanizing impact of such a total invasion of her physical being. How could she begin to communicate the shattering loss of selfhood? It was as if he was the only one there, the only real person, the only sentient consciousness. She opened her eyes and looked around fiercely.

"But I *was* there! I existed! I mattered! And he didn't know it. I actually tried to reach out to him psychically. It was kind of an instinctual thing, I guess. I thought if he could feel my existence, my beingness, that he might somehow be moved to kindness. I didn't understand how committed he was to penetrating, without being penetrated—you know, touched, reached, connected."

The rapist, it turned out, was not the only one who violated Julia that night. After he made his escape, she called the police. Two male officers from the Oakland Police Department came to Julia's apartment. While questioning her, the officers made jokes about sex and asked about the rape with thinly veiled voyeurism—insisting on knowing what seemed to her like pornographic details. The two officers encouraged one another in this inquisition, exchanging knowing winks and raised eyebrows. After completing their investigation of her apartment the police took Julia to a building she could not identify. It was not a police station—more likely the morgue. The only person she saw there was another man, who was identified as a "police physician." The two officers stood behind the "physician" watching the "exam" and continuing with their sexual banter and innuendoes, while the physician probed Julia's vagina, looking for evidence of semen or physical injury. He chatted casually and joined the officers with laughter and jokes of his own. Eventually, he announced cheerily, "Yep, she's been raped!"

"I was never taken to a hospital, nor was it offered to me as an option," Julia continued. "I was never given the support of another woman or consoled in any way. To my knowledge, there was no further investigation of the rape. No one was ever prosecuted. In fact, my middle-of-the-night rendezvous with the officers was my only contact with the police department. I felt like I'd been raped yet again. They were as putrid to me as the smell of semen that stained the sheets of my bed."

Pin-drop silence filled the room when Julia finished speaking. We all sat in this poignant stillness for several minutes, absorbing the impact of her story. Then the group took a break in silence before reconvening back in the full plenary circle.

As the men began reflecting back their experience of the women's truth forum, many acknowledged that they had never before heard a woman speak so candidly about being raped, especially not in a way that captured the physical and psychological dimensions of the experience so vividly. One by one the men spoke, several with tears or visible anguish.

Mark began, his face flush with new realizations. "Never will I hear the word 'rape,' or think about rape, in the same way again," he said. "I had no idea what the experience must be like, until today." Others resonated with this, saying they felt they'd experienced something of the shock and horror of rape.

"It feels like I came as close as possible to living through the experience of rape," reflected Howard, "without actually being a woman, or facing the violation directly."

An older, quieter man named Jim had been relatively quiet through much of the gathering, and had become visibly upset during the rape story. He spoke haltingly, choking back tears. "I have five daughters. My middle daughter was raped when she was nineteen," he said. "At least two of my daughters were physically or sexually abused by their husbands and boyfriends. I never realized, until this day, what they must have gone through." He paused to collect himself. "I always thought . . ." His voice trailed off and he sat in silence, looking devastated. One of the facilitators moved next to him and put an arm around him. Jim began crying and mumbling softly, and then raised his voice slightly. "I realize I can't speak about this now. But thank you, Julia, and thank you to all the women. I'm grateful beyond what I can express."

Charles, the young law student, said that he realized for the first time what it must be like for women to live with the constant threat of sexual assault. "It's a shattering realization. I never really got it before how women and girls are always having to be vigilant—alert every minute of their lives; how they have to go through their daily activities with the perpetual threat of attack—as if they were prey to some wild animal on the loose."

Another man, in his early forties, named Tom, had hardly been able to contain himself, hearing all this. He became increasingly distraught as the conversation progressed, and finally burst in. "I need to—I *have to* interject here!" he stammered. "I know exactly what Julia is talking about! I was raped when I was fourteen—by the priest at our church!" Tom was shaking as he spoke, and his face was glowering, red. "Sodomized! Do you have any idea what that's like?!" he thundered. "There is an assumption here—and in our society—that only women get violated! Only women suffer from the patriarchy. I'm sick of that lie! I've lived with it all my life. It's not just women who suffer from rape!" Tom's rage filled the air, and two facilitators moved next to him, offering containment as well as support for him to move deeper into emotional release. Tom looked around the room, making eye contact with each person, and then dissolved into tears as grief overtook him. Recomposing himself within a few moments, he continued, "My mother was a staunch feminist. She was a leader in the women's movement, and she raised me to feel like a total schmuck, just for being male. All my life, she and her friends constantly engaged in male bashing of one kind or another, and they always made sure I understood every detail about how terrible men are."

Tom explained that he developed a deep guilt and inferiority complex, and grew up feeling constantly apologetic for being male. "It wasn't until I was in my late twenties and started years of therapy that I began to reclaim my own manhood. And with that came all the memories with the priest. It was brutal."

Tom's story ushered in a deeper sense of openness and trust in the group. Several expressed gratitude to both Tom and Julia for their courage and vulnerability in sharing their stories. Then Julia stood up, walked over to Tom, and whispered something to him. The two of them hugged, and tears began to flow freely around the group. The entire room was transported into a space of empathic sorrow and compassionate healing presence, not only for Julia and Tom, but for women and men everywhere who have suffered the excruciating agony of rape or sexual violation.

Despite the unimaginable pain and agony that was being expressed, a growing sense of intimacy was emerging in the group. Each story that came forward, each step into further exposure and vulnerability, brought us closer together as a group. The very act of bringing conscious, compassionate attention to our pain—unraveling and giving voice to these challenging and humbling experiences—was loosening their grip on us. Meeting the need for these long-repressed aspects of our humanity to be unveiled and witnessed was beginning to awaken unique dimensions of mutuality, human forgiveness, and authentic intimacy. We became acutely aware of the profound healing that is needed in our species. We knew with conviction that what we were doing, as women and men *together*, was confronting the cultural dynamics that are killing us all—killing women and men, killing people of every gender and race and ethnicity, killing our children, killing the planet.

Women's group at GERI workshop in Meru, Kenya, 2019

CHAPTER 6

Cure of Grace: The Heart of Reconciliation

The time had come to shift gears entirely [carrying on from the previous chapter]. All the intensive work we'd been doing was profound and transformative, but also demanding emotionally—even draining. It was vital to shift into a different experiential space together—one that would restore and rejuvenate us and consecrate our work. So, the next afternoon the women's and men's circles convened separately to create ceremonies of mutual honoring and blessing for one another. The women created a ceremony to honor the men and the masculine, and the men did the same to honor the women and the feminine. Both ceremonies were presented on the last evening.

Honoring ceremonies in gender reconciliation work are experiential offerings created and choreographed by the participants—as a means to express gratitude and offer blessings of mutual appreciation and forgiveness. The focus and content of the ceremonies are inspired directly by the uniqueness of each group and the particular work that has transpired within it. A true ceremony or ritual is never forced or staged. Both the design itself and its choreographed execution are spontaneously crafted through the power and process of the group that creates it.

An effective ritual ceremony serves as a kind of meta-narrative, helping us to re-structure attitudes and behavior in daily life beyond the ceremonial space itself. It is something we participate in together—a special time out of time—an experience invoked and orchestrated from within our deep selves. Through the ceremony we glean new information, insights, guidance—similar to the way one receives information from a dream that can then be brought into waking life. In gender reconciliation work, the power and beauty of the honoring ceremonies is directly proportional to the authenticity and depth of healing work and truthtelling that has preceded them. In this case, the group had done some extraordinary healing.

As the women's group and men's group embarked upon designing ceremonial offerings for each other, there was tremendous enthusiasm and spirited joy all around. Both groups entered into a rarefied environment of high energy, creativity, and playful tenderness—peppered with frequent outbursts of laughter. Because their hearts were so open, people were willing to risk and stretch themselves in ways that might have seemed unthinkable only days before. Everyone was aware that this was a rare privilege:

to actually take the time and "trouble" to honor, acknowledge, and bless one other across the "gender gap."

The men presented their ceremony first. They were pleased to be offering a ceremony of their own creation, weaving in unique references and vignettes from the foregoing week. The men ushered the women into a beautiful, sanctuary-like setting and seated them in a semicircle facing the men. The room was lit all around with candles. After an opening song and prayer, each man stepped forward, picked up a candle, and stood before the women. One at a time, the men spoke to their complicity in reinforcing the "patriarchy," which had been largely unconscious. Each man named a behavior or characteristic that he no longer found acceptable in himself and committed himself to changing it. These declarations varied greatly according to each man's unique character, maturity, and personal growing edge. Charles, the lanky law student, said "I have learned so much about women's pain this week which I never realized before. I can see how insensitive I've been to some of the women I've been working with and dating at school this year. I am committing myself to listen to them more deeply, to open to them."

Each man had written his behaviors of complicity on a piece of paper beforehand, as the men had planned, and after all the men had spoken they put all these papers together into a ceremonial fire pot and burned them—dramatically symbolizing the release of these behaviors and ritualizing their commitment to personal transformation.

After the papers were burned, the men made personal vows of renewed alliance with the women, coupled with a symbolic offering of summer blossoms they had gathered. Each man stepped forward, spoke his vow, bowed deeply before the women, and then floated his blossom with his personal blessing in a basin of scented water.

When it came to be Howard's turn, he began to speak in halting tones, but his voice grew stronger and more confident as he spoke. "This week . . . has been a major breakthrough for me. I realized something very important: I have been spiritually asleep . . . while dreaming that I am spiritually awake . . ." He paused, allowing his words to sink in. "I have resisted waking up from this comforting slumber. As you know, I've done lots of men's work over the years, and I've been leading it for a long time. Until this week, I had believed that I'd pretty much healed my personal collusion with the patriarchy, and that I was taking full responsibility for it in the world through my men's work."

He paused, making eye contact with each woman individually, and then continued. "But what I've realized here is that there is another whole level of work to be done. Until now, I had believed I was free of patriarchal insensitivity, and that I never took male privilege for granted. Because of these cherished beliefs, I could not see that there was a deeper level of complicity and denial still operative within me. I have been blind to the ways that I am still perpetuating patriarchal dysfunction, on more subtle levels. And I don't think I'm the only 'sensitive, aware man' for whom this is true. There is a huge, uncharted territory here that needs to be explored . . . with great care and sensitivity. And it requires that men and women do this healing work together. I believe this is the next step that is needed in the men's movement. And I vow to find ways to bring this mutual healing work between women and men into the men's community."

Howard silently placed his blossom on his heart and then gently floated it alongside the others in the water. When each man had spoken, the men clustered around the basin and approached the women. They anointed each woman individually with the water, speaking her name, and offering specific reflections of her soul's depth and beauty. The men then stood together before the women, bowed, and prostrated themselves on the ground.

Many of the women wept. The men's ceremony had been startling and beautiful. The women understood that the men were acknowledging the ways in which cultural conditioning creates difficult gender dynamics that women must grapple with, often on a daily basis. The men had expressed personal awareness of these realities in a ritualized manner. And they offered more than an apology; they expressed their commitment to transform personal complicity and become instruments of healing between the masculine and feminine in society.

Deeply moved, with their hearts wide open, the women began their ceremony for the men. Each man was escorted, flanked by a woman on each side, into the community room, which the women had decorated with flowers and candles. The women seated the men in a circle and gave them flowers to hold. Then they began chanting a song of compassion and love, which they sustained throughout the ceremony.

As the women chanted, they moved around the circle. Each woman stopped before each man and thanked him individually by quietly naming that man's virtues, gifts, and beauty, as she saw them. Each woman made her specific offerings to each man in whatever way felt appropriate to her: softly whispering appreciation, grasping hands, giving a warm hug or a sisterly kiss, bowing, massaging the man's face or feet, or simply looking fully and radiantly into his eyes—offering each man her respect, affection, and honor. Words and thoughts dissolved into a profound presence of nurturing harmony and reverence as the women's soft chanting and attentive ministering led the men into a gentle yet stirring ecstasy. The sweet rose fragrance of the burning incense was but a tiny semblance of the loving presence that filled the room and lifted the hearts of all in the spirit of cherished communion. Tears flowed freely on both sides.

The depth of the healing work we had done together was powerfully consecrated in these ceremonies. As Howard put it later, "The pinnacle of our work together in this workshop was, without a doubt, the group ceremonies. It felt like I saw God—or, actually, the Goddess!—in a new way."

In Jerry's words,

> Our ceremony for the women was highly charged. I found tears streaming from my eyes. I truly felt that this outpouring of intent was the least we could do to represent all men—those who are involved in gender reconciliation work, and those who aren't ready for it yet. And then, the ritual in which the women honored us men was sublime. Talk about an altered state of consciousness! The energy of the nurturing feminine was so thick in the room that I felt like each woman, thanking me in her own way, was a unique incarnation of the Goddess. My experience of the ceremony was a magnificent, intensely beautiful evocation of the many facets of the Divine Feminine. It was truly a transcendental experience.

Harriet, who had earlier been so "triggered" during the workshop, later described her experience of the ceremonies:

> I felt all those unresolved issues within myself. And then I saw all the contradictions break apart, and our hearts break open, when in ceremony on the last day the men prostrated themselves in front of us. Many of us were left speechless; there was incredible power and sincerity in that silent, collective gesture. And later I saw tears in the men's eyes as we women circled in honor of them. Out of the ashes of our disagreements and confrontations rose the sacred masculine and the sacred feminine again.

The women and men in this workshop who so courageously attended to each other discovered—and embodied—the essence of gender reconciliation. They opened themselves to the "alchemical" nature of authentic healing and persevered through the agonizing pain buried deep in the collective human psyche until they reached the "gold" of ecstatic loving communion between masculine and feminine.

The Mystical Heart of Healing

Another example is recounted from a woman named Gail at a Gender Equity and Reconciliation Workshop at Ghost Ranch, New Mexico:

> Empty from losses, numb in relation to myself and others, I entered a dark void of mystical transformation. My heart opened that week and my life changed. Cracked like an egg, split in half, I experienced the core of my being. The workshop was the vehicle, the safe space to begin the intense process of self-discovery. It left me with passion burning within, which melted away icebergs of deep-seated emotions frozen from years of wounds buried.
>
> Entering the workshop, I felt poised and self-confident, able to draw from my years of professional training and education to speak my values and opinions

during the group circles. This framework sustained me for the first few days.

Then came the holotropic breathwork. Doors unlocked within me that had been closed for years. Blissful from overcoming my fear and finding strength in my vulnerability, I spent the next day in quiet reflection. I hiked the mountains, walked the labyrinth, and meditated on the opening of my heart. I felt unified and whole as never before.

"You have an edge about you," a large-framed, gray-haired male participant, named Ralph interrupted my reverie during dinner. "I sized you up the very first day."

"What do you mean?" I asked, feeling jarred by what felt like a jolt of sexually charged energy.

"I bet you have men clawing at your door," he continued chuckling.

All week, I had consciously taken care to not even subtly engage romantically or sexually with anyone in the group. My commitment from the beginning was to refrain from any of this, which would stifle the whole experience, and was also the community agreement. I knew I had not flirted or knowingly enticed any man during the workshop. But yet, like radar, this man had sensed my state of tender openness, and was using his power to tap into my life-force and drain my heightened vitality.

"Why are you saying this to me?" I asked as tears welled in my eyes. "You're supposed to leave your judgments at the door when entering this workshop."

"This is just the way I am," he said patting my leg. "I'm too old to change my ways." I felt sexually objectified as he ignored my internal process and devalued the beauty of my unfolding. It was like a bad dream. I strained to stay engaged, desperately trying to understand.

"You're hurting me," I said, forcefully scooting my chair back, repulsed at his touch and his words.

"I'm sorry," he said, appearing slightly affected by my reaction. "No need to bring this up again."

"Oh, yes there is," I said angrily, standing to leave. "That's what we're here for."

Rage heated every cell of my body as the moon lit my path back from the dining hall to the community center. Two other participants walked with me.

"I ran right into a lion's den," I said, disgusted at my naivete.

"Sometimes it's not worth speaking out," said the man who had sat with me during my breathwork. "You should pick your battles wisely," he continued, attempting to console.

"He had no right!" I said, incensed that this cold water was tempering my blaze. "This is what we're here for. I have to speak out." Empathic eyes recognized my fury as I glanced over to the older woman by my side.

"Let's do a quick check-in," said one of the women facilitators when the group reconvened, as her monitoring eyes stopped on me. "Peaceful," "wonderful," "content," the voices rang out as the talking-stone was passed around the circle. Heated by human touch, the smooth, heart-shaped stone filled my hands and grounded me. "Extremely unsettled," I choked out the words through a tight noose of emotion that constricted my throat. A warm, gentle hand touched mine and replaced the stone as I passed it to the next person. Shaking uncontrollably, I held tight to the life raft offered.

After the check-in, the facilitators explained that we would be separating into women's and men's groups and that we would meet separately to honor group time alone. Silently, the men departed. The circle of women drew closer, filling the empty spaces left by the men. Concerned and curious eyes penetrated me hoping to heal the disruption that had occurred. Frozen, my heart raced. "Relax! Stop shaking! Breathe!" screamed my inner voice. The air was thick with silence.

Steaming like a volcano about to erupt, I spoke. Words poured without substance. "What happened?" someone finally said, interrupting my disconnected rambling. Pausing, I took a deep breath, hoping to bring order to the chaos in my head. I began again. After explaining the details, I looked into the eyes of one particular woman and apologized. She was the accused man's partner. Her sympathetic voice validated my story and acknowledged her partner's character. Her friends voiced their agreement. "If you knew him better," one of them said, "you'd understand that's his personality. We all just put up with him." I felt victimized again, but now by women, I shrunk down further into my shell. Self-doubt invaded me. *Was I wrong in what I spoke?* I wondered. *Maybe my feelings weren't valid.*

"Ralph came on to me too," said Allison, a soft-spoken, petite woman with long, dark hair. Relief showered me as I heard the affirming words. "Yesterday," she continued, "he came to me and said, "If I was 30-years younger, I'd be all over you."'

The group sat silently with the news of this second offense.

"Why didn't you warn me?" I demanded. "Why didn't you tell someone?"

"I did tell someone," she bit back. "I told my roommate. Gail, I tried to tell you, but remember you were unavailable."

Torn between emotions of anger and hurt, I sat quietly, trembling as other women shared their feelings. Again, the discussion began to shift toward justifying this man's actions. Again, I felt deserted.

"Damn it!" shouted another woman. "Can't any of you see the pain Gail is in?" Several minutes of anger burst from this woman as she stood-up for me like a protective parent that the child in me welcomed. Others tried to calm her fury.

"I'm embarrassed," another woman said meekly, "because I would have never realized that his behavior was wrong." Fear, guilt, anger, sadness, and hurt inflamed the heart of the community. I sat in the heat of the fire.

"Gail, what do you need from us?" one of the facilitators asked. My body was rigid with emotion. Trembling, I looked around the circle attempting to satisfy the longing of my desire. "I need to know that all of you will stand with me. Right now, I'm not sure." One by one each woman acknowledged her support.

After nearly two hours of further processing, the women's group determined that the community agreements had been broken. A commitment of silence was established until the following morning, when everyone would bear witness to the issue.

Dreams of warriors and dark voids punctuated a fitful and brief night of sleep. The dark and hazy morning sky reflected my mood as I prepared for what was to come. Beaten down from waves of emotion, I attempted to hide my anguish under a mask of make-up applied like war-paint. I hated conflict, but often I found myself speaking out against injustice. But unlike the many times before, this experience was different. On this day, I was having to stand up for myself.

Twice during the week I had walked the labyrinth, once in ecstasy and now in despair. The early morning mist washed over and cooled me as I meditated through the winding stone path to the center. Leading with heart, I opened myself to the spirit of my grandmothers, my mother, and daughter. Images of my son flashed before me. Two ravens flew high above the rocky cliffs. Letting go, I breathed in the strength being offered to me.

Back at the community center, I waited. Gentle hugs and compassionate eyes comforted me and softened my fear. Diane, a facilitator, sat with me in the circle as one of the male facilitators, explained the practice of witnessing. The women would continue the discussion from the night before. The men would sit in a surrounding circle and listen in silence without responding. The tension in my body mounted like the mercury rising in a thermometer.

Again, I spoke the violation. This time all the men, including Ralph, were present, sitting in silence. For over an hour, I listened as the women spoke, and internalized the multitude of emotions coming forth. The further we spoke, the deeper each woman's story resonated within me. Finally, we announced that the community agreements had been dishonored. This man's behavior required some type of response from the community. My heart sank. Everyone was suffering from what I had shared. However, not speaking would have further injured my self-worth and dignity, and my silence would have damaged the integrity of the community.

During a short break, the facilitators spoke with me and Allison and asked if we would be willing to be part of a healing circle with Ralph. Together, we would confront him with our complaint. He could then respond. The rest of the community would bear witness in a surrounding circle. We each agreed to participate. The facilitators had also asked Ralph, and he was willing to participate as well.

"Just don't leave me," I appealed to the two women facilitators. They promised to stay. I desperately wanted to escape. "Raven, show yourself," I pleaded, looking out the window for its deeper mystical message of transformation. All four facilitators gathered in the center circle.

Suddenly, Raven's shadow appeared on the wall before me. I turned and saw Raven through the window in flight against the dark, rainy sky. "Ah," breathing deeply, I felt the calming magic of Raven's visitation. Nature was alive and supporting me. I entered the circle, taking in the energy of the women, the men, and the entire community.

There was an arrangement of cushions set up in the center, and the facilitators asked the two of us and Ralph to each invite a support person from the outer circle to join us by our side. Then the facilitators opened with a beautiful prayer and asked the entire group to focus their hearts and prayers on the three of us in the center of the room, explaining that the outer circle was providing very important silent support for the inner circle.

Listening as the other woman spoke first, I yearned for her power and conviction. I gazed into Ralph's eyes as he absorbed her words. He began shaking. I, too, was trembling. When she was complete, the male facilitator rang a mindfulness bell, then asked Ralph if he wanted to respond. "Not yet," he whispered, appearing crestfallen.

Now it was my turn to speak. Ralph turned toward me, fully present, unarmored, prepared to take whatever punishment I was going to give. In that moment, I realized that Ralph and Allison in the healing circle with me were symbolic of my mother and father, my own femininity and masculinity. I sat between the divisions that had been part of my life for so long. I wasn't feeling anger anymore, mostly just sadness, and lingering hurt. As I spoke, tears flowed from my eyes. And from Ralph's. Watching this man cry, I embraced his pain, and at the same time I more fully understood my own father's suffering. When I finished speaking, the bell rang again, and the facilitator invited Ralph to speak.

Several moments passed, before he attempted to respond. "My tears," he said finally, "are my answer." Ralph was choking on the intensity of his emotion. "My tears say how sorry I am." He paused and took a long breath to help ease his shaking, before slowing to speak again. "I didn't mean to hurt anyone," he said looking at both Allison and me. "I had no idea the impact my words and behavior would have on both of you. I thought it was just playful bantering. I'm not trying to excuse what I did, or the impact it has had." Looking down in anguish, he shook his head and said, "I really just didn't realize this would be so hurtful. But I see now that it was." Looking up with tears continuing to flow he said, "I am so very sorry. I hope you can accept my apology."

Years of bottled-up feelings within were released listening to his words. In hearing him, and knowing that he had truly heard me, my divided heart came back to wholeness. The facilitators rang the bell and asked for a moment of silence. Then they invited Allison and me to share whatever else was still on our hearts. If anything needed to be said. Both of us, one at a time, expressed our gratitude for Ralph's openness to listen and hear us, and we thanked him for the sincerity of his apology. He was moved to further tears by our words. The three of us embraced, and a wave of radiant healing energy—and relief!—went surging through the entire group. Just as we completed our embrace, amazingly, in that moment the sun suddenly broke through the dark winter sky, shedding luminous light, warmth, and loving energy upon us all. We all just soaked it in.

It seemed almost too good to be true, but in that auspicious moment of deep healing and reconciliation, it truly felt as if a veil opened, and the Divine not only was shining *Her/His* light upon us, but actually communing with us in a glorious celebration of all that had transpired. As one man in the outer circle said afterwards, "I saw the mystical heart of Christ in the room."

We had come to a very beautiful resolution, and there was a sense of optimism within us all that truth was spoken for these issues that so often go unaddressed and are just "swept under the rug." As a community we had addressed the issue and confronted what had happened—but had done so with compassion—and we moved through it in a way that was a deep learning and spiritual uplift for everyone.

Healing a Broken Heart

A final example is recounted from a woman in a GERI workshop in Toronto in 2011:

Some of the more riveting experiences of my life have been in GERI workshops, both at home in Canada, and abroad in the magnificent country of South Africa. One experience that comes to mind is a passionate scene, unfolding before my eyes, that still takes my breath away.

At one point during the workshop, we were in the women's truth forum, and a young, powerful woman was standing in the center of the circle, arms raised. She had been badly abused by many men over her lifetime. Her anger was vehement and righteous. She briefly shared two incidents of being violated, and her rage boiled up. She shouted, screamed, stamped, and bellowed. Then she glared at the men, who were sitting in the outer circle in silent witness. Her gaze fell on one of the male facilitators, who seemed to represent all of her abusers. She paced back and forth, shaking and trembling, and said she was afraid.

Then the male facilitator rose gently, and slowly got down on his knees. He shuffled across the circle, on his knees, and stopped right in front of her. She stopped in mid-sentence. Then he bent his head low and said, "I cannot take away your pain. I can't change the past. I cannot undo all the terrible things that have happened to you, at the hands of these men. ... But what I can do, on behalf of these men, and *all* men, is to apologize to you. I am sorry for these horrible things that have happened to you at the hands of men." His eyes welled up with tears, as he raised his head, and his eyes met her astonished gaze. She took a big sobbing breath. She started to cry, and then...she mumbled, "Thank you." She hung her head, still crying, and said, "That's all I ever really wanted . . . an apology." Her whole demeanor shifted. "A genuine apology is all I wanted," She asked for a hug, and they embraced briefly. She settled herself, and for the remainder of the workshop she seemed in a new and better place."

Follow up 8 months later: We hadn't heard from this woman since the workshop. One day out of the blue, we received an email message from her. She wrote:

I just wanted to drop you a note to say hello and wish you a happy holiday season. You have deeply touched my spirit and my heart. Although many things have changed and are changing, I am profoundly grateful for the opportunity of being part of the GERI workshop. The seeds that were planted are still being nurtured and some have developed into little plants!

For the first time in my life I am experiencing a fun, joyous relationship with a man—something I never thought would be possible. Although it is still in its early stages, I firmly believe this would never have been possible without the healing that took place at the Gender Reconciliation workshop. Thank you for helping me appreciate this very special moment in my life.

GERI: The Journey from My Head to My Heart

Mark Greene

I had the great good fortune to become a member of the Gender Equity and Reconciliation International community as a result of my men's work with the ManKind Project. The ManKind Project is a community of men working to heal men's trauma and disconnection. As a result of that work, I received an invitation to attend the GERI workshop. There are faces and stories from the GERI Workshop that remain with me to this day. Although it has been years since I attended, a rainbow-colored friendship string remains tied around my left wrist. The woman who tied it there could not have been more different than me in terms of race, religion, country of origin, and her rich personal history, but the string remains, a reminder of how connected I feel to her to this very day.

In order to fully understand the impact of GERI in my life, there are two pieces of my story that are important. One is that I had already spent over a decade writing and speaking about masculinity and men's issues. In my capacity as a Senior Editor for the Good Men Project I had published hundreds of articles exploring our bullying, dominance-based culture of masculinity, my goal being to deconstruct our angry, reactive, binary-riddled dialogues around gender. My writing created an impact, drove conversations, created change.

Meanwhile, a friend had invited me many times to attend a ManKind Project weekend. I steadfastly refused. It is often said that the longest journey for many men to make is the sixteen inches from our heads to our hearts. I was wary of that journey. My reluctance was rooted in some simple truths about myself. I did not trust men. I did not like men. In fact, I hated men *and* I was sick to death of being alone. A fifty-five-year-old man, with a wonderful marriage, a joyful family, and work I felt privileged to be doing, and yet, beneath all that, this fear and anger towards men was my story.

My men's work with the MKP taught me to address my past trauma and make change. Doing that work changed my life, helped my marriage, strengthened my relationship to my son, and redefined both my long-term friendships and men I am newly proud to call my friends. It changed everything for me. But it also opened the door to another area of work that I needed to engage. Such is the nature of taking on our personal work; it doesn't have a final goal or end point. It is a path leading us where we intuitively sense we have to go. My contacts in the Mankind Project invited me to attend a Gender Equity and Reconciliation weekend. And so, I went.

The vast gulf of silence between men, women and non-binary people, the lack of shared stories and understanding is a testament to the degree to which our culture's rigid and brittle gender binary keeps us apart, distrustful, and out of balance. Our dominance-based culture of masculinity (sometimes called Man Box culture) breaks boys' emotional expression and connection very early in our lives and then slots young men into a dominance-based hierarchical masculinity, in which we are taught we must dominate others or lose status.

How do we train boys out of connection? When a young boy expresses too much emotion, be it tears or joyful giddiness, or when a boy expresses too much need for connection or comfort, we say to that boy, "What are you, a sissy? What are you, a girl?" We take the most universal human capacities for forming relationships, namely emotional expression and the need for connection, wrongly gender them as feminine, and then we use the *denigration of the feminine* to train boys into isolation. What is lost to boys is empathy, caregiving, compassion and connection across difference. Our culture blocks boys from doing the trial-and-error work over the course of their childhoods to learn to express in nuanced, relationally intelligent ways. And because we break that connection to self via the denigration of the feminine, we teach boys beginning when they are too small to even understand what is happening, *that women and girls are less.*

Men will tell you that this is where misogyny is rooted for so many of us. Beginning early in childhood with our parents, our brothers and sisters, the kids in our neighborhood and at school, our coaches, teachers and religious leaders, in movies and media. We were taught the narrow and restrictive rules for being emotionally stoic, tough, dominant males. The disdain we were expected to have for girls and women was pounded into us daily, hourly by the micro policing from the boys around us, all modeling dominance via the denigration of the feminine. We learned to hide away major parts of who we are, those aspects that don't fit the narrow confines of Man Box culture. The result for men trapped in Man Box culture is lifetimes of deep isolation.

In *The Will To Change*, bell hooks writes, "The first act of violence that patriarchy demands of males is not violence toward women. Instead patriarchy demands of all males that they engage in acts of psychic self-mutilation, that they kill off the emotional parts of themselves. If an individual is not successful in emotionally crippling himself, he can count on patriarchal men to enact rituals of power that will assault his self-esteem."[1]

For millions of men, the gulf between ourselves, women, and gender non-binary people, feels too vast to bridge. Which is why, even a man like myself—who had both wrestled and written extensively about the harm done by Man Box culture, who had done men's work—still felt little hope in ever healing my disconnection from the larger community of women. So much harm has been done and continues to be done by men, that I felt I would always be justifiably viewed as a possible threat; distrusted by women and non-binary people. In spite of all that, and pushing against my deep discomfort, I attended the GERI weekend. What I found was a group of men and women sharing their stories, and it was those human stories that proved to be the most powerful bridge of all.

Each person's experience of the GERI workshop is quite personal and distinctive. If my work of the ManKind Project was learning to trust and connect with men, then the GERI workshop helped me discover what it feels like to be trusted, and to find community and connection with women. I was brought into relationship with a diverse group of human beings from all over the world, all seeking to express our trauma and to see each other more clearly and completely. For many of the men in that group, we had an opportunity for the first time to speak to a group of women about our pain, our confusion, the harm we had done to women in the past, and the guilt we all too often carry. And such surprising responses emerged. "I thought you men were made of steel," one woman told us tearfully. "I thought I could hit you over and over and that you could take it. I'm so sorry."

In a culture of violence, it is impossible that violence does not go both ways. Such moments are powerful, revelatory. We, as men, were able to offer apologies that were deeply heartfelt, elevated by the ritual and storytelling of the weekend. We were able to make public commitments to ourselves, commitments to creating a world free of violence and abuse against women, in that moment, freeing ourselves a bit from our own long histories of pain and shame.

The GERI workshops changed my understanding of women's lives and struggles. No longer abstractions, the story telling and the work we did brought women's experiences, their resiliency, their power, and their determination home to me in a deeply personal way. Since that weekend I have carried a heartfelt understanding of what it means to have a shared purpose to make a better world in partnership with women and non-binary people. I understand what my place is in that agreement, which has created for me an immense sense of belonging. In finding that clarity, the journey of sixteen inches from my head to my heart now feels forever completed.

Mark Greene is Senior Editor of the Good Men Project, and author of *Remaking Manhood* and *The Little Me-Too Book for Men*.

Women and men at GERI workshop, Ghost Ranch, New Mexico, 2020

Women and men at GERI workshop, Busia, Kenya, 2025

GERI intensive workshop for Unity Church in Walnut Creek, CA, 2025

CHAPTER 7

Embracing the Beloved: Sexuality and Sacred Communion

Sexual pleasure is "a gift from God" that should be "disciplined with patience."
— Pope Francis

In the sacred epic *Mahabharata* from India, there is a story of a noble young prince named Pandu who, while hunting, takes the lives of two mating deer. His five swift arrows pierce effortlessly to the heart of their unguarded pleasure. As the stag lies dying, he turns to Pandu and begins to speak. He is no ordinary stag, but is in fact the holy rishi *Kindama*, who transformed himself and his wife into wild deer so that they might couple in sublime innocence. The holy stag curses Pandu—not because the hunter has killed, but because he has defiled life's most precious union. "You have taken advantage of the hallowed union that perpetuates and delights all life—henceforth are you cursed. If ever you should lie with a woman again, that shall be the moment of your death!"

This story from the *Mahabharata* reminds us that the sexual act is something sacred, to be protected and honored—and that to take advantage of this most precious of human experiences can lead to our demise. And we don't have to look far in society to find striking examples of such demise. From the Catholic Church, to Capitol Hill, to MeToo downfalls and exploitations in multinational corporations and progressive social change organizations, symptoms of our troubled relationship with sex are everywhere manifest. We live in an environment in which sexuality is often trivialized and defiled, stripped of its emotional depth and divorced from its sacred root. This occurs in different ways throughout our society, and one particularly challenging arena is the complex domain of pornography, which we now examine a bit more closely.

Grappling with Pornography

Pornography has become the default sex education in contemporary societies. Issues related to pornography frequently arise in the course of our gender reconciliation work, and pornography has grown over the years to become a key theme in the lives of many people who come to GERI programs.

The pornography industry today is continuing to expand, enhanced tremendously by the Internet. In the United States, the industry mushroomed from an estimated ten million dollars in the 1970s to around ten billion dollars in 2006, a thousand-fold increase.[1] In 2019, the global online porn market was estimated to be $35.17 billion, and it grew rapidly thereafter due to COVID-19.[2] Pornhub, an explicit-video-sharing site, reports that it gets 2.4 million visitors per hour, and in 2015 alone, people around the globe watched 4,392,486,580 hours of its content, which is more than twice as long as *Homo sapiens* has spent on Earth.[3]

Exactly how much pornography is there on the Internet? Estimates vary widely, but probably the most reliable estimates come from a massive 2010 study carried out by two neuroscientists, Odi Ogas and Sai Gaddam. They report that in 1991, the year the World Wide Web went online, there were fewer than 90 different adult magazines published in America. Just six years later, in 1997, there were about 900 pornography sites on the Web. In another fifteen years, this number grew to 2.5 million pornography websites in 2012. Ogas and Gaddam analyzed several billion Internet searches and found that of the 1 million most visited websites, 42,337 were sex-related—about 4 percent.[4] They also tracked web searches from July 2009 to July 2010 and found the proportion that involved porn was 13 percent. Finally, they interviewed officials at the major search engines about the prevalence of porn searchers, which produced estimates of 10 to 15 percent. Crunching these numbers, Ogas and Gaddam estimate that altogether, pornography accounts for around 10 percent of all the material on the Internet. Higher estimates of 30 to 50 percent or more are frequently seen, which may have been accurate in the earliest years of the Internet (1997–1999), when the vast majority of web users were young adult men. In 1999, about 40 percent of web searches involved porn, but as web demographics expanded to include most of the population, the researchers note, the proportion of porn searches has fallen substantially.

Sexually explicit videos and images are promulgated through cyberspace to ever wider, ever younger audiences, as well as to diverse peoples across the globe, many of whom had little or no prior exposure to pornography. Analysts and critics are divided in their assessment of the phenomenon, but no one doubts that the impact on society is huge.

At the 2003 meeting of the American Academy of Matrimonial Lawyers, two-thirds of attending lawyers said that online pornography is playing a significant role in contemporary divorces. Later studies on divorce have reported similar results.[5] In recent years there has been significant research documenting the addictive powers of pornography, and its ability to ruin sexual intimacy.[6] Gary Wilson has done extensive research on how pornography activates addictive neurological responses in the brain.[7] His popular TED talk, "The Great Porn Experiment," went viral on the Internet.

In 2016, Drs. John and Julie Gottman, two of the world's leading researchers on marriage and relationship, published an open letter on pornography, which summarized numerous studies and their own extensive research, and stated that "we are led to unconditionally conclude that for many reasons, pornography poses a serious threat to couple intimacy and relationship harmony."[8] Shortly thereafter the Gottmans qualified this conclusion somewhat in an update, writing that "When couples use porn in a way to stimulate each other, such as in masturbation and fantasy, porn can be beneficial to a relationship. ... Using porn can lead couples to discuss their sexual preferences, and research does show that talking about sex improves a couple's sex life and leads to more orgasms for women. This is good. But this use of porn is rare, at least in the research we did... While porn use can be a way for couples to openly discuss sex and improve their sex lives, which is a positive outcome, the negative consequences of excessive porn use, such as becoming conditioned to require porn to become sexually aroused or achieve orgasm, are readily apparent."

There have long been advocates for pornography, such as Candida Royalle and Carly Milne who maintain that pornography is a healthy force in people's lives. Royalle received a lifetime achievement award for her work at the Feminist Porn Awards in Toronto.[9] Recently a post-porn movement has emerged as a counterculture body of scholarship and ideals developed within Europe and the USA. The post-porn movement applies a critical lens to corporations producing pornography, and values instead non-corporate pornographic content, as well as pornography that centers queer and gender diverse people, and questions the racialization and reliance on stereotypes in the pornography industry.

Passion and Peril

In the late 1990s, we organized a series of invitational workshops for leaders in the women's and men's movements at the time, and other social change professionals. We experimented with a unique exercise developed by John Stoltenberg, author of *What Makes Pornography Sexy*.[10] The results were challenging but insightful, and helped show how pornography impacts our society, and our unconscious attitudes about sexuality, physical beauty, intimacy, and socially acceptable behavior. We eventually moved on from this exercise, but the insights were valuable, as recounted in the first edition of this book.

Over the years we have heard many stories about the impact of pornography on people's lives, often shared for the first time in our GERI programs. It takes great courage for people to recount these stories in a group, and the result is generally very liberating for the person sharing, and moves the entire group deeply, inspiring a greater level of honesty, vulnerability, and intimacy. Examples from two young adults we shall call Clair and Greg are given below.

Innocence to grief to grace: Clair's story

I was quite lucky growing up. I was somehow kept free and very innocent about sexuality, partly because my Dad and my first boyfriend protected me a lot, especially maybe my first boyfriend who was not as transparent as he could have been.

By age 27, I had spent most of my life feeling like gender equality had already happened. I just never really thought about it. I didn't think gender was interesting or important in any way, and I didn't think women's empowerment was a thing to be concerned about. I felt vaguely disdainful about the whole thing.

At that time, something happened between me and my boyfriend that led to a major shift—one that is still ongoing—that gave me new insight into a collective pattern far greater than just that relationship. I started asking my boyfriend about pornography; if he watched it, and if so how much. I didn't expect him to say yes, but he said, "Yes, of course I do," and he laughed a bit. I don't know how to explain it, but something in me began to divide. I wanted to understand more, so I asked him more, and as we spoke something started rising in me, a very strong feeling of horror and grief that I couldn't make sense of. I thought, "But these women that you're watching and masturbating over, you don't know anything about them! They're just a body to you. How do you rip apart a woman's body from her being?" Even as I write this, I feel so much grief about it, because this is such a relentless force in society. It's something that still causes me a huge amount of grief today.

As we talked more, I went into a state of shock. I'd never really thought about these things before. I'd always thought of myself as highly progressive and very much on the liberal side of things. I never considered myself conservative or moralistic or anything like that, and yet I found myself really troubled by this. On my way home from his place the next morning I had a terrifying moment in the train station. I looked around and saw all these women's bodies on the magazines, and I suddenly realized with horror, *we're just here to sell stuff. We're being used to sell stuff.* At the time it felt like such a strong insight, and the grief about how we are being used was so new and so hard to accept, that I almost fainted.

When I got home I went to the bathroom and started retching. I thought I was going to vomit. My male housemate asked me what was going on. I told him what had happened and he said, "Oh yeah, it's quite common" and he showed me a picture of this naked woman on his laptop screen. He was kind of empathetic, but also presented an attitude that said "Yeah, this is part of life."

Over the next year I sank into a very deep and dark experience of trauma and depression about patriarchy. I wanted to understand what was going on with men, so I stayed in my relationship. I thought to myself, "I'm going to stay, I'm going to understand this." I thought that maybe there is something there that I needed to learn. I wanted to understand what's going on, so I really "pornified" myself in my relationship in sex, even to society itself on some level. I thought, maybe if I do this then it'll be enough for him.

For me, the trauma consisted in the realization that I, and all women, were mere bodies, which were always being scrutinized and evaluated, like walking pieces of meat in a meat market. This dawning realization was a very new and very bleak experience. I questioned my male friends about it, thinking that maybe this would make me feel better, but it actually made me feel worse. I began to wonder if men and women were even the same species, because this disconnect that men seem to be capable of, of separating our physical forms from our selves, felt so unhuman. Nothing in my life has weighed as heavy on me as this experience. It felt like I stared into the abyss of patriarchy. And before this, I hadn't even known there was an abyss.

I engaged in a lot of exploration around these issues through reading feminist writing. Reading bell hooks gave me some hope, and was also the first time I read about masculinity and what's happening for men. I realized that in my sexuality I had learned how to perform for men and to present myself as a lovely object to be consumed, but with very little or no actual desire on my part. My only desire came from being objectified and eroticized. I have begun to find myself and move past this conditioning, but this process has taken decades and is still ongoing. Some of this, of course, is personal and psychological, but a large amount of it has to do with the socialization that we receive as women, and the impact that socialization has had on me.

I separated from my boyfriend and moved to South Africa about a year after these experiences. In the meantime, I'd begun to work for a feminist organization in San Francisco that funded women's groups around the world. That experience was amazing in many ways. I learned a lot about power, and about the relation between the Global North and the Global South. This helped to dismantle some of my mental frameworks that were not equitable enough, but it didn't really heal me. I still didn't understand men. The work was important, but very "rights-based", which just did not do anything for my soul. I learned a lot and I appreciated it, but I hadn't made any progress in my healing, so when I was invited to a gender reconciliation workshop in Cape Town by my boss, I really didn't want to go. I felt a heavy stone in my heart when he asked me to go, but I also knew inwardly that I had to go through with it.

So I went, and it was one of the hardest few days of my life. For the past year I had been in the worst depression of my life, and it was daunting to go to a place where I had to open up about those things. To my great relief, thanks to the facilitators I ended up feeling safe enough to actually share what was real for me. First, I shared my grief with the women only. There, for the first time, I shared my brokenness, and it was held. I wasn't made wrong, I was just held tenderly in that space, and it was just what I needed. Then I shared this same story and more in a circle of women surrounded by men. It was terrifying, but necessary. Something in that sharing and being heard was so relieving. That didn't mean that everyone agreed with me, but I didn't need them to agree with me. It was very powerful and relieving to my soul just to have my experience heard. Of course, we heard the men speak as well. I heard from men who didn't sexualize women in the way that troubled me so much, and who were able to unite their bodies and their beings. That, too, was a great relief for me. At the same time, I heard other things that were going on for men that I had not had empathy for until then, and I realized that they are still human. Men's battles may be different, but we can connect.

Over the years since, I've been in multiple GERI workshops, both as a participant and as a facilitator. For the first two or three years these were still very painful experiences, because I had to confront the incredible grief inside me, which is reinforced on a daily basis due to the constant sexualization of women's bodies in this world we live in. But slowly I have begun to heal. I can't put my exact words on what it is that has helped me to heal, and I still don't feel fully healed. This is still an issue that I grapple with daily and in my relationships. But at least I now know that I don't need to compromise myself, that my experience is real and valid, and that in my relationships I don't need to settle for less than someone who will understand and meet me where I am.

GERI received me fully, without passing any judgment of good or bad on my experience. There is something so natural about being received by the men in these groups. There is something very powerful that comes from being in a space safe enough to express myself from the heart and to have that expression be fully received by everyone, women and men. It has made me understand more fully that men struggle too, and that I can love them in all their humanity. This is very significant for me, having at one point had such a vicious hatred towards them. I've learned also that as human beings we have all had very different experiences, even within the genders.

Clair has remained part of the GERI network for years and is much loved by all as she continues her personal and healing journey. Her professional life is devoted to advancing gender justice in the world, and to the GERI mission and community.

Secret comfort yet uncomfortable secret: Greg's encounter with online pornography

I was raised in the Internet age, which also means the age of Internet pornography. I knew porn existed before I even knew to be interested in it. I had stumbled across it online by age eight or nine. Later, when I began to come into puberty, and into the whole awakening of sexuality, and newfound interest and curiosity in girls, women, and sexuality, the Internet is where I went to learn. Of course we learned the basic biology of things in school, but my real "sex education" as a boy came from watching Internet porn.

In some ways, in the beginning, it really was just a manifestation of my blossoming sexuality and interest in understanding these things. But I pretty quickly found myself hooked into a more compulsive type of use. By the time I was 13 or 14, I was using it almost daily. It became an easy place of escape and comfort, somewhere I could go if I was feeling anxious, or even just bored. Whenever my parents left the house, or if I had a chance to be alone, there it was, always beckoning. A secret comfort—yet also, an uncomfortable secret. It was something always hidden from family, and mostly unspoken amongst my other male friends—we all knew it was something we all did, but it was generally a kind of shameful secret we kept hidden.

One of the other things about Internet porn is the infinite novelty. There is no end to the pictures and videos available, and there is always something "just better" than the last. You can spend hours looking for that perfect image, perfect video, perfect moment. Constant comparison and dissatisfaction.

How did that impact the way I saw actual women and girls in my life?—analyzing and ranking them, seeing them as body parts? I remember, as a teen, when I would walk into a room, one of the first calculations I would do was to rank the girls in order of attractiveness. I would then rank the boys in order of dominance, always very aware of my position—and vulnerability—in the male hierarchy. It's almost as if there was a kind of pornographic filter laid over my eyes, that changed how I saw and looked out into the world.

Today, when I look around now and see boys who are 12, 13, 14, I'm struck by how *young* they really are. And to think of all that I was watching and taking in at that age, and its formative impact on my sexuality... And seeing those young boys—just tender saplings really—and knowing the vast majority of them are doing the same thing today. As a teen, my "sex dreams" at night were not sexual episodes with women, but dreams of myself sitting in front of a computer screen watching porn. That is how embedded it was in my psyche.

I can't help but feel a sense of loss and sadness, that *this* was my sexual formation and "initiation," if you could even call it that. If there had been something else available, something different, a real initiation into genuine sexually, I gladly would have taken it. Even as a teen, I often felt, *this isn't how I want it to be*! But the pornography was too easy to start, and too compelling to turn away from.

It wasn't until I started coming into adulthood, and looking at my life more seriously and consciously, that I began to really be able to put some distance between it and myself. Even then, though, I could feel its influence on me. Even years later, as I began to have more romantic and sexual relationships, I could feel the residue of this formation, right there in bed with me. Of course, those experiences were still intimate and beautiful in many ways, as was the genuine love and care between us, but I still feel the sadness and pain now for what it might have been, for the ways I wasn't as fully present as those moments really called for and deserved.

It hurts my heart to know and feel that I have never truly experienced a sexuality free of any pornographic influence. I don't even know what it would look like, be like... But my longing now is to re-discover that.

I want to know what *real*, original, authentic sexuality is. I want to forget everything I think I "know" and enter into the unknown again—for the first time. I want to reclaim that original wonder, curiosity, and eros that I know is there.

I want this for myself. And I want this for all those other boys and men who have been and are grappling with these same issues. All of us yearn for, and *deserve*, something better.

It is my deep conviction that, if young men and boys were but given the chance, given the opportunity to learn and discover their sexuality in real and healthy ways, *this* is what they actually most long for. We take pornography as our guide and mentor, *not* because it's what we truly want, but because it is—sadly, tragically!—often the only option on offer. But given another, better path, I know that men will line up eagerly to walk it.

In our experience, the majority of accounts relative to pornography are reported as harmful, painful, or destructive. A smaller number of participants say that pornography was neutral or irrelevant in their lives, and a few individuals have considered pornography a beneficial influence. Those who decry the "sex-negative" values of our culture have a legitimate point. Yet pornography hardly seems to be a remedy—indeed, it seems more a symptom, based on what we have witnessed firsthand in gender reconciliation work.

Taking responsibility for past indiscretions

Sexual manipulation takes place in myriad forms. Here is sharing from a woman during the cross-gender truth forum in a GERI workshop, in which she owned her complicity for the pain she had caused men.

I have a whole list of ways I've been harmed and violated by men in my life. Like when I was 13 years old, in a laundromat, and the 60-plus year-old male owner pushed me against a washing machine and started rubbing his body all over mine. Thankfully a car pulled up and I narrowly escaped further assault. Or the time I was date raped at 16-years of age. Or, when my husband—my best friend—of 15 years suddenly told me he wanted a divorce because he needed someone younger. I was 34 at the time and he was 43. There are a multitude of other stories on my list, and I resonate deeply with all that has been shared from my sisters in this circle.

But, I also need to speak to the harm that I've done to some men in my life. When I began dating after my divorce, I held a belief that men knew everything about sex, but I quickly realized this wasn't true. This gave me a sense of self-confidence, which was liberating and freeing for me. "Claiming" my sexuality allowed me to also reclaim my personal power on multiple levels that had been so utterly crushed when my husband left me. But, in so doing, I also hurt several men.

I remember going into the campus bars and immediately sizing up which man I was going to work on seducing. I knew I had the sexual power to bring most any man I wanted to his knees, and I would seize the moment. It was a "fun game" that many of the men were into also, but for some it was very painful.

With any man I began dating, I made it very clear that all I wanted was a casual relationship, nothing serious. My children came first and getting my degree was next, so as soon as any man began "falling for me" or wanting anything more, I would immediately cut it off. I was in control. I had the power, which wasn't the case when my husband left me.

There is one question that I stood for in the Silent Witnessing about if you have ever coerced or manipulated another more vulnerable person into a sexual relationship. When I heard this question, one man, John, who had been a friend immediately came to my mind. Like a flash, I remembered how I seduced him into going to bed with me at an extremely vulnerable time when he had come to me for support. His fiancé had left him and he was thoroughly heartbroken and distraught. Right after having sex, looking at me painfully confused, he said that he wasn't sure it was a good thing to have done. I laughed and shrugged it off. I have a lot of shame about this. He was broken, and I came in like a vulture, with only my own self-interest, and broke his tender heart again. What kind of person does this, much less what kind of friend? I hold a prayer that John was able to heal from the betrayal he experienced from his fiancé, and from me. I want to say to all the men here, as my witness, that I'm sorry for the ways I have hurt men.

A few months later we heard from this woman, who told us that after the GERI workshop, she wrote letters to the men whom she knew she had hurt. She apologized for any pain she had caused them and asked for their forgiveness. The one man she could not find was John.

Sacred Sexuality and Tantra

We hear much today about "tantra" and sacred sexuality, and there is a plethora of books, articles, and workshops about the relationship between sexuality and spirituality. In particular, the "neo-tantric" schools adapted from Hinduism, Buddhism, and Taoism purport to teach the long-hidden practices. A thorough review or analysis of these offerings is beyond the scope of this book, but a brief summary of basic information about spirituality and sexuality is important for several reasons. First, sexuality is clearly fundamental to gender healing work. Second, spiritual aspects of sexuality are particularly important in gender reconciliation, as people strive to heal themselves and their intimate relationships from damaging sexual conditioning, and aspire to create something far better. Finally, there is tremendous confusion, exploitation, and rampant misinformation in relation to spirituality and sexuality, so it is important to briefly outline some basics. As author(s), we by no means represent ourselves as experts or adept practitioners of these disciplines, and our treatment here barely scratches the surface. Our purpose is to offer a glimpse of the profound horizons expanding today, perhaps to dispel a few popular illusory notions, and to direct interested readers to informed sources for further information.

Sexual conditioning in the West has been extreme, and devastatingly effective. Progressive Westerners today often regard themselves as sexually liberated and evolved, having transcended the narrow constraints of the past, but as writer Christine Emba observes, "We're Liberated, and We're Miserable."[11] Many Westerners blithely assume that their experiences and perceptions of sexuality are universally shared by all human beings. Not so. In particular, the West has so commercialized sexuality, and our Abrahamic religious heritage has so oppressed sexuality and distorted its sacred nature, that it is difficult for most Westerners to perceive how damaging our conditioning is, or to conceive of the sexual act as a sacred, religious, or spiritual sacrament. The materialism of our culture is not limited to the excesses of material affluence. It is also reflected in the desacralization of sexuality, reducing it from a form of celebration and worship to the mechanical fulfillment of bodily desires and fantasies. In various other cultures, both ancient and contemporary, sexuality is held and experienced in utterly different experiential and archetypal frameworks; in some cases it is an esteemed vehicle for spiritual purification and awakening.

Though widely popularized and commercialized in the West, the true nature of the tantric traditions of Hinduism and Buddhism has little to do with their mass-marketed misrepresentations. The Sanskrit tantras actually refer to hundreds of specific scriptures and associated complex systems of spiritual training and practices, only a handful of which specifically deal with sexuality. As Daniel Odier describes the tantric tradition of Kashmir Shaivism, "This is a path of incomparable depth and subtlety, and has nothing to do with the product that the West has commercialized under the name 'Tantra.' It stands in opposition to both the hedonistic sexual quest and the ascetic spiritual quest, because it reunites the totality of the person."[12]

The goal of all tantric paths is spiritual liberation (*moksha*) or enlightenment. The underlying philosophy of tantric practice is that the human body and its sensual pleasures can be utilized as a vehicle for spiritual realization. As summarized by Sahaja-yoginicintra, an ancient female tantric Buddhist master:

> Human pleasure,
> with its identifiable
> characteristics,
> Is the very thing that,
> When its characteristics are
> removed,
> Turns into spiritual ecstasy,
> Free from conceptual thought,
> The very essence of self-arising
> wisdom.[13]

She goes on to describe the practice of tantric sexual yoga as a loss of the sense of separate selfhood through a merging of identities in which "one ceases to know who is the other, and what has happened to oneself."

In Buddhist and Hindu tantra, the practice of sexual yoga entails the realization or manifestation of deities within the human body. In the ritual sexual ceremony known as *maithuna* or *Yab-Yum*, a couple unites in sexual intercourse, and ideally they realize together enlightened states of consciousness.

The contemporary "neo-tantra" movement focuses primarily on the lost erotic arts of enhancing pleasure in love-making—drawing upon ancient (often hidden) sexual practices that expand duration and intensity of orgasm, cultivate multi-orgasmic capacity (including for men), and sublimate sexual ecstasy to spread it throughout the entire body, generating 'whole body orgasms.' These practices often catalyze expansive breakthroughs in people's experience of sexuality. The better neo-tantra programs also address psychological, therapeutic, and relational dimensions of intimacy, and can offer substantial benefits far beyond and vastly superior to much of contemporary sexual education and conditioning (e.g., pornography, social media, movies, etc.).

Authentic tantra, or true sacred sexuality, is another matter altogether. The goal of tantric practice is not to enhance sensual pleasures, but to serve as a means for spiritual realization. The tantric adepts sought to manifest full Buddhahood in a single lifetime, something normally believed to happen only after innumerable lifetimes of spiritual practice. In tantric practice, the heart opens at a very profound level, thereby freeing all the knots, constrictions, and obsessions of false views, egocentric emotions, and self-regarding vanities. These energies and fears surface, are fully experienced, and then transmuted and released—permanently relinquishing their hold on the practitioner.

A key purpose of entering into tantric practice is to support the *other* partner to reach enlightenment. In tantra, the experience of intense sexual pleasure or bliss is not the occasion to be swept away by ecstasy, but, instead, the ecstasy is to be "dissolved" in the very moment it arises, through realization of its inherent emptiness. There is nothing ultimately real about the bliss of sexual union; it has no source, no owner, no existence in itself. The tantric practitioner realizes this, and continues to realize this essential emptiness of sexual bliss as it continues to build in intensity. The practitioner eventually enters into a vast, sky-like experience of universal or cosmic awareness.

Of course, words cannot describe the experience. As Miranda Shaw summarizes it,

> In tantric practice, one goes beyond pleasure and follows the pleasure to its root, which is the core of the mind, which is made of pure bliss . . . When you're in this deep level of bliss, it's very easy to become attached to the object of the bliss, or source of the bliss—which is your partner—and also to the experience of bliss itself, and to turn the bliss into yet another experience of entanglement. That is why the experience of bliss is combined with meditation upon emptiness.[14]

Tantric practice is not something that can be learned through books, and certainly not in a weekend workshop. Prerequisites include extensive meditation and breathing practices, realization of emptiness, a purified motivation, and breaking through the illusion of the separate self.

Tantra is a key practice of "inner alchemy" that harmonizes masculine and feminine energies within the human being, regardless of gender identity. In heterosexual tantra, the man honors and worships the woman as the Goddess, and vice versa. Each partner merges with the other as a channel of enlightened energies for mutual transformation. For LGBTQ+ couples the process is basically the same, creating a sacred union of masculine and feminine divinities within both partners. Although tantra was long kept secret, the practices can be taught to sincere practitioners who are sufficiently prepared. As Miranda Shaw describes her experience after years of personal research:

> I changed profoundly on every level from my research and study. . . even on a cellular level. I was completely transformed physically. People who knew me before I started my research and then saw me towards the end of that period did not recognize me.
>
> I discovered a whole form of male celebration of women that I did not know existed. I was also surrounded by images of divinity in female form, and seeing the unclothed female body in a religious context rather than in a commercial, secular context as it is in the West was profoundly affirming for me as a woman. My understanding of what is possible in male/female relationships changed and my understanding of myself as a woman completely changed. I had internalized a lot of the shame-based attitudes of the West, not only the general attitudes of the culture at large but also specific forms of shaming that had been inflicted upon me in my own personal trajectory from which I was able finally to be healed.
>
> I encountered the power and full sacredness of being female, because the tantric teaching is that women are pure and sacred in the essence of their being . . . their very cells, their energy, not simply something that they can attain, but an ontological fact.

Tantric practice activates spiritual energy centers in the body, called *chakras* in the Asian traditions, of which seven are commonly mentioned: the perineum, sexual center, navel (or solar plexus), heart center, throat center, the "third eye" (between the eyebrows), and the crown chakra (top of the head). This system is described differently in various spiritual traditions.

In the articulation given by the Tibetan Djwhal Khul, three key elements to this process are described. First is an "upward trend" of energy moving from the lower chakras upward, a process called *transmutation* that purifies and refines the energy of the lower energy centers. This generally begins with the activation of the Kundalini, the spiritual "serpent" energy that is normally dormant, seated at the base of the spine. Second is a "downward trend" from the higher to the lower chakras in a process called *transformation* that energizes and aligns the upper and lower energy centers. When all the chakras and subtle energy channels are consciously and simultaneously aligned, then a third process, called *transfiguration*, can take place: a form of initiation in which the person's essential being and consciousness are utterly transformed to an altogether higher level and energetic frequency of consciousness.

The intricacies of this process are complex and precise, guided by a deep bio-spiritual wisdom that is hidden and generally beyond the understanding of the pracitioner. As one of William Keepin's spiritual teachers emphasized, the spiritual mystery of the union of masculine and feminine is "a secret so sacred it cannot even be whispered."[16]

Some of the better writers and specialists in tantric sexuality include Miranda Shaw, Nida Chenagtsang, Mantak and Maneewan Chia, Ian Baker, Georg Feuerstein, Ben Joffe, Lorin Roche, Thubthen Yeshe, and others. One of the key guidelines for tantric practice is that it should be practiced under the guidance of an authentic master, with appropriate spiritual and psychological preparation. This holds for many spiritual paths, but is perhaps all the more true of the tantric path, because of the inherent potential for self-deception, ego gratification, or sexual indulgence or distraction.

The *mahasiddhas* were profound non-celibate yogis of ancient India who taught that desire and pleasure are not inherently problematic, ensnaring the disciple with attachments and projections, but can be transformed from passion into profound love. One of the great *mahasiddhas*, Padmasambhava, went to Tibet in the eighth century and established two distinct Buddhist orders: a celibate monastic tradition (red robes), and a non-celibate yogic tradition (white robes). As scholar/initiate Ian Baker affirms, the entire tradition of Tibetan Buddhism came from the *mahasiddhas* of India. Moreover, "although publicly hidden, the oral tradition of Tibetan Buddhism generally upholds the yoga of sexual union in the context of absolute and mutual compassion, to be the most expedient method for manifesting enlightenment in mind and body."[17]

In Hindu Kaula tantra, the ultimate purpose of sexual yoga is transcendent awakening of love in the heart, which fuels profound empathy and compassionate action. Simililarly in Buddhist tantra, *Dzogchen* (the Great Perfection) means "essence of the heart" teachings, based on a heart-centered consciousness, rooted in expansive awareness. The heart is paramount; Buddha dissolving into the light happens from the heart chakra, not from the crown. Non-dual bliss is the transcendent correlate of desire. Desire is dualistic, with a subject and object, but spiritual bliss transcends all dualities. This is also the inner meaning of *sat-chit-ananda* in Hinduism: the realization of ultimate truth entails transcendent bliss.

Tantra originated primarily from female *mahasiddhas*, and it works directly with sensation and expanded awareness, rather than conceptualization or imagination. "Through the alchemy of Tantra," explains Lama Thubthen Yeshe, "the same desirous energy that ordinarily propels us from one unsatisfactory situation to another is transmuted into a transcendental experience of bliss and wisdom." Dynamic breathing practices, such as Tibetan *tummo*, ignite the 'inner fire' of the lower chakras, which moves up the spine and 'melts' the *thigle* or *bindu* (subtle energies) at the crown—which then 'drip' downward through the chakras, galvanizing profound awakening experiences along the entire spinal neuro-endrocrinal axis from the hypothallamus to the genitals (called the 'central channel'). There are 72,000 male and 72,000 female subtle energy 'drops' in the human body, and *tummo* practice brings them into perfect balance. This same inner alchemy is also found in Western esotericism, characterized as "rising fire, flowing waters."

Advanced practitioners learn to circulate these profound energies up and down their own central channel, and also via genital union with their consort, up into and out from the central channel of their consort. This profoundly unites their hearts as one with each other and the cosmos, creating ultimate bliss and intimacy. This is true sacred sexuality, and when coupled with advanced meditation, it can lead beyond sexual bliss altogether to non-dual realization of the transcendent union of spiritual bliss and emptiness.

This closely parallels Taoist sexual yoga, where the energies of the "micro-cosmic orbit" within the practitioners' bodies expand to unite with the "macro-cosmic orbit" of the entire universe. "Tantric consort practice transcends ordinary pleasure and desire and reveals the innate bliss of one's innermost being as a numinous communion with all existence," explains Baker. This is the union of Shiva and Shakti; the human body unveils and opens into the infinite cosmos from within. As the Buddha purportedly said, "enlightenment arises in the body, or it does not arise at all."

The practices of *karmamudra*, or sexual yoga, were long kept secret and said to be highly advanced, far beyond the capacity of monastics and lay people alike. Yet these "completion stage" practices were developed by the *mahasiddhas* specifically for non-celibate practioners and householders. Tibetan Buddhist sexual yoga was recently expounded in detail for the first time by Tibetan doctor Nida Chenagtsang in his pioneering book, *Karmamudra: The Yoga of Bliss*, which details specific practices, including their full applicability for LGBTQ+ persons. The Dalai Lama himself encouraged Baker to write about this hidden tradition, and told him, "The time of secrecy is over. Unless these practices become better known they will be completely lost. That would be a great tragedy." Accordingly, Baker and Chenagtsang co-founded a new initiative in 2023 called The Vajra Path to bring these practices skillfully forward in a contemporary inter-traditional context.

Transcendent Sexuality

It is not necessary to be formal tantric practitioners or adepts to reclaim and cleanse our erotic experiences from the clutches of a culture that has long degraded and repressed sexuality on the one hand, and lauded it in outwardly trivial and obsessive ways on the other.

Ordinary people with no training at all in tantric traditions have experienced the depths and profound openings of sacred and transcendent sexuality. This fact alone shows that exalted sexuality is an innate part of our human birthright. We close this chapter with an article from one of the world's leading researchers on transcendent sex. Dr. Jenny Wade has conducted systematic research on the transcendent sexual experiences of hundreds of people who had no tantric or special training whatsoever, yet in their love-making discovered this other transcendent domain, and had astonishing healing and transformational experiences.

These remarkable stories expand the notion of "sex-positivity" to another whole level altogether. Wonderful as this is, a sad finding in Dr. Wade's research was that most of the people who had these experiences never told anyone else about them. We invited her article in part to recount and honor these profound stories here, both for the auspicious promise they portend for human sexuality, and *also* to uphold the core principle of gender equity and reconciliation—which is to bring forth the *full* truth of our gendered and sexual experiences, not only the challenging and difficult experiences, but also the exalted, uplifting, and sacred experiences. Dr. Wade's research documents the profound and transformative path that is available to ordinary human beings through sexuality.

Sex and the Sacred: Spiritual Awakening and Transformation in Lovemaking

Jenny Wade, Ph.D.

Throughout history people have connected the sacred with sexuality, from the oldest known document in the world, *The Epic of Gilgamesh*, to the present day (for an overview, see Wade, 1998, 2000).[18, 19] Altered states of consciousness arising from sex are part of the human repertory, regardless of spiritual beliefs or practices or sexual mores. These transcendent experiences span an astonishing array of altered and transpersonal states, many of them consonant with the spiritual literature of various traditions, including otherworldly episodes of indigenous religions and experiences associated with various stages of contemplative practice in the esoteric and perennial systems.

I researched the stories of ordinary people who had such experiences without any special sexual or spiritual training.[20,21,22] A few excerpts are illustrative:

> [M]y awareness of us as individuals or as our unified whole also recedes. In this field, there is no content, only a sublime ecstasy. And in joy I know, I know that I am perfect, that he is perfect, that everything is perfect. There is nothing here. And there is everything because the world comes back, but as part of me, not something separate. I move in beauty, and the world moves with me. The world and I are the same, God and I are the same, and we cannot be other than beautiful and whole and perfect.—Naia

> It begins in sensuality and ends in God...., I am simultaneously aware of moving into and then through [my lover] to something beyond, wholly transcendent. I feel as if my body is made of filaments and enormous energy—pure feeling, a kind of primordial bliss—is streaming through it.... I feel as if I am entering God, or God is entering me, that I am blazing with the energy of God and pouring that energy back into my lover, and worshiping her and God at the same time, and then thoughts spin out and there is only That—the utterly inexpressible, the union with the Source of all, and a kind of divine annihilation.—Blake

These are only two of the many types of spiritual experiences people have during sex, the most common of which are presented below. "Naia" and "Blake" were not sexual athletes or spiritual adepts. She is a middle-aged, Episcopalian executive who has struggled with her faith over the years, and he is a retired teacher who rejected formal spirituality and attributed his spiritual awakening to psychedelic experimentation decades earlier. These life-changing experiences are available to everyone: they happen in relationships ranging from casual, even "illicit" couplings to "true love," regardless of sexual mechanics and regardless of sexual or gender expression and partner choice. They even occur for people with histories of sexual abuse, and can be healing experiences. "Eve," an incest survivor, whose mind went blank other than wishing for sex to end when she was in consensual adult relationships, had one miraculous experience that changed everything:

> While we were making love, I felt the most incredible spiritual awakening... like I had actually attained a higher plane, feeling one with—and satisfied with—the whole universe. My partner was an extension of my physical being. I felt like I had received a gift from God....
>
> I have never forgotten it. This one [experience] still makes me feel wonderment and happiness...I felt bathed in a golden light, warm and contented emotionally...that I was part of a greater good that was all around me.—Eve

The following examples illustrate several kinds of ecstatic experiences triggered by sex. Perhaps the most common is the sense of the two lovers' merging into one being physically, psychologically, and spiritually.

Then any sense of separateness between us dissolved. I couldn't even tell whether I was making love to her or being made love to. I can hardly even tell you what our physical bodies were doing because it was like our bodies were part of the flow and ebb of all this energy and Spirit body. We were all mixed together in this mysterious, melting dance....We were one moving, touching mass of energy and awareness, not two separate poles of consciousness....I sort of felt like a woman *and* a man...one being, one love, kind of a melting together.—Kyle

Another is *trespasso*, a visual hallucination common to many esoteric traditions, involving perceiving another face or a succession of faces superimposed on the lover's, usually interpreted as the partner's past-life personalities.

At least half-a-dozen times, I've had an experience with my eyes open where I'd see my lover's face morph into all these different faces. [There] might be 20 different faces....some are more memorable than others, so I'd recognize them when they came up again.—Vivian

People also perceive their partners and themselves to change into animals, typically during rough sex play. When a lover feels overtaken by an animal's psyche, it is a form of identification that can include a sense of shapeshifting.

When she steps into that place, she gets rougher sexually. There's a rawness. She even smells different. And she said my eyes seemed a lot darker.... Her sense was that they weren't my eyes at all.—Lynn

Another form of experience that can occur during sex involves an expanded identification with the psyches of an entire group, pouring through the individual in a way that resonates with the person's experience, though it was clearly not their own.

My identity falls away, and I'm identified with all women now and back in time, and their state of mind. There's not a separation.... A sense of rapture that came from so many different places, and how wonderful it was to have that...and that sense of unity [with all women].—Kristin

Supernatural beings, completely distinct from the lovers, sometimes appeared (e.g., angels, deceased loved ones, demons or deities). In some cases lovers feel themselves or their partners manifesting divine forms. More commonly, they sense an ephemeral Third presence or divine entity that is co-created with and by the lovers, yet also independent of them.

I had a little sister who died when I was ten and she was six. And I felt her presence in the room right then. ... I felt her close to the divine Presence, as if she came from God. ... I didn't have a sense of myself as being just me, but of a divine Presence being around.—Armand

Sometimes when we make love, ... my lover's face ... has that radiant, lit-up-from-within beauty, almost as if she is divine herself in a way. ... It's like looking at images in a church, ... something transcendent even in the vision of her, like when great art gives rise to religious feeling. When she transforms before my eyes, I've been displaced to a different environment where everything has become radiant because *she's* my environment. I'm going into a holy place.—Blake

Many spiritual traditions feature subtle energetic phenomena, such as *kundalini* in Hinduism, especially Tantric practices. Lovers unfamiliar with these traditions nevertheless reported classic experiences, such as sensations of bodily heat and liquefaction, subtle force fields, illumination, and unusual spontaneous movements, such as speaking in tongues (glossolalia), a spiritual hallmark in Christianity.

The light was just going through me.... and shooting out of the top of my head. I had feelings of white lights shooting out of the top of my head.... You think of sunlight or lightning, but nothing like *this!*...I started crying because it was overwhelming, an emotional effect like "Oh, my God, I'm coming *home*. I got home." A feeling that I'd been separated for a long time, like coming together, and finally being *home*.—Suzette

Lovers sometimes demonstrated paranormal abilities they do not normally possess, such as clairsentience, a fully developed cognitive revelation that seems to come from nowhere, which people described as "knowing everything" and "realizing the truth," or telepathy, the ability to access the unspoken thoughts and feelings of others. Out-of-body experiences, in which the individual's point of view and awareness seemed to move to a place above the lovers, were frequent.

I suddenly found myself having for the first time what I would call a transcendent kind of experience. I was out of my body observing me and my lover lying in bed from above, perhaps near the ceiling. I'd never heard of such a thing and didn't know how to explain it, but it was a very strange phenomenon suddenly looking down at the two of us.—Dick

Some seemed to be transported to other locations through altered visual imagery and sensations of weightlessness (floating) and forward motion (flying) through terrestrial or celestial environments. One man said, "It's like going through the galaxies, traveling at amazing speeds. It's visual and physical. I've actually seen stars like galaxies rushing past and also have a physical sense of my body rushing along...."

Some found themselves in a magical relationship with the natural world. Sometimes they seemed identified with an entity possessed of its own intelligence, such as the woman who said, "I can 'become' a tree, a cloud, a lovely smell." At other times they became one with the entire natural world.

There's a connection with the universe...with the flora and fauna, all the other animals [and people] in the world.... the sense of oneness and... union with all living creatures.... for all time and all space.—Terry

In past-life states, people were transported to different locations in previous eras with the bodies and personae of other individuals living through detailed biographical events. For example, during sex on their second date a couple relived Victorian-era lives in which they fell in love, had an adulterous affair that resulted in a pregnancy, lost the child, and split up. The couple initially rejected reincarnation and found the whole experience distressing. When I interviewed them, they were separating after many years of marriage and were beginning to see parallels between their past-life sexual experience and their real-life situation.

The story was dictating to us, like watching a movie, and you don't get to change it if you don't like what's going on....I didn't see any similarity in it with us at that time, though it did say something about why we felt so compelled to be together..., why we felt so familiar, like we'd always been together.... The rational part of me dismissed it.... [Now] I believe we were given an opportunity to be with each other in a different context, but we haven't been able to do it. We made the wrong choices again in this lifetime. It's too painful to continue.—Carolyn

Finally, during sex people can have "enlightenment" experiences, those states of nonduality described in Western and Eastern contemplative religions. Unitive experiences involve the nondual dissolution of time, space and ego in a total identification with the Absolute (God). Awareness is formless, dimensionless, infinite, and suffused with light and bliss, as described in Western mysticism, like Blake's experience above, and the following examples.

At the same time I felt it coming from the outside, it was also coming from the inside.... I participate in divinity in a direct, inclusive way. There's no separation at all. All those mystical incantations about the entire universe being embedded in the person...., it was all suddenly manifest....Was there a face to God? No. Or a presence? The presence was us....We were just there. It just was....Just God is left, and I am that.—Zebediah

It's a very boundary-less time, and then comes the Light, mostly a flood of bright, whitish-yellowish light....It's as though the Light were all the universe ... —Esther

People also experienced realization of the Void of Eastern contemplative traditions. Void experiences involved impersonal, formless, dimensionless, infinite nonduality of time, space and ego sensed as the primordial emptiness that underlies yet constitutes the cosmos. The Void may or may not be accompanied by light and bliss.

There was this dissolvingness, and this losing of boundaries. And then there was this incredible nothingness and everythingness. Out of this feeling of nothingness and no-self, there was yet all possibility and all potentiality.... no time and no space.... Really pure awareness, just no sense of self. The completeness of the nothingness was enormous.—Ann

These adventitious sexual altered states, virtually identical with those attained in religious traditions from shamanism to contemplative paths, changed lives—thus meeting the requirements defining a spiritual experience.[23,24,25,26] According to participants, their sexual altered states produced the following benefits:

1. *Healing*, including the resolution of internal conflict, especially: self-acceptance and loss of shame around sexuality and gender identity; resolution of sexual dysfunction, especially associated with a history of sexual trauma; the resolution of personal loss; and integrating sexuality and spirituality counter to many cultural norms, which promoted more intentional sexual behavior.
2. *Personal growth*, which included positive changes, such as discarding limiting beliefs, ceasing dysfunctional behavior, and quitting unsupportive relationships. It also involved acquiring new capabilities, such as broadening gender expression, and acquiring greater mental clarity, creativity, and even paranormal skills, such as the ability to conduct energetic healing.
3. *Empowerment and purpose*, including feeling confident, revitalized, and motivated to help others realize more completeness in sexuality and spirituality.
4. *Enhanced relationships*, especially greater connection with the partner, decreased defensiveness and increased compassion, which were extended to relationships with others and with nature.
5. *Conviction that Spirit is real*, variously expressed. Often the sexually-produced altered states countered the person's prior spiritual beliefs. For example, Buddhists or atheists might have an experience they interpreted as the Christian Holy Ghost, or Jews might be visited by Kali. The experiences, dissonant or not, often led to a spiritual quest to understand what had

occurred, and the physicality and relational quality of sexually-produced transcendent states made them seem more compelling than other practices.

Sex felt like six different meditation practices...all happening at the same time....this multifaceted thing that... all aspects of my being, emotionally, physically, sexually, intellectually, spiritually were engaged...in an integral, transformative practice.—Ranier

One of the saddest findings in my research was that, with rare exceptions, these individuals had never told another person—not even their partners—about their transcendent sexual experiences, for fear of ridicule or being considered crazy. Most often they had to struggle alone, trying to make sense of these profound experiences that seriously undermined their belief systems, or radically expanded their entire sense of spiritual reality. Acceptance of this type of embodied spirituality through sexual experience remains rare, and very few of these people found their experiences honored or recognized in religious or contemplative traditions, which often overtly discourage any thought of the convergence of sex and the sacred.

In conclusion, the interplay of altered states of consciousness and the felt sense of the numinous creates a variety of sexual experiences that appear to have the same characteristics as those recognized in some of the major spiritual traditions. These experiences unveil a whole new world out there, a vision of sex that goes way beyond more and better orgasms. Just knowing how uplifting and inspiring sex can be may be helpful to those who have suffered sexual wounding and abuse in the past, including those who have been spiritually marginalized for their preference for partners. The fact that there seems to be no difference between the ability of LGBTQ+ persons and heterosexuals to enjoy transpersonal experiences during sex could be extremely beneficial, especially for adolescents and others coming to terms with their sexual identity or orientation.

Sex can provide an accessible medium for extraordinary transpersonal experiences in the lives of ordinary people. The potential for working with such embodied forms of spirituality can open remarkable new horizons of personal awakening, healing, and spiritual development in everyday living and loving.

Love is the water of life. And a
lover is a soul of fire.
The entire universe turns
differently when fire loves
water.

–Rumi

CHAPTER 8

Forgiveness and the Harvest of Alchemical Gold

Do not store up for yourselves treasures on earth, where moth and rust consume, and thieves break in and steal; but store up for yourselves treasures in heaven. . . . For where your treasure is, there shall your heart be also.
—Matthew 6:19-21

Gender reconciliation work is not quite what it first appears to be. Delving deeply into this work inevitably takes people on an inner journey, and, if they follow it far enough, they are ultimately led into an awakening of an expansive, all-encompassing love. In some traditions this is called an encounter with the Beloved—a spiritual form of universal love (sometimes called *agape* in Greek, or *premabhakti* in Sanskrit). This is where gender reconciliation work ultimately leads, but it's rarely what people are seeking when they enter into it. Gender reconciliation work could thus be likened to certain spiritual or mystical paths in which novices are initiated onto the path by "veils of attraction" that draw them in through a kind of grace or divine seduction, and only later do they discover what the path is really about.

In our experience, people come to gender reconciliation work with many different motivations. Some are seeking to heal from past wounds, others are hoping to deepen their professional work as clinical therapists or clergy or educators, others are seeking effective ways to reconcile gender-based challenges in their professional workplace or religious institutions, and still others are intending to become trained as facilitators or trainers themselves. Whatever their initial motivation, if people remain engaged in gender reconciliation work over time, their relationship to the work evolves as they discover its deeper layers.

The spiritual process behind gender reconciliation work bears some similarity to the trickster tradition of Sufi mystical lore. Unsuspecting wayfarers are lured onto the path by whatever their own attachments or "hooks" happen to be. The "Beloved" catches them by these hooks and "drags" them along, and then proceeds to remove the hooks one by one. As the journey continues, the Beloved pursues the dismantling process quite beyond mere hooks, and begins to take the person apart—deconstructing their ego and very sense of selfhood. Carried through to its fullest extent, all that remains of the person in the end is a radiant heart of love, with no blocks or impediments. Pursued over extended time, gender reconciliation work bears a resemblance to this process. In its highest manifestation it becomes a path whereby the "small self" is gradually deconstructed—disabused of false desires and identifications—and what eventually emerges is the true Self, with its profound capacity for universal love.

There are moments in the course of gender healing work when the veils obscuring its deeper mystery are suddenly parted and the underlying omniscient presence of the Beloved, or Spirit, or Love—the force and radiance at the core of the work—is subtly revealed. In such moments there is an inexplicable energetic shift that touches everyone present, and people are moved beyond their usual self-focused attachments into a selfless, universal compassion. Each time this happens something new is given to the work, and the people involved are uplifted and changed in some way—bonded together in a shared experience of divine love.

This may sound a bit dramatic, but the experience of it is very real, and is actually quite natural and inevitable under the right conditions. There are times when the gift of this *collective alchemy* is palpably operative, far beyond mere words or New Age jargon, and the community touches into collective mystery and transformation. When this happens, the uncanny presence of Spirit or Love works through the entire group or community. The love is reflected in each person in the group or community, and everyone present becomes aware of and inwardly connected to this love at the same time. We call these moments "diamond points"—times when there is a conspicuous Presence, an uplifting awe, a magic that everyone participates in and which moves the entire group into a shared experience of the universal heart of love. Such experiences are part of the birthright of the collective human family—when the blinders are lifted and we catch a glimpse of the spiritual fire that fuels this work from "beyond the veils," and pours forth warmth and healing and radiance into everyone present. It is the fire of a universal love that consumes the barriers and illusions that separate us.

In this chapter we attempt to capture a few of these radical and transformative moments, to convey something of their power and grace. These moments are shared experiences that serve as a profound inspiration for what is possible in human community and society—a bright beacon for our troubled time.

"Meltdowns" and Transformative Moments

One of the challenging situations that sometimes arises in gender reconciliation work is an upset or crisis of some kind that precipitates a systemic breakdown in the entire group process. We sometimes dub these situations "meltdowns," because in these moments there is a deconstruction of the group process, which morphs spontaneously from one configuration or context into an entirely different one. This shift can take place quite suddenly, often within less than a few minutes. The scene can transform from a warm and friendly circle of people sitting listening attentively to one another to a highly charged emotional cauldron of collective grieving and angst. Although unpredictable and sometimes cathartic, these moments are frequently junctures of exceptional healing potential and transformative spiritual power. These moments constitute auspicious opportunities for a kind of collective metamorphosis around complex gender issues that can reach archetypal proportions.

The character of these experiences is virtually impossible to describe in words. They are usually intense in the moment, lasting anywhere from a quarter hour to half a day or more. Afterwards there is often a transcendent or numinous quality that leaves everyone present feeling humbled and grateful, with a palpable sense of sacred integration between human and spiritual planes of consciousness. Such moments of group transformation are never planned or orchestrated beforehand—they cannot be; rather, they emerge from spontaneous openings, or perhaps an upset of some sort. They can present a significant challenge to facilitators, who must respond in the moment to the unfolding situation with intrinsic courage, trust, and respect for what emerges—coupled with a triage approach to handling the practical needs that arise in the group. The process demands a high degree of faith, skill, and sensitivity on the part of the facilitators.

A few examples will illustrate the power of these "diamond points" of gender equity and reconciliation.

The Trauma of War

About midway through a GERI workshop, after a remarkably deep process that left the group tender and open, one of the men, Doug, began to speak haltingly. At first, we could barely hear him. Doug was a Vietnam veteran, and as he began to tell his story he grew agitated and started to sob, tears rolling down his cheeks and choking off his words. Doug's story came out in bits and pieces. He had been on patrol with his platoon. They had raided a village looking for nests of Viet Cong, but the men of the village were nowhere to be seen. Only women, children, and a few of the elderly men were there. The platoon had orders to push on across a rice field that they were afraid was covered with hidden land mines. They had taken a number of the village women as prisoners. It wasn't clear why.

As they headed out of the village, their lieutenant suddenly ordered the women to walk out ahead of the soldiers through the field. His logic for this decision was simple: there were likely mines in the field. If the women walked first, they would either step on a mine and trigger it, or they would walk between the mines and mark a safe path. Either way, if the platoon followed precisely in the women's footsteps, they would be safe. It was a reasonable choice from the lieutenant's perspective; his first responsibility, after all, was to his men, not to the Vietnamese women, who were suspected, in any event, to be aiding and abetting the enemy.

Doug had only been a private, a boy of nineteen, yet he held himself responsible for what had happened that day. He kept repeating, as he began to writhe in his pain, that he should have challenged his lieutenant, he should have stopped the action, disobeyed the order—done *something*. Instead, he and the rest of his platoon had watched as the women one by one began making their way through the rice field. After several tense minutes, the lead woman misstepped and was suddenly blown to pieces in front of his eyes. Shortly thereafter, the second woman went down, and then the third, and the fourth, until every woman was dead, their bloody, dismembered carcasses marking the path of safe haven for these American soldiers.

This was a story Doug had never told before, and the wrenching grief and anger that accompanied his telling were chilling. He retched and writhed and gasped for breath, his hands grabbing at his head and chest, as if his heart was literally breaking from the horror of the memory. One of the male facilitators moved in and embraced Doug in a loose bear hug as he thrashed about the floor. This provided Doug enough containment to ensure he would not hurt himself, while giving him freedom to literally writhe in his pain. Doug was exploding with excruciating agony. The two men locked together in what outwardly appeared similar to a wrestling match. Doug's suffering seared all of our hearts precisely because it captured the character of the collective trauma men have carried for thousands of years in war; the trauma that accompanies the organized and strategic annihilation of one's fellow human beings.

Tears flowed from every eye in the room. Gradually, the wrestling men began to exhaust the energy, and Doug became settled enough to sit on the floor with his back against the wall, tears still running down his face. No one spoke. We all sat together in the weighty silence, resting our souls and extending our hearts to Doug. Then, a graceful young woman, who happened to be of East Asian descent, rose from her place on the floor and walked quietly over to where Doug was sitting in his humbled exhaustion. She knelt down beside him and, with the delicate embrace of a healing angel, cradled him and brushed the tears from his cheek with her hand. She looked exactly like a Vietnamese woman as she held him. The poignancy of that moment defies description. We had tapped into the dark chasm of archetypal trauma—*and* the transcendent forgiveness—of our species. It was a healing moment bigger than all of us, for which we all felt fortunate to be present.

A Healing Bow

Another example of a meltdown involves a young woman who remained rather quiet throughout most of the GERI workshop she attended. She was afflicted by an acute awareness of the longstanding violence that has been perpetrated against women by men. She took special care not to project her personal rage and sorrow onto the particular men in the workshop, nor did she hold any of them personally responsible. Nevertheless, this awareness was very present for her, and although she spoke to it from time to time, she remained relatively detached, silent, and soft-spoken. On the last morning of the workshop, one of the men attempted to draw her out by gently asking if there was anything he could do or say to establish a connection with her. She responded to this man, speaking softly, as was her pattern, but then slowly opened up enough to finally share some of her personal story with the group.

Her words were circumspect and insightful as she told of various ways she had been deeply hurt by men in her life. She spoke with a clarity and authority that had not been present in her earlier participation. Everyone was moved by her vulnerability and authenticity, and, afterward, several in the group spoke up passionately, honoring this woman for her honesty and courage. Then, one of the men took the talking stick and said to her, "I don't just want to honor you, I want to pay homage." At which point he kneeled and folded his body forward until his forehead rested upon the ground, in a deep bow, before her. He made this gesture with utmost sincerity and integrity. The woman was stunned, and speechless. Her heart broke open as she vacillated between doubting what was happening—it was too good to be true—and seeing it take place before her very eyes. The man maintained the bow for a full two minutes, during which the woman's eyes softened and opened in a cycle of disbelief and gratitude.

This act led to a yet deeper sharing from the same woman, who made a brief reference to having been raped—the first mention she had made of it during the workshop. Hearing this, another woman in the group let out an involuntary howl and began to cry. Her sobs soon deepened into wails, and then further into wrenching screams of grief. Others too began to weep, and then to bellow and scream. Within one or two minutes the entire group was plunged into a deep collective grieving process—many crying or sobbing in one another's arms. This meltdown process continued for an hour and a half as people accessed deep grief and rage, mutually supporting one another to go through dark caverns of personal and archetypal pain. The facilitators operated in a triage mode, assisted by several interns, supporting those who were in deepest grieving and emotional release. Eventually, the powerful energies began to exhaust themselves, and one by one the participants emerged from their inner realms, tender and delicate, all huddled close together in loving support and surrender. The experience left everyone moved beyond words, far beyond what can be conveyed here.

As mentioned earlier, such moments call forth an uncanny sense that a higher intelligence is orchestrating the entire process, because each person's internal issues are triggered in a manner that precisely suits their particular character. Such a synergistic, multilayered experience—in which several people simultaneously receive precisely what they need for their own unique healing process—cannot be planned or organized. A deeper wisdom and distinctly numinous presence emerges and guides the process.

The man who bowed, a young pastor who had recently graduated from Harvard Divinity School, described his experience of the workshop: "What happened to me has given me more faith, hope, and love than any other single experience in my life. [Given] the epiphanies I've had over the past eleven years, and my mixed experience with group work, this is no small notice."

Synchronicities in the Collective

An example of a different kind of diamond point entails a man and woman whose personal histories contained striking parallels in a way that became highly significant as the workshop unfolded. Their separate personal stories, each unbeknownst to the other, were intertwined in a way that was potentially explosive, although, happily, they were resolved in a powerful healing event.

The synchronicities began when two participants, David and Kathy, were paired at random in an afternoon exercise of holotropic breathwork. The two had never met prior to the GERI workshop, and both were health professionals in their fifties. During the breathwork, Kathy experienced a powerful revisitation of the trauma surrounding her sexual violation by several teenaged boys, friends of her brothers. Kathy was particularly troubled by the role her two older brothers had played in this attack, which was a kind of gang molestation. Her brothers had not engaged directly in the sexual assault, but they had done nothing to intervene, or stop the attack. This had happened when Kathy was ten years old.

David was Kathy's sitter for her breathwork session, and he attended to her process with great sensitivity as she moved through several waves of intensive grief and emotional release in revisiting her childhood trauma. David happened to be a body-centered psychotherapist with many years of experience, and he "held the space" for Kathy skillfully throughout, providing a field of compassionate presence and nurturing support. This interaction led to a strong bond of mutual respect and affection between them, which ultimately proved indispensable for what later emerged.

As the workshop progressed over the next days, Kathy shared her story with the group, and subsequently two more women, Ruth and Susan, came forth with their own stories of incest and childhood sexual abuse. Things shifted radically, however, when, during the men's truth forum, David brought forth a startling revelation from his own past. He recounted that he had, some 25 years earlier, molested his own 10-year-old stepdaughter. A shock wave went through the group, eliciting especially strong reactions from Kathy and the other two women. Kathy was so distraught she was virtually unable to speak. The emotional volatility in the group rapidly escalated and became so explosive that Kathy stormed out of the room in a state of intense turmoil, determined to leave the workshop altogether.

The group plunged into mayhem and confusion. Expressions of unabashed outrage, grief, and misprojections flew around the room. One of the women facilitators followed Kathy out of the room and worked with her individually as she struggled to deal with feelings of betrayal and mistrust that threatened to overwhelm her. Kathy was beside herself with anger and despair. She felt betrayed by David. She sensed duplicity and hypocrisy in his offerings of support for her healing process.

Meanwhile, the other facilitators and interns continued to work with the group, processing the volatile dynamics. Ruth and Susan shared many of Kathy's feelings, although neither had become as close to David. They demanded to know from David why he had brought this story forth into the group when and how he did. He explained that his intention was not to hurt, but to help to heal. He felt a moral obligation, he explained, to disclose his own past complicity in the painful abuses that had been suffered by others in the group. David explained how very difficult and humbling it was for him to reveal this incident from his past, and added that this was the first time he had ever done so in a mixed group. But not to do so, he felt, would make a mockery of the unique and courageous work we were doing together. The men's truth forum had seemed the obvious and appropriate moment for this to come forward. He had actually shared his story first in the men's circle the day before, where he felt safer, but he felt that the women in the group, and perhaps especially Kathy, Susan, and Ruth, deserved to know. He was ready, he said, to "stand in the fire" if that would serve to heal the wounds of such abuses within the group, and perhaps help prevent them in the future.

Kathy finally returned to the group after a lengthy absence. She had decided to articulate her feelings of outrage and betrayal directly to David, with support from the group. She was very nervous as she began to speak, but once the words started to come, she poured out strong, passionate feelings about the incidents of her childhood, the betrayal by her own brothers, and the way in which such betrayals undermine a person's life. She talked about the fragility of the work we were doing together, the necessity of respecting one another completely. She then addressed her confusion about David, acknowledging that he had treated her kindly and respectfully. As she continued speaking, her demeanor shifted, and she came to a place of affirming that in the present moment, she could find no fault in his behavior, and she acknowledged that it was important for her to know about his history and that he had given her that opportunity by volunteering it courageously. During her sharing, Kathy cried and yelled and laughed and sat silent as she struggled with contradictory feelings and perceptions. Ultimately, she articulated her recognition that David's intention was not to harm anyone, and that he had a right to bring his own wounds and complicity into the work we were doing.

The workshop continued into the evening and the next day, with frequent reverberations around these issues. On the last evening, the women's and men's rituals were conducted to honor one another. During the ritual, Ruth, the elder of the two sexual abuse survivors, stood up and picked up a potted plant someone had contributed as a healing presence. She walked slowly across the room to David, kneeled in front of him, and placed the plant before him, then reached out and took his hand. She explained that while she was deeply grieved by what he had done—an act that she herself had suffered at the hands of another—she also honored his courage in bringing this out into the group and seeking to heal from it. She told him it was clear he had done much personal work to heal this past injustice, and that she admired this about him.

Then Susan came forward, and then Kathy. Each of them reached out to David, extending forgiveness and understanding. Each noted his courage and honored the healing impact of that courage on their own lives, not just on his. Then, with tears running down their cheeks, Kathy and David gently embraced. The energy of this interchange was sublime. It was clear that deep healing had become possible precisely because the victimizer had sat down with the victimized, and together they had grieved and borne witness and forgiven the other for their pain.

The entire group was moved deeply as these four human beings—three "survivors" and one "perpetrator"—continued to share and commune quietly with one another, with occasional spurts of tears or laughter punctuating their soft whispers. By this point much of what was said between them could not be heard by the rest of us in the group, but the healing energy radiating out from them was intensely nourishing for all. Eventually, the rest of us moved into a closer circle around the four of them, and we all began to sing and chant songs of healing and forgiveness.

Three years later, during a subsequent GERI event, Ruth told us that this gender workshop had changed her life in a profound way, and that it was one of the most important things she had done. Kathy has made similar remarks to us over the years, as she too has attended several gender reconciliation events. David was also deeply grateful and expressed strong interest in working more closely with gender reconciliation.

Spontaneous Forgiveness

The final example in this chapter illustrates a similar synchronicity that led to a remarkable healing experience. It began when a woman named Sharon shared a traumatic personal account of being forcibly date raped by her boyfriend. Shortly thereafter, another woman, Brenda, followed suit and shared her own story of a date-rape experience. The details in the two cases were different, but the general pattern was the same—both women had been raped by men who were supposedly their special beloved partners, and both had been traumatized not only by the rape experiences themselves, but also by the sense of profound betrayal and confusion afterward.

Meanwhile, there was a man in the group, Mike, who had become increasingly quiet and sullen as the workshop progressed. Finally, one afternoon following a breathwork session, Mike disclosed in the men's circle that he realized that what had happened to Sharon and Brenda was also part of his own life experience. Speaking with deep sorrow, in halting tones, he explained that he had forced himself upon his wife, as well as his former girlfriend, in the exact same manner. "In short," Mike announced quietly, "I have committed date rape. But I never considered it that, until I heard these two women in the group tell their stories." For the first time in his life, Mike faced the reality that he had date-raped two women.

Over the next several hours, the magnitude of Mike's realization came upon him with full force, and he sank into deep grief and anguish. Several women in the group noticed a difference in his behavior that evening, and began asking what was happening for him, but Mike turned his eyes away and did not respond.

The next day, after a fitful night's sleep, Mike took the plunge and shared his realization with the full community during the truth forum. A silent shock wave coursed through the women as Mike disclosed his story. He added ruefully that he had always regarded these experiences as macho sex acts with "his" women, and thus he had never been able to take seriously his wife's or girlfriend's protests about the harmful nature of his actions. When he finished, Mike collapsed into deep, grieving tears.

As the day progressed, Mike's anguish and shame became increasingly evident and extreme. He would not meet the eyes of the women, and he feared strong reprisals, especially from Sharon and Brenda. Many in the group extended themselves to him, particularly among the men's group. It was remarkable to witness Mike's process of healing and awakening, and many were moved by the depth of his remorse.

Toward the end of the workshop, something remarkable happened when Sharon spontaneously went over to Mike at one point and offered him consolation for his grief. Mike was shocked at first and totally disbelieving, because he had especially been avoiding contact with Sharon and Brenda. He continued to carry deep culpability and shame for his past. Sharon took his hand and explained that even though it was painful to be in the group with a man who had perpetrated the same harm that had been done to her, his coming to grips with his own culpability was something that her boyfriend had never been able to do. And so, despite herself, she said it was healing for her to witness a man confront his violent past so genuinely. She said she had never seen a man do this, and she was grateful for it. Brenda followed with a similar gesture a few minutes afterward.

Mike was moved to yet another level of surrender and humility as he melted into sobs of simultaneous grief and gratitude. The two women sat down next to Mike, crying and holding each other while gently holding Mike's hand. The three of them embraced each other softly, creating a spontaneous forgiveness ritual among themselves. Witnessing their process, the entire group was transported, and copious open-hearted tears flowed forth in response to the beauty of this remarkable healing moment.

Exquisite moments of deep healing such as these are a natural and integral part of the gender reconciliation process. People sometimes mistakenly suppose that such jewels of collective healing could only emerge in a group after first completing the huge task of purifying and healing each participant's personal wounds individually. But this is not the case. Rather, these diamond points of healing emerge naturally when even a few individuals are willing to step into the fire and become the instruments for a larger wisdom and love to work through them. And these healing moments serve both to inspire the larger group or community and to deepen the requisite trust and integrity that is necessary for the next unfolding stage of healing to take place. Thus, the gender healing process advances by a kind of unlayering, in stages, of ever deeper material—like peeling the proverbial onion. And at each step the group trust and bonding is deepened, which creates the conditions for the next step to be taken. The growing intimacy and communion is thus an intrinsic part of the process of gender reconciliation and not merely a "gift" or reward that comes at the "end."

Unraveling the Knot of Gender Injustice

What is startling about gender reconciliation work is that its true foundation and inner motivation is the yearning in each of our hearts for spiritual love and union. Such yearning, however, is veiled to a great degree—covered over by all manner and dynamics of gender oppression, relationship dilemmas, power, desire, conditioning, and other convolutions, which we generally experience as a complex knot of "problems" that need to be addressed and healed. What makes gender so powerful to work with is the fact that this knot is a conglomeration of multiple primordial forces that are all bound up and intertwined together. These forces include (a) the patriarchal dynamics of repression and injustice, which are ancient and deeply ingrained in the human psyche, (b) the intimate yearning of the human heart for love, (c) the desire for sexual passion and expression, and (d) the human longing for the deepest forms of intimacy, both with other human beings and with the Divine. This complexity distinguishes gender diversity work from all other forms of diversity work, because it interweaves millennia of structural violence and gender injustice together with the intensity of sexual passion, and with the heart's burning need for deep intimacy.

Gender reconciliation is unique in bringing the most subtle and vulnerable yearnings of the human heart right into the center of the complex issues of power, survival, governance, culture, justice and morality. For this reason, it is our conviction that to unravel the gender knot skillfully in society would greatly facilitate the unraveling and healing of many other structural injustices in our society and culture. Gender disharmony is at the root of much human suffering and societal injustice; therefore, gender healing is foundational to healing our society on multiple levels, and to revealing and transforming the deepest truths of the human condition.

Celebratory moment in GERI workshop for young adults at SOFKIN in Hyderabad, India, 2022

CHAPTER 9

Beyond Words: Transformational Healing in Community

All things true are given and received in silence.
—Meher Baba

Gender reconciliation work elicits challenging emotional, interpersonal, and group dynamics that have longstanding and tenacious psychological and cultural roots. Effective and safe navigation of this sometimes delicate, sometimes volatile terrain requires skillful modalities for group process work that go well beyond verbal communication and dialogue. Other dimensions of consciousness and sensitive awareness must also be engaged, and for this purpose experiential, transpersonal, and contemplative methods are invaluable for facilitating deep transformative healing and reconciliation. Several of these specialized skills and practices applied in GERI programs are outlined in this chapter.

Advances in consciousness research are gradually opening up new doorways for exploring and understanding the deeper realms of human consciousness, many of which were hitherto largely neglected in Western psychology. The emerging field of transpersonal psychology and the burgeoning interest today in spiritual practices, alternative healing modalities, and ritual practices from diverse cultural traditions are creating a fertile field of new possibilities for working skillfully with the challenges of gender healing and reconciliation. Psychiatrist Stanislav Grof, a leading pioneer in transpersonal psychology, emphasizes that modern Western society is the only culture in the world that seems to believe that people can transform their psychological and spiritual dilemmas by merely talking about them; for example, in cognitively oriented psychotherapy. All other cultures across the globe—both ancient and contemporary—recognize that some form of contemplative, spiritual, or nonordinary consciousness is vital to the process of healing and transformation.

This chapter explores three different classes of such modalities utilized in the practice of gender reconciliation: experiential breathwork, contemplative techniques, and ritual processes. The chapter concludes with a highlighted section by Stanislav Grof and Brigitte Grof, describing their experience of a special GERI program held at the Esalen Institute in 2018.

Experiential Breathwork

Breathing practices of various kinds have a vast, time-honored history in many spiritual traditions of the world. Specific exercises to intensify, control, or withhold the breath, or maintain constant awareness of breathing, have been utilized in many cultures to awaken deeper levels of consciousness and spiritual awareness. Traditions that incorporate breathing practices include Kundalini yoga and Siddha yoga (*bastrika*), Raja yoga and Kriya yoga (*pranayama*), Tibetan Vajrayana Buddhism, Sufism, Burmese Buddhism (*tummo*), Taoism, and many others. More subtle forms of breathing disciplines are also found in Theravadan Buddhism (*Vipassana*), Zen, and certain Taoist and Christian practices.

In all these cases, focused breathing exercises (or "breathwork") serve to awaken interior levels of conscious awareness in the practitioner. Some breathwork practices activate powerful healing energies in the body/mind/psyche and shift consciousness to deeper levels where healing and transformation may occur. Breathwork therefore has a powerful application in gender healing and reconciliation work. Yogic forms of breathwork allow participants to stay present and work skillfully in the midst of intense emotions that gender work can trigger. It also allows participants to shift and stabilize their own consciousness and access their own inner wisdom.

In the GERI work we have utilized several breathwork modalities, including contemplative forms of meditative breathing. We have applied holotropic breathwork extensively, which was developed by Stanislav and Christina Grof after they experimented with many different kinds of breathing practices drawn from spiritual traditions, shamanism, and humanistic psychology.[1]

For readers unfamiliar with breathwork, it may be difficult to imagine that merely working with the breath could have significant effects of any kind. However, breathing practices are capable of awakening deeper dimensions of consciousness and awareness in remarkable ways, which is why they are employed so extensively in spiritual traditions. As Grof remarks, "Unless one has witnessed or experienced this process personally, it is difficult to believe on theoretical grounds alone the power and efficacy of this technique."[2]

A full presentation of the principles and practice of holotropic breathwork is presented in several of Grof's books, and so we give only a brief summary here.[3] The holotropic technique combines sustained rhythmic breathing with evocative music and focused bodywork. The process provides a safe, protected environment that enables participants to explore a broad range of experiences and spaces within their inner consciousness. The practice typically activates an "inner journey" or introspective exploration in which breathers become aware of deeper dimensions of their own consciousness, often with pointed relevance or significance for their lives. In practice, the holotropic process is usually done in pairs within the group, so that each person doing the intensified breathing has a designated "sitter" throughout the session. Thus, breathwork is generally done in two consecutive sessions, where half the group are "breathers" and half are "sitters" in the first session and these roles are reversed in the subsequent session.

What are the benefits of applying holotropic breathwork in the GERI process? Breathwork serves to bond and catalyze the group of practitioners in several important ways. First, it supports deep psychological and spiritual "inner work" within each individual, which often brings forth key insights, healing experiences, and new levels of awareness. Second, the breathwork process cultivates a unique form of bonding and intimacy between the breather and sitter, which often constitutes a powerful dimension of the experience. Because there is no verbal communication during the breathwork process, it also serves as an implicit training and sensitization in nonverbal communication, because breather and sitter connect through subtle energetic exchanges and silent relational interconnection. Third, breathwork creates a field of collective awareness and "healing energy" in the entire group—often quite palpable—that enables all participants to bear compassionate witness to the inner work of one another. Fourth, we have repeatedly experienced that engaging in the breathwork process seems to "convene the group soul" of the community in which it is practiced, and thereby helps to build a strong unitive cohesion and sense of shared intimacy and community purpose that is invaluable. Finally, we sometimes ask the entire group to take a collective intention in the breathing process; for example, the intention that the breathwork will support the larger purpose of gender reconciliation and healing. Throughout the breathwork process, these different levels of experience and interconnection operate simultaneously, interweaving and overlapping in intricate ways—often creating a powerful, transformative healing experience in the group.

One of the most crucial characteristics of breathwork is that each person's experience is unique and emerges from their own inner wisdom. Thus, the inner expanse of each participant's psyche is inwardly available for free and unhindered self-exploration. Especially important, even when there is a collective, stated intention, is that the facilitators or group leaders do not steer or shape the participants' experiences in any way, nor do they direct or decide what "should" happen in breathwork. Each person's particular experience is honored and received as the appropriate experience for that person at that time. Psychological interpretations of breathwork experiences by facilitators or other participants are discouraged, since each person's experience speaks for itself from within the breather's own wisdom.

The range of experiences that occur in breathwork has been mapped out in detail by Grof in what he calls a "cartography of the psyche." Breathwork experiences are classified into three broad domains of qualitative characteristics, called the *biographical*, *perinatal*, and *transpersonal*. The biographical realm refers to the individual's personal life history; the perinatal domain refers to experiences relating to birth and death; and the transpersonal realm relates to experiences that go beyond one's personal identity, including mythological and spiritual experiences. The experiential terrain that arises in breathwork is thus vast and rich—analogous to the range of experiences that occurs in dreams, meditation, prayer, and other contemplative or spiritual disciplines.

Skeptical readers may question the value or relevance of such techniques, and particularly their application for gender reconciliation and related healing work. Such skepticism is understandable, especially given that Western science and the disciplines of psychology and psychiatry have not always embraced the profound spiritual and psychological experiences that arise in consciousness practices such as breathwork, meditation, and other contemplative disciplines. In fact, these experiences have often been dismissed, or even pathologized clinically—especially those of a transcendent or spiritual character. As Grof points out ironically,

> Psychiatric literature contains numerous articles and books that discuss what would be the most appropriate clinical diagnoses for many of the great figures of spiritual history. St. John of the Cross has been called an "hereditary degenerate," St. Teresa of Avila dismissed as a severe hysterical psychotic, and Muhammad's mystical experiences have been attributed to epilepsy . . . Many other religious and spiritual personages, such as the Buddha, Jesus, Ramakrishna, and Sri Ramana Maharshi, have been seen as suffering from psychoses, because of their visionary experiences and "delusions" . . . By pathologizing holotropic states of consciousness, Western science has pathologized the entire spiritual history of humanity.[4]

However, this situation is slowly beginning to change significantly in many arenas of the mainstream health professions. The legitimacy and value of spiritual and contemplative disciplines is becoming ever more widely recognized. Meditation and other contemplative practices have been introduced into numerous secular organizations in the legal, academic, and service professions with excellent results and a growing demand for wider application. Experiential modalities, including methods such as holotropic breathwork, are increasingly recognized as indispensable tools for fostering a deep level of self-inquiry, healing, and psychological integration that is difficult to achieve by other means.

Research on holotropic breathwork is still sparse, but results are encouraging. A 1996 controlled clinical study combined holotropic breathwork with psychotherapy over six months, and found a significant reduction in death anxiety and an increase in self-esteem for people who did both the breathwork and therapy, compared to those who did only therapy.[5] A 2013 report documented the results of 11,000 people who participated in holotropic breathwork over 12 years. The results suggested that breathwork helped to treat a wide range of psychological and existential life issues, with significant benefits related to emotional catharsis and internal spiritual exploration. No adverse reactions were reported.[6] Finally, a 2015 clinical study with 20 participants found that holotropic breathwork can induce highly beneficial temperament changes, which can have positive effects on development of character, measured as an increase in self-awareness.[7]

Application of Breathwork to Gender Reconciliation

We have applied holotropic breathwork in all of our longer GERI programs for 30 years, and also as a key component of every module of the GERI Professional Facilitator Training since it began in 2001 (the only exception is in the online GERI certification trainings during the Covid pandemic, when in-person meetings were not possible). Perhaps the best way to illustrate the value of breathwork in gender reconciliation work is to give several illustrative examples. The anecdotes recounted below all took place in the GERI workshops or trainings.

The first example describes a participant's first experience with breathwork, in which she went through a birth experience, followed by a powerful opening into universal love. Such a strong "heart opening" experience, although perhaps dramatic, is not uncommon in breathwork.

> It felt like I was on a very intense ride of some kind, as I twisted and turned, always pushing forward. I heard the music but did not feel connected to the group or the room. It began to feel like birth. I pushed through this small narrow tunnel with much effort. After what seemed like a long time I pushed through this place and exploded out into the most love I have ever felt. I cried in love and profound gratitude. It felt very sacred. Here I relaxed into expansiveness and love. There was no sense of body, only love.
>
> Suddenly I became aware that the music in the room had stopped and I wondered why that was. It seemed only a few minutes had gone by, when actually two and a half hours had gone by. As I opened my eyes I asked, "Am I done?" The room seemed so dark compared to the brilliant place I had been in. My sitter was there and had covered me to keep me warm. It was truly a wonderful experience. As I meditate on this experience in the days that have followed, I have a sense that it was a piercing of the heart . . . I now find myself to be a little stronger somehow. I am a little lighter, and the conflicts of

life do not overwhelm me. I feel grateful for whatever happened.

The next example involves a woman whose father had died when she was six years old. This childhood trauma had colored her relationships with men throughout her life, and she had done extensive psychotherapeutic work to begin uncovering the enormous grief associated with her father's absence in her life. This paved the way for her powerful experience in breathwork.

The experience unfolded for me as a journey to the underworld. First, I was falling down a long tunnel, like Alice in Wonderland. Then I found myself running through a dark underground world with the massive roots of mountains reaching down from above me, and the ground below me writhing with thousands of big black snakes.

With the help of a young man who I recognized as my Guide (someone I have encountered before in dreams and active imagination), I made my way through this ominous landscape to a place deep in the heart of the world. It was a large underground cave with a clear pool in the center. Here I met a dear friend of mine named Dino who died ten years ago, someone who I still miss very much. Dino and my Guide prepared me for the meeting with my father. First, without saying why, Dino suggested that I reach out to my sitter, because I was going to need his support. I was reluctant to do this, but as soon as I did, my father appeared. I think this is really crucial, because that reaching out was the first opening for me, the first sign that I was willing to allow my vulnerability to show, to acknowledge that I needed—and could rely on—a man's support.

The meeting with my father was incredibly healing and cathartic. He encouraged me in the work I am doing now, gave me the sense that he has been watching over and caring for me all these years with great attentiveness, and even gave me advice about my future and some of the relationships I am in right now. After speaking for some time, there was a laying on of hands, with my father, my friend Dino, the Guide, and another male friend of mine laying their hands on my abdomen and my heart in order to heal many old wounds . . . [This] was incredibly powerful and evoked an enormous emotional release. So much grief came pouring out, and I accessed a level of actively missing my father that I had never experienced before.

When the laying on of hands was completed, my father began to pour a red and golden liquid directly into my heart from a beautiful ornate vase. It seemed like an endless flow of compassion and healing was filling up my entire being, giving me the strength to do healing work for myself and also to share it with others. In the midst of this inundation with love, I had the sense of being a little girl again, lying in my father's embrace . . . It felt like the dispelling of years of pain and longing and sadness.

The journey ended in a place which I know only from a painting, but which I have always felt drawn to as some kind of "perfect" place of peace and tranquility. It is a beautiful lake surrounded by trees and dramatic mountains on all sides, with wonderfully expressive clouds filling the deep blue sky . . . I rested there feeling safe and loved.

Later, as this woman integrated the personal insights that emerged from this experience of reconciliation with her father, she found that this visionary encounter also helped her to heal some long-standing emotional and sexual patterns with men.

The incredible heart opening which I experienced with my father—my "open heart surgery"—gave birth to a whole new kind of openness and vulnerability which I have been able to access in my relationships with men. I suddenly realized how much of my emotional self I was hiding from men because I was afraid of being hurt, disappointed, or left . . . For years I have been using this "tough chick" persona (to varying degrees) in my relationships with men and wondering why they wouldn't open up to me emotionally! Now I have to laugh; how could they feel safe opening up to a woman who was herself so well defended? . . . I realized that this persona I have been carrying around for so long, the "tough chick" who hides her emotions behind a sexually provocative, nonchalant exterior, was now obsolete. This is not the way I want to interact with men anymore.

I can honestly say that something important has shifted. I still feel my father's presence every day. He didn't leave me. He's still here, and he's always been here. I just never knew. The more I connect with my spiritual self, the more "real" his presence in my life becomes, and the more I feel I am connecting with some archetypal Father (God?) from whom I draw strength, compassion and understanding.

Over the past 35 years, we have applied holotropic breathwork in many GERI programs, and also in other professional domains for environmental scientists, politicians, mental health professionals, and leaders in academia and NGOs. We have witnessed thousands of powerful healing experiences in breathwork sessions.[8] Although the content and specific details of these experiences vary greatly, what they share is that the breather is opened to a new level of awareness in a way that is unique to their particular life experience, and this catalyzes a specific healing and integration process.

The next example illustrates one possibility for relational intimacy beyond romantic connection, which the breathwork often facilitates in a natural way between breather and sitter. This experience is described by a man in his sixties named Stuart:

During my breathwork I had an experience that continues to bring reflection and wonder. About midway through the session, my sitter, Mary, was moving her hand through the energy field near the top of my head. I could feel the warmth of her hand and was just experiencing the sensation when I was suddenly seized by a powerful desire to feel her touch. My back arched automatically and I thrust my face in the direction of her hand. I urgently said, "Touch my face, touch my face!"

She began to stroke my forehead and face, and I began to weep. There was no sadness in the weeping; the touch felt so good and so right. I had such a longing for it and felt such a release.

> At the end of the session I shared my experience with Mary. I said it had a very different quality than my usual romantic desire for relationship with a woman. This longing seemed to come from a deeper, more archetypal level, from deep down in my physical being, in my bones. . . As I was sharing with Mary I often wept. At some point, a last tear began to roll down the side of my nose. Mary gently reached up with a tissue and wiped it away. This act of tenderness caused another tear to roll, and she wiped that away, which caused another to roll, which she also wiped. I laughed, "Every time you wipe away a tear, it causes another to come."

Such tenderness and intimacy is not uncommon in the interaction between sitters and breathers in breathwork. The process enables participants to enter a unique domain of intimacy and healing with one another in full safety and mutual protection. In this context—which is otherwise rare in our technological society, yet utterly natural and uncontrived when experienced—an unimpeded exchange of compassionate expression and tender presence naturally flows in people from the wellsprings of unconditional love that dwell within every human being. In this touching vignette of each tear wiped causing yet another to flow, a deep truth of spiritual love is represented symbolically: The pain of the heart is the very medicine by which a broken heart is healed. Reflecting on his experience, Stuart observed:

> Later I thought, what a good symbol for gender healing! Every time the feminine wipes away a tear from the masculine, it causes another tear to flow. The tenderness of the feminine causes a successive softening of the masculine, the empowering of the feminine, and their mutual growing together. This experience has caused me to reflect upon the deep suspicion, mistrust, and misunderstanding with which men and women often approach one another. We need one another at such a basic level, yet we often hold ourselves apart, almost intentionally, against our deep desire to be together.

Not only can women "be there" for men, as the foregoing example illustrates, but men can also "be there" for women. Here is one woman's account during a gender reconciliation workshop:

> The most powerful part of the breathwork day for me . . . was observing how most of the men were there for their partners. In my life experience, whenever the going gets tough, especially emotionally, men check out. Today I saw men cry, and hold women while they cried. The men's tenderness, gentleness, and love just blew me away. I absorbed beautiful new memories today, which in turn helped me close powerful gates to the belief system that "all men are bad," or "no man can be trusted."

A final example illustrates another level of breathwork experience that taps into mythological or archetypal dimensions catalyzed by the gender healing process. In this case, after the group had been intensively processing challenging gender dynamics in society, one woman-participant had this breathwork experience:

> Our focus on gender seems to have set in motion some powerful archetypal energies which emerged in my breathwork. As I cut loose in the breathwork session, my body focused on the release over and over again of fierce, fighting energy. As I cut through my own bonds, and the bonds of women over time, I became the fierce aspect of the goddess. The different polarities of Kali—the Hindu goddess of creation and destruction, the demon-slaying, sexual, independent goddess who seems to stand outside all social bounds in India—manifested in me. The all-compassionate mother and the fierce fighter for justice surfaced and were all one.
>
> But there was more. All of this intensity, all of this fury, all of this loving, compassionate energy, even sexual at times, could be held and witnessed by men. This had never happened to me before. And maybe this has seldom happened to women in the last four thousand years . . . I was in tears with the power of it—the new resources of masculine and feminine within me.

The foregoing examples summarize a few ways in which breathwork contributes to gender reconciliation work. Further examples of the impact of breathwork in gender healing are presented later in this book, particularly in Chapter 10 on recent work in South Africa.

Contemplative Practices

"Silence speaks with unceasing eloquence." This aphorism from the Indian sage Ramana Maharshi encapsulates in a single phrase the remarkable gift of contemplative practices and meditation. A related injunction sometimes heard in Quaker prayer meetings is: "Don't speak, unless you can improve upon the silence."

Conscious use of silence serves to facilitate and deepen the delicate process of gender reconciliation work. First and foremost, silence invites people to listen more deeply within themselves, which helps connect them with their own inner wisdom. Learning to listen deeply within oneself is probably the most universal spiritual practice, found in all traditions. Silence also helps participants to integrate complex or conflicting levels of experience, which often characterizes gender work because it combines intensive outer exploration and inner awareness simultaneously.

Meditation and Prayer

The practice of meditation is becoming increasingly widespread as a powerful means to explore and transform the deeper realms of consciousness. There is a plethora of excellent books on meditation in various traditions, so rather than repeat what is beautifully presented elsewhere, we recount a simple teaching story that captures something essential about the nature of meditative practice:

Student: What is the essence of meditation?
Master: Have you ever noticed that between one thought and the next thought, there is a gap of silence?
Student: Yes . . .
Master: Prolong the gap.

Of course, this technique of silencing the mind is just one of many different approaches to meditation, but meditation practice generally entails the need to stop chasing after the incessant waves of thought on the surface of the mind and plunge down into the underlying ocean of consciousness. Numerous forms of meditation are practiced in various traditions; some methods focus on a chosen object of meditation, or on dissolving thoughts in the ocean of love within the heart, whereas other practices entail being fully present and open to whatever arises in consciousness (without identifying with it). The power of meditative practice is profound, far beyond what can be summarized briefly here. For our purposes, suffice it to say that the practice of meditation over time cultivates a deep moment-to-moment awareness, sensitivity, and inner silence within the practitioner, and gradually awakens innate qualities of wisdom and compassion.

In the group context, silent meditation serves to convene and bond the collective community in an intimate, nonverbal way, similar to what is frequently experienced in spiritual or contemplative retreats. Silence also helps to create an atmosphere of authenticity and integrity, which in turn supports each person to connect more deeply inwardly before they express themselves. The judicious use of contemplative silence or group meditation can be especially important at times of broaching sensitive or tricky topics, or when an unusually poignant truth or personal story emerges.

A related practice is the "mindfulness bell" taught by the late Vietnamese monk Thich Nhat Hanh. At certain moments, a bell or chime is rung in the group, at which point everyone stops whatever they are doing and enters into silent meditation for the duration of three breaths. This grounds people in the present moment before continuing again with whatever they had been doing before the chime was rung. We have found the mindfulness bell to be an especially useful tool in gender work.

The term "prayer" is often construed to carry a strong religious connotation. Because the gender work attracts people of many different religious persuasions, including some who have a deep practice of prayer and others who don't identify with any religion in particular, we generally work with silence in the form of meditation or simple contemplative practices, and participants are encouraged to utilize whatever inner practices suit their individual needs. The spiritual context for gender reconciliation work is nonsectarian and embraces the full range of authentic spiritual traditions.

That said, however, if we define "prayer" in a broad spiritual context as the yearning for or invocation of a larger universal wisdom or compassion, then prayer is definitely a key aspect of gender reconciliation work. Not only are various individuals within any given group engaged in internal prayers of their own during the work, but there are times when the entire group enters collectively into states of delicate sensitivity, vulnerability, intensive emotional processing, or exquisite communion with the "Beloved." At these times the hearts of everyone present are completely aligned and subtly intertwined in what can only be described as a deep collective prayer. This creates a field of "heart energy" that is extremely powerful and that serves to catalyze remarkable possibilities for healing and transformation. Seen from this context, both meditation and prayer are fundamental to our gender reconciliation work, and they play different roles at different times.

An advanced form of meditation or awareness practice in various traditions entails "just sitting" with what is. The Indian sage J. Krishnamurti coined the term "choiceless awareness" to refer to this broad category of practice. Notwithstanding the differences among specific approaches in different traditions, such as *shikantaza* in Zen, *jnana* in Vedanta, or *dzogchen* in Tibetan Buddhism, these practices all have something in common. The essence of this practice is to sit in open, receptive awareness and to remain consciously centered in whatever arises. Of course, as with all meditation practice, this is not as easy as it sounds. It requires a degree of sensitivity, presence, and disciplined attention that generally requires years of regular practice to develop. It also requires that no arena of consciousness be explicitly shunned, or preferentially pursued. Painful or challenging insights sometimes arise, which can require great discipline and courage not to push away. At other times extremely subtle levels of awareness emerge which would be missed altogether were it not for the fine-tuned sensitivity of the awareness practice.

Collective Witnessing

Gender reconciliation work could be viewed as a particular form of choiceless awareness practice, carried out in a group setting. If the meditative practice described above is a form of *individual* witnessing in choiceless awareness, then gender reconciliation work can be viewed as a form of *collective* witnessing in choiceless awareness. The major difference is that instead of being a silent individual witnessing practice, the process is conducted in a group setting, which requires a form of witnessing communication within the group.

When a group of people gather to embark upon gender reconciliation work, a powerful process begins—of unraveling into group awareness what was formerly privately held in individual or unconscious awareness. When painful or challenging material arises, the task of the group is generally to face it and go into it, rather than politely avoid it as we do routinely (and appropriately so!) in our public settings of everyday life. For example, in one intensive workshop, a husband chose to disclose to his wife—in front of the entire group—that he had had an affair in the not so distant past. His confession created an intense dynamic that involved not only the couple themselves but the entire group. In another workshop, a woman confided tearfully to the group that she had physically abused her son when he was young. In both cases, these significant disclosures were presented to the group as a whole, and the community was called upon to somehow engage the material with those involved, and to do so from a place of compassionate witnessing and wisdom. In essence, what is essential in these moments is for the community to sit in open and receptive awareness, remaining consciously centered in whatever is arising. This too is not as easy as it sounds. It is not uncommon for one or more participants in the group to become emotionally triggered by what emerges and to respond from a place of projection, judgment, fear, or personal need. Yet, a key to the work—the "work" of the work, so to speak—is for those who can do so to remain in a space of compassionate, focused witness. Their conscious presence helps to hold the space for those who have brought forward painful material in order to work through it to whatever insights and resolution may emerge. The group process thus closely mirrors what happens in individual meditation as one confronts personal shadow material.

Zen master Bernie Glassman calls this kind of group practice "bearing witness," and the associated communication practice he dubs "talking meditation," which emerged within the Peacemaker Order that he founded. As Glassman describes the practice,[9]

> We start from the unknown, we bear witness, and healing arises.
>
> When we bear witness, we become the situation . . . Once we listen with our entire body and mind, loving action arises. And it begins with the state of unknowing, with the vow to let go of our conditioned responses and penetrate the unknown. The broader the bearing witness, the broader and more powerful the healing that will take place.
>
> Certain silences don't help, they hurt. It's important to tell your story, to tell where it hurts. In the Peacemaker order, we call it talking meditation. Without speaking the hurt, the healing won't come.

In the domain of gender and sexuality, the "silences that don't help" are legion. In gender reconciliation work, these silences have a chance at last to be voiced and witnessed—in a safe, skillfully supported and respectful group environment.

As this unmasking process unfolds, deeper and more hidden personal stories and experiences begin to emerge, which catalyze the alchemy of collective healing. This process of unveiling helps the group shift into increasingly authentic and sensitive levels of communication, which in turn engenders more spacious silence. Collective engagement in contemplative practices helps to create an invisible field of "heart energy" that catalyzes the healing process and elevates group interactions to higher levels of meaning, intimacy, and subtlety.

Honoring Ceremonies and Celebration

Honoring ceremonies and celebration are a third essential component of gender reconciliation work. Ritual ceremony entails the intentional cultivation of creative interplay between archetypal or spiritual realms and the everyday material world. Effective ceremonies combine spontaneous creativity with a deep invocation of universal ideals and archetypal or spiritual "presences," applied with a particular purpose in a group setting. In GERI programs for men and women, each gender group creates and choreographs a ritual offering for the other. This provides a rare opportunity for men to truly honor and uplift women, and the "feminine." The women also do the same for the men, and the "masculine." In GERI programs for LGBTQ+ persons, half the group creates a ceremony to honor and bless the other half.

In the West we have largely lost connection with the richness and power associated with ritualized or sacred ceremonies, which form an integral part of many cultures around the globe. Western ideals of rugged individualism and scientific rationalism, coupled with the plethora of mind-numbing distractions in our society have exacted a huge toll, and we moderns have relatively few ways to connect creatively with the larger universal mysteries of life. Gender reconciliation work provides one avenue for reclaiming some of this rich and fertile ground in a relatively natural, nonthreatening way. An example of how ritual-process works in gender reconciliation was given in Chapter 6.

Ritual is sometimes defined as the invocation and embrace of the spiritual domain in the manifest world. Ritual ceremony entails the mixing of different realms or levels of reality, where spirit, soul, and world weave creatively together. To be meaningful, honoring ceremonies must somehow invoke the presence or symbolism of a higher ideal, "archetype," or spiritual energy, and bring it into practical, real-world manifestation. Effective ceremonies combine elements of spontaneity and freshness with openhearted engagement of the participants. The design need not be complicated. In fact, the essential ingredients of an effective ceremony are neither an elaborate setting nor intricate choreography but, rather, sincere intention and enthusiasm on the part of participants. Some of the most powerful ceremonies in gender reconciliation programs have been some of the simplest in structure.

Ceremonial process allows the community, as a whole, to move beyond cognitive and dialogical modes of communication, and to engage intuitive or creative faculties, as well as the body's kinesthetic wisdom. In practice, a typical ceremony might include a simple circle dance, chanting, singing, or rhythmic drumming. The atmosphere might be enhanced by candles or scented with sage and sandalwood, and offerings might include activities such as foot-washing, anointing, or blindfolded "trust walks" in the spirit of sacred friendship.

At times in gender reconciliation work, it happens that something so challenging or pertinent arises in the group that there is an immediate need to create a unique process to address the particular issue. In such a case, a spontaneous healing process or group activity of some kind emerges that is, in effect, a creative ritual to fit the occasion. An example of this is the men's circle discussed in Chapter 4.

The most common use of ritual ceremony takes place toward the end of GERI events, when the men create an offering or gift to honor the women, and vice versa, or one half the group honors the other half. This form of "self-generated" ritual provides a vehicle for spontaneous creativity and group collaboration, in which subgroups are each given a unique opportunity to bestow a kind of "blessing" upon one another—a process that often confers as much upon the givers as the receivers.

Intimacy Within a Community

Transpersonal healing and collective ceremonial processes have a profound capacity to deepen intimacy within a community and cultivate new levels of mutual respect, empathy, and understanding. Once experienced or awakened, these processes often invoke a spontaneous wisdom and power that transcends the group's original vision, and mysteriously transforms the emotional and even physical well-being of all the individuals involved. Such powerful phenomena are an integral element of gender reconciliation and collective healing in community. They serve to evoke wonder and restore an innate reverence for life, a phenomenon well known in other cultures that routinely engage in collective spiritual and ritual ceremony. Gender reconciliation work is one of the doorways for such rich, nurturing experiences to come back into Western societies.

We close this chapter with insights and reflections on the GERI program from psychiatrist Stanislav Grof and Brigitte Grof.

Reflections on Gender and Equity and Reconciliation

Stanislav Grof, M.D. and Brigitte Grof

The crisis in relations between men and women and people of diverse gender identities is arguably one of the most important challenges facing humanity. Will Keepin and Cynthia Brix, and the facilitators they trained, have developed a form of collective healing work that aims to transform gender relations in human societies. Their methodology was inspired in part by the Truth and Reconciliation Commission led by Archbishop Desmond Tutu in South Africa (applied to gender instead of race), coupled with basic principles of transformational group process, and the holotropic breathwork developed by Stanislav and Christina Grof in 1974 at the Esalen Institute in Big Sur, California, which has remained a key component of their program for 30 years, especially in the facilitator training curriculum. In 2001 Will and Cynthia launched the first professional training in Gender Reconciliation, with Diane Haug as co-trainer. Their program evolved over time to become Gender Equity and Reconciliation International (GERI), which today conducts intensive trainings in numerous countries on six continents.

In May 2018, we co-led together with Diane Haug a workshop at Esalen Institute with Will and Cynthia and team, combining their GERI work with holotropic breathwork. It proved to be a wonderful and intense combination; the gender work added a completely new dimension to the breathwork experiences.

The holotropic breathwork process, which entails sustained accelerated breathing, is an extremely powerful and effective modality that can facilitate deep emotional and psychosomatic healing, stress reduction, and spiritual healing and awakening. Experiences in breathwork can provide experiential access to ancestral, racial, collective, and karmic memories, as well as the realm of the collective unconscious that C. G. Jung called "archetypal." These transpersonal experiences are deeply connected to the various universal archetypes of human societies down through the cultures and ages, some of which are intimately connected to gender, sexuality, and spirituality, which is the particular focus of the GERI program. Another frequent result of holotropic work is connection with the numinous dimensions of one's own psyche, and of existence in general, which is also a frequent occurrence in ritual and spiritual practices of many cultures and ages.[10] All these dimensions are also intrinsic to the gender dimension of human experience, which makes for a natural affinity between holotropic breathwork and the GERI program.

We had been aware of the GERI work for years, but this Esalen workshop was for us a unique opportunity to see how Will and Cynthia and their team are able to use the holotropic states of consciousness to increase ecological sensitivity, and gender and political reconciliation. The openness and honesty of both female and male participants (including the workshop leaders and facilitators), and their willingness to share their wounds and witness each other, led to a deep mutual appreciation, understanding, and collective transformational experience between both genders.

In this Esalen workshop, the experiential process with 77 participants entailed moving back and forth between the holotropic breathing practice and the GERI cross-gender exercises, and shifting periodically between various sub-groupings and full plenary sessions. This interweaving of process enabled participants to engage deeply with one another at multiple levels in community, and then deeply within themselves—in a two-step combination that proved to be profound. The alternating experiences of going through the GERI interactive cross-gender exercises and deep truth-telling in community (in the mornings), followed by the holotropic experiences in which participants delved deeply within themselves (in the afternoons), and finally concluding with plenary integration (in the evenings), enabled a remarkable journey into the depths of inner and outer dimensions of individual and collective experience.

The result was a steady deepening of intensive immersion in individual and collective healing over the six days of the workshop. At different times, the men and women met separately, and other times together in concentric circles, in which women spoke truth to their experiences with men in silent witness, and then vice versa with roles reversed. There were plenty of tears of release and acknowledgment, mutual compassion and understanding, and sometimes great laughter and exhilaration, as one deep truth after another poured forth. Engaging in these circles sometimes closely resembled a breathwork session in itself, in terms of the levels of cathartic expressions, release of long-held tensions, and the depths of gender truths excavated.

The workshop process culminated in a remarkable set of ritual ceremonies on the last two days of the workshop, which were some of the most powerful we have seen. The ceremonies were designed and choreographed by the participants themselves, after having gone through several days of breathwork and deep truth-telling in relation to their gendered experiences in life.

This preparation imparted to these final honoring ceremonies a palpable sense of archetypal depth and numinous presence, healing, and creativity—drawing on the strength of the inner and outer processes that had preceded them.

In the final ceremonies, the women created a magnificent "sound bath" of female voices, masterfully choreographed with accompanying instruments and bells. They invited the men to lie down, and during the sound bath the women moved deftly among the men in repose, whispering affirmations and prayers into each man's ears. The men later reciprocated with their own ceremony for the women, reciting blessing prayers and original poetry to honor and uplift the feminine. The men then invited the women into a large circle, and arranged themselves in a concentric inner circle. Facing the women, the men moved gently sideways in unison, with sacred transcendent music playing, as each man made silent prayerful eye contact with each woman, until they came around full circle. The veils of separation between genders seemed to drop away, and the men and women beheld one another soul-to-soul, devoid of the overlays of cultural projection and gender conditioning that are so rampant and debilitating, covering up our true divine nature. These ceremonies had a profound quality of sacred renewal, in which ancient wounds are healed and dissolved in a collective numinous unity, reminiscent of certain legendary visionary and ritual circle dances in indigenous communities down through the ages.

As the GERI team described their work in India and Africa, we heard some of the most powerful and remarkable stories about holotropic sessions we have ever heard. Will gave a talk about the divine nature of the universe, combining relativistic-quantum physics, astrophysics, beautiful Julia and Mandelbrot fractals, and quotes from spiritual teachers and ancient mystics, which was truly inspiring.

We absolutely recommend this gender equity and reconciliation work that is described in this beautiful book. We believe it is an important contribution for world peace.

Stanislav Grof and Brigitte Grof
Wiesbaden, Germany,
December 24, 2021

PART II

Ubuntu in Action

Part II provides accounts of the GERI program and its implementation in different sectors of society, including specialized programs for specific populations and communities. Ubuntu *is an African term that means, "I am because you are." It affirms the fundamental interdependence of all humanity, and was often emphasized by Archbishop Desmond Tutu.*

These chapters are written with extensive quotations and personal narratives to capture the voices of people from these different communities and sectors, sharing in their own words how they have experienced the GERI program and the impacts it has had in their lives. Because there are many voices from different people and diverse cultures, this part of the book by its nature exhibits a chorus of voices and communication styles. The editors have made minor edits for syntax, clarity, and readability, but we have left the tone and local flavor intact as much as possible, so that the individual quality and tenor of these reflections comes through as best as possible.

CHAPTER 10

LGBTQ+ Healing the Gender Spectrum

I would not worship a God who is homophobic.
I would refuse to go to a homophobic heaven.
No, I would say, "Sorry, I would much rather go to the other place."
— Archbishop Desmond Tutu

Over the past 30 years, GERI has paved the way for many people to experience the power of transformative gender healing in community. This includes a long history of working with lesbian, gay, bisexual, transgender, queer, and people of other gender identities (LGBTQ+). The earliest prototype of this program was piloted in a series of intensive trainings that brought gay, lesbian, bisexual, and heterosexual communities together for transformative healing and reconciliation in the mid 1990s in the United States. These programs took place at the height of the AIDS epidemic that was devastating the gay men's communities nationwide. A subsequent prototype program was developed in Cape Town, South Africa for LGBT communities in 2003, and further modified in 2010. Today's continuation of this program is primarily intended for the LGBTQ+ community and for gender healing and transformation outside the traditional categories of male and female, although not excluding them.

LGBTQ+ Needs and Rights

The specific needs of LGBTQ+ populations have been widely under-served, but fortunately this is changing as the gender landscape continues to shift today, and gender identities and expressions expand beyond exclusive male and female conditioning and roles. Just three weeks before Archbishop Desmond Tutu formally announced a partnership with the GERI program in August, 2013, he helped to launch the United Nations "Free and Equal" campaign to support LGBTQ+ rights. At the U.N. press conference he said, "I oppose such injustice with the same passion that I opposed apartheid."

Recent advances to support LGBTQ+ rights are inspiring, although there is still a long ways to go. Many countries are implementing pioneering legislation to sanction same-sex marriages, or at least civil unions. In 2015, the Supreme Court of the United States legalized same sex marriage nationwide. At present, same-sex marriage is legally performed and recognized in 29 countries (nationwide or in some jurisdictions), with the most recent being Costa Rica in 2020. Chile allowed same-sex couples to marry starting in March, 2022, and Switzerland in July, 2022.[1]

Meanwhile, increased attention and awareness has come to intersexed individuals and their unique challenges, experiences of discrimination, and need for legal protections. About one in every fifteen-hundred newborn infants is "intersexed," meaning that their genitalia do not conform to the usual male or female anatomy.[2] Since the nineteenth century, intersexed infants have been surgically altered to make them either male or female (usually the latter). However, this practice has come under intense criticism, as the intersexed individuals have often grown to feel as adults that their sexual identity was mistakenly forced upon them by the medical community. This contentious arena has raised important new scientific and medical questions about male and female biology and anatomy.

Despite growing acceptance, LGBTQ+ populations have been severely persecuted in most if not all societies across the globe, including the supposedly advanced Western countries. LGBTQ+ individuals have also been the target of increasing "hate crimes," homophobia, and long-standing discriminatory policies that constitute systematic violations of their fundamental human rights. These abuses of human rights have been increasingly reported in the media and press in recent decades, and new legislation is slowly being implemented in many countries to protect these vulnerable populations. On June 15, 2020, the Supreme Court of the United States ruled that the protections provided by Title VII of the Civil Rights Act of 1964 are also extended to LGBTQ+ individuals, thereby making it illegal for workplaces (with 15 or more employees) to discriminate on the basis of sexuality or gender identity.[3] In some countries such as South Africa, gender justice is guaranteed as a basic human right for all citizens in the Bill of Rights, including choice of sexual orientation, yet the society has a long way to go in practice to catch up with the ideals of its Constitution.

The GERI LGBTQ+ Program

The GERI LGBTQ+ program creates a dedicated space to address the injustices, oppression, and gender wounding of the LGBTQ+ community, and to explore this emerging aspect of gender healing. The program is geared especially for people who identify as queer, transgender, gender non-conforming or otherwise part of the LGBTQ+ community, including allies and all those interested to explore these expanding gender identities and expressions. The program also creates an intimate and safe space to confront internalized shame, rejection, and loss, which is otherwise often confined to the individual because there is no other place where it can come forward. The GERI LGBTQ+ program strives to restore queer sexuality and identity with dignity, love, belonging, and acceptance within beloved community.

This first story comes from a young adult in South Africa, who shares their challenges of growing up as a gender fluid person, as well as the healing they have found both through spiritual practice and the GERI process.

I attended my first three-day introductory GERI workshop back in 2015 at Chrysalis Academy, a youth development organization. I had hoped to skip the three-day workshop and enroll immediately in the yearlong facilitator training program, because I felt like I was already a "seasoned facilitator" who knew more than the average person on topics related to gender. But I don't regret doing the three-day workshop, because an opening and softening in my heart allowed me to begin the healing journey from within before I reflected on others who may have harmed or helped my gender biography and conditioning. I experienced the divine in each of my peers over those three days.

I feared having to go inwardly because of the many wounds I carried. As a little boy I was very quiet, introverted, and shy at times. Growing up I was often ridiculed or laughed at whenever I spoke because I "sounded like a girl," and there would be moments when I just silenced myself to avoid drawing attention to myself. An important moment happened to me one Sunday at a Pentecostal church service when I stepped up to the altar for a prayer of healing. During the prayer the pastor asked me if I was molested as a child. My response at the time was "no," because I didn't recall ever being molested.

I have sat with that very question over the last eight years. Now, I remember that I experienced my first sexual violation with an uncle. I was nine or ten years old at the time and remember finding him asleep (intoxicated on alcohol) in my mother's room while she was at work. I sat on the bed because our television was in my mom's room. I remember my uncle waking up, taking my hand and placing it on his genitalia. I was curious and frightened at the same time, but I didn't say anything. This was a man I trusted and who would frequently visit our house. The groping went on until my late teenage years. I never spoke about it, but I remember feeling violated and also objectified because I was a queer *boytjie* (South African slang for a young man).

At the time of my first GERI workshop in 2015, I identified as gender fluid and I felt very appreciative of the facilitators for creating a place of safety through this experiential process, but there was a deep longing and desire to be witnessed, seen and embraced by my own community (queer family), as I shared parts of myself that I had denied for many years. The careful holding and articulation of the community agreements was quite helpful. It grounded me to know that I could share painful stories about my gender experience. I was on a very different path when stepping into that first workshop and felt safe enough to be separated with the men, knowing that I carried pain and a deep wounding from my father who was both physically and emotionally absent for nearly 20 years of my life, and I projected that onto men around me. There was also a powerful and transcendent feeling in being present with the masculine within me and around me in the separate gender group.

I could not have stepped into the GERI work without being introduced to the diverse and powerful spiritual practices and foundations of the work. I came from a conservative Christian background where things like mantra, meditation, or contemplative prayer were never mentioned. I chose to break away from the Old Apostolic Church, and for the last eight years have been part of a spiritual community in Pentecostal church, which still needs to do a lot of work to affirm the LGBTQ+ community. As an ordained Reverend in the church, I am the only genderqueer or agender person in the church community, which can often be very isolating. However, being introduced to the spiritual aspects of the GERI work, I feel accepting of my queerness, and even more so in the "house of the Lord." I value GERI's emphasis on spiritual practice, and "brightening one's inner light" through silent contemplation or prayer, and it is through this work that I have been introduced to my own light or my higher consciousness, my true self in the world. I was able to discover a way into the Inner Light by practicing stillness meditation and going inward to connect to the divine and to my own divinity, because I was made in the image of God, or Divine as we call them.

I had denied my queerness before stepping into the GERI work but through the emerging GERI LGBTQ+ program I am grateful to reconnect to this part of my being. I am humbled by the way that GERI work has seeped into my life and heart. The power of truth-telling in community propels us to give voice to the wounded and broken parts of our being. I have experienced through the GERI work that we are all storytellers of our gender biography and it is our divine right and duty to bring these stories of shame and pain forward, and when we are able to confront these stories that we do so with reverence and compassion. Love illuminates, anchors, enlightens, and gives birth to our gender stories. As the transgender rights-activist, author, and TV host Janet Mock said, "I believe that telling our stories, first to ourselves and then to one another and the world, is a revolutionary act."

The next account comes from a young woman, who shares both her pain of having to hide her same-sex relationship from friends and family, as well as her heart's vision for a gender-healed world where this would no longer be the case.

I started dating men in my twenties. In those days, I always introduced my boyfriends to the people in my life, who became friendly with them. I even introduced them to my parents and socialized with them. Then, about five years ago, I met a woman and we became romantic partners. After we became a couple, it was difficult for me to tell my close friends about my girlfriend, and I only told my parents that I had a close friend who was like my older sister. My parents, who don't know that I have a girlfriend, tell me to get married every time I see them. It seemed like a lie to me not to tell my dear parents about the existence of my beloved partner. It is very upsetting.

Then I joined a GERI workshop. At the workshop, the question "What would a world without gender bias be like?" was so shocking to me. It was a question I hadn't even thought of, and when I did my heart fluttered with excitement. I thought that if a gender-equal world came about, I could introduce my girlfriend to my parents, and they could bless the two of us rather than always worrying about me not getting married and my old age. It made me realize that gender bias is affecting many aspects of my life of being in a same sex relationship—from a very deep inward place within me to daily practical living.

At first, I worried about whether this kind of story could be shared at the GERI workshop. But when I did, people deeply sympathized with it, and there were people who shed tears and said that they wished such a world would come.

The reality has not changed yet, but the GERI program has allowed me to meet people who share deeply with each other and dream of a gender-equal world together. That is very touching to me. What had been stuck and rigid in me has been released. Conversations with men are no longer challenging for me. Just like women are all different from each other, men are all different, too. So, I don't think there's any reason for me to avoid all men or feel uncomfortable. Their history and experiences have shaped them, and I now believe that if we talk together and listen sincerely, we will be able to live comfortably in a society where each of us is respected as individuals, regardless of gender.

The story below is from a young man who had a powerful experience during a workshop of reconciling his sexuality and his spiritual journey and relationship with God. He writes:

The Gender Equity and Reconciliation Workshop acted as a significant catalyst in bringing to my awareness the internalized homophobia and shame of my sexuality. Whilst I knew I was gay from the age of 12, it was not until recently, at 25 years old, that I was able to accept the reality, and "own" that I am gay. For years I struggled with the notion of God being unwilling to accept me if I simply embraced the reality of my internal experience. This led me to fight against, deny and suppress my experience of being gay, for many years.

During the Truth Mandala activity, I can recall vividly that moment I entered the room and my eyes fell on a black sheet lying carelessly scrunched on the floor. At that moment, dread filled me, and I had a strong internal reaction to the object. I learned that the black sheet symbolized shame. Each man was given the opportunity to stand and engage with one or more of the symbolic objects and speak about their hidden or unexpressed emotions. When I felt ready, I stood up and put the black sheet over my head. Standing in front of the other men in this way was extremely confronting. Feelings rose inside as I covered my face with this black, oppressive, ugly object. Uncontrollable tears streamed down my face. Words were not required in that moment. It was there I had an experience of the shame within my being. I felt shame that somehow I had disappointed God by "turning out wrong." Believing THIS had led me to pursue changing my- self, in order to be "acceptable to God and to other people."

I was confronted with the oppressive nature of my thinking. The shame had led me to cover my- self, as though I was Adam in the garden of Eden covering my "shame" with cloth, trying to please and earn God's approval. I was painfully confronted with the ways in which the shame led to a desire for change and to be deemed "acceptable." This had manifested in many life decisions in an attempt to change my experience of my sexual orientation. The manifestations of this shame included a decision to pursue a relationship with a girl, to seek out what I considered to be masculine activities and to my denying anything I thought was considered feminine. The amount of energy expended in trying to cover shame, and trying to "change" in order to become acceptable to God and other people, was intensely draining.

The month following the Gender Equity and Reconciliation workshop was an internal battle. I was realizing my oppressive thought patterns and the shame I had been living under for so many years around my sexuality. One of my main struggles was with God's acceptance. I really grieved the extent of losing the connection I had with God/Divine, which had been a source of guidance, and comfort. I was concerned and scared that if I accepted "the reality of who I am" as a gay man, God would somehow disown me. Transitioning through this process is something I am eternally grateful for, as I realized, firstly, how limited my spiritual connection with the Divine had been. The integration of my sexuality through the process of letting go of my shame actually expanded my connection with God. Only a couple of months after the Gender Equity and Reconciliation workshop, I discovered a God filled with much more grace than I could possibly comprehend. I experienced incredible bliss in the realization I didn't have to continue to struggle against my own sexuality any longer; God actually accepts me for me. I had expended enormous energy trying to change, and pleading to God to change me, and sincerely choosing things that I believed would aid the process or "goal"—I could now let go of these. Words cannot describe how amazing this realization is.

In this process, as I came into a new way of being with myself, I had to make some changes in my life, to reflect the change within my spirit. First was to come out in my church. I knew people would be shocked and confused, but it was essential for me to come out there. Afterwards, though, I wasn't able to participate in the community at the same level as before. I had worked for the church, and was extremely involved in a leadership position. But although it was my community, it didn't feel safe anymore.

Leaving the church as my community and my employment was exceptionally difficult. I found myself trying to find some more connective spaces that would support my sexuality. As a gay man, and from conversations with other LGBTQ+ individuals, it is very difficult to find Christian spaces that provide a sense of connection and support around spirituality. I also wanted to find my identity apart from religious expectations. I felt betrayed—even deceived—into having believed these things around my sexuality, and my unique identity of self and of soul—and that was really damaging. This made me very cautious about entering into another religious community, with expectations thrust upon me to conform again to a particular worldview and beliefs. I wanted to find my own identity apart from the expectations of church and religion. My soul was desperately wanting to find that out for myself—finding that out with God, rather than simply with what the church says. . . even what the Bible says—by trusting my own inner soul and divine connection. I felt a sense of grief and loss to leave the church, but I needed to find my identity, to find who I am. And I felt that freedom within my spirit to do that—I even felt that freedom within God to do that. It feels a bit like the prodigal son in the New Testament. Leaving home to find one's identity, and then returning and still being embraced as the son. Each season I am becoming more comfortable with "who I am." I realize how vital it is for me, and all people, to be themselves, and how intrinsic being "me" is to authentic spirituality, and the grace that flows from divine acceptance.

Years later, returning to be involved in GERI as a trainee, and doing the six-month training online, was a real sense of coming home for me—coming home into community, coming closer to home spiritually. I don't think I'm there yet, but it helps me find what my sense of spirituality is, because in the GERI Community there's such vulnerability, humanness, and just a deep sense of beauty in the work and in the people involved. In the training and community, in all its diversity—multicultural, multilingual, multifaith, multidimensional in so many ways—I felt a kind of spiritual flow through it all. Even in the participants who come I see glimpses, I see beauty and the essence of people's vulnerability in their sharing and in their stories, and that is deeply spiritual.

In the following sharing, the Rev. Laurie Gaum, who is a GERI Trainer, shares his powerful story of challenge, heartbreak, healing and transformation after being publicly outed as a gay clergyman in the Dutch Reformed Church, and his legal battle after being defrocked.

I began my studies in theology during the early nineties at the University of Stellenbosch near Cape Town. South Africa was just awaking from its apartheid sleep, while Stellenbosch was the very cradle that intellectually gave birth to the ideology of apartheid. I came from the Dutch Reformed Church (DRC) and was receiving my training for Dutch Reformed ministry; the DRC gave scriptural justification to apartheid. As young, white Afrikaners and future DRC ministers in class, we were grappling with the legacy of apartheid and of the church we would become ministers to. My dad has been in the leadership of the (DRC). I followed in his footsteps, but had to struggle with integrating my sexuality as a queer man, doing so only at a later stage of my life.

As the country was opening up on various fronts to democracy after the unbanning of the liberation movements and the release of Nelson Mandela during the build-up to the first democratic elections in 1994, we were also confronted with other kinds of "awakenings." In our class were six women who were only allowed into full time ministry in the DRC from 1990. Many of them were academically strong and were making a considerable impact on the class. Some of my fellow male classmates along with some male lecturers found it hard to deal with the women and to fully accommodate and accept them as fellow theologians and future colleague ministers.

Being on the progressive side of the class along with most of the women made me experience the pain inflicted on them, since they were also my friends. When I incidentally came upon the Gender Equity and Reconciliation International (GERI) process some fifteen years later, I knew this provided a tool to respond to the wounding intrinsic to my women friends' experience, but also to that of society at large (Nozizwe Madlala-Routledge calls GERI an effective tool to address patriarchy). But I still needed to wake up and come home to my own experience as a gay man.

My church background didn't offer much space to explore my sexuality and, having grown up suppressing it by focusing my attentions on spiritual development and finding some solace therein, it was only during my student years that I started interrogating this hidden side of my being. I had to spiritually and theologically "figure it out" before I could challenge myself to integrate theory and practice to bring mind, body and spirit together.

After I'd reached a place of peace with God and could accept myself as having been created "gay in God's image," it of course did not mean this would be as simple for the church of which I was part.

I was minister to a Dutch Reformed congregation in the inner-city of Cape Town when I was in my first relationship at age 30. It was a rocky relationship at best, which we were living as an "open secret." In a moment of mental aberration my partner of four years outed me to the church and to the tabloid media providing them with personal compromising photographs of myself. Soon afterwards he committed suicide.

The church responded by demanding that I take a vow of celibacy or be defrocked. I lost my partner. I lost my job. I lost my church community. It was an extremely challenging time as I was facing several losses simultaneously.

I successfully appealed this decision to the denomination and was reinstated two years later in 2007. I couldn't have survived this without the immense support of my family and friends. I've been in the struggle for equality on grounds of sexual orientation and gender identity and expression (SOGIE) ever since, in the church and in broader society.

My dad and I struggled a lot over several years as he wrestled with his own son being gay, which was counter to his own beliefs, as well to as his leadership role and responsibilities to the DRC. Over several years, we exchanged extensive letters through email that eventually helped him come to a better understanding, and also about the interpretation of biblical texts regarding same-sex relationships. This long and difficult process bonded us as father and son even more deeply and he came out in full support of me and has been an activist for the LGBTQ+ cause ever since, especially in the church. We published a book in 2010 containing some of our conversations around this subject.[4] He and I were applicants in a civil court case against the DRC which we won in 2019, declaring discrimination on grounds of sexual orientation unconstitutional and leading to a more affirming decision in the DRC.

In 2015 I was part of a delegation representing GERI at the Parliament of World Religions in Salt Lake City when the news came in that the Dutch Reformed Church had reached an historic decision towards full inclusion, scrapping a celibacy clause for its LGBTQIA ministers, and allowing its ministers to conduct same-sex unions (which are legal in South Africa). However, the church not only failed to implement this, but it went ahead in 2016 to reverse the decision. Meanwhile, hate crimes especially against Black lesbians in some of South Africa's townships are rife, along with what is called "corrective rape," which is purported to "cure" lesbians from their homosexuality.

The GERI process, as it links onto my other work with masculinities, has firstly supported me to articulate my own experiences. It continues to encourage me to "drop from my head to my heart" in order to share from there. I'm convinced this is a crucial learning, especially for men who have been socialized to operate "from the head." While discussions on homosexuality have been ongoing in some denominations for the past 30 years, it has mostly been heterosexual males speaking about an issue which to a large degree falls outside of their own experience. They've dissected the phenomenon from all sides, in many cases without listening to the first-hand experiences of those directly affected and without bringing their own experiences to the table.

So [heterosexual] men need to be brought into the conversation by learning the tools to speak to their own experience and emotions. As a gay male I have enjoyed coming home in the GERI processes of the Truth Mandala to what I like to call "the circle of equals" where each man's voice is respected and brought forward equally. But the next step in this process—to "make the circle bigger"—is important for men to find their home within the greater human family alongside women. Here we're privileged to listen to and witness women and trans people giving a first-hand encounter of their experiences within the safe space of an authentic meeting with the other. It's here where the space for genuine transformation is created, making behavioral change possible.

Within the honoring part of a workshop it has been important for me, when issues related to SOGIE have featured strongly, to suggest that from within the male group (therefore from within traditional patriarchy) an honoring of the diversity regarding SOGIE is also registered in some or other way.

Although global mainline churches like the Anglican Communion, the Roman Catholic Church and the Methodist Church seem to be at a deadlock regarding progress on LGBTQ+ inclusion, and while my African continent amongst others plays its role in upholding this, the GERI process offers valuable and finely devised tools supporting men and women to venture toward vulnerability. In so doing, it enables them to find a language for their own experiences.

As GERI aided me into further "awakening," it also continues to help me to come home into the community of men and into the fullness of humanity along with my sisters. I believe this to be a crucial journey for our time.

Reconciliation Between "Queer" and "Straight" Believers in Religious Communities

A study of five inclusive Christian congregations in South Africa was conducted in 2019 by Dr. Selina Palm, a GERI facilitator and senior researcher at the Unit for Religion and Development Research at Stellenbosch University. Projections of "sin," especially in relation to sexuality, had made people feel dirty or unaccepted by God, and especially for many queer people had induced a deep internalized stigma and self-hatred, often for years of their lives, shaping their attitudes toward God. The study concluded that the single most important factor for catalyzing change was the need for tools and safe spaces for embodied engagement between "queer" and "straight" congregants, in order to develop a vision of social justice that reconciles sexuality, human rights and faith.[5] As one Black female congregant expressed the dilemma, "Every time we exclude someone from the community of humankind we are spitting in the face of God, [but are doing it] in the *name* of God, of Jesus."[6]

Responding to this need, a series of workshops applying the GERI methodology with a specific focus on human sexuality and intersectionalites is being implemented by Dr. Palm and Rev. Laurie Gaum of GenderWorks,[7] with support from Tristan Johannes, Desireé English, and others. The purpose is to bring together "straight" and "queer"people in safe spaces (or "safe enough" spaces) in which the cycles of LGBTQ+ shame and hiding can be broken, and webs of relationality are established that generate bondedness and a united sense of 'we' that supersedes 'us and them.' These workshops also offer a complementary "third" dimension to the LGBTQ+ sector that otherwise often focuses either on workshops for LGBTQ+ people, or on diversity and anti-bias training for straight people.

As participants reflected,[8]

> The workshop highlighted that sometimes we can feel so different [as queer people] but if we have more sessions like this, the enlightenment is that we as [all] people are so similar and have the same struggles that should connect us rather than drive us further apart.

An older gay man noted with surprise in relation to straight stories shared that, "We are actually more alike than different." Meanwhile, straight people became more aware of their privilege when asked to listen to the stories of others:

> Even as a straight person, a lot of the bigger themes about body/sacred, sin, pleasure, shame, anger, hurt, etc. all apply to my story, and it was really helpful to reflect on those things. It was also important for me to [realize] as a straight white woman [that] my story has always *mattered*, and often at the expense of others' stories. ... I needed to make much more room for the stories of those around me (white cis woman).

And another:

> I feel so much more comfortable around the language of queerness, and I understand how complex the spectrum of gender and sexuality is.

The workshops opened the eyes of many straight people to the challenging experiences of many queer people. In the honoring ritual ceremonies designed to unite spirituality and sexuality, one group centered their ceremony around coming to "the Altar of Acceptance," and another focused on letting go and "crossing over into celebrating diversity together," which included seeing one another in their diversity, and embodying singing and dancing together as a vision of what the church could be in its worship spaces.

Five key themes emerged from these workshops: the importance of safe spaces, healing and ritual experiences to reconnect sexuality and spirituality, deep connection across multiple differences, enabling courageous conversations to take place, and embracing taboo topics. Other themes included the importance of engaging the fluidity of sexuality and transitions in people's lives, straight people becoming allies, and appreciation for the harmonious modelling by the four diverse facilitators as a cornerstone of the methodology. Several of the participants have continued on to be trained as facilitators within the wider GERI process.[9]

There is an urgent need today in many religious communities for affirming and inclusive spaces. In the United States, for example, refusal to accept LGBTQ+ equality is still creating major divisions in several churches.[10] As one part of the solution, "this evidence-based approach can offer safe spaces for embodied, storied encounters between LGBTIQ+ believers and straight believers that meets a current gap" in most religious congregations.[11] Several of these workshops are currently being conducted for the South African Council of Churches, to support diverse belonging, and ultimately create a gender-inclusive "kin-dom of God" as a form of Beloved Community.

GERI Workshop at The LGBTQ Center of Southern Nevada, Las Vegas, 2024

CHAPTER 11

Intersectionalities and BIPOC Communities

I want there to be a place in the world where people can engage in one another's differences in a way that is redemptive, full of hope and possibility.
—bell hooks

Intersectionalities of gender with sexual orientation, race, gender identity, culture, and ethnicity have long been an important aspect of the GERI work.[1] The crucial need for sensitive and skillful embrace of intersectionalities became abundantly clear when GERI was first invited to India in 2001, and South Africa in 2003. The program has been adapted accordingly to accommodate a broad range of intersectionalities, and today many GERI workshops and events are attended by highly diverse groups, which contributes to the strength of the program itself, and greatly enriches the experience for participants.

The specialized GERI BIPOC programs convene dedicated spaces for Black, Indigenous, and People of Color to do their gender healing work together. The facilitation teams for these workshops are all GERI facilitators of color, and the programs are designed to create rare forums to delve deeply into gender injustice and dynamics in a BIPOC space.

Myra Kinds, GERI Trainer and the BIPOC and Intersectionalities Lead, begins this chapter with her perspective:

There is no such thing as a single-issue struggle, because we do not live single issue lives.
—Audre Lorde

I was once on a panel representing Black clergy. I recall a question posed by a young Christian Black man in the audience. Why do I describe him that way? Because the moment we enter spaces, we are often noticed less by our spoken introductions and more by historical assumptions and biases—our intersections, how we are seen, and what others believe about our lives, based merely on outer appearances.

The participant asked with concern, "How can I step into my role at my place of employment and do my job, without the other parts of my identity getting in the way?"

I met his question with a rhetorical question: "Then who, exactly, is walking through the door?" I then told him that leaving any part of himself at the door would be like walking through the door naked, and that would be a disservice to himself and his organization.

I am a Christian woman—and an African, born in America. I am a wife, mother, sister, minister, and sacred vessel. I identify as "she/her" and embrace and protect my divine feminine. I am the Gender Equity and Reconciliation BIPOC and Intersectionality Lead. As I sit in my role, I sit as my whole self, representing others in our community and those who may desire to join yet are unsure if this is a space for them, and wondering if they will need to leave parts of themselves at the door.

BIPOC stands for "Black, Indigenous, and Persons of Color." In other countries, there are different acronyms that describe individuals whose ethnicity/race makes them the "other" in the room, even in their own birthplace. This added description for our identity has almost guaranteed common lived experiences and disparities. No matter male, female, or orientation, the BIPOC categorization presents the other layer of challenges and stories yet to be fully told. When explaining GERI, we say: "We create safe forums for people of all genders to have intimate and often taboo and sensitive conversations around gender and sexuality, without shame or blame. In this process, we are invited to bring our personal stories of pain and suffering into the open and speak truth to our gendered experience—not as victims, but as witnesses to our lives. The purpose is not to wallow in our pain and suffering, but to bring them forward into the light, and jointly confront them as women and men. Together we heal and transform, and move toward a newfound place of wholeness, mutuality, and renewal that goes beyond equal rights and mutual respect to a place of mutual reverence." This is the heart of GERI.

Intersectionalities are always present but often invisible. When we meet someone for the first time, we typically see that person only at "face value" and through our personal filters of conditioned beliefs, perceptions, and often projections. This happens to me all the time. I can walk through a door just like anyone else does, but most people don't see me first as a woman or even notice what I'm wearing. What they see first is that I'm Black and with that comes all kinds of thoughts, feelings, expectations, and assumptions from the person I'm meeting. So, there frequently are obstacles and barriers—subtle and overt—that have to be worked through before we can even begin to get to know each other on a deeper level.

The flip side is that usually when any one of us walks into a room of strangers, we enter with a certain level of caution and perhaps anxiety, wearing a "mask of protection" and revealing only a small part of ourselves. This is because we need to be sure that the people and the space are safe enough for us to feel comfortable showing other parts of ourselves. So often there are many extensions of ourselves that we don't let others see. This is particularly true for people who have been marginalized on a personal, cultural, and/or historical level. So, as GERI facilitators we are always working to be aware and sensitive to who is in the space, and to ensure that everyone feels welcome and invited to bring their whole selves and their full story—extensions and all—to the table. If we don't open and invite the unseen and invisible parts of ourselves in, we won't heal. Healing is possible but we have to do it in community.

As GERI welcomes in this 30th year anniversary, we are even more committed to creating space and opportunity for all lives to be fully seen and stories to be heard in this healing space, with all its intersections. We look forward to welcoming more BIPOC voices, learning what we do not know and holding space for all who will come. The BIPOC space is fully a part of GERI and does not imply that we must do this work segregated. Instead, we acknowledge that this is another entry place to start on the journey.

The voice of GERI BIPOC can be summed up in this shared experience from GERI BIPOC's online introductory sessions. When we entered the space, we did not realize that we were still holding parts of our stories in our breath until we exhaled. It was like a familiar scene, coming to sit at the family gathering. We had experienced and witnessed each other. During the retelling of stories, we exhaled together. There was no code switching[1] and no hesitation to express our passions in this space. We shouted together and breathed together. We could look around the space and see ourselves in our complexions, hear ourselves in our accents, and reconnect with ourselves and one another in our silence. This is a space that some may not think is even possible, and yet it is.

In 2018, we convened our first North American GERI workshop for People of Color (POC), entitled #WeToo: People of Color Healing the Gender Wound. This workshop was held in Seattle and brought together an intimate group of 13 dynamic and inspiring people across different ethnicities, nationalities, and cultures. Together the group delved deeply into stories of challenge, pain and personal wounding from gender oppression, racism, and white supremacy—courageously opening their hearts and listening intently to one another with compassion and love. The sacred space was both healing and liberating, reigniting the spirit of *Ubuntu* and mutual harmony that lies at the spiritual heart of humanity. Below is a personal account of the workshop.

We were all very excited to be part of the first people of color GERI workshop. For the first time we had a workshop facilitated *by* people of color *for* people of color. I am from Kenya, so I personally do not get the term "people of color." In my view, everyone has color.

The power of this POC GERI workshop was the way it gave us space to see ourselves through our own eyes, rather than the eyes of the system that has labeled us. When we came together, we saw ourselves as whole, complete, and enough as we are. There was nothing to place ourselves against to find a "positioning." We were simply ourselves, speaking our experiences from a place of deep authenticity. There was no "gaze" but our own looking within, to find who we are as women and men in community. The truthtelling was powerful. The tears were real. All voices were heard. Every voice was valid. We were real and true—to ourselves, our pain, our realities, and our communal circumstances. "It was profound being in People of Color space," reflected one female participant, "Seeing brown hands on both sides of me felt good... I felt safer to bring these things up. It's easier to open my heart to men of color knowing you have been targeted by the -isms." This was a deep digging to excavate all the namings and markings upon us as a people and community. It was a process of understanding the systems within which we have lived, and learning how they have marked us, named us, and created a "myth" around who we are. We were unearthing, understanding, and refusing to accept this outside naming and marking as *our* story. It was a time of reclaiming and creating our own new stories as individuals and as community.

One powerful realization we all understood is that gender work cannot be done in the absence of racism. Racism is embedded in patriarchy as a system. Participants at the workshop were clear that breaking the patriarchal code must be done in the realm of understanding how racism feeds patriarchy and how patriarchy feeds racism. In my view, racism is a whole other realm of intervention beyond gender and patriarchy, which are, in turn, a whole other realm beyond racism. However, there are points of convergence that must be addressed, since racism is a systemic conditioning system just like patriarchy. A person who is not white in the United States is not only marked by patriarchy but also by racism. Who someone is as a man or woman in the United States is embedded in a racist social system. For me, disrupting patriarchy was a significant breakthrough to help me see and understand all the other systems that operate in society—religion, economics, culture, education, etc.—and how I can disrupt them in my life and community, too.

As we navigate in GERI workshops the labyrinth of the conditioning we all have gone through within our patriarchal society, we learn and understand all the other systems we live in and see how they have programmed us. We see how who we say we are as women and men is embedded in another's story. GERI is a space where we can choose to reclaim our voice, and who we say we are. We come here to set ourselves free from systemic conditioning and create our new story.

The profound sense of knowing who we are and understanding our circumstances was powerful at the POC GERI workshop. The significance of freeing oneself from the systemic naming and conditioning is a wakeup call for each person. The challenge was how to break that from a societal point of view. We all agreed that more workshops are needed for our people. We also realized how needed these workshops are for those who benefit from patriarchal and racist systems.

GERI has worked for the past 30 years to bring these transformative workshops to many countries throughout the world. Each one has the responsibility to bring it home to our people. The healing of one is the healing of the whole. Healing begins with each of us.

The next account shares the powerful story and background of a man who participated in a GERI workshop with a diverse group of participants in San Francisco, highlighting the unique challenges he faced growing up as a Latin American immigrant in the United States.

I was born in Cochabamba, Bolivia, as the youngest of seven children. I had three older brothers and three older sisters, and at the age of three my father was forced to escape Bolivia due to being persecuted and pursued by the military police. Though I no longer remember it, I believe the first significant trauma in my life happened on the fateful day when my father was chased through our home until he leapt over the courtyard wall, not to be heard from again until he sent the money that allowed my mother and the seven of us move to the USA to join him some ten months later.

We arrived in Providence, Rhode Island in July of 1968 and moved into a home in a predominantly African-American neighborhood during the height of the racial tension of that time. As new immigrants unfamiliar with the language, culture, and norms, we were on the receiving end of targeted violence and assault. Our home was vandalized and the garage of the rental home where we lived was set on fire. It's clear in hindsight that as a sensitive boy of four I was deeply traumatized. I experienced my first assault at the age of five, when two teenage boys attacked me as I walked home from kindergarten. I also witnessed my brothers and sisters get attacked by gangs of kids from the school we attended.

My father and mother were under immense pressure to work multiple jobs to support us. On top of that, they were driven by a mission to save money and buy a home in a better neighborhood. It was in this early childhood environment that my gender conditioning began. My father's discipline was at times extremely harsh, particularly his discipline of my brothers and me. Beatings with belts and harsh reprimands from both my parents were common. In hindsight, I realize that as a very sensitive and empathic boy my tendency to cry easily was a byproduct of the trauma and stress we were all under. I learned early that crying was harshly discouraged. Both my parents and my brothers would often say to me, *no seas un maricon* (don't be a wuss), and *no seas un lloron* (don't be a cry baby). I grew resentful that my parents comforted my sisters when they cried but did not give me the same nurturing response.

We eventually moved to an exclusively white working-class neighborhood, where the violence and discriminatory attacks continued. Given these attacks and targeted discrimination from our school peers, my oldest brother began "training" me to box and defend myself, often roughing me up in the process, in order to "toughen me up." From my adolescent years through my high school years, I responded to discriminatory remarks with fisticuffs, and since I excelled at sports, I often exacted revenge on my aggressors on the field.

I chose to isolate myself rather than develop friendships with my teammates and school mates. I was essentially a paradox in high school, as I excelled in both sports and school but lived a loner existence. Despite being a relatively good-looking young man, I did not date much, which led to an increase in my social isolation. Looking back on it, I realize that my self-isolation was a way of insulating myself from the harsh locker-room banter that most boys engaged in, and my lack of dating was a way of protecting my heart. This social isolation continued into my adult years, and it left me looking for all my social and emotional needs in my romantic relationships. I was very guarded emotionally, and walked around in a suit of armor, never fostering friendships either at work or outside of work. In my marriage I tended to be very domineering and controlling, to protect my heart.

My search for healing was initiated by the sudden passing of my life partner of 29 years, almost 5 years ago. She and I had planned to launch a workplace diversity and inclusion consulting business that never came to fruition. At that stage in my life I had not worked in the diversity and inclusion space for a few years, but her death drove me into an existential crisis that prompted my search for meaningful work in the diversity and inclusion world.

Lo and behold, in August of 2017 I came upon a Facebook post by a friend who had just attended an introductory workshop with Gender Equity and Reconciliation International. The name of the organization piqued my curiosity and prompted me to visit the website. That evening I spent over four hours combing through videos and written testimonials. The work spoke to my heart, and it aligned with my deeply-felt belief that women's equity is the number one most important human rights issue in the world. I decided that evening to attend the next workshop, which was to take place in San Francisco, California. Six weeks later I attended my first workshop. Within the first half day of the workshop, I knew that I needed to become involved in this organization in a meaningful way. Over the course of the workshop, I also experienced profound healing from hearing the "gender stories" of white men, the segment of society that I viewed as my primary oppressors during my formative years growing up in a working-class neighborhood. Completing the weekend workshop opened my heart, mind, and soul in a way no other diversity and inclusion workshop or training I had attended or facilitated had ever done.

This next story comes from a young woman's first experience of a GERI workshop, her distinct experience of womanhood as a woman of color, and her transformative insights into her own story that were revealed and opened through the process.

My father went to prison two weeks after I was born. The nature of his charges, and his African-American heritage, meant that he was given a 40-year sentence, an inordinately long punishment for his crimes. I was raised by a mother who was healing. This was my beginning. I learned that being a woman meant surviving, taking it all on so that no man could let you down. I learned to distract myself from the loneliness by achieving. I learned to take before I was taken from.

During my four-day GERI workshop, I found that my story of womanhood differed from the white women I shared space with. I felt myself drawn instead to the stories of the men, and the narratives of the guilt and shame they felt for harm they've caused. I realized the distance I felt from the grief of my upbringing: the sadness I felt around growing up without a father, my lack of male friendships, my own #metoo stories, and the gap I felt between myself and men I chose to be in relationship with. In listening to these men, I felt the cool wash of the recognition of a rejected side of my identity being illuminated by a side I called another name. I wasn't a victim, I was a survivor, but I didn't realize that "survivor" could be the mask I put over my pain's true quality: that of a perpetrator, one who has caused harm. As I sat in the outer circle and listened to the men share their stories of confusion and shame, constricted by the small box that couldn't contain all of who they are, I cried with them with earnest empathy. And when we created a ceremony to honor them, helping them to move past their pain and the pain they've caused, I recognized my own capacity to not only feel empathy for the shadow of the perpetrator our society demonizes, but also to celebrate these men in all their fullness and complexity. And I realized that if I could celebrate them, even with their capacity for harm, then I could celebrate myself.

After the workshop I decided to visit my father for the first time. Through this reconciliation work, he and I were able to meet each other in the present moment and begin the long journey of knowing each other: me in all my unfinished growth and him 29 years sober and grateful for the freedom to step on the earth without meeting concrete.

There's much I could say about what I learned and its ripple effect in my life. It wasn't a grand epiphany about men or women, or my discovery or separation from any particular narrative... But for me, a major shift occurred when I accepted that I hold within myself the power to harm and be harmed *and* to love and be loved through everything. Is that not the full human experience? This is what GERI gave me in just four days.

In 2010, two year-long GERI training programs were completed in South Africa; one with twenty-three trainees in Cape Town, and the other with ten trainees in Soweto (outside Johannesburg), all of whom were certified as GERI facilitators. The following story is from one of the U.S. GERI facilitators who assisted in both trainings and demonstrates the rich intersectional healing that can occur across culture, race, age, gender, and sexual orientation.

The Soweto GERI training included several young Black men in their 20s–30s, one elder white man (a Christian Brother), Black women of various ages, and one 30-ish white woman from Canada who was starting the training as an intern for GERI. I am a 70-year-old white woman and a GERI facilitator.

Throughout the training I was impressed with the enthusiasm, sincerity, and authenticity of these trainees.

The fourth day of the training was dedicated to holotropic breathwork. One of the young, Black male trainees, Themba, had expressed that he would like to have me be his sitter, so I asked him to sit for me as well. Over the first two days he and I had made eye contact many times, and I felt connected to him. The breathwork session started out in pain as I tried to get settled. At first, I moved a little bit to the music, then I decided to let the pain carry me into the holotropic state. I began to moan, which turned into a sob as I thought about my disintegrating, aging body. I saw a ship where I was waving goodbye to someone on shore. Then at some point the experience shifted, and I began to see vivid images of young African men being loaded on slave ships and carried to the US. I became overwhelmed with shame around my blue eyes and blond hair—symbols of the "Aryan" race which had slaughtered Jews and enslaved Africans. I wept from deep inside myself. I wanted to vomit out my insides and felt the pain that my race has caused to so many others in the world. It felt like I had tapped into the collective guilt and shame of my ancestors. I knew that I could cry forever.

I reached for Themba's hand and asked if he would place it on my stomach, which he did. At some point one of the breathwork facilitators came over and also placed his hand on my stomach. They gently pressed together as I sobbed and wiped the snot from my runny nose. I felt like I was full of the vile from generations of evil. This continued through most of the session. As the music began to lift, I started reaching out to Themba, holding his hand and rubbing his arm. Then, when I began to rouse, I sat up and we held each other for a long time. I kissed his face, he kissed my forehead. As the chant *Om Namah Shivaya* began, I sang and he hummed. I could feel the vibrations of his voice in my body. This was very helpful and healing.

In the small group debriefing at the end of the day, I learned that Carol, an African woman who was breathing beside me, kept having visions of golden sunlight and blue water...which she could not explain, but which seemed to me to be related to my visions of blue eyes and blond hair. My mandala drawing was mostly black with red blood inside a circle, with blue eyes and tears on the outside. This was a very, very powerful breathwork session that I will be processing for a long, long time. As we ended the day, Carol gave me a skirt that I had admired the previous day. This was so very sweet and generous of her. I left looking forward to the next training module and to connecting further with Themba and Carol.

I spent the next two weeks in Cape Town assisting with another GERI training, this time with a large group of activists and NGO professionals. Then we returned to Soweto for the third training module on Spirituality and Sexuality. It was a joyous reunion to be with everyone again, and especially nice to reconnect with Themba and Carol.

During the morning session we were in small groups and were invited to share about our spiritual and religious journeys. It was so interesting to listen and learn about the African spiritual tradition that for several of the trainees is integrated with their Christian religious belief.

In the afternoon, we moved into a truth forum activity that was focused on LGBTQ+ experiences. Two of the Cape Town GERI facilitators, who identify as lesbian and queer, had traveled with us to co-facilitate this particular session. The two facilitators set the context and gave the instructions for the activity. There were five empty chairs in the center of our circle. We were invited to take a chair if we wanted to speak. Everyone on the outer circle was to remain in silent witness. The facilitators led a centering meditation, and then they posed a question: What are your earliest memories and learnings about different sexual orientations or gender identity, and how do you identify?

We all sat in silence reflecting for a few moments, and then one person moved into the center, and then another.

I went next and shared that I had grown up in a fundamentalist Pentecostal family and was taught that women were to be with men, and sex was dirty and a sin until you were married. I then said that after many failed relationships with men, in my later life I have chosen to be in same sex relationships with women. I shared that now I identify as lesbian or bi-sexual.

I put the crystal heart down and as I did so, Themba moved into the center circle and took a chair. He picked up the heart and stared at it for several moments. Then he looked at me and said, "Two weeks ago, if I had known that you were lesbian, I would never have talked with you. I wouldn't have wanted to be near you." He paused briefly, and the silence was poignant. "But, after all we have experienced together, I now know you. I cannot *not* be your friend." There was a remarkable spiritual energy that filled the room as Themba came forward with this. He leaned down and gently placed the heart in the center of the circle, and then he came over and we hugged for several minutes. Everyone sat in silent awe.

After the activity ended, Themba and I talked further. For him it was a deeply transformative experience in relinquishing his homophobia that he had carried all his life and had never questioned. For me, it brought another level of awareness as to the true purpose of my travels to South Africa and deeper meaning in my continued work as a GERI facilitator.

Indigenous Wisdom on Gender

In an early GERI program at Ghost Ranch, we were blessed to have as guest faculty and facilitator Dr. Rina Swentzell, a prominent indigenous elder from the Santa Clara Pueblo in New Mexico. Dr. Swentzell co-facilitated with the GERI team, and she presented remarkable teachings about gender in indigenous traditions, on both human and cosmic levels, as well as third and fourth genders in some traditions.

At the end of the five-day program, Dr. Swentzell made a striking remark about the kiva, the large circular subterranean meeting space that is characteristically found in every Pueblo community. She explained that Western anthropologists generally assert that kivas were used for indigenous "religious ceremonies." This is true, she said, but only about ten percent of the time. The rest of the time, the kiva was used for the very kind of community engagement and healing work that we had been doing throughout the GERI program. She explained this was essential for maintaining the interpersonal integrity and community health of the Pueblo communities yet is something that modern Western societies have largely lost.

We close this chapter with a compelling perspective on gender reconciliation from another prominent indigenous elder, Pat McCabe, from the Diné (Navajo) tradition.

An Indigenous Perspective on Gender Reconciliation

Pat McCabe

The Meeting of Masculine and Feminine Activism

As a woman, indigenous to what some call "North America," who was displaced from my culture due to events unfolding in the course of this land's history, I found I had to question deeply the reality I had been handed. I turned to Indigenous peoples to hear *our* version of the truth, and how we make sense of this life; how we view reality. Among many differences, one that took me on a profound journey was to witness and experience how we hold the spectrum of our gender.

That I am born woman is significant in every single Earth-based culture I have encountered. The dysfunction between masculine and feminine, and between men and woman, is at the core of many difficulties we face. My primary course of what I will call "Sacred Activism" has been to unravel and explore the nature of this malfunction.

How does the functional polarity of masculine and feminine aspects come into the picture of activism, you might ask; isn't looming global catastrophe complex enough without throwing *that* unwieldy can of worms into the mix? Perhaps. And yet, ancient culture—which has known how to live in relative health, happiness, and sustainable harmony for thousands of years—would tell us that the last world was destroyed because Men's Nation and Women's Nation believed they could live without each other.

At one point in my spiritual seeking, as I was confronting my own aging as a female of our kind, and the mysterious way in which modern culture greets this inevitable transformation of half of our population, I called out to my teachers: "What do we *really* mean when we say, 'feminine?' And what are we really talking about when we say 'masculine?' Those words have so much baggage. If we were to not use those words, what would we really be talking about?"

They responded, "Ah, now you're asking a good question." My inner 6th-grade, front-row student beamed. "It's true, you think you know what 'feminine' is, but you don't. And you think you know what 'masculine' is, but you don't. All you really know is how the 'masculine' behaves, and how the 'feminine' behaves, when they are plugged into a power-over paradigm."

But that paradigm is a choice, among many choices. And those two Medicines behave very differently in other paradigms, which humanity has known at other times. In a power-over paradigm, "might makes right," and those with the most brute force take their places in what naturally forms as a pyramid shaped structure. Although violence may not always be present, any time one person chooses power over another, that violence is implied, it is the underlying force in action.

Who Am I?

When activism becomes too convoluted and overwhelming, I resort to this: you have to know who you are, where you are, and how it is. Who I am, in one view, is a female of the human species, or of the Five-Fingered-Ones. Why did I come here as this?

As I am connected to two systems of ancient humanity, the Diné and the Lakota, naturally I inquire in those movements. Here I see that I can call myself Holy Earth Surface Walker, Life Bringer, Life Bearer. Here I see that my design is for Thriving Life, which will bring forth the future in fruitfulness of inestimable variety, exactly as the Mother Earth herself does.

I am told that my biology affords a Spiritual capacity that is capable of profound co-creation and cooperation with the Earth, as well as the Womb of the Cosmos, such that as she infuses me with boundless nourishment and nurturing, I am a fountain of care and generosity in my home, in my family, in my community, and in the cosmos as well. In this connection to her, I stand with her "authority," always, as her agency, speaking on behalf of Life and Sacred Creation of every nature. I am naturally a lucid dreamer, dreaming with the Mother Earth, receiving instruction for how to be here; for how my community can move and keep adjusting to be in alignment with the Thriving Life Plan, specific to where we are planted on her vast body. My language for this knows little about Point A and Point B, moving instead from the center, spiraling out, circular and evolving with each revolution, in the perfect, true and deep efficiency of the natural world around me. Glass ceilings, witch hunts, liberation, equality? Equal to *what,* exactly?

The Sacred Masculine Roles of Protector and Provider

Who are we as Men's Nation? I have heard very little language for the Sacred Masculine in my life. "Patriarchy equals masculinity" is a common calculation of our time. But if I am only witnessing how the masculine behaves in a very particular system, and one with both literal and implied violence as its primary modality, then my inquiry must move deeper and in other directions if I am to come upon the truth of knowing "who I am" and who the Masculine is, relative to the Thriving Life Plan.

Does patriarch inherently mean violence? As many have said before, when we, story beings that we are, do not have language for something, it tends to remain elusive or entirely invisible to us. A primary form of activism for me at the moment is attempting to remember the language but also the song of the Masculine as it is in service to Life.

From ancient human systems' perspective, I might say that there are three primary roles that might be called inherent to the Sacred Masculine. Two of these roles are Protector and Provider—of and for *Life*. The sign of any successful leadership on the part of the Men's Nation is that the children and elders of their community are cared for. As I come from a line of humanity that recently has weathered attempted genocide, I can say from experience that when a man is prevented from fulfilling these two sacred duties, it can change him. Most commonly, the adverse response is that he either becomes a perpetrator of power-over violence, or he relinquishes all belief in his ability to keep his sacred charge. These responses carry forward for generations.

I confess that I cringe as I name these two Sacred roles to modern Men's Nation. How must it feel to a man to be charged with being Protector, when even the most adamant of "free nations" are positioned to move into martial law at any instant? And how must it feel to be charged with being Provider in an economic system that is rigged, so the majority can never win? I cry as I watch this machine that men are indoctrinated into, often father to son, breaking their hearts, and spirits, and bodies too; their noble instincts hijacked by an illusion of false power, false pride, and a false promise of fulfilling a distorted version of their Sacred role. How do we know that these are false? We know because they are not leading to Thriving Life.

The Sacred Fire Keeper

A man in his eighties exclaimed, "Finally, I am released from the tyranny of testosterone." This brings me to the third medicine of the Sacred Masculine: the Sacred Fire Keeper. As nature would have it, I went through a rollicking ocean of midlife hormonal fluctuations, which included a specific Grace for about a month: a massive surge of testosterone. I had never experienced such a fire. Everything that moved, and even certain inanimate objects, were of sensuous interest to me. I remember being profoundly in awe of all of the many men I have known who were nothing but honorable and respectful with the use of this molten blaze that apparently they were holding within.

My respect for Men's Nation, and what they are charged with, grew so deep during this time. Nowhere did I see the true initiation in the modern world for its correct use as Sacred Fire. Seemingly, the teaching of how to hold the confusion and fear of it was to douse it in liberal amounts of alcohol.

The Sacred Hoop of Life

From ancient humanity systems view, sometimes our whole Life construct is held in the symbol of a hoop, the Sacred Hoop of Life. Every Life form, plant, animal, stone, water, sky, star, air, fire, holds a place on the Hoop of Life. Every member of this Hoop has a perfect design to uphold its part. If any member does not uphold their part, the integrity of the Hoop begins to fail.

This Fire held within the Masculine Design is also, assuredly, a part of our Thriving Life Design. If The Plan is Life, then it would only make sense that such a Fire would be profound Medicine for Life, a driving force that assures that Life will most definitely continue on into the future. What a relief to hold this force, so vilified and feared in our time, as deep Medicine to be held with respect and, yes, reverence. Now, to learn the true nature of Sacred Fire tending.

To Men's Nation

To Men's Nation, I find the language arising—at long last!—to say: I sing, dance, and pray for you, wholeheartedly, to be just as powerful as you possibly can be, in body, yes, but also in that laser, at times singular, focus of your amazing mind. In my journey into the Earth and into the womb of the Cosmos I cannot hold that way of mind, nor am I meant to, and so at that time, I rely on this strength of yours to hold us and keep us. I ask for your wonderful wide heart to be as powerful as it can possibly be, nothing moves me now as deeply as hearing you speak, and sing, and pray, with an open heart, rare Medicine to me and to the unknown or forgotten origin of hunger of this Holy Earth, Sky, and Multiverse. I travel deeply within, and also beyond, to encounter the true nature of your Thriving Life Spirit. As I come to understand myself, and all that was hidden from me, I see that we can meet, in perfect, functional and Holy Polarity.

Holy Earth Surface Walker, Sacred Fire Keeper, Guardian and Tender of Life, the One who has a heart that can weep in prayer, prayers of love and adoration for the Life Bringer, Life Bearer, and her fruit, your daughters, and sons—I come before you now.

Keeper of the external Sacred Fire, you watch over the coming of age of the daughters who will bear the Future, vigilant, tireless, meticulous, architects of the Visions coming from Spirit, through the spiritual womb of the Womb'an, to Earth. You watch over your sons as they mature into strength, Sacred Internal Fire growing, growing, as yours has also. That Fire within, the driving force propelling Life forward for our kind, burning with the Sun, Holy Star above, powerful, inextinguishable, you tend that fire also, once again, to serve the flowering of Life, with true and holy strength.

I say to you, I cannot be who I am made to be, without you being who you are made to be. In your very existence, in my very existence, we consummate the great purpose of Thriving Life. None shall drive us apart, ever again, not in my heart, mind or spirit, this is my vow of conjugal bond with you as the Female of our kind. This *is* my most Sacred Activism, now forming the seeds of Truth, which is Life, to be cast into the soil of the future, together, with you.

To speak these words has taken every bit of strength and courage, all of my cunning and vulnerability. The Spirit Helpers have intervened again and again to guide me to this place, and again I would call this Grace descending upon me. To me, this seems to be the root from which any activism needs to arise. The Hoop of Life does not understand "us vs. them." The Hoop of Life only understands "We." Every action then must arise out of a functional polarity from our kind, or we only further the illusion of separation.

Every form of separation must heal, one by one by one, but this one, between Masculine and Feminine, between Men's Nation and Women's Nation and the spectrum humanity holds in between and beyond, is at the core of our course correction. Suddenly, our task doesn't really seem so bad at all.

For all my relations and the continuing story of Creation, that We, all of us together, are telling, right now.

Pat McCabe, known as Woman Stands Shining, is a Diné (Navajo) mother, grandmother, activist, artist, writer, ceremonial leader, and international speaker.

William Keepin and Hopi Elder Thomas Banyacya testifying at the World Uranium Hearing in Salzburg, Austria, September, 1992 (the same month of the first GERI-prototype workshop). Banyacya testified on the devastating impacts of uranium mining on the Hopi and Diné (Navajo) indigenous nations. Keepin testified on clean renewable energy solutions to eliminate uranium mining, nuclear power, and fossil fuels.

CHAPTER 12

Transforming Patriarchy in Religion

Banish the Divine Mother, and Her sacred daughters become secular prey.
—William Keepin

The #MeToo movement precipitated a dramatic awakening of the reality of widespread sexual harassment and exploitation across the globe, and religious institutions and spiritual communities were no exceptions. Devastating revelations of sexual misconduct and exploitation—often enabled by corresponding institutional complicity and cover-ups—are continuing to emerge with alarming frequency today in churches, *sanghas* and spiritual communities of every major faith tradition.

There is a profound irony in this: the world's great religious traditions—all of which purport to uphold the dignity and divinity of each human being, and promise intimate refuge to the human soul of the highest spiritual purity and moral integrity—have also been the places, and even at times the justifications, for some of the most tragic and painful violations in the realm of gender and sexuality. These betrayals which have harmed so many, violate the very spiritual heart of the traditions themselves. Yet, in facing these painful realities openly and honestly, there is a profound possibility to renew, reclaim, and restore the hearts of the traditions, as the great spiritual treasures of humanity that they are, gifted equally to all.

In 2018, we organized an interfaith conference in Costa Rica, bringing together nearly 100 people from 5 continents, including leaders from nearly every major spiritual tradition. During the conference we convened a panel of young spiritual leaders earnestly engaged on the spiritual path. One of the questions we asked them was about the future of religion, and "What is it that you most need from religious leaders today?"

After some silence, one of the young men, Garrett Evans, who is also a leader in the Gender Equity and Reconciliation International work responded,

> Part of what I need is an acknowledgment of the ways that religion has betrayed its highest calling and highest purpose. Thinking about sexuality and spirituality, it seems that, in almost every major world religion, there has been a profound betrayal of the genuine spiritual impulse—particularly in the realm of gender and sexuality.

Coming from a background in the Zen tradition, so many Zen teachers have engaged in sexual misconduct with their students, and we see this in so many other traditions, too.

To come to the spiritual life with this genuine yearning of the heart—a cry of the soul to go Home—and then to have this trampled upon by somebody who is a spiritual elder, to whom you are looking for spiritual guidance; this is so profoundly tragic.

So, we need to acknowledge what has happened here, to acknowledge this betrayal of the spiritual impulse. Because the heart of the religions themselves is *not* polluted. The heart of the traditions is about guiding and protecting and inspiring us on our journey home. To hold the genuine hearts of the traditions while at the same time acknowledging the betrayals opens new possibilities for the future. This actually creates the space where new life can be breathed into the different traditions, so that they don't have to die. Or, perhaps in one form they do have to die, but they get to rise again.

This call for accountability and the promise of new inspiration in the traditions—made in the presence of senior priests, rabbis, Buddhist nuns, imams, indigenous elders, swamis, and other religious leaders and aspirants from across the traditions—was met with resounding appreciation and affirmation by those present. The Gender Equity and Reconciliation process is designed to initiate a whole new gender conversation and accountability within religious and spiritual communities and institutions—to raise awareness of the impacts of gender injustice and patriarchy experienced by people of faith. Religious leaders, spiritual seekers and congregations can come together and discover a mutual harmony, joy and compassion as a spiritual community or congregation through the Gender Equity and Reconciliation work. The GERI work draws on spiritual practices and principles—universal and nonsectarian—and is easily adapted for diverse religious communities. Over the years, GERI programs have been implemented in a wide variety of religious and spiritual contexts—from Zen Buddhist sanghas, to the South African Council of Churches, progressive Evangelical Christians, Anglican clergy, interfaith and contemplative communities, Catholic priests and nuns in India, and others.

In our professional certification training we have had trainees across the religious spectrum, including Catholics, Protestants, Evangelical Christians, Muslims, Sikhs, Buddhists, Hindus, Jews, atheists, interfaith, and people who identify as spiritual but not religious; all of whom found the spiritual foundation of the GERI program refreshing and necessary for the transformation of gender injustice within their spiritual traditions.

In this chapter we bring forth voices of several faith leaders and spiritual activists, from across the religions, naming the struggles and pain of gender injustice within their traditions, and also the hope and promise of gender reconciliation in these communities.

Emily Nielsen Jones is a philanthropist and activist engaged in promoting human equality, justice, and peace around the world. She is particularly passionate and engaged in the nexus of faith, gender, and development, and works to mobilize our faith traditions to more fully and unambiguously embrace gender equality. Emily is actively engaged in the women-led philanthropy movement and is a trained Spiritual Director and author of numerous articles.

With a Brave Love, Transmuting Our World's Intolerable Status Quo

When I first encountered GERI about ten years ago, I was at a low point of utter despair with how savagely low the bar still is around the world for women and girls' basic human rights, safety, and dignity. My husband and I had started a foundation called the Imago Dei Fund a few years earlier, which began addressing human trafficking. My learning curve to understand the drivers of why our world is still enslaving people in the 21st century brought me face to face with the heart-crushing, mind-numbing reality that over 70 percent of the world's enslaved people are women and girls, and that by the time she is "trafficked" she has usually experienced a continuum of eerily normalized violence, neglect, and commodification, which only recently has been aptly named *gendercide.*

At the time, my daughter was a tween, the age when lots of bad stuff starts to happen to girls to rupture their natural and wired-in presumption of equality, and to begin grooming and socializing them into patriarchal norms and customs that see being born female as a second-class status meant for submission, overwork, and normalized oppression. My feminism was reawakened and I became rather obsessed with wanting to understand: how could it be that in the 21st century—after having fought so many movements of liberation and expansion of civil rights for all—the bar was still so low for women and girls' basic human rights, and that in many places, the needle was in fact sliding backwards? Virtually everywhere I visited, I would meet someone who would say something to the effect of, "Here girls are expected to wake up early and serve their brothers and fathers." "Here a husband is like the king of the family and can beat his wife if he doesn't like the food she cooks or something she says." "As a girl, you grow up serving everyone and are usually the last one to eat, and when finances are tight you need to work so your brothers can stay in school." "Gender-based violence and rape isn't a problem, it is a culture here, and sad to say some of the worst domestic violence is in the homes of pastors and other 'great men' who we look up to."

As Charlotte Bunch describes in a 1997 UN Report titled *The Intolerable Status Quo: Violence Against Women and Girls*:[1]

> Imagine a people routinely subjected to assault, rape, sexual slavery, arbitrary imprisonment, torture, verbal abuse, mutilation, even murder—all because they were born into a particular group. Imagine further that their sufferings were compounded by systematic discrimination and humiliation in the home and workplace, in classrooms and courtrooms, at worship and at play. Few would deny that this group had been singled out for gross violations of human rights. Such a group exists. Its members comprise half of humanity. Yet it is rarely acknowledged that violence against women and girls, many of whom are brutalized from cradle to grave simply because of their gender, is the most pervasive human rights violation in the world today.

The more you peer under the hood of our world's gender norms and the culture of gendercide that persists, the more you see that this Intolerable Status Quo is no accident but rather is the manifestation of an ancient Tradition—which goes back thousands of years—and is, still to this day, sanctioned and perpetuated by patriarchal cultural and religious practices and beliefs that continue to persist everywhere around the world. As a person of faith, I had experienced patriarchy throughout my life in most of the churches and ministries I have been a part of, but it was of a "softened" form and I suppose I have had rose-colored glasses on, presuming the needle was just almost automatically moving forward. At the same time that I was learning more about the systemic devaluation of the girl-child around the world and seeing what unadulterated patriarchy looks like in many places, I began to see a disturbing trend happening in my own backyard in Boston, Mass.—all these start-up churches were popping up all over my city that had no women in leadership, and when I began clicking around to find out who is starting these, I found an amped up patriarchal language being used that was encouraging men to step up to resume their rightful place as prophets, priests, and kings of their homes, church, and society. There is nothing more distressing and sad than to see people using their holy books and appeals to God and faith to justify a powered up, entitled masculinity that devalues and treats females as a "lesser than" class of humans.

Deep in my being I became aware that if we don't get our faith traditions on board with the full and unambiguous equality of women and men, the needle will just continue to slide backwards. Thankfully, there is an incredible movement of people and organizations working at this nexus, and a friend and colleague in women's philanthropy kept saying to me, "You really need to meet Will Keepin and Cynthia Brix and learn more about their work!" Thankfully I did and I just loved their vision and had the incredible privilege of helping to organize and participate in two GERI retreats which touched me so deeply. What I experienced was a beautiful sacred space, led by an incredible team of GERI facilitators who invited us all to open our hearts, share our gender pain, and encircle each other with love and understanding. In both of these retreats, there was a beautiful racial and gender diversity and also a range of religious backgrounds from around the world, which made the conversation all the richer. An essential part of the GERI secret sauce, as I see it, that enables people to cross so many dividing lines, is the contemplative dimension that grounds everything in a posture of silent witness, inviting everyone to bring however they understand the Sacred dimension of life into the circle, and to listen and hold one another's experiences in silence and compassionate listening.

I so appreciate that every retreat held, both online and in person, is part of a global movement to extend the work of racial truth and reconciliation that we have witnessed in places like South Africa and Rwanda to the oldest oppression humans have inflicted on one another across the most intimate line of difference that cuts through all human families, tribes, and affiliations. We can do better. But we need to do the deeper work of healing the ancient roots of patriarchal oppression that continue to exist within our cherished cultural and religious traditions, or else that proverbial needle will just keep sliding backwards. Not under my watch! Thank you, GERI, for inviting so many into your work of holding our world's gender pain, and transmuting it from the roots up with love and care. You give me hope that a gender-healed world is indeed possible and on her way.

Imam Jamal Rahman is co-founder of the Interfaith Community Sanctuary in Seattle and a popular speaker on Islam, Sufi spirituality, and interfaith relations. The author of many books, Jamal also collaborates with Rabbi Ted Falcon and Pastor Don Mackenzie. Affectionately known as the Interfaith Amigos, they tour the country sharing the message of spiritual inclusivity.

Infusion of Love, Beauty and Holiness

I attended the retreat program of GERI twice, once in 2016 and again in 2019. It is my heartfelt conviction that the program of gender reconciliation is profoundly beneficial for Muslim men and women.

Let me provide some context. Patriarchal dominance and bias pervade Muslim societies. This prejudice varies from country to country, but it is a fair assumption to say that the Muslim woman is at best a second-class citizen in many Islamic countries. This is profoundly sad because the Prophet Muhammad was radical in his feminist views and championing of the rights of women, and the Qur'an accorded women revolutionary rights regarding property, divorce and inheritance. The men of the

7th-century Arabian Peninsula reluctantly went along with the wishes of the Prophet Muhammad and injunctions of the Qur'an safeguarding rights of women. But when the Prophet died, the male authorities blatantly misinterpreted verses of the Qur'an about women, and fabricated misogynistic sayings of the Prophet to reassert their patriarchal dominance. Over the centuries, the Muslim psyche has become partially paralyzed because the rights of women are repressed. This is a stark truth that must be acknowledged and urgently remedied.

I offer here briefly a few features of the GERI program that in my experience make the GERI retreat unique and special. The program from the outset creates an environment of palpable safety. An aura of sacred protection pervades the space. Many are willing to be vulnerable. The women express their pain and anguish; the men feel moved to acknowledge their conditioned biases, and their own pain. Tears, reflections and conversations stir the souls of the participants. One begins to sense, from within, healing, relief, and hope. This womb of safety is critical. Muslim women say in confidence that at home or work they are reluctant to talk about their pain and distress caused by patriarchal abuse. They fear retribution or reprimand by society members, including their own extended family. Muslim men admit that they are reluctant to firmly object to fossilized and unjust patriarchal customs, for fear of ridicule from male elders and the clerics who are exclusively male, often sarcastically referred to as the "bearded assembly." In the GERI retreat there is an abiding emphasis on compassion and mercy. This resonates in me! The Prophet Muhammad declared that the entire spiritual wisdom of Islam can be distilled into one word: compassion. When pressed to explain further, he replied that the key to fulfillment in life is to practice compassion for self and others.

All the exercises, dialogues and encounters are steeped in mercy and gentleness. With compassion for oneself, participants confront their demons and embrace their angelic nature. Magically, anger transforms, little by little, into inner vigor; fear into mindfulness; sadness into empathy. Some participants report that their experience of compassion brings them closer to their inner higher self and they feel a soul connection to others. During breaks and food intervals, people connect and share stories and insights. Perhaps the cliché is true that in conferences the greatest learning occurs during breaks!

The most touching part of the program for me is the creation of sacred ceremonies by men to honor women and by women to honor men. The energies of creativity, love and veneration that weave into this collective effort are remarkable. The rituals become infused with love, beauty and holiness. The ceremonies by the men and women are a sight to behold and experience! Music, song, poetry, and declarations of commitment fill the air.

Postures of bowing, kneeling, and prostration are accompanied by requests for forgiveness and expressions of adoration and reverence. The entire place comes alive with the glow of Presence. Tears flow and laughter rings out. Everyone feels blessed and transformed. After having gone through such intensive cross-gender truth telling, by the time of the closing ceremony, the participants, male and female, feel a deep soul connection with one another. It feels as though an authentic community has been born and it is graced by love and beauty. I am reminded of the utterance of the 13th-century sage Rumi, who exhorts us to "come out of the circle of time, and enter the circle of love."

Islamic spiritual teachers tell us that, in order for us to enter the circle of love, we must do the inner work of becoming an *insan e kamil*, a perfected human being. To become more fully human, it is crystal clear to me that we must do the work of gender equity and reconciliation. And, for me, GERI is the perfect medium for this sacred undertaking.

Mirabai Starr is an author, translator of the mystics, and a leading voice in the interspiritual movement. She taught philosophy and world religions at the University of New Mexico-Taos for 20 years and now teaches and speaks internationally, focusing on the perennial teachings found at the heart of all the world's spiritual paths, and promoting peace and justice.

Secrets and Epiphanies of the Heart

In the beginning, I wasn't quite sure how this gender work [GERI] applied to my life. I grew up in the counterculture. My parents were 60s radicals, and they removed us from society and went "back to the land" in communal living. I was exposed to a lot of spiritual paths, and I grew up eating and drinking and breathing a kind of openness to all ways of being. So interfaith understanding and orientation is just completely natural to me—or so I thought. I also thought that I was free from gender wounding because my parents were both feminists, and our counterculture world was very respectful of the feminine.

But I also knew that I had been violated in a very serious way by my first spiritual teacher, a man 25 years older than me. He insisted that we keep our "relationship" a secret—how can you even have a "relationship" with a 15-year-old child? During the GERI workshop, I was really able to take the *secret* out of that secret, and take the shadow and bring it to light. That has been extremely helpful to me.

The other important epiphany I had, was that it's all about oneness, and so this gender work is not different than the interspiritual. They both have exactly the same goal: to bring us to that place of oneness, and of unity. All spiritual paths are about that, and this work is absolutely about that. I didn't feel any kind of "sociopolitical psychobabble" going on, ever. There was a very graceful way of continually bringing it back to the heart, where it all is.

I was deeply moved by all this and am eager to see how these two modalities of the interspiritual and the gender equity and reconciliation come together.

Minister Myra Kinds is a GERI Trainer and BIPOC and Intersectionalities Lead. She is a licensed American Baptist Minister to Youth, and a recognized leader in underserved communities, specializing in addiction and recovery, mental health, and domestic violence.

A Space Full of Grace

It was just short of the four-month anniversary of the passing of one of my siblings. I had resigned from a decades long position as a Network Director to be available and by my brother's side in his final days. I had stepped out, relying on faith, and began consulting on projects that resonated with my core values. It was through one of my clients who shared the workshop flyer, with a simple note. "Interested in going?" This is how I found Gender Equity Reconciliation International (GERI).

If I were to begin to assign labels to describe myself, I am a woman of color, wife, mother of four, sister, Christian Minister, and community bridge builder.

The project I was working on for my client, was really a question I had raised while in discussion with her and the organization. The client, a Christian based organization, led me to boldly ask the question, "Are our Churches safe spaces?" As #MeToo, #ChurchToo and centuries of harm were being exposed, I questioned "Were the Churches exempt? Were we the safe space?" To go even deeper, "Are our spaces of worship a place of healing?" Before a response was even uttered, I knew that we needed to unpack, specifically from a lens of faith, what does "safe space" look like?

Day One of the workshop, I entered GERI in my "head space," and very quickly on that first day found myself in my "heart space." Participants immediately started out listening to intimate stories of strangers. These strangers and the weight of their sharing was not initially passed on to the participants, the stories were coming from our facilitators. They did not come to teach gender reconciliation, but to model it, to show us what was possible. Remember what I said about "unpacking" earlier? Well, there was a lot of unpacking in those three days. The holding of the space was brilliant. The transparency of the facilitators was not choreographed but organic, all while we participants seamlessly were being woven into this GERI community.

GERI has created a space, inclusive and judgment free; inviting each of us to bring all of who we were, and are, to the table. It is a space full of grace, all done as an invitation. No pressure to share, and yet we all did, no pressure to go deep and yet we all did. In a short three days we had become a community, knowing more about one another, or at least how our stories affected us, than our own family members and community outside of GERI. Even with our differences, GERI maintains a space of listening to learn, and learning to listen. We are present for one another and hold everyone in love.

By the third day I knew that this was just the beginning for me with GERI. A month after that workshop I was enrolled in GERI's full immersion training. Since that initial encounter, walking through the door in my head space, I have become a GERI Facilitator and Trainer. As facilitators, we are family who are constantly together doing our internal work whether in a GERI module or through peer mentoring. We grow together. As we grow and heal, we hold space for others, accepting of all who come just as they are, wrapping them with love and grace.

It is a true honor to be a part of such amazing work, and to witness a Beloved Community.

Swami Ambikananda Saraswati is a Hindu monastic and student of the celebrated Swami Venkateshananda of Rishikesh. She founded the Traditional Yoga Association in Reading, UK, and is author of several books, including new translations of Hindu scriptures.

Transcending Our Differences

The pandemic that hit our world in 2019 seemed for a while to be something that, although wreaking death and sorrow, would also remind us we're all in this together: an inseparable people, regardless of gender, ethnicity, class—or the many other distinctions we now name—all vulnerable to the same virus. How quickly that myth was dispelled. Inequalities and disparities were certainly exposed, but not transcended. Some were sadly amplified.

Women have broken through the glass ceiling. I live in a country that had a woman prime minister in the 1980s. Women of different colors and ethnicities now head companies dealing with everything from medical research to tech industries. And yet… and yet… women are still attacked and murdered on our streets because they are women; two women a week in the UK, where I live, are murdered in their own homes by a partner or ex-partner. More subtle violence persists—women still feel pressured to surgically distort their appearance to conform to what, they are assured, is required by the male gaze.

There is still work to be done if we are to transcend separatism, including in the field of the religious and the spiritual—indeed, maybe *especially* in these fields.

Just as the male gaze is the preeminent gaze in our societies in general, when it comes to spirituality and religion, it is still the only gaze that counts. Among the Abrahamic faiths, the faiths of the male God, it is men that determine what we are required to be as women to fit their religious model. Even in faiths like Hinduism, where in scripture God is both male and female, men are still the primary authority on all things religious and spiritual, reinforced by a thousand years of colonization, while women are relegated to a supporting role.

I recall speaking with a student some years back, and I made brief reference to one of the highly venerated Swamis I had known in India. She swooned, "Oh my! You actually got to meet *him,* in person? That must have been an *extraordinary* experience!" she exclaimed, her eyes shining with wonder. My smile shifted a bit, to one of irony. "Well actually," I said, "it was an extremely *ordinary* experience, as he was chasing me around the table, trying to get his hands to follow where his eyes were eagerly racing."

None of this means that men are actually having a much better time than women. Their role is as much determined by forces outside themselves as women's roles are. And maybe some men can and willingly do conform to the stereotypes required of them, but most of them do not, and their lives are also filled with pain.

Then, along come dedicated people with a different vision, one that could slowly, and with care and insight, begin to make changes: Gender Equity and Reconciliation International (GERI) emerged.

The physicist Paul Dirac famously said, "Pick a flower on earth and you move the farthest star." The leaders of GERI seem to have a keen understanding of this: that it is not the great and grand gesture that is required now, it is the day-to-day vision of each other that counts; that the greatest change comes from the smallest things, because it is these small adjustments that put us in touch with that part of ourselves that does not divide, that does not see a "me" and a "that." GERI's work is work on the spiritual level because they see that if true change is to take place, that is the level at which it needs to be rooted and sourced.

GERI does another remarkable thing: they work from the bottom up. Groups of men and women, meeting and talking and taking the time to understand and share with each other what it means to be a woman in whatever society they are situated, and what it means to be a man in that society. As men and women meet and come together, of course, so do different ethnicities, different social classes, different cultures. At a grassroots level, transcendence begins among people in these groups—first by talking to each other, and then by supporting each other, and then by supporting and lifting each other up.

In societies where God is a male god and all things sacred and holy are a "he," the people of these groups themselves begin to experience and seek another vision. These small GERI groups are places where the words of the Rev. Dr. Martin Luther King Jr., "Nobody is free until everybody is free," begin to become real.

My prayer is that this work infuses us all and, through it, we all access another way to transcend the differences that now so divide us.

Rev. Dr. Ray Hammond, M.D. is a Harvard-trained emergency-medicine physician turned minister, who co-founded Bethel African Methodist Episcopal Church in Boston with his wife Rev. Dr. Gloria White-Hammond. He is co-founder of the Ten Point Coalition that transforms the lives of Black and Latino youth in Boston by cultivating renewal, reconnection, and responsibility. He serves on the Black Ministerial Alliance, is a Fellow of the American Academy of Arts and Sciences and has received nine honorary doctorates.

Living Radical Love and Community

Let me begin by sharing with you that for much of my adult life as a Christian, I struggled to understand and live out these three verses from the third chapter of the Apostle Paul's letter to the Galatian Churches. He writes, "So in Christ Jesus you are all children of God through faith, for all of you who were baptized into Christ have clothed yourselves with Christ. There is neither Jew nor Gentile, neither slave nor free, nor is there male and female, for you are all one in Christ Jesus." The church seems to me as one place where the bridges between ancient enemies, Jew and Gentile, should be built. A place where racial and radical justice replaces oppression based on race or class, or political or economic status, slave or free. And it should be the place where those who used to be called second class, inferior, and the "weaker sex" are seen as equals, as sisters in faith by their brothers; a place where male and female are powerful partners together in Kingdom building.

But too often the church has failed here. And that's why I celebrate the courage of those who take on the third, and I believe most difficult barrier: male and female. Tearing that barrier down is very hard, but how can we possibly build the body of Christ, the beloved community, or even healthy homes, communities, or countries, if we cannot heal the brokenness between women and men?

In a lifetime of working on and addressing this question, three of the most helpful days were the three days I spent with Gender Equity and Reconciliation International in May of 2018. It was a time of coming to know myself more deeply; a time of hearing and understanding the hearts, the history, and the hurts, and the hopes of my sisters and my brothers. It was hard; there were tears, it opened some old wounds, but for every hurt endured, there was even more healing, and for every wound that was opened, even more walls came down. And it was more than worth it to become the better man, the better husband, the better father, the better pastor, and the better follower of Christ I so much want to be. So I say to you, my brothers and sisters: may the Holy Spirit be with all who undertake this GERI journey toward equity, toward reconciliation, toward a church, a family, and a world where radical love and community is not just what we preach and teach—radical love and community is what we *live*, what we *do*, and what we *are*. God bless you.

Dano Jukanovich fulfills an Executive Pastor role at Christ the Redeemer Anglican Church in Danvers, Mass. He also co-founded the Boston Collaborative, connecting Christians and other people of goodwill to work together in ways that leverage their time, talent and treasure to serve Boston area communities:

A Glimpse of Heaven

I felt loved. When a woman I barely knew wiped tears from my eyes and said, "I see you," I felt loved.

I'm not sure how I got from here to there over three days through the Gender Equity and Reconciliation International retreat in Boston, but somehow, I did. I walked into a room with 21 people, most of whom I had never met, a large number of whom were women, and I was invited to participate in the human growth process.

Clearly God wanted me to be there. I had just come off a weekend with a small group of friends where we spent time in guided reflection about what it meant to be made in the Image of God. It was the first time I had in any serious way contemplated God as represented both in the masculine and feminine, and I was hungry to learn more.

At the GERI retreat, I struggled with the intense level of vulnerability in the midst of people I barely knew. I found myself defensive about whatever culpability I might have in the gender-inequity so prevalent in our world. But I committed to share and engage as authentically as I felt able to do.

I also listened a lot. I listened to the other men in a group of only men. I listened to the women as they shared with the full group of men and women. It was heart-breaking to listen and contemplate the ways we had debased the Image of God in each other.

This was all facilitated by a thoughtful, wise and experienced group of GERI counselors and mentors. One of the questions asked was, "If there was one thing you wanted the women around the room to know about men, what would it be?" My immediate thought, I believe from God, and which I later shared with the group was simply, "We love them." We men struggle and fail—sometimes disastrously—but we do genuinely love our wives and daughters and mothers and sisters and friends.

At the end of the three days, the men had an opportunity to "produce" a ceremony honoring the women, and vice versa. These took a good chunk of time to prepare and were rather elaborate. We men did a decent job, and I believe the women were touched by the theme of putting on a "Garment of Praise," which we enacted with heartfelt sincerity for each woman individually.

But then the women really blew us away with the ceremony they prepared. The men walked into the foyer where there were three bowls set up on a table.

Some of the women guided us through steps to take dried leaves that represented our own grief and crumple them up and let them go. Then they poured water over our hands into a basin, as a sign of releasing the past, and entering a new life.

Then they had us walk toward the meeting room where there was a sign on the door that said, "Welcome back to Eden." After having spent a few days really baring my soul and uncovering my own brokenness, and better understanding the pain others have experienced, seeing that sign made my heart leap with hope at what relationships between men and women were intended to be and *can* be in the context of communion with their creator.

All the men lined up in the room, each standing face-to-face with one of the women at the retreat. Some of the women were narrating a larger story, while each woman facing one of us would periodically repeat, "we see you. . . in your grief," "we see you. . . in your desire to protect," "we see you. . . in your love for the women in your life," "we see you. . . in your strength," "we see you. . . in your fear," and on and on.

They read a version of the Lord's Prayer, modified to be "A Prayer for a Brother." It was overwhelming, and still is, even as I write this. I suppose you would have to be there to really understand what I'm describing.

Prayer offered by the women during their honoring ceremony:

Our brothers of GERI
Courage be your names
Your healing come
God's will be done
In your bodies, minds, & souls

We give you today
Our eyes and ears
Forgive us our deafness
As we forgive those
Who don't hear us

We walk not by ourselves
But together in God's image
For ours is the calling
To God be the glory
Forever and ever. Amen.

I'm so thankful to have been part of the GERI retreat, and for getting to have that small glimpse of Heaven where I will see God face-to-face and know God's perfect and unconditional love.

Michele Breene is a GERI Facilitator with over 25 years of experience in leadership development, team building, and executive coaching in the UK, the USA, and Kenya and East Africa. Today, Michele's primary focus is as mentor, facilitator, coach, and spiritual director in leadership areas relating to spiritual formation and gender equity.

Tim Breene is an experienced humanitarian and business leader, and former board member and CEO of World Relief, a long-established global Christian

Relief and Development organization whose mission is to empower the local church to serve the most vulnerable.

Deep Listening Across the Gender Line

In the wake of the #MeToo campaign and revelations of rampant sexual harassment in our society, Gender Equity and Reconciliation International (GERI) convened an invitational gathering, comprised of 33 key leaders from women's and men's movements across the country. My husband Tim and I were delighted to be invited, and we had no idea what to expect! This subject matter must be one of the most challenging issues of our day and yet with wisdom and sensitivity, our facilitators, an international team from the U.S., India, and South Africa, led us into a safe and beautiful space of sharing and healing. Those attending were a remarkably diverse group in terms of life experience, age, geography and engagement with this issue. Tim and I were both surprised at the extent to which both men and women carry wounding, from mother to son, father to daughter, etc. Not just through physical and/or emotional abuse, but in the unwitting stereotyping passed on in ways that create enormous pressures on young adults. We shared through silent witnessing, the pain and heartbreak of individuals' stories and were moved by the opportunity to listen without judgment, to offer deep and genuine compassion, unconditional love and respect for one another. Tim and I were struck by the immense value arising from the sharing by both genders of how we have each been affected.

Personally, my heart is still resonating with joy and a growing sense of hope that gender equity might actually become a reality during our daughters' lives. We laughed, we cried, and we bonded around our individual experiences of deep wounding and personal shame, sharing the beginnings of our journey towards reconciliation between our genders. To my mind, the strength of reconciliation that took place could not have happened without the skillful guidance of our leaders, down into the deepest pits of our pain, holding attentively each others' grief and distress, through to sincere affirmation and shared appreciation for one another. We recognized that we cannot fix anyone's pain, but we witnessed how we can each be a part of one another's healing.

I was reminded of workshops I've led with Kenyans, Ugandans, Rwandans and South African brothers and sisters, designed to reconcile racial differences and tensions. But this GERI process, which I believe could be replicated to address racially-based injustices, gave me new insight and appreciation for what was missing. This was something unique that goes far beyond an intellectual conviction of the need for change to a whole-hearted emotional and instinctive commitment to collaborate with one another in healing together, driven by a powerful and unified rejection of gender injustice.

Our experience of this approach to gender reconciliation has left us with an overwhelming conviction that now is the time to fully engage and be a part of ensuring this movement continues to act as a catalyst throughout this country and beyond, gathering momentum and scaling up towards deep and sustained change for our grandchildren.

Below is a letter from a group of Christian church leaders in the Boston area, reflecting on the need for gender equality and healing in church communities, as well as the promise of the GERI program in supporting churches into the future and living out an authentic ethic of love.

We are a group of Christian church leaders who have come to the following agreements about what is needed for the future revitalization of our churches:

Christian churches, wherever they are on the theological spectrum of complementarian/egalitarianism, for the most part remain rooted in patriarchal norms. Thus, the voice of women, and the vision of flourishing and fruitfulness arising from the combined gifts of men and women in partnership, is realized infrequently.

Moreover, there remains a considerable amount of unresolved pain for women seeking to fulfill their true sense of calling.

Evangelical churches are one of the streams of Christianity lagging behind in leveraging women's gifts and advocating for their interests in society at large. We believe this is a primary issue in the accelerating disillusionment with conventional church for women and young people.

"Status quo" bias continues, even in seminary training where inherited narrow theological conceptions of the respective roles of men and women in Ministry seem to prevail. Church leaders urgently need new, revitalized approaches, to sow the seeds of change in the churches.

The GERI approach—modeled on Archbishop Desmond Tutu's peace and reconciliation work in South Africa and endorsed by him—offers a unique vehicle for the transformation of both hearts and minds with respect to gender equity through its focus on personal witness, forgiveness, healing, and reconciliation. In alignment with Tutu's TRC principles, the GERI methodology makes visible and lays bare the hurt caused by patriarchy to both women and men. This facilitates a needed reconciliation process, which in turn opens a unique space for new relationships and new beginnings. We believe this humanizing of "the other" is critical to breaking down resistance to change.

There was unanimous agreement that addressing gender equity and healing within the church is mission critical for the future health of the church. Women in ministry is integral to the Church's survival for the next generation. The next generation won't engage in doctrinal issues as long as women continue to be treated as second-class citizens.

1. Churches are at a point of inflection with, for the most part, declining attendance particularly amongst millennials and "gen-xers."
2. Some commentators have observed that spiritual priorities have shifted from "what is true?" (boomer generation) towards "what is just? and "what is beautiful?" As Rev. Ray Hammond put it, "*Radical love and community is not just what we preach and teach, but who we are and what we do.*" This has been the hallmark of the GERI process, and it is what inspired Archbishop Desmond Tutu to endorse this methodology.

A renewed focus on living out an ethic of love, accepting the truth about divisions that tear apart the fabric of humanity (gender, race, sexual orientation, socio-economic, age, faith etc.), and owning our respective parts in that brokenness are foundational to the perceived authenticity and relevance of churches going forward, and to making the church relevant again to younger generations. This is where the lessons of the GERI process can be powerful.

There are obviously multiple reasons why the GERI process is so effective, but a key insight is that it is a heart-based approach. Other approaches that are mind-centered or oppositional will not be effective for making progress with gender equity in the church environment.

GERI is a living example of what we seek to implement in church communities.

GERI workshop for interfaith religious leaders, ca. 2011

Cultivating Harmony in Religions: Bringing Female Voices Back into the Choir

Jetsunma Tenzin Palmo
Dongyu Gatsal Ling Nunnery, India

We all know a very sad truth: that not only in worldly concerns but also in religious traditions, the female voice in the choir has been extremely muted.

All the main scriptures of the world, in all religions, were written by men, for men. So naturally, the scriptures are out of balance. This is not to say that, if only women took over, then everything would get back on track—but simply that in any choir, there should be not just basses, baritones, and tenors; there also need to be altos and sopranos.

This imbalance remains alive today. For centuries women were basically neglected and overlooked, especially their spiritual concerns. It's ironic, because the founders of all these religious traditions were not like that. Virtually all of them were very supportive of the feminine. But through the ages, women were relegated to being second class citizens. In some traditions they were almost subhuman. These systemic gender disparities predated the religious traditions, which then inherited and replicated them.

My main concern and knowledge is of course in Buddhism, so I will mainly speak about that, but you can readily refer what I'm saying to your own traditions—because everywhere it's been the same basic story.

According to the early sutras, the Buddha emphasized the importance of what he called the fourfold Sangha—Sangha meaning community. The fourfold sangha are monastics and lay people of both genders; so you have monks, nuns, laymen, laywomen. And the Buddha said when the fourfold sangha is strong, like a table with four legs, then the Dharma will flourish. And even at the very end of his life when he was about to depart, he said, "Yes, now it's time; I can go because the fourfold sangha is well established." I mention this because according to the sutras, the Buddha was initially resistant to the idea of a female monastic order, but in the end he agreed, and the order of nuns was established. In the sutras, the Buddha often praised the nuns; honoring them individually according to their unique gifts. But in time, because of social conditions in India, it was always difficult for the nuns to get support in the way that the monks did.

One of the problems for women is not just men, sometimes it's other women. Even recently in England, where they now have female vicars, it was suggested among the bishops that women should now become bishops. They put this to the vote of the congregation, made up of mostly women, who voted it down. Women didn't want women bishops; they were not authority figures that women could adore. So it was actually the male bishops who pushed it through, and ordained women bishops. In this case it was the men who helped the women, not the women.

This has always been a problem throughout the world. The men support the men, and the women support the men, but then who supports the women? When I first joined my lama's community in 1964, I was the only nun. Many people say, oh, you must have felt so lonely in the cave [in solo retreat], but I never felt lonely in the cave. I felt lonely when I was the only nun, and couldn't join the monks. And then along came a young American, doing his Ph.D. in Buddhist studies—he was Jewish, not even Buddhist—and they spent hours every day teaching him. He wrote a thick book for his Ph.D. with all that he received from them. And yet, they didn't teach me any of that. Nothing. And when I read his book, oh my Goodness, to see all the rich teachings that were denied me, simply because I was a woman.

So this was my great sadness at that time. I stayed because of my lama, but it felt like there was this magnificent vast buffet, all laid out, and I was given just a little bit of this and a tiny bite of that; and it just made you more hungry, because there was no satisfaction, no meal there.

Eventually I heard about a cave up on the mountain, and I moved there and stayed in solo retreat for 12 years. Afterwards I lived in Assisi, Italy for five years, and then I felt called back to India, where the lamas in my tradition told me, "We want you to start a nunnery—we don't have anything for women." And I thought, yes, this is true. If I don't do it, who will? They won't.

So I said yes, but, I didn't know how to start. I had no money. I wasn't even a Tibetan, I wasn't male, and I wasn't a lama. How was I to raise funds for a nunnery; by giving talks? Why would anybody invite, you know, a boring old English nun? They want exotic Tibetan lamas!

But slowly it began to come together, as I toured more in Asia, America and Europe. Today we're thriving with 100 nuns. And I really thought through, what do I want for these nuns? And essentially the answer was: I want them to get all the training I never got—so they will become much more educated, and much more practiced than I was.

And I put this all together—so our nuns study and debate, they do the rituals, and every year they have a two-month silent retreat. And we also have a retreat center with 12 nuns currently in long term retreat; some of whom have completed 13 years now. In Tibet there were lineages of Yoginis, which had died out in exile. And my lama Khamtrul Rinpoche had asked me, "I always pray that you will renew this very precious lineage of yoginis." So this is what these nuns are doing; re-claiming the Togdenma yogini lineage.

Only 20 years ago, nuns never studied Buddhist philosophy. They learned a few simple rituals, and a few simple practices. They had no opportunities for further study; it was like this for centuries. When I first came to India, I stayed in the only nunnery that existed at that time. One of the other young nuns was highly intelligent and truly gifted, and she begged to go to the newly founded Tibetan University in Sarnath near Varanasi. Finally they let her go. She was the only nun in a class of 100 monks, and each year she finished top of the class. But after two years, the nunnery said, OK, that's enough learning for a nun, now you must come back. The training course was 15 years, but she had to leave and come back; she had no money, and no support. She was so brokenhearted.

About 22 years ago, things began to change. American and European nuns were joining what is called the Dialectic school, and they were debating and training in the Tibetan tradition. Meanwhile the nuns from Tibet had always been told if they study philosophy, their little brains would all boil over. But here were these women studying philosophy and debating with the monks. And the foreign nuns said you can do this too, and so senior students started teaching the Tibetan nuns Buddhist philosophy and debate. And then gradually nunneries were founded with a study program.

Today, in our nunnery, almost all the teachers are nuns. So everything has changed now. And I have to say, who has been teaching the nuns? The monks! Once the monks got the idea that actually it's OK to teach nuns, they went for it like anything, and they have been extremely supportive and helpful.

In Buddhism in general, and in Tibetan tradition in particular, there have been very few female teachers. I went to the International Buddhist Congress, and the 60 people selected to represent Buddhism worldwide were all male. Not a single female. After the conference, the Vice president came to me and said, "Oh, I'm so sorry there were no women on the platform, you were just unintentionally overlooked." I said, "Well, we've been unintentionally overlooked for centuries, we're used to it." But it shows that we still have some way to go.

Yet things are changing. Many of the senior teachers in the Buddhist world now are women—not only in the West, but also in Asia. And in places like Vietnam, Taiwan, and Korea, where nuns are much better educated than in the Tibetan system, there's also a lot of social outreach, as in Catholicism. Nuns run schools, hospitals, orphanages, retreat centers, colleges, and universities.

Any choir, to be balanced, has female as well as male voices—that's what brings the harmony. So it's not like if women get one bigger slice of the cake, the guys get a lesser slice of the cake. The Dharma is not a cake! It brings harmony. Everybody wins. It's a win-win situation for the whole world.

In fact, whether male or female, we are equally human—just two sides of the same coin. So there is no point in considering one side superior to the other. In the ultimate nature of the mind—our primordial awareness beyond self and other—there is no gender distinction. But meanwhile we need to cultivate mutual appreciation and respect to heal the wounds that have been inflicted through the ages and within the various cultures.

Towards this goal the work of Gender Equity and Reconciliation is an essential ingredient for helping to build a new world view which understands and acknowledges its past mistakes and determines to move forward in a more positive and constructive manner. Towards this vision we can all aspire and make our contribution.

Questioner: What advice or wisdom can you offer for our Sangha, as we struggle with the news that the head of our lineage is accused of sexual assault of several female students?

This is a big problem. It's not just Shambhala or Rigpa in the West, it also happens in the East. It's a deep-rooted problem, it's the system, and has involved a number of teachers, not just in Buddhism but other traditions as well.

The problem is not only the teachers' actions, but the whole cycle of concealment, secrecy, and total non-compassion for those who have been victimized by this behavior of the teachers. The sanghas themselves often reject the victims, and instead of coming forward to help and heal, they sometimes create more of a chasm and more pain. Moreover, other senior teachers or lamas sometimes look the other way and don't hold their peers accountable for this kind of behavior, which becomes an enabling complicity.

When you lance a boil, the poison comes out, and then you see it clearly. It is actually the beginning of healing. So too with all these scandals in various Dharma circles. Of course, it's not in all Dharma circles; the majority of the lamas and other teachers are perfectly pure. But there is definitely a problem, and now, it is coming more to the surface. It may be very painful, but this very pain, if we embrace it with compassion and wisdom and understanding and acceptance, can heal.

In saying this, obviously I am not condoning what these spiritual teachers have done, which is awful. It's unbelievable. What were they thinking? Honestly, even in normal society, people don't go around acting like that. There is a whole big system behind it all, a very feudal way of thinking.

But what we can do is to hold with compassion and understanding this problem—on all sides—and allow it to come out into the fresh air and set some boundaries. We need to rethink the whole situation of the commitment between the student and the teacher, and when our deeper intuition says, this doesn't feel right, to trust our intuition.

In the 2019 conference of the Sakyadhita International Association of Buddhist Women, this problem was highlighted because several sexual scandals had recently erupted in dharma circles. Under these distressing circumstances, the goals of healing and reconciliation are essential. At the conference, Gender Equity and Reconciliation International presented a breakout session that provided a skillful example of a forum for addressing these issues in spiritual communities. If we can embrace the lancing of this longstanding boil with courage and compassion, and practice Tonglen in earnest for all parties involved, then the needed healing can emerge.

Jetsunma Tenzin Palmo is a *bhikṣuṇī* (nun) in the Drukpa Lineage of the Kagyu school of Tibetan Buddhism. She spent 12 years in solo retreat in a Himalayan cave. She is founder of the Dongyu Gatsal Ling Nunnery, and President of the Sakyadhita International Association of Buddhist Women.

Catholic nuns and priests completing GERI truth forum, India

CHAPTER 13

God Enters Through a Wound: Implementing GERI Within and Across the Religions

God is not a Christian. ALL of God's children and their different faiths help us to realize the immensity of God. No faith contains the whole truth about God.
—Archbishop Desmond Tutu

Gender Reconciliation Within Religious and Spiritual Communities

Buddhist teacher Jack Kornfield recounts a powerful story from the early days of Spirit Rock Meditation Center in Woodacre, California, which is one of the leading and most progressive Buddhist spiritual retreat centers in North America. Not long after Spirit Rock was founded, they organized an all-Buddhist retreat to facilitate inter-sectarian dialogue and mutual collaboration across the three major schools of Buddhism—the Theravada, Mahayana, and Vajrayana traditions. The gathering was well attended by *bhikkus* (monks) and *bhikkunis* (nuns), and numerous lamas, roshis, Ajahns, Rinpoches, and venerable teachers and lay leaders from across all three Buddhist schools. Most of these people had rarely if ever met with their counterparts from the other Buddhist schools, which is not uncommon in sectarian religious life, not only in Buddhism but other traditions as well, primarily because the demands and schedules of monastic life leave little time for much else. So, this was an unusual and welcome retreat, and was intended in part to build bridges and collaboration across the three Buddhist schools.

Early on in the retreat, as participants began sharing their experiences, including concerns and challenges, a consistent theme emerged relating to difficulties faced by women in these schools. One painful story after another emerged, and to everyone's surprise, women's challenges in Buddhism became a primary theme of the retreat. Even the women themselves were startled to discover how deeply painful—and remarkably similar—their challenges were across all three major schools of Buddhism. The men across the schools were also genuinely surprised and dismayed, and listened intently with sensitivity and compassion, as the retreat became an important learning experience for everyone present. Jack recalled that this experience had emerged entirely unexpectedly, and it was a significant wake-up call for virtually everyone at the retreat.[1]

This story is but the tip of the gender-in-religion iceberg, because the same imbalance holds equally true for other religious traditions as well. Buddhism is not to be singled out here, because all the major religions embody the same structural gender injustice, which is thoroughly embedded throughout their institutional structures and liturgical protocols. This is finally beginning to change in recent years, and much progress has happened over the past 20 years, but there is still a very long ways to go.

For precisely this reason, gender equity and reconciliation work offers a major potential to serve as a profound healing force within each of the major world religions, and if pursued, can contribute tremendously to revitalizing religious and spiritual communities, and infusing them with the light and warmth of genuine beloved community. This vast potential remains largely untapped in nearly every religion, and yet it is deeply aligned with their scriptural teachings. Every religion upholds the Golden Rule in one form or another, yet every religion violates this rule in relation to the women within its own ranks and communities. All religions profess a teaching equivalent to "love thy neighbor as thyself," yet in almost no religion are women treated like unto men, and in most of them, LGBTQ+ people are also treated as less than equals.

Ironically, of all the social and cultural institutions in society, the religions hold the spiritual and moral mandate to lead the way for healing and reconciliation across all divisions of gender, race, class and the various intersectionalities. The time has come to rise to this spiritual imperative. A practical way for religions to begin to live up to this highest ideal—and implement it in a literal way within their *sanghas*, *tariqas*, and congregations—is to pursue gender equity and reconciliation within their communities and clergy.

Few community practices can accomplish so much, with comparatively modest effort, as gender reconciliation work can accomplish in a spiritual or religious community. Why is this? First, because gender injustice is systemic and universal; every human being has a direct personal relationship to some form of lived gender injustice, even if they are not conscious of it. Second, even more importantly, because not only does "God enter through the wound" as Carl Jung said, but God enters more deeply through a deep wound. Gender injustice is one of the deepest wounds in human existence, and the collective healing work practically does itself, *provided* that the all-important requisite conditions are met. What are these? Sincere intention, deep commitment to the healing process, an impeccable container, highly skillful facilitation, properly trained and skilled clinical support, and intensive prayerful invocation. Given these conditions, then "God" (or "Dharmakaya") by whatever Name is invoked, does in fact show up, and the transformative healing unfolds. We've witnessed this happen again and again, over 30 years of this work, in spiritual communities East and West across the globe.

Gender Reconciliation Between Catholic Priests and Nuns

"So much of religion, in *all* religions, has been very male dominated," acknowledges Father Prashant Olekaer, a Jesuit priest in Mumbai, India. "We religious leaders need to be liberated from our male domination. I know many priests who would like to be liberated, but we haven't had a methodology for that."

Between 2002 and 2007 more than 100 Catholic nuns and priests from across India participated in annual GERI programs offered at the Sadhana Institute in Lonavla, India, and at the Medical Mission Sisters in Pune, India. Remarkable healing and reconciliation experiences emerged in these programs, along with heart-wrenching stories of sexual exploitation and pedophilia within the clergy, accompanied by allegations of systematic cover-up by Church authorities. Numerous accounts were aired of priests who had molested or raped nuns and children, and if a nun became pregnant she was summarily excommunicated as morally depraved and cast onto the streets, whereas the priest was usually relocated to a new diocese, where the same pattern was often repeated. A senior church leader told us that the worst repeat offender priests were sent to the United States.[2]

Despite these painful revelations, many instances of remarkable healing and reconciliation between nuns and priests took place, imparting a strong sense of practical hope that oppressive Church structures will one day be surmounted and transformed. After participating in these programs, Fr. Olekaer concluded that "Gender Equity and Reconciliation offers us a major breakthrough." Some of the most creative and liberating moments came during the honoring ceremonies, and also the skits and psychodrama exercises, in which priests and nuns were prompted to create role-play dramas enacting the healing and transformation of the Catholic Church. Highly creative vignettes were generated by these courageous Catholic clergy, in jest but with sincere purpose—including scenarios of nuns being ordained and giving communion to priests, grand weddings of priests and nuns being married in the loving spirit of Christ, and an especially dramatic enactment of a grand papal procession that proclaimed a new woman Pope.

Resolving Cross-Gender Conflict Between Nuns and Priests

Challenges sometimes arise in the context of gender reconciliation work. An example took place in a GERI workshop for Catholic nuns and priests at the Sadhana Institute, founded by Jesuit priest Anthony de Mello. Early in this workshop, the nuns and priests found it particularly challenging to break their silence and speak to the real issues affecting their lives and congregations. However, as the workshop progressed, many poignant stories came forth. In the women's truth forum, several nuns spoke about retaliation against them when they had refused unwanted advances of priests. Numerous tales emerged of sexual overtures or abuses by priests during confessions or spiritual direction, a context in which the females are particularly vulnerable. For many of the sisters, this was the first time they had shared such raw, emotional truths in the presence of men.

In the men's truth forum, further powerful stories emerged, including several stories of sexual abuse. When the priests were asked how many had been sexually or physically abused, over half of them raised their hands. This was a big surprise to many of the nuns, who had assumed that such abuse was almost nonexistent among men.

With each new poignant story, a deepening sense of safety and intimacy emerged in the group, accompanied by a growing tension of undercurrent from a few in the group who were challenged or disturbed by the entire process. Was it really necessary, some asked, for these things to be aired, especially in mixed company? Did the revelation of past wounds truly enable reconciliation, or merely deepen the shame and humiliation? Working through the ensuing dynamics, a deep and rich dialogue and community healing process emerged.

On the last morning, we separated into the women's and men's circles to prepare the honoring ceremonies for one another. A crisis suddenly emerged in the women's circle, when two nuns reported that the previous evening, they had overheard a few priests making disparaging remarks about the nuns, and the entire workshop process, even using profane language. The nuns were distressed and outraged to learn of this, and they decided they could not proceed with the honoring ceremony. Instead, the nuns demanded an immediate, full council process to openly confront this festering undercurrent that had been brewing all week under the surface.

The atmosphere was tense as the facilitators arranged the nuns and priests in two semicircles, facing one another—with four meters separating them. The facilitators opened with silence, then established the ground rules for the process, and for all communications, to ensure utmost integrity in the process, and safety and mutual respect for all. A simple communication process was introduced to carefully balance each side's contributions. The women would be given five minutes to speak, while the men listened, and then the men would be given five minutes to speak, while the women listened. This process would continue, back and forth, until there was some clear movement or other need, or resolution of some kind.

The facilitators opened with a community prayer and re-invoked the collective intention for gender healing and reconciliation, and reaffirmed the community agreements to which we had all agreed, in service of our common purpose for gender reconciliation.

The women began. Several challenged the men with the rumors they had heard and asked for honesty and forthrightness. The two nuns reported what they had overheard the previous evening. Others lamented the sense of hypocrisy that some men were saying one thing in the group during the plenary gatherings, and quite another privately to their close confidants. This, the nuns insisted, was a replay of what often took place within their religious orders—for both nuns and priests—which rendered their religious community lives unsafe, and superficial. No one ever spoke the truth directly; it was generally whispered behind people's backs. How could the priests stoop to labeling the nuns' heartfelt truthtelling and vulnerability as "priest bashing," or "shit"? The bell rang, and the facilitators called for a pause of silence.

It was the men's turn. The priests responded slowly at first, but became increasingly forthcoming. Several priests expressed shock and dismay that this had happened and empathized with the women. The bell rang again, another pause, and the nuns continued with further confrontations from their own experience. Then the priests spoke again, and opened up with ever more candid sharings, expressing strong feelings with eloquence. Several expressed solidarity with the women, and a few apologized on behalf of their fellow priests who had said hurtful things.

As so often happens in gender work, we found ourselves immersed in a complex conglomeration of personal, social, institutional, and historical pain. The frustrations being aired had roots that reached deep into the personal histories, cultural dynamics, and institutional realities that operated in these people's lives. There was a strong fear that we might never find our way through all this "gender muck." We had reached the point of no return, however, and it was clear that the only way out of the situation was by going *through* it, to its natural conclusion. The resolution had to be real; it could not be artificial or genteel for the sake of "niceness," which would only perpetuate the already damaging situation.

As the dialogue continued and challenging feelings were aired, tempers slowly began to cool. A spirit of love and generosity began to find its way back into the dialogue. It was a remarkable process to witness, and most everyone in the room was committed to finding a genuine and authentic resolution. The community was unwilling to gloss over the painful issues, and they continued sitting in the fire with the issues and with each other—sometimes in silence, sometimes in the form of one person's rage or humiliation, but increasingly without accusation and blame.

The turning point came when a priest who had been silent throughout, who we shall call Joseph, quietly revealed that he had made the remark using foul language, which had been so hurtful to many of the women. He said he was feeling extremely vulnerable, and that he had only meant to express his feelings, but never to hurt anyone. Joseph offered a moving and tearful apology, for the pain he had caused. Several of the nuns thanked Joseph for his courage in openly acknowledging his role, and expressed compassion for him, and for the difficulty of what we were all working through together.

The facilitators called for a short break in silence. Joseph's heavy armoring had been cracked open, and he was in considerable distress, and the male facilitators worked carefully with him. His heart had been pierced by what had transpired, and he was distraught and vulnerable. Gradually, and with strong support from the facilitators, he began to recollect himself.

When the group reconvened, the anger in the room had subsided, and a new energy was present. Continuing with the facilitated communication process, compassion and understanding began to flow, and the atmosphere and tone in the group shifted away from confrontation toward conciliation, gratitude, and mutual appreciation. The storm was passing, and the sun began breaking through the clouds of fear and betrayal. The process continued to unfold in mutual appreciation, and gradually morphed into a spontaneous healing ritual. The facilitators introduced a simple Sufi partner dance, in which every priest and nun had the opportunity to offer a blessing to the other. Tears of tenderness and joy flowed as people shared moments of intimacy in pairs as they moved through the dance. We closed with several group songs and chants, punctuated by eruptions of laughter and an atmosphere of celebration.

Following up with Joseph later, his eyes were shining as he shared the deeper learnings from his experience. At first he had felt betrayed by the process, but he came to see that a powerful healing had taken place, in which he had been the (unwitting) sacrificial lamb. He pointed out the irony that he had celebrated mass that morning, invoking the theme of gender healing, and that his prayers had indeed been answered, but not in the way he would have ever imagined or chosen. We honored him for his courage, and in fact he received lots of appreciation from the entire community, both nuns and priests, for what had had done. Further follow up with Joseph later confirmed that he was doing well. We continued to offer GERI programs annually at the Sadhana Institute for several years afterward.

Gender Equity and Reconciliation Across the World Religions

Another equally critical application of GERI work is for inter-religious healing and reconciliation *across* the religious traditions. Just as the principle of "love thy neighbor as thyself" or its equivalent in all religions applies *within* each religious community, so too it applies equally *across* the different religious and spiritual traditions. When well-intentioned, open-minded women and men of diverse religions come together, and speak from the depths of their hearts, they often discover that they are all engaged in a common quest, and are seeking to realize a shared Absolute, which goes by many different names across their diverse traditions. As Desmond Tutu puts it, "God is not a Christian." God cannot be confined to any one tradition, because all traditions are contained in God. Although religious difference has often been the source of tremendous conflict in the world, it can also be a source of mutual enrichment, elevated insight, and remarkable bonding. Gender reconciliation work in spiritual and religious communities has a strong potential to help awaken this unitive insight and experience.

"Love one another, as I have loved you" (John 13:34) is the final commandment Christ gave to the disciples. This same principle can be said to apply to the diverse religious communities themselves. Just as God has loved every human community, through God's grace and gift of different religions to each of them, so this "new" commandment is given to all the religions and their respective communities: to love one another, just as God has loved each of the religions and their respective communities.[3]

As Desmond Tutu puts it, "Instead of separation and division, all distinctions make for a rich diversity to be celebrated for the sake of the unity that underlies them. We are different so that we can know our need of one another." In the Qur'an, this teaching is made explicit that God created human diversity for a divine purpose, so that we can learn from our differences, and thereby grow in love for one another and for God. As the Buddha said, "hatred never ceases by hatred, but by love alone."

How to achieve this in practice? Gender equity and reconciliation has a remarkable role to play in creating unity and healing across the religions. Because gender oppression is universal and is found in every religion, gender reconciliation can serve as a highly effective modality for leveraging systemic healing and unity across the entire religious spectrum. There is a profound irony that the religions of the world seem to meet in both the highest and lowest levels—at the mystical heart of the soul's communion with God or the Absolute, and at the most tragic subjugation and oppression of fully half of the human family. As one spiritual leader wryly remarked, "the religions seem to meet in God and gutter." Indeed, because the "gutter" of gender oppression is a place they meet, it is also another potential site of reconciliation, healing, and restoration of the traditions to their wholeness. For this to be done properly though, we must fully embrace the traditions at once in their most profound promise and deepest truth, *and* at the same time in full accountability for where they have fallen short. To do one without the other would leave something still incomplete, but to do both together holds the profound promise of true healing across the traditions, of reclaiming the genuine spiritual impulse that dwells in the heart of each tradition, and of recognizing each one as its own unique reflection and revelation of the Divine that has been bestowed upon humanity.

Women across the religions share a very similar experience, particularly in terms of their unique challenges in spiritual and religious life. Men are often only dimly aware of this, and even women are surprised to discover the depths of their commonalities. Once recognized, these awakenings serve to bond women *and* men, across the religions, in a new shared quest. As women discover deep and striking parallels in their challenging experiences, they begin to bond over their common affliction, which strengthens their resolve, increases their mutual compassion, and diminishes or dissolves altogether their concerns about the differences across their respective faith traditions. As men become aware of the systematic oppression that has been the lot of women, irrespective of their faith tradition, the vast majority of men are shocked and dismayed by this and are moved to bring a deep systemic change. Thus the gender dysfunction could be said to be deeper than the religious divisions, and therefore the bonding and healing across the gender divide naturally leads to healing and bonding *across* the religions.

We have been fortunate to witness this process take place in our inter-religious applications of GERI program, and also in the interspiritual conferences organized by Satyana Institute's other primary project called Dawn of Interspirituality, which organizes events to bring religious leaders together from diverse faith traditions. In 2009, we convened a women's spiritual leadership conference in Turin Italy, with 75 women from 15 countries, spanning primarily Christian, Buddhist, and Hindu traditions. As the women shared in depth about their spiritual lives, they discovered significant parallels in their experiences, including lack of voice and influence, marginalization within their respective religious institutions, and in some cases exploitation and sexual abuse. These common experiences led to a recognition of systemic oppression of women that was universal across their religions. In another interfaith conference we organized in Costa Rica in 2018, we conducted the silent witnessing exercise in a group of religious leaders from nine different major religions. The result of this was profound, as women and men together realized the vast injustices of gender oppression, as well as the ways that all religions are called to transform this injustice, rather than continue to perpetuate it. The process proceeds similarly to what was briefly referenced above in the scenario at the Buddhist retreat described by Jack Kornfield.

As the men witness these parallels in women's treatment across the religious traditions, and are awakened more fully to the plight of women in religion, the vast majority of men are shocked by the systemic disparities, and are inspired and motivated to take action and do something about it. For example, as described by Craig Parker, a leading member of the clergy in Boston who attended a GERI retreat for religious leaders:

> Rarely have I experienced such vulnerability, rawness, empathy, and grace as I did on this retreat. I will treasure the stories I heard, and I plan to implement the lessons learned as I engage with students, young professionals, prisoners, and fellow ministers. I especially appreciated the honoring and blessing ceremonies we created for each other. I was surprised at how much they moved me to tears.

Another example comes from Rev. Philbert Kalisa, an Episcopal priest from Rawanda who is the Founder and CEO of REACH in Rwanda, which has done remarkable healing and reconciliation work for over 20 years between Hutus and Tutsis, following the horrendous Rawandan genocide. He had this to say:

> The sharing from women to men touched my heart deeply, and pushed me to repent for not speaking out some of the injustices I see often in our churches and societies connected with our culture that doesn't consider women as equal as men. I made my decision not to keep quiet anymore. I will advocate for women created in the image of God as our mothers, wives, daughters, sisters and nieces.

A final example comes from a corporate consultant and trainer who attended the retreat.

> To call my experience transformational is not overstated. I left with a deep and passionate commitment to play an active role in bridging the divide between women and men.

This last declaration came from Jorge Rico, who fulfilled this commitment by joining the GERI professional training, and subsequently he became a prominent member of the GERI leadership team. Jorge is one of the co-authors of this book and is currently helping to take GERI work into the corporate world, and into his native Bolivia and Latin America.

GERI Workshop for the Tanenbaum Center for Interreligious Understanding

In July 2016, Gender Equity and Reconciliation International (GERI) was invited to facilitate a workshop for the Tanenbaum Center for Interreligious Understanding in New York. Tanenbaum is an interfaith organization committed to "combating religious prejudice, and building a world that respects religious difference."

Tanenbaum sponsors the *Peacemakers in Action* Network, a group of prominent religious leaders from across the globe and many different world religions who dedicate their lives to promoting peace, religious understanding, and a safer world. GERI was invited by Nozizwe Madlala-Routledge, South Africa's former Deputy Defence Minister, who co-convened this workshop for Tanenbaum's *Peacemakers in Action* Working Retreat in New York. Nozizwe dedicates herself to gender equality, ending sex trafficking, and promoting the inclusion of women in peacemaking. She is currently the Director of the Quakers United Nations Office in Geneva. A *Peacemaker* herself, Nozizwe invited us to introduce GERI, and she and her husband Jeremy co-facilitated with our GERI facilitation team.

About 45 people, including Peacemakers from global conflict regions including Colombia, the Philippines, Afghanistan, Nigeria, Israel, Syria and Sri Lanka, as well as staff and volunteers from Tanenbaum participated in the workshop. Participants plumbed the depths of the GERI work with a curiosity and willingness to acknowledge the pain and wounding along gender lines that is prevalent in institutions and societies in our world.

Many *Peacemakers* surprised themselves in discovering a new level of intimacy and depth of understanding with each other as a group. The workshop was not without its challenges, however. Participants were encouraged through the GERI process to examine and confront some of the patriarchal attitudes, norms, and systems that perpetuate gender inequality, religious intolerance, and injustice that lie at the root of conflict, violence and war in their various contexts. As *Peacemakers* whose work takes them to the coalface of extremism, violence, terrorism, and countless acts of injustice, the invitation in this program was for them to turn inward, and explore their edges and lived experiences of gender injustice in their own lives. Most participants greatly appreciated the program and new insights, and the heartfelt connections they made with one another. Activist and *Peacemaker* Sakena Yacoobi was especially enthusiastic about the process, and said she wanted to bring the GERI program to her native Afghanistan.

A few participants were challenged by the process, exhibiting the poignancy of centuries-deep wounding around gender, and its diverse manifestations across the cultures and religions of the world.

The facilitators responded accordingly, attending sensitively to the needs of each participant. As one touching example, there was a senior Christian Archbishop from Jerusalem in the group who was unsettled by the cross-gender truth forums. He was indignant, saying that women should not be invited or encouraged to bring forth their painful stories and experiences, especially not in front of *him* as the head of the Church. He explained that he should not have to know about, or hear these stories, nor should the women have to humble themselves by sharing their vulnerable stories in his presence.

Hearing this, Nozizwe sat up in her chair, leaned forward slightly, and sensitively inquired, "Archbishop, may I ask you a question?" He nodded in her direction, and she proceeded. "As the presiding Archbishop, and the head of your church, in service to Christ, are you not called by your position and high office, to effectively stand *in the place* of Christ?" The Archbishop replied in the affirmative, that this was indeed his highest intention, calling, and vocation. Nozizwe nodded, and continued gingerly, "If these women cannot bring their traumatic experiences of humiliation and violation, to you—as the most senior bishop in the church, who stands in the very place of Christ—then where, and to whom, *can* they bring their pain and their brokenness?" She paused, and added, "If Christ himself were here today, would he turn these women away and refuse to hear them?"

There was a deep poignant silence, followed by a quiet, delicate exchange between the two of them, in which the bishop listened, slowly yielded, and finally acknowledged that Christ *would* listen to these women's stories, with compassion, and that he would also take righteous action to rectify the situation. Nozizwe's heart and the Archbishop's heart met in a place of mutual sincerity and commitment to Christ, and their intimate exchange seemed to turn the bishop around. This was an inspiring moment that touched the hearts of all present in the spirit of true reconciliation. In that moment at least, the longstanding boundaries and barriers of both gender and religion were dissolved in a larger field of truth and love.

GERI at the Parliament of World Religions

Given the importance of applying GERI work for interreligious understanding, the authors have maintained a strong commitment to this dimension of our work. We have presented GERI programs at several international interfaith conferences, including the Parliament of World Religions in 2015 and 2018, and we participated in panels and presentations in the 2021 online conference. The sessions in 2015 and 2018 were entitled *Transforming Patriarchy in Religion: The Promise of Gender Equity and Reconciliation*, and nearly 200 leaders from diverse spiritual and religious backgrounds attended one or the other of these sessions, with many of them reporting an important awakening experience to the need for healing gender disharmony in their personal lives, and across their respective spiritual communities.

Sacred Union Human and Divine: An Auspicious Future for Spirituality and Sexuality

Down through the centuries, human sexuality has been profoundly exploited, abused, and pathologized in myriad ways across the cultures and institutions of human societies. Perhaps nowhere has this been more egregious and tragic than in the religious and spiritual traditions, where we have witnessed such unconscionable abuses, blatant exploitation, and destructive doctrines and practices—all within the domain in which we might rightly expect to discover the highest purpose of sexuality revealed, coupled with impeccable protocols of integrity and purity in its practice and expression.

Sexuality remains a profound gift from the Divine to humanity, and despite all the challenges and painful missteps that have occurred and are still continuing today, the shining possibility ever remains that sexuality will one day be fully restored to its rightful place as a vehicle for sacred union between human beings, and between the human and the Divine. All spiritual traditions contain within their hidden and esoteric traditions an articulation of this sacred dimension of sexual union, and its inherent connection to oneness with the Divine. We close this chapter with a few reflections from across the traditions on this sacred possibility, both as a reminder of what is possible, and as a prayer that this will one day become widely realized and practiced in human societies.

Sexuality As Sacrament

Although many spiritual teachings in religious traditions across the ages have rejected sexuality—at worst as a necessary evil, or at best as a distraction to spiritual life—certain spiritual masters have recognized and celebrated the highest, sacred purpose of sexuality.

One such master is Ibn al Arabi (1165-1240), widely recognized as one of the greatest Sufi masters of all time. Scholar Sadiyya Shaikh has provided a masterful study of gender, sexuality, and mystical union in Sufism, based on the teachings of Ibn Arabi. She presents startling insights from Ibn Arabi who "genuinely dismantles some of the foundational binaries of patriarchal hierarchy" throughout his nearly 800 published works. Ibn Arabi frequently invokes the creativity and interplay of masculine and feminine cosmic principles. He acknowledges both the vastness of God (or the divine Source by whatever name), who transcends all gendered binaries, and he also unites the God-human identity with the essence of the masculine-feminine principle.

In Ibn Arabi's cosmology, the origin of all creation is God's desire and love.

Throughout his writings are vivid images of sexuality, marriage, pregnancy, and birth that articulate the intricate cosmic process by which God creates and self-discloses. He maintained that God *needs* creation, including humanity in particular, in order to complete and manifest divine potentiality, a perspective that is also central to other mystical traditions such as the Kabbalah and the Zohar in Judaism. For Ibn Arabi, male and female originated from a single soul (*nafsin wahidatin*), and having been separated, they naturally love and yearn for one another, culminating in sexual union.[4]

Ibn Arabi departs from many other leading spiritual authorities (then and now), who marginalize or dismiss sexual desire as a spiritual distraction or sensual indulgence. Ibn Arabi regarded sexual union as based on a deep existential love, which can be "the greatest self-disclosure of God." However, this is a reality that only a small number of mystics have realized. As Ibn Arabi describes the complete interpenetration of spirituality and sexuality,

> [Each lover] dissolves in the other. There is no part in oneself that is not in the other. Love has suffused all one's parts, so one's entire being is interconnected with the other. For that reason, each [lover] dissolves in their likeness with a complete annihilation, in contrast to their love for anything that is not their likeness. Each becomes one with their beloved, so that each person says, "I am the one I desire, and the one I desire is I," and at the final point of this station says "I am God." So when you love a person who is like you with such a love, then your witnessing [of the one you love] turns you back to God. ... Many of the sages are oblivious to this reality (of the spiritual importance of sexual desire). Indeed, it is one of the secrets that none know except a few of the people of divine favor (*'inaya*).[5]

Ibn Arabi's description could apply equally, word for word, to the experience of transcendent mystical union with God, or the Divine by whatever name. As Sadiyya Shaikh summarizes his teaching: "The pleasure experienced during sex intimates the pleasure of union with God, who is the ultimate beloved. ... Most people are unaware of the theophanic and pedagogic nature of sexual pleasure and do not apprehend the reality that God both takes and gives pleasure" in sacred human sexuality. The potential for Divine participation in human sexuality unveils "a theophanic reality [that] allows for the experience of *conincidenta oppositorum* [sacred union of 'opposites'], which ultimately is also the nature of the reality of God."[6] This is an exalted form of 'inner alchemy' that unifies dualities of matter and spirit, masculine and feminine, and human and Divine.

Similar articulations about the sacred union of feminine and masculine and its relation to the soul's relationship with God are found in esoteric teachings across the traditions. For example, in the non-canonical Gospel of Philip,

> None can be free unless they receive a power which is both masculine and feminine. ... The separation [of male and female] is at the origin of death. If woman had not been separated from man, she would not die with him. Christ came to heal this wound, to rediscover the lost unity. ... Male and female unite in the Bridal Chamber, and those who have known this sacred embrace will never be separated.[7]

In our contemporary social context the question naturally arises: how do these intimate principles apply beyond the rigid "gender binary" of male and female? This raises important current social issues that are addressed elsewhere in this book. However, a key insight found in many spiritual traditions is that each individual person is a unique *combination* of both masculine and feminine aspects, and is a direct reflection and manifestation of the Divine. In short, God is inherently androgynous, so human beings are also inherently androgynous. Just as the Godhead ultimately transcends gender, so human beings are also ultimately "transgender" spiritually— even if most people identify as either male or female based on their biological sex. This androgynous nature of the human being has long been known, and has been frequently exhibited in highly realized mystics, who often transcend rigid gender identification. For example, "Men encountered in St. Teresa [of Avila] a woman who was more fully a man than they were, while she was also fully a woman."[8] Gender-inclusive consciousness often emerges with spiritual advancement, irrespective of biological sex or physical anatomy.

Details of the profound divine intimacy outlined above are intentionally obscured. As one Rabbi explains,

> Those who know the secret of the image, of which it is said, *in our image, in our likeness* (Genesis 1:26) will understand. ... I cannot explain it, for it is not permitted to put this in writing, even indirectly. ... The Kabbalah as a whole is considered to be founded on the secret of this dyad. Sexual difference characterizes the human soul, the "image" in which it was created, as is the divine realm which is its model.[9]

It is a tragic irony that religious institutions East and West have sometimes been among the worst offenders in perpetuating egregious gender-based injustice and sexual exploitation—even unto this day—while harboring this sacred secret within their esoteric traditions! May human sexuality be restored to its rightful life-giving and exalted purposes.

CHAPTER 14

Introducing GERI in the Corporate Sector

We cannot all succeed when half of us are held back.
—Malala Yousafzai

Over the past three decades, Gender Equity and Reconciliation International (GERI) has offered programs in collaboration with schools, universities, prisons, religious institutions, for members of parliament, corporations, foundations, and NGOs. The GERI programs transcend workplace issues and frame the experience in deeper meanings that can afford participants growth on a personal level that has positive residual impact in all relationships, including professional relationships.

This chapter outlines the experiences and aspirations of several professionals working in corporate environments who have experienced GERI programs and are seeking to introduce GERI in corporate contexts. The first story is from Chaya Pamula, the Co-Founder and CEO of PamTen Inc. and Founder of SheTek and SOFKIN, who shares her experiences of gender bias in the workplace and how she continues to work toward a more just system that specifically uplifts women in technology.

Having worked in the Indian corporate world, I experienced gender bias firsthand. I worked in a large manufacturing company as a manager in the Management Information Systems (IT) department. I was the only woman employee among 5000+ employees in the company. I used to be the only woman at the table in the management meetings. My peers would not look at me when I spoke, ignored my voice, and never felt my opinion was important. In fact, they felt awkward and uncomfortable in my presence, as they had never worked with a woman colleague in their lives. Because of this, they didn't know how to treat or respond to a woman at work. I couldn't get confrontational due to lack of support system but had to constantly take up new challenges to prove my knowledge and abilities.

When my family migrated to America, I thought I would no longer have to face these challenges, with the United States being an advanced country. I was surprised to discover that women are still a minority in the technology field, and of course in many other fields such as manufacturing, finance, aviation, etc. A recent workplace survey in STEM fields showed that half of women had experienced some form of discrimination in the workplace, and 20 percent have resigned in the past because of workplace discrimination or harassment.[1] I learned many lessons through my own experiences in corporate America. One of these lessons is that some issues can be addressed through awareness and communication. Not everything has to be confrontational. The individual's awareness, culture, values, and perspectives drive their behavior. Gender equality is something that men must be sold on as well. It is vital for men to believe in this equality to shift the belief systems and organizational cultures.

GERI work addresses these problems at the grass-roots level. A change at the individual level influences the change in the family, the community, and ultimately the legal and policy frameworks. Diversity training programs that only speak about the gender injustice and importance of diversity and inclusion can be effective to some extent, but may not produce lasting change. An experiential workshop with a solution approach can be much more effective in catalyzing a change in people's mindset. I am excited to partner with GERI through our SheTek organization to bring this work to the corporate world. SheTek's mission is to increase the number of women represented in the tech industry. While we offer many technologies and soft-skill programs combined with mentorship, it is critical for all genders to learn to work in synergy. This will not only help individual growth but also organizational growth. Without addressing the issues at the grass-roots level, the corporate initiatives around diversity and inclusion cannot be effective. We need more hands-on, experiential programs that positively influence the overall culture and organizational practices.

The GERI work is essential in today's world that is challenged with gender abuse, racial differences, and inequality. I see tremendous need for GERI work in all sectors and communities across the world. The unique framework of GERI brings outcomes that are significant, measurable, and sustainable, for a more balanced and peaceful world.

The following reflection is from a corporate trainer and Organization Development consultant who discovered a new openness in herself through hearing the genuine stories of men's pain and suffering. She continues holding the possibility of similar transformations and growth of mutual compassion in professional environments.

Within the first hour of participating in a GERI workshop, I knew I was experiencing a new type of gathering. Men shared stories of themselves and family members experiencing physical and sexual violence. They openly expressed their rage, heartbreak, and wrenching hopelessness over these traumatic events. I witnessed the pain they carried in their bodies while simultaneously becoming aware of the patriarchy's power in keeping men silent. My heart opened as I witnessed this rare moment of masculine vulnerability. It is unusual to hear men express the deep vulnerability I encountered in GERI workshops. I was changed by being a witness to the pain and desires of all the GERI participants. It increased my empathy and deepened my intellectual compassion. I knew immediately that I needed to become part of this community and learn how to facilitate these transformational conversations.

As a coach and facilitator in the corporate world, I've seen how this suppression has limited the human capacity for empathy, connection, and personal engagement. Despite the billions of development dollars spent, workplaces still operate from the belief that people are expendable and shareholder value is king. The narrow focus on shareholder value has damaged human lives, nature, and threatens our collective future. There are thousands of "solutions" for the corporate workplace, but the most important—creating compassionate engagement across a team—is one that GERI excels at delivering.

Dismantling the patriarchy's grip is key to addressing the major challenges we face. Our values and our identities must evolve to meet this moment. We need a revolution of our collective heart. GERI has the method, mission, and people to usher in that revolution.

This next story is from a woman participant who writes about the negative consequences she endured after speaking out about her boss who had sexually propositioned her and the important life lessons she learned through the experience.

At age 40 I had a major experience of gender injustice in the workplace. I was a middle manager in a health and wellness corporation in Indianapolis. My duties included supervising and guiding a team of 20+ women. Within a few months of taking the job, I was sexually propositioned by the co-founder of the company, who was also the chairman of the board of directors. He said, "I've enjoyed getting to know you over the past few months. Now it is time to take our relationship to a deeper, more intimate, sexual level." I immediately said "No! I am not interested. Our relationship is and will remain entirely professional." This man, who is world-renowned in the wellness field, did not give up easily. Over the next several days at work he continued to pressure me. When I said "No" again, his response was, "Well, I can see you are just not ready yet."

At that point, I felt like I had only a few stark options. I could lie down and go to bed with him. I could quit my job and leave quietly, never speaking a word. Or, I could speak truth to power and report this man to the company management. Thankfully, I was in a position and had the support of my family to bring this injustice of sexual harassment out in the open. Unfortunately, many women are not in a position to take such action, especially women who are marginalized based on race, culture, socio-economic level, age, and ability. Risking the loss of their job is not usually an option. In my case, my main objective was not retaliation, but rather accountability. I hoped, however naively, that the senior management, all of whom were men, might want to reconcile with me and move beyond what had happened. My boss who had propositioned me apologized for his actions. But the other senior male leaders in the corporation retaliated against me and hired six attorneys to my one. I had the opportunity to take the case to Federal court, but in the end, I decided that doing so was not the answer. I had spoken my truth and found the power of my own voice.

Throughout this experience, I had several major learnings. The first was my awakening to another level of betrayal—from other women in the workplace. Having taken the issue to the senior management, I anticipated that the men in the corporation would turn their backs on me, but then my women colleagues did the same. They stopped speaking to me. I wasn't invited to lunch or on breaks with them any longer. They refused to be seen with me even in work-related situations. The workplace environment and my co-workers became actively hostile. I realized that, sadly, many of these women *had* to turn their backs on me in order to keep their jobs. The threat to their economic livelihood was real and for many they had little choice, because they had families to feed and needed a roof to keep over their heads. For some other women, however, it extended beyond just merely economic and was more about maintaining their position and power within the patriarchal hierarchy. The cut-throat corporate environment that encourages competition and survival of the fittest in order to move up the corporate ladder required these women to step on whoever got in the way of their success. This tearing down of one another is a horrific violation that does so much damage and must stop if we are to achieve not only equality and equity among the genders, but also across all of the intersectionalities. In a healthy and thriving workplace environment everyone— men, women, gay, straight, transgender, queer, Black, brown, white . . . —needs to uplift and support each other in their achievements and mutual advancements.

The second important learning was that, based on the incredible stress that this experience had already caused in my life, I realized the extreme toll it would take on me and my children if I pursued the Federal court case, even if I managed to win. It would have been a very high price to pay for years to come, and inwardly I felt that to go down that track would have most likely ended up becoming a cancer in my body.

Another learning I received after experiencing this violation of sexual harassment and ultimately going through the GERI training was that I began to see how trapped men are in the system as well, and how much they too need liberation from the dysfunctional and injurious system of patriarchy. Patriarchy denies men their humanity, just as it does women.

Over time, I was eventually able to turn my anger, fear, and sense of betrayal from this sexual harassment experience into deeper understanding, compassion, and purpose. My life and career shifted into what I knew was my true path in the health and wellness field, which was to bring healing and understanding between women and men in skillful and more compassionate, life-giving ways. My engagement with GERI increased significantly and shortly after being pushed out of my former job, I began working for GERI as the coordinator of the yearlong professional immersion and facilitator training. In addition to my job responsibilities, I was invited to enter into the training, which was a deep and intensive process of gender healing and reconciliation. The training environment was nurturing and caring and the perfect place for me to land as I continued to heal from the trauma I had endured.

After the whole sexual harassment ordeal had ended and before I even knew about my future employment with GERI, my attorney said, "Do not tell anyone about this and especially no potential employer. If they found out that you were involved in a sexual harassment case, they would never come near you with a ten-foot pole. They certainly wouldn't hire you." She told me that they would consider me a troublemaker, because I had spoken out. To my great relief and delight, GERI was a welcoming environment that allowed—even encouraged—me to share my pain and suffering about the violation and the injustice. This was crucial not only for my own healing, but was ultimately essential in rebuilding my trust of men, as well as with women.

I am so very thankful for finding my true vocation and my home within the GERI community of practitioners. Many years have passed since this extremely challenging and traumatic experience; perhaps needless to say, GERI has totally transformed my life.

The following is a story of awakening and transformation of another woman participant. She reclaimed her femininity after realizing that she was literally killing herself trying to fit into a rigid masculine model within the tech world.

Having experienced my share of navigating the unknown, I am now a coach who helps other people navigate life's uncertainties. After graduating from a prestigious engineering school in Canada, I became a young female engineer living in Silicon Valley, chasing the startup dream. One day, I ended up in the hospital with severe menorrhagia that led to cancer in the uterus. This became the forcing function that got me asking the existential questions about life, purpose, values, identity, livelihood, community and spirituality. Making the shift from an external achievement-based life, valuing the mind and power above all else, towards one connected to the heart, the body, and an internal compass of values takes time. In my experience it has been over a decade of exploration, heartbreaks, uncertainty, anxiety and magic.

It wasn't until my first GERI course, 12 years later, that I was able to look at my life experience through the lens of gender. I was born to a single mom who had six brothers that raised me when we immigrated from Vietnam to Canada. I was sexually abused as a teenager and started to dress like a tomboy. I went into Computer Engineering during the dot-com boom where our class had a ratio of about one girl for every ten guys, and so all my friends were guys. Similarly, in my co-op and full-time jobs in tech, it was normal to be the only female in the team or company.

My *ah-ha* moment in the GERI course was in a one-to-one conversation. It came up very simply, as a few words of truth from within, that made me weep. *I've been trying to be a boy for as long as I can remember!* Being of rational mind, in the past, I've never let myself hear those words because it didn't make any sense—I am a cisgender female and straight and in a loving relationship with a man. But this time around, I couldn't ignore how much shame, how much sadness, heartbreak, and confusion came up. In that moment, I could see a deeply-rooted story that affected all my actions and decisions, my bias that was running unconsciously for decades!

I realized that there was a narrative that, in a patriarchal world, to be free to do what I want, to be successful, to have autonomy, to travel, to create, to have power, there was one winning gender and a losing gender. I wanted to be part of the winning team. Growing up, my single mom struggled a lot to get back on her feet and was very emotional. So I think that early on I connected more with my uncles and vowed that I would never fall for a man who might impregnate me and leave me. I distanced myself from all the women in the family who tried to pass on to me the ideals of being "a good housewife" who served men. I tried my best to fit in, into a man's world—the engineering world, the start-up world, the venture capital world. So I dressed like a man, I approached relationships as transactional, I led with masculine energy at work.

And in that pursuit, the GERI course also helped me own up to how much violence and prejudice I had inflicted on both women and men, and on myself. My gender expression wasn't coherent with my gender identity and there are no winners in that path of fear and survival. I was blown away by this deeply uncomfortable and unraveled perspective on how I had lived my adult life trying to be a gender I was not. And how crazy and beautiful that it was my uterus that intervened!—a physical body part that I secretly wished not to exist was bleeding uncontrollably to near death, to get me to stop doing what I was doing. If not for GERI, the sacredness and safety of this space and community, I'm not sure I would've been able to face the truth, maybe the reckoning of my lived experience. To not hide it deeper in shame, but then to become curious—*oh, wow,* have other people experienced what I experienced? Are there other women in tech who feel the pressure to be more like a man? Maybe dress like a man, or lead like a man? Maybe others had to suppress their emotions, intuition and compassion like me? Maybe instead of women lifting women up, that we have been knocking each other, and ourselves, down?

As a result of my transformative experience with the GERI work, I often coach tech-startup leaders on authenticity, on valuing both the masculine and feminine, on uncovering who is running their inner board of directors, and in what ways they self-sabotage. Whenever I am invited to speak to women in tech, I have started to talk about Authentic Leadership and what embracing feminine leadership looks like. I feel a strong conviction that even in this patriarchal world, we all have the feminine qualities of deep listening, kindness, nurture, warmth, humility, devotion, understanding, forgiveness that are truly valuable and needed in the world today. From my direct experience, what would be helpful is to not suppress but to include these qualities in our authenticity, our way of being and our way of navigating uncertainty. I am also making my way through the GERI facilitation program and am deeply grateful for this transformative work that has brought deep healing and greater clarity on the purpose of my life.

This final writing is from a male participant who is a human resource professional, with a long history working in DEI [Diversity, Equity and Inclusion] initiatives. He shares about the applicability and need of the GERI process within corporate environments.

I had entered the workshop feeling I was as enlightened and informed on gender equity issues as a person could be. I fancied myself a strident feminist and an HR professional who had advocated for gender equity at virtually all my previous jobs. Despite this so-called enlightenment and strong belief in support of gender equity, I was blown away with the heart-opening and mind-expanding experience of my first GERI workshop. The experiential nature of the GERI process and the degree of personal engagement required to participate made me realize that the reconciliation and healing components of such work are essential to advance the cause of gender equity. I realized that this was where my decades of previous work in the diversity and inclusion space within corporate environments was missing the mark. I know through my professional experience and academic studies that people must go through a paradigm shift and have a personal epiphany to be able to shift not only their thinking about gender but also their behaviors, so that they may act as true allies for gender equity within their families, communities, and workplaces.

Within the experiential exercises, GERI workshops require the participants to relate and share their own life experiences with the patriarchy. This is a significant contrast to the academic or theoretical nature of DEI work in corporate setting workshops. GERI workshops, first and foremost, create a safe space, by way of engaging the participants gradually in moments of personal reflection, but equally as important through "sacred listening," whereby one is prompted to set aside their judgements and/or biases and to truly listen to others from the opposite gender, or to people of different gender identities. This, in effect, opens one's heart space and mind to feel and empathize with fellow participants in a way that many DEI workshops do not afford them. This collective experience eases and supports people to show up in a more vulnerable manner and creates opportunities to have breakthrough moments of enlightenment and growth.

Role play exercise in early GERI workshop, Holy Names University, Oakland, California, 2001

CHAPTER 15

GERI in Government and Politics

Whether they are stories of the pain of trauma, or stories of the pain of guilt—that is, whether we are victims, perpetrators or bystanders—we become co-participants in the process of witnessing, and we are moved to participate at a deeply personal level. … [It is] a process of "making public spaces intimate."
—Pumla Gobodo-Madikizela

"We have not even begun to deal with the gender issue here in South Africa!" exclaimed Nomfundo Walaza passionately. Nomfundo was our co-facilitator in a gender reconciliation workshop we were conducting in Cape Town. "We've made significant strides forward in terms of racial integration since apartheid ended, especially through the work of the Truth and Reconciliation Commission, despite its limitations. But we've barely scratched the surface on the massive issues between women and men in this country." Nomfundo was the director of the Desmond Tutu Peace Center in Cape Town, and her words echo what we have heard from other colleagues and friends in South Africa, most notably former Deputy Minister of Health, Nozizwe Madlala-Routledge.

Will Keepin first met Nozizwe in 2003, when she was Deputy Minister of Defence for South Africa. The two were introduced by Bernedette Muthien, an activist from South Africa who had trained in the GERI facilitator training. At the end of an intensive visionary meeting between Will and Nozizwe, she invited Gender and Equity Reconciliation International (GERI) to present our gender reconciliation training to an invited group of Members of Parliament (MPs) in South Africa. Nozizwe explained that unexamined gender dynamics between male and female MPs in the Parliament were significantly undermining the efficacy of their government service work. Despite the fact that women had come into Parliament in much greater numbers after apartheid ended, women still had comparatively little voice. Men largely ran the show and did most of the talking, and the women were marginalized and silenced—not intentionally so, but primarily out of longstanding cultural habit and norms over centuries. By inviting in the gender reconciliation process, Nozizwe sought to begin transforming gender relations in the Parliament, which she hoped might foster a similar transformation in the government, and eventually in the larger South African society.

The need for gender healing in South African society is profound. South Africa has one of the highest rates of sexual violence and gender-based violence anywhere in the world. Not only rape but domestic violence, sexual abuse, and sexual harassment in the workplace are also widespread in South African society. At the same time, South Africa is still a relatively young nation, only having ousted the terrorist apartheid government in 1994, and continues to grapple with the memories and deep trauma of this legacy. The AIDS crisis in South Africa has also been among the worst in the world. Within this larger cultural context, the political climate in Cape Town at the time of our workshop in 2006 included visible drama on several fronts directly relevant to gender work, including the recent passage of a same-sex civil union bill, a series of high-profile political sex scandals, and the AIDS crisis which was at its height, as described in more detail below.

Deputy Minister of Health Nozizwe Madlala-Routledge invited approximately 35 members of Parliament to the six-day workshop. Two days before it began, a highly visible sex scandal broke out when the Chief Whip of the ANC party was accused of sexual misconduct with a young female colleague. A volatile crisis emerged in the Parliament, which caused many of the MPs registered for our workshop to withdraw, to attend to the crisis. Nozizwe opened up the workshop to include leaders from other sectors, including the South African Council of Churches, women's organizations, NGOs, and parliamentary staff. In the end, there were 25 participants in the workshop, including 15 women and 10 men. All but one were either Black or "Colored," the non-pejorative term used in South Africa for persons of mixed race.

Facilitation Team

Given the inherent intensity of gender reconciliation work, plus the challenges of operating in the South African cultural context, it was important to have an abundance of highly skilled facilitators for this event. We had been informed beforehand that many of the participants belonged to the ANC and would likely have suffered imprisonment and/or torture under the apartheid regime. So we needed clinically trained staff on our team who were comfortable working with participants who might regress or become restimulated into past traumatic experiences. Quite beyond these clinical considerations, it was equally crucial to incorporate Black African facilitators in the mix and to have African consciousness and sensibilities integrated into our facilitation team. With these considerations in mind, we assembled a mixed-race facilitation team of exceptional capacity and multiple skill sets, including seasoned African leaders and activists, along with other GERI facilitators with clinical expertise. This gave us confidence going in that our team could handle whatever challenges might arise in the group.

Narrative Account of the Workshop for Members of Parliament

The first evening and full day of the workshop proceeded like most of our gender reconciliation events. The group began to grapple in earnest with gender injustice the second day when we showed the video clips. The silent witnessing exercise was especially powerful in this group, as participants witnessed the magnitude of gender injustice and suffering they had themselves directly experienced, much of it in relation to apartheid. It seemed that such an exercise was new to most participants, especially in a mixed group of women and men.

During the silent witnessing process, when the question was asked of the women, “Please stand if you have ever been hit, or physically abused, by a man,” one woman stood up, all by herself. Elana, a woman in her mid-fifties, explained later that by standing for this question, she had finally found a way to acknowledge her own story without actually having to tell it. Later, we learned that Elana had never

Deputy Minister of Health Nozizwe Madlala-Routledge convenes GERI workshop for Members of Parliament and other leaders, Cape Town, South Africa, 2006.

told her story to anyone before. Even in her women's circle over the years, if she spoke at all about this story, Elana had always referred to it as a friend's story, and never revealed it as her own. So this act of standing for this question was, in itself, a mini-breakthrough for Elana.

On the third day we did the holotropic breathwork process. Many participants had powerful experiences, awakenings, and insights during the breathwork, which served to deepen their participation in the workshop. The breathwork convened the "group soul" and strengthened the invisible glue of the community, as it so often does.

Elana had confided to the facilitators prior to the breathwork session that she was fearful that her abuse experience might come out during the breathing work. She said that she had suffered 30 years of abuse from her husband, which were very painful memories for her, and she seemed afraid of losing her protective shield over this part of her past. During the breathwork, Elana's abuse history did indeed resurface, and she followed the facilitators' guidance to keep breathing through it, and the facilitators worked with her closely. Elana had a powerful energetic experience with lots of tears over the two-hour session, which gradually shifted from tears of grief to tears of forgiveness and healing. Afterward, her eyes were shining, and Elana appeared to be in a place of release and peace. The next morning, when she arrived at the workshop, she said, "Today, I am a better person."

On the fourth day, we moved again into separate men's and women's circles, using the "Truth Mandala" process developed by ecologist Joanna Macy. Many poignant stories poured out into each of these circles, the majority of which came out again the following day in the cross-gender truth forums, so we will move on to describe the fifth day.

Women's Truth Forum

The women went first into the inner circle as the men took their seats quietly around them. After a brief invocation the women began to come forward with their stories and other sharings.

Dana, a Member of Parliament, recounted that her teenage daughter had been raped about one year earlier by two boys. One of the boys was HIV-positive. As a result, Dana's daughter was now HIV-positive. Dana had suspected that her daughter had brought this rape upon herself, assuming that her daughter must have been "sleeping around." However, when her daughter was in the hospital after the rape, Dana learned that she had been gravely mistaken, and that her daughter was a virgin when she was raped. Dana was absolutely devastated—by the horror of the rape, by her daughter becoming HIV-positive, and by her own mistrust of her daughter. "I am so angry with myself for not trusting my own daughter!" she kept repeating.

This story provided a poignant example of how the patriarchal system coerces and manipulates women into blaming themselves or each other for their victimization or traumatization, to such a degree that even a young girl's mother would blame her innocent daughter for "getting herself raped." Moreover, if a girl gets into trouble, it is seen as partly the mother's fault, which could also have been part of the reason for Dana's anger.

After Dana's story, several other women followed suit with their own stories—sometimes standing, sometimes crying, always with passion and sincerity. Some walked to the center of the circle to pick up the "talking Earth" (a miniature replica of the Earth), or one of the other icons from the previous day's Truth Mandala: the stone, dead leaves, empty bowl, shawl, or stick.

In many moments throughout the day the entire room was spellbound by what emerged. The previous day in the women's circle, Elana had shared part of her story. But now, in the cross-gender truth forum, she came forward with her full story. Elana's husband had beaten her and their children regularly. "To protect the children, I used to beg him, 'Hit me instead!' But he wouldn't listen." Later, her husband raped her, which produced their fourth child, a girl. Elana acknowledged that she hated this child because of the rape, which greatly saddened her heart.

At one point, Elana's husband moved another woman into their home to be his lover. He and the new woman lived downstairs, while Elana and her children were relegated to the upstairs, where they had to sleep in the toilet room because it was the only sleeping space available. Elana was forced to work and give all her money to her husband, and to do all the cooking and cleaning. She was basically a slave. "He would never listen to me! Never!" she exclaimed. Her husband would drag her downstairs at times to make her do things for him. Sometimes, in fits of rage, he would threaten to throw her babies off the balcony, with Elana down below desperately hoping she could catch them in her bare hands to save their lives.

As time wore on, Elana became increasingly desperate and miserable. One day she refused to give her husband the money she had earned because she needed it to buy shoes for the children. He flew into a rage and came at her with a knife. Elana was cooking sausages over a hot stove at that moment, and to thwart the imminent attack she reeled around and threw the sausages and hot grease on him. She also hit his live-in lover with the frying pan. Her husband was not wearing a shirt at the time, so his chest was burned. Elana served a jail sentence for this action, and she felt unjustly imprisoned for having defended herself against being potentially murdered. "I didn't know what else to do," she explained. After some time, her husband bailed her out of jail because he wanted her home earning money and doing the chores. The cycle of abuse set in again. It mellowed somewhat over time but never came to an end until her husband died several years later.

More stories emerged, and then Nomfundo moved into the center, picked up the stone, and began to speak about a 12-year-old girl she had treated at the trauma center. "This young girl was kidnapped, raped repeatedly, and then left to die in a grassy field near the Cape Town airport," she began slowly. "Early the next morning, an airport worker stumbled upon the girl lying in the tall grass." Nomfundo articulated her words with transparent anguish and precise diction. "She was naked, unconscious, covered with blood." Nomfundo held out the stone in front of her with both hands, as if asking it to absorb and bear the wrenching pain of the story. "The girl's body required surgical treatment to heal. Her sense of self and identity were completely obliterated by the experience. I've never treated anyone so utterly shattered."

As Nomfundo spoke, her eyes met the gaze of Kieran as he listened intently from his seat in the outer men's circle. Nomfundo moved toward the edge of the women's circle, reached out with both arms, and silently offered the stone to Kieran, as if to say, "Here, you take this. You are a man, and it was some of your male brothers who did this hideous violence to this girl. Please share in the horrific weight of this tragedy with us." Kieran received the stone and held it in his hands for some time while Nomfundo continued, then he silently handed the stone to the man next to him, who held it for a while and then passed it on. The stone slowly made its way around the silent men's circle.

Tears flowed copiously around the room, not only among the women. Several of the men had also been wiping their eyes, occasionally reaching for a tissue. When the stone was handed to Lloyd, he held it for a few moments, dissolved into tears, and then broke into loud sobbing. Given the strong taboo in South African culture against men crying in public, this was a remarkably poignant moment. The room was filled with a spellbound presence, infused with the sound of Lloyd's sobs. Two of the men moved over to join Lloyd at his side, offering hands of reassurance and support as he continued to weep. Nomfundo waited until Lloyd's crying subsided into sniffling before finishing her story.

As the women's truth forum came to a close, the men were given a chance to reflect back what they had heard. Many women reported how healing it was to hear men acknowledging the specific details of women's pain. At one point, Umoja stepped forward and placed his hands gently on each woman's back, in silent gratitude and acknowledgment.

Men's Truth Forum

In the afternoon, it was the men's turn in the inner circle, with the women in silent witness around them. To speak openly about personal experiences relating to gender, women, and sexuality was a highly unusual experience for South African men—indeed, this was a first for nearly all of them. The process of preparing the men to address gender issues in this plenary format was greatly enhanced by the men's Truth Mandala the day before, in which many powerful stories had come forth. Once a few of the men took the bold plunge, the way was made easier for the others.

Several of the men's individual sharings are summarized here briefly:

Isaac is an earnest young man with an angina heart condition that he's had since birth. He began by relating a painful story from three years previously. He was with his three closest friends one day when suddenly a gunfight broke out in the neighborhood where they were walking. Caught in the crossfire, he and his companions scrambled to get out of harm's way as shots rang out all around them. Two of his friends fell to the ground as bullets tore through their flesh. Isaac and his third friend made it, but his other two friends both died that day. Isaac had been devastated by the loss. His soulful eyes welled up with tears as he recounted the story.

Isaac spoke of his mother's response and advice to him about the tragic loss of his friends, which was to simply forget about them and move on. He shared other anecdotes about his mother: how she tried to raise him to be tough, "like a man," but it was against his intrinsic nature. He recounted a confrontation once with his brother in which he refused to fight. Overhearing this, his mother then instructed his brother to beat him up, which his brother proceeded to do. Isaac said the emotional pain of his mother's command to his brother was far greater than the physical pain of the beating itself.

Shortly before the workshop began, Kieran had shared his fear that as an American facilitation team we would come in with all the "answers" and do most of the talking. He referenced his frustration with trainers and facilitators from the United States in previous workshops he had done. He later told us he was pleased to find that we had come in not as experts but as learners.

Kieran opened his sharing by relating several childhood stories. Once, as a young boy, he had become frustrated with his sister while trying to put up a tent, and he started to hit her. He was supposed to stake down the tent, and he whacked her with the mallet, though not very hard, he said. For this he was beaten by his father—"hided until it drew blood," as he put it. "You *never* hit your sister, and you never hit a woman!" his father screamed at him. He was also beaten for childhood sex play.

Kieran holds strong views about the value and importance of gender work, which he articulated eloquently: "This work of gender reconciliation challenges the foundations of every major cultural institution in our society: the military, the church, the government, the corporations, the service professions, the educational system." Kieran paused, allowing the power of his words to sink in before continuing in his calm, confident voice. "In every case, these institutions are lopsided—conferring unfair advantages upon men. But, at a deeper level, these institutions are structured in an imbalanced manner, favoring masculine over feminine values, which is harmful to everyone in society. To embark upon this work of gender reconciliation is to rattle the very foundations of our society, across the board. It is absolutely essential work."

Kieran went on to give a specific example, describing how innocent young men are profoundly betrayed by the military system, an arena he knows well. In every nation state, he explained, the military system soaks up tender young men—so young they have barely left their childhood behind—and conditions them to reject their own innate intelligence and sensitivity as human beings. They are trained to kill, taught to not think for themselves, trained to reject anything "feminine" as intrinsically weak and inferior, conditioned to regard women as objects of sexual pleasure, and drilled to obey superiors' commands without reflection or consideration, no matter how insane or irrational. Their budding sexuality in particular is co-opted to serve military purposes, and their capacity for relational intimacy with women is severely impaired or destroyed. He said that the military system cannot function without this deep structural gender imbalance, which is imprinted ruthlessly and early in the young man's life—at a time when he is innocent, tender, impressionable, and not yet capable of standing on his own as an adult. In this way the young man's adult personality, mindset, and values are precisely molded to fit the needs of the military machine—and his humanity is betrayed. (This account seems akin to the testimony of traumatized masculinity from the U.S. Marine officer in Chapter 21, p. 308).

Other powerful stories continued to emerge in the men's truth forum. One man spoke about his adolescent sexuality, which entailed masturbation with pornographic pictures of girls in magazines. These experiences were deeply imprinted and were later projected onto his relationships with actual women, whose bodies he compared to the idealized pictures in the magazines. Another man shared that many years back he had carried on a secret affair during his first marriage. His wife had trusted him completely, and when the affair came to light she was totally shattered by the betrayal of trust. He concluded his story by saying that they had divorced, and she remarried another man. Although she and he had remained friends afterward, he said the experience had caused her lasting damage.

The men's truth forum came to a close, and the women were given a chance to reflect back what they had heard and what was stirred in them. Verena summarized the feeling of many women when she said, "Just hearing men acknowledge these things helps so much. That's all I ever really wanted from my husband: if only he could have acknowledged what he did."

At this moment, a beautiful process of reconciliation began to unfold spontaneously within the group. It started when one of the women remembered how warm and nurturing it had felt when Umoja placed his hands gently on her back at the end of the women's truth forum. Recalling this, she moved forward and placed her hands on one man's back. The other women followed suit, placing their hands on all the men's backs, one by one. The women began to sing softly—a beautiful South African chant. The men joined in, gently rocking, then stood up, turned around, and faced the women. Everyone continued singing in two concentric circles, which slowly began to rotate, with each woman making eye contact with each man, and vice versa. Radiant eyes and touching smiles filled everyone's hearts as the chant continued. It was an exquisite ritual of reconciliation, inspired naturally by the brave and beautiful work this group had accomplished together, and paved the way for honoring ceremonies the next day.

Men's Honoring Ceremony

The men went first and escorted the women into the room in pairs, carefully seating them in a semicircle. The women sat quietly, glancing at one another with quizzical looks as they surveyed the other end of the room, where the men had built a rather large, curious-looking structure. It was some sort of tower consisting of some twenty chairs, all carefully stacked and balanced, one upon the other. The structure took up more than a third of the room and reached nearly to the ceiling.

As the ritual opened for the women, the men announced that this tower of chairs represented the patriarchy. They proceeded to proclaim their commitment to dismantle and topple this oppressive structure—which holds both women and men in bondage to a system of oppression and injustice. The men then surrounded the tower of chairs. Reaching down in unison, each man pulled out one chair leg from the bottom simultaneously. The entire edifice of chairs came tumbling down with a resounding and dramatic *crash!* onto the floor. The skit was merely symbolic, but the power was impressive. There was an audible gasp from the women, who were moved by the dramatic symbolic gesture.

The men quickly straightened up the chairs, then lined up in a row and stood before the women. On behalf of all the men, Lloyd stepped forward and solemnly delivered the following declaration:

Declaration to Our Sisters:

Acknowledgment of Women's Pain and Struggles, and Our Commitment to Bring Down the Structures of Patriarchy

We have met over the past five days in community as men, and in community with you as men and women. We have listened to each other's stories—some personal, others told on behalf of vulnerable, degraded, hurt, brutalized human beings—all for no other reason than that they are women, sisters, mothers, and girl children.

We have heard, too, that through the social structures of power and decision making, many of our brothers have abused our intended roles of caring and protection—for selfish power, and personal pleasure and gain.

The bonds of humanity have been broken.

We acknowledge that we have shared in the unfair and unjust advantage that has upset the Creator's intended balance of human relationships for love, companionship, and cooperation.

We have been complicit in breaking the intended dream of equality.

So now we come forward to say to you: we are sorry. We affirm that we want to start anew. Therefore, we now mark our foreheads with ash—the dust from which we have come, and to which we shall return—as an act to symbolize our sorrow, our apology, and our atonement.

And we come with a willingness to express, not our guilt—because guilt weighs us down and gives a burden we cannot bear—but rather, our responsibility. So we ask, will you accept our offer to take responsibility, as we commit ourselves to live out—and challenge and support all men everywhere to live and work for—gender equality, and thereby seek reconciliation?

After this declaration was read, the men explained that they would like to invite each woman to have her hands washed and massaged, if she chose. The men lined up with bowls of water, towels, massage cream, and chocolates, and began singing a soft chant as they started gently washing, drying, and massaging the women's hands, rubbing in moisturizing cream, and finishing by giving the women chocolates. They continued in a row, tending carefully to each woman.

Afterward, the men lined up again before the women, and each man stepped forward, spoke to his personal complicity in the patriarchy, and offered his own commitment of personal action to end the unjust oppression of women. The men then brought closure to their ritual by bowing in silence before the women. They departed the room in silence.

Nearly 20 years have passed, and these men have kept their commitments to work for gender reconciliation; several remain engaged in GERI to this day.

Women's Honoring Ceremony

Deeply moved, the women sat quietly for several minutes, taking in the power of the men's ceremony.

A few minutes later, the women came out and escorted each man into the room, seating them carefully in a beautifully prepared circle. The light was dimmed, and stirring music was played as the women began a gorgeous dance of veils—each woman carrying one or more colorful, flowing veils of many different fabrics. The women began to weave in and out among the men, dancing ecstatically, whirling the veils around themselves and all around and between the men, draping them across the men's arms and legs and chests and sensuously sliding them across the men's faces and heads. The men sat enthralled with the colorful spectacle of dancing women, smiling eyes, and subtle sensuality as the women continued their dance for several minutes.

As Kieran remarked afterward, "The women became more and more beautiful as the workshop progressed!" This was even more true now as the women danced with magnificent grace and open-hearted joy, their eyes shining with radiance—unimpeded by fear, contraction, or judgment, offering their heart-to-heart blessings.

This phenomenon is something we have observed consistently over the years in facilitating gender reconciliation work. As the healing work progresses, and trust builds, the inner beauty of everyone is released and begins to shine out—sometimes tentatively at first, like the petals of a flower opening to the sun. But as the gender reconciliation work unfolds, the fragrance and resplendent color of the soul's beauty and inner light is gradually and inevitably revealed—an exquisite emanation of our true nature. And when this takes place, people begin to glimpse what a *huge* price we are paying for gender oppression in our daily socially-conditioned lives, in which this extraordinary beauty, strength, and intangible fragrance of our beloved fellow human beings is covered over by thick layers of social and cultural conditioning, so completely that most people have entirely forgotten that this inner beauty even exists.

After this sumptuous opening, the women stood in a circle alongside the men, and stepped forward, one at a time, each offering her personal testimony and commitment to the work we had all been doing.

The women concluded with a glorious African song, bringing closure to their ceremony. The men joined in, and the whole group was soon engulfed in joyous celebration of song and dance.

Integration and Closure

The final part of the workshop focused on integration, evaluation, and closure. Facilitators outlined some of the major challenges that can arise when shifting back into familiar work and family environments, and summarized practical ways to carry the new skills and insights back into daily life. To support the participants afterwards, several small groups were formed for participants to delve more deeply into the challenges of integration back into the workplace and home life.

The program concluded with a full closing council process, followed by a rousing final African song. The community dissolved into plenty of laughter, warm hugs, shining eyes, gentle tears, and deep gratitude, expressed in joyful reverie and intimacy. Everyone present knew that together, we had blazed a unique trail of gender reconciliation in South Africa. In our hearts, we all hoped that this joyous conclusion was actually the seed of an auspicious beginning for a new, unprecedented form of gender harmony and reconciliation in the great Rainbow Republic of South Africa.

Elana's Follow-up

Elana had come to a place of deep forgiveness by the end of the workshop, and she said she didn't feel hate anymore. Her entire demeanor had changed, and she said she felt her story of abuse was finally out of her.

In a women's circle two days after the workshop, Elana recounted her follow-up story. The day after the workshop she went to visit her husband's grave, and there she was able to forgive him for all the abuse. Afterward, she decided to visit the home of his former lover (the woman who had moved into her home downstairs), with whom she had had no contact whatsoever for many years. When Elana knocked, the woman answered the door in a wheelchair. Elana explained that she had come because she wanted to forgive her. The woman was very grateful for this gesture from Elana, and invited her in. She told Elana that she had been thinking of her intensely over the past several days, and she explained that she believed the reason she was now in a wheelchair was because of all that she had done to her. The two women had a remarkable healing conversation. Elana was able to forgive her, and felt deeply released and free afterwards.

Elana had returned to work the next day and was visibly radiant and peaceful. When her boss began discussing work matters early on her first day back, Elana interjected, "You didn't even ask about the workshop!" Her boss smiled and replied, "You don't have to tell us about the workshop. We can see it on your face!" Elana explained that all her coworkers commented on how different she looked. Then her boss inquired, "Do tell us about the workshop, please." Elana began speaking about the workshop, and she said the ensuing conversation with her colleagues was so engrossing that it lasted nearly six hours, until well into the afternoon.

This workshop was a watershed event for GERI in South Africa. We stayed in contact with a number of the participants over the years, and some of the male participants subsequently became leaders in the gender reconciliation work. This workshop led to many further invitations to introduce GERI programs across the country, which kept GERI busy for years, and eventually led to the founding of GenderWorks in 2012. GenderWorks is a South African non-profit organization that delivers GERI programs and trainings in southern and eastern Africa and is continuing to expand and flourish to this day.

Destructive AIDS Policy in South Africa Is Reversed

Another remarkable story from this workshop relates to the South African AIDS crisis, which was at its height in the years leading up to this program in 2006. As the AIDS epidemic mounted in South Africa, then President Thabo Mbeki denied the scientific consensus and vehemently insisted that HIV was not the cause of AIDS. His government policy effectively banned antiretroviral (ARV) drugs for most HIV and AIDS patients, despite the fact that ARVs were freely offered to South Africa and had proven highly effective in slowing the growth of the HIV virus.

Mbeki's policy was an unmitigated disaster. Deaths from AIDS skyrocketed, and by 2005 an estimated 900 people were dying daily. Archbishop Desmond Tutu compared the loss to a mid-air collision between two fully loaded Boeing 747 jumbo jets every day. Both Tutu and Nelson Mandela urgently implored President Mbeki to abandon his AIDS policy, but Mbeki would not budge. A study from the Harvard University School of Public Health estimated that in the period from 2000 to 2005, Mbeki's policy was directly responsible for more than 330,000 unnecessary deaths from AIDS in South Africa.[1]

Deputy Minister of Health Nozizwe Madlala-Routledge conducted her own investigation into the AIDS crisis and advocated introducing ARV drugs into South Africa. Mbeki's swift response was to silence her, and for over two years she was prohibited from speaking or doing any further research on HIV/AIDS. Her superior, the Minister of Health "Manto" Tshabalala-Msimang, was vehemently supportive of Mbeki's policies.

A Quaker and pacifist, Nozizwe had previously been the Deputy Minister of Defence, and during her tenure she transformed the mission of the South African military to a peacekeeping force. She and her husband Jeremy had been strong activists against Apartheid, and she was imprisoned three times, and spent a year in solitary confinement without a trial. She later became Deputy Minister of Health. Because of the major challenges she faced with the AIDS crisis and being silenced, the GERI program for MPs was repeatedly delayed. At that time, we had no knowledge of all that Nozizwe was going through, because she was extremely discreet about sharing sensitive political matters with outsiders. There were long periods of no contact, as she struggled mightily with her challenges, but each time we were able to reach Nozizwe, she remained determined. It took three and a half years until the GERI program was finally conducted in November 2006.

During the GERI program (summarized above), we conducted two sessions of holotropic breathwork. Nozizwe was a practical person and seasoned politician, and when she heard us introduce the breathwork process, she confided with Will Keepin privately that this process would not likely be effective for her, but she agreed to give it a try. Nozizwe's breathwork session was relatively "quiet" outwardly. Afterwards, when Will checked in with her, she said only that during the process she'd had an experience involving the mother of a colleague.

"African Minister Ends Decade of Denial on AIDS"

Two weeks later, on World AIDS Day (December 1, 2006), the newspaper headlines read as quoted above. Nozizwe Madlala-Routledge officially repudiated President Mbeki's AIDS policy, announced a bold and sweeping reversal of South Africa's AIDS policy, and committed billions of Rand for a new treatment campaign to make ARV drugs widely available.[2] She overturned President Mbeki's AIDS policy, declaring it a "serious violation of human rights." For this, Nozizwe was hailed as a hero in South Africa and in the wider international community. The treatment campaign she launched remains intact today as one of the most successful in Africa, and Nozizwe is credited with saving untold thousands of lives.

President Mbeki was enraged, and eight months later he fired Nozizwe on a specious pretext.[3] This caused a public outcry, and public support for Nozizwe increased dramatically, and declined for Mbeki, contributing to his forced resignation from the presidency in September 2008.

Nozizwe soon became Deputy Speaker of the National Assembly (equivalent to Parliament). In 2009 she gave a keynote speech at a conference on Patriarchy in South Africa,[4] where she spoke about the transformative power of the Gender Equity and Reconciliation process. At the end of her formal speech, Nozizwe put her notes aside and spoke on a more personal and intimate level. She said that, during the Gender Reconciliation program, she had had a remarkable and unbidden visionary experience during a breathwork exercise.

The mother of President Thabo Mbeki appeared to her in a vision. She explained that this was not a dream; Nozizwe was fully alert and awake, and the sense of the presence of Epainette Mbeki (mother of Thabo) was vivid and palpable, even though Nozizwe had never actually met her in person. In this vision, Nozizwe saw a reversal of roles between mother and grown son, where the President shrank in stature to a small boy, and his mother expanded greatly, towering above him.

As the vision continued, a remarkable forthright exchange ensued between Nozizwe and Mbeki's mother, who expressed great love for her son and said she was proud of him as President in many ways. But on the AIDS issue, she said that she and Nozizwe both knew he was woefully mistaken. She gave Nozizwe a firm message of empowerment and admonition to challenge her son. As his mother, she said that she knew Thabo inside and out, and although he was well-intentioned, she also knew very well his stubbornness and manipulative tactics. She admonished Nozizwe not to be intimidated by the President or his antics, and not to be afraid to challenge him and repudiate his disastrous AIDS policy. Nozizwe recounted that this "visitation" from President Mbeki's mother was the needed impetus that gave her the courage and final determination to openly defy the President and overturn his AIDS policy.

The Zulu name "Nozizwe" means "mother of nations." In Nozizwe's breathwork session, the mother of the President called upon the "mother of nations" to defy the President of the nation, thereby saving countless lives among the people of the nation. It was an exquisite example of feminine wisdom speaking truth to patriarchal power.

GERI Testimony in the Parliament of South Africa

In November 2011, a delegation of GERI leaders was invited to give testimony in the National House of Traditional Leaders in the Parliament of South Africa. The GERI delegates—Dorothea Hendricks, Jabu Mashinini, Judy Bekker, Judy Connors, and William Keepin—testified about the implementation of gender reconciliation work in South African communities through the South African affiliate organization GenderWorks. Dorothea Hendricks was the first to give her testimony to the House:

> I bid you greetings, and I pray that your work, and the work we also do, will be blessed by God and by our ancestors.
>
> It is an immense honor to be here today. Gender is a topic which is close to everybody's heart. So much goes wrong, and yet so much can go right as well. We are engaged in a work called Gender Reconciliation, which is a valuable tool, and we believe it could support the work that

you are doing back home in your constituencies as well.

I'm a therapist, but gender reconciliation is not a therapy—it's an incredibly deep journey that begins with a three-day immersion experience in which you begin to listen deeply in new ways, and hear things that probably you have never heard before. In particular, you hear rarely-spoken truths from men, and from women, on what their respective life experiences have actually been, and how our gender roles and gender energies affect one another.

Gender reconciliation has given me the lived experience of a world in which people can deeply respect each other. If you've had bad or difficult gender experiences, for example, in this forum you're able to share your story, and also to learn what the experience has been for the other gender. It's a forum where, for many people, they begin this journey from a place of brokenness, perhaps sharing traumas, or coming from diverse cultures or faiths, and then they are able to really be there for one another, and hear the different accounts of what people have actually experienced.

We have been training both young and mature people in this work, and we believe that these gender reconciliation initiatives can be delivered in schools, to young people, to professional people, urban people, rural people. It has been an amazing journey; it's been the most sacred experience for me to go through. I have never, for example, even as a therapist, thought that it's possible for people to find healing where gender issues and gender energy have gone wrong. Yet this is what I have consistently experienced in this program.

Judy Bekker then spoke about implementation of the GERI work in local communities,

> Part of the GenderWorks intention is to create a community of facilitators who go into their own communities and deliver this work. We are a growing body of facilitators and trainers, as well as a community of people who participate in these gender reconciliation programs. This work provides forums for men and women of all ages, all persuasions or religions, all backgrounds, to deeply hear each other. We listen, we share, we practice certain skills that help us improve our communication and the way we are together. We

> also play and laugh, and there's a building of community that happens. Invariably, men and women who go through these workshops come out with a greater sense of understanding of each other, and actually have a sense of release in having been able to exchange and share in ways that would normally not happen.

Jabu Mashinini spoke to the House about the unique approach of the GERI program, and the importance of working with women and men together,

> This work [GERI] is different from any other gender work that is mostly happening in various institutions. When we hear of group work related to gender, it's usually women or men working separately. If it's men's organizations, we hear either how men should behave differently towards women, or that the men are off working by themselves. And with women's organizations, we hear how women need to get their human rights back, or we hear statistics of wrongdoing by the other gender towards women. Although such work has its place, with both sides, one side doesn't know what the other is doing. What is different about this GERI work is that we work with both men *and* women together, and it's about healing, not blame.

In her testimony, Judy Connors brought forward several key reflections from recent participants in local GERI workshops, recounting in their own words how the program had touched their lives.

> One of the key results we find is that men and women begin to understand one another better. For example, one young man said at the end of this work, "I'm glad to have seen women speaking from their heart about the way they've been violated, because I myself as a man have done many of these things, and today I'm aware of the pain that I have caused." Another woman said, "I used to hate every man. But now as a result of this work, I'm a new person, and I've learned that not all men are the same, and I respect men."
>
> We also find that both men and women begin to get a better understanding of themselves, and become more accountable. For example, one woman said, "Even though I wanted to get back at men because I'm very angry with them, I realized that this work is not about getting back at men, it is about rectifying my wrongdoings, and I have

stopped hurting people's feelings, particularly men."

One man said, "My valuable learning was that you don't need to be tough to be a man, but you need to take full responsibility for your acts, and be man enough to accept your role."

An important question naturally arises: What happens *after* these trainings, when people go back home? It's fine to learn something, but what do people actually do with these new insights and knowledge? Some of our participants have said very beautiful things about this:

One person said, "I now spend more time with my family, and we have a more open and respectful relationship." Another man was very honest, and simply said, "Well, I have stopped beating my girlfriend." And finally, there was a story that shows the power of how men can influence other men, "One day I came home and I found my neighbor's wife sitting outside the door. She had been beaten up by her husband. I intervened and spoke to the husband, and told him that this is not the way to solve family problems, that he should instead talk with his wife, and he agreed. The situation improved after that."

"I have been looking for a long time to find a way to bring healing and reconciliation between women and men here in South Africa," Nozizwe told us after the workshop for Members of Parliament. "This work is the answer," she concluded. "We need much more of this work in South Africa."

One of Nozizwe's important insights that led her to invite the GERI program for Members of Parliament (MP) was that mere gender parity in government was not adequate for deeper social change. Today, 46 percent of the MPs are female in South Africa, which is second in Africa only to Rwanda, which has 61 percent females in Parliament. Even with nearly half of the MPs as women, the actual gender dynamics between women and men had not changed. This insight extends to other government organizations and bodies, including those that are already working towards gender justice, or have already achieved a seeming level of equality or parity. Without transforming gender dynamics *between* women and men, gender parity often either compromises women and replicates dysfunctional and imbalanced gender dynamics, or else forces assimilation into male structures and styles of power and influence, leaving the roots of gender oppression intact.

Gender reconciliation work has broad applicability in the political arena. Just as working across gender differences offers extraordinary potential for transformative healing across religions divisions, it also has strong potential for transcending and healing across deep political divisions, even in situations of highly charged political conflicts (as recounted in the final chapter of this book). In political climates such as the United States, which is increasingly polarized and gridlocked today, the gender angle may offer a breakthrough across the aisle, allowing representatives to meet in their shared struggles, heartbreaks, and aspirations as women and men.

Perhaps the most glaring indication of the vast need for gender reconciliation in politics is the many recent sex scandals in politics, which were highlighted by the #MeToo movement, yet have been a persistent problem long before and since. In 2017-2018 alone, in the United States, there were high-profile sex scandals involving nine different U.S. Congressional Representatives, one U.S. Senator, two Federal Judges, three Executive Branch leaders, and other leading politicians in 29 U.S. states. This is according to a Wikipedia article, which is not a definitive legal record, and many of these allegations have been contested, or are still pending. Nevertheless, the issue is very real, and in many cases there are non-disclosure agreements (NDAs) in place, often involving large sums of money to keep the details quiet, which makes it all the more difficult to assess the full extent and impact of this challenge.

Beyond the high-profile cases, there are also many less visible challenges of sexual harassment and exploitation, microaggressions, and various forms of toxic gender dynamics in the workplace generally, and in politics in particular, which create substantial suffering. These dynamics can be processed in a skillful forum of gender reconciliation, or at least mitigated to a significant degree, which also helps create a safer workplace environment where these challenges arise less often, and can be skillfully addressed when they do.

We have experimented with applying the GERI methodology to other arenas of political or organizational conflict, with encouraging preliminary results. In one case, we conducted a daylong dialogue workshop with a group of about 15 Palestinians and Israeli Jews, evenly divided, who live in the vicinity of Boulder, Colorado. The GERI methods were adapted for this context, and the results were encouraging. Participants from both "sides" reported coming away with a better understanding of the real issues, and a deeper empathy or sensitivity to the challenges experienced by the other side.

In another case, we applied the GERI methodology to a conflict within the environmental activist community, again in Colorado. One party to the conflict was a group of environmental scientists, lawyers, and policy analysts, all of whom were highly educated and lived in the "front range" bigger cities (Denver, Boulder, etc.). Most of them worked full time and lived in nice suburbs, making comfortable salaries. The other party to the conflict was a group of dedicated environmental activists who lived in the mountainous "Western slope" region of western Colorado. They tended to be modestly educated, and were usually paid less, often for part-time work, and many held multiple or part-time jobs. This was partly a class conflict, as well as a division of labor conflict.

Each party was convinced, although it was never spoken out loud, that they were the ones doing the "real" environmental work, and they felt unappreciated and taken for granted by their colleagues on the other side. The "Western slope" activists lived "in the field" close to the sites where the environmental abuses were actually taking place (such as factories polluting rivers, or clear-cut logging, etc.). They were the ones chaining themselves to trees, or facing down bulldozers with their physical bodies, risking life and limb in direct action campaigns intended to stop environmental destruction at its source. Meanwhile the "front range" activists were the ones conducting detailed environmental damage assessments, developing campaign strategies and priorities, engaging in court battles, raising funds, and flying back and forth to Washington and New York to liaise with the national environmental organizations and philanthropic funders.

We adapted the GERI methodology to this context. In the truth forums, the Western slope activists were in the center first, with the front range people in silent witness in the outer circle. These roles were then reversed. Each party had ample time to fully air their perspectives and grievances, and their aspirations for change—without being interrupted. This process alone was immensely helpful, and people on both sides were feeling good that they had gotten their truth out on the table. But the real magic came later. We separated the two groups again and gave them a new task they didn't expect. Each group had to focus, in detail, on what they truly appreciated and valued about the work of the *other* group, and the individual people in the other circle. After an hour of brainstorming on this theme in separate groups, we had the groups come back and repeat the two concentric circles, each group sharing what they valued and appreciated about the other. This melted the hearts of the entire community, as each group realized how crucial the tireless efforts of the other group was to their overall mission, and also that every role and each individual person was essential to the larger success of their work. Many new realizations and insights emerged, awakening deeper understanding and empathy all around. We then closed by having each group create a simple honoring ceremony for the other, which was easy at this point, and the end result was celebration and festivities much loved by all.

Most people, even coming from vastly different political positions or spiritual orientations, are able to connect heart to heart in gender reconciliation work. The process works well with liberals, and equally well with conservatives and traditionalists—all of whom can relate to gender conditioning and can usually access compassion and sensitivity across the gender gap. Of course the process is not always straightforward in practice, and significant obstacles do arise at times that require seasoned facilitation and strong spiritual presence, which are skills that are cultivated and practiced intensively in the GERI facilitator training program.

We have applied these same principles in other contexts with senior government officials in the Federal government and in state agencies in the United States, for which purpose we developed a focused set of "Principles of Spiritual Activism."[5] These principles have found wide application, and were adopted by the Pachamama Alliance as part of their curriculum for their innovative *Awakening the Dreamer* training.[6] Given sufficient dedication and commitment among the participants involved, gender reconciliation work carries a strong inherent potential to transform ruinous divisions within a community and unite their collective hearts into an experience of unity and deep mutual appreciation. This in turn can go a long way toward building a healthy political group, organization, or movement.

We close this chapter with a highlighted section from Nozizwe Madlala-Routledge.

A Practical Methodology for Uniting Women and Men in the Struggle for Freedom from Patriarchy

Nozizwe Madlala-Routledge

I first became aware of the need for gender equality and the liberation of women in the early 1980s when I was supported to serve as chairperson of the Natal Organisation of Women in Durban, South Africa. I say supported because it was a collaborative effort under shared leadership.

I then went on to serve as Managing Secretary of the sub-Council on the Status of Women of the Transitional Executive Council (TEC). The TEC prepared the way for the transition in South Africa after Apartheid, including levelling the playing field for South Africa's first non-racial democratic elections. Our job was to help facilitate the participation of women in the elections and to make recommendations on how to improve the status of women. I then chaired the ANC Women's Parliamentary Caucus and the Multi-Party Women's Group in the first democratic Parliament of South Africa.

I first came across Will Keepin, and later Cynthia Brix, when I was Deputy Minister of Defence, and we discussed the possibility of gender reconciliation programs for Members of Parliament in South Africa. Later when I was Deputy

Minister of Health, I helped organize a GERI workshop for Parliamentarians with Will and Cynthia and their facilitation team. The need for the work was ironically highlighted when a case of gender violence surfaced in Parliament the very week we had organized the six-day program, and most of the Members of Parliament (MPs) we had invited had to withdraw to urgently attend meetings to address the incident of gender violence in Parliament itself. Fortunately, we were able to recruit leaders in the NGO community to fill the gaps.

What I heard and experienced in the GERI workshops was transformative in bringing women and men together to jointly listen and be witness to how patriarchy as a system of male dominance negatively impacted the lives of women and men. I saw that we have a tool that can address patriarchy and unite women and men in a struggle for freedom from the shackles that bind both men and women. I have been able to continue my connection with Will and Cynthia over the years including inviting them to facilitate a workshop for an interfaith network of peacemakers (Tanenbaum Center), which highlighted the need for gender transformation in all sectors of society.

We were also able to make use of GERI workshops in Embrace Dignity, the NGO my husband Jeremy and I had founded to transform the oppressive patriarchal system of prostitution. Using the methodology developed by GERI, we invited men to listen to the survivors of the system of prostitution to share their painful experience of its harms.

GERI has grown and established itself globally as a part of the effort to end gender based violence and oppression, thanks to collective effort led by Will and Cynthia and the GERI leaders over the years. I am now leading the Quaker United Nations Office in Geneva and hope our paths of collaboration will cross here as well.

Nozizwe Madlala-Routledge is the former Deputy Minister of Defence (1999-2004) in South Africa, and former Deputy Minister of Health (2007-2007). She is currently Director of the Quaker United Nations Office in Geneva.

CHAPTER 16

GERI at the United Nations

Gender inequality is the overwhelming injustice of our age and the biggest human rights challenge we face. Patriarchy is not easily defeated.... I ask you to hold us to our promises. Do not let us in the UN off the hook. Keep our feet on the fire.
—António Guterres, Secretary-General of the United Nations

This chapter summarizes a series of trainings that Gender Equity and Reconciliation International conducted for the United Nations (UN) community and affiliated organizations. Gender equality is a key priority of the UN, which established in 2015 a set of 17 Sustainable Development Goals (SDGs), designed to serve as a "blueprint to achieve a better and more sustainable future for all." Goal No. 5 is specifically Gender Equality, which is described as "not only a fundamental human right, but a necessary foundation for a peaceful, prosperous and sustainable world."[1]

Every year since 2015, GERI presents a session at the NGO forum of the UN conference of the Commission on the Status of Women (CSW), held in mid-March each year in New York City. These sessions consist of a brief overview of GERI, followed by introductory experiential exercises to give the delegates who attend a taste of the GERI process itself. These events provide a unique opportunity to introduce GERI's work to a broad range of gender equality leaders and activists engaged in the larger UN community.

In 2019 a new series of GERI trainings was initiated for the UN community, in collaboration with the UN Committee on Spirituality, Values, and Global Concerns, chaired by Ken Kitatani, who was our chief collaborator in convening the first three-day intensive UN GERI training. Ken Kitatani provides a summary outline of this training in the special highlighted section below. Other collaborators and co-sponsors of this program included the Forum 21 Institute, Beth Blissman of the Loretto Community at the UN, the ManKind Project USA, and the Nathan Cummings Foundation. Additional key players who helped bring about this UN GERI series include Jon Levitt, Paul Samuelson, and Julien Devereux, all of the ManKind Project.

A second UN GERI training was conducted in December 2019, in which we collaborated closely with co-organizer Saphira Rameshfar, who had attended the first

UN GERI training. Saphira serves on the Executive Committee of the NGO Committee on the Status of Women in New York, and is also a UN Representative of the Bahá'í International Community to the United Nations. Venues were graciously provided free of charge by The Sukyo Mahikari Center for Spiritual Development for the first training, and the Bahá'í International Center at UN Plaza for the second.

The following highlighted section is by Ken Kitatani, who is Director of the Forum 21 Institute, and was formerly Chair of the UN Committee on Spirituality, Values, and Global Concerns. The Forum 21 Institute has engaged with UN specialized agencies, governments (UN member states), accredited civil society organizations, and academic institutions—focusing on the intersection between ethics, values and sustainable development. It has made consistent efforts to introduce values and ethics into the UN Sustainable Development Goals (SDGs) in various ways.

Gender Equity Reconciliation International (GERI) at the United Nations

Ken Kitatani

As a close friend, colleague, and collaborator with Gender Equity and Reconciliation International and its founders William Keepin and Cynthia Brix, it gives me great pleasure to share my reflection on the first GERI training that was carried out in 2019 with the United Nations (UN) community.

Gender equity, gender balance and gender justice are an important part of the United Nations Sustainable Development Goals (SDGs) in many ways. There is also an inextricable connection between gender imbalance and climate change, as shown by the work of Women In Need International (WIN). For gender equality, the UN Commission on the Status of Women (CSW) plays an important role, functioning as the UN organ that promotes gender equality and the empowerment of women. Likewise, there are many gender-related initiatives that various UN agencies carry out in order to promote gender equity.

At the same time, it cannot be denied that the UN is struggling with many gender-based issues such as sexual harassment incidents within its own ranks, some of which were high profile cases reported in mainstream media like the *New York Times*[2] and CNN.[3] The #MeToo movement has only heightened scrutiny, and UN Secretary General Antonio Guterres has made this a top priority in the UN.

Regular sexual harassment trainings are conducted by all agencies within the UN and staff members are required to attend such trainings. Despite these efforts, staff members will privately say that it hasn't helped resolve the fundamental cause of gender bias, discrimination, and harassment. Perhaps this is because such trainings focus primarily on the legal and procedural aspects of sexual misconduct (symptomatic therapy), and not on the holistic approach that is grounded in ethics and values (causal therapy).

The Gender Equity and Reconciliation International training has had global success in various stakeholder settings and is endorsed and promoted by notable figures such as the late Archbishop Desmond Tutu. When Will and Cynthia approached me with the idea of carrying out a GERI training with the UN community, I thought that it would provide a golden opportunity to bring together many people from the different sectors of the UN and work together in a very profound way. Together with a team of colleagues from the UN civil society and professional staff of the UN, we reached out to as many representatives of the UN community as we could, inviting them to join us in the GERI training.

The three-day GERI training was very successful in many ways. It achieved what the training set out to do; enable all participants to experience a transformational change deep within themselves. It allowed participants to question the fundamental existential questions of life such as, "What is gender?" "What am I?" "How do these different perceptions and understanding of gender play out in my daily life and society as a whole?" "How are gender issues related to other issues of society, such as racial injustice?" and so on.

The training resulted in each individual leaving with a deep sense of respect for oneself and every other participant, being freed from the intellectual and emotional shackles bound to categorizations such as gender—male or female or otherwise—that have been instilled in us since our birth. It also instilled a new vision and practical hope for actually achieving gender equality. For example, Saphira Rameshfar, Executive Committee Member of the UN NGO Committee on the Status of Women (NGO CSW/NY), summarized her experience as follows:

> The GERI training brought to light for me the power of understanding, and how central the role of unity is in advancing the work of gender equality. At the international level, there is an attitude of "fighting" for women's rights, which is important, and I am grateful for the gains won by those who have gone before us. Yet, to push us to the next stage of development, our ends must be

coherent with our means. If we are working for a world that is based on understanding, justice and love, then the way that we get there needs to be characterized by these qualities.

Women and men must come together to design a new structure, to create a new culture in which all can flourish, and the foundation of this process must be trust and understanding. The GERI training created the safe space to hear one another, to strive for insights and compassion, to work on our individual transformation, and to commit to building a new gender-equal civilization together, in unity. It is a unique space, unlike any other I have participated in. A must for anyone committed to the work of gender equality.

Secondly, the success of the training was proof that a new door had opened—a door to gender reconciliation in the UN community. All of the participants who were part of the UN community felt inspired and emboldened to take this method of GERI to all parts of the UN.

Since this training, a second training was carried out and presentations made at the CSW conferences. GERI continues to grow and spread in the UN community.

I will continue to support and wish for the further growth and success of GERI within the UN community, and will remain forever grateful to the leaders of GERI for guiding us on the path of gender reconciliation.

Ken Kitatani
Director, Forum 21 Institute

Several reflections are offered below from some of the other organizers and attendees in this program.

The first is from Beth Blissman, who is the Representative to the UN for the Loretto Community and serves as evaluator and consultant for numerous educational and non-profit initiatives in social and ecological justice.

At the 2018 Parliament of the World's Religions in Toronto, Canada, my friend Ken Kitatani called my attention to a session by a group called Gender Equity Reconciliation International (GERI). "Check out this session," he said, "you'll like what these people are doing." Indeed, I was impressed by that session where I witnessed the potential of men and women talking openly and honestly about the possibility of ending thousands of years of oppression and cultural conditioning, in short: ending patriarchy.

The following week I was invited to a meeting with the GERI founders to brainstorm future possibilities. The day we met happened to be my birthday, and it felt like a new birth indeed, as we shared ideas of how to assist the United Nations in fulfilling its promises of a better world for all.

Our first collaboration was on a parallel event during the 2019 Commission on the Status of Women entitled "Breakthrough in Transforming Patriarchy: The Promise of Gender Equity and Reconciliation." At this event, Phil Vivirito, GERI Trainer, and Chaya Pamula, GERI board member, presented the GERI methodology in an engaging and active session attended by 19 women and men. One participant observed "I was surprised and amazed at the power of simply being witnessed," following the short experiential taste of the GERI process. Another woman shared her realization of the gender-based lack of safety she had felt throughout her life, and her re-energized vision for a safe and gender-healed world.

Even before the CSW event in March 2019, those of us who had gathered in November 2018 sensed that GERI's work might provide those of us working as representatives of non-governmental organizations (NGOs) at the United Nations, as well as UN staff and governmental delegates, with deep insight into new tools for disentangling ourselves from patriarchy through healing and reconciliation.

So, several of our organizations co-sponsored an invitational training with Ken Kitatani of the U.N. Committee for Spirituality, Values, and Global Concerns (CSVGC) in May 2019 entitled "MeToo to WeTogether: Reconciling Relations Between Women and Men." The training was designed specifically to facilitate skillful forms of mutual healing, respect, and creative collaboration and partnership across the gender divisions in society.

There were 29 of us together, all willing to jointly confront the challenge presented by the #MeToo movement. We shared our gender stories, discovered ways for women and men to reconcile gender relations, and envisioned possibilities to collaborate together in seeking a world where the Divine feminine and masculine were valued equally.

At that training, it literally made my heart sing to meet and journey with leaders from the ManKind Project who are dedicating their lives to educating and supporting other men to build higher emotional intelligence and begin healing from past trauma limiting their lives. After three days of GERI exercises, rituals and deep sharing, all participants seemed lighter, happier, connected, and feeling a bit more hopeful and whole.

We convened a second "MeToo to WeTogether" GERI training in New York City in December 2019, in which we experienced glimpses of how the work of GERI is essential for the UN to meet its gender equality goals. Historically, the UN has not only struggled with providing equality for women, but it has also not been tremendously supportive of LGBTQ+ individuals. As someone who arrived in New York as an "out" lesbian woman serving as a UN Representative for a faith-based community, I've been witness to much pain in both religious and secular settings due to a lack of understanding of sexual orientation and gender identity by those in positions of power. I'm grateful that GERI offers focused programs for LGBTQ+ and BIPOC communities, as so many cultures around the world awaken to the multiple factors of human advantage and disadvantage (such as race, ethnicity, class, sexual orientation, gender identity, religion, physical ability, age, etc.) and how they intersect. These intersecting and overlapping social identities may be both empowering and oppressing, depending on the situation, and it's high time that we discussed them honestly in safe spaces.

As the #MeToo movement continues to unmask the long-hidden exploitation and harassment of half of humanity, it is clear that neither women nor men (nor people who identify outside the gender binary) can resolve this crisis on their own. There is currently an urgent need for profound transformation in gender relations between men, women, and gender non-conforming persons in our society and around the globe. My colleagues and I were grateful to share about GERI's innovative methodologies at another workshop we gave entitled "Educating for Gender Justice: Stepping Stone to achieving the UN Sustainable Development Goals (SDGs)," at a conference hosted by the UN Department of Global Communications in August 2019.

I deeply appreciate the GERI approach because it's not about one-sided solutions, or women *versus* men, but it is a rapidly growing movement for people of all gender identities to vision what an inclusive, just, gender-healed future might look like. This approach is quite consonant with the UN SDGs and the UN slogan of shaping the #WorldWeWant: "If we don't dream it, we'll never do it." (I often say to myself: "If I don't dream it, I'll never do it.") So, it was a true gift to find GERI and the opportunity for us all to dream a better future for ourselves and all life on Earth.

We live in a unique moment in our cultural evolution, and it's prime time for men and women and people of all gender identities to be working together—co-creating new pathways of relational integrity among the sexes.

This next reflection comes from a woman who attended the second GERI training with UN collaborators. She shares how her heart was opened through the process and how she left with a renewed hope for gender relations.

When I first heard about the Gender Equity and Reconciliation training, I knew I wanted to be involved. I joined a three-day program held at the United Nations. I couldn't believe how dramatically people were transformed in such a short time. By working through a carefully curated series of experiences, we were able to see our own gender biases and move past them. I was most affected listening to the trauma inflicted on cisgender men, which often began at an early age. After my first three-day training, I felt my heart open toward men and a deep empathy flowed through me. I could no longer witness the damage inflicted on women because of gender stereotypes and limitations without also seeing how men suffered under the same toxic, patriarchal system.

My heart opened after hearing honest testimony from men about how they'd been taught to shut down their feelings of vulnerability and had often been bullied and in other ways pressured to deny parts of themselves. I saw broken boys inside the men, and realized how we are *all* victims of a system that needs to change. I believe my future relationships with men have been forever changed, and I left the training feeling more hopeful about finding a healthy intimate partnership.

The GERI methodology is a way to shift people's perspectives on gender that is powerful and long lasting. I was personally changed by the training. I knew I was in capable hands from the first moment of the program; I felt I was being nurtured and that the space created for the work was safe. Considering how emotional and traumatic people's experiences can be around gender, I was impressed with how the facilitators handled the material and the participants, who came from many different backgrounds. I've now been involved with GERI as a facilitator and I see that the program works in different countries, too. When it comes to gender conditioning, we have more in common across the globe than we may realize.

In this same training was a senior leader in men's work, with decades of experience facilitating men's circles. He was deeply moved by the training. As he later recounted,

Afterwards I shared with my wife about the training, and about hearing so many painful and harrowing experiences that the women in particular had gone through. I said to my wife how grateful I was that she had not had to go through these kinds of traumatic experiences. She looked at me like I was a crazy man, and said, "What are you talking about? Of course I have!" And I said, "Well, you never mentioned any of these things before." This led us into a whole new conversation together, in which she told me things that had happened to her that she had never told me before—in 30+ years of marriage! My jaw was dropping from some of it. This further ignited my passion and determination to take action and help change this dysfunctional gender legacy we've all been subjected to.

Another senior leader in men's work, who participated in both UN trainings, reflected:

After thirty years of exploration and work with women and men in human development, personal growth and expansion into issues of inclusion, equity and belonging, Gender Equity and Reconciliation provided me a profound depth of insight into the lived experience of women and men. The exquisitely constructed witnessing spaces and exercises allowed me to deepen and unfold, listen and understand, awaken and remember the experiences of my sisters, brothers and friends arising from unhealthy gender socialization and the costs and impacts of that socialization. When women and men come together with deeply respectful intention, so much can happen to advance our individual journeys and humanity as a whole. GERI's community, learning experiences and connections are a critical element of gender *re*-training.

It was heartening to experience this work in person with UN personnel, with leaders from all walks of life and from many organizations—shifting, deepening and evolving their understanding of gender, and seeking to extend those understandings for the benefit of all of us.

A Bahá'í woman participant in the training spoke of her experience and the importance of the spiritual dimension in gender healing work:

> My experience in the GERI training was nothing short of remarkable. To be allowed access behind the curtain of masculinity and femininity as experienced by women and men in today's society, and truly understand the vulnerability and strength of both men and women is indispensable to creating lasting solutions to gender issues. The program allowed participants to bear witness to the debilitating effects of gender inequality, and then find ways to heal and transform. A key feature of the GERI program is its incorporation of inclusive spiritual principles and practices, which shows how interfaith knowledge and practice can be utilized to advance work in this gender equity field.

Less than three months after the second United Nations GERI training, the Covid-19 pandemic burst onto the world stage. Our enthusiastic plans for further UN GERI trainings were reluctantly brought to a halt and placed on hold. We will resume them in-person once the pathway again becomes clear.

In the meantime, Saphira Rameshfar convened a special invitational session to introduce GERI to leading gender-equality activists and other members of the Executive Committee of the NGO/CSW NY in March 2021. This session was convened as part of the NGO forum of the 2021 CSW conference, which was held online due to Covid-19. A group of nearly 60 gender-equality leaders, activists, scholars, philanthropists, and jurisprudential and religious leaders came together for this special online session, which provided an experiential introduction to the GERI online program. As one participant reflected, "The authentic dialogue and connections really are a step towards fostering unity and equality... Thank you for renewing my faith in humanity and restoring a sense of hope!"

Another colleague, Tschika McBean, Human Rights Officer for the U.S. Bahá'í Office of Public Affairs in Washington DC, organized an invitational three-day online GERI training in January of 2021, bringing together other leaders at Bahá'í Office of Public Affairs, gender activists, academics, and UN colleagues in the DC area. As one woman reflected after this online training,

> I experienced an amazing shift of awareness. . . I had no idea how the structures around gender had impacted me, and still played a part in how I viewed my personal power. This was eye-opening and I felt an amazing compassion for the experiences of others, men and women. Truly, I felt an experience of the depth of human connection that I will carry with me into all that I do.

We are enthused to continue implementing UN GERI trainings. As illustrated in this chapter and elsewhere, gender activists who experience the GERI process often find themselves emboldened, reinspired, and renewed in their hearts, with fresh hope for the genuine possibility of a gender healed word. As one woman-activist reflected, the GERI training gave her a glimpse experience of what a "post-patriarchal world" might actually look and feel like. In the midst of the struggles, trials, and tribulations of gender activism on the global level, these glimpses offer an essential rejuvenating force that activates our inspiration, and enables us to bring our hearts fully into our activism.

The Future of GERI and the UN

Notwithstanding its limitations, the United Nations is a vitally important institution for implementing gender equality. Gender injustice is a global systemic affliction that oppresses all of humanity, and therefore a global unified response, such as the UN can potentially provide, is essential. There is a long way to go, but it is also helpful to see how far we have come. In the course of human history, human rights related to gender are still a new awakening and recent phenomenon. We close this chapter with a brief historical overview of UN resolutions to support gender-based human rights, and to end gender discrimination and injustice around the world.

Although couched in the dry language of legal proclamations, each of these resolutions represents a major and unprecedented step forward in the liberation of humanity from the shackles of gender oppression that have persisted for thousands of years. When coupled with community-based transformational processes that GERI and similar modalities provide, the results can be nothing short of profound for the future of human civilization.

Women's Rights and the UN

The UN General Assembly adopted an international treaty in 1979 called the Convention on the Elimination of all Forms of Discrimination Against Women (CEDAW). It was analogous to an earlier treaty adopted in 1965, the International Convention on the Elimination of All Forms of Racial Discrimination (ICERD).

Described as an international bill of rights for women, CEDAW contains 30 articles focusing on non-discrimination, sex stereotypes, sex trafficking, women's rights in the public sphere, education, employment, health, equality in marriage and family life, and various protection and reporting measures. CEDAW has been ratified by 189 member states. (The United States signed but did not ratify the treaty. The United States has also not ratified the Equal Rights Amendment to its own Constitution.)

The United Nations held its Second World Conference on Human Rights in Vienna in 1993 (the first conference had been in 1968). The agenda for the Vienna conference initially did not mention women or recognize any gender-specific aspects of human rights in its prospectus. Therefore, the Global Campaign for Women's Human Rights organized a Global Tribunal on Violations of Women's Human Rights, which was formally presented in the parallel NGO conference, held concurrently with the main conference at Vienna's UN complex. Over 950 women's organizations from across the globe were represented at the NGO conference, and hundreds of women came from around the world, many of whom presented powerful personal testimonies on a vast range of abuses: some personal, others political, and others cultural. The campaign was inspired by the slogan, "Women's rights are human rights."

As a result of this campaign, women's rights gained a strong and effective presence at the 1993 Vienna conference, and violence against women was officially recognized as a human rights violation. The final conference statement issued by the 171 participating governments—The Vienna Declaration and Programme of Action—devotes several pages to treating the "equal status and human rights of women" as a priority for governments and the United Nations.

This was an unprecedented breakthrough. It was the first time that the human rights of the female half of humanity were formally recognized by the United Nations. "For the first time, women's groups can now make demands on the United Nations," said Reed Brody of the International Human Rights Law Group, "and for the first time the United Nations will have to deal with them."[4]

The 1993 Vienna conference was a tipping point in gaining international acceptance of women's rights as human rights. Six months later, the UN General Assembly adopted the Declaration on the Elimination of Violence Against Women (DEVAW) in December 1993, which was the first international instrument explicitly addressing violence against women. Two years later came the watershed UN Women's conference in Beijing in 1995, with its Platform for Action.

The first ever UN Security Council Resolution (UNSCR) on women, resolution 1325, was adopted in 2000. This was the first time the Security Council recognized the disproportionate and unique impact that armed conflict has on women and girls. It recommended four pillars of action—participation, prevention, protection, and relief and recovery—emphasizing that women, and a gender perspective, are essential to negotiating peace agreements, planning refugee camps, peacekeeping operations, and reconstructing war-torn societies. The UN Secretary-General's in-depth study on violence against women was released in 2006, the first comprehensive report on the issue. In response to persistent public pressure, the United Nations adopted nine more Security Council Resolutions (UNSCR) on Women, Peace, and Security—beginning with resolution 1820 in 2008, which recognized rape and sexual violence in warfare as a crime. The remaining resolutions promote gender equality and strengthen women's participation, protection and rights in wars and post-conflict reconstruction.

LGBT Rights and the UN

In 2011, the Vienna Declaration was extended to protect LGBT persons, affirming that "LGBT rights are human rights." In a resolution hailed as historic, the U.N. Human Rights Council passed the first resolution ever focused exclusively on the human rights of LGBT persons.[5] The resolution produced a report "documenting discriminatory laws and practices and acts of violence against individuals based on their sexual orientation and gender identity."[6] The resolution called upon UN member states to repeal laws that criminalize homosexuality, to abolish the death penalty for consensual same-sex relations, and to enact comprehensive anti-discrimination laws. In 2014, a second resolution was passed on "human rights, sexual orientation and gender identity," which updated the 2011 resolution to include sharing best practices for overcoming violence and discrimination in the application of international human rights law and standards.

In 2013, the United Nations High Commissioner for Human Rights launched the UN Free & Equal campaign, with an inaugural press conference in Cape Town with Archbishop Desmond Tutu as a major spokesperson, as summarized in Chapter 10.[7] The Free & Equal campaign has reached over 2.4 billion social media feeds annually through multiple social media channels, supports national initiatives for LBGTQ+ rights in many countries, and has also organized several high level events at the UN in collaboration with the UN LGBTI Core Group.[8] As the campaign states, "more than a third of the world's countries [still] criminalize consensual, loving same-sex relationships, entrenching prejudice and putting millions of people at risk of blackmail, arrest and imprisonment," as well as being constantly subjected to bullying, discrimination, targeted violence, and hate crimes. UN Free & Equal campaigns and events have been organized in almost 30 countries, with strong support from UN, political, community and religious leaders and from celebrities in all regions of the world.

In 2016, the UNHRC passed a resolution to appoint an Independent Expert to find the causes of violence and discrimination against people due to their gender identity and sexual orientation, and to discuss with governments about how best to protect these people. This has been seen as the UN's "most overt expression of gay rights as human rights."[9]

UN and Racial Discrimination

In 2021, in the wake of the murder of George Floyd, the UN High Commissioner issued a groundbreaking report on racial justice and equality, pursuant to an earlier Human Rights Council resolution 43/1 that was adopted by consensus in 2020 to address "current racially inspired human rights violations, systemic racism, police brutality and violence against peaceful protests." The report introduces a four-point agenda to end systemic racism and human rights violations by law enforcement against Africans and people of African descent.

GERI and the UN

GERI was founded one year before the 1993 Vienna conference. Much of the key data and testimonies from the Vienna Tribunal became a standard part of the curriculum in the GERI programs and trainings for several years. GERI adopts a complementary approach to the legal and policy approaches to social justice that are normally followed by the UN, and government bodies. Both approaches are urgently needed. By addressing root causes of gender injustice, GERI supports the implementation of key UN policies and other legislation against gender-based violence, and promotes peace and security for people of all gender identities.

The commitments reflected in the noble UN resolutions of CEDAW, the 1993 Vienna Declaration and 1995 Beijing Platform of Action, the ten United Nations Security Council Resolutions (UNSCRs) on women, peace, and security, and the LGBTQ+ resolutions and Free & Equal campaign—all reflect the highest aspirations of the human spirit to create a truly healed, peaceful society that meets the needs and rights of all.

Taken together, these UN achievements point to the urgent need for an altogether transformed set of new gender and intersectional relations throughout human societies. These new forms of relating between the sexes and across gender identities and intersectionalities cannot be mandated out of thin air by laws and policy resolutions, important as these are. They must also be proactively seeded and carefully cultivated over time, in a dynamic process that gives birth to new forms of relational authenticity and integrity in community.

Toward this end, GERI offers a unique contribution that can make an inspiring difference within UN networks and its affiliated organizations. The GERI experiential learning methodology complements traditional rights and policy-based activism, and lays out a pragmatic pathway for re-establishing trust, understanding, and right relations between women and men, and people of all genders. This opens new doors and creates new possibilities. As one young woman shared tearfully, after witnessing the depths of men's stories, pain, and authenticity in the UN GERI training, "You have opened parts of my heart that I didn't even know were closed."

PART III

Transforming Gender Injustice into Beloved Community: Voices of Victory from Around the World

Part III provides accounts of the GERI program and its implementation and impacts in different regions of the world. There are different chapters here for several specific countries and regions, and one chapter for four countries in which the GERI work is currently emerging.

Like Part II, these chapters are written primarily in the voices of local people from these various countries, sharing in their own words how they have experienced GERI and its impacts in their lives. Because there are many voices from different people and diverse cultures, this part of the book by its nature exhibits a chorus of voices and communication styles. The editors have made minor edits for syntax, clarity, and readability, but again we have left the local flavor intact as much as possible.

The GERI program is more developed in some regions than others, based primarily on the length of time the program has been operative in the various regions. The chapters reflect these differences accordingly. The regions where GERI has been operative the longest have tended to provide considerable assistance for getting the program going in new regions.

CHAPTER 17

South Africa

GERI began its work in South Africa in April 2003 when we were invited by the Quaker Peace Center in Cape Town to give the first GERI workshop in the country. This invitation was arranged by a local gender activist, Bernedette Muthien, who had attended the first GERI training in the United States.

Toward the end of this first workshop, Bernedette Muthien arranged a meeting with Nozizwe Madlala-Routledge, then Deputy Minister of Defence, who invited GERI to come back to South Africa to introduce GERI work for Members of Parliament. This took nearly four years to implement, because of challenges that emerged in relation to the AIDS crisis in South Africa. We returned to South Africa in November 2006 to conduct this workshop, by which time Nozizwe had become the Deputy Minister of Health.

The workshop for Members of Parliament and other leaders was a watershed event for GERI in South Africa. It is described in Chapter 15 on Government and Politics. Afterwards, we received invitations from many different organizations around the country, including the South African Council of Churches, the University of KwaZulu-Natal, and Phaphama Initiatives outside Johannesburg. We also launched the first GERI professional training at Phaphama Initiatives in 2007. This was followed by the first Cape Town training in 2008. Six more professional trainings were conducted between 2010 and 2021.

In 2012, we were invited by Professor Pumla Gobodo-Madikizela to present at a conference entitled *Engaging the Other*, which she organized at the University of the Free State. We presented a daylong GERI workshop there, which led to conducting a series of GERI programs at the University. That same year, one of our board members, Dorothea Hendricks, introduced us to Reverend Mpho Tutu, who attended a GERI workshop in Cape Town. This led to a series of meetings that in turn led to several meetings with Archbishop Desmond Tutu, and the establishment of a partnership with the Desmond and Leah Tutu Legacy Foundation and Stellenbosch University.

Young men at the Chrysalis Academy in Cape Town, South Africa engaging in a 2-day father-son workshop utilizing the GERI methodology, 2025

In 2012, GenderWorks was founded as a non-profit organization in South Africa by a small group of individuals in Cape Town who had completed the GERI training and were committed to carrying the GERI work forward in South Africa. With its core emphasis to implement Gender Equity and Reconciliation workshops, GenderWorks is going strong with five areas of focus: In-person and online workshops, Community Workshops, Religious Sector, Human Sexuality, and Facilitator Trainings.

The following writing is from Judy Connors, co-founder of Phaphama Initiatives, an organization that GERI partnered with to implement gender reconciliation in schools, prisons, and in Soweto and other township communities in the province of Gauteng.

> In 2008 the direction of Phaphama Initiatives changed, and we started a partnership with GERI. For the previous 19 years, we had been a grassroots NGO focusing on conflict transformation workshops and the teaching of African languages in a young democracy that dawned in 1994 in South Africa, where the divisions between races were wide and worrying.
>
> Equally as intractable, and rearing its head in almost every workshop, was gender disharmony. While our work knew how to teach people the skills of dealing with interpersonal conflict, we were not equipped to handle gender injustice. For a long time we searched for a program that would align with Phaphama's ethos: one of bringing together people who may not normally have engaged

with one another, to learn from and with one another. What a wholesome and restorative channel was opened (through GERI) when men and women from township communities could sit with one another reflecting honestly on our gender biases, our cultural gender conditioning and our intergenerational experiences of gender violence. And always in the stories, the gender inequity was exacerbated by the intersections with other forms of discrimination, such as economic or racial oppression. Sometimes it felt like the river of pain would swallow us all up. As one participant visiting from Canada described a poignant moment during one of our GERI workshops in a township:

> In the woman's breakout group, many women were telling stories about rape. One beautiful young woman was encouraged to tell her story, and she did, haltingly and with embarrassment. She had been raped only two weeks prior, had not gone to the hospital because she didn't understand and was afraid, and now she was HIV positive and likely pregnant. The story was vivid and gripping. Unfortunately, it was not unique. As the topic shifted to HIV, the facilitators decided to take a count of who was, in fact, HIV positive. *Everyone!* (except the facilitators). The pall of the dark horror of this reality enveloped me.

But despite the intensity, the pain didn't swallow us up. Instead, there are many, many testimonies of how the courage to speak up, and the relieving acknowledgment of being listened to without judgment, enabled a life-giving stream to begin flowing again through the stagnant, choked waterways of anger and hurt. In the monthly GERI Heart Circle follow-up meetings after workshops, current events in the country were used to help participants further explore their gender conditioning. The empathic resonance unleashed in these programs created a strong field of mutual healing and community support. The Canadian visitor continued to attend further workshops and participated from a place of humility and love.

We even experimented with new settings where GERI had not been attempted yet—prisons. Who would have thought that the format of the work could be successfully adapted to an all-male correctional facility, where the voice of the feminine was upheld only by the three women facilitators? Many men could, for the first time, get in touch with their anguish at not knowing their fathers, and their remorse at how they had treated the women in their lives. And for some, their time in prison was not too early to begin rebuilding their relationships with mothers, fathers, partners, and children.

Today, under new leadership, GERI is mainstreamed into most of Phaphama's interventions. For me personally, the spiritual significance of this work has been the most enduring. So many lived realities in our world today provoke intensely polarized dualities. The GERI work holds out a powerful invitation to continually strive to embrace these dichotomies with full attention of the mind and compassion of the heart.

Through the GERI work, I am now also much clearer about the distinction between being "cured" and being "healed." The scars of the gender conflicts we have experienced in our lives will never leave us, but we can, with the support of a loving community, learn to integrate the wounds into the fullness of who we are as we become more healed and whole.

This next story retells an experience from one of three women GERI facilitators who were on the team facilitating a workshop in a Johannesburg prison with 36 male inmates all convicted of violent crimes. This woman shares the story of speaking her raw, heartfelt truth during the workshop and the important awakening she received.

One of my experiences was when our GERI facilitation team was in South Africa and facilitated workshops in prison and communities there. The male prisoners were offenders in gender-related cases, and they had killed, beaten, or raped women. It was in that prison that I first shared that I was date-raped and how that had impacted my life. I have never understood why men cannot take a woman's no to sex as a NO, or how they think that women enjoy sex when being raped. In my sharing I was adamant that I did not enjoy it and it was not something I had asked for. I wanted these men in prison to understand that rape is wrong, a brutal violation of a person, and exceedingly painful both emotionally and physically. I just hoped these men understood that the issue of harming women just because they were women was something that needed to be looked at both from an individual and societal perspective. Society had a role to play in creating who they had become and they needed to understand that, and to acknowledge their own role in buying into the societal conditioning that taught them that men could do whatever they wanted to women as a way to show they were real men. When the consequences of these actions catch up with us, the individual pays a price, but the society as a whole pays also. That is why we have prisons and mental houses! So many damaged people—from children to adults. If there is to be healing, individual healing must be linked to the healing of the whole community. We all have a role to play. I have a role to play for the healing to take place.

I started growing my understanding of the systems we live in—patriarchy being the foundation of all the others—and how these systems have shaped who we/I think and say we are/I am. The more I engaged in the GERI work, the more I understood that patriarchy has wounded both women and men. In hearing men talk about their experiences with women in their lives—their mothers, sisters, female cousins, girlfriends, aunties, grandmothers—I was shocked to learn that men are also harmed by these systems. What was really shocking for me was to see the pain men live with from the wounding they get from patriarchy in the process of being "shaped" to be "real" men in the society through the very same system that has privileged them over the years. The whole process is like a conspiracy episode in a drama, where those who fail to conform are shamed and tortured through various ways, both physically and mentally. It is a vicious system and brutal in its punishment of those who do not conform, and those who conform lose themselves and become tyrants. There is no escaping the effects of the system, either way. The tyranny of the system produces tyrants.

I understood this and much more in my experiences with GERI. I had begun the journey of reconciling my experiences in a patriarchal society with the harm it has done not only to me but also to the men it privileges. In this understanding I could find space to open my heart further to hear their stories, as I deepened understanding of myself and my own story.

This piece from a male GERI Trainer is a poignant sharing about the importance of having the safe forum within the GERI process to express and transform his emotions of anger, shame, longing, and sadness in order to be a more conscious man and loving husband, and father.

I have been very involved with Gender Equity and Reconciliation International (GERI) from the early days of its appearance in South Africa. I went through the program, and then the facilitator training, and have since been a GERI trainer of other facilitators. I want to share about my experience of the GERI program and its impact in my life.

As a husband and a father to three children, the most important thing for me in being exposed to GERI is that it has both challenged and supported me at the same time. It has challenged me in the sense that through participating in the GERI work I have come to recognize that I have disappointed my wife many times. But it has supported me in that while being challenged, I have also been forgiven. In the GERI program I have been able to share my story in a space that is safe enough to be honest and to be listened to.

There are four emotions that have been elemental for me in this work. Accessing them in the safety of the GERI space has allowed me to share my own story, and feeling them in myself has helped me to listen sympathetically to the stories of other men and women. The first of these is *anger*, the anger I carried in my youth, and even as a grown man, because of what I didn't get as a young man from my male role models, including my father. Second is the *shame* that comes with seeing the pain created in the world by men like me and knowing that I, too, have played a role in bringing about that pain. The third feeling is the *longing* to have male role models who can demonstrate the way to be a man with integrity. I've never had a conversation with my father about what it means to be a man. I've never had this conversation with my uncles, either. My education came from the streets. But "streets" doesn't mean just being in rough places. It also means life experiences like GERI, in which I expose myself to scenarios that allow me to gain new perspective. Fourth, and last, is the *sadness* and pain that I've been carrying. I hadn't been able to express my sadness and pain because there hadn't been a space for me to do so. GERI has helped me to do that.

When I managed to share these emotions for myself, I realized that if even I had these struggles, as a person who was not as traumatized as some, then what about those who are continually traumatized in the worst possible ways? What about those in prisons, in dysfunctional families, in places where they are never safe? Recognizing all these forms of pain is what made me commit to support this work, to train others to continue learning, and to continue reflecting in my own life, thinking: How can I be a better husband? How can I be a better father? How can I be a better mentor to the many young men who look up to me in the place I come from?

That commitment became a responsibility that I wish to be accountable for, and it has been a great support to know that I have a system, a process, knowledge, and a community that will help me to support those that look up to me. I've used this information to support mostly young men in the township where I come from called Soweto, one of the biggest townships or locations in South Africa for Black people. I've also done this in corporate spaces where men realize they're struggling but don't know how to get out of the conditioning that they've had from their own families, from bad associations, and so on. I continue to do this in different spaces such as NGOs, international corporations, and international agencies like the United Nations Food Foundation and the Nelson Mandela Foundation, to make people aware of the subtleties of gender trauma and pain, and to help people discover how we can address these issues within our organizations. I am grateful to have been given this knowledge and support by the GERI community and to have been mentored in this work for some years.

The following is from a participant who shares her gender story as a survivor of sexual abuse from childhood and her process of speaking this deeply hidden secret in her first GERI workshop, and the healing and forgiveness that unfolded after.

"You will never know what he does to me behind that closed door." My mother spoke these words in the heat of yet another episode of domestic violence in our home. I was 12 years old. On that day, I noticed for the first time the cracks of physical, emotional, mental, and spiritual exhaustion showing in my mother's voice and on her face. I had heard the arguments between my parents before and had seen the physical beatings, but until I was older and understood more, I always wondered what she meant. I feared my father, and I hated him for a very long time.

I am the fourth of five children and the only girl. I was born on Christmas Day and was given a name that means "so long hoped for." From the moment of my birth, I was drenched in pink and bows and frills and curls. My father used to speak boastfully about me being born on Christmas Day, as if it was his achievement. With a father and three older brothers around I had thought that I'd be safe and protected, but my lived experiences from early childhood to adulthood were very different. When I did a reflection exercise on my life, it is striking how often I used words like "fear," "abandoned," "betrayal," "secrets," "alone," "lonely," "unworthy," "undeserving, "not loveable," or "not wanted."

Between the ages of four and eleven, I experienced abuse that I held within my being as a deeply buried secret. Living under the threat of physical violence and harm to my brothers, I never spoke of the abuse I endured. The stories in books, my imagination, and my single-character role-plays as a make-believe social worker who wielded the full power of the law on perpetrators became my safe place. There, in fantasy, I was free, I was powerful, I was safe.

I was an obedient child, not doing anything to bring attention to myself, though I defended my brothers fiercely when my father would make them strip down naked and then beat them violently. I would beg and plead for him to stop, and I tried in vain to pull him away from them. I hated him so much more then, and I was so confused about why things never changed or became better, especially after church priests visited. These experiences impacted my life in profound and long-lasting ways, and I now know and understand that they were deeply traumatic. I subconsciously carried all those emotions and beliefs deep within my being. Becoming an adult, navigating relationships, being comfortable around men, and being in the presence of anyone who was drunk or drinking alcohol were all deeply challenging and disturbing experiences.

I was introduced to the GERI work when I attended my first workshop in 2014. It was a life-changing experience. For the first time, I felt safe enough to share some of the secrets buried deep inside me. The truth poured out from me unexpectedly as I shared my experiences of sexual abuse between the ages of four and eleven, the fear and hatred I had towards my father, and my complete distrust of men. That was the beginning of the unraveling of my inner threads of shame, guilt, fear, sadness, and anger. It was like my "industrial-strength" suit of armor was being gently cracked and taken apart, bit-by-bit. The GERI workshop process created a rare experience and place of safety where I could speak my truth and be seen, heard, and witnessed by the women and men in the circle. I also listened to all the women's stories and, for the first time, felt validated and less alone.

The most profound moment was when I heard the men share their stories, and my heart started to soften. I felt an energy lift and leave my body. At that moment, something in me changed forever. When I heard the pain and suffering the men shared, I could see them as human beings in pain who also been through profoundly traumatic experiences, just like I had. My question of "Why?" about the behavior of men became a compassionate inquiry that asked, "What happened to you?" I also knew that I had found the answer to the unspoken question of where my career was heading. I had found another part of my divinely orchestrated purpose. I knew I needed to become a facilitator of the GERI work. I needed it for myself and for every young child, woman, and man, for all people. I needed it for my mother and all the women going back generations who could not speak the truth of their gender wounding and pain.

Through the GERI process, the layers of pain and suffering are dissolved, not only for each individual but also for the collective, and for the generations that came before and will come after. As I've participated in the GERI work, the hatred I've carried towards my father has dissolved as the stories and experiences of other men, husbands, and fathers brought me understanding, compassion, and ultimately forgiveness for my father. The work continues to be an integral part of my way of being and my practice of being human.

My path towards forgiving my father started when I was sitting on the floor in the Truth Mandala, holding the stick of anger in a tight grip and the bowl of emptiness nestling in my lap. When I felt complete in my sharing, I paused and took in a deep breath. The woman facilitator, who was sitting at the end of the half-circle of chairs, gently called my attention with a question, asking me what I would say to my father at that moment. She sat close to me, and as I lifted my gaze to meet her steady and present eyes, I felt my grip on the stick relax, and I heard myself say, "I would tell him that I had forgiven him."

This sharing comes from a social worker who joined the online facilitator training. Through a deepening of her relationship with the men in the GERI program, she experienced significant breakthroughs and healings that changed the perceptions and judgment that she has held about men.

When I first joined the GERI as a trainee I was working as a gender-based-violence social worker. During my social work consultations with the clients, I realized that I was being both judgmental towards and biased against men. I always assumed they were in the wrong and women were their victims, which is not always the case. For years before this work, although I worked as a gender-based-violence activist, it took me participating in the GERI workshop to realize that all these years I had been an angry activist. I always thought that it was "us women against men," and my approach was very harsh on men in general. This is because of my past victimization as a woman and the victimization of my mother by men and by her in-laws. I come from a patriarchal society, community, and family, and all my life I fought to make men see me, acknowledge me, and stop looking at me as an object they can abuse or use as their doormat. I have seen abuse in communities, in churches, and in the workplace, where men do not beat you physically but belittle you with their words or actions. This had made me declare war on them.

Participation in GERI changed my perceptions. I reached a breakthrough, and when I bowed and cried, I was really getting my healing. After that I had an encounter with the men, the encounter that made me recognize and acknowledge their pain. I realized that they were wounded, too. Their transparency, and their non-defensiveness when we shared our truths with them, really humbled me. I always hated a man who is defensive. The men in the GERI workshop listened, and no matter how I presented myself, they never walked away but heard me with compassion. From that day onwards, I vowed to try and be gentle to them and try not to be judgmental. I am not fully there yet, but every day I try to be a better person than the one I used to be. I realized that it is not us *against* them but us *and* them both being the victims of our past traumas. I realized that we need to reconcile and heal and wish to continue spreading the message of healing and reconciliation.

It is not easy sometimes, coming from the country that has such a high incidence of gender-based violence and femicide. It is not easy being in the center of it daily as a social worker. I have to separate out my own emotions and feelings and focus on the healing of women and men. Every day I listen to couples and function as a mediator in their marriages. Our society is still unfair towards women, patriarchy still rules, and cultural practices harmful to women and girls are still an issue. I try everyday *not* to go back to the hate I used to have for men, but instead motivate myself to spread the GERI work so that in the end we all heal and reconcile. We cannot change the past, but we can surely change the future. This is not going to happen in one day, but I know that one day our influence and workshops will change the world. Yes, we can!

This next reflection is from Jeremy Routledge who shares about discovering through the GERI process what was missing in his life.

When I attended my first GERI workshop in 2006, I experienced something that had been missing in my life, and that I have been working on ever since. It was hearing women, in a safe space, share the pain they have gone through as a result of violence in all its forms: physical, sexual, emotional, and structural. The workshop was also a place for men to share their pain, which was new to me. Understanding the pervasive system of patriarchy that oppresses women (and also men), and seeing that there were other men in the workshop and elsewhere who were allies in overcoming this system, enabled me to continue on this path. I subsequently completed the facilitator training and it has been wonderful being part of both the local and global GERI community over the years.

I am also a facilitator in the Alternatives to Violence Project (AVP), a group that complements the work of GERI. Through AVP we were able to run the first, and probably the only, GERI workshop for women and men serving sentences in Pollsmoor prisons.

GERI has also helped me in Embrace Dignity, an NGO my wife Nozizwe and I started in 2010. Embrace Dignity addresses the patriarchal harms of the systems of prostitution by supporting survivors and providing them the means to exit the sex trade, and we also advocate for legal reforms.

The following sharing is from a GERI facilitator who relates experiences of his first workshop, which gave him an experience of inner peace as he was able to speak openly about the pain he had carried for so long.

My journey with GERI began in an unlikely place: Medium B Male Section at Pollsmoor Prison where I was serving a ten-year sentence for armed robbery. The year was 2007, and for the first time female and male inmates at Pollsmoor were allowed to come together for what was the most transformative process for me. It was a forum where I was able to speak to my own pain as a man. Prison is not that kind of environment. The workshop was an opportunity I used to release all that I had been carrying even from before prison, growing up without a father. It was my space. I felt safe. The facilitators held the space. This was what I had prayed for. I was able to speak about my family, growing up without a father...and I listened to other people open up. Other men opened up. I saw the healing taking place. You don't know until you experience it. I began to see my father in a different light, never having had an understanding of who he was. I developed more compassion for the prison warders. I looked at people differently. Everyone needs help and goes through their own pain.

The GERI workshop gave me a sense of freedom and relief in speaking truth to my pain. It gave me a feeling of true inner peace. I could speak as a victor and not a victim.

This GERI participant was released on parole in 2008, has since completed the GERI facilitator training and is now a certified GERI facilitator. He is currently a leading facilitator of GERI workshops and Alternatives to Violence programs that work with prison inmates and other socially challenged groups in South Africa.

This next piece by GERI Trainer Lucille Meyer, who is Chrysalis Academy Chief Executive Officer, shares the powerful impact of the implementation of GERI work with young adults at the Academy. A partnership between GERI and the Chrysalis Academy was established in 2017.

"Love is always the place
where I begin and end."
- bell hooks

"The three-day Gender Equity and Reconciliation International (GERI) program allowed me to be in the company of male elders, something I longed for all my life, as my father was never there. I have no words to describe how their words pierced my heart."

These are the sentiments shared with me by a Chrysalis Academy graduate about five years ago after he experienced a three-day GERI program. To this day, his words remain etched in my mind as a testimony to the transformative nature of the GERI experience.

The Chrysalis Academy is a youth development organization based in the Western Cape, South Africa. It is widely regarded as a model of excellence in holistic and trauma-informed programming for young people. The mission of the academy is the provision of a three-month residential program for youth ages 18–25 from the Western Cape, aimed at unleashing their potential, deepening their resilience, and fostering active citizenship. The academy has wholeheartedly embraced the GERI program as central to its work. Eight GERI facilitators and two GERI trainers, who are either staff or graduates of the academy, form part of the GERI global family. The gender equity and reconciliation piece closes the holistic loop for the Chrysalis Academy, in that much of the wounding endured by young people relate to issues of gender and sexuality—the *absent father wound,* leaving young people without male role models and with a yearning for belonging; *gender-based violence,* leaving deep scars of fear, self-hatred and lack of self-worth; and the search for *identity*.

The resonance of the GERI program stems from its experiential nature and heart-focused approach. The activities that constitute a three-day GERI program meet youth where they are at. Their lived experiences and inner knowing are recognized, not diminished, and their voices are amplified by having their stories deeply listened to by other participants. The magic happens within a carefully woven safe container, within which youth feel no judgment, blame, or ridicule—responses that they generally encounter in their families, the education system, and society as a whole.

From the academy's experience over the last 21 years, youth and even older adults require physical and psychological safety to share their stories. GERI's approach and carefully-designed activities and architecture, including participants and facilitators sitting in a circle as equals, provide the perfect catalysts for this safety to emerge. There is something alchemical that emerges when people are witnessed as they bring to the fore their wells of pain and wounding. Participants have spoken of a "freeing up, a lifting of the weight on their shoulders, and feeling lighter." They have spoken about the beauty of being seen and heard. For youth, who are often on the margins of society and invisible to many, it is a transformative experience to be seen and heard. Participants have remarked that the spaciousness that emerges when the truth is spoken serves to remind them that they are so much more than their pain and wounds. It is as if within the spaciousness, they are able to see more clearly the systemic nature of gender oppression and conditioning.

Another attraction of the GERI program for youth and older adults is the skillful use of rituals. Rituals are features of families, communities, and societies, and can be regarded as a set of activities executed in a specific way to achieve particular objectives. At the academy, we have found that youth love rituals, regardless of their religious persuasions, as rituals speak to their innermost longing, with many having said that they feel the resonance of the rituals directly in the space of the heart. The rituals serve in many ways to cement the collective agreements and create a more durable container of safety, while at the same time forging connections beyond the physical. We have found that the GERI program, while following a structured approach, is sufficiently flexible to include country-specific examples of songs, rituals, games, and ways of honoring, all of which are very attractive to youth. The honoring ceremonies choreographed by youth have been deeply moving, with a palpable sense of dignity, grace, and care in their execution. The design of these honoring ceremonies by participants, to seal the work that has been done, instills a deep sense of commitment to continue the work of gender healing beyond the workshop and enact their vision for a gender-healed world.

At the Chrysalis Academy, we do not introduce our students to any program that we have not experienced ourselves. My own personal journey with GERI began about six or seven years ago. I was invited to look back and reflect on my own conditioning with respect to gender and sexuality. This has not been easy, as I had to share my own encounter with inappropriate advances from an educator at a very young age. I also had to consider my own complicity within the patriarchal system in raising my daughter and son. Above all, I was invited to listen deeply to stories by men of how they have been socialized, particularly by their fathers, into not expressing the feminine side of themselves. Yet, I learned to sit with discomfort and patiently witness how those uncomfortable emotions evolved into compassion, kindness, and a greater understanding of our collective and systemic trauma. The journey has been a liberating one. I have shed many tears and experienced a felt sense of joy and hope. I have also felt the rage within my bones when listening to many stories of childhood trauma.

GERI recognizes that we cannot heal overnight thousands of years of gender oppression, marginalization, exclusion, and silencing. However, through stepping into these carefully crafted activities and honoring each step of our progress, we pave the way for the seeds to be planted for ongoing connection, truth-telling, expansion of consciousness, healing, and hope. It is in doing the work, sharing stories that perhaps we may never have shared before, and listening deeply to others, that participants can sense into what a beloved community potentially feels like, where each one can be held in their truth, and there is a commitment to foster healing, equity, and justice for all.

In South Africa, my motherland, the freedom and beloved community that we longed for during the apartheid era have not materialized to the extent that we had hoped. It is evident that freedom and beloved community are not guaranteed by having the best constitution in the world or well-crafted policies. Beloved community is carved in practice when people of all genders sit together, connect heart to heart, without fear of ridicule or judgment, and open themselves to the alchemy that is possible. Without hesitation and with a deep inner knowing, I am convinced that the Gender Equity and Reconciliation work is key to individual and collective transformation, spurring us on to become instruments for reshaping our families, communities, countries, and society as a whole. It is in practice where we begin to experience what a beloved community is like. It is in sharing our wounds and listening to the pain of others in community that we discover our oneness—our humanity—despite all the boundaries, conditioning, and systemic injustices. *Umuntu ngumuntu ngabantu! (A person is a person through others*). This is the overwhelming experience of participants in GERI sessions.

I have been through many different gender trainings and programs over the last 40 years, including postgraduate training, and the GERI program is the one that has touched me the most. It has radically shifted the entire lens through which I view issues of gender and sexuality, and more importantly, how I now choose to show up in the world. In fact, it would not be an exaggeration to say that the GERI program cracked my heart wide open. I think this is because the GERI work is centered in the heart where we are all connected as one, both to one another and to the Supreme, whether we call it God, Spirit, Brahman, Universal Love, or the Infinite Reality. After all, it all begins and ends in Love!

Honoring Ceremonies

The honoring ceremonies in the GERI workshop process invite participants to be creative, playful, authentic, inclusive, and meaningful. Participants bring together their musical talent, dance, crafts, and poetry skills. In a short time, they co-create a ceremony to honor, acknowledge, celebrate, and express gratitude for the shared experiences during their time together. A poignant moment in the honoring ceremonies is when personal commitments are offered, most often individually when, for a few moments, all attention is on the person speaking a heartfelt commitment to the other group. This commitment often reflects new personal insights or understanding of the other gender and is offered as an intention of a new or different way of being going forward.

In Africa, music is a social activity in which almost everyone participates. Significant events are celebrated with rituals and music, bodies moving and swaying to the weaving rise and fall of the volume and rhythm. Beating drums, stomping feet, and clapping hands can add to the intensity of the moment. A unique African sound is ululation, a wailing or a high cry used to show emotion at a ceremony.

In one workshop, the women formed a pathway from the door entrance, and one by one, the men were led into the room, through this pathway, to the sound of the women singing, clapping, and rhythmically swaying and moving their bodies. Some ululating, some were humming. As each man entered, they lifted their hands and wiggled their fingers in a swaying movement to signify the blessing flowing over them. The women used the tune of a song called "Never give up" and changed some of the lyrics to incorporate the elements of anger, grief and sorrow, shame, emptiness, and fear, which they heard and witnessed in the Men's Truth Forum process. It was a way to acknowledge what they had shared and offer encouragement on their way forward.

The song's lyrics became, "*In times of sorrow, never give up. In times of fear, never give up. In times of sadness, never give up. In times of anger, never give up. When you feel empty, never give up.*"

It is a song that you cannot sit still and listen to. It invites you to join in the

Boys eagerly anticipating their ceremony to honor the girls; GERI high school workshop, Etatwa Township, South Africa

singing, swaying, clapping, and moving of your feet. All the men had joined in the song in no time, and the volume rose joyfully in the room. The men were smiling in recognition and acceptance of the women's wish and blessing, and the women were beaming with the sheer joy of giving.

In the men's honoring of the women, they created a birthing scene in their ceremony. The men enacted the process of childbirth to symbolize their role in creating and birthing a gender-healed world. This was a very touching and emotional experience for the women in the group. They saw and heard the message from the men that they will do what is needed to incubate and birth the change that is needed, however painful it may be.

In another workshop, the women used a specific song and changed the lyrics to incorporate each man's name. This was a powerful experience for the men when they realized their names were being used. The looks of recognition on their faces were beautiful to behold as the message of the song began sinking in. The lyrics of the song were changed to, "*Who is this man? This man is* (insert the man's name). *Have you ever seen a man like this? Let's celebrate and honor this man* (insert the man's name)." They sang this song whilst walking rhythmically around the men in a circle, and before long, all the men were sitting with big smiles on their faces, almost in disbelief that the women had chosen to honor and acknowledge them in this way.

In the men's honoring, they escorted the women into the room while softly singing a song, and led each one up the few steps in front of a stage to chairs placed in a semicircle. Each chair was adorned with a scarf draped over it, and as they guided the women into a seat, they paused to hand over an artfully decorated card to which two sweets were attached. With this action, they elevated the women above them, standing on the ground below the stage. One by one, each man stepped forward, with the others softly humming a tune; he knelt on the lower step, looked up at the women and offered his commitment of what he intends to do to fulfill his part to bring about a gender-healed world. Soft gasps of surprise and appreciation were heard from the women throughout the ceremony. One woman said, with tears running down her face, "No man has ever done something like this for me. I have never felt so honored and respected as a woman." Another said, "When we did that ritual, I felt so positive and energized. And when it happened, seeing how genuine it was, I sat there and imagined, 'Have other women experienced getting a gift and receiving it as genuinely as these men gave it before? No hidden agendas; I'm just doing this for you.'"

Young adults at GERI workshop in Cape Town, South Africa

CHAPTER 18

India

The Gender Equity and Reconciliation International (GERI) work was first invited to India in 2002 to facilitate a private workshop with Catholic nuns and priests at the Sadhana Institute in Lonavla (see Chapter 13). In 2010, we were invited to offer our first public workshop in Mumbai. In 2016, we convened a yearlong professional immersion and facilitator training in collaboration with Dream a Dream, an NGO in Bangalore, and graduated our first cohort of Indian GERI facilitators. One of them, Ansar Anwar, became the Lead for GERI in India in 2021, and his work continues to expand GERI in India through multiple workshops and trainings, especially for youth and young adults.

In the past several years the violence against women in India has gained more media and public attention. For example, the 2012 Delhi gang rape and murder of Jyoti Singh sparked national and international protests and condemnation, receiving widespread media coverage. The subsequent 2015 BBC documentary film, *India's Daughter*, was aired around the world, although it was banned from showing in India. Although painful, the effects of this heightened attention to gender-based violence in Indian society has been beneficial in terms of awakening greater awareness and activism.

The first public GERI workshop in India came as an invitation from Prashant Olalekar, a Catholic priest in Mumbai, organized by his colleague Hazel Lobo, who later completed the GERI facilitator training. This intergenerational 3-day program had over 30 participants that included NGO professionals, journalists, religious leaders, software professionals, corporate workers, and activists ranging from 23 to 65 in age. In the cross-gender forums, heartbreaking stories were shared of sexual harassment, betrayal in relationships, divorce, pornography, rape, molestation, and bullying. The men listened courageously to the women's experiences and pain—something rarely addressed in mixed gender forums anywhere, and particularity in India. They also opened up and shared vulnerably about their own pain, which touched the women deeply. The honoring ceremonies were an exquisite mix of nurturing blessings and deeply moving singing from the women, and the men concluded their ceremony with a Bollywood-style dance performance that had the women in stitches and tears both.

"This process was very deep and opened up a space that has been so transforming, so healing; giving me so much hope," reflected a therapeutic counselor from Mumbai, who also served on the Vatican Family Council in Rome. "It opened up another world for me."

This workshop was the first time that Sr. Lucy Kurien, founder of the Maher Ashram, experienced a GERI program."I work mostly with women, and I've been listening to women's stories for 25 years," she reflected, "so I did not even realize that men also go through [gender challenges]. And here in GERI, in a matter of days, as I was listening to the voice of men, I realized how much I have been missing out on. After I went through the GERI program, I understood how much men suffer."

Commitment to change oneself and ultimately society's beliefs and behaviors is not easy, but the women and men in this workshop stepped up and showed their commitment through their participation. Some of the participants have stayed engaged in the GERI work and community ever since, including Sr. Lucy Kurien and Mangesh Pol, who continue to implement GERI programs in Maher's extensive network of homes across India.

One of the Indian men made an astute observation about India at the end of the workshop. "Nowhere in the world are women celebrated at a divine level as they are in India. But, as much as they are celebrated at a spiritual, metaphysical level, the denigration of women is extreme."

This profound irony is dramatically expressed in the ancient story of Draupadi in the Sanskrit epic,*Mahabharata*. By way of brief background: The crown Prince Yudhishthira gambles away his kingdom in a rigged dice game, and after losing all his possessions he puts himself up as a stake and loses, and finally even stakes his wife, Princess Draupadi, and loses her as well. So Draupadi suddenly becomes a slave, and she is dragged by her hair into the Royal Court by the winning party, the Kauravas, led by the evil Duryodhana. Draupadi makes a bold appeal for justice to the assembled Kuru elders. She argues that because Yudhishthira lost himself *before* he put her up as a stake in the dice game, he had no authority over her. She further declares that the dice game was unfair because the opposing party did not put up equal stakes in the game.

Draupadi is clear and forthright, her arguments brilliant, her logic impeccable. No one can refute her. Yet none of the esteemed Kuru elders intervenes on her behalf. Unprotected by the very pillars of society who should be jumping to her aid, Draupadi is defenseless against the lustful tyranny of the Kauravas. A jubilant Duryodhana orders his deputy Dushasana to strip Draupadi naked before the assembled multitudes in the Royal Court. The venerated Kuru elders—the highest political and military statesmen and religious leaders in the land—merely cast their eyes downward, paralyzed in impotence. Vidura, one of Duryodhana's 99 brothers, appeals to the assembled elders to do their duty and intervene to protect the royal daughter-in-law, but none of the leaders makes a move. Bhishma, the senior statesman and normally a man of the highest ethical standards, offers a pitifully inadequate response, saying that "morality is subtle."

The Kuru elders' crippling silence bespeaks a profound betrayal of Draupadi, and symbolically the betrayal of the feminine. Whenever any woman, anywhere in the world, is violated or unjustly oppressed and then turns to the social and religious authorities, only to find justice thwarted or denied by patriarchal institutions, she is symbolically reliving this disturbing drama of Draupadi. She is doubly betrayed, first by the violation itself, and second by justice denied.

Utterly bereft, Draupadi appeals directly to the divine Lord Krishna, who works a miracle to save her and protect her honor. Draupadi cannot be stripped. In her moment of crisis, Draupadi fulfills one of the key teachings of the *Bhagavad Gita*, which is to abandon all *dharmas* [practices] and take refuge in the Divine alone—here symbolized by Krishna. The flagrant violation of Draupadi is a major cause for the war that ensues after the Pandavas' 13-year exile. Despite being vastly outnumbered, the Pandavas, led by Yudhishthira's brother Arjuna, are ultimately victorious.

The Kuru society is unable to protect its women, including even the royal princess Draupadi, from the corruption and rapacious violence within its own ranks. This is the condition of contemporary societies as well, not only in India. Like the blind king Dhritarashtra and the other Kuru elders, many contemporary men exhibit a similar, complicit denial of the profound violations of women in a patriarchal society. It's not that the majority of men *approve* of women's oppression, any more than Bhishma or Drona approved of Draupadi's violation. They may even give lip service to women's emancipation. But if men are not willing to directly confront these issues and take decisive action to deconstruct the patriarchal system, they become passively complicit in the resulting injustice. The role of Krishna in this story bears some similarity to the role of Jesus when he intervened to protect the woman accused of adultery. Had Jesus stood idly by, as the Kuru elders did, the woman would have been murdered on the spot, and those who stoned her would have gone off scot-free, reinforced in their ruthless self-righteousness.

The timeless teachings of this epic are as relevant today as they were thousands of years ago, and offer essential lessons for engagement in the world, encouraging men to behave more like Arjuna, willing to stand up for what is right and just, and less like Duryodhana and Dushasana, the macho, lustful, bravado type. Similarly, it points to the need for older men to take proactive responsibility for mentoring younger men into becoming responsible, compassionate servants of society and protectors of women and girls, rather than turning a blind eye—as Bhishma, Drona, and Dhritarashtra do—to the reckless behavior of aggressive immature masculinity that can so easily degenerate into rash violations of women.

The model of Draupadi also serves as a teaching and inspiration for women to stand up for themselves in the face of injustice, and to support one another in speaking their truth, rather than suppressing their sisters, daughters, and mothers—as women sometimes do. This is important in today's world where many women, in India and across the globe, are still no safer than women were at the time of the *Mahabharata*. Indian women today tend to model themselves after Sita, with her devotional reverence and humble service to Rama. This is very beautiful, of course, but seems most appropriate only when their men behave in a loving and dignified manner like Rama. When men start behaving like Ravanna, or become aggressive or act out like foolish boys, Draupadi's example teaches women not to submit to their will, but instead be true to themselves and stand up for what they know is right. This can be challenging or even dangerous for women at times, but when acting with pure motives and integrity to transform the unjust conditions of society, higher spiritual forces and protective energies can and will work "miracles" on women's behalf, just as Krishna did in Draupadi's case. The inspiring story of Sr. Lucy Kurien and the Maher Ashram at the end of this chapter is a powerful contemporary example.

Stories of Transformation in GERI Programs

We begin with one woman's story of growing up in India, and subsequently founding both technology companies and nonprofit organizations to care for orphans and underprivileged children in India.

I was born and brought up in a large family in India. My father was the eldest of 16 siblings and took the responsibility of supporting the family after my grandfather's death. I grew up learning many family values from my parents.

In India, men are traditionally expected to take financial responsibility for the family, while women are expected to take care of the home. This is fairly common in many middle-class families and in small towns in India. However, the culture in metropolitan cities is slowly starting to change, and women are more often becoming educated, and financially contributing to the family. I come from a traditional family where most women are homemakers, and the men are the breadwinners. Most financial decisions are made by men in the family, and women don't even imagine that they have the potential to have a career or to make financial decisions. My mother was a very smart woman, and she had extensive influence in the family due to her compassionate and caring nature. But she had to end her education in middle school due to added responsibilities at home when she lost her mother, and she never thought about empowering herself through continued education. She thought her total life's purpose was to stay home and care for the family, and she was still very happy with her life. But I strongly feel that if my mother had been given the education and opportunities that most of us have today, she could have been a great leader for the country.

Every woman should have the means and information to make the decisions about her own life. The women in many communities do not even think they have the potential to progress their education, build a professional career and gain financial independence. I see this as a lost opportunity. I grew up thinking the same way. My family was more interested in getting me married than sending me for higher education. My mother understood what she missed in her life after my father passed away, and she encouraged me to educate myself to be financially independent before I get married. This is what motivated me. I am one of those few fortunate women to have family support in this, and that helped me to become what I am today.

Through my not-for-profit organization, SOFKIN (Support Organization for Kids in Need), I learned that there is still so much injustice that happens to women in underserved communities. Most of the children that are brought to our organization come from abused families. The men in the families are alcoholic; they beat up and abuse the women; they do not provide for their families. These children are left without food, medical care, or education. Many girls and women still lack access to basic services, and women remain under-represented in these communities. How can we change the status quo to build and nurture a safe and equal society?

Achieving gender equality will not happen overnight. We need programs with proven models to influence this thought process at the individual level. GERI is one such program in which women and men (and people of all genders) jointly share core gender wounds, find solace in each other with mutual understanding, and emerge into a newfound space of forgiving and healing in a safe container.

When I first attended the session of GERI, I did not expect myself to be openly sharing my personal experiences. The first day itself was a great experience in meeting individuals at the human level, without the outer shield of their race, religion, social status, or professional titles. The conversations in the safe space created by the facilitators helped to peel away the layers of confusion, fear, and isolation. We were all listening to each other's stories, and the pain, feeling love for each other without consciously realizing that the positive energy from each other is what was truly allowing us to forgive and move forward. This is the most powerful healing process that I ever witnessed and experienced. This cannot be expressed in words, but only experienced through the work.

The next narrative comes from a man. He recounts his experience and trials growing up as a boy in India, demonstrating some of the unique challenges faced by Indian men, especially those who are part of religious minorities. He also shares the transformation he has experienced over the years and his work with young people.

Childhood was a dark time in my life, filled with many struggles and challenges. I came from an underprivileged and targeted Muslim community in South India and I witnessed much violence. I am the first person in my family who had the opportunity to go to school and college, something my sister and four brothers could not do. In the early years of my life my biggest struggle was hunger. In those days the only thing I wanted was simply a full belly. But at the age of 11 or 12 these challenges were compounded when I started being sexually victimized by my uncle. I was fond of him, and he gained my trust by giving me money for food. But after gaining that trust he used me for his sexual satisfaction. Those days were completely blank for me. I was very distressed, but I didn't know how to react to the situation. I told myself that it was my own problem, and that I could not share this information with anyone. But I was like a tiny, scared fish who had to escape from the big shark in my life.

My challenges didn't end there, but only increased more and more. When I was 19, I experienced communal violence and religious conflict for the first time. People whom I had trusted and considered friends began to treat me differently. I was prohibited from wearing my Topi (Muslim cap), faced suspicions of belonging to terrorist groups, and was called many derogatory words. There were bombings in my neighborhood. On top of all this, people even called me by derogatory names related to my body, because I was thin, short, and had less hair than normal. As a boy, I had to be strong. I was supposed to be strong and muscular, but my body was skinny. I was deeply depressed and in a state of shock. But I could not express my emotions or my feelings to anyone. I could not cry, because I was a boy. There were so many issues, so many problems that I could not share with anyone. I felt unable to respond to these events and to the things that people said to me. That's how I grew up. After so many years of hiding all of this within me, I began to think I had done something wrong, that I was the reason these problems were so unstoppable, and that I should just terminate my life.

It was at that point that I decided to not give up on myself, to fight back and raise myself up again. I began to seek out organizations that work in the realm of intersectionality. A couple of years after I had begun working for an organization that introduced me to GERI, I had the opportunity to attend my first workshop. That was a turning point in my life.

Up until then, I had never spoken about the sexual abuse I experienced. But in GERI, I found a place where I could express myself, share my emotions, and cry. For the first time, I spoke about the abuse, the violence, and all the emotions I had never expressed in my life. I was given the chance to say everything I needed to say. The workshop felt like entering into a different world, a new world where people saw me differently. I felt so happy, so blessed to discover that it was possible to live in a different way. And that is exactly what happened. From the beginning of the workshop, I thought, "my Lord, these people are here to listen to me!" People who didn't know me hugged me. They cried with me. They shared my feelings and my emotions. This was my first time seeing that I am not alone in this journey, but that there are other people going through these things.

It was also the first time I truly heard women's voices and saw that they have their own issues and challenges. I saw that the experiences they go through are very different from what I had gone through. I got to know about women, and I got to know about myself as a man. I actually understood the life of a woman in society, and in my family, and I actually understood *their* emotions and experiences. In all these ways, I found empathy through this gender reconciliation work. It was really surprising. It was shocking to see myself within this group, and to recognize myself as a person who had held back so many emotions and been so burned up by the challenges I had experienced. From then on I stayed involved and kept moving forward with this work.

I've now been involved with GERI for seven years and have become a facilitator. In my work in the social sector I see many children, young people, and teachers, and I am proud to say that I am doing my small part to better society by spreading my GERI work in this community. I strongly believe that this work can help everyone. I try as much as possible to listen to young people and create space for them. I still remember my first training, which involved young people from different backgrounds involved in a local youth organization. I remember witnessing them, just listening to them. Their stories, their journeys and experiences were totally different from mine. Seeing those young people through the lens of a caring, empathic, and compassionate adult perspective brought me strength, and gave me a sense of togetherness. Looking at those young people really changed my way of seeing.

So that is a little of my journey. Along my path, the most powerful tools I have found are *empathy, inclusivity, trust*, and *equity*. I am deeply grateful for GERI, and I feel honored and blessed to be taking part in this gender reconciliation work, which is making a big difference in the lives of young Indian people, and in the lives of many people around me.

This next story comes from a woman in her sixties who experienced the GERI work in Mumbai. She shared the devastating impact of pornography and prostitution in her life and marriage.

I attended a three-day Gender Equity and Reconciliation Workshop in Mumbai, India in 2010. It was an extension of a trip in which I was facilitating Women's Art and Writing workshops. I mention this because this workshop was not my focus, or even something I had previously considered. In other words, I went with no agenda or preconceived expectations.

It was a large group and I am by nature an introvert, so while I am happy to share in breakout groups, I do not normally speak in such a large setting. The incident I am about to describe occurred during a whole-group gathering. We were seated on the floor in a large circle. One man was speaking about his personal struggles with pornography. I was suddenly quite overcome, and when he finished talking I spontaneously began speaking from a very deep and hurt space about the dissolution of my 20-year marriage over my husband's fascination with porn and prostitution. I do not remember what I said, only the depth and grief of the feelings that rose up within me. This speaking was not coming from my head but from my heart, my gut. I also remember the feeling of being held, cradled almost, by the male and female facilitators. Not physically, but emotionally. Later, during a break, a young woman came up to me and said that my story made her rethink what she had been told—that men just do this and to accept it. She was studying to be a counselor. I remember feeling grateful that perhaps some perceptions had shifted, at least for her. For myself, it is not so clear. I would characterize the experience as cathartic but also unsettling.

This was the first and only time I have publicly told my story. I had told a few other people prior to this, but never to people I did not know well. When I came to the workshop I had no intention of doing this, it literally just happened. It welled up and came out. I do think people need to hear the impact this can have on a life, a marriage, a relationship.

Sharing my story did bring an acute appreciation of the work GERI is doing in bringing awareness to these issues. With ongoing therapeutic support, trust and intimacy can be rebuilt. The three days was a taste of what might be possible. What was most beneficial was being heard, affirmed. I was taken aback by how intensely I still felt about this after three years, how much grief had been pushed down and bottled up. The workshop was quite powerful in unlocking these emotions.

The following reflections were shared by a middle-aged man who recounts how the GERI process of truthtelling helped to restore and heal his trust with other men in particular.

Growing up in a small town in India, my experience transitioning from my teen years to young adulthood was the most challenging part of my life. I was witness to many horrific incidents of bullying, physical abuse, derogatory remarks, body shaming, and violence. As a result, I had confused and misplaced attachment in my relationships. I reached a point where I could not even trust other men. I spent most of my time isolated. I found excuses not to attend social events due to fear of abuse from the same gender. I led a stressful life, with low self-esteem. I didn't feel safe interacting or socializing with women or men. My gender wounds were deep and painful.

I started my GERI journey in 2006. Since then, I have had a shift in my whole outlook. Through GERI, I have found a platform and community that has helped me heal my past gender wounds and become able to speak out and be heard in a safe and non-judgmental, sacred space. Through the process of truth-telling exercises, I have been able to share stories of the gender wounds that were buried deep within me for years. I was able to feel better when a safe space was created around me. It allowed me to let go of all the suffering.

One of the insights I discovered in this GERI work is that I need to take the first step to recognize what is stirring within me, and to find out how I can give voice to my pain and suffering, to be able to name the feelings, and experience the sensations within me. Through making this shift, I have been able to express my own stories and experiences around gender more confidently. I have also learned to hold space for others in this healing journey, and be gentle to myself, too.

I have also witnessed that my whole perception and perspective around gender has shifted. I treat women and other genders more respectfully, and I advocate the same to my two young boys, whom I have taught to respect and treat women as equals. I have been able to shift my stereotypical view of the world, and I am now more open to empathy, equity, compassion, and love.

As a GERI facilitator, I have been able to connect with people from many different cultures, languages, races, genders, and countries who inspire each other and hold a safe and sacred space for each other to heal. This GERI work and process around heart-centered practices connects people from all walks of life.

GERI's work in India has provided a safe space and platform for many people, who through this work can heal past gender wounds and lead a more meaningful life.

This story is from Mangesh Pol, a GERI Facilitator whose life was radically transformed the day he met Sr. Lucy Kurien. He shares how he moved from a place of hating men, due to his father's behavior, to a place of compassion, understanding, and acceptance of all people.

I was born into an "untouchable" family. In India we have so many religions and so many castes, and untouchable is the lowest of the lowest caste. As an untouchable, you don't have any rights. You can't go to school for an education. You don't have the right to have clean drinking water. You don't have the right to walk on the same street where people of higher castes are walking.

It's a very hard life. And the untouchables are the poorest of the poor. When I was a child, we were barely surviving to just get our daily bread. My father was an alcoholic and did very little work, and whatever money he earned went to buy his alcohol. He would drink and he would beat my mother. This was the everyday routine.

I have two older sisters and I'm the youngest child. By the time I was born, my father had already left the house. I used to ask my mother what happened to my father, and she told me that when she was pregnant, my father used to kick on her stomach. He would drink and he would beat her, and the violence never stopped. From that day on, I started hating men, because of my father.

When I was six years old, an angel came into my life—Sister Lucy Kurien, who is the founder and director of the Mahar Ashram in Pune. When Sr. Lucy brought me to Maher, I thought, "I am born in an untouchable family. There are so many people here that will hate me and they will not give me the chance." But I didn't find that. I found that everyone was kind and compassionate toward me.

This was my second birth, coming to Maher. From that point on, I started my journey. I started going to school; I got my own hairbrush; I got my own blanket; I got hot food. The people who I've met on this journey are such blessings in my life. They are loving people and caring people.

When I finished my 12th-grade education, I thought, "Now that I have graduated, I can get a job and work to help so many people. I can help my mom. I can help my sisters." This was true, and I also realized that there is still so much to learn. The same year of my graduation I was selected for the best student of India. I received a gold medal from the President of India and the University

Grants Commission head. What a very beautiful journey for me—a child who thought he would never be able to go to school.

I'm 28 now, and when I joined the Gender Equity and Reconciliation International (GERI) program several years ago, I was really open to learning. During my training as a facilitator, I learned to listen and be present to the feelings of other people. Many of the trainees and participants in the GERI workshops have never had the opportunity to share their stories. For me, GERI is a space—an inner journey—where you can share your emotions, your feelings, your thoughts. Where you can connect with people and listen to each other's stories. I feel like every story is important, not only *his* story, or *her* story, or *their* story. Each and every person has a story that is very important.

Poet Muriel Rukeyser said, "This universe is made of stories, not atoms." It's very beautiful to listen to the gender stories of people in the GERI work. When I listen, I don't judge them. I practice being with the story and the person. I listen with compassion. Doing this started changing my thought process. It started changing me inwardly.

GERI gives an opportunity, a platform, where people listen compassionately to your story, to your thoughts. And there is no one judging you. When I started the GERI program, I experienced people in a new way. I witnessed people's emotions and I saw how they were working on themselves to change their lives in positive ways. All this gave me an energy to live my life to help others.

When I traveled to the United States and experienced the GERI work there, I learned that yes, it's a different culture, but the people there are no different. Wherever you are in the universe, people are people. And it's very good to hear them, and to listen to them, and to learn from them. The same was true when I was in Nepal and doing the GERI work there. Traveling as a GERI facilitator has been a beautiful experience to listen to new people and learn about different cultures.

I've also facilitated the GERI work in India. In India, men give the orders, and women and children are supposed to listen. This is the culture and the way of Indian society. In a GERI workshop we did with young people, in the beginning some of the men in the group were just going through the activities like it was a task, and when sharing they talked from an intellectual place rather than from their feelings. But as the workshop continued, they started to speak more and more from their hearts. By the time we got to the honoring ceremony, the men weren't just going through the motions, they were really offering the ceremony to the women from their hearts. When the women and girls saw this, they were just crying; nobody could stop the tears. The men were really there with the women and girls in their hearts.

This is the journey. This is the GERI healing process.

Through all this, I really experienced that, "Yes, I am part of this universe and I want to give back in service for all that has been given to me." As a GERI facilitator, I know there's a lot to learn, a lot to give, and a lot to share. I keep working with my emotions and I continue my learning to see and speak from my heart. Some things we can see with the physical eyes, but others, you can only experience from the heart.

Honoring Ceremony

The following sharing is of an honoring ceremony that the men offered to the women in a GERI workshop at Dream a Dream in Bangalore.

The scent of rose and tranquil sound of soft music filled the room as we were each escorted in by a man and invited to take a seat in the circle of chairs. Once we were all seated, the men formed an outer circle standing around us. The music changed to *Jab Koi Baat Bigad Jay*—a beautiful Indian song whose lyrics mean "Whenever something goes wrong. Whenever there is a problem. Stand by me, my beloved."

As the song played, the men began moving and dancing around, rotating behind us. Then suddenly, small pieces of colorful paper like confetti were showering down upon us. It took only a moment before one woman picked up one of the papers that had gently fallen on her lap and exclaimed with delight, "There are messages on the paper!" All of us started quickly gathering the papers sprinkled around us as if they were nuggets of precious gold. *You are special . . . You are wise . . . You are loved . . . You are light . . . We hear you . . . We respect you . . . We honor you.* There must have been 40 or more different

Women's honoring ceremony for men, Bangalore, India, 2015.

blessings, each handwritten with special care and attention. As the music came to an end, one by one the men stepped into the center of the circle, knelt before us and gave his personal commitment for continuing to bring harmony, reconciliation, and gender justice into their families and communities. The music began again as the men approached us with a bow offering a hand and inviting us to dance together. The women were deeply touched by the tender and meticulous care the men had taken with preparing the ceremony and honoring them, and the loving spirit of the experience brought another level of healing after all we had been through together.

Maher: A Model of Hope for Oppressed Peoples Everywhere

Sister Lucy Kurien
Maher Ashram, India

I was working with a project called HOPE, training women in economic development skills in a poor neighborhood. One day in 1991, a pregnant woman knocked on our convent door, and asked to take refuge with us. She said that her husband was threatening to kill her because he wanted to bring another woman into the house, so she was fearing for her life. My religious superior was gone that day, and I was not authorized to take anyone in to spend the night. I spoke with the woman and learned she was married for three years and lived with her husband that whole time, so I felt one more day would be no problem. I told her to come back the next day, and I promised to try and do something for her.

That night, my prayers were suddenly interrupted by agonizing screams outside. I rushed out to the street to see what was happening, and suddenly a woman came running around the corner—totally engulfed in flames! When she saw me she ran toward me, screaming, "Save me! Save me!" I realized with abject horror that this was the very woman who had visited me earlier that afternoon. Her husband had poured kerosine on her, and set her on fire.

I helped put out the fire and took her to a hospital, but the doctors said she was already 90-percent burned. I asked the doctors if they could save the baby, and they operated, but when they brought me the seven-month-old fetus, it was, *how can I say it*, a fully cooked baby. Both mother and baby died that night.

I was absolutely devastated. I wanted to run away from this world and its cruelty. I continued living at the convent, but I was not the same. I was so sad and heartbroken. And I was so angry with myself for not helping this woman when she was in need, and with the rules that prevented me from helping her. I would look at the women and children begging on the street and be so frustrated, because they were suffering and here I was living in comfort and isolation. I had joined the convent to help people, but what was I doing for them?

Some of my friends told me, "Lucy, you are not the same." I was becoming an angry person, irritated even for small things. I was never like this before, I had been a very joyful person. They encouraged me to go for counseling, and I started meeting with Father Francis D'Sa. He was a Catholic priest, and he also used to teach Hinduism and the Bhagavad Gita, and was very open-minded. After some time, he said to me, "Instead of sitting and mourning, waiting for the convent to do something for the poor, why don't *you* do it?" I listened and said, "Father, I have no education. I have no money. What will I do?" And he turned around and said, "If you have love in your heart, you will be able to do something."

This struck me very much. I came home and wrote to my religious superiors and told them I wanted to do something for these people who are suffering on the street. My letter got no response. So I went to visit them and explained what I wanted to do. They said "No, we can't do anything." Again and again, I kept writing to them, and finally they understood that I was serious with my decision. Finally they allowed me to go. They told me that I could go and do whatever I thought I wanted to do, but they would give no money or personnel. I had to sign a memorandum of understanding, stating that although I was still a member of the congregation, the work I was doing did not belong to the congregation. I was left alone to work on this project, but they did allow me to continue staying in the house with the other nuns.

This was a big challenge—no money and no personnel. All I had was 20 rupees pocket money (about 40 cents). I started talking with people to find support for the project, and it took years. Finally, Fr. D'Sa put me in touch with an Austrian man who gave me enough money to buy a small piece of land and build our first home. We built our first house in 1997, and called it Maher, which means "mother's home" in the local Marathi language. The day we opened, two women in distress came that first night.

Today we have 63 homes in 6 states across India. More than 4,000 women and children have been through Maher. At present, over 900 children and 300 women are living in the Maher communities. The children we rescue from the street were begging, or were sold into prostitution, or were born to a prostitute. Hundreds of these children from Pune who were begging are now going to school. Women come to us fleeing from abuse and violation, and whenever possible we work to reconcile them with their husbands and families, which is successful about 80 percent of the time. Other women we rescue from the street are outcasts because they had been raped, or widowed, or rejected by their husbands' families because they couldn't pay their dowries. Some of them are mentally disturbed, and we have created special homes for these women. We also started homes for men rescued from the streets.

Our work is not just giving these people food and shelter, and a new home in an institution. What they need from us is love. If they have the support and love that they need, they can come up in life. And the children need education, not just sending them to school to sit quietly, but giving them an all-around education to come up in life. We teach our children not only what they learn in school, but also meditation, how to respect the Earth, how to manage with little, and still be happy.

Of course, it's not always easy. It can be very difficult to work with the moods and likes and dislikes of hundreds of people. But if we are connected to the Divine, we can do it. People ask me, "Lucy, with all the challenges, how can you still smile at the end of the day?" Yes, I can still smile, even in the midst of all our difficulties, because I believe that if we give love to these people, everything is possible and we can do wonders.

From the beginning I wondered, what is the type of spirituality that we can offer in Maher? I come from a very traditional Catholic family, and I'm a Catholic nun. But the people who come to Maher are from all different faiths—Hinduism, Islam, Buddhism, Christianity, indigenous religions, and more. How shall I teach them? How can I lead them into spiritual life?

One night, a beautiful image came to my mind of all the major world religious symbols in a big circle, with a flame of love and light burning in the center. You will see this banner in every Maher home, because every religion is teaching us to go to the Divine. So we honor all the religions. If you come to us during Christmas, you might think we converted all the children into Christians; or, if you come during Diwali, that they all are Hindus; or if you come during Eid, that they are all Muslims. We have a lot of joy and spirituality celebrating the major religious festivals, and we celebrate them from all different religions. The children sit in meditation, they sing, they pray. When I pick up a woman or child from the street, how would I know which caste or religion they belong to? So what? Give them love. That's what I believe in. Care for them at whatever stage they are in. We try to create an atmosphere of joy, peace, and love, and give this to the people who most need it.

GERI at Maher

I have attended Gender Equity and Reconciliation International (GERI) programs several times, and we've had several GERI programs in Maher. Each time I attend, my eyes are opened more and more. The work of Gender Equity and Reconciliation is very much needed in India. It is a powerful program to make people aware of what's going on, especially the women who suffer unnecessarily around gender issues. This work is an eye opener for men and women to learn what each other goes through.

We have conducted several GERI programs for teenagers and young adults at Maher, and a special GERI program for our staff of housemothers. Several Maher staff and community members are GERI facilitators, or in the training program. We are planning to expand GERI programs in the Maher communities, and we also want to introduce GERI programs to the local colleges and universities with whom Maher has a connection.

I feel that Gender Equity and Reconciliation could also play a very important role if it is done within the religious communities; for both males and females. I wish the Church would recognize this work, give importance to it, and take it forward. Unless people go through this program, they don't understand how much value it has.

Sister Lucy Kurien is the founder of Maher Ashram in India, which is internationally recognized as one of the most remarkable projects for rehabilitation of battered and abused women and children (and more recently, men) in India.

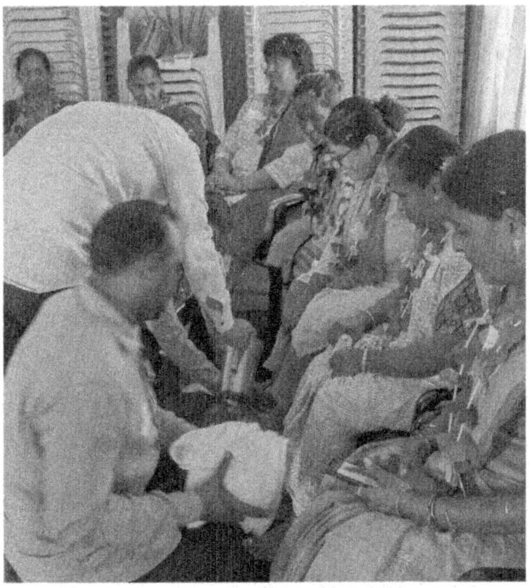

Men honoring women at GERI workshop at Maher in Pune, India, 2024

Celebratory moment at GERI workshop at Dream and Dream in Bangalore, India, 2025

CHAPTER 19

Kenya and East Africa

Dr. Karambu Ringera is the founder/co-director of Tiriji Foundation in Meru, Kenya, which empowers orphans, women living with HIV/AIDS, survivors of violence, and other vulnerable community members via education, advocacy, and leadership development. Over 80 children live in their Children's Home, and over 600 women have been through their skills training programs. GERI's collaboration with Karambu goes back many years, and she co-facilitated several key early GERI programs on the African continent. The first GERI training in Kenya was held in Nairobi in 2011. Below, Karambu describes the deep need for gender healing in Kenyan society, and some of the jewels of transformation that have emerged through the work.

Dr. Ringera: On the Need for Gender Healing

Kenya is a highly patriarchal society. Until very recently, men owned every business, held all prominent positions in government and the Church, were the leaders in every facet of life, and the ones who spoke on behalf of women and children. The systems in which we live—religion, politics, culture and traditions, education, economy, etc.—are premised on a male-centric worldview. In a world created by men for men, women, youth, and children have no say. The systemic, patriarchal oppression taking place in homes, religious spaces, educational institutions, offices, and hospitals is a silent pandemic that has killed many people both literally and metaphorically. And it is very alive in my present day.

Sophie, one of my older children, who has done an online GERI workshop and lives away from home, called me recently and told me that a man who cleans their compound will not take instructions from her because she is a woman. She was so taken aback she asked him to repeat what he had said. This is her story:

Where I live right now, women have no say. It is very traditional and there are no programs to teach men or help them see the world in a different light other than a patriarchal perspective. Women's programs teach women to bear the abuse from men for the sake of their children. When homes break up, most children become drug abusers and petty thieves. Men remarry and forget their children. On this particular day, our compound cleaner was making too much noise. I decided to ask him what the problem was. He told me to mind my own business, that I am a woman and I should not be talking to him. He said I am a woman who lacks respect because I dared stand facing him to talk to him, a man. "You cannot tell me what to say, you woman. Even my wife has never spoken to me like that. Whoever married you, you useless woman?"

Sophie told me no one had ever spoken to her like that before. She explained:

The woman in me who was disrespected stood my ground and answered him back. In this incident, I experienced what being called a 'useless woman' feels like, simply because of my gender, and I dared answer a man back. I also answered him in a way that made him know that in my community, men who want to be respected by women do not speak to women or treat them the way he does. Lastly, I wanted him to know there are women who are different. He did not like it, but I had to speak my truth. My courage to speak to this man the way I did came from understanding that things do not have to be the way they are, and from my promise to myself that I will never be a man's doormat. I have a voice, and I will use it. Now I know first-hand why it is critical to have GERI programs all over Kenya. When I complete school, I will join Dr. Karambu Ringera to bring GERI to this part of Kenya.

Another of my girls goes to a church where the order of seating is as follows: elderly men sit in the front pews, then young men, followed by elderly women, then young girls. The people who sit at the back of the church are young girls and unmarried young women. "Women have no say and are taken as second-hand citizens. They cannot stand up in church to say anything. If you need to say something, you tell the elders, and the elders will tell the church. In her church, men literally own women. Once married, the man owns you. If you have a conflict with your husband, you appear before a council of elders (*baraza*) that reads your wrongs before everyone. But if the husband has a conflict, the wife has to leave the room. So she never gets to know what her husband was told."

In our language, to marry or to be married means to "purchase" or "to be purchased." The man marries (purchases) and the woman is married (purchased). It is a system literally premised on the notion that since the man pays dowry, he has purchased the woman. Many of my married friends have shared how they are raped within marriage because the man will say: "I paid for this, so it is my right to have sex with you anytime, anywhere I wish. And you have no say in the matter!" (Marital rape is legal in Kenya.) Imagine women having no say over their bodies, no place in church, and no right to air their opinions even when a male cleaner is not doing a good job.

Growing up as a girl, I observed that women were not the equals of men in the home. My mom worked on the farm where we grew coffee and foodstuffs like corn and beans. My father would receive all the money from the coffee we delivered to the factory since it was sent to his bank account. When the corn and beans were in the granary, he could just take it to the market and do whatever he wanted to do with the money. I remember that my mother once forged my dad's signature and got money from his account. That must have been because she did all the work and when the money came, my dad would spend it in bars. He was an alcoholic, which eventually killed him.

Growing up, we were taught that girls were good only for marriage, especially if they did not excel in education. To become eligible for marriage, girls had to go through a rite of passage to become women—circumcision or female genital mutilation (FGM). This is a procedure that has the clitoris chopped off, and in some cases, once cut off, the vagina would be half sown so that the husband of the woman could open the woman up when he married her. When I was in primary school, I remember seeing girls with a glazed look in their eyes when they came back to school as *ngutu*—circumcised girls. Many of them never completed primary school because they got pregnant or got married. Once the girls had been deemed a "woman," men took advantage of them, impregnating them and never marrying them. Most girls of that time were married with a child born outside the marriage. Most of those kids were left behind to be brought up by grandparents. They carried a sense of abandonment for the rest of their lives.

In school, photographs of doctors, engineers, and pilots in textbooks were of men. Women were always depicted in the role of caregivers, as housewives, teachers, or nurses. For the longest time I thought women could not be engineers or pilots because those were men's jobs. When a girl was good at math or science subjects, even teachers would tease her in class. There was no place for a girl to excel other than in being a "good girl," meaning you did whatever you were told and never asked questions. Even when married and your husband beat you up, you were supposed to keep quiet and bear it like a "woman." Everyone thinks mistreating women and the girl child is "normal."

Covid-19 made 2020 the year that brought to light the extent of abuse for the girl child and women in our society. The saddest part of the Covid-19 story was that most of the abuse was meted out by family members—fathers, brothers, uncles, and close family friends. Statistics of teenage pregnancies and early marriage in 2020 and 2021 were astronomical in comparison to the years prior to Covid-19.[1] The media routinely show pregnant teenage girls, but they never show or talk about who made them pregnant. The erasure of men from the picture makes it look like the girl got pregnant on her own, while men are shielded from the consequences of their actions.

Here is a story from a Kenyan woman participant in a GERI workshop:

When I had just completed my bachelor's degree, I was date-raped and I got pregnant. I felt I had let my parents down and so I never went home during my pregnancy. None of my siblings or parents asked me where I was or came to visit me. I could not tell anyone that I was raped because they would not have believed me. I lived with my shame and blamed myself for a long time. It seemed to me that men never have to care about raping people because the onus is on the victims (most of them women and girls), whom men are taught are theirs to "play" with. Women have to bear the brunt of men's animalistic behavior and deceit. Within patriarchy, the system gives men all the privileges in spite of their being so badly behaved. Something did not add up for me in this picture. It still does not. I developed a very negative attitude towards men and the marriage system. Although I eventually got married, it did not last long and it was easy for me to walk away because as far as I was concerned, men were and would always be unreliable, unfaithful, and untrustworthy. The guy I was married to was all these things. I had promised myself that I would never allow myself to be a "slave" of the marriage system. And I never did, although I still did not understand many things, because even in walking away from an abusive marriage, there was (and still is) a lot of judgment and stigmatization.

From all the above observations and experiences, I have been searching, all through my life, for the answers as to why society is structured the way it is. In my Women in Development classes in South Africa I started glimpsing the enormity of the problem. It was not merely a problem in my community and country, it was also an African continental problem. When I went to study in the USA, I found that it was also a global problem. I started looking for alternative ways of overcoming these systems and ways of navigating my life as a woman in the ocean of patriarchy.

When I first came to the world of Gender Equity and Reconciliation International (GERI), I was ready for answers to these myriad questions. I was interested in understanding this "thing" about women and men, but I was not sure there ever was going to be reconciliation between the genders. Inside of me, I never felt I could reconcile, heal, or bridge this enormous gaping hole that patriarchy had dug in my soul. Moreover, I could not see a gentle and loving way of doing the reconciling, healing, and bridging work to birth "beloved community."

I've now been involved with GERI for over 16 years, participating in and facilitating many workshops and trainings, both in Africa and globally. A wonderful example of the power of the GERI process in transforming individuals and systems and bringing healing to people came alive for me in the first Kenya GERI workshop held in Nairobi in 2011. It was attended by young professionals from various walks of life. One of the young women (we shall call her Winnie) shared the very sad story of how her mom was treated inhumanely by her husband's brothers, and when the husband died, Winnie's uncles started harassing her mercilessly, because they were interested in her family's land. The uncles really tortured her mom, who had been left with 7 small children, in the hope that she would leave the family land. Winnie shared, in tears and deep pain, how her mother and the kids suffered terribly at the hands of these men. But her mother wrestled with them for years and refused to leave. Although the uncles were wealthy, they refused to help her educate the children. One of the uncles wanted to inherit her mom. When her mom refused, the torture got worse. When Winnie finished telling her story, there was no dry eye in that room.

Then one man, Emmanuel, stood up, went over and knelt down in front of Winnie. That gesture alone was astounding; for a Kenyan man to kneel before a woman is totally unheard of. And he said to Winnie: "As a man, I kneel before you to apologize and ask for forgiveness, on behalf of your uncles, for all that they did to your mom and your family." We were all stunned. You could have heard a pin drop in the silence that ensued. Winnie looked at the man; she heard and saw his sincerity, and broke into tears. She wept for some time as we all sat in silent witness. Then wiping her tears and taking a deep breath, she looked at the man and said, "Thank you" and knelt down next to him and gave him a hug. Everything stood still. That was a defining moment for all of us. The GERI process works! Gender healing and reconciliation is possible. We saw it happen right in front of our eyes.

Soon after the workshop, I asked Emmanuel what had prompted him to do what he did. He said, "In hearing the deep hurt in Winnie's story and their suffering as a family, my heart was torn because in her crying, I also saw my mother crying." Here is his story:

> Personally, my mother had passed through a similar experience. My dad died when I was only four years old, and mother went through hell in the hands of my uncles and close family members who took our land and have never given it back to this day. Although I was only four, I remember my mother used to cry a lot. When Winnie shared her story, I remembered my mother and our story. My mom used to cry every day, but she had no shoulder to lean on. When I saw Winnie cry, I saw my mother crying and that is what prompted me to provide a shoulder for her to lean on, something my mother never had. I knew from my experience that, for healing to take place, someone has to stand in the gap. I stood in the gap for my mother when I grew up. And I knew I could do it for someone else.

How does GERI work bring reconciliation and lasting change? The impact of GERI on Emmanuel's life has been profound since those days. He shared this with me recently:

> One, I learned to forgive easily in order to release myself from carrying the weight of the offenses done against me. Two, I became more responsible to the people close to me, my children and my wife, to ensure that no one goes through that kind of painful experience in their life. The pain of getting your property stolen

by someone is deep; seeing my mother cry every day was torture. I wish upon no one such a painful experience and I have done all I can to protect my loved ones and others from it. Thus, wherever I go, I know I can be a shoulder to lean on for someone who is hurting because of patriarchy. As a man, I can, and I do, stand in the gap.

Here is the follow up from Winnie today, 12 years later:

GERI had a great impact in my life. When I shared my story, a heavy burden was lifted from my shoulders. When Emmanuel knelt down and apologized on behalf of my uncles, I forgave my uncles. I released a hatred I had carried for years. I was able to clear out something that had been a weight within me for a very long time. The anger just faded away and I felt a new spirit in me. The experience also made me realize that forgiveness heals the soul, the mind and the heart; and no matter what anyone does to me, I have power to change it through forgiveness. My life has changed since then because I have a heart for helping other people heal their wounds. I created a magazine to capture stories of women who have gone through difficult times but have been able to overcome those obstacles. My uncles eventually came back to apologize to us.

The workshops touch both men and women deeply. We come to terms with our individual woundedness, understand another's woundedness, and we intuitively recognize and understand at a deep level that our individual and collective healing is up to each one of us. This is what happens in the sacred space that we create together within the GERI workshop space. From there, we take the healing out to the world by choosing to live our lives in ways that bridge the gender gap and bring healing every day. Everyone who attends a GERI workshop is deeply moved by what happens in that space and the depth of trust, sharing, transformation, and healing that happens within the three days of the workshop. Since societal conditioning takes place within the community, the healing, too, will happen within the community. The healing begins with me.

Hence, I have a role to play in enabling this transformation to take place. That is why I am a GERI trainer and facilitator, holding the mantle for the East Africa region, with the vision to take the GERI work all over our continent. The GERI process is powerful, real, and it works!

In the next account, a young Kenyan man shares his poignant gender story, and the challenges he and other young men face coming of age. His transformative experiences through the gender-healing work has allowed him to step more deeply into his humanity and become an empowering leader within his community supporting other young men to do the same.

I feel very fortunate to have come across Gender Equity and Reconciliation International. I did my first GERI workshop in 2019, and it has been one of the greatest transformational programs I have participated in.

I live in a very patriarchal community, and I have always wanted to see my community heal from the harm patriarchy has caused not only to women and children, but also to men. Before I came to the work, I was in deep confusion about how I should live, and I felt called to a different way of showing up as a man in my community. In my community there is a lot of patriarchy that is passed on to young men, especially in circumcision rituals performed on adolescent boys, and in the way boys are taught how to become men in that context. In some ways I was fortunate, because when I was circumcised I didn't belong to any family or community, and so I was fortunate that I was not indoctrinated into how to be a man in that way. Still, in the community that I live in right now the system of patriarchy has been very destructive, not only to women but also to men, in terms of how we are conditioned to relate to others and express ourselves. I came to GERI with a lot of confusion, because in my heart I felt drawn to be a different kind of person than how men here are taught to be. For example, I wanted to be able to interact with women and young children, but in my culture I'm not supposed to interact with women or children because they are supposed to fear me. Fear is seen as respect here, but in my heart I felt, "No, I don't want to live like this."

As a boy I lived with my mother, but when I was 11 or 12 years old she had a stroke, so I had to start taking care of her. We were very close. I would wash her clothes, I would look for money for food and for her medication, and I would generally care for her. We remained homeless for 13 years, and during that time I experienced continuous domestic violence at the hands of my father, which caused me to hate him. For over 20 years I carried a deep woundedness due to the way my father treated me and my sickly mother. Just recently, when I attended a GERI workshop, I had a dramatic experience of healing, because I was able to forgive my father and step into a better manhood for myself.

Being so close to my mother gave me a lot of compassion for women, and so I didn't feel that I belonged in my culture, in which people wanted me to fear and not trust women. So I carried this burden of wounding, not being allowed to simply go stand with a woman and talk with her. I'm not supposed to play with small children, either, and yet I feel very drawn to children and women because my transformation in life has come through women. This burden was always difficult for me to bear, and so I was happy when I came to GERI and found people who encouraged me to be more human than "man." That has always been my greatest desire, to be more human than man. Because being more human for me means being more free, and through the work of gender equity and reconciliation, I have felt great freedom interacting with everyone and just being *me,* regardless of where I am showing up. I now get to show up more fully as a human being in my community, and also provide a safe space for women and children in my culture, and for men, too. This has given me a whole new freedom, because now when I'm in a gathering in public spaces, I don't need to worry about who I'm interacting with; I can just be there as a human being interacting with other human beings. I used to think sometimes that maybe I wasn't man enough, because I felt I needed to be with women and I felt happy when I was with children, but my fellow young men were not like that. But in the transformation brought about by this process, I feel great joy, like my heart is healing from all that doubt and damage.

GERI has broadened my perspective and helped me to discover that it is not just a matter of talking with people, but of integrating human consciousness, humility, and deep compassion to create a safe space for both men and women to step into their own journey of healing. I now see all people, men and women alike, as pure and complete, and I respect the humanness in each one of them. I recognize the Divine in each person, regardless of their gender. This work has supported me in breaking out of the box of patriarchy and becoming a freer human being, able to live my life fully and powerfully, thus impacting not only myself but also women, children, and the other men in my community. And that freedom is attracting more men in my community to also join in this work and step into their humanness, and into the genuine beauty of manhood, while at the same time respecting that we are fellow human beings along with women and children

I have recently started a new project, Kenya Men Circles, which brings men together for conversations to facilitate their healing. I am happy that there are several other men from my community who have joined in this work. Together, we are creating a space to show up differently and to help younger men see that there is a different way to live. Together, we come to understand that we cannot live by inflicting pain on women and children so that they fear us, mistakenly thinking that fear is respect. It is so beautiful to see my fellow men joining me in this work as we continue to grow ourselves and to step into our power and our humaneness, so that we can become a light to other young men who are still growing up, and also to the older men in this community.

I am happy for what we are creating together, and I am so grateful that I came to this work because it involves not only my own transformation but the transformation of my whole community. I know that my own heart is healing, that I am becoming freer as a man, and that this is enabling me to support others in my community who are on the same journey. We are building a community in which no one is higher than anyone else. Instead, we live together in harmony. That cohesion brings forth the beauty of our culture—*the original culture*—which brings people together and creates trust and true respect based in love.

I am so happy for all my "mentors and femtors" who have supported me to become who I am today. Words may not fully convey the real transformation that GERI has brought in me, and my community. I am forever grateful.

The next sharing is from a young woman who writes about forgiveness and embracing her "true self."

Knowing who you are can be an easy thing to say, but working on it is a scary thing to do. For the longest time I thought that I knew who I was, but as time went by, I knew I was lying to myself, because I was living my life based around the anger I was carrying within. I was unable to forgive myself and the things that happened in my life, including violent acts and the opportunities that were denied to me because I am a woman. I would always come second in a family of men. This really affected me, and I thought I was supposed to be like my brothers, to think like them and be masculine.

Growing up I was always upfront, and masculinity ruled my way of life. I could never take any ideas from a man, and I always wanted to be the one standing out in the midst of men. I thought this was normal, but at the same time I didn't have many male friends. Males were often scared and intimidated by me. In school I was always controlling others. Later I worked in an institution full of beautiful men with amazing souls, but I still wasn't able to see them. Then a moment of truth came.

When I first attended a Gender Equity and Reconciliation workshop, I was not sure what I was getting myself into. I let myself accept the unknown of my gender healing journey, and I felt an urge to replenish my relationship with my father. I hadn't been on good terms with my father from the moment he looked at me and decided I was no longer his daughter. His words hurt me for the longest time of my adulthood, but through GERI I was able to know myself better by accepting forgiveness and forgiving myself and my father. I embraced freedom, freeing myself from the woundedness of my past. I learned that when something mean is said to me, it does not define who I am. Freedom gave me compassion and authenticity, and my heart, mind, and body felt lighter.

I am still on my journey continuing to know who I am as I unpack all that is stopping me from fully embracing who I am. I am working on healing the wounds that have been hard to let go. Life is a journey of so many colors. It takes time to find the right color that reminds you to come back to your inner self. GERI helped me find my color.

In the next story a participant recounts the important emotional process she moved through during the workshop that culminated in a powerful healing and transformative experience that shifted the way she sees men.

I stepped into the segment of the women's Truth Mandala with the stick, representing anger. I sat down, holding the stick in my hand, and told the story of what happened, and what I was angry about. I was holding anger due to the fact that I was the one left feeling shameful, feeling guilty for letting it happen to me, while what I had done was trust this person. I was angry to be part of a world and conditioning and education that leaves me feeling guilt and shame. And knowing that they are out in the world, probably not aware of what they did, not aware of how much impact that had in my life.

And then also, I had this sense of collective anger towards this world we've created, where sexual violence is such a reality. That it's a way people exert power and control, and that the female form has received and holds in our collective memory the pain of it, the powerlessness, the helplessness, the shame, and the guilt.

After I was done telling my story, the facilitator looked at me and she said, "You have told us the story while holding the stick. I feel like there's more that needs to come out. Tell us that story *through* the stick." For a second, I didn't quite know what to do, but then I felt a shaking and rumbling beginning to happen in my body, and gripping the stick tightly, I started to speak.

I said, "My parents split up when I was ten, and because of that, I grew to be a protector and ended up holding a lot of my mother's pain. I grew to hate men deeply while also desiring a relationship with my father. The dissonance was ripe. I was date raped some years ago, and I haven't healed from it. I didn't even know how ill it has left me, until this moment."

When I stopped talking, my face was covered with tears and snot. I was shaking hard, but the anger had left me. A lot of the anger I had held in my womb space had been released. I could feel it.

I had just come out of a relationship that had left me feeling so lost and small. All I wanted to do was release that frustration, but I hadn't had a place to do it. I struggled with feeling connected to the men in the GERI workshop, until I shared what had happened to me, which broke my shell open and I was able to let the anger out. It helped me clear a lot of those feelings. I was able to release just enough of my anger to step into the next process of healing, in which I could begin to share space with men in a way that allowed me to see them as human beings first. Seeing men as human has taken me a while, and will continue to take time to grow. I feel like I'm still a long way away, but there is something happening, and speaking my truth was a major step in my healing. Before this experience, I had all these things to say to the men. But after the activity, I realized my anger was not going to serve. I no longer had anger to direct at men. I went back into the witnessing circle, grateful that there were men who were willing to be vulnerable and raw and honest and open. It comforted me to know that these men were here and showing up. That, although the one man who harmed me may never know, *these* men heard me, and now they understand more about what I and many other women have been through. When these men hear their friends and other men talking about what they want to do to women, hopefully this will embolden them to say something. So, when it came my turn to share in the witnessing circle, I just thanked them for being there, and I left that space feeling more love and feeling more connected to my brothers.

The first time I attended a GERI workshop was in 2018, since then it's been a slow regenerative process. I'm learning to first see the person before seeing the pain I have held; to see that we all have trauma and pain to hold each other through, as well as gems and gifts to offer each other. The ability to hold the kind of deep healing space for another as was held for me is why I chose to join the GERI deep immersion training and continue my healing journey, and work toward becoming a GERI facilitator.

Honoring Ceremonies

Because Kenya is a very patriarchal society, it is all the more powerful to see men honoring women. When men hear the suffering that women go through at the hands of men, most are shocked because such suffering has been hidden from them. In sharing our stories, we all see how both men and women have

GERI Facilitator Meggy Nakibi and GERI Trainer Garrett Evans presenting at the 12th Chuka University International Research Conference in Chuka, Kenya, 2025

GERI workshop outside Nairobi, Kenya, 2021

suffered at the hands of the systems we live in. Women also are shocked to hear the suffering of men, because patriarchy largely benefits men. To understand that men, too, have been harmed by patriarchy is a sobering truth. Hearing these stories opens the door to a powerful time of forgiving ourselves and those who have harmed us, because now we know better that people of *both* genders are suffering, and we are all embedded in this system together.

This remembrance of our interbeing is then enacted in the honoring ceremonies: The men invited us to gather outside the workshop room where we had been meeting the past three days. As we waited, the women quietly chatted and giggled together in excited anticipation of what was to come. Then, one by one we were invited into the room.

A man came for me, and with a bow, invited me to follow him. He asked me whether I was okay with wearing a blindfold, and I said I was. Once blindfolded, he took my hand, placed it on his arm and guided me through what felt like a "wash of fresh air"—the other men had made a tunnel with their arms and bodies through which we walked. They had scarves that they were swaying up and down, creating a gentle breeze touching my face like a soft caress. Another man took my hand and led me to a chair. He guided me until I was safely seated on the chair. I was still blindfolded when someone gently asked me whether I was okay being touched on my feet. I said I was okay. My feet were then tenderly lifted from my shoes and placed in a basin of warm scented water. Then this man washed my feet, dried them, and oiled them, and oh all this was done so gently and lovingly! Then he ever so carefully put my feet back into the shoes. I was invited to remove the blindfold and in front of me stood another man, smiling with eyes shining brightly and a with a piece of paper in his hands. He proceeded to read the sweetest words I had ever heard spoken from a man. "The story you shared and the stories from the other women opened my eyes and touched my heart deeply. I had no idea of the challenges that women face. I heard you! I see you! I will never be silent again!" Tears, tears, tears—tears of a deep wash that felt like a cool balm on a burn; the sincerity with which the words were uttered sunk them deep within me. The words landed right into my soul. I knew from that moment on that, I will always see every man I meet in my life differently. Even if I forget for a moment, I have that moment that I heard those words from that voice, and I will be able to forgive and heal, over and over again. The men then stood before us and made a commitment for how they would personally continue to bring gender healing and reconciliation into their lives and the world.

That was a profound moment of deep healing for me. It was a major turning point in my life. I had always found it hard to trust men in my life. But there is something deep and amazing that happens to men and women who go through the GERI workshops. Something happened in me, too. One sees themselves in a very different light. There is a "lifting of the heart" that happens that brings a freedom of being—like coming up from under water to breathe again; like coming into life anew! For me it felt this way: if this level of authenticity is possible for these men (and women), it is possible for any person. There was a sense of relief in knowing that *truly* we can transform our lives in real tangible ways. *Real* healing is possible! *Real* freedom from the shackles of patriarchy is possible. After being in the dark tunnel of patriarchy for so long, this experience was like coming out from the tunnel into light. This has continued to give me the hope that I need every day to go on doing the gender equity and reconciliation work. I am fully convinced that this is a powerful tool for human transformation and regeneration. I am eternally grateful I found GERI and GERI found me. My commitment is to bring it to all corners of Africa and our globe. And so it is.

Seeds planted in Kenya many years ago are now sprouting and hold great promise for the development and growth of the GERI work at a new level. The vision is to create a powerful GERI presence in Africa in general, and specifically in Kenya and Eastern Africa, and the 11 Nile Basin countries, plus Congo, Rwanda, Burundi, Malawi and Zimbabwe.

CHAPTER 20

Latin America

Latin America is a region with warm beaches, spectacular mountains, and vast indigenous history and cultural heritage. Unfortunately, gender-based violence and gender inequity have been growing at alarming levels in the past few decades, and the *machismo* culture is still very prevalent. As Alicia Bárcena, Executive Secretary of ECLAC (Economic Commission for Latin America and the Caribbean) expressed it,

> Gender violence occurs systematically in our region. It knows no borders, it affects women and girls of all ages and it happens in all spaces: in the workplace, in the framework of political and community participation, in transport and on the street, at school and in the educational centers, in cyberspace and, without a doubt, in their own homes. It is what we in the United Nations system have called a "shadow pandemic."[1]

The Pan American Health Organization conducted surveys on violence against women between 2003 and 2009 in 12 Latin American and Caribbean countries (Bolivia, Colombia, the Domincan Republic, Ecuador, El Salvador, Guatemala, Haiti, Honduras, Jamaica, Nicaragua, Paraguay, and Peru). In these countries, the percentages of women reporting physical or sexual violence by an intimate partner ranged from 17.0 percent in the Dominican Republic (2007) to 53.3 percent in Bolivia (2003).[2] Countries like Mexico and Brazil have the highest numbers of femicides[3] —murders of women and girls because of their gender.

GERI's work in Latin America began in 2012 with the first in-person workshop in Bogota, Colombia, with 25 women and men participants, organized and co-led by GERI facilitator, Natalia Margarita Cediel, a professor at the Universidad de La Salle. In Bogota, GERI co-founders Cynthia Brix and Will Keepin also gave two introductory experiential presentations on GERI at the Universidad Javeriana, and the Universidad Nacional de Colombia, with the participation of more than 60 people.

Further doors were opened in 2014 and 2015 when GERI co-founders Keepin and Brix gave presentations at the U.N. University for Peace, outside Ciudad Colon, Costa Rica. In 2018 Silvia Araya Villalobos organized three events to introduce GERI in San Jose, Costa Rica. GERI leaders Keepin and Brix gave presentations at the Universidad Latina, the Universidad Autónoma de Centro América, and the Inter-American Institute for Cooperation on Agriculture. A frontpage article about GERI was published in the Sunday *CRHoy* newspaper *(Costa Rica Today)*, where the need for reconciliation between men and women was reported as a priority. As one professor from the Universidad Latina who attended the program said, "Costa Rica doesn't have an army, but we're living a war in every household."

The GERI project in Latin America has continued to grow and the first online course in Spanish was launched in 2020 with five facilitators from Argentina, Bolivia, Colombia, Costa Rica and Venezuela. The implementation of online programs circumvented many of the financial and logistical challenges and barriers previously faced, and opened the possibility to a significant expansion into Latin America. More people have access to the courses now as the Latin America GERI community is strengthening.

Women in Latin America are still frequently subjected to catcalling in the streets, and generally feel unsafe when walking alone at any time of the day. Little girls in Latin America learn very quickly how to dress and how to behave to avoid being attacked or molested. For boys and men, the "machismo" culture conditions them from childhood to always be strong, to base their value and status on the amount of money they earn, and to compete with other men for the attention of women.

Highlights, Stories, and Personal Narratives

"You have broken my faith in love! And in men!" The young woman raised her voice in outrage to her father. Then she broke down in tears, as her fiancé and parents looked on in anguish. After a couple minutes, she said in a tone of defeat, "Now, I'm fearful about even getting married."

This was the heart-breaking declaration made by a young woman to her father during our first GERI workshop in Bogota, Colombia in 2012. The young woman and her fiancé had come to the workshop, along with both of her parents. Her father had had an extramarital affair about five years earlier, which had caused tremendous pain within the family. The ensuing family drama around this re-surfaced over the course of the workshop, and led to intensive processing between husband and wife, between daughter and fiancé, and between the parents and their daughter. The GERI facilitators worked carefully with each of these family members, supporting each in their particular process, and facilitating dialogue between them, as their story emerged into the group. The full group was also supportive of the various family members, and skillfully held them in compassion, which was much appreciated. This was the first time the daughter had ever expressed to her father the anger she felt for his betrayal of her mother. She also said this instilled in her a trepidation about marriage, and a lack of trust for men. The father became contrite, and acknowledged her pain, and his wife's pain, while also affirming his deep love and commitment to them both. After intensive processing all around, including a few sessions outside the main meeting space with the various family members, the daughter and her parents came into a place of understanding, acceptance, and mutual appreciation. Follow up with them later confirmed that the experience, though challenging, had been helpful to them, and they all felt especially grateful for the support.

As workshop organizer Natalia Cediel said afterwards, "The work done here these three days has healed a lot of my family lineage. The whole experience was to feel embraced—in a sacred temple—of the hearts of all who shared the experience."

The following personal stories come from women and men who have been part of subsequent Latin American GERI workshops and courses. The first story is from a 42-year-old woman who shares an experience she had as a child that shattered her trust and sense of safety in the world.

When I was 12 years old, I lived in a middle-class neighborhood in Bogotá, and even though it was a big city, I felt safe and hadn't ever really thought about the possibility of being harmed. One day when I was walking to the store to buy something to eat, a man driving by slowed down and asked me for directions to a street that passed through my neighborhood. I told him how to get where he wanted to go, but the man didn't move. He sat there in his car staring at me. I was looking at him wondering why he wasn't leaving and then I kind of zoomed out from his face and I saw that he was masturbating. I was shocked and really scared. I quickly looked away and started walking as fast as I could to the store.

I went in and bought my food, but when I came out the car was coming down the street again. I started walking faster and tried to ignore him, but this time he lowered the passenger window and pointed a submachine gun at me. I was so scared. I still remember the scene so vividly even today. He told me to get in or he would kill me. I lost my breath for a moment, but I stared him straight in the eyes and without thinking I said, "Kill me, but I won't get in." It was a survival reaction. I didn't know what was going to happen, but he didn't shoot me. Instead, he simply told me to wait for him to finish masturbating.

This was one of those very horrific times in my life when I was so thankful to God for being saved. Even worse, after the man drove away, I went to the police station, which was three blocks away, and with all my strength and my ability I tried to explain to the policemen what had happened. Instead of taking their radiophones to try to find the guy, they made fun of me. They said, "Oh, that guy showed you his two pistols—the submachine gun and his other gun." They made fun of me right in my face. I was a 12-year-old girl asking for help, and instead I got taunted. It was like a slap in the face. I was feeling so afraid.

From that moment on I have felt totally insecure in my city. I don't feel safe as a woman walking alone in my own neighborhood. And, now that I have a daughter, I'm even more afraid for her safety.

The next story is from Hugo Sanchez, a GERI Trainer originally from Venezuela, who shares about the machismo behavior that as a child he tried to reject, but which he still inherited from the elder men in his family. He shares about the ways he took on that conditioning, and the pain he inflicted on others before ultimately shedding and transforming the cultural patterns of male socialization in his own life.

From early in my childhood, I noticed the division of roles and the physical separation between men and women in my family gatherings. The men would sit outside in the backyard drinking beer and badmouthing their wives (i.e., my mother and my aunts). The women would stay inside, sitting in the living room or working in the kitchen. One of the privileges these men enjoyed, among many others, was to do nothing in the house and be served by the women. Among the men it was okay to talk about one's numerous sexual adventures outside their marriage, and they took a lot of pride in it. The code was mostly unspoken, but I was told one day to "never ever step on another fireman's hose." Meaning that whatever another man did—especially sexually—I should look the other way and not say anything. I had to be a partner in crime to whatever the group of men did or said. If I broke this code, I would never again be let into the group of men. I would not be a real man. I learned that a man must be strong, take what he wants, conquer, and dominate. But, growing up, this never made sense to me. Why marry somebody only to talk behind their back and treat them like a servant? Women were so beautiful, kind, and intelligent. There was something in the women of my family I didn't see in the men.

So there I was, in my teenage years, thinking I had matured and that I had my "own criteria" for being a man, but the patriarchal attitude was embedded in me early on, with little chance to refuse or even recognize it. I had no real choice, and no role models of sacred masculinity to look to. I learned to be a good sexual performer, but not a good lover. Besides, if I fell in love I would become "weak" and suffer, so why bother? I had girlfriends, and this was celebrated by both the men and the women in my family, but if any girl in my family had a boyfriend she would be reprimanded and told to wait until marriage.

As a young man I always thought to myself, "I will not be like my father and uncles. I will never cheat on my wife or become an alcoholic." So, I grew up to marry and have children, living a "clean life." And one day . . . let's just say I didn't go fishing but I was on the boat and a fish jumped in the boat. I had the choice to return her back to the water, but I didn't. That's when that patriarchal programming reactivated. "Why not?" I told myself, "I am a good husband and a good father. I am not an alcoholic, and I take care of my responsibilities. Therefore, I can afford a little adventure, right?"

Little did I know the amount of pain this would cause to the people who love me the most and whom I love the most. Lies snowballed, and things got very messy for everyone involved. It was a period of darkness and a feeling of betrayal and unworthiness settled in for a long time. But that was not the man I wanted to be, the man that I know I am inside, and so I engaged in a process to face my shadows and reclaim my integrity. My process of healing started with the New Warrior Training Adventure with The ManKind Project (MKP), the most powerful transformational experience I ever had in my life. That weekend with the MKP broke the chains of my past, and I regained my accountability and integrity. I realized that the MKP work is needed among men's circles and I became a facilitator to help the project reach as many men as possible.

I was introduced to GERI by one of my MKP brothers, and I am so grateful for it. Being in a circle with both men and women brings another level of healing. For me, it is very difficult to talk with men about things that may be embarrassing or shameful. Speaking the truth in the presence of women during my GERI workshop, while incredibly difficult and vulnerable, brought me a degree of healing impossible to achieve in men-only circles. To be heard and held compassionately by people of the gender I have inflicted harm upon made me realize the depth of love I was disconnected from. Hearing the women's stories was and still is the fuel to my commitment to equity. To be able to see the impact my actions and those of other men have had in women's lives is truly awakening. This awakening anchored me in my responsibility and commitment to honor every human being as an equal.

GERI has been a core means for me to help bring about equity and create an opportunity to reconcile with the feminine, to be accepted and heard without judgment, and to be seen for who I am. Being a GERI facilitator for my beloved Latin American community brings me back full circle, because I know firsthand what Latin American men and women have experienced growing up, I know what their family gatherings look like, and I know the incredible violence with which both men and women are raised in the Latino community. GERI is a platform through which I can co-create a legacy for generations to come, a legacy of commitment to shifting the patterns of patriarchy, a legacy of purification, work, vigilance, advocacy, authenticity, and integrity. A legacy of a world in which all women, men, and all gender identities and sexual orientations can live a life in peace and harmony, without fear.

In one course, two men shared about the pain of being divorced fathers and how they wanted to be more active in their children's lives, but are prevented from doing so because the laws normally favor the mother. They shared that divorced fathers are often legally forced to be a distant figure and are sometimes even prevented from seeing their children for long periods of time. As one male participant reflected, "For me, after sharing my story, it was very healing to hear the women in the course honoring the role of the father as valuable." This is his story.

Fatherhood is a form of happiness that I hold—not as romanticism, but as a genuine enjoyment. I've lived this happiness as a father, and, as a stepfather, as a godfather, and mentor figure. I've been in this role for a long time and for many people who have seen me as a kind of surrogate father, fatherhood has always been attractive to me. Even as a child, I had a doll that I liked to take care of, and my sister helped me to make clothes and such for the doll. I enjoyed taking care of my doll and pretending to be a daddy. I learned a lot about empathy and love playing with my doll.

I work in education, and sometimes there are boys and girls who need some extra help or caring support. I have always felt gratification and satisfaction of serving, however briefly, as a "papá substitute" for these children who have seen me as a male figure with whom they could have a caring and trusting relationship, similar to that of a father.

When I met my ex-wife (who I was married to for 15 years), she had three children from another relationship. When we became a couple, the children were eleven, five, and two years old. I had a very close relationship with the children, and they saw me as a father figure. I so enjoyed being Papi to these three children. Seven years into our marriage, my wife and I had a child together.

Some years later we made the decision to divorce. At that time, my biological son was five years old and the relationship between us was very strong. When my wife and I stopped living together, I moved into the house next door so we could be neighbors and stay connected. My son made the decision that he wanted to primarily live with me. Even before then, I had been doing much of the child rearing myself, and really enjoyed this part of life. Around the time when he came to live with me—about three years ago—his mother began a new relationship and moved away from us. So I took on much more responsibility than before. Instead of sharing the parenting duties equally, I was doing 80 or 90 percent of the parenting, or even 100 percent of it on some weeks, living with my son who depended fully on me.

I never felt this as a burden though, or something overwhelming. The only thing that is strange and at times uncomfortable is the perception that some people have of me in this role, as if I'm an extraordinary person or father. This can be uncomfortable for me, because in reality I don't do more or less than any woman, any single mother in my same position. Women are not applauded and are not deified for doing the same thing that I do as a single father. But in my case, I'm often seen as some kind of extraordinary person and given special respect and admiration, when all I do is what any caring mother would do.

During this time though, I was always afraid that there might be a legal dispute, and that I might lose my son. In my country, when there is a separation or divorce, the standard practice is that the child stays with the mother.

Many men in this macho society feel more comfortable this way—that the mother is granted custody and they can continue to live their separate lives with a more distant relationship with their children. They like this because it allows them to continue looking for other forms of personal fulfillment and success. In our society being a father is not seen as a great achievement for a man. It seems to me that our task as men is to change the vision that society has of us as fathers. Society sees us as something like an accessory, something dispensable, or as someone whose role is simply economic. I'm a man who enjoys the role that most men were taught is not acceptable. My invitation to other men is that we live and enjoy fatherhood, and fully give, and receive, the blessing that it is in our lives.

On the other side of this experience, a young woman participant shares how she has risen above and transformed her challenges, disappointments, and the broken heart of being a single mother into strength, clarity, and wisdom.

Recently a good friend asked me why I described myself on my Instagram profile as "a survivor of Covid-19 and patriarchy." My answer to my friend's question can be summarized as follows:

By the time my daughter arrived, I had already learned to die, but of all the deaths I have faced in my life, the mourning of my daughter's father's relationship with her has undoubtedly been the most difficult to process of my entire life, and at the same time the one that has opened my heart the most. He did not literally die, but since the fourth month of pregnancy, he has been absent from his role as a father. In my gender biography, nothing has hurt me as much as this.

Suddenly, I woke up as a single mother at the age of 39. My eyes were opened to the reality of many women around the world, and especially those in my country, where men often decline their responsibility as parents. Nothing was enough to make my daughter's father understand the miracle that had come into his life—not the DNA testing, nor approaching his family, nor knowing that I was in a coma with a high risk of mortality for a month from a coronavirus infection.

Being an example and role model for my daughter while her father has been absent has been the most important challenge I have faced in my life. I decided not to engage in a legal battle for the recognition of paternity, not because I do not know the rights of my daughter, but because I want to free myself and free her from the storm of having two parents who fight and cause endless suffering. I decided not to force him to contribute money for her support, because money is not what I value in a father figure. An affectionate and emotional connection would be most important, but I no longer desire for a connection between my daughter and her father because I understand the negative impacts that an emotionally unstable father figure can have. I decided not to hate him for his voluntary absence in her life, not because I don't feel his behavior is unacceptable, but because by hating him I could stain my daughter's heart. Even though being a single mother is sometimes very difficult, I think it would be harder for my daughter to feel the confusion of loving and expecting something from a person who cannot give back what she needs. I decided not to think or speak ill of him, not because I feel that he does not deserve it, but because through him, God gifted me with my daughter.

Whenever I feel anger, frustration, and loneliness, I try to practice self-empathy, mindfulness breathing, and focus on my needs as a woman as well as the needs of my daughter. In short, I am a survivor of patriarchy, because my heart has not stopped loving and trusting.

Several times I have proudly said that I am a single mother, even though this is not well regarded in some conservative circles. I have assumed my responsibility for my mistakes. The difficulties in my relationships have not closed my heart or my aspiration to have a loving home for both my daughter and myself. I promote gender equality with even more passion than before without looking for culprits and without carrying anger toward the men in my life, my work, and my family. I have survived. From the pain and disappointment of gender wounds, I have emerged, like a phoenix, with strength, clarity, and wisdom.

This next writing is from a woman participant who shares how she has had to overcome what she learned as a child about repressing her emotions from witnessing her parent's behavior and finding a balance of the masculine and feminine within herself.

The adventure began when I received an invitation to participate in the first online GERI workshop for Latin America. This gave me the opportunity to process my gender history, particularly involving the rigidity of gender roles within my Latin American patriarchal culture. Males are trained to show themselves as strong, to face life without showing their emotions (with the exception of anger), so they do not express what they feel or need. On the other hand, females are trained to be emotional, welcoming, containing, and dependent.

In my family of origin, this differentiation of gender roles was very clear. As a child, my dad lacked a family environment where he was allowed to cry and express his fear, sadness, and needs. For him, the only acceptable emotion was anger. When he had disagreements with my mom, he would stop talking to her for several days, which for me was like living in an ice castle.

When I was in elementary school, I often wondered, "Why don't you just hug and kiss? That way we can be happy again!" The situation of conflict was increasing between my parents until they decided to attend couple's therapy. When they came back from one of those sessions, I remember my dad told us this: "Every Friday we will come and sit down as a family to talk about what we feel and what we need." This was the best news I could receive back then! Yet when Friday arrived week after week, this resolution was never kept.

A few years later my parents separated, and my heart broke. Growing up I chose to dedicate myself professionally to the personal development and integral well-being of people. I was attempting to heal the wound of abandonment, which originated when my mom decided to leave my dad and take me and my three sisters with her. My dad responded with anger and stopped providing financial support. My mom took complete care of her four daughters, but as we grew up, she treated us as if we were "boys," cultivating masculine qualities of strength, determination, and independence. In my case, this included not allowing myself to show vulnerability.

Arriving at that first GERI course and listening to other participants share their experiences expanded my own perspective. I remember the story of a male participant who shared that he recognized himself as very sensitive since he was a child. It was very hard for him as a child that his father hugged and welcomed his sister when she cried, while his father rebuked him if he saw him shed a single tear. Listening to this story helped me empathize more with men, who were not allowed to contact or express their sadness or fear. How can men be vulnerable and express their feelings and needs if they are emotionally castrated as children?

Later in the course, I also recognized that the way I had lived and related to the world was primarily from my masculine energy. I did not allow myself to show vulnerability, especially in my romantic relationships. I felt that the man who was my partner could not really love me, nor could I truly trust him. When I shared these feelings in another session of GERI, a colleague asked me if he could make a comment, I agreed, and he remarked: "Do you realize that continuing to believe that men are not trustworthy is taking away the possibility of recognizing that reliable men do exist?" It was eye-opening for me!

My healing process through the GERI workshops continues and has allowed me to reconcile and integrate the feminine and masculine energies within me. This has helped expand my experience of being whole and rounded, and it gives me the opportunity to recognize and honor these energies in others as well. I also feel a deep respect and empathy for human beings in general, because regardless of where we were born, we have likely been raised within a patriarchal culture. I know that living in union and peace as human beings, we can overcome patriarchal conditioning and live in resonance with our highest essence.

This next account is from a woman participant who writes about the healing and transformational experience that has happened for her from men who truly listened to and appreciated her story during the GERI programs.

Over the past five years, I have participated in three GERI programs, one in-person and two online courses during the pandemic. Each program has been powerful in the way it has brought about a higher level of awareness for me in relation to my own life and the larger human family.

A GERI workshop goes well beyond the typical gender issues that are present on a surface level.

For most of my life, I had always blamed myself for failures in relationships. I felt that my own personality, my own personal shortcomings, were the cause of so many failures. Little did I know that in most instances, I had not had a chance to do things differently. I had been forced and pushed to act in a certain way by a cruel and senseless system of patriarchal toxicity that called all the shots, and it had punished me every time I had not conformed to those patriarchal authorities, whether they were men or women.

Participating in the GERI workshop opened my eyes to the sad fact that those men and women in positions of authority who hurt me so much were also victims of the same patriarchal wounds they were inflicting on me. This understanding aroused compassion for them in my heart. This is the power of the healing that GERI brings; it is the power of forgiveness. Understanding this truth has allowed me to recover my lost pieces; the ones that I pushed away, was not allowed to express, or had neglected. This recovery is a dynamic process that has continued long after the workshops and become an integral part of my life.

Sharing my story in the women's group was transformative for me, as I moved through the emotions of shame, fear, anger, grief, sadness, and emptiness. With each emotion I embraced, I felt they were healing me. Acknowledging those emotions, naming them, and recognizing their value in the story of my life allowed me to be grateful for their support to my higher Self as I passed through life's challenges. Hearing the other women tell their stories through those same emotions and feelings was also very moving for me, and brought me closer to them and deepened our relationship as sisters. Our sharing has taught me that I am not alone in the world, that my life story has many things in common with women of different ages across the continents. As a Mexican woman in my sixties, when I heard a young Korean woman in her twenties tell me: "What you just said resonated deeply with me because that's exactly what I have always felt," it showed me how similar our gender experiences are all over the world, despite the isolation we feel sometimes.

GERI work is very needed in Mexico. Toxic masculinity has been so normalized in this culture. I am Mexican, but I lived in the United States for more than 20 years. Now that I am back in my country, it strikes me how constantly toxic masculinity is displayed, even among "well educated" men. And yet most women don't seem to care. They block themselves and stay at a surface level.

In my life, and in my Latin American culture, men rarely listen to women. They seem to always be in a hurry for you to speak faster and take less of their time. I have encountered very few good listeners in my life. So, when a group of men in a GERI workshop listens to my story attentively, I feel I am being accepted and that my story is important to them. This has been very healing. Just having their attention is very soothing to my heart. During one of the workshops when I shared my story some of the men actually responded by apologizing on behalf of all men, even though they were not the perpetrators of the violations that caused my pain and suffering. Those moments have been incredibly healing and transformative. Recognizing the offense and the hurt, and caring enough to apologize for something they didn't do personally and to express their regret and their care for me, has been very, very soothing and healing to my heart.

The following is from Jorge Rico, a GERI Trainer originally from Bolivia, who shares how the GERI work has helped him heal from his own childhood wounds, and about the importance of offering gender healing and reconciliation work throughout Latin America.

In my years of training and growth as a GERI facilitator and now trainer, I have been privileged to serve as co-lead for the Latin America region and Spanish language expansion. The shift to online trainings due to the COVID-19 pandemic has provided us with an opportunity to hold many more workshops while engaging people from around the globe. With each workshop I have co-facilitated, I have continued to grow in my knowledge and appreciation for this work. I have had the privilege of facilitating several workshops in English for participants globally and in Spanish for participants from Mexico, Argentina, Peru, Costa Rica, Colombia, and Brazil. The GERI mission and work is profoundly needed in Latin America, where patriarchy and machismo culture are quite prevalent, and women's rights are not quite as advanced as they are in the USA, Canada, and some European countries.

The work translates well to the Latin American setting and is equally impactful, and heart and mind opening. The opportunity to facilitate GERI workshops in Spanish allows me to advance my own personal healing from the wounds and scars I have from my formative years being raised in a Latino home surrounded by macho attitudes in the Bolivian American community in which I was raised. As a GERI facilitator, the gift of hearing people from their twenties to their sixties exclaim that the workshop has been "life changing" and "transformative" has become food for my soul, and it fuels my desire to increase my involvement within the organization. I long to expand this work into corporate settings, and I plan to continue my GERI work and personal journey of healing with each new workshop as long as I am able.

Silvia Araya Villalobos is a GERI Trainer and the program manager for Latin America. Here she shares her own awakening to men's pain and how important being in co-gender circles has been in her own healing journey.

When I first encountered GERI, I was working as a clinical psychologist and facilitating women's circles. I started doing this type of work because patriarchy had taught me to reject my femininity as if it was something negative, a weakness I had to carry around; and the more painful part for me was that it implied a separation between me and other women, because judgment, competition, and comparisons were the norm in many female-to-female relationships.

With all of this in my heart, I started to work with my fellow sisters, and while I felt the sorority and camaraderie grow, I also noticed that the problems with the rest of the society and the separation with men were continuing to grow bigger. I began to feel disappointed with the ideal that I had about healing our pain as women. I realized that what we were doing—even though very beautiful and full of heart—had a limit, because we were excluding the "others" from the process. And even though I believe deeply that the work of healing between women is very important, and possibly the first step for many, I also think that if we just stay there, the pain will continue, for we cannot evolve unless we do work on healing and transforming together, as one human family.

This is what keeps me in this work: the vision of seeing humanity as a big community, with diversity, differences, correspondences, commonality, and everything in between. I believe we have the capacity to feel each other as one and heal together as our ancestors knew how to.

I've been on the GERI path for several years now and being with men in the circles has opened my eyes even more to the pain that men carry. Before coming to this work, I knew as a clinical psychologist how the system has castrated men from their emotions. However, it's been important for me—and for other women—to actually see the pain we have inflicted on men as mothers, sisters, spouses, girlfriends, or just as silent accomplices who have helped perpetuate violence against men.

Stepping out of the victim role and becoming witness to the many times I've also hurt others, both men and women, have been integral parts of my healing journey that continues every time I join a GERI group. Even as a facilitator, my wounds, my edges, and my issues are all on the table along with those of the other participants.

Every group is different, and every history is unique. But what keeps amazing me is that even with all the pain and separation we've experienced, in just a few days people's lives can start to transform, tears held back for years start flowing, smiles and hugs emerge and, in these moments, my faith in humanity gets renewed. I feel blessed to be able to experience this with more and more people every year: it's possible to heal and to be together as family.

Honoring Ceremony

The following ceremony was offered from the men to the women in a workshop with The Center for Sharing in Pasco, Washington. In this particular workshop, the majority of the participants were Latinos/Latinas.

Together, as women, we were invited into the room and asked to sit in front of an empty table. On the other side was the group of men who we had journeyed with over the past three days, having shared our gender stories of the pain we had all endured. Behind the men were piled a heap of small boxes—each one about the size of a brick—and each one with a word written on it. One man stepped forward, carrying one of the boxes, and said:

"We, as men, stand before you today to acknowledge that we each have played a part in building the 'wall' of patriarchy. This wall separates men from women. Each of these 'bricks' represents a behavior that contributes to this wall. We will now place these 'bricks' and speak out loud the behaviors—both those that we have heard in your stories, and those that we are committed to changing in ourselves and in the world."

Then one by one the men stepped forward and built the wall. With each "brick" laid, a word or phrase was spoken:

Man-splaining. Not listening. Aggression. Sexismo. Objectification. Abuse. Machismo. Misogenismo. Sexual harassment. Lust. Withholding affection. Exclusion. Not taking responsibility. Idolizing. Minimizing contributions. Apathy. Lack of respect. Conditional Love.

When the wall was completed, each man stepped forward and offered his personal commitment for supporting gender healing and ending injustice,

Women honoring men at GERI workshop in Juchitan, Oaxaca, Mexico, 2022

often making reference to one of the bricks beside him.

Once the men had completed their individual commitments, they said in unison: "Women, we hear you. We hear your pain and suffering. Today, with you as our witnesses, we commit ourselves to knock down this wall that stands between us, and no longer uphold this division."

At that moment, all the men together tore down the wall, sending the paper "bricks" flying and toppling onto the floor—much to the spirited satisfaction of the women. The men then invited us to join them in the newly opened space, a full circle where, with music playing softly in the background, they individually honored each woman, thanking her for her sharing over the previous days, and reflecting back her unique gifts and qualities. They presented each woman with a flower and a chocolate as a blessing, representing our unity as brothers and sisters on the path of reconciliation. As the honoring ceremony came to a close, we all began singing, dancing, and sharing hugs as together we celebrated our personal renewal and new beginning as a community together.

The Latin America GERI team is a dynamic committed group that meets monthly, and is steadily building the GERI work in their homeland. We close this chapter with a brief vignette from a three-day in-person workshop in Juchitan, Mexico, co-organized by a local non-profit service organization, Centro de Compartimiento, and sponsored by the Vista Hermosa Foundation. The workshop unfolded in the usual manner, and on the last day just before the final closing, as GERI trainer Silvia Araya recounts:

I was walking outside for some air, and I noticed one of the young women sitting all alone at the corner of the building.

She was crying. I went over to check in with her, and gently asked what was happening. She was holding a flower in her hand which had been given during the men's honoring ceremony. I felt a bit concerned that something had happened that triggered her. Instead, she lifted her face to me and said, "I'm crying, because never before has a man seen me so deeply, and tenderly likened my essence to the beauty of a flower." I proceeded to confirm that these were indeed happy tears, and she nodded as she leaned again on my shoulder, and continued crying softly.

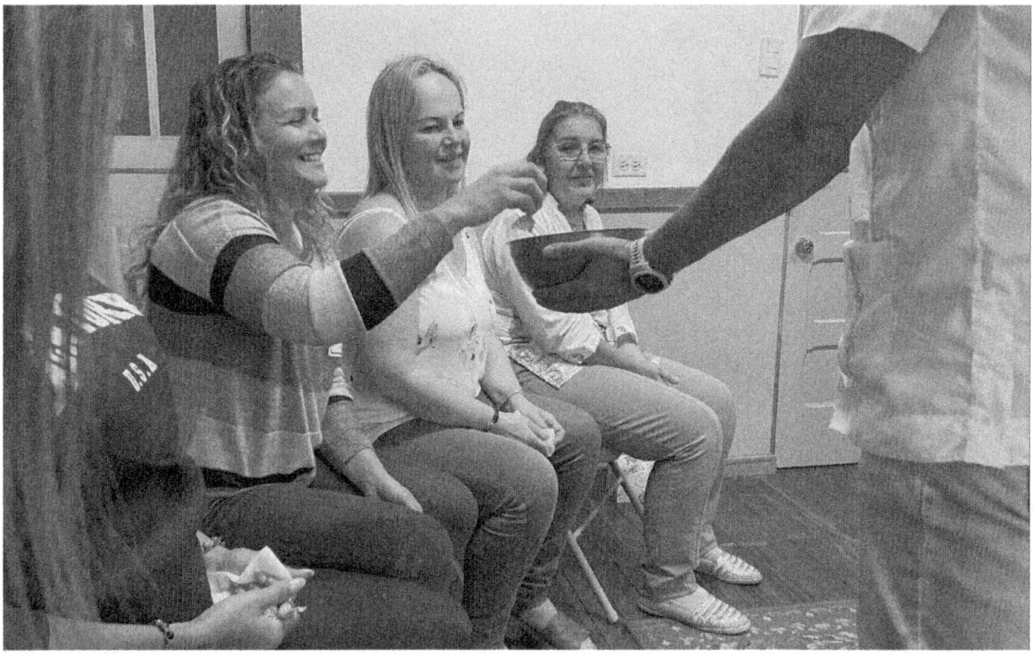

Men honoring women at GERI workshop in San Jose, Costa Rica, 2023

GERI workshop at Universidad de la Salle in Bogota, Colombia, 2025

CHAPTER 21

United States and Canada

This chapter opens with a woman's experience of receiving back her female sovereignty.

A small green piece of paper folded like a tiny book rests in my living room. On the cover is a gold spangled heart. Inside, the handwritten words read: *We stand with you!!* I have kept it on a table since the Gender Equity and Reconciliation (GERI) workshop. In morning prayers, I return to it again, and remember the sincerity of that declaration. When I read that card again, I see the faces of the men who wrote it, and the experience radiates out into my life and continues to live on. It's crucial to keep it alive and fan the flame.

How unspeakably rare is it to gather at a common fire like this—this circle of women and men seated around a centerpiece of candles who have come here to speak deep truths. How many circles are there in the world, or how many down through the ages of patriarchy, where women and men come together to return and remake true reconciliation and recommitment?

From the opening circle of the workshop, we were enveloped in social safety that came from a deep, enduring, spiritual place. The power of this work is not only that it creates a place to tell our truth. It provides a place for each of us to contact our hearts and actively hold ourselves and each other in deep respect. We create a place for painful truth to be expressed and heard, and out of this arises our longing for what can be. This longing grows into action. In that very group we took part in restoring the Sacred Covenant between the genders.

Towards the middle of the workshop, each person had a chance to bring forward a time of pain and suffering related to gender, and be witnessed in their process and truth of their story. We helped each other climb out from the affliction of these wounds, to "lift out of" mutual ensnarement. To use a Buddhist term, it was a co-arising of healing. Reflecting back, we broke through some of the key, unwritten rules of patriarchy:

- *Don't love yourself. We are in charge of who has value.*
- *Don't open your heart and give love to anyone except your family and prescribed partner.*
- *Don't tell the truth around men, or else someone could get killed.*
- *This problem is yours alone to handle, and the fact that you have problems of self-doubt says you are unworthy as a human being. In fact, you brought it on.*

We loved each other. We opened our hearts. We spoke truth. We lifted the burden of the effects of patriarchy on each of us personally, and threw it off.

Reclaiming Sovereignty

We were invited to return to our separate gender groups and create ceremonies of honor, blessing and commitment for each other.

The men led us (the women) into a semi-circle with a green velvet high-backed chair in the center. A colorful sign above the chair read "Throne of the Feminine," which though simply crafted, was awe-inspiring in its power and elegance. One by one we were lifted to stand by a man's hand, in a gesture of respect and exquisite care. We were each brought forward to have our own turn sitting on the throne.

The men knelt before us, bent on one knee, leaning forward to give full and earnest attention to the woman on the throne. Then each of the men took a turn speaking to what he saw and appreciated about the woman. *"I celebrate your wisdom. . . I celebrate your outstanding leadership. . . Thank you for your radiant heart. . ."*

In patriarchal culture we are taught to narrow our regard and give our light of attention based on rank or status or sexual relationship, but here we were fully celebrated. Each man shone from his heart a full-spectrum light. With sincere attunement, they gave full and equal focus to each woman. Our ages spanned from 24 to 67, and we were each accorded the respect given a valued elder. One of the men described it later as a ceremony of giving back female sovereignty—we were being seen and reinstated in our sovereign place as women.

It was in this part of the ceremony that all the women received those handwritten green cards: *We stand with you!!* These words carried potent force, as I could feel that the men remembered hearing the painful personal experiences we'd shared earlier, and they wanted fervently to show us that we were truly held, supported, and loved.

In the ceremony created by the women, we led the men through a birth canal created by a tunnel of hands. Tones sounding like the sea brought the transformational feeling of the ocean. Each woman then gave a blessing and affirmation to the men, and took turns sharing a personal commitment (as the men had also done). We ended the ceremony singing and dancing together.

Back on the first day of the workshop, we had been invited to envision a "gender healed world." What I had pictured was that around the world, there could be a special moment each morning when a re-commitment to creating gender reconciliation would be declared out loud. To remember the workshop, I decided to do this in my own home. Along with re-reading, "We stand with you!!" I hold a pink-quartz heart-shaped stone each morning, and ask *"What will I do today to live inside a world of gender reconciliation?"* May this work of reconciliation, healing the traumas of centuries, continue far and wide.

Like the story above, the visceral experience and imprint of remarkable healing moments of gender reconciliation resonate and reverberate heart-to-heart long after the program ends. Participants from around the world often share how the special blessing they received during the honoring ceremony—a handwritten note, a heart stone, words of appreciation, a song, a poem—is like a sacred covenant that has been etched on their heart. On the final day of the workshop, participants, in pairs, tie colorful string bracelets on each other's wrists as a symbol of their connection and commitment to gender reconciliation inwardly and outwardly. These blessings and commitments are not made lightly, or as mere flattery, but are sincere heartfelt offerings. Years later, people sometimes report with great joy, "I still have my bracelet from my GERI workshop."

Speaking truth with the intention of healing is at the heart of the GERI process, and the depth of truthtelling is directly linked to the depth, beauty, and meaning of the honoring ceremonies. Without the truthtelling, the honoring would be empty. Without the honoring, the truth-telling would be incomplete. Just as we each need a place to bring forward our unheard stories of challenge, pain, suffering, we also need a space to bring forward our heartfelt appreciation, aspirations, and visionary prayers for those who have journeyed with us, and for all those who yearn for this reconciliation but have not had a chance to experience it.

At times, we may not even realize how deeply we really need to be heard, or how much we need the truths of others. As one man reflected after hearing the women, "I *need* your stories. Hearing them opens something in me—a doorway into a greater wholeness that I couldn't find without them." This holds just as true in North America and other industrialized countries as elsewhere in the world. Despite the important and very real progress that has been made towards gender equality in these regions, the depth of truthtelling that happens in GERI circles is still almost unheard of.

At the same time that the GERI process was first being conceived in 1991, the reality of workplace sexual harassment was just coming to the forefront. Anita Hill's testimony before the United States Congress regarding the sexual harassment she experienced while working as an intern for Clarence Thomas, a Supreme Court nominee at the time, made a huge impact. We had hoped that this might be a watershed moment when gender injustice would emerge to center stage on the social agenda. Sadly, despite the integrity, honesty, and power of Hill's testimony, the core issues were again swept under the rug, not to emerge again in full force until the #MeToo movement in 2017.

The #MeToo campaign dramatically revealed rampant sexual harassment and the urgent need for profound transformation in gender relations between men and women in most societies across the globe, laying bare the raw pain of gendered dysfunction in contemporary society, and dispelling any illusion of having gone beyond this legacy of oppression. First sparked in 2006 by U.S. activist Tarana Burke, the movement went viral when actress Alyssa Milano tweeted, on October 15, 2017, that anyone who had been "sexually harassed or assaulted" should reply

#MeToo and post about their experiences on social media. Half a million people responded within 24 hours, and by early November, #MeToo had been retweeted 23 million times from 85 countries. These personal accounts of sexual harassment and exploitation of girls and women came from experiences in nearly all walks of life—from Hollywood and media industries, to university campuses, to everyday encounters on public transit, to #ChurchToo with sexual exploitation and harassment exposed in Christian, Jewish, Buddhist, Hindu, Islamic, and other religious and spiritual communities. The #MeToo movement was an unprecedented turning point and historical moment in cultural evolution that went viral, and led to a global outcry for transforming longstanding violation and dysfunction between the sexes.

Over the past 30 years in the United States and Canada, GERI has convened workshops and trainings in a wide variety of contexts and key metropolitan areas including: Boston, Boulder, Dallas, New York City, San Francisco, Santa Fe, Seattle, St. Louis, Toronto, Vancouver, and elsewhere. Multiple collaborations over the years across North America have flourished, and significant partnerships with The ManKind Project, Illuman, Bioneers, the Charter for Compassion, and other organizations have been established, enabling GERI to touch the lives of many more people.

Stories of Transformation

We now present various personal accounts from people throughout North America who reflect on their formative experiences around gender and sexuality, and the healing and transformative impact the GERI process has had on their lives.

The following is from a male participant who shares how he was shaped as a boy and young man by what he calls a "traumatized masculinity." He recounts how this cut him off from the fullness of his humanity, which was exacerbated as an officer in the U.S. Marines, and how he has grappled with coming into a more healthy, integrated masculinity.

I inherited a traumatized masculinity. The expression of masculinity I received was formed culturally and epigenetically by men who had experienced war, or had been trained to fight in wars, or by men who had themselves been raised by such men. Women cooperated, more or less. I call this masculinity *traumatized*, because it cut us off from our full humanity, our wholeness and health as men. If I thought at all about this process while growing up, it simply seemed like a necessary adaptation to "the way life is." My wife, my daughters, other women who have challenged me in love, and men who have walked the journey themselves, all helped me recognize this traumatized masculinity and the patriarchal system it serves. Participating in Gender Equity and Reconciliation International (GERI) work has also helped me clarify how this masculinity affects others, and how to heal it.

I was five years old when a girl not much older than me said, in front of other kids, that my name was a girl's name. My young body experienced shock and embarrassment which turned quickly to outrage. I protested that my name was certainly NOT a girl's name. Now I realize that I had already unconsciously learned the cultural truism that a man is not a woman, and a boy like me most definitely better not be a girl, or girlish. To say otherwise questioned the very foundation of my identity and belonging. At five I was already *all in* on being a man, like my father and the men I saw on the edges of my female-dominated world. I was already on the quest to be a real man.

To a large extent, culture has given me a negative model for the object of my quest: a boy is *not* a girl; a man is *not* a woman. I watched and learned what happened to those boys who transgressed gender norms. So, like most boys and men around me, I arranged my psychological and emotional world based on what I should *not* be: afraid, tender, sad, confused, sensitive, vulnerable and a host of other stances deemed weak or too emotional. My own emotional vocabulary became limited to feeling good or bad, or mad. Male modeling encouraged me to exhibit anger and aggressiveness in asserting my identity and place, especially in the face of any suspicion of weakness or vulnerability. I shunned anything within me associated with women or femininity. The world told me in myriad ways to grow up and be a man—the kind of command that I never heard directed at my sisters or girlfriends. And I was all in for the project of being a man, an attitude that worked swimmingly in a patriarchal society. Until ... it didn't.

My persistent search for acceptable manhood led me through prolonged years in educational formation and athletic endeavors, professional and military training. It led me to graduating from a military academy and becoming a Marine officer engaged in some of the most brutal training in the United States military. I attended Army Airborne and Ranger trainings, was assigned to special forces, supervised Marine Drill Instructors and recruits. I embodied the military objective of developing the personal capacity to inflict lethal violence on others, while at the same time being the target of deadly violence myself. Pursuing that goal by nature cut me off from my full humanity. Most painful of all, it diminished my ability to appreciate beauty, in myself and others. The "toughness" I developed became a serious obstacle to healthy human relationships. It hid my trauma behind patriotic slogans. It nurtured a distorted sense of brotherhood based on shared suffering, and the shared willingness to inflict suffering.

It would be straightforward if I could point to one dramatic event or key turning point that transformed my male-identity and healed my traumatized masculinity. But for me it hasn't been like that. It's been more of a slow slog, working through self-serving deceptions and biases and cultural assumptions. There was a period of studying for a divinity degree when I struggled mightily with what I was hearing from women friends. I was particularly distressed by their pain concerning the patriarchal church, and the exclusively male priesthood. I simply could *not* understand how women felt called to priesthood. At the same time, I readily acknowledged their extraordinary charisms and spirituality. Then there was the day when I realized that I was trying to press into a patriarchal model *their* sense of vocation, when in fact they were themselves the evidence that it was *my* image of priesthood that needed to be transformed. This may seem elementary now, but at the time it was revolutionary for me.

Seeking my identity in manhood eventually led me to men's rites of passage. Within a ritual container created by compassionate elder men, I faced my own trauma in ways I was unable to alone or even with women partners. The men's work I experienced healed much of the wounding I had received at the hands of other men, beginning in my family of origin. In time, I served as national Chairman for Illuman, an international men's organization dedicated to supporting men on their spiritual journey and toward healed masculinity.

While serving in Illuman leadership, I participated in several GERI events. I experienced healing of the relationship between men and women, and how it can be a powerful, even central, aspect of men's work. My experience with GERI helped digest and integrate the men's work I was already doing. My male privilege now became the opportunity to sit and hear how patriarchy has deeply wounded women, and to see that wounding in myself as well. Through skilled and experienced facilitation, GERI leaders created a space for gender awareness, mutual understanding and personal transformation.

My name is not a problem for me anymore. I no longer fear gender confusion or identity loss. I have many names. I understand my maleness as an opportunity to fully inform my life as husband and father and man who works to embrace the blessed and broken aspects of the journey. GERI helped develop my willingness to step with empathy and humility toward others' fluid experience of gender. It enlarged the possibility of doing the work of healing not only relations between men and women, but most meaningful to me, relations between men. For me, GERI work heals relations between men, because I also understand patriarchy as broken relationships between men as brothers, between men as fathers and sons. To see how patriarchy operates between men and women helps men to realize how it oppresses all their relationships. I see GERI work as the extension and deepening of this real "men's work"—work that I embrace as a lifetime of deconstructing the patriarchal structures that keep us separate and afraid. For this I am grateful.

The next story is from a woman participant who shares poignantly about her experience of and healing from childhood trauma, and the important "tools" she learned for navigating her emotional responses, and insights that allowed her to release shame. She also writes about the unexpected and powerful healing she received from hearing the stories both from other women and men in the GERI work.

I attended my first GERI workshop in 2014 without really understanding what I was getting into. GERI work feels like a spiral to me. Every workshop contains most of the same components or activities, but each time, the levels of understanding, healing, and connection go deeper.

In my first workshop, I shared a story that I had never shared publicly before. My mother was schizophrenic and a single parent, and when I turned 12, she attempted to traffic me. During the next year and until just after I turned 13, she would periodically send me out the door to acquire food, money, or cigarettes, by whatever means I could muster. My first thought had been to do what she did. I thought of going to the bars, but I was innocent and did not really know how to do what she did. So I went door-to-door, and our neighbors helped us out of those times. Shortly after I turned 13, my mother beat me for a final time, and people we had encountered at church happened to come by and intervened. I went into foster care and never returned to live with my mother.

When I first started sharing my story in the GERI circle, I felt like I understood myself and my own story pretty well. I'd done a lot of therapy, and I thought I was open with others about my experiences. However, that first workshop cracked open a part of my heart that had never really let anyone but a therapist know exactly what happened, and how traumatizing it was to have my mother betray me over and over again, violently and cruelly. I realized after that workshop that I had inner layers I had not yet explored. I also became aware that I had hidden the details from others because they felt too horrifying and shameful to reveal. In telling my story, I began to realize that the shame was not mine, it was my mother's. I discovered that letting others into my story created a powerful opportunity for healing. I learned tools to moderate my trauma responses and to consider how others were responding to what I said. I did not want to cause harm in the sharing of my story, and the GERI work taught me tools for managing my own trauma responses. Eventually, I attended the training to become a GERI facilitator, and I learned how to help others modulate their own responses and care for a group when trauma was present.

But my own story was not the only one that brought me healing. I heard other women speak about their own suffering, including sexual abuse, trafficking, and sex work. I began to realize that even women I knew had experienced this. I realized I was not alone. That was a powerful realization, and it healed my sense of isolation. I began to feel a restoration of my interconnectedness with the human race through the telling and hearing of these stories.

What surprised me, also, was the men. I confess I had had a sense that women were the victims of men in society. I'd heard the stories from my mother of the abuses she'd suffered as a child and that the women in her family had suffered. My mother's mother and sister also prostituted. My mother's grandmother, Mary, was sold into indentured servitude when she was a little girl. In telling and thinking about these stories, practicing compassion toward myself and my own suffering, I slowly recognized that the wounds went back generations and had been passed forward. But when I heard the men's stories, I had an awakening to their suffering that blew open my heart.

I had always thought that since men were at the top of the patriarchal pyramid, they were happier, in control, safer. But as I heard men share their stories, my heart opened to the stories of how afraid they were. As boys they had been beaten, shamed, raped, abused, and belittled for any weakness. Every day of their lives, they lived in the fear that by revealing their softness, tenderness, emotions, uncertainty, receptivity—all the things society tends to associate with femininity—they would lose what little respect and safety they had fought for. I realized that men and women were in this pain together, and that we had to heal together.

At present, I am a last-year master's student in mental health counseling and expressive arts therapy. I am working as an intern at a jail that also serves as a medium-security prison. My clients there are all addicts, serving time for crimes ranging from possession of drugs to murder. I work with men who have raped women, tortured animals, and hurt children physically and sexually. Some have certainly done less violent crimes, but we see it all in the prison.

I call upon my experience with the GERI work every day in this work. I am reminded on a daily basis that these men did not become who they were in a vacuum. They tell me their stories of being abused and neglected, and because I've done GERI work, I can really see their suffering and have an open heart toward them. In fact, a shift that has happened for me in this work is to realize that work with offenders must start earlier and more intensively. Work with victims is needed, of course, and they're more likely to actually seek help voluntarily. But as long as the men perpetuate the violence, we're never going to have an end to the line of victimized women and children. Most definitely, I could not work in the field I'm in without the personal healing work I've done in and through the GERI community. I simply did not have the tools and the community connections to deal with my own or others' overwhelming trauma before I came into GERI.

This work has not only affected my professional life, GERI has also helped deepen my marriage and heal it. I am able to approach my husband through eyes of compassion rather than seeing him only through the lenses of my childhood and ancestral victimization. My husband has also attended GERI workshops, and it has softened our hearts and given us tools to care for one another. I used to get "stuck" between irresolvable forces: his needs or my needs? His solution to the problem or my solution? I have found through GERI and through working with other GERI facilitators that there is a third way. It's the way of the heart. Every time we face one of these seemingly irreconcilable tensions, I fear there will be no resolution. But as we stay in a heart-centered place, a third way emerges. It feels a little like being born, each time. There's a lot of pressure and a tight squeeze, but so much new emerges from staying in our heart spaces. My own fear has shifted into greater confidence that, when we face something like this, the heart way will lead us into something new and beautiful, together.

This next account is from a middle-aged male participant who writes about his healing as an adult from the severe abuse his father inflicted on him as a child, and his subsequent awakening—through men's work and GERI—to how this had impacted his relationships with both men and women.

Realization. It's a continuum. Some realizations are greater, some smaller, covering different subjects and concepts, and together they are a continuum, each building on or somehow fitting in with the others, like a web of lights coming on.

My father fought with the U.S. Army's 10th Mountain Division in WWII. He was a young man from Kansas, and he found himself in a brutal, close-up, hard-fought campaign that threatened his body and assaulted his senses and sensibilities in ways that he had no idea what to do with. Psychotherapy was a rare commodity then, and the Army thought even less then than they do now about helping soldiers re-adjust to civilian life. The result was that Dad brought the war home with him.

I came to see my father's anger as a series of steps. There was always a great deal of criticism and verbal abuse. I believe my dad was truly trying to teach me and my siblings and bring us along to help us do better in the world. At times he had patience and was a good teacher, and when he was at all irritated or angry, he would raise his voice. Dad had been a woodworker and believed strongly in physical discipline. He kept a hardwood stick in the kitchen windowsill. If he were madder than yelling at us, he would threaten to "get the stick" and beat us with it. If he were madder than that, he would take us downstairs to beat us, so the neighbors wouldn't hear us screaming. If he were madder than that, he would have us pee first, because he knew he was probably going to beat us till we were incontinent, and he didn't want the mess. If he were madder than that, he would flatten us on the spot.

Think about one of those for a minute. Imagine what it's like to have your father stand over you as you empty your bladder into the toilet, knowing what that means—you know what is coming. As a kid, I came to understand exactly what it meant to "have the piss beat out of you."

When I left the house and struck out on my own as a young man, I didn't know how to process the abuse from my childhood. I eventually found places and ways to process the events of my childhood, and one of the most impactful was an acting and singing coach who could see people energetically. Shari could see where the energy flow was blocked. After three and a half years of working with Shari in singing classes, I got reconnected to my body (after retreating into my head as a kid) and made great strides in processing what was stuck from my childhood.

One day when I was five years old, I was supposed to be napping but wasn't able to sleep. Mom was doing something in the bathroom just around the corner from my room when she got a phone call. She went into the kitchen to take the call, and I got up and went into the bathroom. There I found a bare razor blade on the side of the sink. I had some idea of what it was and knew it was sharp, so I picked it up by grasping it on either side with my thumb and index fingers. I looked at it and wondered what it was capable of. I went to the wood trim on the side of a door and used the razor blade to cut out a small notch. I was fascinated and did that five times, at which point I realized I couldn't undo what I had done and panicked. I put the razor blade back and ran back into my room, feigning sleep.

When Mom came back to the bathroom after her call, it wasn't long before she noticed the notches I made in the trim and came in to ask me about it. She was mad and got the stick. She had me put my hands on my bed, palms down, and she beat the backs of my hands with the stick. Mom didn't have the anger Dad did, and I remember many times she would try to run interference between Dad and us kids. This time I believe she beat my hands so she could tell Dad she had punished me. I have no memory of what happened when my dad got home that day, so I asked my sister about it when I visited her.

She said that Mom told him what happened, and he saw the notches in the trim. "He took you into the bathroom and beat you until you could hardly breathe," she said.

I told Shari and the class about that, and I looked at Shari and said "Five's little, Shari. Five is little." She took a moment, then said, "What would it take for you to beat a five-year-old like that? If he burned down your house, if he wrecked your car—what would it take?"

I took time to think through those scenarios and search in myself to see if there was anything a five-year-old could do that would have me react that way. I said to Shari, "There is nothing a five-year-old could do that would make me beat him like that." She replied, "That's the difference between you and the people who raised you."

I have continued that work in many ways, including years of men's work with Illuman, which has helped me be able to have close relationships with men, something I wasn't able to do when I left home as a young man. Through that work, I saw how my relationship with my father had kept me from trusting men—how could it not? The man who was supposed to love, protect, and nurture me was someone I needed protection from.

All that work led me to Gender Equity and Reconciliation International (GERI). In my work with GERI, I got immersed in the idea of gender conditioning and how that has affected me. When I had previously thought about the abuse from my childhood, I thought of it in terms of the mental, physical, and emotional toll it had on me. I didn't think about it as much in terms of gender, asking the question "What did the man in my life, my father, who I naturally learned about masculinity from, teach me about what it is to be a boy and a man?" And I didn't ask the obvious follow-up question to that: "How have I carried that forward in my life and my relationships?"

I had been previously made aware of how society and culture reinforce gender roles and conditioning, but my GERI work has expanded my consciousness around these aspects of gender in ways I hadn't imagined. I was not aware of the depth and breadth of this type of gender conditioning, and the immense harm it causes.

My work with GERI has led to healing in me along gender lines, and I have witnessed much healing in others.

I am honored to continue my gender work as a GERI facilitator and look forward to continued growth in how I see and approach gender, gender reconciliation, and the healing that is possible there.

Realization. It's a wonderful happenstance, and I remain open to GERI work expanding my realization continuum, adding more and more lights to that web.

The following was written by a young woman participant in her twenties who attended a GERI workshop with a friend. She shares how during the women's circle, her friend told—for the first time—her story of being raped, and the powerful and healing support that she then received from the group of women. The writer continues sharing part of her own gender journey, and how through the GERI work her spiritual practice has been strengthened and her faith deepened.

In my first GERI workshop, I remember being in the women's circle and listening to a participant, who was also my friend, share a story of being raped by a man in a position of power. I remember the intense anger and sadness I felt, which only multiplied when she told the group she had never shared this with anyone before. I remember approaching her as she sat on the floor, wrapping my arms around her as she cried, while the other women in the room echoed "it's not your fault." Eventually, we were all embracing her, and each other, and the collective power of sisterhood allowed her to feel everything she had been holding in for years.

Later that night, the facilitator of the session brought her aside to make sure she was okay. At some point I was called in and I sat with my friend, who I knew was overwhelmed with emotion, but I could also see she was lighter. There was a weight that had been lifted—the fear of being at fault was stamped out by the outpouring of support and grief and validation she had been met with. She expressed gratitude for being empowered to share, and to be received with love and grace and acceptance and power. I knew this was only the beginning for her, but the change was evident.

I saw before my eyes the incredible healing impacts one GERI workshop could have. So when one of the trainers called me a few weeks later to see if I would be interested in joining facilitator training, I knew in my heart the answer would be yes.

Since then, I have been able to share more of my own gender journey—the pressure I felt to be perfect; the deeply rooted belief that my brothers were smarter than me; the constant struggle between being a "good feminist" and having feelings of inadequacy or a desire to be attractive when around men; the second-hand trauma I inherited from my mother who was raped by her brother and then her high school boyfriend; the body insecurity I also inherited from her; the need to be enough and not too much, always.

At various points throughout my time with GERI, I have been able to voice these pieces of my gender journey to the community. I have been heard, and seen, and reminded of my worth. I've been challenged to sit with my own thoughts; to meditate and pray; to have faith.

The last piece in particular—meditation, prayer, and having faith—was difficult for me at first. But my fellow GERI community members never rushed me. They made space for my doubt. They held the door open for when I was ready. And they welcomed me in when I became more in touch with my spiritual side in a way that was separate from the strict Catholic upbringing that had kept me away for so long.

In being given grace and patience and acceptance, I've in turn been able to provide that for others. I've been able to offer validation, and also harsh truths. I've been able to tell men why I mistrust them, why I fear them, why I want to please them. I've been met with love and acceptance and sympathy and empathy.

I will never forget the time in a GERI training when one of the men was standing before the women in the group, sobbing his apologies for all the harm men had done to us. I was sobbing too, as I said, "You aren't responsible for all the harm men have done. The patriarchy hurts us all." And I knew that he wouldn't take that as a way out, or an excuse for his own personal harm. I knew he would understand that I had empathy for him the same way he had empathy for me. And he did.

GERI has expanded my empathy in ways I didn't know were possible. I see the effects in my everyday life. The inclination to go back to those moments where I saw men sob, where I saw women scream, where I saw all of us come together in pain and love—that has helped me through countless situations. GERI has truly changed my life.

This story is from a young man who shares how a group conflict and crisis during a GERI program awakened in him a new level of accountability and inner honesty.

I experienced GERI as part of a unique 5-day workshop incorporating the GERI process with holotropic breathwork, in a group of nearly 80 participants. Each morning the group would engage in the GERI process, and then each afternoon we did holotropic breathwork. Both modalities have their own unique intensity and combining the two of them brought the group into a whole new type of alchemical cauldron.

On the evening of the third day, one of the women in the group unexpectedly brought forward a significant piece of information, bringing the group into a kind of crisis. She shared that, even here in this gender reconciliation workshop, she had experienced two instances of unwanted sexual advances from individual men. She began to very powerfully and incisively articulate some of the kind of gender shadows and hidden agendas around sexuality that were taking place right then and there *in* the workshop—basically calling out a couple of (unnamed) men who had, essentially, sexually propositioned her in the previous couple of days.

As this was being revealed, I felt an intense charge and potency come into the room, and into myself. I (like I imagine many of the men did) began to very carefully comb through and replay my every interaction with this woman, every word I had spoken, and every glance we had shared; all the while wondering, "*Is there any way that she's talking about me?*"

As she finished sharing, there was a charged energy in the group, as each person grappled with what had just been revealed. The facilitators called for a short break in silence, while they met with the woman, who revealed to them the two men involved, and they also met separately with the two implicated men. The facilitators then convened a facilitated process, with a smaller circle in the center with several of the facilitators, with the woman and her support person, along with the two implicated men. In the outer circle, the rest of us—the remaining 70 participants—were sitting in silent witness and in support of the process in the center.

After moving into this configuration, the facilitators opened with a short prayer and invocation. They laid out the ground rules for a facilitated dialogue process, and got permission and agreement from those in the center circle. Then the woman directly confronted these two men. Sitting in the outer circle with the rest of the group, I continued to grapple with the intensity of my own experience, and with the careful review I had done of my every word and thought, right down to my eye movements and the length and quality of my gaze towards her throughout the three days. She was an attractive young woman, and I was deeply questioning myself: have I *really* been impeccable in every way? I very strongly had the feeling that, while she was calling out and naming these two particular men and their particular incidents of transgression, that she was also naming something that applied, more broadly, also to me.

While it was not me sitting in the hot seat in that center of the circle, there was something about this whole process of her sharing and what was happening in the center that was shining the light into the dark recesses of my own inner being. I sat with this question, "Is there some small part of me that also belongs there in the inner circle? And if there is, how would I be called to show up there?" As the process in the center continued, each of the two men—much to their credit—acknowledged the truth of what she was bringing forward, reflecting on their own unconscious and unintegrated behavioral patterns around sexuality.

Even with this admission, however, the charge and discomfort in the room—and in me—was still there. This level of admission had not satisfied the woman in the center, it had not satisfied the group as a whole, and it had not satisfied what was unresolved within me. Seemingly, the truth had been revealed and confessed, and yet, we were not set free.

Sitting in the outer circle myself, in a kind of attunement and empathic resonance with what was happening in the center, I continued to ask myself, "How would I be showing up? What's really being called for? What is being asked of me?" I continued to struggle with the disturbing intensity of my own experience and questioning. As I sat in this inner turmoil, it suddenly dawned on me the level of accountability that was being asked for, and something in me that I had been struggling against began to open. Beyond the fact of the sexual advance itself that was being named and acknowledged, there was a deeper level that still wasn't being spoken to. I realized that there is a way I can still be "hiding out" and holding out from full accountability, by saying, "Yes, I did this, but it wasn't my intention." Or "Yes, it happened, but it was an unconscious pattern."

There was another level of accountability that was actually being called for. Something like, "Yes, I did that. And in that moment, I *chose* to do that. It actually *was* my intention." At one level, yes, it is true that these patterns are unconscious. At times we do things that are against our highest self and highest aspiration. On another level, there is a choice and a decision that's actually being made, if almost imperceptibly. To acknowledge that moment of choice; *this* is the process of bringing what's unconscious into consciousness. This is another level of responsibility, another level of bringing the light of consciousness into that area of murkiness and mixed intention, and shining the light *there*, to dispel that unconsciousness.

This all this came to me in a moment. This was the level of truth that was being demanded. If I was really going to be fully honest with myself, this was the level of truth I needed to hold myself to. As soon as this realization came into me, all that inner division and inner conflict and inner struggle that I had been feeling just began to release. I was no longer struggling against myself, trying to protect myself or fearing what might be revealed. Instead came a genuine feeling of having nothing to hide—a lightness and ease of allowing myself to come out of hiding. I also felt a relief of knowing that this tension and conflict that we were going through, we were going to find our way out of, just as I had in myself. Something had released in me, and I felt that we as a group would find our way through also. As the dialogue continued in the center, they came to a closure and a kind of mutual resolution, which included a sincere apology and the acceptance of that.

The next day, when I had the opportunity, I thanked this young woman for her sharing, and then very delicately shared some of what my own experience, process, and insight had been with her, and through the process. I was very careful of my intent and motivation, but knowing how important this whole process had been for me, I thought it might also be important for her. She reflected back that it was very much this quality of unprotected accountability that she was asking for and needing to hear, and we shared a beautiful moment of mutual appreciation and a kind of recognition of one another that we had deeply seen each other through this exchange.

I reflect back often on this experience and insight, and call into remembrance both that quality of unprotected honesty, as well as a deepened faith that if I bear with my own process in sincerity and earnest intention, I will be led through to the other side.

This next story is from a woman who entered into her first GERI workshop with deep questions she wanted answered about her relationship with her three boys. Within the first hour of the first day, her heart was opened to new hope and possibility.

I did my first GERI workshop at Ghost Ranch in New Mexico. I was terrified and kept reaching out to the GERI program coordinator, in the weeks before the workshop, with the need to know that everything was going to be okay. I knew I had complex PTSD, and my condition had been improving for over a decade. Still, I suffered from feelings of isolation and not belonging, and I had intense fear of others, of speaking in a group, and of being seen. I carried a belief that I did not belong in the world. After all this time, I desperately wanted to know what was still wrong with me and if it could be healed. I had so much resentment and anger towards men of power and privilege. I truly detested them and wanted to, first, lure them in, and then, second, see them fry. My relationship with men was like an addiction. I loved them, I hated them, I needed them to survive, but I also wished that I didn't need them. So I went to GERI with specific questions I wanted answered: how is this anger affecting my relationship with my three boys? If I hate men, do my boys feel I hate them, too? If men are evil, are my boys evil, too?

I will never forget the very first GERI exercise. I was partnered with a man, and we were asked to say why we were there, and then introduce our partner to the group. The man I was paired with was a white man in his late sixties. He had been a captain in the Navy. He had grown up in a different time, and it was surprising to see this kind of man (note my judgment) in a workshop like this. We sat across from each other. In my life, most of my relationships have had a hint of power struggle in them. I knew I did not have much power over the men in my life, but I did have my looks and my sexuality. However, this time was different. The man before me said, "I am a white man of privilege and I want to know what I don't know, and how I can do better in the world. What can I learn in order to show up differently?" He was so genuine and innocent, and the fact that this was my first introduction to the work was truly mind blowing, or might I say, heart opening. I burst into tears. But they were tears of hope and relief. It was the first hour of the first day of a five-day workshop and I had already been given the greatest gift possible. In that moment, one man's admission and honesty seemed to be the great salve my heart needed to open up for the journey. He was the sign I needed to tell me this was the way, and no matter how foreign and frightening it was, if I continued through the unknown and leaned into the hurt, in the end I would finally be able to feel again, because my heart had been cut off, but now was reconnecting to its own inner source. And this has led me reliably on such an important, loving journey that hasn't stopped since. Now I am in the process of training as a GERI facilitator.

This next woman participant describes her first workshop, her visceral realization and experience of the unity of the human family, and the deep sense of shared humanity that came through hearing the genuine stories of both men and women.

I've attended several GERI workshops, but there's nothing quite like your first one. I had never been in a space before where people sat together and shared their lived experience of being identified as a "man" or as a "woman." It was very eye-opening. As you listen and witness peoples' stories, it's like the veils of conditioning and stereotypes fall away and you really see—oh my goodness, we *all* have suffered under this repressive and restrictive gender system! Men have suffered trying to be "good men." Women have suffered trying to be "good women." And we have suffered in deep and shocking ways, across the board.

At one point in the workshop, it struck me with great force and clarity that we all have the same heart, the same nervous system, the same capacity to be hurt, to be angry, to love, to hope, to fear, to feel shame. Instead of looking around the room and seeing men as "men" and women as "women," I was struck with such a deep sense of awe at the universality of our shared human experience. This may be something you *think* you know, but it's a different thing entirely to sit in a circle with others and really see, and hear, and witness it reveal itself around you. In so many ways, whether we identify (or have been identified) as a "man" or a "woman," we are having more of a significantly similar experience than I had previously thought possible.

On the final day of the workshop, we ended with a ceremony. I had never experienced anything like it before. When it came time for the men's honoring ceremony for the women, I was very nervous. I didn't know what to expect or how I would feel about it. It turned out to be a very beautiful experience. My heart was melted by the care and thoughtfulness the men brought to their creation. In one part of the ceremony, the women stood shoulder to shoulder forming an inner circle looking out. The men stood in an outer circle facing the women. Before that moment, I had never had a man (let alone a group of men) who was essentially a stranger to me look me in the eyes and acknowledge the pain of my lived experience as a woman. I had never seen a group of men state with such sincerity and conviction that they wanted to transform their manhood—for the women in their lives, for each other, for themselves, and for a more gender-healed and just world.

My whole body was shaking with the intensity and intimacy of that moment. One of the women standing next to me had to literally hold me up, as I had so much energy flowing through me that I thought I might faint. The support of that woman and standing shoulder to shoulder with the other women in that inner circle was another beautiful and tender healing moment of the ceremony. That honoring ceremony, and the workshop overall, fills me with hope and a conviction that we can make a difference when we take the time and have the courage to face the realities of gender-based violence and trauma.

This sharing is from a woman participant who began to restore trust in herself and others, especially men, after feeling safe enough during a GERI workshop to speak of her childhood traumas from abusive parents. She writes about the profound healing she received from the men's witness, appreciation, and honoring of her as a woman.

There are experiences in life which are truly life changing. Gender Equity and Reconciliation International (GERI) has unquestionably been one of them for me. Over the years I had done a lot of therapy, but GERI work was unique and different, a singular kind of healing modality. My home environment growing up was filled with random verbal cruelty and frequent physical abuse. I never felt safe. My parents' interest in us was primarily as an appendage of themselves. Space for exploration, learning, and making mistakes seemed almost non-existent. My father was the disciplinarian, meting out punishment with violent slaps and brutal leather straps. My mother believed that children should *not* be seen or heard. There were nine of us, and I was just one of a loud cacophony of competitive voices, struggling to be seen and heard. I learned very early that my authentic voice was decidedly unwelcome. Isolation and silence seemed my only refuge.

Prior to my work with GERI, in gatherings of people I often felt uneasy and defended. Though time and experience had somewhat softened my attitude, I was always waiting for the other shoe to drop. I didn't understand that gathering in groups triggered unconscious associations with my experience as a child. Through my ongoing participation in GERI, I learned that groups could be compassionate, encouraging, and inspiring. GERI workshops modeled for me that groups of women and men could be loving and supportive. My authentic voice not only felt welcomed but honored as an integral part of a loving mandala of tenderness and healing. For perhaps the first time in a group of people, I felt cared for and even cherished.

As the eldest girl, I was about six when my mother instructed me on how to hold, feed, and diaper a baby. I was called the "little mother." But being little mother did not protect me from my father's capricious anger and verbal tirades. I lived in terror that something I would say or do would ignite his unchecked brutality. When his rage wasn't directed at me, I watched helplessly as my siblings begged him not to hurt them, while he beat them over and over with a leather shaving strap.

Before working with GERI, I felt my experience as a girl/woman was rare and unique to me. But in GERI work I discovered I was not alone. Many women and men have experienced similar, terrible trauma. Though a few close friends knew of my family history, before GERI, I had never spoken so deeply of the trauma I had experienced as a child. In my first GERI workshop and in subsequent ones, I began to understand the impact of the lived reality of ongoing verbal and physical abuse. The violent perpetrator, who was supposed to love and protect me, continuously violated that sacred trust. I realized that the experience of this abuse felt life threatening to me and to my siblings. For the first time, I understood the depth of my parents' betrayal of us, and the shame I carried for betraying the siblings in my care. Most importantly, I understood that in a misguided effort to protect myself, the fear and hatred of my father set me up for a lifetime of choosing weak, angry, or passive-aggressive men. That evasive strategy created powerful and long-lasting repercussions. While distancing me from my fellow human beings, it also made me oblivious to men's experience.

GERI work blew apart my assumptions and stereotypes about men. It opened a window into the reality of gender conditioning in men's lives and experience. I learned that, contrary to my ingrained beliefs, men are victims, too. In GERI workshops, men shared stories of physical, emotional, and sexual abuse. I realized for the first time that men experience victimization, neglect, abandonment, and betrayal, and that their relationships to women and other men can suffer greatly as a result. Hearing their stories deeply touched me. They softened and opened my heart. In GERI workshops, I began to move beyond my stereotypical constructions of men and experienced them in all the beauty and complexity of their being. I experienced the amazing alchemy and wonder of vulnerability as my defenses and preconceptions about both genders fell away and were transmuted into profound emotional and spiritual healing. I felt more open and deeply connected, not only to the men in the workshops, but to all the men in my life. As a result of GERI work, I resolved that, going forward, I would carry that awareness into every relationship in my life.

Part of that alchemy, and for me one of the most surprising aspects of GERI work, was the incorporation of ceremony and ritual into the integration/healing process. I confess that prior to my work with GERI, I avoided even the suggestion of ritual. I felt they were generally meaningless, and overall a waste of time. But my work with GERI has shown me the vital importance of ceremony and ritual in gender healing. In one of the ceremonies, as each man spoke, the lifetime burden of fear and anger began to melt. I felt my soul's armor crack as the curtain of invisibility quietly lifted. Tears flowed as the men gently whispered healing words of love and comfort. *I honor your truth. . . I value your wisdom. . . I see your inner beauty . . .* The ceremony touched a part within me that bypassed the sentries of judgment and went straight to my heart, which opened wide to receive the profound blessings. In conjunction with my new sisters and brothers, I felt empowered and moved to embody the truth of my full being in the world.

This next sharing is from Julien Devereux, a longtime colleague and friend of GERI who writes about his 25-year journey in the work that has brought conscious awareness and transformation of his white male privilege. Julien has been instrumental in finding and supporting efforts to introduce North American men to the GERI work.

While staying at home these last few years and caregiving for my wife through her experience of medical challenges and disability, I have had time to reflect on life and how I became who I am. Looking back, one of the most fateful events in my life was meeting Will Keepin and a bit later Cynthia Brix, the co-founders of GERI, and participating in the organization's development since the late 1990's. I was in a training Will was conducting called "Leading with Spirit," and Will asked if I wanted to come to a retreat exploring gender inequality. It was the early stages of this work, and it was very experiential and experimental, but it was clearly an important focus for any kind of social change. As a Southern white male and a product of that ubiquitous but silent system of unearned privilege, and having others defer to me, I struggled in this new and unknown territory. I thought of myself as a fairly conscious man, but during the first workshops women did not defer to me, rather they courageously named my unconscious behaviors when they saw them. This was painful, but so necessary in helping me to transform my old and well-established patterns of habits that were oppressive to others. Early in the work, the intersectionality of race, culture, sexual identity and economic differences were less emphasized because the primary focus was on gender. Now, these and any other intersectional differences are included. As a social worker, group facilitator, and organizational manager, I became committed to offering my skills and experience to GERI to help it grow and develop. I trained as a facilitator in the work, completing the first GERI training program, held in the early 2000s. I worked on establishing a foothold for the work in a place that really needed it, my home state of Texas. We held four workshops over the next several years and each one was small but very powerful. Many of those who attended those early workshops are still involved in the work today. We also established some of the first ongoing GERI Heart Circles that are groups of participants who have attended a GERI workshop or course and want a supportive community to continue to ground their transformational experience with others. These were very meaningful to me, and I created a format and structure for these groups that is still being used by GERI as a framework for this small group work. It is through the GERI Heart Circle groups of like-minded and like-hearted people that we can create and grow a culture based in compassion for the suffering of others, mutual respect, and appreciation of difference, grounded in a shared divine love.

The three-day-workshop model GERI has utilized over many years has become a reliable and replicable method for creating deep transformation and healing. As it developed over the years, the GERI team has developed and refined it continuously. Due in part to the COVID-19 pandemic it was necessary to create a virtual version, and this has expanded to a global community reaching across culture, language, and geographic limitations. I believe this is possible because the process touches what we all share in common, one heart of divine compassion for all people.

I hold the GERI process in what I call the three "H's". First, we create a container to *hold* the participants and facilitators in a safe but evocative way to encourage exploration and truth telling. Second, we *hear* the stories of all the participants and facilitators that speak to our common human experiences told from their unique perspective. Third, we *honor* each participant's courage and experience without judgment, critique, or debate. As the work has grown and been adapted to different formats, cultures, language, and groups, these three H's are still intact.

Another important event in my development was accepting a challenge from a woman in an early GERI workshop—Dr. Susan Bailey, then Director of the Wellesley Centers for Women at Wellesley College. She asked me during an exercise, "Where are the other men in this conversation?" I myself wondered where they were. So, I went looking for men conscious enough about their socialized oppression to join with the GERI community. I had friends who were part of The ManKind Project (MKP) and participated in that training for many years. Through MKP, I found that these were the men I was looking for. I took leadership positions in that organization and finally became Chair of the Curriculum Circle, and then national Chair of MKP-USA. In these roles I was able to create an opportunity for MKP men to join in GERI trainings, and many of them have continued and are now part of the facilitator teams. I consider this cross-fertilization to be one of the high points of my life and my most significant contribution to the expansion of the work.

Seeing gender in this new way has completely changed the lenses in my worldview glasses. As I now operate from a more traditionally female role as the primary caregiver to my wife, I see how much weight falls on these feminine roles to just keep life going.

Cooking, cleaning, laundry, family relationships, emotional support for my wife and daughters is a constant with no days off. I deeply appreciate all the days that my wife did this for me and my daughters and kept us whole as a family. Even attending a three-day workshop is a privilege that not all people can afford. I hope that we can keep finding the support needed to offer the GERI work to anyone who is open to healing from centuries of abuse and oppression inherited from our cultural gender legacy, and find a new way of being together.

Honoring Ceremony

We close this chapter with a short, but poignant retelling of the honoring ceremonies from a workshop held in Toronto, Canada with a group who had been in personal and professional relationship for 15 years and thought they knew each other very well. Many of the stories that were shared were being told for the first time and thus naturally brought a deeper trust and intimacy within this group of friends and colleagues.

After an intensive cross-gender healing process that included heartrending stories of violation and betrayal, the men created a spontaneous ceremony to honor and bless the women. The men gave each woman a lighted candle, knelt down, and offered this apology:

> On behalf of mankind, we would like to apologize to you
> for all the pain, the suffering, the hurt, the anguish—
> for the moments of loneliness that you have had to feel,
> for the powerlessness, and for the atrocities that men have created on this planet.

The women's ceremony was equally powerful. The women reflected back the pain and suffering that they had heard during the men's truth forum and acknowledged the men's challenges of the male socialization and conditioning they had received, often unwittingly. Then the women draped a shawl around the shoulders of each man and said, "These shawls symbolize the restoration of the love, care, and nurture that was stripped from you as boys and young men when you were told to *be tough. . . to not cry. . . to man up. . .*"

Then the women formally addressed the men:

> As women, we invite you into a new covenant of manhood, that honors the fullness of your humanity, in all the infinite beauty and wisdom—both individually and collectively—integrating masculine and feminine alike.

As each man accepted the invitation, three women stepped forward and approached each man, one by one. As they repeated his name three times, the women ceremonially knighted each man, tapping his shoulders with a small tree branch that had been adorned with colorful ribbons. Then they bestowed a handmade crown upon his head. When they finished, the women and newly crowned men together sang a harmonious chant, and then danced and celebrated.

The sacred sovereignty of the entire community was thus re-established.

Men's honoring ceremony, GERI workshop in Seattle, WA, 2015

The GERI program is continuing to grow in multiple directions across the United States and Canada. GERI leaders recently presented an introductory training for 27 graduate students and two associate faculty members at Royal Roads University in Victoria, BC, Canada, in June, 2022. This was an invited training session in the university's new Master's Program in Executive and Organizational Coaching. As Associate Faculty Member Carollyne Conlinn described it, the purpose was to create an academic experience "that would be intellectually stimulating while also creating an environment where deeper levels of personal transformation could occur. The GERI introduction to gender equity and reconciliation offered both. The depth of connection to each other in the learning circle was palpable. Students referred to it as one of the highlights of their academic journey."

Other GERI initiatives are continuing in the Boston area, with the UN community in New York, and with several partnership organizations.

GERI at the Parliament of World Religions in Toronto, Canada, 2018—with interfaith religious leaders from India, and North and South America

CHAPTER 22

Emerging Regions

In this chapter we explore several emerging regions where the GERI work has been introduced and is continuing to build and expand. In each case, we were first invited and introduced to the country by a few dedicated individuals who saw the value of GERI for their particular culture and context. With the support of the global GERI community, and these peoples' determined commitment and vision to bring gender healing to their countries, local GERI chapters are created and nurtured. These emerging regions provide illustrative examples of the different ways and stages that GERI is introduced and takes root in new contexts. Several stories below offer inspiring motivational accounts of how individuals or a small group of people can do much to bring transformative change and healing to their lives and communities.

As the GERI work expands, we strive to honor the unique cultural context of every new country we work in, and adapt the program accordingly. Our general policy is to go only where we are invited, and to work closely with local leaders to implement the work appropriately within their cultural context. When the work continues to grow in a particular country or region, we eventually implement a professional GERI facilitator training program in that region to train local leaders, and empower them to take the GERI work out to their fellow citizens and communities. In this way, the GERI work is uniquely adapted and embedded into each new cultural context, by local leaders.

GERI in Australia

Esther and William Diplock are a married couple, both therapists and university lecturers, who trained in the GERI work together. They are GERI facilitators and trainers, and also coordinators of the Gender Equity and Reconciliation work in Australia.

Esther: Like many workshops in our country, our Australian Gender Equity and Reconciliation workshops start with a "Welcome to Country" honoring and acknowledging the need for reconciliation in Australia with our indigenous heritage. We then open the space for each new circle of women and men, gay and straight, from a diversity of cultures and spiritualities, to begin engaging with and speaking to their own personal stories and collective history of gendered experience, in our process of working together for gender equity and reconciliation.

The GERI work in Australia is in its infancy and growing. Starting in 2013, we have been running annual three-day workshops and frequent introductory evenings. There is now a growing community of past participants who gather periodically throughout the year for support and ongoing growth and development.

This work is vital in Australia. In our country, awareness of the need for this kind of work is at times subtle and implicit, with many people not directly conscious of the hidden impacts of patriarchy on both women and men. Perhaps one of the most insidious impacts is the subtle and powerful pressure on both men and women to not express emotions openly and cleanly. For example, there is an epidemic of suicide amongst Australian men, which many link to a deeply-rooted suppression of their emotions. We suspect this is exacerbated by the deeply entrenched patterns in much of "Aussie" culture of putting down and disparaging the "other" gender. GERI workshops help to provide an alternative to old cultural patterns, and a much-needed new and healing meeting between the genders.

Now in my mid-forties, one of the strongest connecting threads across my life is seeking for places of intimacy and community where I deeply and honestly reveal myself, and am known and know those around me. Many of my experiences from childhood contained feelings of being deeply lonely and unknown. I grew up in the midst of a busy household with many visitors and much social activity, however with very little honest revealing and expressing of emotions. The GERI work has been deeply rewarding, as a place where I have witnessed a depth of intimacy and connection, which follows the honesty of being deeply witnessed in our gender stories. The gifts of the GERI process are still unfolding in my own life.

A profound moment of truth occurred for me in my first module of the GERI Facilitator Training. Sitting in the inner circle of the Truth Forum with the women, and witnessed on the outside by the circle of men, I touched a level of grief that welled up into tears, as I looked around at the faces of these beautiful women, who I was beginning to fall into loving community with. It was the powerful and painful awareness of an old story of mistrust, anger and dislike of women, which I had not been letting myself become aware of. Suddenly in that moment, I realized I had an inner dialogue about women, including myself, of being weak and dangerous. Lifelong patterns of pursuing a career and denying my own feminine body suddenly took on new meaning, as I realized I had wanted the power and permission I had witnessed men receive. This opened up space in me to share into the women's circle my pain and grief about the recent death of a close woman in my life, who had gotten under my protective barrier. She was a woman, both strong and safe for me, who offered me a deep and healing love during the four years of our friendship. Somehow, in the midst of this Truth Forum of open and honest sharing, and in light of having been loved and embraced by my female friend, I was able to let myself see more of the damaging story that my culture, family and upbringing had modelled for me about women being weak and dangerous, particularly sexually. And I began more consciously to claim the truth of my beauty, gentleness and safety, whilst daring to step more fully into my own form of sensuality and power.

This has been a significant and fundamentally important realization for me in moving into the facilitating role. Over the ensuing years, I have diligently committed to unearthing the old stories about who and what women can be. I have planted myself into new friendships and women's circles where I have met and shared myself, in my weakness and strength, my safety and my dangerous edges. In myself, and the women who are surrounding me, I see deep diversity and also a common humanity. My childhood mistrust, anger and dislike of women, and myself, has dramatically shifted, as I have allowed myself to nurture and love myself. This is freeing me deeply in my facilitating role to stay lovingly and compassionately present with all the many and varied stories and experiences the women and men share into our workshop circles.

William: For me, facilitating a three-day GERI workshop is a challenging invitation into my own gendered story. It is important, as a male facilitator, to bring the "right balance" of gentleness, clarity, sensitivity, challenge and compassion to the role. One of the key reasons for this is the innumerable ways patriarchy has negatively affected both genders. In my experience, patriarchy has affected women much more overtly destructively, whilst men have often been in positions of apparent privilege and power in comparison. Therefore I, as a white, male facilitator, who has had great privilege in my life, take seriously my responsibility for the welfare and wellbeing of others in the workshop. Not in a condescending way, nor a patronizing way, but in a way that loves, frees, is centered and fair minded. In taking facilitation seriously, I keep the women in mind in the workshop, at the same time I am supporting and holding the men. I work in a way that is not shaming, guilt inducing, humiliating or embarrassing, and yet at times is deeply confronting. I am required throughout to make facilitator interventions and I need to be on my game when challenging any unhelpful or potentially-damaging behavior from participants, in both the single gendered sessions (men only) and even more so when both genders are together in a combined session.

It is the stories of personal transformation that have been so powerful to witness. They feed our ongoing commitment to this work. Both of us have been emotionally moved and have found our own voices and courage growing as we see individuals making powerful and life affirming choices for themselves following the GERI workshops. One of the women found the courage to make changes in her working life, after expressing her anger at men into the full group. A year and a half later, she wrote about her experience:

> During the GERI workshop there were several first-time experiences for me. One was expressing my anger at being abused by particular men in my life, and also my anger for being ignored and compartmentalized in the workplace because of my gender. I took time within the group space to step out of my typical, understanding, patient, conciliatory role (i.e., nodding while

> my boss took up an hour of our weekly meeting in monologue)—to express my anger. The amazing thing was that the men in the workshop group gave appreciation to this expression, not disapproval. As a result, later when I went back to work, I was able to be more assertive with my boss. I felt the workshop community was with me, supporting me and cheering me on. I was not rude, just assertive, asking for a two-way collaborative conversation with my boss. Since then, on several occasions at work, I have been able to speak out more about decisions and directions I feel are immoral or misguided. I have also made decisions not to follow these directions. This may have contributed to my work contract not being renewed. I did not reapply for the position when the new contract came out. I have stepped away from working for a wounded man with too much power and too little self-reflection, and have given myself a chance to see what else is out there. This is a financial risk to myself and my family, and yet I live in hope, and I am applying for jobs that have both integrity in the work and appreciation of the workers.

Another woman shared afterwards about the impact of the workshop on her relationship with her son.

> The Gender Equity and Reconciliation workshop helped me to shift in my interaction with my son. I saw the tenderness and the uncertainty in the men in the workshop as they spoke of past and current struggles with their mothers, and with their gender, and I witnessed the profound effect that mothers have on their sons. I also experienced the loyal and deep love the men have for their mums. By hearing several of the men share about the way their mother's criticism or non-acceptance was so crippling, when they were trying to work out their own identity growing up, I was able to transfer this understanding onto my own mother-son interaction. I started the journey of becoming more of a listener, and reflecting back feelings, rather than blaming my son for his mistakes. Since the workshop I have also been working towards stepping back and trusting my son to make his own decisions, even when he may make mistakes and suffer the consequences. As his mother, I can still be present for him in a kind way when hard lessons are learnt. In this way I am stepping out of the way and letting him grow. I now envision myself more as a support person for him, on the side, ready when needed, rather than his team manager.

A significant aspect of the growing Gender Equity and Reconciliation work here in Australia has been the ongoing connection and follow-up in the GERI Heart Circles we have run for past participants after they have completed the

3-day introductory workshop. These have proved to be a valuable and rich way of supporting the participants to share openly about their experience of living gender equity and reconciliation in their own individual worlds. Feedback from these gatherings has indicated that participants greatly value the growing sense of safe and honest community with others who are like-minded, where they can grapple with the very real challenges they face in working towards reconciliation in their workplaces, families, and social world.

Our Earth and the citizens of our country, Australia, are thirsty for and in need of many forms of reconciliation. It is our privilege and commitment to serve in this way, working towards Gender Equity and Reconciliation for our people, and for the generations that come after us.

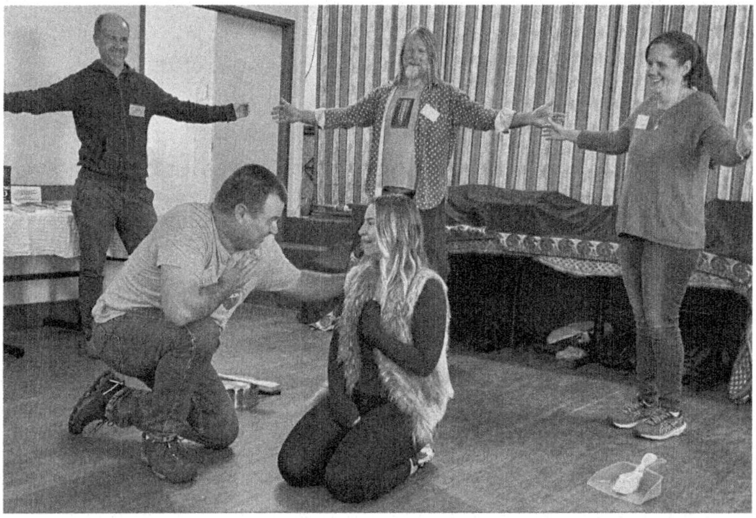

Men honoring women at GERI workshop, Brisbane, Australia, 2023

GERI in South Korea

> *I am dreaming of the day when this program is introduced in Korea. In Korea, anger is rising as men and women dislike each other. I feel sick and sad when I think of it. I would like to introduce GERI to Korea. Your language moved me and made me cry. Korea really needs healing.*

This was the first email we received from Harin Jeong in Seoul, Korea, who had experienced GERI at a conference presentation and subsequently read the first edition of this book. Over the past several years, Harin's passion and commitment to gender healing continued to grow, and she organized a circle of committed GERI practitioners in South Korea, which has grown to include a facilitation team of Koreans able to offer GERI programs in their native language. Harin has also convened several book-study groups in Seoul, bringing together people from all walks of life to experience GERI and share their stories together.

Several reflections and stories from South Korean participants and facilitators are shared below, recounting their experiences with GERI. This first account is from a Korean woman who shares her experience of the power of collective witnessing, and how her own heart continues to open through the work.

I was the first daughter of a family of conservative Christian Presbyterian pastors in Korea, and I am the mother of two children. This way of introducing myself has long been familiar, but behind these familiar identities are the stories, experiences, challenges, traumas, and triumphs that make up a life. It is very painful to live as the daughter of a poor pastor in Korea, and a mother who is bipolar. I have always wanted to understand my father, reconcile with my mother, and connect with my younger brother. But for a long time I didn't know my real heart, and I just wanted to be away from my family.

I learned of GERI in 2018, and I bought the book *Divine Duality* and then started a book club because I wanted to share it with others. The stories in the book caused tears to pour out of me when I read them. These were living stories; not made-up, or merely instructive. The book was very humble, sincere, and provided just a small clue, but it was the small clue I desperately needed. My anger felt uncontrollable. I had tried various things to try to change the world by the power of love, but it hadn't worked out well. I had many sad and challenging experiences that I couldn't understand: sexual violence at the age of 18, an ex-husband who kept giving me messages that I was not enough of a woman, the unknown death of my sister, a mother who was always angry. I left in search of that little thread that would crack the wall of the hard wasteland on one side of my chest.

In 2019, I went to Nepal and the United States to participate in two GERI in-person workshops. Coming into the GERI space was physically and psychologically unfamiliar, but I could feel the energy of this space. It was dynamic but safe, not sticky but warm. I can never forget my first experience of the Silent Witnessing activity. It was an experience of not being alone, with people who shared their true experiences, while also witnessing and acknowledging my experiences. I had gone through a deep depression in my relationship with my ex-husband, and received personal psychological counseling for two years, but this was my first collective therapeutic experience. People were honest, men shed tears, and I witnessed women of different skin colors and ages feeling the same anger and sadness as me. I felt the pain of countless generations of women in my own anger and sadness.

These experiences inspired me, and my heart began to crack open. What kind of life did my father, younger brother, mother, and grandmother live? The loneliness, fear, and frustration they actually experienced needed to be mourned, but they could only express it in tragic ways.

After that, I gained strength inside me. I was able to look at men more comfortably, and escape from my identity as a victim of the past. I have now completed the facilitator training program to continue the GERI work in South Korea. My colleagues and I organized the translation and publication of *Divine Duality* in Korean, and we have hosted more book clubs. We continue to share with people this path towards wholeness, and someday I hope to do this GERI program with my parents and two sons.

This next man shares how he was impacted by his realization that his experiences and challenges around gender were not merely personal issues but were personal manifestations of cultural gender conditioning that affect everyone and the entire society; and how opening himself to the stories of others gave him a new, deeper understanding and empathetic perspective.

I first learned about the book *Divine Duality* in 2018 through a friend and participated in a group reading of it through a book club. At the beginning of the book, I found the following sentences, "In the privacy of every couple's bedroom, the entire archetypal history and drama of the 'battle of the sexes' is present. Every couple is saddled with a burden they can barely discern or comprehend, much less transform on their own."[1] When I read this, I felt like I was hit by lightning. At that time, I was divorced, and I was a good person, and my ex-partner was a good person, but I could not understand why our marriage had become so difficult, and full of pain. I thought that the cause was only personal factors, such as the personality of the other person and myself during and after the marriage. And naturally, it was easy for me to place blame on the other person.

But after reading the above passage, I realized that the pain I experienced during my marriage could be caused by more than personality problems. Having grown up as a man in Korean society, I started to become conscious of my conditioned behaviors—whether conscious or unconscious—and the conditioned femininity that I demanded from my wife.

Becoming aware of this was in itself a big change for me, and it was the start of an even bigger transformation. Since then, I have been steadily participating in book clubs and GERI workshops. The experience has given me the strength to tell my gender story honestly to others, and to share the pain and difficulties I have experienced living as a man in Korea. I also gained the strength to look at gender conflicts occurring in society from a new perspective, and experienced ways of moving forward to reconciliation and healing through collective healing methods rather than punishment and prohibition. My hope is that everyone in Korea, men and women together, can do the work to be free from gender oppression.

Since that first beginning, I have continued to explore the conditioning inside me, the pain I suffered because of it, and the ways I have tried to ignore such pain. And I am meeting people from various countries who have similar experiences and pain. I was surprised that women from various countries around the world were telling such similar stories, and I learned that the problem of patriarchy is not just a problem of Korea. Through this process, we have confirmed in our own experience that the pain caused by gender conditioning is universal. With that understanding, I have found a new ability to be generous in accepting other people's actions when I meet them. I have become a much more relaxed and softer person than I had been in the past.

I can now understand, accept, and empathize with other people's actions, which were not understandable to me in the past, as an expression of the pain caused by that person's conditioning. This has made a big difference in both my personal and work relationships. Also, even when I am with women, I can comfortably relate to the other as a person without any awkwardness or tension as before. As a result, I can actually feel in my body that both men and women think of me differently and relate to me more comfortably and naturally than before.

In the midst of these changes, I have met a new partner with whom I have been able to explore love, free from my past conditioning, and through that, I am enjoying a completely new relationship to, and experience of, love.

The final sharing comes from a young woman who shares about the newfound feeling of safety and heart-opening she experienced through the GERI process.

When I participated in the three-day GERI workshop, I was surprised by the enormous sense of ease and safety in my body. Every part of my body became so relaxed that I felt my soul finally settled into my body. For the first time in my life, I have felt safe inside my body, as a woman in the presence of men. The level of safety was something I never had experienced with any other healing work. We often hear "GERI is not therapy but it's therapeutic," and that is true for me. Since then, every time I engaged in the GERI training I would find my body relaxed and my heart open.

GERI is trying to rectify the imbalance that's been going on in the world, and I felt that the same principle is applied during the GERI course for participants who are from "minority" cultures. As a non-English-speaking Asian, I'd never experienced this level of genuine respect for my culture. I feel GERI's goal of a gender-healed world, or just a human-healed world is actually embodied within its workshop design.

Participants in GERI workshop at the Sakyadhita International Association of Buddhist Women Conference, Seoul, South Korea, 2023

GERI in Nepal

In March 2019, GERI was invited to conduct a three-day workshop in Pokhara, Nepal. The workshop was hosted by the Lions Club of Pokhara Talbarahi and attended by 39 professionals and business leaders from Pokhara and surrounding communities. The convenor was Mr. Lok Bhandari from the Lions Club, who diligently organized the workshop after having earlier experienced the GERI program at Omega Institute in the United States. The facilitation team consisted of five GERI facilitators from India, plus Will Keepin and Cynthia Brix. Responses were enthusiastic, and the workshop was featured in the local news in Pokhara, Nepal.

One middle-aged man in the workshop—a development worker and gender equality advocate—shared deeply in the GERI process about a health problem he has struggled with for years, and his fears of how his family and wife might react to learning about it. This lifted a burden for him, which allowed him to later share his story with his family for the first time. He said, "I'm now feeling comfortable to share the health problem that I never shared with my family or relatives—even with my wife—thinking they will treat me differently if they knew my reality. I'm very much obliged to the GERI community who encouraged me to share my deep-rooted fear, which is now completely healed, and I'm very much relieved to share this problem with my wife." He reflected how his experience of being in a deep cross-gender process dramatically changed his attitude and perceptions towards women, allowing this new level of communication and sharing with his own wife and family. Another woman participant reported, "After sharing I feel so light and healed inside...This [workshop] is so usable, lively, and precious for a better life."

Participants also particularly reflected on the power of the honoring ceremonies, which touched their hearts and shifted their relations with the other gender. As one male participant reflected, "I found total change in my daily regular activities after this workshop. I feel a lot of relief and healing as a result. I found it so fruitful... The last session of honoring touched me so much." Coming together as a Hindu community, each gender incorporated elements of Hindu philosophy in their honoring of the other gender; inviting, hosting, and honoring them, as if they are God and Goddess, who protect them from insecurity of all kinds and bring love, peace, and prosperity to their lives.

In the closing honoring ceremonies, the gender groups blessed each other with flowers, candles, scented water, sweets, colorful scarves, and bracelets of friendship. As the women entered the room, the men greeted them with flowers, water, and *Aarti* ("the ceremony of lights" or waving of lighted lamps before an image of a god or a person to be honored). The women were invited to sit, and the men honored each woman individually with words of appreciation and affirmation of her unique character and contribution, giving each one a carefully created artwork on paper affirming her particular qualities and gifts. Finally, the men offered flowers to the women, and closed the ceremony, bowing in the *Namaste* posture to the women. The women's ceremony for the men was similarly beautiful, and closed with an exquisite dance performed by the women in celebration of the group of men. As Lok later reflected on the honoring process, "As witnesses and participants, we all could not stop the tears of happiness. We are truly obliged to the men and women groups who performed such a profound contribution to honor each other in line with gender transformation."

Lok Bhandari and the Lions Club colleagues began planning with GERI for a subsequent workshop, and implementing a facilitator training program in Nepal, but these plans had to be put on hold due to the Covid-19 pandemic, and will resume when conditions permit.

Participants in GERI workshop, Pokhara, Nepal, 2019

GERI in the United Kingdom

This next account comes from Natalie Collins, a UK activist who organized two intensive GERI workshops in the UK.

I was raised in an evangelical Christian home with few gender stereotypes but lots of cultural messages about gender, relationships, sexuality and power. At 17, I entered a 4-year relationship with an abusive man who harmed me deeply. He destroyed everything I was. I escaped from him after he assaulted me, and my second child was born three months premature. It was during my abuse-recovery journey that I became aware of patriarchy and the ubiquity of male violence.

Due to several miraculous coincidences, I began delivering domestic-abuse education programs to women who had been, or were being, subjected to abuse by a partner. The women were awesome and the program worked brilliantly, but it became crystal clear that women and girls really needed to get this information earlier in their lives, *before* being subjected to abuse.

Those ponderings led me to bring GERI's work to the UK and to organize a three-day workshop. Although I've been working on gender justice for many years, elements of the workshop gave me new insights into key issues. For me personally, it was a revealing and important few days, and I was not alone in my enthusiasm. As William, a male participant, wrote of the workshop:

> The language and form of the course was amazingly inclusive and I think everyone felt welcome. The process—taking apart, looking at, and putting back together the ways gender conflict has affected my life—was emotionally demanding in a way that has never been asked of me before or since, and having that support system in place was key. I have always been conscious of sexism and misogyny in a general sense, but the workshop helped me not just understand but feel how the fault lines in the relationship between men and women has hurt us both.
>
> The exercises within the workshop created opportunities to reexamine events in my life and allow myself to name and explore how they impacted me. To me the most powerful form of this was the "Truth Forum," which allowed both men and women to see how each group talks about these things in a single-gender environment. Finally, the two circles could communicate what they had drawn from listening to each other, which helped bring the groups back together. I cannot overstate how important it was to hear women talking to other women about their experiences of gender conflict in a way that was inevitably different from how they would talk about it in a mixed-gender setting. I hope that the women in the workshop learned something similar from the men's circle.
>
> The approaches of the Gender Reconciliation workshop felt truly innovative and I believe it could make a huge impact on how many people view sexism and gender conflict, because, for me at least, it opened a window onto what a gender-reconciled world might actually look like.

Aspects of William's positive feedback were echoed by many of the participants. Following on from this workshop, we immediately began planning a workshop for June 2017. Although there were some challenges over the three days, I was again extremely impressed by the facilitators' openness and immediate positive response to feedback. The group shared, in the final activity, how life-giving and positive the experience had been for them.

A local artist, Caroline, wrote the following about her experiences of the second workshop:

> The most important experience

> for me was in the cross-gender "Truth Forum" when I found I was able to contact long buried anger about the separation of female sexuality from humanity. For some reason it was possible for this to surface—and to be enacted safely—within the form of the Mandala. It was significant for me that men were present in a respectful way. When it was the men's turn to speak in the Truth Forum, one of them said that he wished women would express their anger clearly. This remark made me feel okay about my outburst.
>
> I was absolutely shocked to see the young women hesitantly speaking about their relationships in a way that conveyed their uncertainty about their own value and RIGHT to say no or to say yes. They still have no great cultural images that would affirm their whole humanity. They are still, it felt to me, dictated to by decorative, passive, erotic images, just as I had been 45 years back.
>
> Yet in spite of these horrible truths about the separation of sexuality from the humanity of both women and men, the honoring ceremonies on the last day gave me a sense of hope that we are at last willing to listen and to change. Three parts of the men's ritual especially touched me. First, coming in and seeing the men all standing up in a row—like soldiers—or like hostile all-male committees I have had to face in my professional life. But then they welcomed each woman, and then they sat down, so that we were looking down at them and not up as usual. Thus the fear of repression and aggression was reversed. Second, the somber extinguishing of the four candles, one at a time, with a spoken regret for each flame as it was blown out, representing a particular quality of woman that had been crushed or damaged. Somewhere there was even a reference to the problem of not paying women properly, which has been a problem all my life. I think it was something about "talents that have been crushed due to lack of money." That was very close to the bone. And then third: there was the re-lighting of the candles, and with each new flame the symbolic invocation and regeneration—and the specific NAMING—of how women can contribute as whole human beings. I have never before seen men make such ritual gestures. I was also very touched by the personal message of appreciation that the men gave to each of us women.
>
> Overall, the workshop seems to me to be an opportunity to become aware at a feeling level of the damaging myths about gender and the attempt to create new ones that allow the full dignity and humanity of both women and men to flourish.

GERI's work brings fresh hope and potential transformation. The way GERI's work enables men to bear witness to women's experiences and listen to women's voices, and vice versa, is unique among current gender justice work in the UK. GERI creates, with integrity and great skill, sacred spaces for deep change that go beyond conceptual awareness and discourse. Personally, my experience with GERI has strengthened my resolve to see this work flourish within the UK, and the workshops have been hugely transformational for me.

Participants in GERI workshop, London, United Kingdom, 2016

GERI in Mainland Europe

In recent years, we have also been invited to expand the GERI work in mainland Europe, including: two 3-day workshops in Spain (Valencia and Tarragona), workshops in Steinen, Germany, in Linz, Austria, as well as University programs in Pescara Italy, and several shorter programs across Austria, Italy, Spain, and Portugal.

Participants in GERI workshop, Tarragona, Spain, 2025
Invited by Rai Crespí Ripoll and Lara Terradas of *EntreHomes* and *EntreDones*

Men honoring women in GERI workshop,
Prague, Czech Republic, 2025
Invited by Pavel Hrdina of *Fortna*

Women honoring Men in GERI workshop,
Tarragona, Spain, 2025

Two Italian television stations reported on a GERI introductory presentation conducted for faculty and staff at the University degli Studi G. d'Annunzio, Pescara, Italy, April 29, 2025.
Invited by Fabrizio Paluzzi

Participants in GERI workshop, Steinen, Germany, 2024
Invited by Ken and Petra Sloan of *Synergeist Institut*

GERI co-founder William Keepin and GERI facilitators Antonia Porter and Valentín Oller were interviewed on a radio station in Palma de Mallorca, before conducting the first introductory GERI session in Mallorca, Spain

William Keepin, Yolanda Lucas, and Antonia Porter presented on GERI at the Forum Against Gender-Based Violence, Barcelona, Spain, 2023

GERI session in Palma de Mallorca, Spain
Invited by Valentín Oller, 2023

Participants in GERI workshop, Linz, Austria, 2023
Invited by Klaus Muik of *Mannsein* in Vienna

CHAPTER 23

GERI Online

After 27 years of conducting in-person workshops and trainings on 6 continents, GERI was faced with the unexpected emergence of the Covid-19 pandemic in 2020, and the abrupt halt of in-person programs worldwide. While GERI had for years convened shorter events, planning meetings, and follow-up groups online, the full experiential programs up to this point had almost always been conducted as 3-6 day in-person intensives. Like many organizations, we suddenly had to speed up our online implementation to deliver a comprehensive online program.

Moving the GERI program online meant adapting the highly experiential and sensitive processes to the online format and reorganizing the course structure to flow over seven weeks rather than as a several-day intensive. Given the sensitivity, volatility, and delicacy of issues around gender and sexuality, and the vulnerable space of entering into a process of uncovering and healing sensitive gender issues, we took great care in maintaining the safety of the process as we modified activities for an online format, and constructed the course flow to support and skillfully hold participants through the experience. Technical adaptations had to be made to maintain GERI's holistic methodology, and not limit the online program to dialogue, but rather continue to include movement, play, contemplative practices, music, art, and other experiential modalities.

For example, in the normal in-person Silent Witnessing process, the women's and men's groups sit on opposite sides of the room, facing one another. As described in Chapter 3, a series of questions is asked sequentially of each group relating to their gendered experiences, and individuals are invited to stand briefly in silence if the answer to that question is "yes" in their personal history. This experience greatly deepens mutual awareness of gender issues, and people are often struck by the power of witnessing the other gender standing for their experiences directly across from them, which brings the reality of painful gender conditioning openly into the room and community.

But how to meaningfully re-create the power of this experience online? We cannot sit opposite each other, and may not even be in the same country, much less the same room. How do we stand for our experiences in this new virtual space? What questions are appropriate to ask in the online context? What is our protocol if a person becomes upset or re-stimulated enough by the process to leave the session? Each activity raised new questions and challenges for the online adaptation, and our leadership team grappled with these questions in modifying the activities and constructing the overall course. We experimented with a prototype model internally with our trained facilitators, and added to the team a specially-trained tech facilitator whose primary role was to seamlessly manage the online technology involved in the facilitation (breakout rooms, music, tech support/instructions, videos, etc.). From this we developed a pilot course, refined it further based on extensive feedback, and finally offered our first public online course in May of 2020.

The results of our online program have been remarkable. We were pleasantly surprised to discover that a substantial degree of complex and delicate psychological transformative work is feasible in the virtual space. Joining together online across multiple time-zones and countries, oceans apart, a deep level of connection and presence is still possible. With skillful facilitation, we enter into that liminal, transformative space, in which deep sharings and mutual healing flow forth. The transformative spirit and intimacy of the GERI process is maintained online.

As GERI Trainer and Online Facilitator Lucille Meyer writes:

> Knowing the intimacy and deep truth-telling that occur in face-to-face GERI courses, I wondered how the courses would pan out on a virtual platform where participants are abstractly located in square boxes on a computer screen, rather than sitting in-person in a circle as equals, oftentimes hearing each other's breaths and sighs of despair as stories are shared.
>
> I was dumbfounded that online we have still been able to weave a safe container and hold each participant as they share their stories. In other words, it is possible for public virtual spaces to become intimate, safe, and sacred. An added bonus is that we have been able to connect virtually with people across the world in one workshop, which ordinarily would not have materialized for many. Connecting with people across the world has been even more poignant, as we have collectively shown up with a common felt-sense of the tragic consequences of the Covid-19 pandemic, including the deaths of loved ones and the economic hardships experienced by many.
>
> Why is it possible for us to continue this heart-felt work on a virtual platform? I think much has to do with the power of a healing intention that each participant and facilitator commits to. An intention for healing orients our whole way of being to show up in a particular way. Once an intention is set, one becomes more deliberate and purposeful about the course of action one has chosen. When participants in a community set an intention individually and collectively, a web of deep connection is forged. Dr. Will Keepin often speaks of the "Inner Net of the Heart," which is a beautiful description of connection beyond words. It is evident that heart-connection does not require face-to-face physical presence. Holding someone's story in one's heart does not require face-to-face presence. It feels to me that there is a radiation of empathy,

trust, respect, and love that envelops everyone who participates in a GERI course, regardless of physical proximity. There have been many moments over the last six to seven years that I felt held as a facilitator, both by the founders of this work, even in their absence, and an invisible presence, that I can feebly only describe as Grace.

As of this writing, we have conducted dozens of online programs in weekly formats, and as three-day intensives. The course has evolved into a 7 or 8 session program, totaling approximately 20-25 hours. These courses have been successfully implemented in a wide range of contexts including: in rural Kenya and East Africa, in South African Universities, with teenagers in India, in courses across Latin America, and through global cohorts bringing together participants from diverse cultures and continents. We have also conducted invitational programs for leaders at the United Nations NGO CSW, and for the Bahá'í International Community. Beyond this, we also developed a full-immersive, online, professional training program for GERI Facilitators that takes place over 6-8 months of weekly meetings (see Chapter 25 for details).

As Lucille notes, one of the sweetest gifts of the online implementation has been a deeper connection in community with our sisters, brothers, and friends worldwide. Our GERI facilitators across the globe had heard about each other over the years, but due to geographic distance many had never met. The online format naturally lends itself to rich cross-cultural collaboration and deepening of community connection. The online GERI programs have created entirely new opportunities, undreamt of in the past, for our facilitators to work together as international teams spanning the globe. Another wonderful blessing is that, in many cases, the online format gives greater access and removes geographic and economic barriers, allowing more people to come into GERI courses and experience this transformative work. This has created an unprecedented opportunity to reach large numbers of people with effective forums and practices to heal the systemic injustice of gender oppression across intersectionalities.

We now share a few personal accounts of people's experience of the online GERI program and its continued impact in their lives. This first account is from a South African man in his early forties who participated first in the online course, and then the online Professional Immersion and Facilitator Training:

I started my journey with GERI when I attended a few online introductory courses and then joined a GERI Heart Circle group. This sparked my interest in the work, and I wanted to learn more about it. The opportunity then arose to do the online facilitator training. When I started, I was a bit nervous, because I didn't know what to expect. I just knew bits and pieces of what the work entailed, but I decided to take the plunge anyway and join the training. This was one of the best decisions I have taken in my life.

The training was conducted in such a caring and thoughtful manner and created the space to truly explore myself through experiential exercises. I felt extremely safe, seen, and heard. This is something that was rare in my life growing up.

I grew up in a home with my submissive mother and very patriarchal father. I also have a brother and sister. Growing up I was taught very opposing lessons from my parents, which caused me to question many of these teachings.

My father taught me that men were to be feared to be respected. I was not allowed to show emotion. Violence and dominance were to be used if I didn't get my way or to resolve issues. He believed this, and it was his method of teaching me as well—I was abused physically, mentally, and emotionally on an almost daily basis. This caused me to have very deep self-esteem and anger issues that dominated most of my life in the decisions that I made regarding career and relationships, inevitably leading to a failed marriage.

My mother on the other hand taught me that it was alright to show emotion regardless of my gender. We spoke about many topics from relationships to kindness and caring about others. Many nights, as a young boy, I remember sitting on the edge of the bathtub consoling her because my father had just abused her. This caused me to have an awareness that I didn't think was meant for an 11-year-old child. However, what I did gain from my mother is a great respect for women. I loved how I felt inside when I practiced the lessons I learned from her. I saw her as a very strong female figure. I was not a violent or abusive person and preferred showing my emotions and caring about others. This was difficult though, because I had to hide the latter for fear of being ridiculed by my father and other male figures in my life. My mother's strength provided more of a feeling of safety for me than my father's intimidating stature or physical presence.

This confusion between male and female roles caused a lot of internal conflict for me. A big turning point came when I was 17 years old and went to a party that I was not meant to be at. It ended up with me being drugged and sexually assaulted by two girls who had heard I wanted to wait for marriage to have sex. When I came to, they were sitting and laughing and were quite smug about what they had done to me. This caused turmoil for me on the one hand, because it felt as if my choice to not have premarital sex was taken away from me. On the other hand, I had held a huge respect for females up to that point in my life, and because the perpetrators were female, I lost that respect. I could not speak to anyone about how this made me feel. In the male community, this instance would have been seen as "cool." This event led to much trauma and wounding in my life, most of which was suppressed.

Going through the GERI work helped me to unpack and uncover all these wounds and trauma that had plagued me for most of my life. I took on the role of perpetrator, believing that I had to hurt others before they hurt me. I struggled to trust people in general and always felt like everyone just wanted something from me. I became selfish and self-centered, not truly caring for others but instead always thinking in terms of what I could gain from them to benefit myself. I took on abusive relationships knowing that they would fail, because I believed that it was all I deserved and that I was not worthy of true love. This not only affected my relationships with partners but also my relationships with friends and work colleagues. I ended up not only hurting others in the process but also myself. The shocking part was that when I joined the GERI work, I didn't even realize how "messed up" I was.

Through the work I was able to break through these beliefs and the conditioning that I had from growing up in such a patriarchal context. Instead of seeing my role as only a good male figure, I also learned what it meant to be a good human being. I learned that I could tap into my masculinity and use it to cultivate safety and sensitivity instead of dominance and fear. I also learned respect for all gender identities without needing to force my opinions onto anybody. I learned that I could even tap into my feminine side, which was comical to me, because growing up I believed that I only had the masculine within me. I learned to respect everyone, not just in terms of gender but as human spirits and sentient beings of this earth. A big learning point for me was that we all have strengths and weaknesses and that this differs from person to person. It is not determined by gender, race, or class. If we could put aside these labels and tap into the abilities of one another as members of the human species, I believe that there would be a profound change in the world.

Sharing with women and people of different gender identities in a safe and open space allowed me to truly open up and be vulnerable without feeling judged. This changed my view on so many aspects of my life. I found that my relationships with others improved as I learned, through the GERI work, to listen more attentively and without judgment. I had struggled before then to meaningfully connect with men, as my relationship with my dad was so traumatic. It had also been hard for me to relate with people from the LGBTQ+ community, as this group was frowned upon. Through the GERI work this changed drastically for me, as I could speak and share openly about how I felt. It was enriching to me to be able to get feedback, and this showed me what healthy relationships could potentially look like. I now find myself getting along much better with men and have also made some good friends in the LGBTQ+ community. I don't feel the resentment or shame that I carried before.

Hearing other people's stories also gave me a greater appreciation for what we go through as human beings, regardless of gender, race, or religion. I feel this has made me more empathetic to the struggles of others and also have more compassion towards the healing that needs to take place in the world. I heard a woman sharing a story about the abuse she endured as a child while she attended a Catholic school and how it affected her outlook on life. I heard the story of a man who was bullied by his peers because he was considered "different." I heard stories of roles being forced onto people, not by choice, but based on their gender or race. This impacted me especially since I was a child growing up in apartheid South Africa. I was often told that I couldn't go to certain schools or attend certain events or even partake in certain sports due to the color of my skin and my gender. It has been profound for me to learn that even though we come from different backgrounds, countries, races, or cultures, there are so many similarities in the suffering that we endure as human beings, regardless of these factors.

So much clarification took place for me on an internal level. I felt less bound by the rules of society. It became clear to me that I had the freedom to act with respect and kindness towards others and also toward myself. Through the GERI work, I heard so many painful stories but also experienced so much care, love, vulnerability, resilience, and strength. The most significant transformation that I noticed within myself was that, through unpacking my "baggage" and healing my wounding, I have been able to feel peace within and connect with others on a deeper level. I feel less defensive and guarded. I have also been able to tap into my spirituality again. The GERI work fills me with so much hope for the future. I have seen what is possible if we show up authentically and be true to ourselves and others.

In this same spirit, this next account is from a middle-aged man in North America who recovered a deeply buried traumatic memory during the online course, which became an important healing encounter as he processed and integrated this experience:

A close friend of mine shared with me that it may be meaningful to do an online course with GERI, but it took a year before I finally decided to step into the process in the summer of 2020. Once I chose to join, I felt nervous in that "fear of the unknown" kind of way.

The seven-week course began, and the support and compassion from the whole facilitation team was immediately clear. I felt fragile and yet safe, and it helped that the others who were in the process were also opening and sharing honestly as well.

I had many breakthroughs during the process: the realization of the trauma that women are subjected to, as well as the trauma that men are indoctrinated into perpetrating on themselves, and others.

Within the container created by the safety and compassion of the facilitators, I found myself becoming open to sharing a deep wound I had never shared in depth with anyone.

When I was a boy, I delivered newspapers every day in a large apartment complex near my home. One Sunday morning, it was cold outside and I stopped by a convenience store to get some hot cocoa. A man, seeming to want to support my efforts to warm up, offered to take me back to where I folded my papers. After some time and some convincing, I said yes and got in his car. I was kidnapped and raped. He told me to never tell anyone about this, threatening to harm me if I did. Afterwards, I went home and did not tell anyone about this for years. My innocence was shattered by this trauma, but there was no one I could tell.

After sharing this story in the course, I was emboldened to do some research in the local news of nearly 40 years ago. I found out that there was a serial rapist who had kidnapped children for years in the area I lived. He would follow them for a long time and find out where to break in to homes at night. I saw his photo in one of the articles, and it was indeed the same man who had attacked me.

From these news accounts, I discovered something I had deeply forgotten: this assault took place when I was 16 years old, whereas my adult memory had always been that it happened when I was only 10 or 11. This was a powerful realization in itself for me, because it validated my utter innocence at the time. My boyhood innocence was still fully intact at 16, when this devastating attack occurred.

I contacted the friend who had invited me to join the GERI process (he is also a facilitator for GERI, but just not in our course on this round). He listened and held sacred space for me to completely let down my guard, and experience all the feelings I had been holding, and running from, for 40 years since this event. Even though we were on the phone and 700 miles away, I felt so supported and spent at least an hour just feeling, crying and releasing.

My friend contacted my GERI team and I connected with Will Keepin a day later and I will never forget when he said, "It wasn't your fault." That realization is still a big deal for me, as I had carried for too long the judgment that I was responsible for what had happened to me.

Now, I am free from the story I used to tell myself and my life has become less anxious. I would like to express my deepest gratitude for this program and all of the facilitators and participants who also were sharing their own experiences.

This final story from a woman in South Africa recounts her heart-opening and healing experience in the online course as she recovered from burnout after decades of working in the social service sector:

After nearly 40 years of women's and gender studies, workshops, and experiences that culminated in a post-graduate degree, even though I worked in diverse communities, with the most vulnerable, LGBTQ+, and spiritual spaces, I often left those spaces more disturbed and distressed. Some voices were often marginalized, depending on who was paying for the workshop, who was facilitating the session, and how confident or not the participants were. I found myself drained, frustrated, and distressed. Then came the pandemic, and the way humanity behaved was the pinnacle of distress, causing me to withdraw from humanity and simply weep. My soul was disturbed. I needed something more, something that went deeper than the superficial work being done in our communities. I was deeply concerned about the state of humanity and had decided that I would take a break. I needed time to heal, meditate, and focus on my health and wellbeing. I had cancer and COVID at the same time, and the toll on my physical body was debilitating, to say the least.

I could never have imagined the difference when a caring colleague shared an advertisement for an online course by Gender Equity and Reconciliation International. Something stirred within my being, and my interest in spirituality, sexuality, and healing resonated. What could I lose?

Like a breath of fresh air, the kind and compassionate way the course was facilitated healed parts of me that I didn't even know needed healing. I was impressed with the community agreements, and the diversity of the participants from across the world—male, female, and all the spectrum of humanity, along with a diversity of races, spiritual beliefs, and education. Every person showed up authentically. With each session, each question, and each breakout group, some things in me shifted and changed me forever. Since doing the course, I have engaged in a much deeper way in work related to gender, healing, and spirituality. I understand now that the need to create more compassionate spaces is imperative. Holding space for my colleagues in the group and being held by others as I shared deep truths brought such intense recalibration to my life. In my own facilitation of programs for life coaches and others, I have incorporated many of the aspects of the course. It was overwhelmingly powerful to sit and simply listen without judgment, and to speak knowing there would be acceptance. Recognizing that we all have challenges was incredibly healing for me. When we go through intense times, we often think we're the only one with those challenges. But the universality of the stories that were shared demonstrated that we are not alone in our struggles.

My family immediately noticed a change in me, in the way I spoke to my grandsons, and in my understanding of my daughters' and sons' various relationships. I learned to hold space for their truth.

Maya Angelou once said, "When you know better, you do better." This rings true for the experience I had with this course. I am forever changed.

These are just three accounts from among the hundreds of people who have experienced Gender Reconciliation work online in the past few years, but they demonstrate the connection, depth, healing, and transformation that is possible in online programs. The integrity and purity of each person's aspiration connects the group in the "Inner Net of the Heart," and opens the door for genuine transformation and a beloved community not limited by physical distance.

Men Honoring Women at GERI workshop near Aswan, Egypt, 2022

PART IV

Academic Research on Gender Equity and Reconciliation

Part IV presents two academic research studies on the Gender Equity and Reconciliation International (GERI) process.

The first research study was carried out by Dr. Samantha van Schalkwyk and Professor Pumla Gobodo-Madikizela, both of whom are currently at Stellenbosch University in South Africa. This was a longitudinal research study conducted with a cohort of 28 university students at the University of the Free State in South Africa. The students completed two three-day intensive GERI workshops, plus monthly follow up sessions over a full academic year. All sessions were audio recorded and transcribed, and the resulting data was meticulously analyzed using a unique research methodology that renders explicit the underlying interrelational dynamics of the transformative process that takes place in GERI, and revealed its impacts over time in a university setting. The study concludes that the GERI program has the potential to transform the deeply embedded infrastructure of gender oppression, promote a safer life for all genders, and should be mandatory for all students entering the university environment.

The second research study was carried out by Dr. Konyka Dunson at the University of the District of Columbia in Washington, DC, USA. This study posits that gender inequality is deeply rooted in social norms, and explores how GERI's methodology of deep cross-gender dialogue can potentially expose and challenge these norms, leading to personal and social change. Based on in-depth interviews with past participants in GERI programs, the study reveals that participants experienced the transformative power of witnessing harmful gendered experiences of others in cross-gender dialogue, which in turn enabled participants to create new experiences of gender equity together. The study concludes that GERI had a lasting beneficial impact, and is a proven catalyst for social change.

CHAPTER 24

Academic Research Studies on GERI

[Students] began to free themselves ... from the lifelong shackles of patriarchal conditioning.
— Dr. Samantha van Schalkwyk, Stellenbosch University

The (GERI) dialogue process is a proven catalyst for social change.
— Dr. Konyka Dunson, University of the District of Columbia

Disrupting the Logic of Patriarchy: Research on Transforming Gender Relations at a South African University

Samantha van Schalkwyk, Ph.D.
Stellenbosch University, South Africa

In completing the final version of this article describing our research on the GERI process with students at the University of the Free State (UFS), South Africa, I reflected on the early stages of setting up this research project. Two examples from my personal experience stand out. When working on the proposal for this research, I went through the necessary processes of obtaining approval from the student affairs office and the university ethics committee. At my meeting with a top manager at student affairs I presented my plan for the research project that would facilitate and explore students' intimate stories of their gendered existence. I motivated the research approach as follows: students would learn from witnessing the stories of others, especially those of different genders.[1] The student affairs representative responded that telling personal stories and the in-depth methodology for setting up such a space would be unnecessary and perhaps harmful for the students. He suggested I rather distribute pamphlets on campus to "teach" students about gender "issues." This is telling of the lack of understanding around the socially constructed nature of gender; a closing down of any understanding that the effects of patriarchal power run deep through the threads of life, molding our realities. Gender work for real change cannot be "taught" or facilitated through the presentation of "facts" on a pamphlet. Harmful social constructions of gender can only be undone through deep reflection on intimate experiences. I was concerned that such understandings were not part of the repertoire of this top manager who was tasked to address student life on campus.

In another encounter during the permissions hurdle, the ethics committee commented that gender dialogue of this nature may pathologize students who "already have reflexive identities and who might not be in need of healing." Such ways of thinking are deeply problematic as they are structured on the premise that certain people have healthy identities and others do not; and worse, that it is these "unhealthy" identities which are responsible for gender violence. We must avoid the tendency to view violence as individualized, as *only* visible, and physical (Henkeman, 2022).[2]

My research aligns with the GERI philosophy in that we understand that symbolic violence linked to patriarchy, and intersections of sexuality, race, class, ability and so on, colors our existence on all levels. Thus, everyone benefits from gender transformative work as our subjectivities[3] have necessarily been shaped by various amalgamations of gendered social conditioning, which are restricting at best, and which serve as what Nicola Gavey (2019)[4] calls the "social scaffolding" of violence. What is unhealthy, then, is the social system of patriarchy which structures and provides feeding ground for harmful relationships between genders. From a feminist perspective, gender-based violence is not only about harmful individual behaviours; we need to examine "the underlying social ordering within which such behaviours are performed and tolerated" (Finchilescu & Dugard, 2018: pg. 20).[5] My proposed research approach, which the ethics committee misunderstood, was not a process that would disrupt "unhealthy" students and "pull" them into correct ways of thinking. What is disrupted in these spaces is harmful patriarchal discourses which shape the experience and subjectivities of all humans.

I open with these experiences not with the aim of negatively reflecting on university approval processes which are a valuable part of any research, albeit as seen above they are often structured by deeply embedded ideologies. Rather, for me, these examples powerfully illustrate what it means to do such gender research in the South African university context. These examples illustrate institutionally embedded *denial* of the workings of patriarchy and its pervasive effects in everyday life. South African feminist academic and activist, Pumla Dineo Gqola (2015)[6] contextualises this well: In a country like (racialized and patriarchal) South Africa where violence is so prevalent, it is easy to slip into denial where we fail to see the way in which violence is so embedded in our social fabric. Also writing from a decolonial feminist perspective in South Africa, Sarah Malotane Henkeman (2022)[7] reminds us that denial is a critical dimension of the landscape of visible/invisible violence; denial is the thin line separating visible (read physical) violence from invisible forms of violence perpetuated through psychological, cultural, and structural spheres. Denial is also a factor that sustains invisible violence. Therefore, it is of crucial importance to engage with gendered processes that will break through such denial, offering spaces for moving deeper, for addressing the darker, vulnerable side of our subjectivities.

This research was eventually approved following a special in-person meeting with the ethics committee at which I explained my case in depth. Our collaboration with GERI began before this in 2012 in the form of a pre-conference workshop for the international "Engaging the Other" conference held at UFS, convened by Professor Pumla Gobodo-Madikizela. The GERI facilitators led the workshop participants through activities and dialogue that facilitated narratives about their gendered lives. Most importantly, this sharing took place between men and women in a safe and supportive space. Anecdotal evidence showed that this work resulted in changes in the way that participants perceived their gendered subjectivities in relation to others. Although the founders of this work come from North America, the work has strong links with South Africa, being based on the central tenets of the Truth and Reconciliation Commission (TRC)—public acknowledgment of traumatic experience, social healing that invokes a common humanity, and cultural and attitudinal change (with the goal, of course, of political change) (Scanlon, 2016).[8] In addition, many of the invited facilitators come from the African continent bringing with them cultural, community and linguistic insights that speak more closely to many of the participants in this context. This work sparked our interest and we wanted to document this collective dialogue process. We wanted to learn about the potentially transformative moments that emerge through women and men's encounters with each other. It is out of this intellectual pursuit that the research project was born.

This research was initiated by the Trauma, Forgiveness & Reconciliation research unit at the University of the Free State, Bloemfontein, South Africa, under the leadership of Professor Pumla Gobodo-Madikizela (now at the Centre for the Study of the Afterlife of Violence and the Reparative Quest (AVReQ), Stellenbosch University). This article describes the background, process, and findings of the research. The data generated in this year-long project was rich and extensive, covering all aspects of gendered life, including sexuality, gender fluidity, race and racism. For this article I focus specifically on the patriarchal logic around the *denial of gender violence as "everyday" violence,* and the possibilities this collective work holds for breaking through such deep-rooted layers of denial—a process akin to acknowledging and interrogating patriarchal power.

What Is the Texture of This "Skin" That Surrounds Us?

South Africa, a country that has often been dubbed the "rape capital" of the world, is sadly known by most across the globe for its brutal levels of violence against women and LGBTIQ people, coupled with deep cycles of intergenerational trauma and dehumanization, racism, and poverty. The patriarchal-racist and classist agenda which blames such violence on "deviant others," hides from view the fact that violence can be part of anyone's repertoire and that we are all implicated in different ways in producing and reproducing patriarchal logic.

Hegemonic gender discourses are part of the logic of patriarchy and underpin violence

Gqola (2021)[9] provides us with the terminology of the *female fear factory* to understand what she considers as one of patriarchy's most efficient tools. "In patriarchal societies we are socialised into the female fear factory in ways similar to how we have been made fluent in language." (Gqola, 2021: p. 69). Following Gqola, patriarchal societies teach a specific *logic* around gender. As children witness the ever-going performance of gender around them—explicit messages, warnings, and also symbolic statements—they learn to behave according to patriarchal rules ("boys will be boys") (Gqola, 2021). Sticking closely to patriarchal norms promises women (and men) the hope of safety, a hope which is "tattooed on our very skin and psyche as we are taught to inhabit patriarchal gender identities" (Gqola, 2021: p. 115). Moving beyond these gender expectations poses the risk of ridicule, blame, shame, and often violence on one's body—this is how patriarchy keeps women (and men) in line. Gqola says that the key to unlearning this fluency is to maintain our mastery of the system but to interrupt our participation in it, and also to refuse to occupy the roles set out by this system. Interestingly, Bronwyn Davies and colleagues from another context (Australia) also draw richly on the skin metaphor. They liken gendered socialization to a layer of skin surrounding us—something that is always there and shapes us, but which is such an established part of our being that it is difficult to acknowledge or interrogate it. The title of this section borrows from Davies' metaphor to illustrate the ubiquitous nature of gendered socialisation in everyday life.

Patriarchal scripts of masculinity and femininity, or what Morison and colleagues (2021: p. 2)[10] call "the cultural familiar," form part of our gendered social conditioning and guide and shape gendered relationships. Such scripts have a negative impact on the way men, women, and gender non-conformative people construct their sense of self and identity in relation to others. There is consensus among scholars in the field of gender studies that these patriarchal gender scripts are intrinsically linked to issues of power and subordination, and to the problem of violence against women, and violence against LGBTIQ people.

Hegemonic masculinity refers to the "embodiment of the culturally most valued way of being a man or boy, and against which all other men and boys measure their practice in a particular place and time" (Ratele, et al., 2010).[11] As Schrock and Padavic (2007)[12] state within the context of their work on a battering intervention program in the United States,

"Drawing on cultural notions of manhood as superior to womanhood, many men believe they are entitled to receive male privilege and to control women in their lives, and such expectations are psychological preconditions for choosing violence."

"Appropriate" femininity, or emphasized femininity, is seen as typically dependent, passive and (aways) sexually submissive/available. "Acceptable" women are passive and neatly feminine while at the same time responsible for their own safety and monitoring conservative sexuality (otherwise they are constructed as "deserving" the abuse they suffer). These discourses shape ideas about sexuality and entitlement which culminate in disrespect, coercion, and violence at the hands of heterosexual men toward women and gay men (who are often perceived as feminine because they refuse to adopt the standards of hegemonic masculinity). South African studies have shown that patriarchal ideologies are instilled from a young age (see for example, Morison, Macleod & Lynch, 2021[13]; Shefer, Kruger & Schepers, 2015[14]; Shefer & Macleod, 2015)[15].

Finding strategies that can open space for the interrogation of toxic masculinity is crucial for disrupting the destructive consequences of patriarchy in educational settings. Equally important, though, is an interrogation of dominant scripts of femininity and the creation of new forms of femininity that move beyond patriarchal strictures. Healing and transformation of gender oppression and violence necessarily entails interrogation of these harmful gendered scripts and the creation of new ways of understanding what it is to be a woman and a man in the world. New narratives are needed to disrupt the unequal power dynamics infused through patriarchal discourse and practice. Such work will go a long way in eliminating violence against women and achieving a just and safe world for all genders.

Gender Oppression and Violence at South African Universities

Universities are microcosms of society. That is, universities reflect and mirror broader values and practices. As violence against women has increased in South Africa, so has oppression and violence increased in university settings (Hames, 2011).[16] Scholarship indicates that South African university settings are spaces in which patriarchal scripts dominate and gender violence thrives. Such scripts are deeply embedded, restricting the movement of women and LGBTIQ students around campus—a type of symbolic violence that infuses into all aspects of campus life.

In her article *"We live in fear, we feel very unsafe": Imagining and fearing rape in South Africa,* Dosekun (2007)[17] found that fear of rape was prominent among a sample of female university students that self-identified as never having experienced rape. These findings powerfully illustrate the culture of fear that shapes students' lives—rape culture and incidents of rape on campus set up an environment that is constantly traumatic for all female-identified students because rape is always a possibility. Evident here is the workings of Gqola's female fear factory, as described in the section above—rape becomes a message about the threat of violence, rape is part of the language of the female fear factory.

All this points to a bleak picture. Nevertheless, it is important to note that the findings of the above studies also showed narratives of strength and agency, community, and energy to promote change. Narratives of fear and powerlessness in relation to men, in relation to patriarchy, never sit alone (van Schalkwyk, Boonzaier & Gobodo-Madikizela, 2014).[18] There is always the possibility for agency, and here lies the possibility for change.

What About the Men?

A key underpinning of the current research is an acknowledgment that the system of patriarchy oppresses men as well as women. This is not to excuse men who perpetrate violence, rather it is to acknowledge that men's entanglement within the patriarchal system, which demands the quest for power, control, and the suppression of emotion, denies men their humanity and results in deep levels of suffering, the gravity of which is not often discussed or understood in everyday settings. This is not a new concept. In her book *The Will to Change: Men, Masculinity, and Love (2004),*[19] the late bell hooks wrote about how patriarchal culture keeps men from knowing themselves through a constant and vigilant psychic self-mutilation. hooks (2002)[20] writes that patriarchy wounds men by imposing a masculine identity that denies their wholeness (they are taught not to love), thus, to know how to love and be loved, men need to challenge and resist patriarchal norms. In the South African context, masculinities scholar Kopano Ratele (2016)[21] eloquently argues that African men need to be liberated from cultural forms of masculinity that are injurious to their being. Whatever men "gain" in terms of patriarchal privileges, they lose far more in the sense of their denied humanity.

The consequences for men of having to suppress emotion, trauma and vulnerability are significant. For me, this is not just a theoretical understanding. During the GERI workshops with the UFS students, I saw men in new ways that changed the shape of my feminist views about men's power. I witnessed the raw pain which men face in relation to patriarchal expectations as well as the devastating consequences of their treatment by men and women who ascribe strictly to patriarchal rule. Often this came through in male participants' narratives of shame, abandonment and emotional isolation resulting from their relationships with their fathers. At other times, this was evident through narratives of deep contradictions between men's need to have better, more loving relationships with women on the one hand, and on the other hand, patriarchal expectations which restricted ways of doing this. The gender research clearly brought home bell hooks' statement, "Knowing that both women and men are socialized to accept patriarchal thinking should make it clear to everyone that men are not the problem. The problem is patriarchy."

The "Everyday" Traumas of Patriarchy—For Women and Men

The core assumption here is that gendered trauma refers not only to catastrophic events such as rape and battering but may also be constellated through an accumulation of experiences that reduce self-dignity and feelings of worth. These "small acts of violence" have an impact through the very denial of people's subjectivity and disregard for their humanity. This follows from North American feminist scholars such as Maria Root (1992)[22] and Laura Brown (1995)[23] who highlight the insidious trauma that occurs through the devaluing of social identities—it often happens subtly yet continuously and has the capacity to erode the human spirit.

Forter (2007)[24] names this the trauma of "patriarchal identity formation," and says,

> These are emphatically social disturbances but have been thoroughly naturalised in ways that make it necessary to excavate and "estrange" them in order to see them as social traumas.

If we want to get to the heart of healing in South Africa, we need to facilitate spaces through which men and women can tell their stories of pain and trauma: these stories need to be heard.

People who adopt alternative gendered behaviors are often subject to ridicule or even overt danger. Active resistance of patriarchal gender norms often may entail fear of losing one's patriarchal privileges; a fragmentation of the self; or a fear of living a life of less certainty (Crawford, 1996).[25] However, the results of living chained within the gender system are even more devastating. Those who do practical work in the field of gender transformation can attest to the deep dehumanization and erosion of the spirit that often accompanies gendered trauma. These negative effects are all the more dangerous because they are most often not recognized and acknowledged by people on individual, collective, and professional levels.

U.S. trauma specialist Janice Crawford (1996)[26] says that rigid reinforcement of what is acceptably masculine and feminine lead to an inevitable sense of inadequacy, incompleteness, and a lack of trust of self and other. This, she says, causes a "severed self," due to the fact that one can never completely fulfil these cultural requirements of appropriate gender. The consequences of such gender-traumatized selves may be confusion and pain, seen through the multiple expressions of violence that are evident throughout the world today—self-hatred, psychic numbness, and physical and sexual abuses that signify rage towards the "other." South African gender scholars have argued for a healing approach that acknowledges the multiplicity of layers of identification with patriarchal gender norms and identities as well as the recognition of essential sameness among human beings—this entails a reconstruction of our entire reality (Shefer & Foster, 2009).[27]

Theorizing How Patriarchal Gender Norms Might Be Disrupted at South African Universities

As Ratele, Shefer, Strebel and Fouten (2010) discuss, there are other forms of masculinity, "competing masculinities" (p. 558) to use their term, that offer alternatives to these dominant ideas about what it means to be a man. Such competing masculinities are crucial for the project of disrupting patriarchy and for creating new realities for human beings.

Femininity is constructed in relation to masculinity and patriarchal norms (see Davies & Gannon, 2006).[28] As Connell (1987: p. 186)[29] contests, "Several points about masculinity also apply to femininity at the mass level. These patterns too are historical: relationships change, new forms of femininity emerge, and others disappear." Femininity and masculinity are constructed in relation to each other, and truly transformative work should look at the constructions of men and women *together*. There are real risks posed when one fails to meet the expectations of hegemonic discourses of gender: Interpersonal risks such as sexual coercion and violence and social risks of humiliation and shaming (Morison, Macleod & Lynch, 2021).[30] For this reason, it is of critical importance to facilitate safe spaces where such work can be done.

A Collective Biography Methodology

Our observations from the practical GERI work conducted at the university was that these workshops promoted change in the ways in which participants understood gender and their identities in relation to others. We wanted to explore the deeper processes at play. The first step was incorporating the GERI workshops into an academic research methodology. Drawing on the collective biography methodology outlined by feminist poststructuralists Davies & Gannon (2006),[31] this research project explores the truthtelling dialogues across the genders. It examines the sites of psychological connection and sites of resistance at which participants disrupt patriarchal power. The research questions guiding this project are as follows:

- How do the students navigate the GERI workshop space?
- What significant moments of connection emerge from this work?
- In what ways do participants produce or challenge patriarchal power in these spaces? How does the *denial of gender violence as "everyday" violence* feature in these intimate tellings?
- What theoretical and practical insights can we glean about the usefulness of the GERI workshop model for facilitating a change in gender relations?

We incorporated two three-day GERI workshops, spaced about six months apart, after which a series of smaller follow up discussions were held monthly with the students at Bloemfontein and Qwaqwa[32] campuses in the Free State. The project took place over one year, and this longitudinal methodology aided in the promotion of deeper reflection and engagement on the part of the participants who established strong connections and moved into deep familiarity of each other's stories. The research project obtained ethical approval from Faculty of Humanities: Research Ethics Committee at the University of the Free State. Informed consent for audio and visual recording (photographs) was signed by all the participants prior to the sessions, and pseudonyms were used instead of the students' real names to strive towards anonymity.

The student participants for this project were recruited via university media channels and through networks with various student organizations. Interested students were scheduled for interviews during which the details and procedure of the research project were discussed. A total of twenty-four participants participated in the study, all of whom were Black South Africans of the Sotho and Zulu cultures. One man was from the neighbouring country Lesotho.[33] All participants were undergraduate university students of various disciplines. It is interesting to note that two of the students were studying a gender-related topic, which could have informed a more feminist lens.

Process and Preliminary Analysis

Two three-day GERI workshops were conducted with the larger group of students, the first broadly on gender, while the second focused on gender with sexuality as a core focus.

The workshops were audio-recorded, including plenary and breakout sessions, and photographs were taken throughout the process. These workshops stood as the first phase of data gathering. The activities such as role plays, life mapping, truth forums and symbolic work with objects mobilized a critical awareness of gender among our participants because they were beginning to engage with their memories in different, more creative ways.[34] The storytelling sessions were particularly beneficial in the process of interrogating gendered social conditioning and the way it shapes experience. As the students began to tell parts of a particular experience over and over again, they begin to perceive the experience in different, more manageable ways.

Through the audio and visual recording, I captured the raw meanings about gendered experience and personhood which emerged in the workshops. I transcribed the audio recordings and read over the texts several times, identifying preliminary themes. There were two types of themes—narrative (excerpts of the students' stories) and visual (the photographs). These themes were then taken back to the students in the second stage of data gathering—the small group discussions. These discussions took place every month and were also audio-recorded. They were spaces within which the students engaged with the data and moved into deeper analysis of their gendered experiences.

In-Depth Analysis: A Narrative Thematic Approach

A narrative thematic approach, as outlined by Reissman (2008),[35] was utilized to analyse the research data. The focus is on the ways in which knowledge is constructed through storytelling. Subjectivity is understood "as/in knowledge and power defined according to cultural discourses and cultural textuality" (Reavey & Gough, 2000: p. 341).[36] Thus, attention is turned from identifying "internal" problems or "disorders" to looking at the external discursive matrix and culture shaping experiences.

A narrative thematic analysis offers three core analytical ground points for making sense of the students' voices. Firstly, *narratives are contextual.* The content of what is told is shaped by the broader socio-historical climate within which the telling takes place, but is also shaped by the micro-context of the listeners—here the facilitated space of the GERI workshops. Secondly, *narratives are infused with the narrator's values.* The taken-for-granted discourses and values that people draw on in their narratives tell us about the circulation and functioning of discourses in their lives. Lastly, *narratives reveal socially constructed identities.* We cannot "see through" narratives and identify an essential self "behind the scenes." Rather, narratives provide us with insight into how identities are constructed socially and the personal and political purposes of these various identity constructions (Reisman, 2008).[37] It is important to acknowledge the political work narratives serve. Stories have very real effects beyond the meaning for individual storytellers, creating possibilities for new social identities (Reissman, 2008).[38] Through the act of listening, the audience is given the opportunity to engage with the experience of the narrator, to enter the narrator's world and see things from their perspective. Reissman (2008: p. 9)[39] attests that the act of listening "moves us emotionally through imaginative identification."

Conducting thematic analysis requires close attention to language, power, and positioning in the narrators' stories. The analysis for this research is driven by the understanding that people have the capacity to resist patriarchal meanings by narrating their own story, on their own terms, using their own definitions. Central to this notion of agency is the act of authoring one's own story, and the capacity to re-imagine the self by transcending harmful patriarchal meanings that have been imposed by society. From a feminist post-structuralist perspective, a person exhibits agency through engaging with their capacity to go beyond the given meanings in any one discourse, and forge something new, through a combination of previously unrelated discourse (Davies, 1991).[40] Davies says that such linguistic work captures a shift in consciousness that is beginning to occur, through the individual (collaborating with others) imagining what is not, but what might be. Through this process individuals can, in effect, re-invent themselves and their identities.

The analytical focus is on what was *said* (the content) rather than how the narratives are relayed. It does not aim to yield in-depth information about individual biographies, but rather insights about categories of power and subordination in participants' lives (Reissman, 2008).[41] Below I present the analysis of multiple layers of narratives that emerged through the GERI workshops and follow up sessions as "windows" through which we can understand the process of sharing intimate stories of gendered life. I centred my analysis on particularly powerful moments that speak to men and women engaging deeply—moments that illuminated deep reflection and mo(ve)ments (Davies & Gannon, 2006)[42] within, and in relation to, patriarchal power. In this way it was often possible to pinpoint the precise moments and process of transformation of consciousness.

Decolonizing Gender Through Collective Engagement: The Students' Voices

Scholarly ideas about how gender oppression can be transformed are based around notions of challenging and disrupting dominant and harmful constructions of gender (see Davies, 2000).[43] The first step is becoming conscious of the ways in which ideas of gender have been socially constructed. Davies and Gannon (2006)[44] describe what such collective processes entail: it does not mean transformation into new subjects in linear time, rather the site of transformation lies in attention to the remembered moment—such attention makes the subjects' vulnerability to discursive power visible, while also making visible the constitutive power/potential of the subject-in-process. The movement they speak about lies, "in the process of making visible the discursive powers of particular discourses and the modes of subjection they entail. It is that visibility that makes transformation possible, not just of ourselves as individuals, but of our collective and discursive practices, of our social contexts, of our capacity to imagine what is possible." (Davies

& Gannon, 2006).[45] The key is to make visible—and hence conscious—what was formerly hidden or unconscious.

In the analysis that follows, I give substance to these theoretical ideas by examining what such a process would mean theoretically and practically. I document the key findings and provide an illustration of the essence of the process of change that emerged throughout these collective engagements. For this article, particular focus is placed on the rich *sites of dislodgement*—the key points at which harmful patriarchal structures can be broken away from—as illustrated in two core themes that emerged from the narratives. These two themes—elaborated below—are (1) reflexively examining *gendered interiority,* and (2) *sites of psychological connection* with others. Both themes provide important information about participants' process of disrupting patriarchal logic.

Reflexively examining gendered interiority: Narrating the shaping of the gendered self

Noncedo first told her story in the women's Truth Mandala. She had been raped five times in her life; the first rape taking place when she was a young child, the next in her early teens, and one of the most recent on the very university cam pus at which the research dialogues were taking place. The most recent rape had left her vulnerable to having to physically walk past her rapists every day on her way to class.

> I felt scared when I was a child because I always wondered when I saw an older man approaching me what was going to happen next...and then I thought about adults; I wonder what it is that they are seeing in me. And at [that] moment I am feeling scared because I am wondering "what am I inside?" "What is it that I represent; this body that I was born with?" Once somebody's looking at it to be seen as something that deserves to be hurt, something that deserves to be destroyed. I fear the trust issues that I have. I've been a rape victim for three times. My first perpetrator was actually a woman. The second time was a family member—my brother—and that was many times because everyone was not only once, it was many times. So, by the time I was 16 it happened with a stranger. I felt that I am used to it by now. If somebody who was closer to me, somebody who was supposed to be loving and caring for me could not think twice of hurting me, then why would a stranger think twice?
>
> I started feeling maybe the common thing here [is that] it has been me for many times and so maybe being a girl, being a woman is what is wrong with this whole thing. I feel that as I've been growing up that maybe if I sit tight enough with my legs closed then whoever is looking at me won't be thinking anything that is sexual. I felt when I was growing up that maybe if I wear my brother's clothes, then I am not showing anything that is feminine, and then maybe they will just forget me, they will just stop...." [crying]
>
> (Noncedo, black cisgender woman; Women's truth mandala, GERI workshop one)

In this deeply moving excerpt, Noncedo conveys a rich sense of her gendered interiority growing up as a young girl who was continually violated by both men and women. Her story paints a picture of what the world is like inhabiting her female body as an object of the sexual gaze. She gives voice to the disconnect between her sense of humanity and her body seen through her statement, "what am I inside?". We see what Connell (1987)[46] describes as the double context within which femininities are formed—on the one hand in relation to the image and experience of the female body and on the other hand the social definitions of women's place in the world. Noncedo narrates a visceral sense of shame that is connected to her feminine self because her body is a symbolic representation for an invitation to danger. The trauma of such shame is connected to her body and this trauma has been powerfully reinforced by the ongoing violence that she has experienced. Noncedo is fluent in the female fear factory which requires women to modify their behavior in order to remain safe in the world (see Gqola, 2021).[47] She speaks about her constant vigilance over her body—her thoughts that if she engages in different behaviors like "closing her legs tightly" or wearing her brother's clothes to avoid revealing "anything that is feminine," then possibly older men will "forget" about her. She constructs her gendered subjectivity as vulnerable, but also as deeply shameful. The shame is infused in her narrative of self, suggesting accountability for the violence directed at her body. Patriarchal rules shaped her early childhood understanding that she was somehow to blame for the abuse and violation. Her narrative illuminates the "everyday" workings of patriarchy. She critiques patriarchal power through narrating for us, the audience, the very workings of such power—thus also disrupting the denial infused into patriarchal ideology.

Noncedo narrates she was also raped by her brother many times. Someone who was close to her and who should have loved and cared for her. Significantly, she constructs this experience at the hands of a loved one as de-sensitizing her to the subsequent violation she experienced at the hands of a stranger ("I felt that I am used to it by now"), in a way also leading her to expect such treatment ("why would a stranger think twice?"). Sara Ahmed (2000)[48] writes about "stranger danger" as a discourse that conveys meaning that the familiar is always designated as safe—it is the unknown man encountered in public spaces that is to be feared. The projection of danger onto the figure of a stranger constructs violence to be extraordinary, coming from outside the safety of the home and community (Ahmed, 2000[49]; Brodie, 2020[50]). This is not what we are hearing from Noncedo. The excerpt above clearly contradicts the "stranger danger" discourse by shedding light on the reality of women's subjective trauma at the hands of those they love. This is consistent with much of the cross-cultural data on sexual violence, which frequently entails perpetrators personally known to the victims. Shedding light on the inconsistencies and falsity of dominant discourses, as seen here, is an important component of these intimate cross-gender tellings. Illuminating the cracks/fissures in patriarchal discourse serves to destabilize patriarchy's power bit by bit—for Noncedo as she breaks the silence for herself and for the other students witnessing such tellings in the workshop space. The recognition that violence is structured and legitimated by home and community (see Ahmed, 2000)[51] holds the possibility for a peek beneath patriarchy's cloak of denial that the familiar can be, and often is, deadly.

Another student, Tolo, recounted how his father's shame as a perpetrator of rape became his own shame.

> My shame is that when I was young, my father was committed for rape. So I have always felt everyone walking around is like "there's that son of a rapist," things like that you know. So I felt like his shame became my shame. So then I carried on my life. I carried on with that burden around, but I [have] never tried to speak about this. Now, I am opening up. Like it has affected me a lot. And then this led to my anger because of how in my life I've probably struggled with my relationships. I think that because of that rape I've always had that position like I will go to jail and what has happened to my father will happen to me. So that has led me to be insecure.
>
> (Tolo, black cisgender male, Men's Truth Mandala, GERI workshop one)

Tolo speaks about his sense of shame that resulted from his father's perpetration of rape. He narrates that his father's shame was transferred onto him, seen through his words, "my shame" and "I felt his shame became my shame." There is a strong sense of the intergenerational transmission of shame due to his shared position of manhood. He suggests that his father was a figure of shame in his eyes and that he has absorbed such shame into his subjectivity. In their introduction to a special Feminism & Psychology issue on the politics of shame, Shefer and Munt (2019)[52] discuss that shame often serves the function of policing people to comply with patriarchal expectations. People who break the rules risk deep shaming, othering, or silencing. However, as we see above, shame seems to have a different meaning for Tolo. He represents shame in two important narrative moments. Firstly, he utilizes shame to distance himself from patriarchal values, seen through his description of his shame and anger directed at his father, the rapist. Secondly, he utilizes shame to voice the negative effects which patriarchal power has had on his sense of self. All through which he constructs himself as a victim. The making of his gendered self has been shaped and burdened by this system of power, as someone who must bear the weight of the actions of his father (and perhaps also other men). The language of shame affords him the voice to call out patriarchal power and give voice to *his patriarchal trauma*. At the same time, it allows him to distance himself from this very same power which, he says, contradicts his own values, thus taking on a very specific moral positioning within this research space.

The excerpts above speak to the way in which the students were able to acknowledge aspects of their gendered experience that were previously silenced by societal structures. The space facilitated an openness of expression to speak about these sensitive or taboo topics and for them to theorize about the power of patriarchy in their lives. They narrated fragments of their social lives—significant moments—which eloquently convey the shaping of their young selves, as women and men in the world. In this way, they develop a language of patriarchal trauma, a means for the embodied and intuitive aspects of their lives to be disclosed. They "call out" patriarchy, developing a critical consciousness of such power in their lives. During this process the students began to make visible what had been previously invisible—something akin to what Davies & Gannon (2006)[53] term "rupturing the skin of silence." This is a process that affords the narrator more power through the act of validating their humanity. At the same time their narratives stand as testimony to the gendered trauma experienced in a patriarchal world. Engaging with these voices offers the speaker (and the listener) a different vantage point for understanding the unequal power dynamics that are infused into all aspects of relationships. Hence, in this sense, one of the sites of dislodgment is the very moment of naming the process through which patriarchy has shaped their lives. In short, breaking the taboo of silence, and speaking truth to personal gender-based violations—*in a community of peers*—helps liberate the speaker from the damaging effects of those violations, while also initiating a process of new identity formation. Such deconstruction of gendered social conditioning constitutes an entryway for further critical engagement and critique. These crucial moments can also be key learnings or even breakthrough moments for the listeners—many of whom have similar personal histories—as they realize for the first time that their particular experiences are not unique to them, but are in fact the shared and systemic consequences of gender trauma in a patriarchal society.

Sites of psychological connection: Personal histories collide

For the follow up sessions I introduced a series of quotes and images taken from key moments during the two GERI workshops and highlighted these as invitations for further exploration and group analysis. Participants were prompted to choose quotes or photographs that particularly stirred their heart. They were asked to share what others' words depicted in their chosen quote mean for them at the current moment in their lives, emotionally and intuitively. Something about engaging with others' experiences—through quotes and images—provided a certain distance that (ironically) allowed for a deeper opening up in terms of emotionally connecting with the material.

To illustrate, a woman, Lebogang, at our first small group follow-up session chose the following quote from the themes that we presented. It had been spoken by a man at the previous GERI workshop:

> *Follow up session prompt taken*
> *from men's Truth Mandala,*
> *GERI Workshop 1*
> "When I saw my niece naked,
> her mother told her to run
> and hide, because her uncle is
> watching. 'Run and hide in the
> bedroom, because you do not
> know what your uncle might do
> to you.' I felt shame because as a
> man I might not be able to wash
> my own daughter. Just because
> I am a man it means I'm going
> to rape her? I'm ashamed to call
> myself a man."

Lebogang elaborates on why this specific quote "spoke" to her on an emotional level. She says the following,

> And this one really speaks to me because it's from a man's perspective... I think of this man who is saying this and talking about his shame, and I think, and it's really made me realize that, yes...I put men in a certain categories, and even if you're educated and know about these stereotypes and categories, they sometimes can be so deeply engrained to the point where it's not even cognitive; it's a feeling that you don't trust men.
>
> And I've often put that onto men for no reason, especially men in intimate relationships. And I've put that on in ways that I don't trust men. I immediately think the worst of men. I immediately think they lie. So this really made me realize how I often hurt men by presuming that they are not trustworthy in some sort of way. So that's how, you know, listening to a man's perspective, where he sort of made me think about my own process.

She continues as follows:

> So hearing a man say this really makes me question my own assumptions and what my own behavior and beliefs could be, [and] how it could be influencing other men's lives, or men's lives that I interact with.

Lebogang witnesses the man's story of pain and confusion at being labelled a potential perpetrator. The quote that she identified and then picked up from the circle of quotes on the floor in the middle of our circle is a vehicle through which she connects to this man's story of pain. She catches a glimpse of the shame that this man experiences every day because he is branded always as a possible perpetrator who is viewed with mistrust and fear. Lebogang's acknowledgment of the man's shame is in essence an acknowledgment of his full humanity and the complexity of his being that lies outside any rigid boundaries of what it means to be a man, or of stereotypes about how men usually behave (the perpetrator label). Importantly this witnessing moves her to reflect more deeply about the experience of men in the world. She interrogates her own conditioning ("I put men in certain categories"; "I often hurt men by presuming that they are not trustworthy in some sort of way"). Through her narrative she examines her patriarchally-enforced role of cautious woman who must maintain distrust in men in order to protect her safety. She constructs a self that is questioning these patriarchally-enforced ideologies that no longer serve her. Lebogang's narrative sheds light on Connell's statement (1987: p. 186)[54] that, "The ideological representations of femininity draw on, but do not necessarily correspond to actual femininities as they are lived. What most women support is not what they are."

One of the men, Lusanda, responded to the same quote above in a separate men's follow up session. Lusanda had disclosed in the GERI workshop truth forum that he had raped his young female cousin years earlier. He told us he is not sure what this experience means for his cousin, or whether she even remembers the rape. Such a telling was powerful, as he told this story in his own gender circle, he was surrounded by a larger circle of women who silently witnessed the telling. He narrates the way the quote "spoke" to him:

> On this one, for this man who feels that he's been painted with a brush just because he's a man: I feel the opposite because I have done something to my younger cousin. And so, for me, this brought back what came up for me at the workshop. And ever since then I've been processing, and I've been speaking to people and working through this. I've been working towards seeing a counsellor, to work through this.
>
> I think, in my life I had a lot of moments of deep depression. And there were no symptoms so there was nothing ever wrong. And I've been wondering whether this particular incident with my younger cousin has been something that has been suppressed for so many years, and needs now to, you know, to be resurfaced on purpose, and dealt with. So that's where I am.

Lusanda narrates that the details included in the chosen prompt, the man's story of his shame as a man who is always judged as a possible perpetrator, made him aware of silences in his own life story. This silence is around his experience of raping his young female cousin. He clearly sets himself apart from this man ("I feel the sort of opposite because *I have* done something to my younger cousin"), but at the same time feels connected to the story due to a shared narrative of shame. These moments allow Lusanda to acknowledge and speak about his complicity in the patriarchal system but at the same time reflect on the ways in which his act of perpetration has negatively affected his existence ("in my life I had a lot of moments of deep depression"). He positions himself as mobilized to change for the better through therapy and "dealing" with his act of violence. This narrative move signals a breaking through of patriarchally-enforced denial whereby Lusanda illuminates the complexity of his complicity with patriarchy and the ways in which this complicity has hurt him by fostering dark secrets. He says, "there was nothing wrong" and then came the workshop, which facilitated the surfacing of the memory of the rape he perpetrated, a memory that he had since "been processing." His narrative suggests that his perpetration was the cause of his depression, and that from the current moment he is struggling with taking up the position of perpetrator. The collective gender process has made apparent the contradictions in his life. His narrative conveys the sense that the resurfacing of the memory of his violation against the body of his young cousin has mobilized an energy of change, thus reflecting Davies and Gannon's (2006) mo(ve)ment whereby Lusanda engages with the patriarchal-enforced denial in a way that prompts personal change.

> *Follow up session prompt taken from the women's Truth Mandala*
> "I think about older men and I wonder what is it that they are thinking. And what is it that they see in me. And I'm scared because I wonder what am I inside. What is it that I represent; the body that I was born with? When someone is looking at me they see something that they could hurt. Something that has to be destroyed."

In the men's follow-up session, Aphiwe narrates his response to the prompt above:

> Because actually, after the workshop, what I told myself that you know what, it's I think it's about time that we, as males, change our mental attitudes in a sense. In the sense that I started developing this sense of seeing women for who they are. Not what they can actually offer in a (sexual) way....Maybe I think it's that we sometimes do not concentrate. Like seeing women as sex objects. When you look at the breasts and be like: oh my god, you know, that's how it is. And you look at them talking. They're wearing their skirts. You just look at them and say: okay how can you tap that? Be cool. Like the workshop on its own changed my way of viewing things and changed my way of thinking.

A common feature of masculinity across the globe is that men are socially conditioned to regard feminine bodies as objects of sexual pleasure, as is articulated eloquently in several earlier chapters in this book. A central feature of objectification is that women's bodies are separated from their personhood, that is, "women are treated as *bodies*—and in particular, as bodies that exist for the use and pleasure of others." (Fredrickson & Roberts, 1997: p. 175).[55] In the extract above, Aphiwe provides a glimpse of his gendered socialization, his way of viewing women as textured by his words, "When you look at the breasts": "And you look at them talking"; "They're wearing their skirts. You just look at them and say: okay how can you tap that?" However, in response to his witnessing of this woman's narrative of her violated and shamed body, Aphiwe, positions himself as moving through new ways of thinking about women. He uses the collective "we" to signify his call to all men to change. He powerfully resists the patriarchal male sexual drive discourse (see Hollway, 1998)[56] through his narrative of gaining a sense of who women are, a sense that women are human beings not merely sexual objects. This realization also prompts an entirely new way of *relating* to women, if tentatively—as Aphiwe begins to move *beyond* a self-serving transactional exchange relationship that is focused on what he can get from women or what they can give him, and instead begins to relate to women for *who they actually are* in their unique personhood, as fellow human beings with whom he can relate (perhaps for the first time) as ontological equals ("I started developing this sense of seeing women for who they are. Not what they can actually offer").

The words of Sylvia Tamale (2011)[57] provide a useful framing for the process above whereby the men's narrative disclosures about private and silenced aspects of their lives were prompted by a *collision* between their personal histories and the personal histories of others (represented through the quotes of text and the photographs). Tamale (2011: p. 5)[58] describes transformative learning as requiring us to:

> ...apply our intellect, *unlearn* deeply entrenched behaviour patterns and beliefs and *relearn* new ones. It requires us to acquire the vital skills to critically analyse internalised oppression and complicity with patriarchy and capitalism. It further requires us to step out of our familiar comfort zones and enter the world of discomfort and anxiety associated with change.[59]

At the same time, she says that such processes allow us to confront issues society has labelled taboo, to "unclothe" inhibitions and silences, to give all these things a voice. Ultimately, it is about realizing that sexuality and desire are not private issues, rather they are shaped by patriarchal power.

The narratives discussed here thus speak closely to the process of Tamale's transformative learning. They illuminate the enmeshment of the participants. Stories acted like a mirror reflecting onto others, pushing them into a kind of pedagogical movement. Witnessing others' narratives prompted the young men and women to engage in a more critical analysis of gender relations. When personal histories collide through intimate dialogue, deep moments of reflection occur that signify sites of pedagogy, learning through witnessing others' stories. In many cases this connection seemed to signify a point of "dislodgment" for the narrators in the sense that, at these moments, they began to interrogate the grip that patriarchal ideologies hold on their own lives and psyches. They took a reflective turn back on their own learnings about gender, and the corresponding impacts on their sense of self and identity. This is one of the most powerful aspects of the GERI process. It functions at multiple levels simultaneously, as each participant's story penetrates the heart of all the other listeners, each in a unique way. Thus, in a group of 21 participants, each person's story stimulates 20 different specific responses, each of which is a unique insight trajectory that creates its own learning, for the person, and within the collective psyche of the group. In the workshop as a whole, there are 21 x 20 = 420 of these psychic "tunnels" or pathways of learning, each of which penetrates the patriarchal wall of obscurity and overlay of cultural conditioning. As a result of all these insights and tunnels, the patriarchal edifice itself begins to collapse. It isn't real, and its shackles are made of clay, so they crumble.

Concluding Reflections and Future Potential

In their editorial for the Feminist Africa edition "Rethinking Universities," Mama & Barns (2007)[60] write that modern universities are "exhibitions" of a liberal kind of patriarchy, and they ask the important question: "If the universities remain unequal and difficult places for women, what kind of male and female citizens are they now turning out?" (p. 6). This question is still relevant now, over a decade and a half later. It is time that universities seriously took on the task of addressing gender violence. The South African Department of Higher Education and Training (DHET) has been developing a policy and strategic framework to address gender-based violence at universities. However, Treffry-Goatley and colleagues (2018)[61] rightly state that for such policies to succeed the underlying patriarchal rape culture needs to be disrupted, as it is these very patriarchal meanings that undermine the implementation of policies designed to protect students from sexual violence. Beyond policies, what is needed is practical ways of working towards transformation. The GERI work outlined here is a valuable step in the right direction.

This project fills a significant gap in research on the African continent—and globally—by working with men and women *together*, to capture the relational aspect of the currents of transformation. This research brings with it a richness to the blind spots identified through years of gender research—one of the important unanswered questions being, "what potentials are there for moving beyond theory and analysis, to actually *erode* patriarchal ideologies in practice?" The findings shed light not only on deeper issues surrounding the trauma of gender relations, but also on how participants may break through entrenched layers of *denial* about the pervasiveness of patriarchal trauma in everyday life. These dialogues facilitated an "opening up" through presence; a deepening as the participants "tapped" into their own truths and made visible the oppressive force and violence of patriarchy and the negative effects it has on their lives. These were moments where students became unstuck from hegemonic gender ideologies. The act of presenting their experiences to others in an open and honest way seemed to result in a different sort of engagement with their experiences, as if through this (re)-telling the participants were able to view their own memories with different eyes. Witnessing their own and their peers' painful gendered experiences in a compassionate, non-judgmental space allowed for shared afflictions, hitherto hidden, to be named and unmasked. The students "excavated" their experiences (to borrow Forter's term), peeling away various layers of socialization and silencing, and thereby began to free themselves—collectively and individually—from the lifelong shackles of patriarchal conditioning. Importantly, the act of resisting patriarchal discourse and carving new discourses is not a mere theoretical observation. Nicola Gavey (2019) reminds us that such constructions have very real material implications for shaping narrators' ongoing sense of themselves in the world.

Any analysis of "doing gender" is specific to the cultural and historical context within which gender dialogue takes place (Connell, 1987).[62] The findings of this study thus cannot be generalized to other contexts beyond this specific group of students at UFS. Nevertheless, the findings suggest that the GERI work with its strong gender-inclusive approach and ethos of respect for shared humanness carves open something crucial for our time. Pumla Gqola (2015)[63] and other scholars eloquently reiterate the risks of testing the waters and moving beyond boundaries patriarchy sets for us—shaming, dehumanization, aggressive violence at the hands of those who are rigidly stuck in the mindset of patriarchy. Such risks fade in significance when one is submerged in the context of the supportive GERI workshop spaces. However, the risks must always be acknowledged through mentorship and support provided to participants outside and beyond the workshop spaces.

Brodie (2020: p. 208)[64] reminds us that "understanding, undoing and repairing the fractures of our violent society is the work of generations." Patriarchal influences run deep. The process of disentangling from the shackles of patriarchal logic is complex and takes lifelong commitment, more than a series of workshops can offer. As researcher, I witnessed the challenges of this gender work, the "slipping back" into patriarchal ways of thinking when students went back out into the world unsure of how their knowledge would fare with others who had not taken part in the process. Such is the "strong pull" of patriarchal cultures.

The challenge for GERI, as well as other initiatives that aim to promote change, is to establish ongoing programs at universities, thus generating sustainable support and safe communities. These programs should be mandatory for students entering into the university environment. At the same time, such initiatives should be tailored to the voice and needs of students in particular contexts, opening space for the acknowledgment of the intersections of symbolic traumas linked to race, class, heterosexuality, and ability, to name a few. Finding ways of explicitly bringing race into the methodology would be promising for the South African context.

If applied widely on a long-term basis this work would equip young students to become change agents in the world—to model fair, compassionate leadership in their professional and personal environments. In essence this work has the potential to change realities and to promote a safer life for all genders. It is all about transforming the deeply embedded infrastructure of gender oppression. This work signifies a powerful move towards (re)discovering the humanness of gender work, in that it creates spaces whereby people can engage on levels beyond denial and face head on the realities of gender oppression—in all its forms and facets. The hope for true transformation lies in such processes that facilitate a breaking down of the *mindset* of patriarchy and a move towards the realization of our full, uninhibited shared humanity.

University students in GERI program at the University of the Free State; men honoring each woman individually in closing ceremony, Bloemfontein, South Africa, 2016.

GERI as a Catalyst for Social Change: Research at the University of the District of Columbia

Two peer-reviewed research articles published in 2024 document the academic research studies on GERI conducted by Dr. Konyka Dunson at the University of the District of Columbia in Washington, DC. Dunson posited that gender-based inequality is deeply rooted in social norms, and her study explored whether dialogue between women and men could potentially expose, challenge, and transform these norms, and thereby catalyze personal and social change. The research protocol entailed in-depth interviews with two women and two men from the United States, and a man and woman from South Africa, all of whom had participated in different GERI programs.

One of the key findings from this study relates to cross-gender *un*awareness:

> All participants noted they were profoundly unaware of what women and men experience differently from each other. ... The process surfaced an awareness that *while men and women exist in the same spaces and communities, their understanding of each other's experience is shallow.*[65]

This shallowness was mutually transformed:

> Participants were universally surprised by the experience of the other gender. [M]ale participants were surprised at how sexist social norms and behaviors impacted women. ... [W]omen were surprised by men's emotional experiences and realized that men's feelings had been largely stifled, not addressed, or voiced.[66] Significantly, *the women and men mirrored each other's responses.* ... [T]he men noted that they shared during [GERI] in ways they had not done before about the depth of their emotional, painful feelings and experiences. As men were surprised by women's experiences, including the impact of sexist harm, the women acknowledged they had rarely shared the depth of painful personal experiences with men or anyone. The [GERI] dialogue created a profound opening for *unburdening* [via] deep sharing in community with each other. ... Significantly, in the [GERI] process they bridged the gender gap, defined by this study as the *assumed* knowledge that covers and obscures what men and women *do not know or realize* about one another's lived experiences.[67]

The study developed a conceptual framework to assess how dialogue can generate social change: DABAS (Dialogue, Awareness, Belief, Action, Society). The essence of this framework is that transformative *dialogue* expands mutual *awareness*, which changes participants' *beliefs*, causing them to engage in new forms of *action* that ultimately transforms *society*. Key to the applicability of this social change model to GERI is that the impacts of the GERI work extended well beyond the program:

> In gender reconciliation, participants experienced an egalitarian experience, with no hierarchy, all voices and experiences, men and women having

equal standing. ... Gender reconciliation, steeped in loving compassion, left participants with a willingness to lead with openness and engage less in polarized gender stances. ... *[W]itnessing harmful gendered impacts through the experiences of others ... enables [participants] to create new experiences of gender equity together*, which is more effective in creating change than [merely] being informed about the problem. ... [B]oth men and women noted that witnessing the harm of gender bias changed their awareness and caused them to act differently beyond the dialogue process.[68]

As just one example of this process: listening to the women's stories, one of the men reflected on his past behavior toward women as a young man, which he said was primarily sexually motivated. While not physically forceful, his mindset at the time was "persuasive" and not respectful of the woman's personhood:

It was a competition for me. 'We're going to make love, and you're going to like it!' ...And the biggest thing for me when I got involved with GERI was the shame and guilt that came up in sharing and hearing the stories of women who had been impacted by predators. But then the healing came where these women were able to forgive me, even though they weren't the ones that I've had the sex with physically.[69]

His vulnerable honesty and owning his own culpability touched the women deeply, most of whom had never experienced such radical truth-telling from a man before. Several of the women felt moved to extend forgiveness to him.

Summarizing this study's main findings:

- Gender reconciliation [GERI] created a rare, transformative experience where women and men gained awareness of their unconscious gender assumptions and biases. ... Participants gained a heightened awareness and "critical consciousness of existing inequalities," essential to creating new pathways for social change. This prompted, amongst all participants, a lasting new stance toward openness and listening in conversations with family, colleagues, and community.[70]

- Gender reconciliation [GERI] left a lasting impact: the women and men forged a commitment to gender equity. ... The gender reconciliation process generated change within a small group of people, which the participants extended through their personal leadership and communication beyond the process. Therefore, the powerful impact of a small group of women and men in transformative dialogue must not be minimized.[71] Rather, dialogue is a significant, essential transformative factor, as a change in social norms happens interdependently (UNFPA[72]). [Hence, GERI] offers a strategy to disrupt harmful social norms.[73]

- The (GERI) gender reconciliation dialogue process is a proven catalyst for social change.[74] ... [A]s with the Truth and Reconciliation Commission, bearing witness to what socially transformative dialogue can accomplish plants massive seeds for social change. ... In gender reconciliation, [participants] can transform prevailing power dynamics into the power of the entire humanity together, dialoguing in a beloved community.[75]

PART V

Re-Writing the Gender Future of Humanity

"If we don't change the way we're going, we will end up where we're headed" (attributed to Lao Tzu). The gender future of humanity does not have to be a replication of the past—but it will be unless we proactively transform gender oppression.

The final Part V begins in Chapter 25 by presenting the GERI training program, which is creating a whole new generation of GERI leaders who are already taking this work forward in remarkable directions. These leaders will in turn train others as the work continues to evolve in new ways.

Gender oppression is a human invention, and it can only be transformed by human inter*vention. The concluding Chapter 26 outlines the major lessons from this 30-year initiative, and the auspicious vision and path forward to replce gender oppression with beloved community everywhere.*

CHAPTER 25

Training the Next Generation of Leaders

Training is everything. The peach was once a bitter almond.
—Mark Twain

Peoples' experiences related to gender and sexuality are uniquely sensitive, intimate, vulnerable, and potentially volatile. There is perhaps no arena of human life that has constellated more widespread and profound wounding, violation, and injustice. Yet, for this very reason, there is perhaps no other arena that offers such a profound opportunity and doorway into wholeness, healing, a restoration of the inner life, and a reconnection to the wonder, mystery, and magic of the world. In GERI work, we seek to tap into both of these dimensions—bringing forward our painful experiences of gender oppression and sexual violation into the open, grappling together with the devastating realities, and also opening ourselves into an alchemical process to transmute this disastrous legacy of oppression into profound new possibilities of beloved community. Needless to say, the process and facilitation must be held with a deep level of skill, care, and integrity, not to mention a high degree of psychological maturity and emotional integration on the part of each facilitator.

In the formative years of the GERI program, it quickly became clear that this methodology and process required its own unique professional training program for facilitators. We observed that even seasoned leaders from the women's or men's movements—often with years or decades of experience working deeply with the same gender—could suddenly struggle as facilitators when cross-gender dynamics and projections enter into the group dynamic. Furthermore, while the GERI processes both online and in-person have detailed structures and outlines, with carefully written instructions, this process is by no means a "canned" program. Facilitators of the GERI work cannot stand fully outside the process they invite participants into, but must learn to immerse themselves into the alchemy of the gender healing process, while also remaining centered and present as facilitators to the full group and their needs. Facilitators also need the sensitivity to closely track individual and group process and dynamics, as well as have the requisite knowledge and skill to read what is unfolding at visible and invisible levels in the group, and intervene and guide the group through uncharted waters.

Since 2001, GERI has convened 20 Professional Immersion & Facilitator Trainings, most lasting 12-15 months. Most of these were in-person trainings, conducted in North America, South Africa, India, and Kenya. Online forms of the professional training have been conducted in Latin America/Spain, and in South Africa/Kenya. Future facilitator trainings will continue in all these regions, plus Europe, Australia, and Korea.

Diane Haug is a longtime global leader of holotropic breathwork, and she co-taught with psychiatrist Stanislav Grof for nearly 30 years delivering professional trainings. She is also the co-founder of the Grof Legacy Project. In 2000, Will Keepin invited Diane to be the first female Trainer in the GERI Professional Training. Diane shares below some of her experiences with the GERI work over the decades.

It is difficult to believe that it has been 19 years since *Divine Duality: The Power of Reconciliation Between Women and Men* (2007) was first published. Given the critical need for collective healing and the profound and pioneering nature of the GERI work, the revision of this important book is timely and greatly anticipated.

Will Keepin and I first met as a result of a powerful three-year experiential training program with Stanislav Grof, M.D. and Christina Grof in the late 1980s. That training program, an alchemical process in its own right, sealed a friendship that now spans over 30 years. Both having roots in northern New Mexico, Will and I began collaborating on various workshops, retreats, and trainings by the late 1990s.

While the theme of gender reconciliation has not exclusively defined my professional life since that time, I am immensely grateful for the rich opportunity to have been included in the early years of the GERI work. It has been an incredible privilege to bring my background in transpersonal psychology and the modality of Grof holotropic breathwork into the context of such socially and culturally relevant training. And, as we discovered in our powerful collaborative retreat at the Esalen Institute in 2018, the theory and practice of Grof breathwork in the context of the courageous Gender Reconciliation process is a potent cauldron for personal and collective healing—for the participants and staff alike.

In my experience, the Gender Equity and Reconciliation work stands alone in terms of creating the strongest, safest, and most ethical container possible for radical truth-telling between people of all gender identities and expressions. It is an alchemical process that transforms darkness (e.g., our wounds, traumas, and "errors of omission") into light. Will, Cynthia, and their skillfully trained facilitators, fearlessly witness and hold a dynamic process that unfolds organically and often unpredictably. Their willingness to trust the intelligence of that process is astounding.

Also quite remarkable is the fact that GERI has continued to grow and to expand its work all over the globe even in the midst of a global pandemic. I attribute that expansion to the GERI leaders' clear intention and vision, heartfelt prayer, generosity of spirit, and tireless service. Clearly, the time has come for this giant leap forward on behalf of healing gender injustice.

The professional training is designed to holistically train and prepare facilitators for the unique challenges, intensity, and beauty of gender healing work. The training process itself dedicates much of the first third of the training process to experiential learning and personal immersion—including a special emphasis on spirituality and sexuality—where trainees dive deeply together into unpacking their own experiences related to gender and sexuality. This not only bonds the training group into a "transformative learning community," but gives trainees time and space to deepen their own personal gender healing, psychological and emotional integration, and spiritual practice. This experiential immersion into the GERI process lays the groundwork for the subsequent phases of the process where trainees gain hands-on facilitation experience with their peers, work together in role-plays, and hone their skills in responding to challenging and sometimes volatile gender situations, while also offering and receiving feedback with their peers and GERI Trainers.

Below, we share the reflections of one trainee on his journey into the GERI training, and the important personal learning, growth, healing, and transformation he experienced through the training process and community.

Like so many men, I had climbed the ladder of outward success but had reached a point, after 30 years, where I was in a mounting inner crisis. I remember standing on the observation deck of the Empire State Building, looking down at my tiny office window in a building nearby. I thought to myself: I've made it to the top, but I've had one failed marriage, I've been separated for a time in my current marriage, and I've had a heart attack that almost killed me. And I am only 53. I feel hollow inside, depressed, and lost. Who am I? Why am I here? Where am I going?

Where does a privileged, white, Western man go to be heard on a deeper level, to be able to say in a mixed group, "I'm wounded, too," without feeling judged?

That was in 2007, four months after my heart attack. When the economy crashed in 2008, I was left unemployed and sinking into an abyss, my own dark night of the soul. I eventually got back on my feet, and I started a men's circle in 2012 to find answers to the fundamental life questions I was still asking myself.

"Men nurturing men" is not a phrase often heard, but that is what we were about, and for our purposes, it was successful. Long-term relationships grew among us. We were going through the difficulties and joys of life together. We witnessed and held space for one another through such things as cancer, addiction, depression, the death of a child or a wife, financial struggles, and so on—all while trying to heal.

Over time, many of us realized that to continue our own healing and growth, we needed to find a forum where men and women could come together in a similar way and heal together. However, the dynamics would be much different, and none of us had the background or experience to facilitate such a circle.

Once again, I felt stuck. There did not seem to be a path forward. I wanted to be heard and to hear from others along the gender spectrum, but where could this 64-year-old former Marine officer and corporate executive go to heal the childhood trauma I never dared to share with another?

When Will Keepin and I first talked in 2018, it took only a few minutes to recognize that the GERI program was the answer I had been seeking. Within days of this meeting, I traveled to experience a weeklong module of the facilitator training.

Looking back on it, I cannot believe how unaware I was. Within the professional environment where I had spent my career, I was considered ahead of my time in servant leadership and organizational change, which included gender awareness and sensitivity. I quickly realized that the widely diverse international group of trainers and trainees in GERI exposed me to a whole other world I had been sheltered from.

But the environment was much like our men's circle, and my ego melted more and more throughout the week. The unconditional love of the others opened me to change on many levels.

When it came time for me to share my own deep woundedness, it was cathartic, but more importantly, what brought me to tears was what one woman shared privately afterward. She explained that my sharing was transformative for her. When I asked how, she replied that she had always looked at older white men with disdain, thinking that men had everything going for them and that they did nothing but walk on others, especially women, to get ahead. My sharing helped her realize that men are wounded too, and that they are looking for the same understanding and consideration that she was looking for herself.

I will never forget what took place later in that week. There is a point in the transformation from a caterpillar into a butterfly when the cocoon is filled with nothing but caterpillar goo. Then at some point, the imaginal cells begin doing their work, and a few days later the butterfly emerges in its glory.

In the experience of Grof® Breathwork, I entered into a state of metamorphosis to the point of melting into a fetal position of goo, flooded with every emotion imaginable, crying and shaking —but I felt incredibly safe.

The flood of emotion had become a gentle flow of peace, making its way into every cell in my body. When the session was complete, I crawled out from under the blankets and slowly stood up, and with the help of my sitter, I stepped outside. I stretched my arms high and wide, and I could feel the rays of the sun warming my wings. I had transformed.

There were many more healing moments that occurred, and when the week was over, I knew my trajectory in life had changed. I had touched into the deeper healing opportunity I had been searching for and discovered discovered how healing it was for others to witness my story as they held space for me.

I learned what both Cynthia and Will meant when they would say, "An alchemy occurs when women and men share their deep wounds in a safe and sacred space. It is an alchemy that can be felt which often goes beyond words." For this, I am forever grateful.

Providence has continued to speak into my life journey. Twelve years after standing on the observation deck of the Empire State Building, I was back in New York City. This time I was there to help facilitate the first GERI workshop in partnership with the United Nations Committee on Spirituality, Values, and Global Concerns.

The session was held downtown about three blocks from my old office. On the morning before flying home, I took the subway to Park Ave. and 32nd Street to see my old office building, and then I walked over and went back up to the observation deck on the Empire State Building. I looked down at my tiny office window about 80 floors below. This time, the words I spoke quietly to myself were different. "I know who I am. I know why I am here. I know where I am going."

Training for Individual and Group Safety

One of the foundational goals across the entire GERI program is to create group spaces, or "containers," with a high degree of personal, psychological, and spiritual safety—so that people feel safe enough to stretch themselves, become vulnerable, and delve into the challenging arenas of gender, sexuality, and spirituality. Without this, the GERI process cannot really take off and soar. This safety is essential in all GERI programs and trainings because we are deliberately going against long-standing cultural taboos of exploring issues of gender and sexuality in "mixed" groups with men and women together, or with people of diverse genders together.

To create this level of safety requires a high degree of mastery and experience among the facilitators and trainers, as well as multiple levels of support in the group that is structured in layers: GERI companions, GERI facilitator interns, GERI facilitators, and the GERI trainers themselves. In every GERI program it is important to always have at least two lead facilitators (or trainers) in the group, one man and one woman, who have years of experience in the work. There is also the GERI Mental Health Resource Team, comprised of seasoned, clinically-trained professionals who are available on call as needed, if challenges arise.

In this way we have found that it is possible to create containers of remarkable levels of safety, in which participants are able to bring forth their vulnerable truths, and delve deeply into the process, while feeling supported. The process is similar to an intimate spiritual group, which also requires a level of safety in order for people to truly go deeply inward. As we all know, that safety has sometimes been violated by the spiritual teacher(s) themselves, which is a profound betrayal of the entire process. And in the GERI work, that possibility also potentially exists, yet despite some significant challenges over the years, it has never happened, in part because we always have teams of multiple facilitators and trainers, who are mutually accountable to one another. There is never one single authority in a GERI program, but always a gender-balanced leadership team, and this creates a community of facilitators and trainers who are accountable to one another. This same structure of mutual accountability is replicated on every level from the GERI companions to the interns to the certified facilitators, up to the senior trainers. This structure has worked well over the years, and people deeply appreciate the high degree of bonding and mutual shared responsibility it engenders.

William Diplock of Brisbane, Australia is a senior GERI Trainer, and a seasoned counselor and member of the GERI Mental Health Resource Team. He reflects below on the GERI process and training, and how the GERI work dovetails with mental health praxis, enriching it with awareness of and sensitivities to unique gender dynamics in ways that support counseling practice:

I have been practicing mental health counseling and therapy for 30 years, and specifically relationship counseling for the past 15 years. My involvement in the GERI work has led me to consider various aspects of relationships in a newer and fresher way. The GERI process itself and the new awareness it has instilled in me about the power dynamics inherent in *all* relationships has gently and subtlety massaged the whole approach I take in my clinical work.

Being involved in the GERI workshops and professional training program exposes me, as a white, middle-class, educated male, to the distinct gendered experiences of women, of other men, and of people of diverse gender, race, and cultural identities. Opportunity is given to listen deeply from the heart and witness the stories and narratives of brave women and men who recognize, own, and take responsibility for their often very painful experiences in relationship to the other gender(s). This takes place in a very safe container that allows for this vulnerability to come forth, which in turn develops empathy and compassion in ways that one does not normally get in a formal, therapeutic, professional-training program for mental health workers. This is "bottom up" experiential learning for all involved.

Over the period of a three-day workshop, as a participant—and certainly as a professional who works in clinical settings—one simply cannot ignore that in some profound way, both women and men are either latently or blatantly damaged by a cultural system that creates violence in "one-up, one-down" relationships which do not work for either gender. On the surface it may appear this system is working for the person (usually the male) in the one-up position. However, given what is increasingly happening for men in this world—through higher suicide rates, addiction, the level of violence in men's relationships with women, and even worse in their relationships with other men—the cultural system is clearly not serving men well, internally or externally. When men are willing to get honest with themselves, they too know something is not working for them, even though they may not be clear in how to name it, let alone change it. I believe there is a part in the psyche of most men that knows their socialization and conditioning is not healthy for them.

Experiencing GERI workshops brings all these things home, in the tangible sharings that participants are willing to bring forward in this safe space. This changes people internally, and therefore these changes also come out in my practice as a counselor (mental health worker).

My continued experience of the GERI work has added dimensions to how I now listen in my therapeutic work.

I was a good listener before. However, now I am more attuned to listen for the way that gender plays out in intimate relationships. It's not that I was unfamiliar with power and control tactics in relationships—through training in Domestic Violence work, for example. But, the GERI work has assisted me to see the way the everyday person in relationship has been culturally formed to think, feel, and act in ways that create harm for intimacy, and love. Being now attuned to this through GERI work makes me more effective as a counselor, and mental health worker.

In the GERI work, I can take in the experience of the other very personally, because at a kind of corporate consciousness, or what Carl Jung might call an "oceanic consciousness," I can perceive that I too have perpetrated, or been complicit in the specific cruelty of this system. This probably happens more so when I hear women's experience; however, sometimes in the men's sharing I can feel such a deep sadness for what my gender (male) has perpetrated on men. I would initially feel a level of toxic shame about this. However, I have now come to experience what I call "healthy shame" without losing myself in it, nor going to a space of deep toxic shame, nor going to a grandiose place and thinking I am superior, but just coming into deeper compassion and empathic resonance with my fellow human beings.

There is no doubt that the GERI work has deepened my empathy and compassion for myself, and deepened my empathy and compassion for the other. This has been important as it has taught me clinically, when working with clients, that sometimes my interventions need to challenge injurious behavior related to gender conditioning. The essential nature of most people is usually well intentioned, and it is only perhaps a family of origin background, or a trauma background, that has led them to engage in harmful behavior. At the heart of who they are, they are good people, so in clinical work it means acknowledging this, while inviting and at times even challenging them, that their harmful behavior needs to stop; otherwise, it will continue to damage their relationships with their partner, their children, and other people.

For people to achieve real intimacy in relationships, the truth of the relational dynamics and imbalances must be clearly and courageously named—and heard—and both people must be led out of their limiting gender conditioning and into an authentic intimacy and equal relating. The GERI work offers a framework and method for this process, which has also supported me in my counseling and relationship counseling work.

Training Design

The full training experience is designed to be an engaging, intimate, and an inspired journey of individual and collective transformation and learning, covering a rich and diverse range of topics including:

- Spiritual basis and principles of GERI
- Building a beloved community of practice
- Gender and spirituality across the faith traditions

- Advanced and creative group facilitation skills
- Ethics for facilitators in gender healing work
- Silent meditation, prayer, breathing practices
- Inner and outer alchemy
- Creating safe (or safe enough) space and maintaining integrity
- One-on-one and group mentorship
- Working with emotions, trauma, and PTSD
- Gay, lesbian, bi-sexual, transgender and queer sensitivities
- Expanding gender landscapes, expressions, and fluidity
- Intimate communication skills and presence
- Sexuality (sacred and profane) and spirituality
- Conflict transformation and collective alchemy
- Holotropic breathwork experience (in-person)
- Tricky and volatile gender issues and pitfalls
- Transmuting shadow aspects and unawareness
- Ceremony and celebration skills in community
- Intersectionalities awareness and sensitivity (race, gender, etc.)

These different elements are woven throughout the training process as a whole to support trainee facilitators at each stage of the process. As the training progresses, trainees are invited more and more to step into the live practice of facilitation, facilitating their fellow trainees in the processes and activities the group had experienced together in previous parts of the training. From the ethical guidelines, to the silent witnessing, to the truth forum, and honoring ceremonies, trainees lead and participate in a full GERI workshop together. Trainees practice telling their stories, embodying gender balanced facilitation teams, and fully inviting each other into the depths of the process.

Each period of practice facilitation is followed by a detailed three-tiered process of review: self evaluation, feedback from peers, and feedback from trainers. Trainees learn to sensitively and skillfully give feedback to their co-facilitators, including at times compassionately naming and addressing imbalances and challenges within their own teams. All of this strengthens the mutual accountability among the trainees, and continues to bond and deepen the group into beloved community.

As the practice of facilitation continues, new and more challenging elements are introduced, including the facilitation of "curveballs" or simulated situations of individual or group crisis. Each of these curveball simulations are based on real challenges that have arisen during GERI workshops or courses over the years. Various individuals in the group are given certain roles to play during the facilitation, to simulate these crises, and the trainees must respond to and facilitate the unexpected emergence of conflicts, resistance, or of individuals needing extra support.

Facilitators are also given one-on-one mentorship during this period to support them in identifying and attending to any "growing edges," so they can continue to stretch and learn as facilitators.

This first phase of training consists of weekly online meetings over six-eight months (for online facilitators), or four six-day in-person modules over twelve months (for in-person facilitators). Those continuing after this initial phase move on to the practical field internship program. Here, trainees begin by serving as "GERI Companions" on workshops and courses, later moving into co-facilitation roles where they are paired with more experienced GERI facilitators and trainers. They continue their learning process in the field as they are increasingly given facilitation roles and continued mentorship from more senior facilitators.

This field internship and continued mentoring is rich in learning and growth opportunities for new facilitators, both as they continue in their personal work, and as they expand their capacity to hold and lead groups. As one intern facilitator reflects on her personal experience and growth over the years—from her first GERI workshop, to the training and into her field internship—she highlights the unique ways that the internship and collaboration with other facilitators, particularly other women, has supported her:

A lot has shifted for me since I first entered a GERI workshop, and later continued into the facilitator training. Since then, I have been fortunate enough to facilitate workshops with some seasoned and special beings. There are many reasons I continue. One is a bonus I never even knew I was missing out on. Because of the relationship with my mother and my own ongoing trauma, I missed out on the sublime experience of sisterhood, mentorship, and friendship from other women. I used to see women as threats, as creatures I didn't relate to. Now, not only are they invaluable parts of me, but they are also my support systems, my mirrors, my inspirations, teachers, and most enjoyably, my friends. What was lost in childhood has been gained through this experience. And though I often still feel the awkwardness of this new endeavor, my heart tells me this is the way, and that healing between women and women is real, and it is very real for me. I noted that while I kept referring to Cynthia as a mentor, she referred to me as a friend. In a way she brought me to her level, and by doing so, she empowered me to be the woman I wanted to be. I also had this experience when facilitating with Lucille Meyer, another GERI lead facilitator. I was in awe of her grace and felt privileged just to absorb her presence. Her comments and her personal communications with me were so nurturing and nutritious. Her actions and words cause me to feel worthy, capable, seen and, honestly, so honored to be a sister and collaborator. These types of women are the models I aspire to emulate. They have become my north star, my vision for what womanhood looks and feels like for me. Coming from the competitive world of Hollywood, these women offer me a way to the surface.

This training and internship process as a whole typically takes a minimum of two years from the beginning of the training to full certification as a GERI facilitator. As of this writing, GERI has graduated over 330 facilitators around the world, including cohorts of facilitators in many different regions—North America, Latin America, South Africa, Kenya, India, Australia, and South Korea—who are able to work together to locally implement GERI programs for their communities. The depth of shared learning and connection from these immersive training programs beautifully weaves and connects these facilitators from diverse cultures and contexts in a beloved community of their shared work towards transforming gender relations.

Our aspiration is that the learning and transformation from these training programs not only create skilled facilitators of the GERI work, but also individuals and communities able to transform gender relations in all that they do. As one GERI facilitator and trainer shares of her experience,

> I have grown in my skills as a facilitator by leaps and bounds. Not only in the GERI work but also in other areas of my life. I'm inviting more and instructing less. I listen deeply, and not to respond, just to listen. I have grown in my capacity to hear the painful stories of others compassionately and remain present and in heart connection with them. I have learned that I do not need to understand the language of someone sharing their stories, my heart recognizes their emotion, and I can empathize with them.
>
> I remember a particular experience when I was sitting on the floor with a group of young women in a workshop in Bangalore in India. A young woman sitting directly opposite me started sharing her gender story, and she kept looking straight at me. She would look away and then return her gaze to me. I made eye contact with her, and for the next few minutes, she poured her heart out in sharing her story in a language that I did not understand. When she came to the end of her sharing, she had tears in her eyes, and a gentle smile had formed on her face. My heart knew that she was saying thank you for seeing and hearing her. During a break, she came to sit next to me quietly, and we just sat and smiled at each other. No words were spoken; none were necessary.
>
> Being in the GERI work is not "hard" work; it is *heart* work, and I am deeply grateful for the gift of being part of the global community of facilitators, trainers, and spiritual seekers. I have learned the value of being held and supported by a sustained spiritual practice and how my most significant and best "doing" is leaning into the ever-present grace of the divine.

With all of our care and attention to safety and integrity, this is not to suggest that we never have difficulties. Challenges naturally arise from time to time, and there have been a few attempts to compromise the integrity of the training or GERI programs, which have not succeeded. On rare occasions, we have had to ask certain trainees or facilitators to leave the program, but this is not common because usually unsuitable candidates choose to leave themselves, long before we have to ask them, based on the challenging feedback they're receiving from their peers, or interactions with the rest of the team. In general, either they correct or adjust their challenging behaviors, or else they choose to leave of their own accord. In this way, the process itself tends to weed out those who are not appropriate for this work.

Moreover, the training proceeds in stages, and trainees at one stage are not invited to the next level unless they have demonstrated substantial capacity in the practical skills and integrity required for each stage. In this way, the trainees are constantly being vetted by their peers, and by the process itself. The senior trainers are people who have proven themselves over the years, and they form a leadership team that has developed complete confidence in one another, and together this leadership teams makes the decisions about when the individual trainees are ready to advance to the next training stage.

People sometimes ask why the GERI facilitator training "takes so long." The basic introductory four-module facilitation training takes a year, or six to eight months for online facilitation, at which point one becomes a Level 1 Facilitator. This is followed by a practical internship that takes typically one to two years to become a junior support facilitator, or Level 2 Facilitator. We advance people according to their skill and capacity, so some people can move through this process more quickly, and we don't hold anyone back who is ready to move to the next stage. It generally takes another year or more to move from Level 2 to a Lead Facilitator, which is Level 3. Then it's usually at least another year, and more commonly two or three years, to become a GERI Trainer, which is Level 4. We also have a few senior trainers (Level 5).

There are three primary reasons why the training takes time. First, trainees need to do their own personal work in relation to their own gender history and conditioning, and most people have significant personal work to do in this arena, even if they have done extensive psychological and therapeutic work in the past. The nature of the GERI work is to delve into arenas of gender conditioning that are often not explored, or are taken for granted in our civilization, or have not been actively processed in the way that GERI does. The second reason is because this particular form of group process work is unique, and it takes time for people to fully explore and adapt to it. In general, people in our training programs are not in a rush, and instead, they quite enjoy the training process, and engaging with the community. The third reason is that the trainers want to have sufficient time with the trainees, in order to witness how they actually function and perform in the field. So the trainers are also not in a rush. In this way, people are certified when the council of senior trainers decide they are ready, and thus far we have not had any major problems with certified facilitators breaking ethical or community agreements.

In all this, we maintain the *minimal* bureaucracy and institutional structure to support the integrity of the training, and the delivery of our programs. In generosity of spirit, if we could, we would prefer to offer the GERI program and all our methods and protocols as freeware on the Internet, and give it away for anyone to use. But we cannot do this, because the process and the tools are powerful, and they can create harm if not applied skillfully by seasoned people of demonstrated capacity and integrity. This is as true here as it is in many other forms of deep transformative and spiritual work.

Spiritual Practice Commitment for GERI Facilitators

There are certain obvious requirements for facilitators of GERI work, which include that they must be sincere in their aspiration and commitment to the mission of transforming gender injustice. They must bring a strong personal or professional background and commitment to the GERI process, be psychologically mature and grounded, and motivated beyond their own ego to act in service to the communities and groups they serve.

Beyond these key qualifications, GERI facilitators must also have a committed and disciplined spiritual or contemplative practice, in a spiritual tradition of their own choice. This goes above and beyond traditional group facilitator qualifications and is connected to the second principle of gender reconciliation, which affirms that the gender crisis is a collective spiritual crisis—for which psychological, social, and political reform are insufficient (although of course necessary).

There are several reasons for this requirement of a spiritual practice:

1. Facilitators of the GERI process, and especially the lead facilitators, need to be able to hold and contain the entirety of what is unfolding in the GERI process at all times—and to do so without losing their center, or collapsing into their own personal psychological issues or trauma history. This is absolutely crucial, and to do this well, the facilitators must not only remain grounded psychologically and clear mentally, they must also maintain a deep spiritual awareness and openness to "higher" wisdom and presence throughout the process.
2. Facilitators must maintain a commitment to doing their own inner personal work, which is necessary to stay inwardly clear and clean, free of distractions or personal psychological concerns. This enables them to remain open inwardly to identify and relate with something larger than themselves, and larger than the group, which holds the entire group in a profound spiritual embrace of healing and wholeness. The unity of the entire group must dwell in the heart of the facilitator as a conscious presence and prayerful intention.

3. A committed spiritual practice cultivates a capacity in the facilitator to serve as the *instrument* of a larger healing or spiritual power, which works *through* those who are suitably developed and aligned spiritually. This enables the facilitator to "drawn down" or "channel" a transcendent spiritual presence and power, which is the essence of the healing energy itself. This is a form of supra-conscious or higher transformative energy that is needed for, and guides, both inner and outer alchemical processes. This higher energy comes to the entire group, but it must be consciously engaged and recognized by the GERI facilitators; otherwise it may not find a suitable portal to enter and anchor fully in the group.
4. Spiritual practice cultivates presence, humility, deep inner listening to higher wisdom, and unconditional, universal love in the heart of the facilitator. These qualities enable the facilitator to hold sincerely the larger intention of the GERI work, and manifest the highest purpose and integrity of the work, and finally to serve as a kind of spiritual lightning rod across the various planes of higher spiritual awareness and consciousness, supporting their skillful manifestation and integration in service of the transformative work at hand in the GERI process. The facilitator can then be used as an instrument for these higher forces to do the necessary transformative work.

GERI Heart Circles: Expanded Post-Program Delivery, Ongoing Learning, and Community Training

Another form of "Community Training" we've implemented for those who want continued engagement, learning, and community practice is called "GERI Heart Circles." After attending the primary three-day GERI workshop or seven-session online course, participants are encouraged to join in-person and online follow-up "Heart Circle" groups. The in-person (off-line) follow-up groups meet monthly or bi-weekly, and over time often become effective communities of practice in which men and women and people of diverse genders working together often forge new modes of renewed gender relations.

Each Circle typically comprises 12–15 people who wish to continue their inner work and interpersonal engagement with others committed to transforming gender conditioning, and to deepen their bond within the GERI community. Facilitation is provided initially by GERI facilitators, and after a suitable training period (usually 12 sessions over 24 weeks), the groups continue as self-organizing and self-facilitating communities of practice. During these first 12 sessions, the group is supported by the certified GERI facilitators and led through an experiential process that also includes a curriculum of teaching elements, resources, frameworks, and practical skills that help to prepare the group to self-facilitate and continue on after the 12 sessions, should the group decide to do so.

These follow-up communities of practice have continued to meet for varying lengths of time after GERI programs, and a number of these groups have met regularly for several years or more after the three-day GERI program. Over the past 30 years, over 80 of these Heart Circle GERI groups have been convened (under various names). A number of groups have continued to meet for one to five years or more after the initial workshops, including in Cape Town, Bloemfontein, and Johannesburg, South Africa, Dallas, Texas, and St. Louis, Missouri. On-line groups enable GERI participants from across the nation and around the world to connect and engage in substantive conversation in relation to crucial gender issues and to build vibrant national and multi-cultural networks of people committed to reinventing gender relations together. Together, these small groups create new forms of friendship and integral relating across the genders, where people can honestly bring forward their everyday grappling with issues of gender and sexuality, fostering a "beloved community of the heart" as they practice the GERI principles in their lives.

The GERI Professional Training, the GERI programs, and the follow up Heart Circles are in a continual state of evolution, with refinements and innovations integrated over time as appropriate. The GERI leadership team and network of facilitators seek to maintain a spirit of perpetual learning and openness, as together we strive to implement our shared mission in the most effective way possible.

We conclude this chapter with an inspired yet realizable vision from Stuart Sovatsky for the future of human sexuality and relational intimacy. This vision is sourced in the Tantric tradition of India, yet it is broadly applicable to all of humanity.

A Profound New Pathway for Gender and Romantic-Erotic Love

Stuart Sovatsky, Ph.D.

In *The History of Sexuality*, social historian Michel Foucault identifies "two great procedures for producing the truth of sex": *ars erotica* and *scientia sexualis.* Ars erotica refers to the highly developed practices of "the erotic art" developed in numerous societies—China, Japan, India, Rome, and the Arabo-Moslem societies. Scientia sexualis refers to contemporary understandings of sexuality—both the Roman Catholic Church's moralistic, marriage-only, rhythm-method-only type of erotic "truths," as well as the "scientific truths" and psychoanalytic theory of the sex drive, the function of the orgasm, and so on, and the version of sexual liberation made possible by safe contraceptive/abortion technologies.

Shared-Gender Mystery

Today we urgently need a new fundamental ecology of gender and a romantic and erotic sense of this ecology in our relationships. For shared gender is not just a partnership, as proposed by Riane Eisler and others.[1] This cooperative metaphor has its place of course, but it misses the profundity of how deeply and indistinguishably the roots of gender entwine and tendril into the very ground of our existence. Partners who cooperate together, get paid equally, and worship goddesses as well as gods might never know in their bones how deeply *shared*, and *alchemically mutually empowering* human gender is, despite the intermingling closeness of sexual intercourse.

Give-and-take partnering belongs to the realm of economic and psychological exchange, and fails to access the more ontological-generative potencies from which gender manifests.

There is another kind of intimate knowing that provokes a spiritual response of each partner to the other: a temperament of devotion and reverence that trails into shy astonishment and ever-more-empowering displays of passion, with the entheogenic (ecstatic) response of allowing our lover to make us feel we are completely beside ourselves, witnessing god or goddess in human form, radiating all the charms of the universe before our very eyes, loving us with a love supreme, evoking play-of-the-gods' dances.

Instead of wonder and awe at the reality of shared gender, we usually seek literal answers to our questions about this Mystery. We believe knowledge comes from demystification, which, in the domains of eros, can be fatal. We do not relate to gender as Shared Mystery but as specific need-fulfilling commodities (we are to "meet needs"), explanatory resources, and vested-interest groups.

Contemporary gender problems—abuse, phobias, sexism—are supported by commodified, over-differentiating gender conceptualizations. Gender *as* gender-differences is persuasive but inadequate to describe the profound interactivities of gender. Western sexology has over-defined erotic meaning. The phenomenology of Mystery—"that which allures uncertainly, excitedly and suspensefully"—is the noumenal substrate of the erotic, rather than some clear-cut "drive" or "bio-instinct" (*a la* science), or "fallenness" (*a la* religion), or even "liberated" category-focused understandings of gender.

Gender is not to be defined by "differences" between people, nor by "attractions" between people, nor even by "my true identity." All such belongs to the scientific method of measuring and establishing a set truth or theory—striving for a "true gender" or a "true-explanation" that one gives oneself and others about "what gender I am/am not."

Instead, consider living from Gender as Shared Mystery: intimacy revealed, yet hidden, tangible yet ineffable, alluring by degrees, pointing to Great Powers of Cosmos. The opportunity is not merely to find or attain the "right" gender, among many; it is to sense the Generative Source of Gender Itself, and live in a kind of spontaneously interactive bliss, close to this Source where the Union is always alive and creating, singing with Wisdom.

Third gender, or fourth? How about infinite genders-fluctuating-always? When will we describe gender in the refined, accurate way that gender *is* and *lives* (like how quantum physics describes matter as vibrating possibilities)? Of course, this will transform Eros as well. Go deeper into Gender, and today's problems of eros evaporate into a Vibrant Mystery. While Yoga, Tantra, Buddhism, Sangoma and Christian-Judaic mysticism are understood as paths of "enlightened consciousness," all such paths could also be seen as paths of "Enlightened Gender Mystery"—the tracing to living as the Generative Source of All Genders, where all spiritual sentiments and physical hormones like testosterone, estrogen, etc. first emerge as Bliss and the Wisdom-Power [Siddhi] of Creation.

Gender Awe

The inequities between the genders, currently discussed as the history of patriarchal dominance and sexism, cannot be reversed merely through scholarly research or political initiatives. Spiritual problems require spiritual solutions. Sanctity can be neither proved nor legislated, and lies beyond politics altogether. Reverence is always an unrequested *response* to another who is perceived as being beyond all of our material concepts and estimations.

Reverence does not belong more to one gender than the other, for it is not the form or gender of the Deity that matters, but the depth of the reverence that devotees *bestow* upon It. We can recover the birthright or trust given us as gendered creatures only through the holy recognition of an utterly shared gender. Indeed, none of us would be here without the powers of Gender being shared (even if artificial methods were utilized). Typically, forgiveness, contrition, and reconciliation wash through worshippers in these moments as well, and relationships can become renewed and even stronger.

These feelings are not some kind of rare luxury that only a few select individuals deserve, nor are they reserved for special occasions. The situation is in fact the reverse: reverence is the only sentiment we do not earn. It is the universal response to the other as Mystery, just for being "the other," the starting point for ars erotica of mutually provocative wonders. This is the deepest erotic opportunity we provide each other: to be humbled and exalted reciprocally. Quietly watch the other's sleeping face for one minute. The mystery is not far away. This overlooked nearness is our tragedy.

Gender Worship

Worship is what even the immortals long to do; they long to worship the other, not themselves. Thus, the immortals become the other—that is, mortals—in order to carry out their sacred rites. They become us, we become them, over and over.

We also allow ourselves to be worshiped, not as a great person but as Mystery. Meditative worship is the opportunity for each of us to transcend our conditioned beliefs about each other for some moments, even amid the most trying times of a marriage or relationship, and to experience the Mystery that lives in spite of the dramas and crises. It is a return to the possible *as real*, and to the hidden *as a promise*.

Even the notion of one's "own" sexuality is a politicized derivation or appropriation of eros, through which one hopes to attain a sense of being an autonomous agent. We would like to own various powers, and popular psychology supports these aspirations, but the erotic powers of sexuality—love, attraction, arousal, fertility, families, and surrender—are entrusted to us, not "owned." Although the image of an owned sexuality can be a temporarily effective prosthetic tool, it should not be used in mapping the intimate contours of erotic space. We cannot pass through the eye of the needle of intimacy carrying our "own" sexuality with us, unless it is exalted by *both* partners and *shared creatively*. In this shared-sense, mutual empowerment can occur, even in times of self-exhilaration or of "setting boundaries."

When two give to one another, love becomes infinite. Respect for each other is most authentic when it is a secondary response to feeling the awe and vulnerability of the other or oneself. When charismatically energized, respect for one another gives back one hundredfold in mutual entheogenic rasa interactivities; we become god/goddess dancing endlessly with one another. Indeed, *Respect* accomplishes in a Heart-to-Heart way what the structurally-separative metaphor of "maintaining healthy boundaries" tries to aim for, but without emphasizing tonalities of a separative isolation.

Reclaiming Sacred Gender Worship and Erotic Love

Over the past 40 years of clinical and psychotherapeutic practice, I have seen a widespread need for more holistic approaches to human sexuality and intimate relationships. Indeed, a whole new psychology is needed that revives the heart and soul of romantic-erotic love itself. I found just such a psychology in the yogic, lifelong developmental path known as *urdhvaretas* ("deeply-rooted-to-full-blossoming-of-all-seed-potentials")—an ancient yogic tradition with abundant offerings that speak to many aspects of our modern distress, especially in the realms of our most important relationships.

Urdhvaretas is the living infinity of life's wild genetic diversity. It offers profound depths of meaning, feeling, and consciousness that encompass tumescences and orgasms unknown even to us sophisticated liberated moderns, and loves and marriages that easily last a lifetime, or many—the kind of relationships that support unbroken family lineages generation upon generation. With urdhvaretas, there is always another realm of seeds-within-seeds-within-seeds.

In the urdhvaretas developmental schema, the maturation of body-mind-heart-soul continues through a lifelong series of adult puberties. As with the teenage first puberty, each of these later puberties transforms one's identity, sense of life purpose, and erotic bodily capacities for lovemaking. These adult puberties are as yet unmapped in the West, with "kundalini awakening" just beginning to enter Western discourse. The maturations within this complete "up-blossoming and down-rooting" of the seed potentials include bodily secretions, tumescences, and modes of orgasm that are not only far beyond Freudian sex-liberation theories, but also largely unknown even within contemporary "neo-tantric sexuality." Looking at contemporary advertising, entertainment, and social media, it seems we moderns have based the entirety of human psychosexual maturation on the foundation of the puberty of the teenage years. The well-meaning Freudian-Reichian-Burning-Man overcorrections to the church's body-negating teachings are essential critiques, to free us from the negative impacts of both the moralistic strictures of Western religions and the limited "liberational" scientia sexualis. Yet beyond all this lies another, far more profound liberation.

The continuation of transformative puberties involves the entire cerebrospinal core and endocrine system, from perineum to pineal gland, which is capable of the "oceanic feelings" of love and oneness, which Freud criticized as mere womb-regressive delusions, whereas the ars eroticas regard them as the most matured enlightenment of embodied consciousness itself.

When the whole body is moved by these spinal awakenings—tumescences of the Great Mother Kundalini—we enter a whole new world. Nascent signs of these deeper potentials ripple throughout the esoteric and spiritual traditions of all times, worldwide. Of all traditions, Shiva-Shakti paths of urdhvaretas yoga from India have traced the unfoldment of charismatic (literally, "gifts from the divine") bodily and consciousness awakenings in exquisite detail, which can be summarized as four main types of physical-spiritual maturation:

- The first is effected by practices involving the perineum and spine, both kundalini awakening and the more controlled, upright-sitting, spinal-energy-flowing meditation, which is found in Buddhism and other contemplative paths.
- Second is the path of the heart, *grihastha*: lifelong, compassionate, devotional, unbreakable marital-romantic and whole-lineage familial love, wherein procreation uplifts each human pair to godlike awe of creating and caring for life itself.
- The third, *pariyanga*, is that of fully matured, "naturally entheogenic" and pineal-orgasmic, conjugal eroticism, most of which has not yet entered the popularized neo-tantra.
- The ultimate *divya sharira*, "divine, whole-body, inner marriage puberty" maturation arises from *nirbija samadhi*, also known as *nirvana*. In India the resulting supremely happy inner marriage (with or without a partner) has been the *sine qua non* criterion for fully matured enlightenment for at least five thousand years.

Within the ever-maturing capacities of urdhvaretas, lovemaking emerges from a "perineum to pineal" neuroendocrine maturity of natural entheogens—our own secretions at successive urdhvaretas puberties, which utterly transform both our physical and consciousness being. Where does this maturing and consciousness-expanding power come from that can transform our bodily "elixir chemistries" into inner "foods of the gods" (entheogens)? From untapped maturational potentials within the siddhi-seed-fertilities of life itself. Why untapped? Because moralistic religions failed to fully explore their own esoteric traditions, and contemporary scientia sexualis naively presents its truths as "final."

Identifying one's gender as "Source of Gender" is not yet easily possible—and yet how strange, because this "Gender" is the very foundation of all Yoga, Buddhism, Christ-himself, and the esoteric traditions. So it goes, when the famed gender specialists get entrapped by the science (scientia sexualis) and politics of the day. The well-meaning yet futile attempts to demystify eros and gender—whether by science, biology, religion, psychoanalysis, or politics—will one day thankfully cease. The ars eroticas of the world, of all ages, will once again reemerge, inspiring a wave of profound liberation and unity beyond the current gender and politico-erotic divides. You, dear reader, already hold the "key" to these profound mysteries right where Mother left it, at the base of your spine after She formed your body in utero. In fact, there are tiny charismatic keys moving within every cell of your body, quivering in hidden recesses, capable of entheogenizing consciousness—like a thousand-petaled lotus radiating ecstatic seed-keys everywhere!

Who was I, who you?
For those hours, it no longer
mattered who was who, loving
each other's hungers as
one's own.
I looked out my eyes and was you,
but you floating in us.
Happy feeling how beautiful you
are from the inside,
not the slightest worry of losing
my way back,
what difference would it really
make?
We would as well be each other as
ourselves,
so in love in awe of each other
were we.

Stuart Sovatsky, Ph.D., is a psychotherapist and advanced yogi and kirtan leader for 45 years, professor for 25 years, Director of the Kundalini Clinic (successor to Lee Sanella), and author of several books including, *Your Perfect Lips* and *Advanced Spiritual Intimacy*.

GERI Professional Training group in United States, 2019

Online GERI Professional Training group, 2021

GERI Professional Training group in Bangalore, India, 2024

GERI Professional Training group in Cape Town, South Africa, 2021

CHAPTER 26

The Future of Gender: Reconciliation, Reverence and Interbeing

The most vital issue of the age is whether the future progress of humanity is to be governed by the modern economic and materialistic mind of the West, or by a nobler pragmatism guided, uplifted, and enlightened by spiritual culture and knowledge . . .
—Sri Aurobindo, *The Life Divine*

Tension was visceral in the room as the Catholics huddled together on one side and the Protestants on the other. Stone faces and tight jaws around the room mirrored the deep impasse in this Northern Ireland community.

Activist Danaan Parry was facilitating a series of workshops to reconcile the bitter differences that were fueling open warfare in Northern Ireland during the early 1990s. Over the previous weeks, Parry had already facilitated several sessions with this group, during which grievances and accusations had been aired at length on both sides. "Today we're going to do something completely different!" Parry announced cheerfully, catching the group off guard. "For a good while now, we've been hearing the challenging issues on both sides of this conflict. But today we're not going to focus on all that," he continued forcefully. "What I want to know from you today is this: What is it like to be a woman in Northern Ireland?" Parry paused, then continued with a slight twinkle in his eye, "What is it like to be a man in Northern Ireland?"

The people glanced at each other with quizzical expressions, wondering what this could possibly have to do with their troubles, which were all about religion, the war, and the pain of lost family members. But Parry persisted, "I really want to know, what exactly is it like to be a woman in Northern Ireland? And what's it like to be a man in Northern Ireland?" Walking around the room, Parry began to motion with his arms. "Let's have all the women move over to this side of the room," he instructed, pointing with one hand, "and all the men on the other side."

When the group was reconfigured, Parry asked the people in both groups to take turns telling their individual stories about their lives in Northern Ireland. The women began telling their stories, bringing forward wrenching tales of husbands and sons killed in the violence, fears for the safety of their children, the constant threat of new violence breaking out. As the Catholic and Protestant women looked at one another and listened to each other's stories, they soon discovered that they were all living through the exact same nightmare. A natural empathy emerged as they identified with one another's sorrows, horror stories, and fears—and before long they were in tears, holding each other, commiserating in mutual grief and compassion. The men had a parallel heart opening and healing experience as they listened to one another and discovered their shared pain across the religious divide, as men living in a war-torn society.

By the end of the afternoon, there were many long, healing hugs within the women's and men's groups. Through the doorway of gender, a profound healing bridge had been created across the devastating religious chasm in this community. Both sides came to realize that they had thereby taken their first major step toward mutual healing, understanding, and peace.

Gender and Interbeing

The heart of gender equity *is* reconciliation, and the process of reconciliation takes place *inside* the heart. The anecdote just recounted from Northern Ireland provides a clear example, illustrating one of the most fundamental principles of gender reconciliation work:

> **A key turning point occurs when individuals perceive the pain and truth of the "other" as their own experience.** Through this doorway of empathic identification, a deeper underlying unity is discovered; a bridge of hearts is created across difference, and people discover that ultimately, *there is no "other."*
>
> Gender equity and reconciliation provides a practical doorway for awakening to the oneness of humanity. Oneness does not mean identity, but rather what Thich Nhat Hanh calls "interbeing." Each human being is intrinsically intertwined with the being of others. This is closely related to the principle of *ubuntu*: I am because you are. All beings are inextricably linked. Because of this, when the heart melts in empathic resonance, an inner doorway opens, and people are awakened to a profound underlying unity. Gender reconciliation can facilitate this awakening, regardless of participants' religious faith, cultural background, gender identity, philosophical belief, or spiritual orientation.
>
> The human heart is universal, and when it opens, union happens. When the clouds clear, the sun cannot help but shine, and it becomes self-evident that the source of light is one, was there all along, and illuminates everything equally. An analogous realization takes place for human beings when the shared heart opens in community: the essential oneness of humanity becomes self-evident; it was there all along, and unites all hearts equally. In these moments, it doesn't

make any difference what religion or beliefs people hold, what their gender identities are, or what their professions are. None of that matters when the oneness of humanity is revealed.

The foregoing anecdote also illustrates how gender reconciliation can be applied in arenas of human conflict quite beyond gender injustice. Northern Ireland was embroiled in an ethno-nationalist war that had already claimed the lives of thousands, and the conflict was constellated along religious sectarian lines. Parry ingeniously bisected the group according to gender, which was effectively "orthogonal" to the religious division, and in half a day, the result was a powerful healing bridge in this deeply divided community. Clearly, this same process has wide potential application in other war-torn regions of the world.

What Have We Learned in 30 Years of Gender Equity and Reconciliation?

The short answer to this question is simple: There is a brilliant light shining at the end of the long tunnel of gender oppression. Here are some of its rays of hope:

- ***Gender oppression is thousands of years old, but only a few days deep.*** Men cannot hear the deep truth of women's pain and remain the same men. Women cannot hear the deep truth of men's pain and remain the same women. People cannot hear the deep truth of LGBTQ+ persons' pain, and remain the same people. Through skillful facilitation and structured support, groups of sincere individuals can face challenging gender issues together that are ordinarily taboo, go through a remarkable depth of transformation and reconciliation, and begin to transform the insidious wounds of pervasive gender injustice that are still widely regarded as intractable. A new relational dynamic emerges of empathic resonance, deep compassion, mutual respect, and even *mutual reverence.*

  As people of all sexes and genders directly comprehend their respective betrayal from millennia of gender injustice, the longstanding structures of gender oppression literally begin to disintegrate. An altogether new kind of intimacy, integrity, and newfound covenant of trust and oneness between women and men—and across the gender spectrum and all sexual orientations—is born. A new vision dawns, and participants glimpse a post-patriarchal, gender-healed world. All this can take place within a few days, and is greatly reinforced and fully integrated by skillful follow-up afterwards.
- ***Ordinary women and men, and people of all genders, have a profound capacity to transform "patriarchy"***—given the appropriate conditions. Safe forums for women and men to jointly confront gender injustice are urgently

needed everywhere, yet exist almost nowhere today. Why? Because untold stories keep oppression invisible, and intact. This is the core strategy of the patriarchal system for eons: keep the dark truths of gender and sexual injustice buried—*forever.* Hence, deep truth-telling between women and men, and people of all genders, has long been taboo in every major institution of society. Until *now.*

Social and cultural conditions are finally shifting, and long-standing patterns of keeping systemic gender oppression hidden are crumbling. Meanwhile GERI and similar programs have been quietly developing practical alternatives. So, just as our culture is finally beginning to confront its appalling scourge of gender injustice and oppression, GERI programs are rapidly emerging and expanding as a skillful new beginning on an unprecedented scale.

- ***Pain is the alchemical medicine for the pain.*** If we avoid our individual and collective gender pain, we merely prolong it, and it never goes away. The needed alchemical transformation cannot take place without facing and embracing the dark and difficult truths. In GERI programs, men and women and people of all genders enter skillfully and sensitively into the pain—together—and discover that "our pain is the medicine by which the inner physician heals us" (paraphrasing Kahlil Gibran). It is a temporary pain, compared to the permanent, debilitating pain of *not* doing this work, which is the sad, frozen, and depressing condition of most human societies today in relation to gender and sexuality. By embracing and moving *through* the pain—neither minimizing it, nor wallowing in it—its crippling effects are slowly but surely transmuted. In its place comes a whole new spirit, fresh healing, nurturing energy, and new life. Indeed, if "God enters through a wound," then God enters more deeply through a deep wound.
- ***Gender equity and reconciliation work has a longstanding impact.*** People often report to us, sometimes years afterward, the profound impact of GERI programs in their lives. We received an email recently—out of the blue—from a woman who had attended one of our very first workshops thirty years ago. She writes: "I have been forever grateful for that experience as it taught me, profoundly, how to transform rage into compassion.... This understanding has been a factor in various choices I've made along the path. ... The compassion I got from this understanding is immeasurable, and one of my best gurus."
- ***Gender oppression cannot withstand the twin powers of truth and love.*** The human heart and spirit are more powerful than the tyranny of gender oppression, by which we've all been conditioned. Convene the proper forum, invite the deep truths forward

with skillful facilitation, confront them with courage without fleeing from the pain or denying the unmitigated disaster of gender oppression—and the chains that bind us all begin to collapse. We've witnessed this time and time again, as documented throughout this book. We've often seen the boundaries and veils between men and women fall away, as together they behold the transcendent radiance of soul-to-soul communion. This unitive experience flows naturally when women and men each discover the magnitude of suffering and betrayal that the other has endured. Women discover that men are *not* the enemy, and many sincerely yearn to co-create gender harmony. Men discover that the greatest male privilege is not any of the social advantages afforded to them. Rather, the greatest male privilege is to actively participate in deconstructing the unjust system of gender oppression itself.

- ***The GERI model of gender reconciliation has proven highly effective in widely diverse contexts and cultural settings.*** Taken together, the data and stories presented in this book, and their broad consistency over 30 years in all the cultures and sectors in which we have worked, demonstrate that the truth telling and community transformation that takes place in GERI programs has a vast contribution to make toward transforming systemic gender dysfunction in most if not all human societies around the world. This work is evidently needed *everywhere*, yet today still exists almost *nowhere*. The time has come to implement the GERI methodology (and related transformational approaches) far and wide.
- ***It takes a global village to heal a global crisis.*** Remarkable groups of people on six continents are working collaboratively in GERI to transform gender relations within their respective societies. To our knowledge, this global network of emergent GERI circles—comprised of women, men, and people of all genders, focused specifically on transforming gender injustice—is something new and unprecedented. These circles are actively seeding fertile ground to foster a new culture of integrity, love, and mutual respect across the gender divisions of society. The inspiration guiding them is not wishful thinking, but skillful means and practical connection in small groups of committed people that constitute living examples of beloved community—interlinked around the world. A new humanity is in the process of being born.

Let us be careful not to overstate the case. Transforming gender oppression is a massive undertaking that entails unprecedented healing and major institutional and cultural restructuring at all levels of society. GERI's programs are but one healing modality in an enormous ocean of vast need.

Nevertheless, GERI programs serve as alchemical crucibles in which the ubiquitous "gender apartheid" that so deeply divides the human family can finally be transmuted, one group at a time, into living incubators of Beloved Community. These groups are planting seeds of a new civilization of love and unity in the human family.

A few more general observations are important to outline:

- Gender injustice and intergenerational trauma are universal; the basic dynamics are largely the same across different cultures, although the specific manifestations differ in form and intensity.
- Effective gender healing and reconciliation requires methods and facilitation skills that go well beyond mere dialogical and psychological approaches, to tap the deeper wellsprings of the human spirit. "Talking through the issues" is not enough; effective modalities for trauma healing and experiential reconciliation are necessary, coupled with sustained, skillful follow-up in community.
- The key to successful gender healing and reconciliation is not dependent on how well versed the participants are in current gender politics and trends, but rather on their sincerity of intention and willingness to engage in the process, allowing it to unfold in its own integrity.
- By addressing challenging gender issues in a group or community a "collective alchemy" occurs that greatly enhances the transformative power of the work. This remarkable synergy goes well beyond what can happen in a one-on-one interpersonal context, be it between intimate partners or spouses, client and therapist, parishioner and priest, or student and teacher. The synergy of community greatly amplifies the potential for healing, which is indispensable for healing collective gender trauma. Cultural gender oppression and dysfunction can only be fully healed and transformed in groups or community settings.

Gender Reconciliation, Integrative Medicine, and Trauma Healing

The growing field of integrative medicine strives to synthesize Western modalities with Eastern approaches and traditional indigenous systems of healing. We have presented on our GERI work at the World Congress of Integrative Medicine multiple times, and the resonance with certain emerging advances in integrative medicine is clear.

A prominent model of integrative medicine was developed by Dietrich Klinghardt, M.D., who posits five fundamental levels of healing based on Patanjali's yoga sutras. These are: the physical body, energy body, mental body, intuitive body, and the soul level. These levels are hierarchically organized, meaning that healing at any particular level has beneficial healing effects on all the levels below it, but *not* on levels above it. Healing on the physical level—which is the primary focus of Western medicine—affects only the physical body. However, healing on the soul level has cascading healing effects on each of the lower levels (physical, energy, mental, and intuitive bodies).

Gender healing and reconciliation could be viewed as operating largely on the soul and intuitive levels, with beneficial effects on the three lower levels. Many of the healing experiences reported in earlier chapters of this book seem to support this interpretation, and Klinghardt's work provides a kind of independent clinical validation of the crucial importance of healing at the soul and spiritual levels, without which a true and complete healing of the individual and the human community is not possible.

Another key innovation in integrative medicine is an effective new form of psychotherapy that has emerged known as "family constellations," developed by the German psychotherapist and former priest, Bert Hellinger. The basic premise is that when a particular family member is violated or marginalized in a significant way, the entire family system is afflicted, often for several generations afterward. The resulting family system remains "constellated" in a particular way that often produces various psychological challenges and symptoms for later family generations that cannot be healed or transformed, until the violated person or experience is somehow recognized and reintegrated back into the conscious awareness of the family system.

Although Hellinger's work is primarily focused on family systems (and to a lesser extent on organizational systems called "systemic constellations"), it seems that Hellinger's basic framework can be profitably expanded to encompass entire human cultures and civilizations. For example, the denial and exclusion of sacred aspects of gender and sexuality in Western society could be seen as having created a "cultural constellation" of gender injustice and dysfunction—one that cannot be healed or transformed until the sacred aspect of gender is reintegrated back into the society. Whether or not such a generalization of Hellinger's ideas is legitimate, the basic principle here is sound: when something essential is denied, the result is a dysfunctional system that cannot recover until that essential element is reclaimed or restored. This is basically what has happened in virtually every human society in relation to gender.

Another important recent development is the Collective Trauma Integration Process (CTIP) for healing intergenerational trauma developed by Thomas Hübl and various colleagues.[1] Hübl's work bears a significant similarity to our gender reconciliation process, particularly in his recognition of the crucial importance of the spiritual and mystical dimensions of healing. The stages of his CTIP model—characterized as cohering the group, inducing the collective wave with its substages, discerning the collective voice and group clearing and integration, and meta-reflection—are all broadly aligned with the stages of the GERI model. Several of the contemplative and meditative practices and group-process exercises are closely aligned with methodologies we have applied, with a few exceptions (breathwork, ceremonial rituals). The overall flow of the group transformative process that unfolds, and its spiritual and healing currents, are quite similar to what takes place in the GERI process, which is not surprising given that both models are working intensively with the dynamics of collective healing of intergenerational trauma, and both models draw explicitly on the community dimensions of transformation ("we space"), and the spiritual and mystical dimensions of healing and transformation. Given these close parallels, there is a potential for collaboration between these two models in the future.

Gender Oppression and Warfare

If humanity is ever to achieve lasting peace and evolve beyond warfare, it is essential that we also evolve beyond gender oppression. War and gender injustice seem to be tightly correlated since antiquity.

According to historian Gerda Lerner, the systemic oppression of women was established gradually over 2,500 years from about 3,100 to 600 BCE. Lerner's historical analysis takes account of many complex social and cultural factors, and a few fundamental patterns emerged clearly from her research. In ancient warring societies, whenever one tribe was victorious, the men of the conquered tribe were killed, and the surviving women and children were captured and enslaved. This was a major cause for the division of all women into "respectable" and "non-respectable" categories, as the captured women were brutally subjugated and freely exploited sexually and economically by the victors. Over time, women's sexuality and reproductive capacity became commodities, and male-dominated family structures were established with full legal and state sanction. Another pivotal pattern emerged during the second millennium BCE, when "the dethroning of the powerful Goddesses and their replacement by a dominant male god occurred in most Near Eastern societies." These currents of structural gender imbalance strongly influenced the early Biblical scriptures written during the first millennium BCE. "This symbolic devaluing of women in relation to the divine became one of the founding metaphors of Western civilization."[2] A second founding metaphor, upheld by Plato and Aristotle, was that females were regarded as inherently inferior human beings. According to Lerner, these two metaphorical constructs came to be seen as "natural," hence invisible, which finally established the subjugation of women firmly as an actuality and as an ideology.[3] Other scholars have given broadly similar accounts, including Anne Baring and

Jules Cashford, Marija Gimbutas, Riane Eisler, and Merlin Stone.

Lesbian and gay sexuality, and the presence of "third gender" people, are also clearly documented within nearly all ancient civilizations.[4, 5] Oppression of LGBTQ+ people also goes way back; for example, the earliest known law condemning male-to-male intercourse in the military was in Assyria in 1075 BCE.[6]

Following these trends down through the ages, many of the early civilizations that survived and expanded over time tended to be both militaristic and gender-oppressive. As Lerner concludes:

> The system of patriarchy is an historic construct; it had a beginning; it will have an end. Its time seems to have nearly run its course ... and in its inextricable linkage to militarism, hierarchy, and racism it threatens the very existence of life on earth.[7]

Gender Inequality and Militarism

Although Lerner's research focuses on ancient civilizations, the correlation between gender injustice and militarism seems to hold true still today. Extensive statistical research conducted by Valerie Hudson and her colleagues has demonstrated the following correlations for contemporary nation states:

- Nations with greater gender inequality are more likely to engage in warfare, more likely to be the aggressor, and more likely to resort to higher levels of violence in conflict.
- Nations with higher rates of domestic violence are more likely to resort to war.
- The best predictor of a nation's peacefulness is *not*: its level of wealth, its degree of democracy, or whether it is rooted in any particular religion. *The best predictor of a nation's peacefulness is its level of violence against women.*[8]

As a case in point, at the time of this writing (March 2022) Russia just invaded Ukraine in a major unprovoked attack. Whatever the eventual outcome of this dangerous war will be, it is striking to note that Russia strongly fulfills the three criteria above, with one of the highest murder rates for women. In a 2019 study of the most dangerous countries in the world for women, Russia came out *third* in a list of 50 nations that have the greatest number of international tourists. Journalists Asher and Lyric Fergusson ranked the 50 countries based on detailed statistics compiled for the following eight factors: street safety for women, intentional homicide of women, non-partner sexual violence, intimate partner violence, legal discrimination, global gender gap, gender inequality index, and violence against women attitudes. In 2017, Russian President Vladimir Putin signed into law a bill that *de*-criminalized many forms of domestic violence. This means that beatings that leave bruises, scratches, or bleeding, but that do not cause broken bones or a concussion, are *no longer* a criminal offense. As Russian researcher Yulia Gorbunova of Human Rights Watch lamented, this is "a huge step backwards for Russia, where victims of domestic violence already face enormous obstacles to getting help or justice."[9]

Of course, correlation does not imply causation, and Russia is but one example. For perspective, it is also important to note that the United States came out number 19 on the above list, and was the only Western country in the top-20 most-dangerous countries for women (due largely to high U.S. rates of intimate partner violence, and non-partner violence against women).

Finally, on a hopeful note, Hudson's research showed that: Nations that have improved the status of women are as a rule healthier, wealthier, less corrupt, more democratic, and more powerful on the world stage.

As Valerie Hudson concludes in her *Foreign Policy* article,

> The evidence is clear: The best predictor of a nation's stability is how its women are treated. … The primary challenge facing the 21st century is to eliminate violence against women and remove barriers to developing their strength, creativity, and voices. A bird with one broken wing, or a species with one wounded sex, will never soar.[10]

We must add to Hudson's agenda the elimination of discrimination and violence against LGBTQ+ people and BIPOC peoples—and the active cultivation of their strength, creativity, and voices. The species of humanity can only truly soar if the entire human family takes flight *together*. May it be so.

Spiritual Wisdom: Unity Beyond Diversity

The gender crisis is ultimately a collective spiritual crisis. As Martin Luther King, Jr., emphasized in regard to racial inequity, the issue was never Blacks *versus* Whites, but rather justice versus injustice. So too in the case of gender inequality, the issue is *not* men versus women, nor hetero versus LGBTQ+, nor transgender versus feminist—but justice versus injustice. Yet gender activist movements have sometimes tended to frame issues in polarized terms, and confine their analyses to conventional psychological, sociological, ideological, or political paradigms. The larger spiritual dimension has often been ignored or minimized. For example, contemplative monk and author Bede Griffiths observed that much of the men's movement has been "all on the psychological dimension—there is nothing beyond the psyche. That is where most Western people stand today—imprisoned in the psyche. We have lost the awareness of the spirit." Spiritual feminist Carol Lee Flinders made a similar observation about the women's movement: "Feminism catches fire when it draws upon its inherent spirituality—when it does not, it is just one more form of politics, and politics has never fed our deepest hungers."

The prevailing view of the "gender wars"—as various conflicts among diverse gender subgroups, whether segregated by sex or by gender identity—is misplaced. Gender disharmony is, at root, a collective spiritual crisis: a war waged by humankind against itself. It is manifest at every level of society, from the individual human psyche, to the family, to community, nation, and finally to the entire human family, and our relationship to our planetary home.

We are divided, and therefore "conquered," as it were. We must reunite as one, and thereby overcome these false gender divisions, rather than allow them to keep us "divided and conquered." This is not to deny the legitimacy of the pain and injustice that has been perpetrated along the fault lines of gender. It is rather to affirm that the human heart has the capacity to transcend and heal these rifts.

By invoking a "higher" or "spiritual" dimension of consciousness, the gender crisis can eventually be resolved—or, rather, *dis*solved. Only on this level can the duality of opposites, and the multiplicity of genders, be transcended in a higher unity. Without this possibility of transcendence, the debates and struggles across gender divisions will be endless, and hopes for a genuine resolution are futile. Einstein's oft-quoted observation is applicable here: a problem can never be solved on the level of consciousness that created it. So too, the "battle of the sexes," and the conflicts among gender divisions, will never be "won" by any particular "side"; another level of consciousness must be brought in that is well beyond that which gave rise to the conflicts in the first place. Such consciousness is cultivated in the wisdom traditions of all human societies. Yet, this unitive dimension of human consciousness has been denied or largely deemphasized in Western civilization for at least several hundred years. This is why the Indian sage Sri Aurobindo has observed that the key question of our time is whether humanity will continue down the materialistic path mapped out by the West, or follow a nobler paradigm that invokes the spiritual wisdom of humanity, uplifting and reuniting the human family.

Because the rise of gender oppression was closely correlated with the suppression of the Goddess traditions, a crucial aspect of ending gender oppression is to fully reclaim the feminine aspect of the Divine. New insights about the universal Divine Feminine are emerging across the major world religions and spiritual traditions, with profound implications. While this is clearly important for women, it also applies more broadly. As men reconnect more deeply to their own divine nature, they tend to become more loving, more committed to serving others, and more prepared to take responsibility for their key role in healing and transforming gender oppression. This also implies a fundamental link between "feminism" and spirituality, and more broadly between gender and spirituality, which has long been known in the esoteric spiritual traditions and is slowly being reawakened today.[11] As one example, the "greatest master" of Sufism, Ibn Arabi, articulated profound teachings about the deep inter-connection between the union of masculine and feminine, and the union of soul with the Divine; and he affirmed that sexuality can serve as an aid rather than a hindrance to spiritual development.[12]

Denial of Divinity

To deny the sacred has long been the signature strategy of the "patriarchy," and it has been devastatingly effective over many centuries. Through systematic denial of the divine or sacred dimension of life, the direct connection to the divine Source—innate in every human being—is blocked or thwarted, and the forces of temporal power and material "worldly" influence can then take over all aspects of human society. With the divine thus usurped, human society is beholden to, and easily manipulated by, the major institutions of social and cultural power: politics, religion, corporations, government, military, education, economics, the media.

Denial of divinity is essentially what Gerda Lerner was surprised to discover in her cross-cultural research on the origins of women's oppression. Yet this strategy was applied not only to women, it is one of the oldest tricks in the book of systemic oppression: deny the sacred and take control. This fundamental strategy has been applied, in one form or another, to every dimension of human society. It was used by religious institutions to ruthlessly eradicate mystical wisdom and the feminine mysteries, replacing them with the ecclesiastical authority of priests and clergy. It was adopted in market economics to reduce the Earth to a mere physical object, thereby enabling relentless exploitation of natural resources and unbridled pollution of the natural environment, to fuel an insatiable appetite for material wealth. It is consistently applied by governments, corporations, the military, and other social institutions to render strong and sound human beings into unthinking, compliant pawns—mere cogs in a soulless machine. It is used to control sexuality—desacralizing the inherent divinity of *eros*—by rendering it immoral in the case of religion, or reducing it to lustful indulgence in the case of secular institutions such as the military or the corporate media. This collective forgetting of our sacred origins and the divine essence of humanity has become so deep and all-embracing, especially in the West, that we have forgotten that we have forgotten.

Throughout the past few thousand years, systematic denial of divinity has served to trick and delude otherwise ethical, upstanding citizens into betraying their own souls and condoning unspeakable evils at times. Entire societies or nations have sometimes been swept up in the grip of a collective delusion or demonic trance, unleashing tremendous forces of destruction. The Nazis are a prime example, which transformed Germany from one of the most advanced to one the most depraved nations in the world in less than a decade. The power of these systematic manipulations and dark forces in human society must never be underestimated, and they have been the lament of many prominent social analysts and scholars, such as Reinhold Niebuhr in his potent book *Moral Man, Immoral Society*.

Cure of Grace

Yet this bleak, disturbing picture is *not* the whole story! Nor is it the most important or the deepest truth of human existence—far from it. For as Martin Luther King, Mahatma Gandhi, Desmond Tutu and many other voices have contended emphatically, pessimists like Niebuhr and others, however brilliant, have missed one absolutely fundamental factor: the power of love and its immense capacity for transformation in society. In King's words, if "pessimism concerning human nature is not balanced by an optimism concerning divine nature," then we "overlook the cure of grace."[13]

Indeed, love is the greatest power in the universe. Love can transform every darkness and bring in a profound grace that reawakens the magic and sacred in life. And for this, it is *not* necessary that the masses of humanity all suddenly awaken to love. All that is required is for a critical mass to awaken to love, and this relative minority of people will, over time, expand and effect a transformation that can eventually touch the hearts of billions.

"The mystic is the pupil in the eye of humanity," as Sufi mystic Ibn Arabi observed, and just as physical light enters the body through the tiny pupil of the eye, divine light enters humanity through its relatively small (but growing!) number of sages, mystics, and sincere devotees of divine love in every tradition across the globe. Working through individuals of pure heart in every land, a web of light and love is being woven all across the planet that will become the foundation for a new civilization of love. This "inner net of the heart" is laying the invisible groundwork for a major transformation of consciousness—through a subtle "inner net" of light and love that vibrates at a higher frequency than collective darkness. Love functions at higher orders and more refined levels of energy that quietly undermine and dissolve the lower orders of energy that comprise darkness.

Gender and Spiritual Identity

Gender equity and reconciliation naturally and inevitably leads to fundamental questions about who we are as human beings, and what is the true nature of our identity. Gender identities are rapidly expanding today, as people are breaking free from longstanding rigid and limiting gender norms. This liberation is taking place not only for LGBTQ+ persons, but also for heterosexual men and women as they break free from traditional debilitating socialization as males and females. In this process, gender identity politics has become a hot-button issue, which continues to play out in various ways, some of which are addressed in the Appendix. Yet gender identities are inherently relative, not ultimate. Even if one identifies as the Source of Gender, as suggested by Stuart Sovatsky, this ultimately leads *beyond* gender to identification with the Source of existence itself.

The question of gender identity can be viewed as one form of asking the question "Who am I?" and seeking the answer somehow in relation to gender. This question—"Who am I?"—is the right question to ask, as reflected for example in the profound self-enquiry practice of the great Indian sage, Ramana Maharshi. But to restrict this question to the domain of "gender identity" alone arbitrarily limits a profound inquiry to a relative dimension. The question "Who am I?" is the beginning of a deep spiritual journey, which, when pursued far enough, will eventually leave behind all questions of gender and move into the realm of pure being, awareness, and spirit. The question of gender identity, carried far enough, thus becomes a vehicle for awakening to deeper levels of self-realization, and not an end in itself.

The Heart of Reconciliation

As participants engage in the GERI process, their hearts open and gradually merge into one another, advancing steadily toward becoming one, large, shared heart. The separations of gender, race, and every intersectionality are gradually dissolved, until all are uplifted together as one. Dr. Howard Thurman, a key mentor of Dr. Martin Luther King, Jr. articulates this process eloquently:

> I had to lay claim to the very root of my being, and hold it and experience it, taste it, feel it. You move down into it, and what you do is you come up *inside* of every other living person. . . The religious person goes down into their self, and what they discover there, they universalize—so that when they look into the face of another, they see their [own] face.

This realization is available to all of us if we follow Thurman's call to move down deep into the root of our own being. This may seem too good to be true, or too simplistic or pollyannaish to be practical. But as Thurman elaborates further on the process:

> The deepest part of me connects with the deepest part of the other. . . . The deeper "down" that I go, the more *into* God I find myself. No categories of classification—faith, belief, etc.—have any standing in the presence of this transcendent experience. Whether I'm Black, White, or of [whatever religion], in the presence of God, all these

> categories by which we relate to each other fade away, and have no significance whatsoever. I am a part of [God], being *revealed* to [God]. Whenever, in my experience with my fellow [humans], this can be awakened, then a door between us is opened, that no one can shut. Because the only and ultimate refuge that anyone has, in this world, is in another person's heart. So my heart must be a swinging door.[14]

This is the heart of reconciliation. It is the innate condition of the spiritually pure heart, in which all differences and distinctions are dissolved in the ineffable supreme presence, by whatever Name it is called.

"Love pierces the heart of every lover. Blood flows, but the wound is invisible." In this one line, Rumi captures the essence of the alchemy of the heart. This is especially powerful when applied in a group: As one person shares their heart's truth, this light-ray of truth pierces the other hearts, each in a particular way. This creates an invisible thread of heart connection,and "spiritual lifeblood" flows from each pierced heart back to the person who shared their truth. As others in the group share their truth, this same process happens again. In this way, each person's heart is pierced multiple times by the deep truths of every other person in the group. This weaves an invisible "internet" of light and shared "lifeblood" among all the mutually "inter-pierced" hearts.

From this emerges a magnificent network of heart-threads of different hues and brightness, linking all the hearts, which we call the "inner net of the heart." Although invisible to the physical eyes, this numinous web of light is radiant to the eyes of the soul, and transforms the community from a collection of people to a communion of souls (or beloved community). In a typical GERI group of 25 people, there are 600 distinct energetic threads of light and love, linking each heart to every other (25 x 24 = 600). For every pair of people, each person's truth pierces the heart of the other, creating two threads or energy channels between them that function like a circuit, with spiritual energy flowing in both directions between their two hearts.

The spiritual "lifeblood" flowing through this network is in turn suffused and empowered by the supreme Source, which is the spiritual "grace" that Martin Luther King speaks of, which fuels the entire net. Each heart is connected 'horizontally' to every other heart, and is also connected "vertically" to the ineffable transcendent Heart of the Supreme Source, by whatever name this is called. This is the union of the outer alchemy (of beloved community) and the inner alchemy (of communion with the Beloved)— which creates the astonishing power and intimacy of humanity transformed and liberated. This is the ultimate beloved community, and the highest destiny for the human species.

Spiritual Androgyny and Mystical Union

In this process, male and female, and all gender categories, are revealed to ultimately contain one another. They are inter-beings. The hearts of heterosexual and LGBTQ+ people contain one another. People of different races and cultures are *contained* in the hearts of one another. The human heart is infinite—and is bigger than gender, bigger than race, bigger than cultural difference and identity politics.

As Rumi famously says, "There is a field out beyond right and wrong, I'll meet you there." Applying this same principle of meeting beyond opposites, we can say: "There is a field out beyond male and female, out beyond hetero and LGBTQ+, out beyond Black and White. Let's meet there." In this meeting, we become one, across all divisions of gender, race, and culture.

This is not to deny the reality of social injustice, but simply to affirm that the categories of Black vs White, or male vs female, or hetero vs LGBTQ+ are not *ultimately* real. They are important, but spiritually they don't actually exist, because there is no separation in the infinite depths of the heart.

In the end, we are not ultimately man or woman, LGBT or hetero. We are not "gendered" beings at all, because gender is partial, and we have become whole. We no longer identify with only a part, or just one side, when all parts and all sides dwell within us. Male and female become united within us in a sacred androgyny. The coupling of sexual intercourse is a physical symbol of this larger union. Sexual union provides a temporary, finite glimpse of this eternal, infinite union.

In this unitive realization, we recognize that it was always so; we were never separate. Masculine and feminine were never really two. Such an integral androgyny is often found naturally in highly-realized spiritual masters of either sex. For example, as J. G. Bennett observed about the great Christian mystic St. Teresa of Avila, "Men encountered in St. Teresa a woman who was more fully a man than they were, while she was also fully a woman."[15] This experience of unitive androgyny is closely related to mystical love, in which there is a loss of the separate self—the identity of I, me, and my personality—followed by a radical union with the Divine. As the Sufi mystic Alansari put it, "Know that when you lose your self, you will reach the Beloved. There is no other secret to be learned, and more than this is not known to me."

Thus the lover sacrifices their life to the Beloved, and the two become one. All duality is dissolved in a higher unity. With this realization comes the startling discovery that the lover always *was* the Other, there never were two in the first place. The separate self never actually existed; it was an illusion all along.

The pinnacle of gender reconciliation work bears a resemblance to this mystical union, though perhaps not always so esoteric or exalted. Yet, not infrequently in gender reconciliation work people discover a kind of uplifting revelation in which the sacred feminine and divine masculine are experienced as dwelling in glorious dynamic union together, deep within the heart. The veils of separation are lifted, and the ecstatic dance of masculine and feminine divinity is suddenly unmasked and revealed. As one participant who is a longstanding Sufi practitioner described it, "I saw God, in a whole new way."

Gender reconciliation work inevitably leads us to, or toward, this unitive experience. It's one thing to read about the experience or hear about it, but when it actually happens to you, it's quite a different thing. Suddenly you glimpse the real miracle of the masculine and feminine. You behold this glorious, cosmic, interpenetrating, inter-receptive tapestry—alive and shimmering before you, and *within* you—and you are part of this scintillating tapestry. You *are* the tapestry, and the tapestry is you!

Gender reconciliation is ultimately a work of love that leads to the eventual dissolution of identification with gender. Notwithstanding the value of today's expanding spectrum of gender identities that are breaking free from the repressive norms of the past, gender healing work ultimately leads to liberation from "gender identity" altogether. All human beings are both masculine and feminine—and neither. All dualities merge, and we become one whole being, and one humanity.

Healing the Past and Birthing the Future

The larger purpose of Gender Equity and Reconciliation is not only to forgive and reconcile the past—but also to *transcend* the past and *rewrite* the gender future of humanity. The future is whispering to us—in every moment—with the promise of a radically new, exceedingly refreshing, uplifting, and nourishing experience of gender relations and sexuality in the human family. This reality is becoming available now, as people engage in this transformational work.

Gender Equity and Reconciliation work reveals a precious secret: when we come together in human community, and move through this collective alchemy skillfully together, something amazing happens. We depart our ordinary social reality, enter into the liminal space of alchemical transformation, and eventually come out the other side into a new radiance and grace—a tangible awakening of renewed authenticity and intimacy, sublime depth, and an oasis of beauty that is part of our birthright as a human community. This becomes the basis for reinventing ourselves and our relationships, and for building a new "beloved community." As Rumi expresses this process, "we exit the circle of time, and enter the circle of love."

Telling the untold stories of gender oppression, in an appropriate forum, releases their hold on us, and renders the oppression visible. This frees us from the past, and clears the ground for a whole new story to be written, and *lived*. Together we *become* a new and renewed community, and begin living into the new gender future—now. This is happening today, and explains why so many people find themselves deeply moved by the power and force of the GERI programs. There is a current of something remarkable moving through the entire human family, which is manifesting in the GERI spaces.

Crucibles of Beloved Community

The past cannot be fully healed unless we also create a new reality, in which the past will not be repeated. Healing the past and actively creating a healthy future go hand in hand; they are two sides of the same transformational coin. Transmuting the past becomes the alchemical fuel for inventing the future and living it now.

GERI Heart Circles (discussed in Chapter 25) provide spaces for participants to continue working with the principles and practices of gender reconciliation in a like-minded community setting. These GERI Heart Circles function like "crucibles" of alchemical transformation that provide a contained, on-going community space for people to bring their challenges and aspirations, and practice the new ways of relating that have been introduced in GERI programs.

Every GERI event creates one of these crucibles, many of which are nurtured over time, each one focused on a local process of healing, yet interconnected with the larger web of other GERI Heart Circles, and the GERI global community. Each Circle functions as a unique experimental follow-up community, in which people continue exploring the practices learned in the GERI program, and engage in deep truthtelling, and in contemplative practices together.

These crucibles are planted like seeds in the "implicate order" (to use David Bohm's term) of collective human consciousness. They are experimental consciousness laboratories, focused on gender reconciliation and transformation, in which people continue to deepen their relational experiences and collective wisdom together. Slowly but inexorably, these crucibles are incubating a new civilization of gender-healed equitable harmony, and its expression in new forms of gender relations and beloved community.

To our knowledge, the GERI initiative documented in this book is unique in its scope and scale. We are a global community of dedicated women and men, and people of all genders—across six continents and various cultures and races—who are not merely "allies" but are fully collaborating *partners* in deconstructing the foundations of gender oppression, and its related intersectionalities with race and class and culture. We are collectively transforming and reinventing gender and intersectional relations in practice. The rare levels of cross-gender truth-telling and mutual safety created in the GERI process enable people of vastly diverse cultural backgrounds and gender identities to navigate seemingly intractable gender wounds and conflicts, and reestablish mutual respect, trust, understanding, and partnership across the genders, races, and cultures of the world.

Toward a New Civilization of Love

Gender oppression is universal. The whole of humanity is in profound need of a kind of "Truth and Reconciliation Commission" in regard to gender injustice and associated collective trauma. Humanity as a whole must one day face unflinchingly the full agonizing truth of gender oppression and sexism in our consciousness, our societies, our families, our relationships—our very legacy as a species.

We must cultivate a vast forgiveness for the ruinous violations of women and girls, the profound betrayal of men and boys, and the persecution of LGBTQ+ people who have departed from narrow, rigid heterosexual norms and stereotypes. Humanity will never be able to move fully forward into its next phase of evolution, toward a new civilization of love and harmony, without first reconciling gender imbalance at a far more profound level than has yet been achieved in any contemporary society.

A Higher Destiny Beyond the Legacy of Gender Oppression

The price we are paying as a human species for our millennia-long legacy of gender oppression is immeasurably vast and devastating. It is impossible for most of us to even imagine the transformed and elevated condition that humanity would be in today, if we as a species had followed a path laid out for us in the key teachings of *any* of the major world spiritual teachers and masters. Had we done so, the very evolution of the human species would have unfolded in very different and advanced ways over the past few thousand years, and the ordinary human being today would be a far more refined, aware, and spiritualized creature.

Coupled with this would be a radically different and more expansive relationship to gender and sexuality. The sacred aspects of gender and sexuality, and the advanced psycho-physical-spiritual development of the human being, would have become prevalent by now in human societies. The average human being would be far more advanced spiritually, physically, mentally, sexually, and psychologically (as presaged in the remarkable vision put forward by Stuart Sovatsky, pp. 390-395). Human experience of gender and sexuality would be vastly expanded from today's norms, as is already glimpsed even today, as shown in Jenny Wade's research (pp. 107-113). All this, in turn, would create human societies that are far more peaceful and attuned to the deeper currents and rhythms of life, and the average person in society would be living in far greater joy, wisdom, and mature spiritual awareness.

This "higher" destiny has always been humanity's birthright, and so it remains—patiently waiting and beckoning for us to choose the path that will lead us there, yet which we have continued to forego. So here we are, still mired in ancient dysfunctional patterns and behaviors that have oppressed us for thousands of years. Rape and war and all manner of widespread injustices *could* have been a thing of the past by now, or nearly so, but such is not yet the case.

In saying this, our purpose is not to taunt with a vision of "what could have been," but rather to emphasize that *this glorious destiny still awaits us*, and we can still choose it. A major prerequisite, and one of the most critical first steps, is to transform the disastrous legacy of gender oppression head on, at its roots. We *can* do this by speaking and standing for truth and following the process that leads to a newfound freedom. This freedom is twofold—a genuine *freedom from* the past, and also the *freedom to choose* and live into our bright and auspicious future.

Most human beings have never truly considered the possibility that gender relations in human existence *could* be radically different. When it comes to gender-based oppression and violence, most people assume that this is an innate and inevitable part of the human condition, and that it's always been this way and will never change. Not true!

A new level of conscious evolution is now awakening in humanity—a new era in our understanding and expression of gender, intimacy, and sexuality—for which all gender healing work to date has been but preparation. A new dawn of a higher form of love is coming—one that is already beginning to show itself. This nobler and more universal form of love—between human souls, and between the soul and the Ultimate Reality—does not deny the expression of physical intimacy and love but will elevate the erotic impulse from largely physical and emotional bonding to a form of profound spiritual communion. The intimate interplay between archetypal manifestations of Divine Feminine and Divine Masculine will become more accessible to suitably prepared souls, and this in turn will bring a magic and delight back into humanity and to the earth that has been lost for millennia. This is our birthright as human beings, and it is coming back to re-enchant our lives once again.

Perhaps this seems like pure fantasy, but in fact we have directly and consistently witnessed the seeds of this process taking place across the globe for thousands of people in our intensive GERI retreats and programs, and in the on-going follow-up Heart Circles. By the end of these gatherings, the participants are genuinely focused on honoring and serving the needs of the other, more than advancing and protecting their own needs. The GERI alchemical crucibles of beloved community are forging new ways and models, for women and men and people of all genders, that will one day spread to become the norm on a much larger societal scale. This process is the Hermetic principle operating in reverse: "As below, so above."

Recall what Thich Nhat Hanh said: the next Buddha will emerge not in the form of an individual, but rather in the form of a community of people living in loving kindness and mindful awareness. The global community of people practicing Gender Equity and Reconciliation is one of these communities. What is now taking place and emerging on a small scale within the microcosm of GERI groups, and other like-minded spiritual groups and communities, will one day become a lived reality in the larger human family. These dedicated pioneers of truth and compassion are planting holographic seeds of grace that will infuse society and eventually transform it from within.

Because every person is affected by gender conditioning, the process of gender reconciliation is one of the most powerful vehicles for awakening the collective heart of a community or group, and indeed the entire human family. This work naturally awakens a community's capacity for compassion and forgiveness. It also serves to restore a sense of the sacred interconnectedness of all life, including humanity's interdependence with the nonhuman world, and with our sacred planetary home, Earth. A startling power emerges when human beings gather to explore and reconcile their differences in community. The potential contribution that gender equity and reconciliation offers to the future of humanity is enormous, and has only just begun.

The Truth Sets Us Free

When we embrace the truth, we are set free. This profound teaching is found in John's gospel and in various other forms across all the major spiritual traditions of the world. The Buddha's final teaching was to take refuge in the truth. A saying attributed to Christ in the non-canonical *Gospel of Thomas* articulates how the process works: "Let one who seeks not stop seeking until that person finds. And upon finding, the person will be disturbed; and after being disturbed, will be astonished. Then the person will reign over everything."[16]

We have lived these successive stages in our collective journey of gender equity and reconciliation. Thirty-four years ago this project was launched, inspired in part

Celebratory conclusion of early GERI workshop, Mill Valley, California, 1997

by the insight from Thich Nhat Hanh quoted in Chapter 1: *What we most need to do is to hear within our hearts—the sounds of the other gender(s) crying.* Thus we began, and we have heard many disturbing revelations over the years. Yet this very process also awakened new depths of mutual compassion and empathic resonance with one another. This in turn opened our hearts profoundly to one another, which led to deep bonding in the universal heart of love. And this has been nothing short of astonishing. We have followed the path of gender truth, which brought deep disturbance at what was revealed, yet also led to mutual astonishment as we have been freed from debilitating gender patterns, and discovered a newfound sovereignty born of mutual reverence in the awakening of beloved community.

Staying true to this process, the path that Thich Nhat Hanh put us on has transformed us from the inside out: *We now hear the sacred music of the other gender(s)—singing in the depths of our own hearts.* This is the astonishing experience of the interbeing of gender—heart to heart, soul to soul—in the oneness of humanity, and in union with the supreme Source.

As this book goes to press, the "Epstein files" have just been partially released by the U.S. government, exposing egregious sexual exploitation of countless women and underage girls by a vast network of leading corporate executives, government officials, celebrities, and spiritual leaders. This is the latest in a long series of disturbing exposés: the MeToo Movement, sex scandals in major religious institutions East and West, and in sports and service organizations, schools and universities, scouting and youth organizations; the list seems endless. In all cases, the perpetrators include complicit leaders in the highest echelons of power who will stop at nothing to keep the truth hidden and protect the perpetrators. All this underscores the core premise of GERI: not only will the truth set us free, but revelations of these deeper darker truths will ultimately set our entire culture more deeply free. Until then, these horrific scandals will continue unabated. Three decades of GERI work across the globe have convinced us that these outrageous abuses can be systematically confronted and transmuted, to help birth an astounding new civilization of love on Earth.

Let us close with a prayer, which is adapted from the same mystical poem we opened with in Chapter 1 (p. 29) written by the Indian poet Jnaneswar:[17]

Without the God,
There is no Goddess,
Without the Goddess,
There is no God.
How sweet is their love!

Embracing each other,
They merge into One,

When we discover their
Unity
All words and all thoughts
Dissolve into silence . . .

APPENDIX

The Shifting Gender Landscape

Over the three decades of Gender Equity and Reconciliation International's (GERI) work—and especially in the past ten years or so —there has been a significant expansion of the "gender landscape," with gender identities, sexual orientations, and gender expressions becoming increasingly diverse and complex. This is a crucial and historically unprecedented process, as contemporary societies are striving to advance beyond the rigid gender conceptions and norms of the past, and create an expanded and liberated gender culture that will better serve humanity. This process is inherently complex and controversial, with high stakes, deep commitments, and intensive feelings on all sides. Much of this material is hotly debated today, and is also changing rapidly. Language and ideas that are current today may be replaced and outdated in just a few years' time. Against this complex and shifting background, this Appendix briefly unpacks the state of some of the cultural discourse on this topic (as of mid-2022).

We begin with some terminology and definitions to lay the groundwork for the current gender conversation. The term "gender" today is defined and used in several different ways, including: a synonym for biological sex; a term for the social norms, expectations, and stereotypes for women and men; a term for the gendered social role that is projected onto a person; or, a shortened version of "gender identity," or the way that a person relates to their own self psychologically, unrelated to biological sex.[1]

When it comes to biological sex, there are three primary definitions or scientific models, all of which affirm sexual dimorphism in the human species, and each of which provides a unique set of criteria that specify what makes a person male or female. The first is the *gamete* model, which sees sex primarily related to the production of sex cells—eggs or sperm for us humans—with a person being male or female based on their developmental pathway to produce small or large gametes for sexual reproduction (regardless of whether the gametes are successfully produced). The second is the *chromosome* model, which defines human females and males by their chromosomes. In this model, a human female is a person without a Y chromosome, and a human male is a person with a Y chromosome. A third view, the *cluster* model, looks for a cluster of endogenous morphological traits—primary and secondary sex characteristics—which are ordinarily relevant to identifying males and females. In this model, no individual characteristic is considered essential for being female or male, nor must an individual show all characteristics of a given cluster. Instead, what makes a person female or male is that they exhibit enough of the important features of their sex-associated cluster.[2]

Together, these three models of sex can readily categorize over 99 percent of people into the division of female or male, including even most people who exhibit "differences in sexual development" (DSDs). Still, ambiguity can arise in borderline cases—such as for certain subsets of DSDs (about 0.018 percent of people)[3]—where these models may struggle to categorize them neatly, or may even contradict one another's classifications. This ambiguity around the edges of categories is not unique to the dimorphic categorization of humans into male and female. Indeed, nearly all attempts at categorization will generally encounter certain unusual cases that cannot be easily settled one way or another based on present understandings, and so it is not surprising that this also holds true for sexual classification. Taking all this into account, these three models of sex present a picture of sexual dimorphism in humans, and for 99.982 percent of the population there is a naturally occurring separation into females and males.[4] The intersexed minority is nevertheless very real, and they have special needs and rights that must be upheld and protected like the rights of any other group.

When it comes to the concept of "gender identity," first coined by John Money and Robert Stoller in the 1960s, the conversation becomes more muddled. According to Stonewall, a prominent British LGBTQ+ activist group, gender identity is defined as "a person's innate sense of their own gender, whether male, female, or something else… which may or may not correspond to the sex assigned at birth."[5] For some, the "innate"-ness of gender identity has a biological and medical correspondence as a permanent and structural fact of a person's brain. Others, seeing gender as fundamentally socially constructed, de-emphasize the idea of an "innate" gender identity, but instead focus on gender identity as something fluid, impermanent, and changing over time. Others attempt to expand and offer perhaps a more nuanced way of understanding gender identity by concentrating on the psychological process of "identification," wherein gender identity is seen as the psychological process of strong identification with a gendered person or ideal. Identification, in this sense, "is constructed on the back of a recognition of some common origin or shared characteristics with another person or group, or with an ideal, and with the natural closure of solidarity and allegiance established on this foundation."[6] Some conceptualizations assert that all people have a distinct gender identity, which is either aligned or misaligned with their biological sex, while by other definitions, many people do not have a distinct gender identity at all.

As for the psychological and spiritual nature, or "soul" of human beings, the situation is more expansive and nuanced. Masculine and feminine characteristics are present in all human beings, and the more developed and evolved a person is, often there is an integrated balance of what are traditionally understood to be feminine and masculine traits. Across the world's religious and spiritual traditions, for example, it has long been recognized that people of advanced spiritual development are often "androgynous," and they integrate a balanced mix of both masculine and feminine qualities, regardless of what their biological sex is. For example, as noted earlier, it was said of the Christian mystic St. Teresa of Avila: "Men encountered in Teresa someone who was more of a man than they were, while also being fully a woman."

Current Events, Tensions, and Controversies

There is much debate, controversy, and conflict in contemporary discourse on these topics, particularly in relation to notions of sex and gender identity, and how society might be arranged for the benefit of women, transgender, and gender nonconforming people. On one side are a subset of trans-activists and many Third Wave feminists, and on another side, gender-critical activists and radical feminists. On yet another side are "LGB" activists, some of whom are seeking to distance themselves from some aspects of transgender activism. And on another side altogether are those approaching from a more conservative or traditionalist perspective, wanting to maintain what they regard as valuable in traditional understandings of sex and gender. Much of the cultural discourse has become quite heated and now resembles a battlefield, with various sides becoming entrenched in their positions, and at times seemingly more intent on "winning" than entering into good faith dialogue to serve the needs of all.

For example, "women-only" spaces have long existed, and have traditionally been considered exceptionally safe spaces in which women and girls can gather among themselves. Now there are battle lines around what constitutes a "woman-only" space, and who, exactly—depending on the model of sex and gender identity—is permitted to be there. This conflict extends to the bathroom controversies that are widely raging today, and how to accommodate the needs of people of all gender identities while also maintaining a sense of safety and security for everyone. Girls and their parents are concerned about girls' safety in school bathrooms, and there have been incidents of sexual assault of girls in bathrooms. At the same time, transgender teens are also particularly vulnerable to sexual assault in bathrooms.[7]

Other arenas of conflict include: the question of women's sports, and who is permitted to compete; or the extent to which a person can expect—or legally compel—others to recognize their gender identity and use their preferred pronouns. Another important domain of controversy is the appropriate care, treatment, and process for trans individuals and those seeking medical transition, particularly for individuals under the age of 18 (discussed below). Indeed, these debates seem to coalesce anew whenever grappling with the question, and practical implications, of what exactly makes a person a "woman," or a "man," or any gender at all. Below, we summarize a few recent key conflicts in this arena, demonstrative of the current trends and cultural conversations and developments.

LGB Alliances and Emerging Tensions

The British charity Stonewall developed the Diversity Champions programme for LGBTQ+ inclusion and safety in the workplace, which was widely adopted by hundreds of organizations. In September 2019, twenty-two members of Stonewall signed an open letter to *The Sunday Times* accusing Stonewall of having "undermined women's sex-based rights and protections" through its policy on transgender issues.[8] Another major concern was that primary school children are too quickly encouraged to question or doubt their gender identity. One of the letter's signatories was the co-founder of Stonewall, Simon Fanshawe, who cited their "intolerance of disagreement and discussion."

One month later, a new charity called the LGB Alliance was founded in October 2019 by several of these signatories. The Alliance describes its objective as "asserting the right of lesbians, bisexuals and gay men to define themselves as same-sex attracted," and states that such a right is threatened by "attempts to introduce confusion between biological sex and the notion of gender."[9] The LGB Alliance opposes the "disproportionate" focus on gender identity in schools,[10] raises concerns about medical transition for children reporting gender dysphoria,[11] and challenges gender recognition reform that focuses on the primacy of gender identity over sex. Naturally there have been strong objections to the LGB Alliance, which has been labeled anti-trans,[12] and chastised for the removal of the "T" from LGBT, but the Alliance affirms that it remains supportive of trans rights.

In early 2021, several UK organizations began to withdraw from the Stonewall Diversity Champions program, including the Equality and Human Rights Commission (EHRC), citing concerns about trans rights, and policies that may be harmful to women.[13] In November 2021, the BBC withdrew from the Diversity Champions scheme,[14] and other organizations that have withdrawn include Ofcom, and the UK Cabinet Office, Equalities Office, Ministry of Justice, and University College London.

On the other side of the Atlantic a parallel organization was founded, the LGB Alliance USA, which is currently seeking to amend the Equality Act, a federal legislative bill that seeks to incorporate protections against LGBT discrimination into the Civil Rights Act of 1964. On February 25, 2021, the Equality Act was passed by the U.S. House of Representatives, but the bill continues to face an uphill battle in the Senate (at the time of this writing).

The LGB Alliance USA is striving to amend the Equality Act, because they claim:

> The Equality Act as written enshrines as law this premise that self-declaration of one's gender identity takes primacy over biological sex. ... More importantly, "gender" or "gender identity" is conflated with "sex" throughout the bill without clearly defining either term. ... As written, the Equality Act erases sex as a protected class in law, weakening protections as well as undermining the existing rights of females as a unique class and will erase the progress women have made toward achieving equality with men.[15]

Young People Experiencing Gender Dysphoria

One of the most important, current, and controversial topics related to sex, identity, and trans rights relates to the best practices for care, treatment, appropriateness, and proper medical and psychological processes for people under the age of 18 who self-identify as transgender, and are seeking puberty blockers or medical transition. These questions are relatively new in contemporary culture, so it is natural and appropriate that there is much active debate, especially in this arena where the issues are complex, and the stakes are high because of the major consequences of various decisions.

Particularly in the West, the number of adolescents reporting gender dysphoria or seeking related medical care has increased dramatically in recent years. According to *WebMD Health News*, "One recent U.S. survey found a 4000 percent increase of gender dysphoria in adolescents since 2006, and there have been similar large increases in Finland, Norway, the Netherlands, Canada, and Australia."[16] A recent CDC survey shows that nearly 2% of high school students in the United States now identify as transgender.[17] Meanwhile, the UK's Gender Identity Development Services (GIDS) reported a nearly 20-fold increase in referrals from 2010-11 to 2020-21, with teenage girls representing approximately two thirds of those referred. Some patients are as young as just three-years-old.[18]

For many, these developments are cause for concern, both in seeking the underlying cause of this trend, and in clinics' ability to provide an appropriate standard of care for each patient. Whether from the rapidly increasing rate of referrals, or from other causes, a significant number of pediatric gender clinics are no longer following the standards of care recommended by the World Professional Association for Transgender Health (WPATH), which recommends mental health support and comprehensive assessment for all dysphoric youth *before* starting medical interventions.[19] A recent study of ten Canadian pediatric gender clinics found that half of them did not require psychological assessment before initiating puberty blockers or hormones.[20]

According to a 2021 article co-authored by Erica Anderson, a former WPATH board member, "we find evidence every single day. . . that the field has moved from a more nuanced, individualized and developmentally appropriate assessment process to one where every problem looks like a medical one that can be solved quickly with medication or, ultimately, surgery. As a result, we may be harming some of the young people we strive to support—people who may not be prepared for the gender transitions they are being rushed into."[21]

Anderson, a transwoman herself, feels so strongly about this that she resigned in 2021 from her senior leadership positions in two prominent trans activist organizations, WPATH and USPATH (US Professional Association for Transgender Health). She has emerged as a prominent voice encouraging trans people to undergo more psychological assessment and care before opting for medical transition. She maintains that some young people are transitioning because it's "trendy," or because of peer influence and "social contagion," a driving force prevalent particularly among teens. "I couldn't be more gender affirming," says Anderson, "[but] having had many, many hundreds of interviews with kids and families, I don't give a 13- or 14-year-old carte blanche. ... What I want always is individualized evaluation and a comprehensive bio-psychosocial evaluation. ... To just say that if a kid says they're trans, they're trans, and so treat them as such, and expedite gender-affirming medical support? No. [This] ignores the long history we have of issues in child and adolescent development, and it is a disservice to the patient."[22]

The conversation about the nature and kind of therapeutic support and care for trans and gender non-confirming youth is itself fraught with conflict, especially when it comes to efforts to rightly protect young people from harmful or potentially coercive tactics that attempt to impose a heteronormative gender identity or sexual orientation. At the same time, psychologists warn against an overly simplistic binary categorization of "affirmation" versus "conversion" that is beginning to take root in common discourse around therapeutic interventions. Strictly "affirmative" therapeutic approaches tend to support the self-proclaimed gender identity of the youth struggling with gender dysphoria.

> The notion that all therapy interventions for [gender dysphoria] can be categorically classified into this simplistic binary betrays a misunderstanding of the complexity of psychotherapy. At best, this blunt classification overlooks

> a wide range of ethical and essential forms of agenda-free psychotherapy that do not fit into such a binary; at worst, it effectively mis-categorizes ethical psychotherapies that do not fit the "affirmation" descriptor as conversion therapies. Stigmatizing non-"affirmative" psychotherapy for [gender dysphoria] as "conversion" will reduce access to treatment alternatives for patients seeking non-biomedical solutions to their distress.[23]

Meanwhile, puberty blockers for young people, often promoted as a kind of "pause button" for teenagers with gender dysphoria, are increasingly being called into question. Potential benefits, as well as adverse effects of puberty blockers and the ultimate "reversibility" of the treatment remain hotly debated, and research in this arena is still lacking. A recent GIDS study of 44 children (age 12-15) who took puberty blockers showed mixed results for mood and quality of life, and no changes in self-harm indexes, psychological function, or degree of gender dysphoria. At the same time the study did show certain adverse effects, particularly suppression of bone mineral density and growth.[24] Other studies have reported results suggesting that puberty blockers, combined with psychological support and care, correlate with improved outcomes.[25] At the same time, scientists and researchers themselves are not free from their own biases and influences, and certain individual articles or studies have later become contested as the methodology, analysis, or motivations of the researchers are called into question.[26,27,28]

Nonetheless, a number of these studies do share in common the finding that nearly 100 percent of those who took puberty blockers continued afterward to medical transition, often with cross-sex hormones associated with irreversible effects, or surgeries such as breast augmentation for transwomen, or double mastectomies for transmen.[29] The apparent impact of puberty blockers and an interventionist model stands in stark contrast to a "watchful waiting" approach with comprehensive assessment, mental health support, and gender-exploration therapy (as per WPATH care standards). While longer-term studies of youth who did not take puberty blockers are limited, studies do suggest that a substantial proportion (60-90 percent) of youth with gender identity disorder come to a natural resolution, and stop identifying as trans after puberty.

In a longitudinal study of 25 girls believed to have Gender Identity Disorder (GID), when they were assessed as young girls (mean age 9, ranging 3-12 years old), 15 of them (60 percent) met the DSM criteria for Gender Identity Disorder (the other 40 percent were subthreshold). Years later in the Follow-up, however, (mean age 23, ranging 15-36) only 3 of them (12 percent) were judged to still have GID or gender dysphoria.[30] In a similar study of

139 boys deemed to have Gender Identity Disorder, when they were assessed as young boys (mean age 8, ranging 3-13 years old), 88 of them (63 percent) met the DSM criteria for Gender Identity Disorder (the rest were subthreshold). However, years later in the Follow-up (mean age 21, ranging 13-39 years old), only 17 of them (12 percent) were judged to still have GID or gender dysphoria.[31] Such studies call into serious question not only the wisdom of puberty blockers and medical transition at early ages for young people, but also suggest other underlying possible causes (and hence other types of treatment) for young people struggling with their gender identity.

There are plenty of transgender people who have undergone medical transition, and are grateful for the positive, lasting results in their lives. At the same time, the potential consequences of rushed gender-affirmative treatment are severe, and are becoming more evident. In December 2020, Keira Bell, a 24-year-old British woman, won a lawsuit against GIDS. As a teen, she had received puberty blockers from the clinic after just a few visits, and a year later began injecting testosterone. By the time she was 20, she had undergone a double mastectomy. Bell says the clinic and medical staff should have challenged her more about her decision to transition to a male as a teenager before beginning medical treatment.

> I was an unhappy girl who needed help. Instead, I was treated like an experiment. As I matured, I recognized that gender dysphoria was a symptom of my overall misery, not its cause. Five years after beginning my medical transition to becoming male, I began the process of de-transitioning. The consequences of what happened to me have been profound: possible infertility, loss of my breasts and inability to breastfeed, atrophied genitals, a permanently changed voice, facial hair.[32]

Bell is among a number of "detransitioners" who regret their medical transition to the other gender, many of whom believe they did not receive an adequate evaluation from a doctor or mental health professional before starting transition. A recent study of detransitioners showed that nearly 40 percent of them believed their original dysphoria had been caused by "something specific, such as trauma, abuse, or a mental health condition." While it is difficult to know the exact numbers or percent of young people who regret their transitions (three-quarters of those who reversed their gender transitions did not report this change to their doctors),[33] these studies along with Bell's story—and others like her—are important to pay heed to in the effort to provide appropriate support and care for young people who are seeking treatment.

A recent assessment of the scientific research on medical interventions for trans-identified youth concludes that, "Despite the precedent of years of gender-affirmative care, the social, medical and surgical interventions are still based on very low-quality evidence. The many risks of these interventions, including medicalizing a temporary adolescent identity, have come into a clearer focus through an awareness of detransitioners."[34] Three major reviews of the literature conducted by government agencies in Finland, Sweden and the UK found an alarming lack of data supporting early treatments.[35]

The scientific research on these issues is hotly debated, and can also be subject to bias or distortion in the charged political climate in this arena. For example, a year-long clinical study with 104 transgender youth aged 13–20 was recently completed at the Seattle Children's Hospital by researchers from the University of Washington. The press release announced: "Gender-affirming care dramatically reduces depression for transgender teens, study finds." The study reported its key finding that "receipt of gender-affirming care, including puberty blockers and gender-affirming hormones, was associated with 60% lower odds of moderate or severe depression, and 73% lower odds of suicidality over a 12-month follow-up."[36] On the face of it, this would appear to be a definitive clinical demonstration that gender-affirming medication (GAM) greatly reduces depression and suicide, which is one of the primary concerns for transgender youth. A major publicity campaign publicized this finding widely. "It's huge," declared the lead researcher.[37]

However, two months later a critical review of this study came out, showing that the study's own data demonstrated no substantial improvement in either depression or suicidality among the youth who took the gender affirming medication (GAM).[38] The impression widely conveyed, that taking GAM reduces suicidality and depression, was *not* found among those who took the medication. The reported improvement was only in comparison to a subset of the teenagers who had *not* taken the medication. However, there was major attrition in the latter group; by the end of the 12-month study, 80 percent of the latter group had dropped out of the study, leaving only six youth in the comparison group. The same review raised concerns about the statistical methods utilized, and criticized the researchers for not making the raw data publically available. All this brought into serious question the validity of the reported statistical results, as well as the integrity of how the study's findings were disseminated and presented in the ensuing publicity campaign. As the reviewer concluded, "It's frequently argued that if kids don't have access to this medicine, they will be at a high risk of killing themselves. ...These researchers, firmly enmeshed in this debate, found that kids who went on these medications did not experience relief—and yet they don't mention this worrisome fact anywhere in their paper."[39]

Other studies exploring this question present a mixed picture. Data from the Tavistock clinic in the UK did not show a statistically significant difference between completed suicides in the watchful "waitlist" vs. the GAM "treated" groups.[40] A major longitudinal study from the Netherlands concluded that suicides occur at a similar rate at all stages of transition, from pretreatment assessment to post-transition follow-up.[41] Although in the short-term, some studies indicate that gender-affirmative interventions can lead to improvements in some measures of suicidality,[42] neither hormones nor surgeries have been shown to reduce suicidality in the long-term.[43]

At the same time, it is important to note that completed suicides are far less common than attempted suicides. "Data from the world's largest clinic for transgender youth over 11 years yield an estimated annual suicide rate of 13 per 100,000. This rate was 5.5 times greater than the overall suicide rate of adolescents of similar age, adjusting for sex composition."[44] This indicates that suicide rates are higher among trans-identified youth, although other studies have reached more equivocal results.[45] Nevertheless, "the proportion of individual patients who died by suicide was 0.03%, which is orders of magnitude smaller than the proportion of transgender adolescents who report attempting suicide when surveyed." The researchers conclude that "The fact that deaths were so rare should provide some reassurance to transgender youth and their families. … It is irresponsible to exaggerate the prevalence of suicide."[46] Another recent assessment reaches a similar conclusion: "The "transition or die" narrative, whereby parents are told that their only choice is between a 'live trans daughter or a dead son' (or vice-versa), is both factually inaccurate and ethically fraught. … [It also] falsely implies that transition will prevent suicides. … We consider the "transition or die" narrative to be misinformed and ethically wrong."[47] In summary, "Suicidality among trans people is incredibly complex; relating to multiple individual, systemic and structural factors. It cannot be located solely within the individual, and any exploration of this must consider intersectional sources of oppression to fully capture its nuances."[48]

All of the above points to the simple yet uncomfortable fact that these important research questions, and their profound implications for clinical practice and medical treatment of gender dysphoria, are still unresolved. By way of summary, we close this topic with an excerpt from an op-ed in the *Washington Post* co-authored by Erica Anderson, a transwoman herself and strong advocate of transgender rights.

> Trans youth, more than most patients in the health-care system, require an interdisciplinary approach: Their doctors rely on mental health colleagues for direction, and it is crucial that those therapists take the reins. Without proper assessment, many youths

are being rushed toward the medical model, and we don't know if they will be liberated or restrained by it...

Many trans activists want to silence detransitioners or deny their existence, because those cases do add fuel to the conservative agenda that is pushing to deny medical treatment to all transgender young people. (Those conservative views are unacceptable, and medically unsound.) Instead, we should be learning from them and returning to the empirically supported careful assessment model recommended by WPATH. And none of this means that we shouldn't be listening to the views of gender-diverse teens; it only means that we should listen in the fullest and most probing way possible.

The pressure by activist medical and mental health providers, along with some national LGBT organizations to silence the voices of detransitioners and sabotage the discussion around what is occurring in the field is unconscionable. Not only is it harmful to detransitioned young people—to be made to feel as if their lived experiences are not valid, the very idea that the gender-transition treatment is meant to remedy—but it will undoubtedly raise questions regarding the objectivity of our field and our commitment to help trans people. The fact that some people detransition does not mean that transgender people should not receive the services they need.

The energy currently spent fighting this political battle would be much better directed toward improving care for all gender-diverse young people. They deserve nothing less."[49]

Divergent Views and Freedom of Thought

Another important area of cultural attention has been around issues of language, belief, and ideology when it comes to sex, gender identity, and the supremacy of one over the other. In the heat of the cultural moment, perspectives can lose their nuance and flexibility, crystalizing into rigid ideologies, with little room for genuine discussion and learning. This at times can devolve into the denigration of people's characters and motives, with unjustified accusations of transphobia or hate coming from one side, and cruelty or dehumanization coming from the other. At times, anything less than total agreement with the prevailing orthodoxy may be met with outright hostility, and people with divergent views find themselves in the crosshairs.

One recent case demonstrative of these back-and-forth swings is the story of Maya Forstater, a tax researcher in the UK, who lost her position at the Centre for Global Development (CGD) after tweeting that people cannot change their biological sex. Her 2018 tweets were made in opposition to a proposed reform of the UK's Gender Recognition Act to allow people to declare their own gender. The CGD alleged that Forstater's tweets—where she stated her belief in a binary sex, and that "men cannot change into women"—were "offensive and exclusionary." In 2019, she appealed the Centre's dismissal to an employment tribunal on the grounds that she was discriminated against because of her beliefs, which include "that sex is a biological fact, and is immutable. There are two sexes, male and female. . . It is impossible to change sex." The initial judge found in the Centre's favor, ruling that her stated beliefs did not meet the criteria for protection as philosophical beliefs by the UK's equality laws, and that her views were "not worthy of respect in a democratic society."[50]

Forstater appealed this initial ruling to the Employment Appeal Tribunal, which reversed the prior decision in 2021, and concluded that her belief that "biological sex is real, important and immutable" does meet the legal test of a "genuine and important philosophical position" protected under law. Importantly, not only did the panel note that Ms. Forstater's views are widely shared, including by respected academics, but that while her words or beliefs may be offensive to some, they did not demonstrate direct attempt to harm others.[51] On one hand, this case and its initial ruling highlights the increasing influence (and perhaps overreach) of a subset of trans activism not only on people's prospects for employment, but even into legal frameworks and decision-making bodies themselves. On the other, its ultimate reversal, does signal an important legal protection for genuinely divergent views, even if inconsistent with the prevailing orthodoxy.

In another recent case, Kathleen Stock, a British philosopher, writer, and professor, resigned from her position as a professor of philosophy as Sussex University in late 2021 after controversy over her challenging the notion that gender identity is more socially significant than biological sex.[52] Stock, who is also a trustee of the LGB alliance, was accused of "transphobia" and "harmful rhetoric" by students and other academics. She declares herself supportive of trans rights, and maintains that "Trans people deserve lives free from fear. They deserve laws and policies that properly protect them from discrimination and violence." But she also says that "laws and policies based around gender identity are not the right route."[53] Stock says that she faced a campaign of harassment over her views that made it impossible for her to continue in her position, and that her personal safety was at risk. The UK's Minister for Higher and Further Education, Michelle Donelan, said: "It is absolutely appalling that the toxic environment at the University of Sussex has made it untenable for Professor Kathleen Stock to continue in her position there. No academic should ever have to fear for their personal safety."[54,55]

When Stock was awarded admission to the Order of the British Empire (OBE) in recognition of her services to higher education, over 600 philosophers signed an open letter criticizing the decision.[56] Later, in response to the controversy at Sussex University, more than 600 other university staff and professors signed an open letter of support in solidarity with Stock.[57] This demonstrates the magnitude of the ideological split in academic communities around these issues, though it is worth noting that the letter of solidarity did not publish the list of the names of the signatories with the letter, citing concerns over the pressure faced by those who had signed similar letters in the past. While academic perspectives clearly differ widely on these issues, this does suggest that those who hold "gender-critical" views are more hesitant to publicly voice their views out of fear of reprisal.

A similar on-going case is Professor Jo Phoenix who founded the Gender Critical Research Network (GCRN) at the Open University.[58] In an open letter signed by 380 people, the network was criticized as "hostile to the rights of trans people," although Phoenix has stated formally that she supports "the rights of trans individuals to be fully protected by the Equalities Act." Phoenix was harassed to the point that she resigned her position, and filed a lawsuit against the Open University for not protecting her from harassment in the workplace. She hopes that her legal case will "make it clear that baseless accusations of transphobia simply for standing up for the rights of women is harassment, especially when made in an academic context." She took another professorial position at Reading University.

Stock and Phoenix are but two of several controversies happening in many universities in the West, as academic debates heat up around sex, gender identity, and academic freedom of ideas.[59] Another example is Professor Donna Hughes at the University of Rhode Island. These disputes are affecting pay and pension plans for academics,[60] and the larger ethical implications for academic freedom remain far from resolved.

Maintaining Women's Rights

Transgender activists have rapidly secured many positive and significant gains in recent years, and public awareness of trans issues, at least in the West, has grown significantly. Recognizing the many important and necessary improvements in this area, another area of important concern comes in preserving the rights and protections that women have made in the past hundred years. One area of contention is around "women-only" spaces and services designed for the protection of women and girls, and exactly who is included in these spaces, and how that is decided. At times, this entails removing the words "women," "woman," and "girl" from the language used by many of the organizations and services designed to help them, or by redefining spaces that were previously "women-only" as "gender-neutral." In her op-ed in the *Economist*, Kristina Harrison, a transwoman herself, maintains that systems of self-identification—that impose the supremacy of gender identity over sex in defining who is a woman—risk undermining women's sex-based protections.[61] It is worth noting that this primarily impacts women and girls, whereas transmen using male bathrooms and changing rooms or playing on male sports teams, has a negligible impact on men. Harrison concludes that, "We need to protect single-sex provision for women ... while simultaneously acting to improve trans lives, systems and services in ways that do not undermine women."[62]

In 2021, a consortium of gender activist organizations circulated widely an online statement entitled "An Affirmation of Feminist Principles," inviting others to sign on. The document asserts, as a tenant of feminism, that "sex, gender and sexuality are social constructs." The document of nearly 1,500 words mentions "women" only twice; once in reference to a "Western binary construction of gender and sex" as the cause of oppression and structural discrimination, and the other as a note that "feminist power analyses go beyond binaries." There is no reference to "girls" in the entire document. Not surprisingly, this Affirmation was not universally well-received by feminists, particularly "gender critical" feminists. One group, Women's Declaration International (WDI), responded with a sharp criticism of the document and has published their own "Declaration on Women's Sex-Based Rights,"[63] with nine Articles, based in part on the U.N. Convention on the Elimination of All Forms of Discrimination Against Women (CEDAW) of 1979.

Intensive dialogue and debate on these matters will surely continue, and much remains unresolved today. These are not easy issues and questions to grapple with, and each "side" has valid and important points and positions, with the very real need for protections and rights for transgender people, as well as the essential importance of maintaining the sex-based protections that women have only recently won. Similarly, as Kathleen Stock notes, each side also has its own responsibility for the breakdown in dialogue and increasing polarization.[64] At the same time, despite this polarization, these "sides" need not be opposed to each other in moving forward towards practical solutions and policies that serve and benefit all.

Moving Forward in Stormy Seas

These examples offer but a small glimpse of the complexity and magnitude of substantive debate today, and the wide spectrum of divergent and often highly contentious positions that are vying for supremacy in the charged atmosphere of the contemporary gender conversation. Tensions within the LGBT movement itself are strong and controversial, as indicated for example by a recent remark from longtime LGBT activist Jonathan Rauch, who cautioned that "unless more trans [moderates] find their voices and rescue their movement from the extremists who have captured it, the future of LGBT equality will be in jeopardy."[65]

The culture is still battling, dialoguing, and researching these topics, which have become a locus of conflict in a larger "culture war" in many contemporary societies. This debate will surely continue well after the publication of this book, with the pendulum swinging perhaps far to one side, and then back again to the other, and it could take several more years or even decades to come to an appropriate equilibrium of balanced understanding, nuance, and widespread acceptance of policies and protocols.

A recent commentary in the *New York Times* on the "transgender culture war" suggests that the current debate is constellated around three conflicting camps, and that many people today are averse to stating their position publicly, for fear of either the wrath of cancel culture, or the uncomfortable bedfellows they may find themselves aligned with.[66] While acknowledging the tremendous uncertainty and unknown outcome of this debate, the commentator offers a prediction: "Within not too short a span of time, not only conservatives but most liberals will recognize that we have been running an experiment on trans-identifying youth without good or certain evidence, inspired by ideological motives rather than scientific rigor, in a way that future generations will regard as a grave medical-political scandal." Regardless of whether this prediction comes true or not, it points to the magnitude of the stakes and ethical issues involved.

Finally, how does all this relate to GERI? Although these complex issues and debates are an important process for the culture at large to go through, they are not the explicit focus of the GERI program or process. The need for compassionate collective spaces for deep personal truth-telling and sharing around gender and sexuality existed long before these debates began, will exist throughout their tenure, and will continue long after these issues have come to an acceptable resolution. The need for GERI programs and similar initiatives continues unabated, irrespective of the outcome of these debates, important as they are. Every human being—regardless of gender identity (or lack thereof)—has a personal story, a unique voice, and an important contribution to make to the larger emerging gender conversation and healing across the genders. The purpose and vision of GERI is to create unique spaces to meet this need, to cultivate the currents of individual and cultural transformation that organically emerge from within these spaces, and as best as we are collectively able, to midwife the corresponding birth of a new gender-healed civilization.

Endnotes

Introduction

1. William Keepin, *Divine Duality: The Power of Reconciliation Between Women and Men*, (Prescott, Arizona: Hohm Press, 2007, 25).
2. https://www.inquiringmind.com/article/1002_41_thich-nhat_hanh/

Chapter 1

1. William Keepin, *Divine Duality: The Power of Reconciliation Between Women and Men* (Prescott, Ariz.: Hohm Press, 2007, 9).
2. Riane Eisler and David Loye, *The Partnership Way: New Tools for Living and Learning* (San Francisco: Harper, 1990).
3. "Devastatingly Pervasive: 1 in 3 Women Globally Experience Violence," World Health Organization, March 9, 2021, https://www.who.int/news/item/09-03-2021-devastatingly-pervasive-1-in-3-women-globally-experience-violence.
4. Emiko Petrosky, et al., "Racial and Ethnic Differences in Homicides of Adult Women and the Role of Intimate Partner Violence — United States, 2003–2014," *Morbidity and Mortal Weekly Report* 66, no. 28 (July 21, 2017): 741–746. DOI: http://dx.doi.org/10.15585/mmwr.mm6628a1.
5. "Impunity for Domestic Violence, 'Honour Killings' Cannot Continue – UN Official," United Nations, March 4, 2010, https://news.un.org/en/story/2010/03/331422.
6. Indira Sharma, "Violence Against Women: Where are the Solutions?," *Indian Journal of Psychiatry* 57, no. 2 (2015): https://www.ncbi.nlm.nih.gov/pmc/articles/PMC4462781/.
7. "Depression in Women: Understanding the Gender Gap," Mayo Clinic, January 29, 2019, https://www.mayoclinic.org/diseases-conditions/depression/in-depth/depression/art-20047725.
8. Martina Schwikowski, "Africa: COVID lockdowns blamed for increase in teenage pregnancies," *Deutsche Welle*, November 13, 2021, https://www.dw.com/en/africa-covid-lockdowns-teenage-pregnancy-increase/a-59166242.
9. "COVID-19: A Threat to Progress Against Child Marriage," UNICEF, March 2021, https://data.unicef.org/resources/covid-19-a-threat-to-progress-against-child-marriage/.
10. Maria Cohut, "Men's Mental Health: 'Man Up' Is Not the Answer," *Medical News Today*, June 21, 2020, https://www.medicalnewstoday.com/articles/mens-mental-health-man-up-is-not-the-answer.
11. Vanessa Roma, *Boy Scouts Of America Reaches Historic Settlement With Sexual Abuse Survivors,* NPR, July 2, 2021, https://www.npr.org/2021/07/01/1012388865/boy-scouts-of-america-settlement-with-sexual-abuse-survivors-victims, accessed April 10, 2022.

12. Robert H. Shmerling, "Why Men Often Die Earlier Than Women," *Harvard Health Publishing*, June 22, 2020, https://www.health.harvard.edu/blog/why-men-often-die-earlier-than-women-201602199137.
13. Rach Dowd, "LGBT People Nearly Four Times More Likely Than Non-LGBT People to be Victims of Violent Crime," the Williams Institute, UCLA School of Law, October 2, 2020, https://williamsinstitute.law.ucla.edu/press/ncvs-lgbt-violence-press-release/.
14. Wyatt Ronan, "New FBI Hate Crimes Report Shows Increases in Anti-LGBTQ Attacks," Human Rights Campaign, November 17, 2020, https://www.hrc.org/press-releases/new-fbi-hate-crimes-report-shows-increases-in-anti-lgbtq-attacks.
15. U.N. Free and Equal Campaign, https://www.un.org/en/fight-racism/vulnerable-groups/lgbtqi-plus, accessed April 10, 2022.
16. Catherine E. McKinley, "How Gender Norms Can Make Domestic Violence Worse for BIPOC," *Psychology Today*, November 16, 2021, https://www.psychologytoday.com/us/blog/the-well-woman/202111/how-gender-norms-can-make-domestic-violence-worse-bipoc.
17. Black Women's Blueprint Institute for Gender and Culture, "Protecting Every Child: A Guide to End Child Sexual Abuse," 2017/2018, https://www.blackwomensblueprint.org/black-feminist-resources
18. André B. Rosay, "Violence Against American Indian and Alaska Native Women and Men," National Institute of Justice, June 1, 2016, https://nij.ojp.gov/topics/articles/violence-against-american-indian-and-alaska-native-women-and-men.
19. "A Public Health Crisis Decades in the Making: A Review of 2019 CDC Gun Mortality Data," The Education Fund to Stop Gun Violence and the Coalition to Stop Gun Violence, February 2021, https://efsgv.org/wp-content/uploads/2019CDCdata.pdf.
20. Sharon G. Smith et al., "National Intimate Partner and Sexual Violence Survey: 2010–2012 State Report," National Center for Injury Prevention and Control of the Centers for Disease Control and Prevention, April 2017, p. 3, https://www.cdc.gov/violenceprevention/pdf/nisvs-statereportbook.pdf.
21. *Measuring the Shadow Pandemic: Violence Against Women During Covid-19*, U.N. Women, Nov. 24, 2021, online at https://data.unwomen.org/publications/vaw-rga, accessed Jan. 24, 2022.
22. *Violence against women is like second 'pandemic' in South Africa: President*, online https://www.aa.com.tr/en/africa/violence-against-women-is-like-second-pandemic-in-south-africa-president/2427879, accessed Jan 24 2022.
23. *Police Response to Domestic Violence*, 2006-2015, U.S. Dept of Justice, 2017; online https://bjs.ojp.gov/content/pub/pdf/prdv0615.pdf, accessed Jan 24 2022.
24. Martin Luther King, Jr., "My Pilgrimage to Nonviolence," in *The Papers of Martin Luther King, Jr. Volume IV: Symbol of the Movement*, January 1957-December 1958, Univ. California Press, Clayborne Carson, Susan Carson, Adrienne Clay, Virginia Shadron, and Kieran Taylor, eds.
25. *Dhammapada*, Eknath Easwaran (transl), Nilgiri Press, 1986.
26. Dr. Martin Luther King, Jr., quoted in "Why the Beloved Community?", https://medium.com/@Beloved_US/why-the-beloved-community-b41c87a10bce, accessed April 12, 2022.
27. Jnaneswar, quoted in *Essential Mystics*, Andrew Harvey, Ed. (New York: Harper Collins, 1997).

Chapter 2

1. Thomas Keating, "The Points of Agreement," Introduction in *The Common Heart: An Experience of Interreligious Dialogue*, ed. Netanel Miles-Yepez (Lantern Books: 2006, xvii-xviii).
2. Rainer Maria Rilke, *Letters to a Young Poet*, Joanna Macy and Anita Barrows (transl), (Boulder: Shambhala, 2021).

Chapter 3

1. Sue Nathanson Elkind, *Resolving Impasses in Therapeutic Relationships* (New York: Guilford Press, 1992)
2. Peter Rutter, *Sex in the Forbidden Zone* (Los Angeles: Jeremy P. Tarcher, 1989).

Chapter 4

1. This workshop was co-facilitated by William Keepin, Heart Phoenix, Jeffrey Weisberg, Harriet Rose Meiss, and hosted by a team of assistants.

Chapter 6

1. bell hooks, *The Will To Change: Men, Masculinity, and Love* (New York: Washington Square Press, 2004, 66).

Chapter 7

1. J. Hanus, "The Culture of Pornography Is Shaping Our Lives," *Utne Reader* (Sept/Oct 2006): 58-60.
2. https://www.prnewswire.com/news-releases/covid-19-update-global-online-porn-market-was-estimated-to-be-us-35-17-billion-in-2019-and-is-expected-to-grow-at-a-cagr-of-15-12-over-the-forecast-period-says-absolute-markets-insights-301043437.html, accessed Jan 28, 2022.
3. Belinda Luscombe, "Porn and the Threat to Virility," *Time Magazine*, 187(13):40-47, April 11, 2016.
4. Ogi Ogas and Sai Gaddam, *A Billion Wicked Thoughts: What the Internet Tells Us About Sexual Relationships* (Plume, 2012).
5. Samuel Perry and Cyrus Schleifer, "Till Porn Do Us Part? A Longitudinal Examination of Pornography Use and Divorce," *J. Sex. Res.* 55(3):284-296, Mar-Apr 2018.
6. Gail Dines and Liz Walker, *You'd Be Surprised to Hear What Porn Is Doing to Sex,* https://verilymag.com/2017/07/porn-is-ruining-sex-say-recovering-sex-addicts.
7. Gary Wilson, *Your Brain on Porn: Internet Pornography and the Emerging Science of Addiction* (Commonwealth Publishing, 2014).
8. https://www.gottman.com/blog/an-open-letter-on-porn/
9. Carly Milne, *Naked Ambition: Women Who Are Changing Pornography* (New York: Carrol and Graf, 2005); Candida Royalle, *How to Tell a Naked Man What to Do* (New York: Fireside Simon and Shuster, 2004).
10. J. Stoltenberg, *Refusing to Be a Man* and *What Makes Pornography Sexy* (Minneapolis, Minn., Milkweeed Editions, 1994).
11. Christine Emba, *Rethinking Sexuality*: *A Provocation* (New York: Sentinel, 2022).

12. Daniel Odier, *Desire* (Rochester, Vermont: Inner Traditions, 2001, 8-9).
13. Sahajayoginicinta, quoted in Miranda Shaw, *Passionate Enlightenment* (Princeton, N.J.: Princeton University Press, 1994, 188).
14. Miranda Shaw, "Everything You Always Wanted to Know About Tantra . . . but Were Afraid to Ask," *What is Enlightenment?*, Lenox, MA, Issue No. 13, Spring-Summer, 1998.
15. Ibid.
16. William Keepin, "A Secret So Sacred, It Cannot Even Be Whispered: The Wisdom and Bliss of the Divine Feminine in Interspirituality," Ch. 10 in *Philo Sophia: Wisdom Goddess Traditions*, (Twin Lakes, WI: Lotus Books, 2021, 211-236).
17. Quotations from Ian Baker in this paragraph and remainder of this chapter are from Ian A. Baker, *Tibetan Yoga: Principles and Practices* (Rochester, VT: Inner Traditions, 2019), pages 168, 174. The quotation from Lama Yeshe Thubthen is from Baker's *Tibetan Yoga*, p. 174. The Dalai Lama quotation is from: https://hyperallergic.com/252891/tibets-secret-temple-the-long-hidden-tantric-murals-of-lukhang-palace/, accessed March 23, 2023. See also Nida Chenagtsang, *Karmamudra: The Yoga of Bliss* (Sky Press, 2018), as well as podcast interviews on www.guruviking.com with Ian Baker, Nida Chenagtsang, Glenn Mullin, Ben Joffe (who includes a valuable queer perspective on tantra), and others.
18. J. Wade (1998). Meeting God in the flesh: Spirituality in sexual intimacy. *ReVision 21*(2), 35-41.
19. J.Wade (2000).The love that dares not speak its name. In T. Hart, P. L. Nelson, and K. Puhakka, (Eds.), *Transpersonal Knowing: Exploring the Horizon of Consciousness*, pp. 271-302. Albany, NY: State University of New York Press.
20. J. Wade (2001). Mapping the courses of heavenly bodies: The varieties of transcendent sexual experience. *Journal of Transpersonal Psychology 23*(2), 103-122.
21. J. Wade (2003). Discovering transcendent sex: Otherworldly adventures behind closed doors. *Exceptional Human Experience 17*(1), 35-39.
22. J. Wade, *Transcendent Sex: When Lovemaking Opens the Veil* (New York: Simon & Schuster, Pocket Books, 2004).
23. Hinterkopf, E. (1994). Integrating spiritual experiences in counseling. *Counseling and Values, 38*, 165–175. https://doi.org/10.1002/j.2161-007X.1994.tb00834.x
24. Mencken, F. C., Bader, C. D., & Kim, Y. J. (2009). Round trip to hell in a flying saucer: The relationship between conventional Christian and paranormal beliefs in the United States. *Sociology of Religion, 70*(1), 65–85. https://doi.org/10.1093/socrel/srp013
25. Myers, J. E., & Willard, K. (2003). Integrating spirituality into counselor preparation: A developmental, wellness approach. *Counseling and Values, 47*(2), 142–155. https://doi.org/10.1002/j.2161-007X.2003.tb00231.x
26. Prest, L. A., & Keller, J. F. (1993). Spirituality and family therapy: Spiritual beliefs, myths, and metaphors. *Journal of Marriage and Family Therapy, 19*(2), 137–148. https://doi.org/10.1111/j.1752-0606.1993.tb00973.x

Chapter 9

1. Grof®Breathwork is another name for holotropic breathwork.
2. Stanislav Grof, *The Adventure of Self Discovery* (Albany, NY: SUNY Press, 1988, 171).

3. Stanislav and Christina Grof, *Holotropic Breathwork: A New Approach to Self-Exploration and Therapy* (Albany, NY: SUNY Press, 2010).
4. Stanislav Grof, *The Psychology of the Future* (Albany, NY: SUNY Press, 2000, 215-217).
5. Sarah Holmes, et. al, "Holotropic breathwork: An experiential approach to psychotherapy." *Psychotherapy: Theory, Research, Practice, Training* 33(1):114-120, March 1996.
6. James Eyerman, MD, "A Clinical Report of Holotropic Breathwork in 11,000 Psychiatric Inpatients in a Community Hospital Setting," *MAPS Bulletin* (2013), online: https://maps.org/news-letters/v23n1/v23n1_24-27.pdf, accessed Feb. 6, 2022.
7. Tanja Miller and Laila Nielsen, "Measure of Significance of Holotropic Breathwork in the Development of Self-Awareness," *The Journal of Alternative and Complementary Medicine,* Vol. 21, No. 12, 2015.
8. For several examples, see William Keepin, "Breathing New Life into Social Transformation: Holotropic Breathwork for Social, Cultural, and Political Leaders," *Psyche Unbound: Essays in Honor of Stanislav Grof* (London, UK: Synergetic Press, 2022, 199-222).
9. Bernie Glassman, *Bearing Witness* (New York: Harmony/Bell Tower, 1999).
10. For more details on Grof Breathwork, see Stanislav Grof, *Healing Our Deepest Wounds*, Stream of Experience Productions (2012), and Stanislav and Christina Grof, *Holotropic Breathwork: A New Approach to Self-Exploration and Therapy* (State University of New York, SUNY Press, 2010).

Chapter 10

1. "Same-Sex Marriage," Wikipedia, https://en.wikipedia.org/wiki/Same-sex_marriage, accessed Jan 25, 2022.
2. This number reflects the frequency that a child is born with sufficiently atypical genitalia that a specialist in sex differentiation is called in. The whole arena of intersex is complex; see "How Common is Intersex?" Intersex Society of North America, https://isna.org/faq/frequency/, accessed Feb. 12, 2022.
3. Lawrence, Hurley (June 15, 2020). *"U.S. Supreme Court endorses gay, transgender worker protections,"* Reuters.
4. Book in Afrikaans. *Praat verby grense: uit die e-pos van,* Laurie Gaum & Frits Gaum (Dialogue beyond boundaries), (Umuzi-Random House, Cape Town, 2010).
5. Selina Palm, "From Exclusion to Embrace: Re-imagining LGBTIQ belonging in local South African church congregations," 2019.
6. Ibid., p. 13.
7. Selina Palm and Laurie Gaum, "Engaging Human Sexuality: Creating Safe Spaces for LGBTIQ+ and Straight Believers in South Africa," *J. Theologica in Loco, 3*, 2, October, 2021, pp 161-181.
8. Ibid.
9. Ibid.
10. Ed Kilgore, "Refusal to Accept LGBTQ Equality is Still Causing Divisions in Churches," *New York Times Magazine*, March 6, 2022.
11. Palm and Gaum, *op cit.*

Chapter 11

1. The term "intersectionality" describes the way peoples' social identities can overlap. It was coined by Kimberlé Crenshaw, a law professor at Columbia and UCLA. Intersectionality includes gender, race, class, sexual orientation, religion, ability, and other identity markers.https://time.com/5786710/kimberle-crenshaw-intersectionality/
2. "code switching" involves adjusting one's style of speech, appearance, behavior, and expression in ways that will optimize the comfort of others. https://hbr.org/2019/11/the-costs-of-codeswitching.

Chapter 12

1. Charlotte Bunch, "The Intolerable Status Quo: Violence Against Women and Girls," in *The Progress of Nations*, UNICEF, 1997. https://www.unicef.org/media/85591/file/Progress-For-Nations-1997.pdf.

Chapter 13

1. Jack Kornfield, personal communication, ca. 2001.
2. Several Indian priests in the United States have been accused or convicted of sexually abusing minors, according to the watchdog group Metamorphose, which also reports that these cases received scant attention within the Catholic Church in India. See https://ephesians511blog.com/2017/06/23/rape-and-sexual-abuse-of-nuns-and-girls-and-boys-by-indian-priests-02/, accessed January, 2017.
3. For examples of teachings across the religions that encourage respect and love for the other religions, here are some key passages from various scriptures:

   Christianity: And Peter opened his mouth and said, "Truly I perceive that God shows no partiality, but in every nation anyone who fears God and does what is right is acceptable to God." (*Acts* 10:34-35).

   Islam: "Those who believe in the Qur'an, those who follow the Jewish scriptures, and the Sabeans and the Christians—any who believe in God and righteousness—on them shall be no fear, nor shall they grieve." (*Qur'an* 5.69) "We believe in what has been sent down to us, and in what has been sent down to you. Our God and your God is one, and to God we surrender." (29:46)

   Hinduism: "As seekers approach Me, so I receive them. All paths, Arjuna, lead to Me." (*Bhagavad Gita* 4.11)

   "The wise person accepts the essence of different scriptures, and sees only the good in all religions." (*Srimad Bhagavatam* 11.3). "Truth is one; sages call it by many names." (Rig Veda *Samhita* 1.164.46)

   Confucianism: "In the world there are many different roads but the destination is the same. There are a hundred deliberations but the result is one."—*I Ching* (Appended Remarks 2.5)

   Sikhism: "The Hindus and the Muslims have but one and the same God." (*Adi Granth*, Bhairo, p.1158)

   Buddhism: The Buddha says, "To be attached to a certain view, and to look down upon other views as inferior; this the wise call a fetter." (*Sutta Nipata* 798)

4. Sadiyya Shaikh, *Sufi Narratives of Intimacy: Ibn Arabi, Gender and Sexuality* (Chapel Hill, North Carolina: University of North Carolina Press, 2014, 220).
5. Ibid., 186-88. Ibn Arabi's quotation has been edited for gender inclusivity.
6. Ibid., 189-90.
7. Leloup, Jean-Yvres, trans., *The Gospel of Philip* (Rochester, VT: Inner Traditions, 2004).
8. Bennett, J.G., *Sex and Spiritual Development*, (York Beach, ME: Samuel Weiser, 1981, 50).
9. Rabbi Todros Abulafia (1222-1298), quoted by Charles Mopsik in Leloup, *The Gospel of Philip* (Rochester, VT: Inner Traditions, 2004, 26).

Chapter 14

1. Agarwal, D. P. "Gender bias in STEM: Women in tech still facing discrimination," *Forbes*. March 5, 2020. Retrieved January 31, 2022, from https://www.forbes.com/sites/pragyaagarwaleurope/2020/03/04/gender-bias-in-stem-women-in-tech-report-facing-discrimination/?sh=196f10f170fb

Chapter 15

1. Chigwedere P., Seage G.R. 3rd, Gruskin S., Lee T.H., Essex M. "Estimating for the lost benefits of antiretroviral drug use in South Africa," *Journal of Acquired Immune Deficiency Syndrome*, 1;49(4):410-5, December, 2008.
2. Available online: http://www.telegraph.co.uk/news/health/news/3346075/African-minister-ends-decade-of-denial-on-Aids.html "
3. M. Wines, "AIDS activist Nozizwe Madlala-Routledge Keeps Her Convictions but Loses Her Job," *New York Times*, September 7, 2007 (avail online: https://www.nytimes.com/2007/09/07/world/africa/07iht-profile.4.7423546.html).
4. "The Cancer of Patriarchy in the Church, Society and Politics in South Africa" conference in Cape Town, 5 - 6 March 2009.
5. W. Keepin, "Principles of Spiritual Activism," in T*he Love That Does Justice, Spiritual Activism in Dialogue with Social Science*, Michael A. Edwards and Stephen G. Post, Eds, 2008.
6. "Awakening the Dreamer," Pachamama Alliance, https://landing.pachamama.org/awakening-the-dreamer

Chapter 16

1. https://sdgacademy.org/goal/gender-equality/, accessed Feb 28, 2022.
2. Cumming-Bruce, N. (2018, December 7). "U.N. Aids Agency is in 'state of crisis' and needs new leader, report says." *The New York Times*. Retrieved March 2, 2022, from https://www.nytimes.com/2018/12/07/world/europe/unaids-abuse.html
3. *The UN has its 'Me Too moment'* - CNN video. CNN. Cable News Network. (2018, March 30). Retrieved March 2, 2022, from https://www.cnn.com/videos/world/2018/03/30/pkg-amanpour-united-nations-unaids-martina-brostrom.cnn
4. See https://www.nytimes.com/1993/06/16/world/women-seize-focus-at-rights-forum.html, accessed Feb 28 2022.

5. Frank Jordan, "UN backs gay rights for first time ever," Associated Press, June 17, 2011, *Times Leader*; available online: www.timesleader.com/archive/166732/stories-un-backs-gay-rights-for-first-timeever103981
6. Ronald Holzhacker, "Gay Rights are Human Rights: the Framing of New Interpretations of International Human Rights Norms," in G. Andreopoulos and Z. Arat, *The Uses and Misuses of Human Rights*, (London: Palgrave MacMillan, 2014), 29-64.
7. "UN unveils 'Free & Equal' campaign to promote lesbian, gay, bisexual, transgender rights," *UN News*, July 26, 2013. Available online: https://news.un.org/en/story/2013/07/445552-un-unveils-free-equal-campaign-promotelesbian-gay-bisexual-transgender-rights
8. https://www.unfe.org/wp-content/uploads/2021/06/UNFE-2020-Annual-Report.pdf
9. Morello, Carol. "U.N. council creates watchdog for LGBT rights." *The Washington Post.* Retrieved 2016-07-05.

Chapter 19

1. Martina Schwikowski, "Africa: COVID lockdowns blamed for increase in teenage pregnancies," *Deutsche Welle*, November 13, 2021, https://www.dw.com/en/africa-covid-lockdowns-teenage-pregnancy-increase/a-59166242.

Chapter 20

1. "The Persistence of Violence Against Women and Girls in the Region and its Maximum Expression, Femicide, Is Troubling," United Nations ECLAC, November 24, 2020 https://www.cepal.org/es
2. Pan American Health Organization; Centers for Disease Control and Prevention, *Violence Against Women in Latin America and the Caribbean: a comparative analysis of population-based data from 12 countries.* Washington, DC: PAHO, 2013.
3. According to Gender Equality Observatory for Latin America and the Caribbean, CEPAL, United Nations 2020.

Chapter 22

1. Will Keepin, Cynthia Brix & Molly Dwyer, *Divine Duality: The Power of Reconciliation Between Women and Men* (Hohm Press, Prescott, Arizona, 2018, 22),

Chapter 24

1. At times I describe this work as "encounters between men and women" because this language serves the purpose of illuminating how the identities of "man" and "woman" are enmeshed with experiences of power within the system of patriarchy. This use of language is not meant to exclude and by no means refers only to cisgender people, but rather anyone who self-identifies along the lines of these linguistic and socially constructed categories.
2. Henkeman, S. M. "Towards an Expansive Conceptual/Methodological Approach to Everyday Violence," in S. Kessi, S. Suffla, & M. Seedat (Eds.), *Decolonial Enactments in Community Psychology* (Cape Town: Springer, 2022, 234-252).

3. Weedon defines subjectivity as "the conscious and unconscious thoughts and emotions of the individual, her sense of herself and her ways of understanding the world." Weedon, C., *Feminist Practice and Poststructuralist Theory*. (New York: Basil Blackwell Ltd.,1987, 32).
4. Gavey, N. *Just Sex? The Cultural Scaffolding of Rape.* (New York: Routledge, 2019).
5. Finchilescu, G. & Dugard, J. "Experiences of gender-based violence at a South African university: Prevalence and effect on rape myth acceptance." *Journal of Interpersonal Violence, 36*(5-6), 2018, 1-24.
6. Gqola, D. *Rape: A South African Nightmare.* (Johannesburg: MF Books, 2015).
7. Henkeman, S.M., *op. cit.* (Footnote 2).
8. Scanlon, H. "Gender and the Politics of Reconciliation," Occasional paper (19). (Cape Town: The Institute for Justice and Reconciliation, 2016).
9. Gqola, P. *The Female Fear Factory.* (Cape Town: Melinda Ferguson Books, 2021).
10. Morison, T., Macleod, C. & Lynch, I. "'My friends would laugh at me': embedding the dominant heterosexual script in the talk of primary school students." *Gender & Education,* Vol. 34 (3), 2021, 329-345. https://doi.org/10.1080/09540253.2021.1929856.
11. Ratele, K., Shefer, T., Strebel, A. & Fouten, E. "'We Do Not Cook, We Only Assist Them': Constructions of Hegemonic Masculinity Through Gendered Activity." *Journal of Psychology in Africa, 20(4),* 2010, 557-568.
12. Shock, D.P. & Padavic, I. "Negotiating hegemonic masculinity in a batterer intervention programme." *Gender & Society, 21(5),* 2007, 625-649.
13. Morison, T., *et al., op.cit.* (Footnote 10).
14. Shefer, T., Kruger, L.M., & Scheepers, Y. "Masculinity, sexuality and vulnerability in 'working' with young men in South African contexts: 'You feel like a fool and an idiot...a loser.'" *Culture, Health & Sexuality, 17,* 2015, 96-111.
15. Shefer, T. & Macleod, C. "Life orientation sexuality education in South Africa: Gender norms, justice and transformation." *Perspectives in Education, 33(2)*: 2015, 1-10.
16. Hames, M. "'Let's burn the house down!' Violence against women in the higher education environment." *Agenda, 23,* 2011, 42-46.
17. Dosekun, S. " 'We live in fear, we feel very unsafe': Imagining and fearing rape in South Africa." *Agenda, 21(74),* 2007, 89-99.
18. van Schalkwyk, S. Boonzaier, F. & Gobodo-Madikizela, P. " 'Selves' in contradiction: Power and powerlessness in South African shelter residents' narratives of leaving abusive heterosexual relationships." *Feminism & Psychology, 24(3),* 2014, 314-331.
19. hooks, bell. *The Will to Change: Men, Masculinity, and Love.* (New York: Washington Square Press, 2004).
20. hooks, bell, "Choosing and learning to love." In Gloria Watkins (Ed.), *Communion: The Female Search for Love* (New York: Harper Collins, 2002, 90-104).
21. Ratele, K. *Liberating Masculinities.* (Cape Town: HSRC Press, 2016).
22. Root, M. "Reconstructing the Impact of Trauma on Personality." In L. S. Brown and M. Ballou (eds.) *Personality and Psychopathology: Feminist Reappraisals.* (New York: Guilford, 1992).

23. Brown, L.S. Not outside the range: "One feminist perspective on psychic trauma." In C. Caruth (Ed.), *Trauma: Explorations in memory* (London: John Hopkins University Press, 1995,100-112).
24. Forter, (2007). "Freud, Faulkner, Caruth: Trauma and the Politics of Literary Form." *Narrative*, 15(3), 259-285.
25. Crawford, J. "The severed self: Gender as Trauma." In A. Goldberg (Eds.), *Basic Ideas Reconsidered. Progress in Self Psychology Volume 12* (Hillsdale, New Jersey: The Analytic Press, 1996, 269-283).
26. Ibid.
27. Shefer, T. & Foster, D. "Heterosex among young South Africans: Research Reflections." In M. Steyn and M van Zyl (eds.), *The Prize and the Price: Shaping Sexualities in South Africa* (Cape Town, South Africa: Human Sciences Research Council Press, 2009, 267-289).
28. Davies, B. & Gannon, S. "Prologue." In B. Davies and S. Gannon (Eds.), *Doing Collective Biography* (New York: Open University Press, 2006, x).
29. Connell, R.W. *Gender and Power.* (Oxford, U.K: Basil Blackwell, 1987).
30. Morison, T., *et al., op. cit.* (Footnote 10).
31. Davies, B. & Gannon, S., *op. cit.* (Footnote 28).
32. The Qwaqwa campus is a branch of the University of the Free State based in the Eastern Free State. This campus plays an important role in providing higher education to the rural poorer communities.
33. The fact that all participants were black students opens space for important questions and critique. The most pertinent here is the critique that a focus on disrupting gender norms among a sample of black participants may be reifying ideas that gender violence is a problem for black people (in other words, not an entrenched problem for white people). This aligns with inherently racist essentialist ideas about black people's "violent nature." However, the recruitment of participants did not intentionally focus on black students. Black students were the only group who responded to the advert and signed up to take part in the study. I see this as an indication of the increased sensitivity that black students experience in relation to gender and power, due to the "double oppression" they face in university contexts.
34. The GERI workshop processes and methods such as silent witnessing, gender biography mapping, psychodrama and truth forums are detailed in chapters 2-6 of this book. I therefore do not go into detail here.
35. Reissman. C. K. *Narrative Methods for the Human Sciences.* (London: Sage, 2008).
36. Reavey, P. & Gough, B. "Dis/locating blame: Survivors' constructions of self and sexual abuse." *Sexualities, 3(3),* 2000, 325-346.
37. Reissman, C. K., *op. cit.* (Footnote 35).
38. Ibid.
39. Ibid.
40. Davies, B. "The concept of Agency," *Social Analysis, 30,* 1991. 42-53.
41. Reissman. C. K., *op. cit.* (Footnote 35).
42. Davies, B. & Gannon, S., *op. cit.* (Footnote 28).
43. Davies, B. *A Body of Writing 1990-1999.* (Walnut Creek: AltaMira Press, 2000).

44. Davies, B. & Gannon, S., *op. cit.* (Footnote 28).
45. Ibid.
46. Connell, R.W. *Gender and Power.* (Oxford, U.K: Basil Blackwell, 1987).
47. Gqola, P., *op. cit.* (Footnote 9).
48. Ahmed, S. *Strange Encounters: Embodied Others in Post-Coloniality.* (London: Routledge, 2000).
49. Ibid.
50. Brodie, N. *Femicide in South Africa.* (Cape Town: Kwela Books, 2020).
51. Ahmed, S., *op. cit.* (Footnote 48).
52. Shefer, T. & Munt, S. "A feminist politics of shame: Shame and its contested possibilities." *Feminism & Psychology, 29(2),* 2019, 145-156.
53. Davies, B. & Gannon, S., *op. cit.* (Footnote 31).
54. Connell, R.W., *op. cit.* (Footnote 46).
55. Fredrickson, B.L. & Roberts, T. "Objectification Theory: Towards understanding women's lived experiences and mental health risks." *Psychology of Women Quarterly, 21,* 1997, 173-206.
56. Hollway, W., "Gender difference and the production of subjectivity." In J. Henriques, W. Hollway, C. Urwin, C. Venn, and V. Walkerdine (Eds.), *Changing the Subject: Psychology, Social Regulation and Subjectivity.* (New York: Routledge, 1998, 223-261).
57. Tamale, S. "Introduction." In S. Tamale (Eds.), *African Sexualities* (Cape Town, South Africa: Pambazuka Press, 2011, 1-7).
58. Ibid.
59. The italic emphasis is my own.
60. Mama, A. & Barnes, T. "Rethinking Universities." *Feminist Africa, 8(1),* 2007, 1-7.
61. Treffry-Goatley, A., de Lange, N., Moletsane, R., Mkhize, N., & Masinge, L. "What Does It Mean to Be a Young African Woman on a University Campus in Times of Sexual Violence? A New Moment, a New Conversation." *Behavioural Sciences,* 8, 2018, 67-87.
62. Connell, R.W., *op. cit.* (Footnote 46).
63. Gqola, D., *op. cit.* (Footnote 9).
64. Brodie, N., *op. cit.* (Footnote 50).
65. Dunson, Konyka, "Closing the Gender Gap: Women and Men Creating Social Change through Dialogue," *Advances in Social Sciences Research Journal,* Vol.11 (8), August, 2024, pp. 161-183, DOI:10.14738/assrj.118.17356; p. 169 (emphasis added).
66. Ibid., p. 169.
67. Ibid., p. 170, 169 (emphasis added).
68. Ibid., p. 175, 176 (emphasis added).
69. Ibid., p. 170.
70. Ibid., p. 161,176.
71. Ibid., p. 161, 177.
72. United Nations Population Fund (UNFPA, 2020). *How Changing Social Norms is Crucial in Achieving Gender Equality.* https://www.unfpa.org/social-norms-change

73. Ibid. 65, p. 161.
74. Ibid. 65, p. 179.
75. Dunson, Konyka, "Dialogue to Dismantle Gender Inequality and Ignite Social Change: Examining the Impact of Gender Reconciliation," *Social Science and Humanities Journal*, Vol. 08 (05), May, 2024, pp. 3709-3723, DOI:https://doi.org/10.18535/sshj.v8i05.1089; p. 3721.

Chapter 25

1. Riane Eisler and David Lowe, *The Chalice & the Blade* and *The Partnership Way: New Tools for Living and Learning* San Francisco: Harper, 1990).

Chapter 26

1. Thomas Hübl, *Healing Collective Trauma: A Process for Integrating Our Intergenerational and Cultural Wounds* (Boulder, CO: Sounds True, 2020).
2. Lerner, Gerda, *The Creation of Patriarchy* (New York: Oxford Univ. Press, 1986, 11).
3. Ibid.
4. "LGBT History," in Wikipedia, https://en.wikipedia.org/wiki/LGBT_history, accessed Feb. 24, 2022.
5. "Third Gender," in Wikipedia, https://en.wikipedia.org/wiki/Third_gender, accessed March 31, 2022.
6. "The Code of the Assura, c. 1075 BCE", Fordham University, https://web.archive.org/web/20141028165014/http://www.fordham.edu/halsall/ancient/1075assyriancode.asp, accessed Feb. 14, 2022.
7. Lerner, Gerda, *op. cit.*, 228-9, (Footnote 2).
8. Valerie Hudson et al, *Sex and World Peace,* (New York: Columbia University Press, 2012).
9. https://www.forbes.com/sites/laurabegleybloom/2019/07/26/20-most-dangerous-places-for-women-travelers/?sh=5c6cc5e3c2f4
10. Valerie Hudson, "What Sex Means for World Peace," *Foreign Policy*, April 24, 2012, available on: https://foreignpolicy.com/2012/04/24/what-sex-means-for-world-peace/
11. W. Keepin,"A Secret So Sacred It Cannot Even Be Whispered," Ch. 10 in *Philo Sophia: Wisdom Goddess Traditions*, (Twin Lakes, Wisc.: Lotus Books, 2021).
12. Sadiyya Sheikh, *Sufi Narratives of Intimacy: Ibn Arabi, Gender, and Sexuality,* (Univ. of North Carolina Press, 2014).
13. King, Martin Luther Jr, "Pilgrimage to Nonviolence", Ch. 6 in *Stride Toward Freedom*, orig. 1958 (New York: Beacon Press, 2010).
14. *Conversations with Howard Thurman*, Parts 1 and 2, interviewed by Landrum Bolling. Online, https://www.youtube.com/watch?v=KvJVxsezAwc, accessed June 1, 2019.
15. J.G. Bennett, *Sex and Spiritual Development* (Deep River, Conn.: Bennett Books, 1999).
16. *Gospel of Thomas*, Saying 2. See the translations available here: http://www.earlychristianwritings.com/thomas/gospelthomas2.html, accessed Feb. 20, 2022.
17. Jnaneswar, quoted in *Essential Mystics*, Andrew Harvey, Ed. (New York: Harper Collins, 1997).

Appendix

1. Stock, Kathleen, *Material Girls: Why Reality Matters for Feminism* (London: Fleet, 2021).
2. Ibid.
3. Leonard Sax, "How Common is Intersex? A Response to Anne Fausto-Sterling," *Journal of Sex Research,* 39(3):174-8, August, 2002.
4. Some thinkers have posited that sex itself is socially and linguistically constructed, with categories of male and female being nothing but social meaning. We won't address these philosophical questions in this chapter, but for a more complete treatment of these issues, see Kathleen Stock's book *Material Girls, op. cit.* (Footnote 1).
5. *List of LGBTQ+ terms*. Stonewall. (2021, October 25). Retrieved January 28, 2022, from https://www.stonewall.org.uk/help-advice/faqs-and-glossary/list-lgbtq-terms
6. Stuart Hall (1996), "Who Needs "Identity'?", in S. Hall and P.DuGay (eds.), *Questions of Cultural Identity*, SAGE Books (2011, 2).
7. https://www.hsph.harvard.edu/news/hsph-in-the-news/transgender-teens-restricted-bathroom-access-sexual-assault/
8. Hellen, Nicholas. "'Anti-women' trans policy may split Stonewall." *The Sunday Times.* 22 September 2019. London. Retrieved 20 February 2022.
9. Hurst, Greg. "Transgender dispute splits Stonewall." *The Times*. 24 October 2019. London. Retrieved 20 February 2022.
10. Tominey, Camilla. "Lesbians facing 'extinction' as transgenderism becomes pervasive, campaigners warn." *The Telegraph*. 25 December 2020. London. Retrieved 20 February 2022.
11. Hunte, Ben. "Trans teen in legal action over gender clinic wait" *BC News*. 23 November 2020. Retrieved 20 February 2022.
12. Parsons, Vic, "LGB Alliance warned by advertising watchdog over 'potentially misleading' claims about gender recognition laws."*PinkNews*. 6 February 2020. Retrieved 20 February 2022.
13. Francis Churchill, *Why are Employers Leaving Stonewalls' Diversity Program?*, July 15, 2021, https://www.peoplemanagement.co.uk/news/articles/why-are-employers-leaving-stonewall-diversity-programme#gref, accessed March 25, 2022.
14. "BBC Pulls Out of Stonewall Diversity Scheme," Nov. 10, 2021, https://www.bbc.com/news/entertainment-arts-59232736, accessed March 25, 2022
15. *LGB Alliance USA Newsletter*, March 17, 2021, https://lgbausa.substack.com/p/equality-act-amend-and-pass, accessed Feb. 8, 2022.
16. Quoted from "Transition Therapy for Transgender Teens Drives Divide," *WebMD Health News* https://www.webmd.com/children/news/20210427/transition-therapy-for-transgender-teens-drives-divide, accessed Feb. 3 2022
17. Michelle M. Johns et al., "Transgender Identity and Experiences of Violence Victimization, Substance Use, Suicide Risk, and Sexual Risk Behaviors Among High School Students — 19 States and Large Urban School Districts, 2017," *Morbidity and Mortality,* Weekly Report 68, no. 3 (January 25, 2019): 67-71, https://www.cdc.gov/mmwr/volumes/68/wr/mm6803a3.htm, accessed Feb. 3 2022.
18. "Referrals to GIDS, 2010-11 to 2020-21," Gender Identity Development Service, May 3, 2021
19. "The mental health establishment is failing trans kids," *Washington Post,* https://www.washingtonpost.com/outlook/2021/11/24/trans-kids-therapy-psychologist/

20. Lawlson et al., "Pathways to care for trans youth accessing gender affirming medical care in Canada: New research from Trans Youth CAN!. Panel presented at World Professional Association for Transgender Health; November 7, 2020," https://transyouthcan.ca/results/wpath-2020-5/
21. Quoted from "The mental health establishment is failing trans kids," *Washington Post*, https://www.washingtonpost.com/outlook/2021/11/24/trans-kids-therapy-psychologist/, accessed Feb. 3, 2022.
22. Lisa Davis, "A Trans Pioneer Explains Her Resignation from the US Professional Association for Transgender Health,"*Quilette*, Jan 6, 2022,https://quillette.com/2022/01/06/a-transgender-pioneer-explains-why-she-stepped-down-from-uspath-and-wpath/, accessed Feb 4 2022.
23. D'Angelo, R., Syrulnik, E., Ayad, S., Marchiano, L., Kenny, D. T., & Clarke, P. (2021). "One Size Does Not Fit All: In Support of Psychotherapy for Gender Dysphoria." *Archives of sexual behavior*, 50(1), 7–16. https://doi.org/10.1007/s10508-020-01844-2
24. Carmichael, P., Butler, G., Masic, U., Cole, T. J., De Stavola, B. L., Davidson, S., Skageberg, E. M., Khadr, S., & Viner, R. M. (2021). "Short-term outcomes of pubertal suppression in a selected cohort of 12 to 15 year old young people with persistent gender dysphoria in the UK." *PLOS One*, 16(2), e0243894. https://doi.org/10.1371/journal.pone.0243894
25. Mahfouda, S., Moore, J.K., Siafarikas, A., Zepf, F.D., Lin, A."Puberty suppression in transgender children and adolescents." *Lancet Diabetes Endocrinol.* 2017 Oct;5(10):816-826. doi: 10.1016/S2213-8587(17)30099-2. Epub 2017 May 22. PMID: 28546095.
26. Costa R, Dunsford M, Skagerberg E, Holt V, Carmichael P, Colizzi M."Psychological Support, Puberty Suppression, and Psychosocial Functioning in Adolescents with Gender Dysphoria."*J Sex Med.* 2015 Nov;12(11):2206-14. doi: 10.1111/jsm.13034. Epub 2015 Nov 9. PMID: 26556015.
27. Bartram, D., A Letter to the Editor Regarding Costa et al. (2015) and Biggs (2019). *J Sex Med.* 2021 Apr;18(4):838-839. doi: 10.1016/j.jsxm.2021.01.179. Epub 2021 Feb 26. PMID: 33642236.
28. Biggs, M., A Letter to the Editor Regarding the Original Article by Costa et al: "Psychological Support, Puberty Suppression, and Psychosocial Functioning in Adolescents with Gender Dysphoria."*J Sex Med.* 2019 Dec;16(12):2043. doi: 10.1016/j.jsxm.2019.09.002. PMID: 31785710.
29. "Transition Therapy for Transgender Teens Drives Divide," *Webmd Health News* https://www.webmd.com/children/news/20210427/transition-therapy-for-transgender-teens-drives-divide
30. Drummond, K. D., Bradley, S. J., Peterson-Badali, M., & Zucker, K. J. (2008). "A follow-up study of girls with gender identity disorder,"*Developmental Psychology, 44*(1), 34–45. https://doi.org/10.1037/0012-1649.44.1.34, accessed Feb. 3 2022.
31. Singh,D., Bradley, S.J., & Zucker,K. J.(2021)."A Follow-Up Study of Boys with Gender Identity Disorder." *Frontiers in Psychiatry, 12*, 632784. https://doi.org/10.3389/fpsyt.2021.632784, accessed Feb. 3 2022.
32. Quoted from "Keira Bell: My Story," https://www.persuasion.community/p/keira-bell-my-story
33. Littman L."Individuals Treated for Gender Dysphoria with Medical and/or Surgical Transition Who Subsequently Detransitioned: A Survey of 100 Detransitioners." *Arch Sex Behav.* (2021) Nov.;50(8):3353-3369. doi: 10.1007/s10508-021-02163-w. Epub 2021 Oct 19. PMID: 34665380; PMCID: PMC8604821.

34. Stephen Levine *et al*, "Reconsidering Informed Consent for Trans-Identified Children, Adolescents, and Young Adults," *Journal of Sex and Marital Therapy*, 17 March, 2022, online: https://doi.org/10.1080/0092623X.2022.2046221, accessed April 10, 2022.
35. Jesse Singal, "What the media gets wrong on gender reassignment," online: https://spectatorworld.com/topic/media-wrong-gender-reassignment-transgender/, accessed April 10, 2022.
36. Diana Tordoff et al,"Mental Health Outcomes in Transgender and Nonbinary Youths Receiving Gender-Affirming Care," *JAMA Network Open*, Feb 25, 2022, online: https://jamanetwork.com/journals/jamanetworkopen/fullarticle/2789423, accessed April 1, 2022
37. *Science Friday* podcast, March 4, 2022, online: https://www.sciencefriday.com/segments/anti-trans-legislation-texas/#segment-transcript, accessed April 10, 2022.
38. Jesse Singal,"A Critique of Tordoff et al," online: https://jessesingal.substack.com/p/researchers-found-puberty-blockers?s=r, accessed April 10, 2022.
39. Ibid.
40. Biggs, M.,"Suicide by clinic-referred transgender adolescents in the United Kingdom."*Archives of Sexual Behavior* 51, 685–690 (2022).
41. Wiepjes, C. M. *et al*, "Trends in suicide death risk in transgender people: Results from the Amsterdam Cohort of Gender Dysphoria Study (1972–2017)", *Acta Psychiatrica Scandinavica*, 141(6), 486–491 (2020).
42. Kaltiala, R. *et al*, "Adolescent development and psychosocial functioning after starting cross-sex hormones for gender dysphoria," *Nordic Journal of Psychiatry*, 74(3), 213–219 (2020).
43. Bränström, R., & Pachankis, J.E., "Reduction in mental health treatment utilization among transgender individuals after gender-affirming surgeries: A total population study." *American Journal of Psychiatry* 177(8), 727–734 (2020). (See also the authors' correction, p. 734)
44. Biggs, M, (2022), *op cit.*, (Footnote 40).
45. de Graaf, N. M, "Suicidality in clinic-referred transgender adolescents." *European child & adolescent psychiatry*, 31, 67–83, (2020). See also Toomey, R. B. *et al*, "Transgender Adolescent Suicide Behavior." *Pediatrics*, 142 (4), (2018).
46. Biggs, M, (2022), *op cit.*, (Footnote 40).
47. Levine, Stephen (2020), *op cit.*, (Footnote 34).
48. McNeill, J. *et al*,"Suicide in trans populations: A systematic review of prevalence and correlates," *Psychology of Sexual Orientation.* DOI:10.1037/sgd0000235, 2017, p. 26., accessed from https://scholar.google.ca/scholar?hl=en&as_sdt=0%2C5&q=Suicide+in+trans+populations%3A+A+systematic+review+of+prevalence+and+correlates.+&btnG=
49. Quoted from "The mental health establishment is failing trans kids," *Washington Post*, https://www.washingtonpost.com/outlook/2021/11/24/trans-kids-therapy-psychologist/
50. "Judge rules against researcher who lost job over transgender tweets," *The Guardian*, https://www.theguardian.com/society/2019/dec/18/judge-rules-against-charity-worker-who-lost-job-over-transgender-tweets
51. "Maya Forstater: Woman wins tribunal appeal over transgender tweets," BBC News, https://www.bbc.com/news/uk-57426579

52. BBC. (2021, October 29). *Kathleen Stock: University of Sussex Free Speech Row Professor Quits*. BBC News. Retrieved February 8, 2022, from https://www.bbc.com/news/uk-england-sussex-59084446
53. BBC. (2021, November 3). "Woman's hour—professor Kathleen Stock; Royal Ballet principal Leanne Benjamin; Richard Ratcliffe." *BBC Sounds. BBC News*. Retrieved February 8, 2022, from https://www.bbc.co.uk/sounds/play/m001153q
54. Quoted from BBC. (2021, October 29). "Kathleen Stock: University of Sussex Free Speech Row Professor Quits." *BBC News*. Retrieved February 8, 2022, from https://www.bbc.com/news/uk-england-sussex-59084446
55. Guardian News and Media. (2022, February 7). "BBC rebukes Justin Webb over comment on Kathleen Stock Row." *The Guardian*. Retrieved February 8, 2022, from https://www.theguardian.com/media/2022/feb/07/bbc-rebukes-justin-webb-over-comment-on-kathleen-stock-row
56. "Open Letter Concerning Transphobia in Philosophy." *Philosophy Transphobia Letter*. (January, 2021). Retrieved February 8, 2022, from https://sites.google.com/view/trans-phil-letter/
57. "Statement of Solidarity with professor Kathleen stock." *GC Academia Network*. (2021). Retrieved February 8, 2022, from https://www.gcacademianetwork.org/statement-of-solidarity-with-professor-kathleen-stock.html
58. "A backlash against gender ideology is starting in universities," *The Economist*, June 5, 2021, https://www.economist.com/international/2021/06/05/a-backlash-against-gender-ideology-is-starting-in-universities, accessed March 25, 2022.
59. Judith Suissa and Alice Sullivan, "The Gender Wars, Academic Freedom and Education," *Journal of Philosophy of Education*, 10 March 2021, https://doi.org/10.1111/1467-9752.12549, accessed March 28, 2022.
60. "Transgender disputes threaten to split university unions," *University Business*,| January 6, 2022, https://universitybusiness.com/transgender-disputes-threaten-to-split-university-unions/, accessed March 28, 2022.
61. Harrison, K. (2018, July 3). "A system of gender self-identification would put women at risk." *The Economist*. Retrieved February 5, 2022, from https://www.economist.com/open-future/2018/07/03/a-system-of-gender-self-identification-would-put-women-at-risk
62. Ibid.
63. https://www.womensdeclaration.com/en/declaration-womens-sex-based-rights-full-text/, accessed Feb. 8 2022.
64. Stock, Kathleen, *Material Girls: Why Reality Matters for Feminism* (London: Fleet, 2021).
65. Jonathan Rauch, "Walking the Transgender Movement Away from the Extremists," *American Purpose*, April 1, 2022, online: www.americanpurpose.com/articles/walking-the-transgender-movement-away-from-the-extremists/, accessed April 10, 2022.
66. Ross Douthat, "How to Make Sense of the New L.G.B.T.Q. Culture War," *New York Times*, April 13, 2022.

Acknowledgments

If the only prayer you ever say in your entire life is thank you, it will be enough.
—Meister Eckhart

We give deep thanks to everyone engaged in the GERI community, beginning with the many thousands of participants who have experienced GERI, all of whom demonstrate tremendous courage and vulnerability as they step into this transformative journey. GERI is deep community healing work, and would be impossible without the engaged hearts, heads, and hands of many.

A postscript to Margaret Mead's famous quip might be: Never doubt that a *larger* group of committed people can change the world more *quickly*. We express our deep gratitude to the more than 330 certified GERI Facilitators and Trainers around the world, all of whom have contributed in important ways to this movement to transform gender oppression at its roots. We also honor and thank our many GERI Intern Facilitators and GERI Companions, most of whom are in the process of becoming certified facilitators, as well as our innumerable GERI Friends who have attended GERI programs and are supporting further GERI work in their communities. We are grateful beyond measure to the 20 co-authors of this book for their tireless efforts to implement GERI programs and trainings in their respective communities, and for modeling pioneering leadership and collaboration in beloved community.

The GERI project has been sustained and enriched both inwardly and outwardly by our spiritual teachers and mentors who hold us and the whole GERI community in their prayers. We are grateful beyond words, knowing that this work demands spiritual integrity, and that what transpires on the material planes is first constellated on the spiritual planes.

We owe a profound debt of gratitude to our beloved teachers and spiritual mentors:

- Stanislav Grof for his crucial contributions to our work; both the holotropic breathwork and intensive training in transpersonal psychology, and his invaluable personal friendship and support for nearly 40 years,
- Sr. Lucy Kurien for her unwavering love and deep friendship over decades, and the profound inspiration of her work demonstrating the power of love in action,

- Jetsunma Tenzin Palmo for her spiritual guidance, mentoring, friendship, and prayerful love and support of us and our work for over 25 years,
- The late Fr. Thomas Keating, for his enduring spiritual direction and creative inter-spiritual collaboration over 20 years, and his profound support on inner and outer planes,
- Nozizwe Madlala-Routledge for her longstanding support, and inviting GERI into remarkable new arenas of application,
- Imam Jamal Rahman for his enduring love, support, and creative collaboration,
- Swami Ambikananda Saraswati for her constant love, remarkable insights, and fruitful collaboration,
- The late Joanna Macy, for her work and its contribution to GERI, her earlier collaboration (with William Keepin) on nuclear energy issues, and her personal blessing of GERI and this book.

We thank other spiritual mentors who have offered their blessings to this work, especially Ravi Ravindra, Llewellyn Vaughan Lee, the late Angeles Arrien, and a profound spiritual teacher from India who wishes to remain anonymous.

Our gratitude goes to Regina Sara Ryan, our Editor at Hohm Press, who did her usual conscientious editing job on a complex manuscript. Thanks also to Dasya Zuccarello, and to Bala Zuccarello and Becky Fulker for their work on the layout. We thank our assistant editors Elizabeth McAnally and Aaron Weiss, who worked tirelessly on a tight timeline to edit many stories in the book.

Many individuals contributed greatly to the development of GERI over the years, without whom it would not be what it is today. A special expression of gratitude goes to the following:

Judy Bekker made a major contribution to GERI for several years as Director of Training in South Africa, and she also co-led GERI programs in Kenya, India, UK, Australia, and USA. She continues to this day as guest trainer.

Judy Connors in collaboration with Jabu Mashinini of Phaphama Initiatives organized many GERI programs over several years in schools, townships, prisons, and also organized a GERI professional training in Soweto that produced several GERI facilitators. She also graciously hosted our many visits to Johannesburg.

Richard Paine contributed greatly as board member, strategic advisor, and facilitator, drawing on his decades of experience in transformational trainings. Rick has also been a close travel companion and confidant for the GERI leadership team.

Emma Oliver served the GERI mission and GenderWorks in multiple capacities for nearly 20 years, and she continues to this day as the tireless treasurer of GenderWorks. Her late husband, Rev. John Oliver, also promoted GERI and helped to establish it in South Africa.

Jeremy and Nozizwe Madlala-Routledge have been longstanding allies of GERI, and they introduced GERI into their various collegial networks, which has been a major boost to advancing this work.

Professor Pumla Gobodo-Madikizela invited GERI to her 2012 conference, Engaging the Other, and in 2015 launched a two-year academic research project on GERI with Dr. Samantha van Schalkwyk.

The late Archbishop Desmond Tutu endorsed the GERI program and launched our partnership with the Desmond and Leah Tutu Legacy Foundation and Stellenbosch University. His gracious friendship warmed our hearts, and he also gave his blessings and endorsement to our Dawn of Interspirituality conferences.

Rev. Mpho Tutu van Furth orchestrated the partnership between GERI and the Desmond and Leah Tutu Legacy Foundation and Stellenbosch University, and she organized GERI events for clergy in the Anglican Church, and with the South African Faith and Family Institute. She also graciously wrote the Foreword.

Dorothea Hendricks has been a champion for GERI in numerous capacities, and initiated a three-year contract with the University of the Western Cape, and introduced us to Mpho Tutu.

Julien Devereux has served GERI diligently in many capacities for 30 years, and he brought many men to the GERI programs, especially in his capacity as Chair of ManKind Project USA, where he facilitated a formal partnership with GERI. Subsequent ManKind Project Chair Paul Samuelson followed suit, as did Terry Symens-Bucher and other leaders in the Illuman men's organization. Jon Levitt of the ManKind Project has been an invaluable support and advisor to the GERI leadership team, providing strategic advice, organizational wisdom, and mentoring support. Phil Vivirito has advanced GERI within his ManKind Project networks in the St. Louis area, and led GERI Heart Circles for years, as did Julien Devereux in Dallas. All these men (and numerous others) have worked tirelessly to bring conscious men to GERI, which benefited greatly as a result.

Chaya Pamula has unwaveringly supported GERI for years, and introduced GERI into her corporate and non-profit organizations.

Gard Jameson has been a remarkable supporter of GERI, and sponsored a series of GERI workshops for the LGBTQ+ Center of Las Vegas.

Emanuel Kuntzelman and Laura Rose have been generous in their support of GERI, and have orchestrated a unique collaboration between GERI and their Holomovement initiative.

We are deeply indebted to our 20 co-authors, whose full bios are given at the end of this book. All are GERI Trainers or senior Facilitators, and we will refrain from sharing the many superlatives they richly deserve—but having already acknowledged three of them above, we are compelled to honor the others, highlighting just a small portion of their invaluable contributions to GERI:

Lucille Meyer has been instrumental in implementing GERI into training curriculums for young adults, and she initiated the partnership that brought GERI to thousands at Chrysalis Academy.

Desireé English has been a pioneering and consummate GERI leader for years, and as our Director of Training, she applies her multiple talents with focused dedication.

Silvia Araya does a magnificent job leading GERI in Latin America and Spain, and brings her diverse gifts plus her translation skills to many GERI events.

Hugo Sanchez serves as co-coordinator of GERI Latin America, and is a valued mentor and eloquent advocate for all things GERI.

Ansar Anwar is providing strong leadership for GERI in India, in collaboration with Vijaya Lakshmi and others, and he is spearheading new innovative pathways for GERI.

Michele Breene is courageously leading a unique initiative to implement GERI within Christian churches and communities, and she contributes much to GERI trainings, particularly in Kenya.

Garrett Evans is often nicknamed the hub of GERI, serving as trainer, facilitator, operations manager, chief of tech support, editor; the list goes on.

Tristan Johannes leads the GERI LGBTQ+ program with eloquence, grace, and wisdom, both online and in-person.

Myra Kinds serves GERI in multiple capacities as the BIPOC and Intersectionality Lead, and she is a constant wellspring of spiritual inspiration.

Antonia Porter has written several proposals for GERI programs at the UN NGO CSW conferences, and led a successful fundraising campaign for the GERI Training in South Africa.

Harin Jeong launched GERI in Korea, translated *Divine Duality* into Korean, and leads GERI programs in Seoul with her partner Soonho Lee.

Esther and William Diplock launched GERI in Australia, and have graciously served as trainers and in various capacities for years.

Laurie Gaum has pioneered with Selina Palm a unique application of GERI for healing between straight and queer believers in Christian religious congregations.

Jabu Mashinini helped launch GERI in South Africa, and remains a dedicated consultant and trainer.

Jorge Rico facilitated several GERI programs in the U.S. and Mexico, and introduced GERI in podcasts for HR professionals in collaboration with Ariana Blossom.

Karambu Ringera co-facilitated several early GERI programs with us in South Africa, and she first brought GERI to Kenya in 2010, and has remained a tireless advocate for GERI, especially in Africa.

We readily acknowledge that there are also a number of other GERI leaders—current and past—who could also have been co-authors on this book. Some have made major contributions to GERI but are no longer active, others are making important contributions and are more recent arrivals in the GERI community. Many of these people are acknowledged below, and our gratitude goes out to them all.

We honor and thank the ten wonderful mentors and leaders who accepted our invitation to write the special highlighted sections of this book, each of whom made an invaluable contribution, shedding light on a crucial aspect of this work.

Beyond our co-authors and trainers, we are also very grateful to other aspiring individuals who have taken the bold initiative to organize and collaborate with us to launch inaugural GERI programs in their respective countries: Natalia Cediel in Colombia, Lok Bhandari in Nepal, Kristin Lietz in Mexico, Natalie Collins in the United Kingdom, Fr. Prashant Olekar and Hazel Lobo in India, Mohamed el Mongy in Egypt, Ticha Masai and Amina Juma Adelaide in Western Kenya, Sr. Lucy Kurien and Mangesh Pol in Maher (India), Klaus Muik in Austria, Ken and Petra Sloan in Germany, Pavel Hrdina and Klaus Muik in the Czech Republic, Fabrizio Palluzi in Italy, Ignacio Falcon and Alejandra Warden in Argentina; Jacob Garcia de Rueda, Yolanda Lucas, Valentin Oller, Rai Crespi, and Lara Terradas in Spain; and Janet Laughton Mackay, Tom Pickens, Karen McAllister, and Carollyne Conlinn in Canada.

Many other people have made major contributions to GERI:

Kara Salter has made important contributions to GERI communications and outreach, administrative support, and social media; and she supports the expansion of GERI in Australia.

Annette Williams serves GERI in multiple leadership capacities, and she has also helped to reorganize our database and documentation systems.

Sarah Flournoy and Leila Scott Price have done a wonderful job launching GERI programs in Houston, Texas. Sarah also convened a special contemplative retreat in Basalt, Colorado.

Phil Rogacki has skillfully launched new GERI workshops in the United Kingdom, and is helping to expand GERI in Europe.

Diane Haug was the first female GERI Trainer, and faithful colleague for 35+ years in bridging GERI with Grof Breathwork.

Linda Cunningham provided support and organizational advice on multiple levels, and helped to advance the three-day GERI program.

Ken Kitatani led the way for GERI within the UN community, and has remained a strong advocate for this ever since.

Saphira Rameshfar helped organize two workshops for the UN community in New York, in collaboration with Beth Blissman. Saphira also organized a special invitational presentation for GERI at the UN NGO/CSW conference (online) in 2021.

Mike Oreskes consistently promotes GERI within his professional networks, and he and Beth Blissman co-facilitated a GERI workshop at the 68th UN Civil Society Conference.

Carl Murrell has strongly advocated for GERI programs in the UN community, and the Parliament of the World Religions.

Tschika McBean has organized GERI events and panel presentations with prominent leaders in her networks in the Washington, DC area.

Kenny Ausubel and Nina Simons invited GERI to present multiple times at Bioneers conferences, and have long been steadfast allies of GERI.

Imam Jamal Rahman has hosted GERI programs in his Interfaith Community Sanctuary in Seattle, and he promotes GERI for Muslim communities.

Linda Lancaster invited GERI to present at several conferences of the Global Foundation for Integrative Medicine.

Lucille Lückhoff hosted most of our visits to Cape Town with tireless grace, and introduced us to many key colleagues and friends in South Africa.

Máire Callan has selflessly offered her administrative support to GERI and Satyana Institute for 18 years.

Kathy Lavine has served GERI beautifully for 17 years as graphic designer.

Sarah Gardam served as editor for the GERI training manual, and numerous other documents.

Ariel Patano has been an exemplary selfless servant to GERI, managing important practical details.

Marilyn Turkovich and her colleagues initiated a fruitful partnership between the Charter for Compassion and GERI.

Les Thomas and Xolile (Pro) Zulani have been instrumental in implementing GERI programs in township communities of South Africa.

Max DeArmon produced a short documentary film about GERI, and has helped organize and facilitate GERI programs in California.

Kosha Joubert has graciously invited GERI into a collaboration with the Pocket Project, co-founded by Thomas Hübl and Yehudit Sasportas for collective healing and restoration.

We are also grateful to many others for their crucial contributions, including but not limited to: Alka Arora, John Guy, Rev. Kristin Powell, Stephen Picha, Shirsten Lundblad, Diane Salters, Clay Boykin, Lora Williams, Janine Turner, Shelli Lether, Shivaprasad Kumarswamy, Evans Njoki, Naomi Mwangi, Kanghei Lee, SeiFu Anil Singh-Molares, Kenna Cormie, and Dominie Cappadonna.

We gratefully acknowledge our generous funders and supporters, who not only make GERI possible, but also hold it with us in their hearts, including: the Imago Dei Fund, Vista Hermosa Foundation, S.C. Rain Foundation, International Community Foundation, Roy A. Hunt Foundation, Silicon Valley Community Foundation, American Endowment Foundation, Loretto at the UN, RSF Social Finance, Lumbard and Paine Charitable Gift Fund.

We are deeply grateful to major individual donors, including Margaret Schink, Emily Nielsen Jones and Ross Jones, Lynnaea Lumbard and Richard Paine, Albert ("Rick") and Julie Lawrence, Suzanne Lerner, Christopher Hormel, Gard Jameson, Emanuel Kuntzelman and Laura Rose, Julien Devereux, Linda Cunningham, Terry Hunt, Laurie McMillan, LoWell Brook, Jon Levitt, Dave Brown, John Steiner and Margo King, Fr. William Treacy, Sarah Flournoy, Ruth Flournoy, Charles Terry and Betsy McGregor, Shelli Lether and Judd Abrams, Michele and Tim Breene, James and Shirley Vollett, Carollyne Conlinn, Miguel and Melanie Lopez-Grewal, Bill Melton, and several anonymous donors.

Margaret Schink has been a profound supporter of GERI in material and spiritual ways for nearly 30 years. Emily Nielsen Jones of the Imago Dei Fund hosted invitational GERI programs on the East and West coasts in response to the #MeToo movement, and has remained a close friend to GERI in numerous capacities.

Suzanne Broetje invited GERI programs into her community, and was instrumental for GERI being introduced in Mexico.

Suzanne Lerner has been a longtime supporter of GERI, and introduced us to many key colleagues.

Terry Hunt has been an enthusiastic and dedicated supporter of GERI since the mid-1990s.

We also thank past funders including: Nathan Cummings Foundation, Kalliopeia Foundation, Shaler Adams Foundation, San Francisco Foundation, Novo Foundation, Threshold Foundation, The Philanthropic Collaborative, Seed Fund, Cunningham Family Foundation, Tides Foundation, Hidden Leaf Foundation, East Bay Community Foundation, Selby-Fong Spirit in Community Fund, Global Environment Projects Institute, Rockwood Fund, Further Foundation, Giant Steps Foundation, Gaia Trust (Denmark), and numerous individuals and anonymous donors.

Lynnaea Lumbard and Rick Paine have been remarkably supportive friends and supporters in innumerable ways.

Albert ("Rick") Lawrence and Julie Lawrence have been wonderful friends and supporters of the GERI initiative, graciously hosting us frequently in their home.

The late Sara Campbell was a dear friend and profound supporter of GERI, and left a generous bequest to GERI.

We are grateful to the Board of Directors of the Satyana Institute: Bernard Zaleha, Richard Paine, Chaya Pamula, Karambu Ringera, Dorothea Hendricks, Ravi Ravindra, Matthew Wright, and Jed Swift (emeritus).

We thank several key leaders for their contributions as Guest Faculty in GERI professional trainings, including Carol Lee Flinders, Christopher Kilmartin, Rina Swentzell, Peter Rutter, Andrew Harvey, Vanya Kent, and the late Lucia Ticzon.

We are indebted to many people who made important contributions to GERI in the past, a few of whom include: Shell Goldman, Elizabeth Peterson, Bernedette Muthien, Zanele Khumalo, Keith Vermeulen, Carlotta Tyler, Rob and Shameima McLeod, Rudi Buys, Nomfundo Walaza, Hazel Lobo, Hetal Jobenputra, Lindiwe Tshabalala, Janet Coster, Alan Strachan, Molly Dwyer, Heart Phoenix, Jeffrey Weisberg, John Seed, Andre Carothers, Allen Kanner, Amy Fox, Patrick Fischer, Royda Crose, Michelle Andipatin, Francis Padinjakkara, Selma Nalloor, Biata and John Walsh, Jane Calbreath, and others.

We thank our network of colleagues and friends, beyond those mentioned above, for their encouragement and mentoring, including Robert McDermott, Richard Tarnas, Kurt Johnson, Vincent Harding, Cedar Barstow, Becca Tarnas, Ross and Hildur Jackson,

Jack Kornfield, Adam Cummings, Swami Atmarupananda, Rabbi Rami Shapiro, Fritz and Vivienne Hull, Anne Stadler, Mahnaz Afkhami, Dena Merriam, Suchetta Bhat, Vishal Talreja, Fr. Guillermo Marco, Omar Abboud, Rabbi Daniel Goldman, Rev. Don Mackenzie, Rabbi Ted Falcon, and many others. We also thank our families for their loving support, including our adult children Patrick Fischer and Emily McIntire.

We also express our heartfelt gratitude with a deep bow to the many spouses, life partners, and family members of our GERI trainers and facilitators—for holding down the home front, when their beloveds are away facilitating GERI programs.

Many other people have served GERI in myriad ways, too numerable to mention by name. If there are others who should have been named here and were inadvertently omitted, we ask your forgiveness. Our deep gratitude to all in the GERI community for your courageous contributions and commitment; you have carried the living flame and demonstrated the triumph of the human spirit.

Index

Page numbers *in italics* indicate photographs; page numbers that include n indicate notes.

Author Biographies

Rev. Cynthia Brix, Ph.D. (hon) is co-founder of Gender Equity and Reconciliation International. An ordained interfaith minister with a background in women's issues and racial diversity, she co-organized seven international conferences on interspirituality, including two on women's spiritual leadership across diverse religious and indigenous traditions. Cynthia holds an honorary doctorate from California Institute of Integral Studies, M.A. in wellness and gerontology, M.Div. from Iliff School of Theology, and she is certified in Grof Breathwork. She is an Evolutionary Leader, and co-author of *Divine Duality: The Power of Reconciliation between Women and Men*, and *Women Healing Women: A Model of Hope for Oppressed Women Everywhere.*

William Keepin, Ph.D. is co-founder of Gender Equity and Reconciliation International, and Satyana Institute. A mathematical physicist with training in contemplative spirituality and transpersonal psychology, his research on global warming and sustainable energy influenced international environmental policy. He has published widely on environmental science, quantum physics, ecology, archetypal cosmology, comparative mysticism, divine feminine theology, and principles of social change leadership. He is an Evolutionary Leader, a Findhorn Foundation Fellow, and Board member of the Grof Legacy Project. His previous books include *Divine Duality, Song of the Earth,* and *Belonging to God: Spirituality, Science, and a Universal Path of Divine Love.*

Karambu Ringera, Ph.D. is a Senior GERI Trainer and GERI Coordinator for Kenya and East Africa since 2006. She founded International Peace Initiatives and the Tiriji Foundation based in Meru, Kenya, which empowers orphans, women living with HIV/AIDS, survivors of violence, and other vulnerable community members via education, advocacy, and leadership development. Several Tiriji orphans have grown up to become leaders in their communities. Karambu has received many awards, including the 2022 Kenya National Diversity and Inclusion Awards & Recognition (DIAR). She earned her Ph.D. in Intercultural Communication from the University of Denver, and M.A. in theology from Iliff School of Theology.

Garrett Evans, B.S. is International Program Officer and Trainer for GERI, where he has worked full time since 2017. He has contributed greatly to developing the GERI infrastructure, programs, research, marketing, and was instrumental in developing GERI online programs and training. He received his degree in conflict resolution from Portland State University. Garrett began intensive practice in the Zen Buddhist tradition in 2011. Through GERI, he feels called to combine his love for the world's contemplative spiritual traditions with healing and reconciliation work.

Desireé English, B.A. is a Senior Trainer and GERI Director of Training in Africa, and is Chair of the Board of GenderWorks, GERI's affiliate in South Africa. Desireé has conducted GERI programs in South Africa, Kenya, India, Egypt, and the United States. She has over 20 years' experience facilitating healing and empowerment of women and youth in communities. She is a Trauma Release Exercises (TRE) Certification Trainer, Integrative Trauma Healing Practitioner, and independent learning and development consultant.

William Diplock, M. Soc. Sc. (Couns) is a Senior GERI Trainer and Program Coordinator for GERI, in Brisbane, Australia. William is a counselor in private practice with 30+ years of experience in individual, couples and family therapy and clinical supervision. He also has ten years of experience in men's work, and serves as a teaching Elder in Men's Rites of Passage in Australia. William received his M. Soc. Sc. in Counselling from Queensland University of Technology, completed a four-year training in Spiritual Direction at St. Francis Theological College, and holds an Advanced Diploma of Integrated Somatic Psychotherapy.

Esther Diplock, M. Couns. is a Senior GERI Trainer and Program Coordinator for GERI, in Brisbane, Australia. Esther is an individual and couples' therapist in private practice, and an educator and supervisor, specializing in Body Psychotherapy and trauma-informed practice. Esther holds a B. Occ. Thy. in Occupational Therapy from University of Queensland and an M. Couns. from Christian Heritage College. She is a Kundalini Yoga teacher, and holds an Advanced Diploma of Integrated Somatic Psychotherapy from the Institute of Body Psychotherapy.

Lucille Meyer, Ed.D. is a Senior GERI Trainer in Cape Town, South Africa. She is Chief Executive Officer of Ch rysalis Academy, an award-winning residential academy that graduates 620 young adults each year who complete an intensive curriculum of skills development and holistic education. Lucille has integrated GERI into the Chrysalis curriculum. In 2017, she received a Lifetime Achievement Award for Excellence in Youth Development. She is also a Certified Trauma Release Exercises Provider and Yoga Therapy teacher. She received her Ed.D. from the Cape Peninsula University of Technology.

Silvia Araya, Psy.D. is a GERI Trainer and the GERI Latin America Lead. She received her degree in clinical psychology from Universidad Fidélitas in Costa Rica, and practices as a Clinical Trauma Professional, specializing in anxiety and panic attacks. She is a certified practitioner of Family Constellations and a Trauma Informed Yoga Teacher. Silvia is author of three books including *Trust and Live without Pani*c, and her new book entitled, *Is This What I REALLY Want?: How to Go Beyond Trauma into the Relationship You Deserve.*

Minister Myra Kinds is a GERI Trainer and BIPOC and Intersectionalities Lead, based in Boston, MA. A licensed American Baptist Minister, she serves as the Minister to Youth at the Peoples Baptist Church, and serves on the advisory board at Gordon Conwell's Campus for Urban Ministerial Education (CUME). She is a recognized leader in underserved communities, specializing in youth programming, addiction and recovery, mental health, and domestic violence. She holds numerous training certificates in Mental Health First Aid, Recovery Coaching, and Trauma First Responder. Myra collaborates with The Black Ministerial Alliance and MENTOR, and consults with faith-based groups around women in ministry, youth, and gender-based violence.

Jorge Rico, M.A. is a GERI Trainer based in Providence, Rhode Island, and co-leads the GERI Latin America project, and GERI corporate training program. Originally from Bolivia, he has 25+ years of experience in Human Resources. Jorge has extensive experience with leadership and employee development programs, and developed and led numerous Diversity, Equity & Inclusion (DEI) initiatives, while championing gender equity throughout his professional career. He holds degrees from Boston College and Cambridge College, and leads the Men's Ministry at Concordia Center for Spiritual Living in R.I.

Samantha van Schalkwyk, Ph.D. is Research Manager and Deputy Director of the Centre for the Study of the Afterlife of Violence and the Reparative Quest (AVReQ) at Stellenbosch University, South Africa. Her research focuses on repercussions of gender violence in post-Apartheid South Africa; transforming harmful patriarchal narratives underpinning violence; addressing patriarchal trauma; and the psychosocial aspects of violated women's agency. She and Professor Pumla Gobodo-Madikizela conducted a longitudinal study on the GERI process. Her latest book is *Narrative Landscapes of Female Sexuality in Africa: Collective Stories of Trauma and Transition* (Palgrave Macmillan, 2018).

Ansar Anwar, B.A. is a GERI Facilitator and Program Lead for GERI in India, where he organizes and delivers GERI programs to young people. Based in Bangalore, Ansar is Associate Director of Design and Development at Dream a Dream, a youth training organization where he has 15 years of experience. Earlier, Ansar managed ten learning centers for holistic development of young people at Makkala Jagriti. He executed a research project on rehabilitation of minority communities, and presented the report to a judge on the Supreme Court of India.

Antonia Porter, MA, studied theology at Cambridge and political and international studies at UC Berkeley. Her work focuses on peace, conflict, and gender equality, with a particular focus on masculinities. She has worked with NGOs in South Africa and internationally, and with the UN and other multilateral bodies including the Intergovernmental Authority on Development (IGAD). Antonia has published in national newspapers including the UK *Guardian*. Her peer-reviewed research synthesizes psychosocial and therapeutic responses to conflict and structural violence, and is published in several journals, including the *Palgrave Handbook of Peacebuilding in Africa* and the *Journal of International Peacekeeping*.

Rev. Louis ("Laurie") Gaum, M.Th., M.A. is a GERI Trainer and activist theologian focusing on gender and sexual diversity freedom. An ordained minister in the Dutch Reformed Church of South Africa, he co-led a 17-year struggle that culminated in winning a landmark court case against the church, which helped establish it as an open and affirming denomination. In 2022 he received an award from the Andrew Murray Prize Fund, citing his leadership as "a facilitator in "Gender Equity & Reconciliation" and human sexuality … [to] guide churches and congregations on creating a safe and healing space between 'straight' and 'queer' believers."

Harin Jeong, M.A. is a GERI Facilitator and lead coordinator for GERI in South Korea, based in Seoul. She is the CEO of the Center for Courage and Renewal Psychology Counseling, and is a counselor focusing on sexual and gender-based violence survivors, and LGBTIQA+ clients. Harin earned her degrees from Ewha Womans University and Duksung Women's University. She has experience in organizational development, is a certified sociocracy coach, and consults on gender equality conflict management. Harin is establishing GERI Korea as a non-profit organization.

Jabu Mashinini, B.A. (Hon) is Trainer for GERI and GenderWorks. He is Executive Coach at Leadership Pathways based in Gauteng province, South Africa, and a leading consultant in diversity training, counseling, peace studies, and the Alternatives to Violence Project. He conducts Diversity, Equity, & Inclusion (DEI) trainings in corporations, and for the United Nations Human Rights Council, and the UN Charity Organization. Jabu teaches DEI courses at the University of Cape Town, and has served in as a Lead Facilitator of the Nelson Mandela International Dialogues.

Hugo Sanchez, B.A., is a GERI Trainer and co-lead of the Latin America/Spain Program. He earned his degree in Social Communications from La Universidad del Zulia, Venezuela, and spent 19 years with major advertising agencies in New York City before leaving the corporate world to pursue his passion for collective change. An experienced yoga teacher and founder of Pacha Yoga, he is also a Yoga Alliance Continued Education Provider and Teacher Trainer. His leadership extends to The Mankind Project, where he has led programs empowering men to live with integrity, authenticity, and service.

Tristan Johannes is a GERI Trainer and the LGBTQ+ Project Lead, and serves on the Board of GenderWorks, GERI's affiliate in South Africa. He trained youth for over ten years, and served as an administrator and trainer at Chrysalis Academy. He holds an Advanced Diploma in Adult and Community Education Training from the University of Cape Town, and is an ordained minister in the Pentecostal Church of Africa, and a certified Integral Yoga and Mindfulness Teacher. Tristan was selected for the 'Leading for Humanity' program of the Desmond and Leah Tutu Legacy Foundation in 2023.

Michele Breene, M.A. is a GERI Facilitator with 25 years' experience in leadership development, team building, and executive coaching in the UK, USA, and globally, in corporate and NGO sectors. Michele has designed courses and led workshops in seven African countries (including Kenya where her family lived for 40 years), and in India and China. She is a mentor, facilitator, coach, and spiritual director in leadership development relating to spiritual formation, mentoring and gender equity. She received her M.A. in Education from the University of London.

Julien Devereux, Ph.D. is a Senior GERI Trainer based in Dallas, and has served GERI in multiple capacities since 2002. He is former Chair of the ManKind Project (MKP-USA), a men's organization that has trained tens of thousands of men in emotional maturity, per- sonal accountability, spiritual awareness, and relational skills. Julien holds a Ph.D. from the California Institute of Integral Studies, and is a certified facilitator of Integrative Breathwork. He is a licensed clinical social worker (LCW) with 30+ years of clinical and managerial experience, including extensive background in the criminal justice system.

Mpho Tutu van Furth is a South African Anglican priest, author and activist. She is the daughter of Leah and Archbishop Desmond Tutu. She co-authored a biography about her father with journalist Allister Sparks. She was ordained in 2003, but due to regulations of the Anglican Church of South Africa, she was not permitted to function as a priest in the church after marrying a woman in 2015. She began preaching in Amsterdam in 2022. Mpho is author of *Forgiveness and Reparation*; and co-author with Desmond Tutu of *The Book of Forgiving* and *Made for Goodness*.

Contact Information

GERI

For more information about **Gender Equity and Reconciliation International (GERI)**, and to learn about upcoming programs, please visit our website or contact us:

www.geri.global
email: info@geri.global

HOHM PRESS

HOHM PRESS is committed to publishing books that provide readers with alternatives to the materialistic values of the current culture, and promote self-awareness, the recognition of interdependence, and compassion. Our subject areas include parenting, transpersonal psychology, religious studies, women's studies, the arts and poetry.

Contact Information: Hohm Press, PO Box 4410, Chino Valley, Arizona, 86323; USA; 800-381-2700, or 928-636-3331; email: publisher@hohmpress.com

Visit our website at www.hohmpress.com